For the library of the
University of Shanandoah,
With warm wishes,

John Huddleston

THE SEARCH FOR A JUST SOCIETY

THE SEARCH FOR
A JUST SOCIETY

by

JOHN HUDDLESTON

GR
GEORGE RONALD
OXFORD

GEORGE RONALD, Publisher
46 High Street, Kidlington, Oxford, OX5 2DN
© JOHN HUDDLESTON 1989
All Rights Reserved

British Library Cataloguing in Publication Data

Huddleston, John
  The search for a just society
  1. Society
  301

ISBN 0–85398–288–0

Printed in Great Britain by
Billing & Sons Ltd, Worcester

This book is dedicated to
Madame Ruhiyyih Rabbani
who has taught me, through the example of her life,
the real meaning of the phrase
'unity in diversity'

Acknowledgements

This book has come about largely in response to a conversation with Mme. Ruhiyyih Rabbani, and I am most grateful to her for her confidence that I could undertake such a project. I am also immensely grateful to May Ballerio, who has been a most patient and skilful editor, and to my wife Rouhi, who has been a full partner in the enterprise, both as a developer of ideas and as a giver of unflagging encouragement when it seemed that the project would never be completed. In addition, I wish to express my thanks to three other friends: Colleen Dawes for her professional advice on the development of international law, and Foong Oy Yeong and Djenane Elie-Goodall for retyping extensive and complicated revisions to the original draft.

Contents

Preface   xiii

PART I
THE PAST

	Introduction	I
I	Peace through Empire: Egypt and Mesopotamia	7
2	Judaism: Monotheism and Ethics	II
3	Zoroastrianism and the Persian Empire	17
4	Hinduism: A Perspective of the Universe	22
5	Buddhism and the Mauryan Empire	25
6	Confucianism and the Middle Kingdom	28
7	Greece and the Rational Philosophers	33
8	Pax Romana	39
9	Christianity: The Concept of Brotherhood	43
10	Islam and the Idea of Equality	52
11	Three Revolutions	63
	The English Revolution	63
	The American Revolution	69
	The French Revolution	74

PART II
THE PRESENT AGE

	A: GREATER POLITICAL AND SOCIAL EQUALITY	83
12	The Abolition of Slavery and Serfdom	84
13	National Self-Determination and the Building of Nations	94
	The Nineteenth Century	95
	Between the Wars	108
	After World War II	110
14	Democracy and the Rule of Law	119
	Constitutionalism in the Nineteenth Century	126
	Constitutionalism between the Wars	137
	Constitutionalism after the Second World War	139

The Emancipation of Women   144
The News Media: The Fourth Estate   157

B: REDUCING MATERIAL POVERTY   165

15   Trade Unions   168
16   Cooperative Themes   176
     The Cooperative Movement   176
     Profit Sharing   179
     Anarchism   181
     Syndicalism   183
17   Socialism   184
18   The Welfare State   198
     Income Maintenance   200
     Public Health   209
     Housing   215
     Conditions of Work   222
     Universal Education   224
     Crime and Punishment   231
     Cost Sharing   241
19   The Consumer Society   251
     Pluses and Minuses   252
     The Temperance Movement and Similar Causes   256
     Protection of the Environment   263

C: FROM WAR TO PEACE   271

20   The Congress System 1815–1914   275
     Congresses and the Hague Conferences   275
     The Growth of International Cooperation   282
21   The Forces for War   293
     Nationalism   293
     Imperialism   294
     Militarism   297
22   The League of Nations 1918–1939   301
     The First World War   301
     The Fourteen Points   303
     The Versailles Treaty   305
     The League Covenant   307
     Successes and Failures   315
     The Collapse of the League   322
23   The Creation of the United Nations   325
     The Second World War   325
     The Nuremberg Trials   327

The Organization of the United Nations   329
The Declaration of Human Rights   338
The United Nations Compared with the
      League of Nations   342
24 International Relations since World War II   346
      The Background to the Work of the United Nations   346
      The Cold War   347
      The North–South Conflict   352
      Regional Developments   357
      Changes in the Balance of Influence between Nations 359
      Global Village   361
      Initiatives by Voluntary Organizations   365
25 The United Nations at Work   368
      Adjustment to Reality, 1945–1962   368
      New Directions, 1962–1975   372
      A Time of Doubt, 1975–1985   379
      Multilateralism: New Hope, 1985 to the Present   386

PART III

THE FUTURE

26 Where Do We Go From Here?   395
27 The Big Picture   402
      Science and Religion   403
      The Nature of Man   406
      The Cycles of Religions   411
      The Spiritual Dimension to the Progressive Movement 414
28 Preparing for a Just Society   417
      The Individual   417
      The Family   421
      Collective Action   424
29 A Vision of World Peace   434
      Political Unification   434
      The Economy   439
      A Realistic Vision?   446
30 The Programme in Action   450

Appendices
1 World Population since the Beginning of Civilization   470
2 Independent Nations and States of the World
      by Continent and Population   471
3 Winners of the Nobel Peace Prize, 1901–1988   474
4 Text of the Universal Declaration of Human Rights   481

Bibliography 487

Index 496

Illustrations

(*between pages 248 and 249*)

1 Hammurabi
2 Confucius
3 Socrates
4 Jean-François Marie Arouet de Voltaire
5 Thomas Paine
6 John Locke
7 'Mad Tom – or the Man of Rights'
8 Abraham Lincoln reading the Emancipation Declaration to his cabinet
9 Frederick Douglass
10 Harriet Beecher Stowe
11 Mahatma Gandhi
12 Martin Luther King
13 Elizabeth Cady Stanton
14 Suffrage cartoon by Blanche Ames Ames
15 Nineteenth-century reformers: Octavia Hill; Anthony Ashley Cooper, Earl of Shaftesbury; Robert Owen; Frances Willard
16 Jean-Henri Dunant
17 Jean Jaurès
18 Jane Addams
19 Eleanor Roosevelt
20 Thomas Woodrow Wilson
21 First session of the League of Nations Council
22 Women's International League for Peace and Freedom
23 Signing the United Nations Charter, San Francisco 1945
24 The United Nations Security Council, 1946
25 The International Court of Justice in session

26 The United Nations Secretariat, a representative group
27 Delegates to the International Bahá'í Convention
28 'Abdu'l-Bahá

Maps

1 The slave-holding states in the
   United States of America, 1860   88
2 Achievement of national independence in the nineteenth
   and twentieth centuries   96
3 The overall status of women in the 1980s   155
4 Nations with above-average practices with regard
   to human rights   389

Tables

1 The world's religions 1987: number of adherents   4
2 Participation in democracy: voting in national elections   122
3 Date of achieving key characteristics of constitutionalism
   in selected countries   136
4 Numbers of democratic and non-democratic nations   143
5 Women's pay as a percentage of men's pay
   for the same work   154
6 Indicators of media distribution   163
7 Extremes of wealth and poverty within nations   166
8 Number of physicians per million of population   212
9 Life expectancy at birth, and infant mortality   214
10 Levels of education: literacy, primary school enrolment,
   graduates   232
11 Changes in volume of violent crime in OECD countries,
   1950–1970   240
12 Sources of central government revenues   246
13 Government expenditures as a percentage of GDP   247
14 Defence expenditures as a percentage of GDP/GNP   248
15 Changes in the earth's physical condition   264

16 Known and estimated diversity of life on earth   270
17 The United Nations system   332
18 Secretaries-General of the League of Nations and the
      United Nations   335
19 Nuclear weapons of the superpowers   352
20 Rich and poor nations of the world: GNP per capita,
      1985   354
21 Net transfer of resources to all developing countries   356
22 Growth in world production and international trade,
      1780–1985   364
23 Growth in membership of the United Nations,
      1945–1985   373
24 Official development assistance for selected nations,
      1960–1986   376
25 Population growth   381
26 Impact of population growth on standards of living   382
27 Sharing the cost of the United Nations between
      157 members   385
28 Membership of the United Nations analysed by population
      and GNP   388
29 Statistics on the Bahá'í world community   458

Preface

THIS book is about the search for a dream. It is an ancient dream, aspired to by countless men and women down the ages. Sometimes manifested in a new religion, sometimes led by far-sighted and noble-minded statesmen or philosophers, sometimes emerging in the spontaneous rebellion of ordinary people against tyranny: the search for a just society recurs throughout history, undeterred by cynicism or past failure. For long the search was episodic and scattered, and concerned itself only with limited aspects of a just society as we would conceive it today. Often an aspiration, beginning magnificently, would deteriorate and sink into the sands of history. Yet all these struggles – the failures as well as the successes – have become part of the collective heritage of mankind and have inspired and given strength to those who came afterwards and carried forward the dream, and the search:

In the passage of time a state of collective human consciousness has been progressively evolved which is inherited by each succeeding generation of conscious individuals, and to which each generation adds something. (Teilhard de Chardin, *The Future of Man*, p. 33)

Slowly but surely the drumbeat of history has quickened. Attempts to achieve a better society have become more frequent and the range of concerns has become more comprehensive. A crescendo was reached in the nineteenth century and has continued ever since.

What do we, in the last years of the twentieth century, mean by the 'just society'? Generally, when the term is employed in this book, it means a society which gives freedom to all its citizens and encourages them to achieve their full potential – physical, mental and spiritual. Such a state of affairs has various implications now gaining acceptance by the community of nations as the century draws to its close.

The first and most important of such implications would seem to be an ethical system that inspires a sense of the oneness of mankind, intellectual integrity, and responsibility both for development of the self and for promoting the welfare of others; that creates a balance between rights and duties. From this basic requirement all others follow.

The provision of physical security, both for the person and

necessary personal property, is the second requirement of a just society. This implies the rule of law in relations between communities (including international relations), between the community and the individual, and between individuals. The law should be in accord with the ethical system mentioned above, and must be seen to be just. It cannot be arbitrary or capricious. It should serve the interest of all, it should apply equally to all and should be known in advance to all. It should be administered by an objective and informed judiciary, fairminded, and concerned for the general well-being. Against those who have been found guilty of breaking the law, it should apply sanctions which are both proportional to the offence and an encouragement to the human spirit rather than a burden on it. The judiciary should be supported by a police force which is itself subject to the law and which views itself as the servant and protector of the community – not an oppressor.

The third broad requirement of a just society is that all citizens have a say in the management of the affairs of their community. This may be achieved directly (as in a referendum) or indirectly (as in the election of representatives to act on behalf of citizens in the supervision and management of government). All adult members of the community should have the right to take part in elections and to vote secretly so that they are protected from intimidation. Equal weighting should be given to the votes of all electors and elections should take place at reasonable intervals. The government should be open in its administration and accountable for its actions to the community which it serves. Citizens should be free to think as they wish and to express themselves freely. However, in exercising these rights the citizen should recognize that abuse of privilege, and failure to live by the spirit and rules of the game, will undermine the open society to the cost of all.

The fourth and final requirement now generally agreed as essential to the just society is equal opportunity for all citizens. There should be absolutely no negative discrimination on account of sex, race, culture, economic status or religion. To make this a realistic goal there are at least two subsidiary needs. The first concerns material resources. There should be no extremes of wealth and poverty, and for the benefit of present and future generations there should be protection and conservation of the natural resources of the planet. Secondly, all members of the community should have access to education for the development of the body, the mind, and the spirit.

The first part of this book touches on some of the highlights of the search for a just society from the beginnings of civilization to the end of the eighteenth century. The second part attempts a general description of the main concerns of progressive movements in the nineteenth and twentieth centuries, and their successes and failures in taking the human race towards a more just society. This part has three sections which deal in turn with progress: (a) towards greater political and social equality; (b) towards elimination of poverty; and (c) towards world cooperation and the abolition of war. The third part of the book starts with a summary of the position today and the alternative paths forward which are available. In conclusion, it suggests that the logical successor of the progressive movements of history is the Bahá'í Faith. With its broad vision, practical approach, and accumulated experience, this movement does indeed give a unique promise of fulfilment of that age-old dream: the coming of the just society.

The best beloved of all things
in My sight is justice.
Bahá'u'lláh

PART I

The Past

Introduction

PART I of this book discusses some highlights in the search for the just society from the beginning of civilization until the end of the eighteenth century. It is divided into eleven chapters, six of which focus on some of the great religions of the world. That perhaps requires a word of explanation because in western society, at least, there has been a tendency in recent decades to downplay the importance of religion. Karl Marx spoke for many when he dismissed it as the 'opium of the people'.

Such scepticism is an understandable result of the experience of religious institutions in moral and intellectual decline. It is with good reason that religion has been associated with superstition, division, fanaticism, authoritarianism and oppression. Nevertheless, such scepticism – no doubt intellectually and spiritually healthy in moderation – should not be a barrier to a fair-minded reading of history or assessment of human society today: the vast majority of the world population still has deep feelings about religion. The fact is that religion has been an extremely powerful force in human history since at least the beginnings of civilization; it has played a very significant part in the evolution of the idea of the just society. There can be little question, for instance, that justice in its broadest sense was central to the personality and teachings of Jesus, Muhammad, Moses, Buddha and Zoroaster.

The contribution of religion to the evolution of the concept of the just society has been its role in the development of ethics: the basic motivations of the individual and the community, and a sense of distinction between right and wrong. Ethics drawn from the great religions of the past have moderated human greed, selfishness, violence and destruction – all characteristics of the unjust society. Religion has reduced the importance of material considerations, too, by showing them to be ephemeral and of limited significance in relation to the vastness of the universe, both in terms of space and time, and in the perspective of the spiritual side of existence.

This does not imply that the great religions have been unworldly. A second aspect of their teachings has been concern for the physical and mental well-being of the individual – key elements of the just society (for instance cleanliness, healthy diet including avoidance of things which can harm the body and mind, literacy, education, and opposition to superstition and ignorance). Another aspect of the religious approach, of vital importance to the just society, is the concept of the brotherhood of man – perhaps better stated as the

TABLE I

THE WORLD'S RELIGIONS, 1987: NUMBER OF ADHERENTS

Religion	Millions	Percentage of Total	Number of Countries[1]
Christianity	1,644	32.9	254
Islam	860	17.2	172
Hinduism	656	13.1	88
Buddhism	310	6.2	86
Chinese folk religions	188	3.7	56
New religions[2]	111	2.2	25
Tribal religions[3]	108	2.1	108
Judaism	18	0.4	125
Sikhism	17	0.3	20
Confucianism	6	0.1	3
Bahá'í Faith	5	0.1	205
Jainism	3	0.1	10
Shintoism[4]	3	0.1	3
Zoroastrianism	>1[5]	–	10
Other religions[6]	8	0.2	170
No religion[7]	1,061	21.3	220
Total World Population	**4,998**	**100.0**	**254**

[1] Includes dependencies as well as independent nations.
[2] Followers of Asiatic 20th century new religions.
[3] Includes Shamanism; religious beliefs centred around the medicine man.
[4] State religion of Japan.
[5] There are fewer than 200,000 Zoroastrians worldwide.
[6] Includes 50 minor religions and a large number of spiritist groups.
[7] Atheists, non-believers, agnostics, freethinkers, etc.

Source: David R. Barrett, 'Religion: World Religious Statistics', *1988 Britannica Book of the Year*.

human family because it embraces women as well as men – and the spiritual equality of all, no matter what an individual's status may be in the world. This sense of family has two sides. The first is to be attractive to others: honest, truthful, reliable, responsible, hard-working. The second is to care about others: to be kind, charitable, sympathetic to the poor and oppressed, stable in sexual and parental relationships, tolerant of others.

Although the development of ethical values at all levels of society was the single most important element in the evolution of the just society over the long period of time covered in Part I of this book, several other key factors were beginning to emerge. In some instances there is an identifiable and direct link with religion; at other times there appear to be independent and secular causes. The one factor that is perhaps most noticeable from the earliest times and in a multitude of contexts is the idea of the rule of law: systematic statements of the obligations and rights of the individual and the state, protection against criminals and against excessive cruelty on the part of the state, even the beginnings of the idea that the state is there to serve the people. Another aspect which began to emerge early on was the maintenance of peace over a wide geographic area and embracing large numbers of people. Such peace, however, was regional and imposed by force from above by a powerful state, such as Rome; not until recent times has there been real discussion of a universal peace based on voluntary acceptance by all. Other characteristics of the just society which occurred occasionally during the period under consideration include the concepts of community assistance of the poor, cultural freedom and self-determination, and public participation in the choice of government and its activities.

The seeds of the just society can be detected in the earliest human communities. The early groups of hunters and gatherers, totally preoccupied as they were with the struggle for physical survival, had no time for the development of human potential in the widest sense. Nevertheless, the very pressure of struggling to survive forced cooperation, on the basis of division of responsibility and function, and this in itself is a basic concept of the just society. The next stage came with the emergence of pastoral and crop-growing communities at the end of the last Ice Age, around 10,000 BC. Some of the earliest evidence of pastoral societies pertains to sheep-rearing by tribesmen in Iraq by 9000 BC, and the rearing of other domestic animals in China by 5000 BC and in India by 3700 BC. With regard to crop-growing communities, there is evidence that millet and rice were cultivated as early as 10,000 BC in south-east Africa, and that maize was cultivated in central America by 5000 BC. By that time too, there were extensive settlements in Iran and China. Such societies tended to be more secure materially than the more primitive hunter and gatherer communities, allowing greater opportunity to individuals, though this positive development may have been tempered for many by a growing distinction between the rich and the poor.

From these early societies there gradually evolved large permanent settlements or cities, with complex structures of labour division, an accumulation of wealth, and eventually the written word – this was civilization, the third main stage in human development. The first civilizations of which we have some historical record were: in the Tigris–Euphrates valley of what is now Syria and Iraq (about 3500 BC) developing into the Sumerian kingdom about 2400 BC; in the Nile valley of what is now Egypt (about 3200 BC); in the Indus valley of what is now Pakistan (about 2500 BC); in China (about 2500 BC); in Crete (about 2000 BC); in eastern Mexico (about 1500 BC); and in the Sudan (about 1000 BC). There is a good case for arguing that initially 'civilization' was a backwards step from today's perspective of the just society – it was associated with an intensification of armed conflict, greater extremes of wealth and poverty, autocratic government, slavery, and a lower status for women than in rural societies. Nevertheless, as pointed out by J.M. Roberts in his *History of the World*, civilization brought with it a promise for the future which was entirely new:

Civilization is the name we give to the interaction of human beings in a very creative way, when as it were, a critical mass of cultural potential and a certain surplus of resources has been built up. In civilization this releases human capacities for development at quite a new level and in large measure the development which follows is self-sustaining.

CHAPTER I

Peace through Empire:
Egypt and Mesopotamia

THE earliest civilizations consisted of multitudes of small city states which had no formal borders and were often in armed conflict with one another. The first successful imposition of peace over an extended area came with the establishment of the Egyptian monarchy which, under King Menes (about 3200 BC), united settlements in both the upper and lower Nile regions over an area some 600 miles long and several miles wide. This remarkable state was to last for 2,500 years, surviving various periods of instability until its defeat first by the Assyrians and then by the Persians and the Greeks.

Early Egyptian civilization is remembered for its skills in the use of herbs for medical purposes; for the establishment of the present-day system of recording the calendar year as 365¼ days; and for the invention of the hieroglyphic system of writing,[1] papyrus which made books possible, and the fraction in mathematics. The Egyptian Empire not only kept the peace over a large area, but developed a professional bureaucracy which provided such services as storehouses where provisions were kept for use in years of bad harvest. The state also had the virtue of being relatively non-militaristic, perhaps because it was geographically isolated from other advanced societies, at least during the early centuries. In contrast with other early civilizations it did not suppress women unduly, and in consequence quite a few women were literate; some of them worked as scribes for the state.

On the other hand, the Egyptian state was undoubtedly deeply flawed in several respects. Perhaps the most fundamental defect was the fact that the king (or pharaoh) had virtually unlimited powers and was treated like a god. There were no written laws and the pharaoh's subjects were effectually at the mercy of his every whim. The state religion served to strengthen his power and gave no moral

---

[1] It is believed the first script came into use around 3000 BC.

leadership to society. The one attempt to establish monotheism and an ethical religion (by King Amenhotep IV in the fourteenth century BC) was crushed immediately after his death. Another flaw from the perspective of the just society was that, like all the states of the ancient world, Egypt was heavily dependent on slavery. The state became increasingly rigid and sterile and at last suffocated the initial creative characteristics of Egyptian society. Inevitably, the mighty Egyptian pharaohs succumbed to the more dynamic states to the north.

The second large state in history was Sumer, a Semite kingdom established by King Sargon I around 2400 BC with its capital at Ur. Uniting the warring cities of lower Mesopotamia (present-day Iraq), the new kingdom established a legal system of mutual obligations with its citizens, whereby each citizen contributed to the cost of the state but in return could draw on the state's resources during times of difficulty. Initially women were relatively well-treated; for instance they were given certain rights in case of divorce. Later their position deteriorated as the veil was imposed and a one-sided emphasis on sexual purity developed, manifested in the punishment of death by stoning for an adulteress but not for an adulterer. The Sumerians are given credit for inventing the wheel (for use on a four-wheel chariot), glass, and the baked brick (stones for building were not readily available in the region), and for being the first to manufacture bronze. They also created the first cuneiform script, which was used initially for keeping records of financial transactions. In this script was recorded the oldest extant story in history, the Epic of Gilgamesh, which includes an account of a great flood, perhaps the one later associated with Noah. The Sumerians are also believed to have been the first civilization to make alcohol, in their case from barley. In the view of many, including this writer, the latter was a negative rather than positive contribution to the evolution of civilization and the just society. This issue is discussed in Chapter 19.

The Mesopotamian state endured in different forms for some 2,000 years before being finally overthrown by the Persians. Sumer itself began to decline in the early part of the second millennium BC and was subsumed into the kingdom of Babylonia whose centre was in upper Mesopotamia. The greatest of the Babylonian monarchs was Hammurabi, who lived around 1800 BC. His kingdom was some 700 miles long and about 100 miles wide (i.e. substantially larger than the kingdom of Egypt). Hammurabi's great distinction in history, however, was not his military prowess but the fact that he was the first monarch we know of who systematically codified the laws of the state and then had them made generally available to all his subjects on eight-foot high steles (or pillars) erected around the country. The principle that people should know in advance what is expected of them and what sanctions will apply if they fail to follow such expectations is one of the essential features of a just society. Hammurabi is recorded as having said: 'Let the oppressed man who has cause come into the presence of my statue and read carefully my inscribed stele.'

Hammurabi's legal code had 282 clauses dealing with three broad subjects: property, the family, and punishments for crime. The clauses on property implicitly recognized the right of individuals to own property (in itself a limitation on the power of the state) and included the requirement that all sales be properly recorded. They also made it clear, on the other hand, that property ownership brought certain responsibilities vis-à-vis the community: land had to be used to produce crops, the landowner had to maintain irrigation canals in his area and to keep in good repair houses which he rented out, as well as to keep a record of his profits for inspection. The rules concerning the family were heavily in favour of the male head of the household. He had, for instance, a right to control his children until they were married and could even sell their labour. His rights were dominant with regard to marriage contracts for any of his children. A wife who failed to produce children was obliged to find a concubine for her husband, and though she was entitled to sue for divorce in case of cruelty, if she failed to prove her case she would be put to death, which was quite a deterrent. But there was at least equality in the punishment of adultery: death for both parties. Punishments for crime prescribed the death sentence not only for murder, brigandage and criminal negligence, but also for theft, shirking of social responsibilities and false accusation. Nevertheless, criminal systems were relatively mild for the time and included provision for monetary compensation to the injured party as a substitute for physical punishment.

The Babylonian monarchy was overthrown by the Assyrian Empire which, with its capital at Nineveh (in present-day Syria), came to dominate the Tigris–Euphrates region from around 1400 BC to 1200 BC, and then again from about 900 BC to 600 BC. At the peak of its second period the Assyrian Empire included both Palestine and lower (i.e. northern) Egypt in addition to Mesopotamia. The Assyrian state was harsh, even by the standards of the time. It controlled subject peoples through appointed governors, rather than through the normal system of tributary and subservient local rulers, and there was no compunction about deporting whole nations in order to crush opposition – as in the case of Israel and the deportation of the ten lost tribes (732 BC). Nevertheless, the regime did have some progressive qualities, including the establishment of one language (Aramaic), one legal system for the whole region, and the construction of a network of aqueducts to bring fresh water to the population. King Ashurbanipal (699–630 BC) built a huge library (the first ever recorded) that is the source of much of today's information about the ancient world.

This emphasis on learning (in the long run an essential feature of a just society) was continued by the succeeding Second Babylonian Empire which replaced Assyria when the latter was overthrown by the Medes of Persia, and which survived for about 100 years before being defeated in its turn by the Persian king, Cyrus the Great. A highlight of this regime was the great interest in literature taken by King Nebuchadnezzar (605–562 BC).

To summarize, the Egyptian and Mesopotamian states made at least four broad contributions to the heritage which was to develop into the idea of the just society. First, both states maintained relative peace over significant areas for a considerable period of time; second, Egypt set an important example in the relatively liberal treatment of women; third, the Mesopotamian states pioneered a common code of law and justice; and finally, there was encouragement of learning.

CHAPTER 2

Judaism: Monotheism and Ethics

THOSE early empires were to be outshone by the three new civilizations that came into being in Palestine, Persia and India – inspired by monotheistic and ethically-centred religions – during the last millennium-and-a-half BC. The general raising of ethical standards in society which resulted from their influence is one of the greatest factors in the evolution of civilization and the development of a just society.

It is possible that other early societies were inspired by religions which were originally monotheistic and ethical, but if this is the case, there is now no historical record. By the time such societies had emerged from the obscurity of pre-history their belief systems were riddled with superstition and were polytheistic in structure. Gods and goddesses proliferated, mostly associated with various aspects of nature. Sometimes there would be an effort to make one god dominant in the interest of the state power, as in the worship of Marduk in Babylonia and Ashur in Syria. Such systems might be considered cryptic-monotheistic. However, like the fully polytheistic religions they offered little – if any – ethical guidance and for that reason had virtually no lasting influence on the development of civilization and the idea of the just society.[1]

Such was not to be the case with the great monotheistic faiths we will now consider. The first of these came to the Hebrews, an obscure pastoral tribe having apparently migrated from Sumeria at the beginning of the second millennium BC and settled in the land of Canaan, later to become Palestine. The religion of the tribe was founded by Abraham, but there were traditions linking it with an earlier religion associated with Noah and one even earlier associated with Adam, perhaps going back as far as the fourth millennium BC.[2]

[1] As mentioned earlier there was an attempt to establish an ethical religion associated with the worship of one God, the Sun God Aton, in fourteenth-century Egypt, but this only lasted for a few years.

[2] It is interesting that this calculation gives a date for Adam which coincides approximately with the coming of the first civilizations.

The traditions, though obscure, indicate some very early concepts of ethical religion. The story of Adam, for instance, can be seen as the first time man began to understand the difference between good and evil, right and wrong. The story of Noah can be seen as demonstrating the consequences for society when it fails to act on such distinctions. With Abraham, the religion took concrete shape in the form of a covenant between God and man whereby God would give guidance for man's spiritual development on condition that man would abide by God's laws. If man did not abide by the agreed Covenant he would be punished. Implicit in the religion, though not often mentioned, was belief in a spiritual life after death.

In the seventeenth century BC during a period of famine, one part of the Hebrew tribe (the Israelites) followed Joseph to the prosperous empire of Egypt where they were allowed to settle. By the fourteenth century the tribe in Egypt had fallen into bondage, from which it escaped by migrating back to Canaan under the leadership of a new prophet, Moses. In His youth, Moses had been outraged by the injustice of the Egyptian treatment of the Israelites and had once killed an Egyptian overseer to save a slave who had been badly beaten. Fleeing into exile, He received the first intimations of his station as a Messenger of God. The new prophet inspired a spiritual rebirth in His people by renewing the Covenant of Abraham and restating it in terms of specific teachings centred around what came to be known as the Ten Commandments.

A major concern of the teachings of Moses was to keep the religion of Abraham – monotheistic and ethical – pure of the corruptions of the decaying religions of the region, particularly those current among the Canaanites and the Philistines who were polytheists. Common practices of these decadent religions included blood sacrifice, temple prostitution (the story of Sodom and Gomorrah is perhaps a reference) and other fertility rites such as the cooking of sacrificed kid in the milk of its mother. The first four of the Ten Commandments made the distinction clear and put emphasis on the need for continued reminders – an emphasis which was to prove all too valid almost immediately, in the incident of the golden calf, and later when on various occasions the rulers of Israel compromised with other religious practices so as to placate their neighbours.

Thou shalt have no other Gods before me.
Thou shalt not make unto thee any graven image . . .
Thou shalt not take the name of the Lord, thy God in vain: . . .
Remember the Sabbath day, to keep it holy. Six days shalt thou labour . . .[3]

[3] *Exodus* 20:3–9.

The practice of male circumcision and dietary laws, though primarily of importance from the point of view of the physical health of society, also served the purpose of strengthening the distinction between pure and corrupt religion. With regard to social teachings, the Mosaic law put emphasis first on spiritual detachment and the idea that earthly goods are a divine trust. A second theme is the injunction to treat one's neighbour as oneself (*Leviticus* 19:18) and to serve one's fellow human beings; to be concerned for the poor and the weak, the afflicted and oppressed. There should be a limit set on the power of those who are strong. The misfortune of others should not be exploited and free loans should be made to those who are in trouble. Every man has a right to life, work, leisure, clothes, food and shelter. Some of the key standards of behaviour required are spelt out in the last six of the Ten Commandments:

Honour thy father and thy mother . . .
Thou shalt not kill.
Thou shalt not commit adultery.
Thou shalt not steal.
Thou shalt not bear false witness against thy neighbour.
Thou shalt not covet thy neighbour's house . . .[4]

The new religion of Moses was a powerful inspiration to the Israelite tribes. They became united, and there eventually emerged a vibrant civilization which manifested itself in the kingdoms of David and Solomon. These monarchs held sway over a large area of Palestine and Syria in the eleventh and tenth centuries BC at a time when there was a temporary eclipse of the power of the Mesopotamian states. With the help of the skilled Phoenicians the once pastoral people built a new capital city – Jerusalem. Here were to be found many fine edifices, including the pride and joy of the Israelites: the 'First' Temple (also known to history as Solomon's Temple) that housed the Ark of the Covenant. This was the greatest time of peace and prosperity for the Israelite people, 'and Judah and Israel dwelt safely, every man under his vine and under his fig tree, from Dan even to Beersheba, all the days of Solomon'.[5]

After the death of Solomon the unity of the tribes was lost; Judah, the largest, broke away from the rest to form its own southern kingdom with Jerusalem as its capital, whilst in the north the remaining tribes were confined to a rump kingdom of Israel. Slowly the new kingdoms went into decline and eventually Israel was

[4] *Exodus* 20:12–17.
[5] *I Kings* 4:21–25.

conquered by the revived Assyrian Empire in 732 BC. A large part of the population was deported and became lost to history (the ten lost tribes). Judah endured approximately another 140 years but then, in 587 BC, succumbed to the Babylonians who razed the walls of Jerusalem and the Temple itself, and sent a large number of the 'Jews' into Babylonian exile.

During this tragic period, when the Israelite people fell from heights of glory to depths of bondage, there emerged a series of prophets who held up a metaphorical mirror to their nation. All were shown the failings, not only of the people, but of their rulers as well. This was unprecedented; hitherto religions had always been subservient to the state. The Old Testament prophets presented the revolutionary concept that all men were equal in the sight of God, that kings might not do simply as they liked, and that the moral code was God-given and independent of the state's authority. This heritage is the basis of Western liberalism and the concept that state power must be confined within a moral framework independent of the state.

Elijah taught that God was a God of righteousness, and also the God of all peoples, not just a tribal God. Amos spoke for the poor, denounced religious hypocrisy and said that God can see all our actions; there was hope for all if the laws were obeyed. Isaiah (one of the first in history to speak out against alcohol) denounced hypocrisy by making a distinction between ritual and piety. He promised that one day a Messiah would appear and bring justice and peace for all men. Jeremiah and Ezekiel spoke of personal responsibility to God for one's actions, and said that worship could take place anywhere: it did not have to be reserved for the Temple.

A temporary respite to the woes of the Jewish people occurred at the end of the sixth century BC. Babylon was defeated by the Persians, whose king allowed the Jewish exiles in Babylon to return to Jerusalem and rebuild the 'Second' Temple (518–516 BC). This period ended two hundred years later when Alexander the Great defeated the Persians and took control of the whole region. After Alexander's death, Jerusalem and the surrounding areas were dominated by the Ptolemys of Egypt and the Seleucids of Syria, both essentially Greek dynasties. In the long run this was advantageous to Judea, as it brought it into contact with the widening and dynamic world of the Mediterranean; the Torah was translated into Greek and so became available to a much larger audience than before. In spite of this, many Jews bitterly resented Greek culture which they saw as an assault on their own religion and culture. They took particular exception to the Greek style of dress and to the sports hippodromes.

Matters came to a head in 167 BC when Antiochus IV profaned the Temple by rededicating it to Zeus. A popular rebellion broke out, led by the Maccabee brothers who drove out the Greeks and for a time re-established an independent Jewish state where their religion could be practised without interference. This was the only time in the entire history of the ancient world when a successful revolt took place in defence of a religion.[6]

In an effort to maintain its independence from Greece, the new state allied itself with Rome, the rising power of the region. This strategy only worked for a short time. Soon the new state was to be swallowed up by its Roman ally as the latter expanded to dominate the whole Mediterranean world. Though at first tolerant (they worked through tributaries such as Herod the Great who extended and embellished the Second Temple), the Romans soon showed the same insensitivity as the Greeks had done towards this talented but 'fanatical people' who numbered about one sixth of the population of the Empire. Examples of Roman arrogance included the taking of money from the Temple in lieu of arrears of tax, and asking for sacrifices on behalf of Rome. The Jewish people rose up once again and drove the Romans from Jerusalem. After some delay (this was the time of the succession struggle in Rome following the death of the Emperor Nero) the Romans recaptured Jerusalem (AD 70) and destroyed the Second Temple as a punishment. The rebellion held out under the leadership of Eleazar ben Jair at the hilltop fortress of Masada for another three years, until finally in desperation the last 960 committed mass suicide rather than surrender.

There was yet another Jewish revolt (AD 132–135) after the Emperor Hadrian ordered Jerusalem to be rebuilt as a Roman settlement and renamed Aelia Capitolina. This was also crushed with typical Roman ruthlessness and the Jewish people were expelled from the city and forbidden to return.

It is easy to dismiss these failed revolts against the Romans as the unreasoning acts of reactionary religious fanatics. Some of those involved were indeed fanatics, but the events represent far more than that. They are among the earliest and best known struggles in history of a people determined to be free to practise their own religion and culture without outside interference. Without such freedom men cannot be truly themselves. The Jewish revolts demonstrated for the first time that no state can be considered just until it has the self-confidence to allow and encourage all its peoples to develop their own culture. When this is achieved there is enrichment and

[6] Celebrated at the Feast of Hanukkah and remembered through the seven-branched candelabra.

deepening of the whole human experience. The Maccabee revolt and Masada will ever be bright lights shining in the annals of human freedom.

The expulsion from Jerusalem was the formalization of a process of dispersal which had been going on for several centuries. It was to continue nearly 1,800 years until the recreation of Israel in 1948. During this period when the Jewish people spread to all parts of the world, often suffering the fiercest persecution, their religion gave them strength and sustenance not only to survive as a people but to make major contributions to the world's heritage in the arts and sciences. One of the greatest of many very distinguished personalities in the history of this period was Maimonides (AD 1135–1202), physician to the great and noble Muslim warrior king, Saladin (1137–1193). Maimonides rationalized and highlighted the teachings of Judaism in 'Thirteen Articles of Faith' which were listed in *A Guide for the Perplexed:* the existence of God, the Creator of all things; His absolute unity; His incorporeality; His Eternity; His omniscience and foreknowledge; the spiritual resurrection of the dead; the superiority of Moses over all other Judaic prophets; the Torah as God's revelation to Moses; the Torah's immutability; the obligation to serve and worship God alone; reward and punishment according to deeds; the existence of prophecy; and the coming of a Messiah.

Though the religion of Moses continues to show remarkable vitality despite its three thousand years, it is clear that for the last two thousand, at least, it has deteriorated into a tribal or national religion despite the breadth of its original teachings. It has been a means for keeping unity in a relatively small nation, but it no longer has the power to bring together in unity people of all backgrounds, which may be seen as a prime purpose of religion. Though the Jewish people became disillusioned with the teachings about the Messiah, particularly in the seventeenth century because of the appearance at that time of a false prophet who temporarily persuaded many of his genuineness,[7] what in the writer's view is most potent now in this Faith is, in fact, the promise of a Messiah who will unite mankind and establish a new Jerusalem.

[7] Sabbati Zevi, who claimed to be the Jewish Messiah, subsequently recanted under pressure from the Turks (he lived in the Ottoman Empire) and became a Muslim.

CHAPTER 3

Zoroastrianism and the Persian Empire

FOR over a thousand years one of the world's most influential religions was Zoroastrianism, the second of the monotheistic and ethical faiths. When exactly Zoroaster[1] lived is a matter of dispute: some argue for the seventh century BC and some for a much earlier date around 1500 BC. Zoroastrians themselves claim the earlier of the two dates, which would make their faith slightly older than the religion of Moses, though later than that of Abraham. But even if the latter claim is true, Zoroastrianism does not seem to have had a significant impact in the world until nearly half a millennium after David and Solomon.

Zoroaster is reputed to have been the son of a priest of the old Aryan polytheistic religion who lived in the region to the east of the Caspian Sea (Parthia). After being married and having children He underwent a series of visions which compelled Him to preach against the prevailing violence and injustice of society. He was at first imprisoned, but was later released for curing the sick horse of King Vishtaspa: in consequence the king became one of His followers. Zoroaster was eventually murdered at the age of 77 by a priest of the old order.

Zoroaster's teachings are recorded in the Gathas, the oldest section of the Avesta, the holy book of Zoroastrianism. They revolve around the concepts of one God and a spiritual life after death. His main concern was the establishment of peace, order and justice. Life is a struggle between the forces of good and evil. All men are responsible for their own actions throughout their lives and deathbed conversions will not change the record when accounting to God. No distinction is made between the souls of men and women, and consequently in the Zoroastrian Faith women have been treated more equitably than in most other cultures.[2] He puts great emphasis

[1] Zoroaster is the Greek version of the original Zarathrustra.

[2] For instance, a woman has the same rights as a man until she is married; she can refuse a suitor; she has the same right to a divorce; and no distinction is made with regard to the laws of inheritance. The main difference is that only men can be priests.

on truthfulness (in the language of Zoroaster, the same word is used for a lie and for evil); honesty and reliability are essential in a just society; and greed and anger are equally deplored. Cleanliness is also given a high priority; the teachings including the particular injunction to keep the home free of dirt and decayed matter, which represent the evil force of death (disease) against the good force of life. He advocated moderation in all things, and condemned both asceticism and selfish concern for the material things of life. Great emphasis is also placed on educational work:

Be diligent for the acquisition of education, for education is the seed of knowledge and its fruit is wisdom,[3] and wisdom is the order of both worlds (i.e. the material and the spiritual) . . . education is an ornament of prosperity, a protector in adversity, a helper in difficulty and a profession in adversity.[4]

. . . work is the salt of life. Without work our life is idle and useless.[5]

It is incumbent on all men to be concerned with the well-being of others and to be generous in their actions:

If one practises many duties and meritorious deeds, but does not give anything to the poor then it is impossible for the soul to go to heaven.[6]

These teachings can be summarized as three broad principles: good thoughts, good words, and good deeds.

Virtually nothing is known about the new Faith in its early period. However, by the sixth century BC it is apparent that it was widely accepted among the Persians although it was not an official religion and had already to some degree become mixed with polytheistic elements from decadent Aryan beliefs. It first became of significance in world history when the Persians under Cyrus the Great and the Seleucid dynasty established their empire after defeating all the great states of the region: Media (549 BC), Lydia (547 BC), Babylon (539 BC) and Egypt (525 BC). The new empire was by far the largest ever established up to that time in any part of the world, and included modern-day Iran, Iraq, Syria and Turkey as well as ancient Thrace, Palestine and lower Egypt. The Persian monarchs indeed had justification for claiming the title 'King of Kings', ruler of a world state. With its capital in Persepolis, the Persian Empire was divided into twenty provinces, each with its own governor. It was united by a network of roads which made for rapid communication and central

[3] The name given to God by Zoroaster was 'Ahura Mazda', or the Lord of Wisdom.

[4] John R. Hummells, *Zoroastrianism and the Parsis*, p. 35.

[5] Ibid.

[6] Ibid.

control. The Empire was noted for its tolerance of the cultures of its component nations, a policy which has been described as being without parallel in the Near East. An example was the release, as noted in Chapter 2, of the Jewish people from the Babylonian Exile and assistance in rebuilding the Temple, acts which earned Cyrus and his successors the high regard of the beneficiaries. The civilization of the Persian Empire has been admired for its beauty and gentleness: the love of flowers, gardens and poetry – a tradition which continues in Persian culture to the present day despite the onslaught of narrow-minded fanatics. Though there were often bloody power struggles at court, the Empire itself brought peace for a period of some two hundred years to a huge region which at the time was in many ways the most advanced part of the world.

Following the victories of Alexander the Great in the last third of the fourth century BC the Persians and cousin nations were temporarily eclipsed. They re-emerged less than a hundred years later with the establishment of Parthia, a new and powerful state which was to become the strongest opponent of the Roman Empire. During this period Zoroastrianism had a significant influence on both the Greeks and the Jews, and it is credited with having more adherents at the time of Jesus than any other religion in the Middle East. The religion was also linked with Christianity through the legend of the three wise men, the Magi, who were of the Zoroastrian Faith.

Parthia was subsumed into a revived Persian Empire ruled by the Sassanian dynasty from AD 225 to 651. The new Empire initially continued the tradition of tolerance towards other religions: Christianity, Judaism and Buddhism. Two developments eventually undermined this policy. First, Zoroastrianism became the formal state religion of Persia, complete with a supreme priest, a portrayal of God as a national God dressed as a warrior king, and the formalization of a large number of rituals such as worship in front of the sacred fire (a symbol of purity) and exposure of the dead on mountain tops to be devoured by vultures. This last was in obedience to the injunction not to pollute the sacred elements – earth and water – with decayed matter, and is, according to some, a final act of charity. (It is also seen today as an egalitarian mode of disposal, making no distinction between rich and poor.)[7] In common with later practice in medieval Europe, it was the priests who became the

[7] This was the period when the holy book of the religion, the Avesta, was compiled. In addition to the ancient Gathas which recounted the discussions, exhortations and revelations of the Prophet, it contained many sections on ritual and religious practices. The Avesta is the only part of the early literature of the religion which has survived; and it is now known only in outline through the Dinkard, a much later record from the 9th century AD.

scribes and recorders of the Empire because they were the main body of the literate. The second factor which mitigated against tolerance was the adoption of Christianity as a state religion by the Roman Empire in the fourth century AD. As a result of this development the kings of Persia came to see anyone who was not a Zoroastrian as non-patriotic, and Christians in particular as traitors.

It is interesting that at this time an attempt was made to build a bridge between the two religions by a Parthian named Mani (AD 216–276) who claimed to be an apostle of Jesus and who tried to found a new universal religion based on the teachings of both Zoroastrianism and Christianity. At first Mani won some acceptance, but eventually he was executed at the instigation of the Zoroastrian priesthood. For several centuries remnants of Manichaeism survived in various parts of the Middle East and the Mediterranean but eventually it died out under persecution from Zoroastrians, Christians and Muslims alike. One of the last strongholds in the West was the neo-Manichaeistic sect of Christianity known as the Albigensians, centred in southern France, who were crushed in a 'crusade' at the beginning of the thirteenth century.

The decline in the spiritual power of Zoroastrianism (which had already begun) speeded up as a result of its adoption as a state religion and the growth of a complex system of ritual. This process was greatly augmented by the overthrow of Persian power by the Arab followers of Muhammad and then by the conversion of most Persians to the new religion. Nevertheless, the tradition of moderation and culture associated with the Zoroastrian Faith had a moderating impact on the followers of Islam, as the flowering of the Persian arts during the Middle Ages bears witness.

There are today only two hundred and fifty thousand or so Zoroastrians left. Most are in Bombay where they are known as Parsis, descendants of those who fled persecution in Iran; there is also a smaller group in central Iran and communities scattered across North America. They are known for their higher than normal standards of education, their honesty, cleanliness, the absence of begging, high sexual morality (reputedly there is no such person as a Zoroastrian prostitute) and their charity and care of the poor. Zoroastrianism is now a matter of inheritance from one generation to the next, and, as with Judaism, its adherents long ago lost interest in converting others and bringing about the era of peace and justice for which Zoroaster worked. Yet the spiritual qualities of the present-day community are an example to the rest of the world, a reminder of the religion's once-great spiritual power and its contributions to the advancement of civilization. Perhaps the most important aspect of its teachings today is the expectation of the coming of a new Prophet (the Shah Bahram) who will found a true universal religion which will unite all mankind:

When a thousand two hundred and some years have passed from the inception of the religion of the Arabian and the overthrow of the Kingdom of Iran and the degradation of the followers of My Religion, a descendant of the Iranian Kings will be raised up as a Prophet. (Dinkard)

CHAPTER 4

Hinduism: A Perspective of the Universe

IN THE Indus valley over an area of half a million square miles lived a people belonging to an advanced civilization. There were cities, built on a grid system, whose populations numbered up to 30,000. There were houses with baths, plumbing and good drainage, made of uniformly-sized bricks. Arising around the 24th century BC, the Harappa civilization invented the Sanskrit script and a standard system of weights and measures; it made use of cotton cloth and constructed public buildings for the storage of grain. It is not clear whether its peoples were ever united into a large state or remained a collection of independent city states, nor is it known if it had any trade contacts with nearby Sumeria.

The Harappa civilization collapsed in the period 1800–1500 BC apparently under the onslaught of Aryan invaders from the north and west. The Aryans brought with them their own Vedic polytheistic religion; over time it merged with the religion of the earlier inhabitants to become the Hindu religion.[1] Very little is known of the origins of this great and rich Faith, but a tradition recorded in the Bhagavad Gita (Sacred Story),[2] the Upanishads (Commentaries), and elsewhere in Hindu literature, tells of a great Prophet named Krishna who was believed to be the incarnation of Vishnu (the Preserver), one of the three facets of the universal God (the other two were Brahma the Creator, and Siva the Destroyer or Cleanser). Of when or where Krishna lived there is no record, though tradition has it that He was a prince. He is associated with teachings of a universal personal God and the idea of renunciation through action. Two main themes run through Hindu belief: to always seek the truth and to live a harmless life.

In pursuit of the search for truth, there have developed six aspects or facets to thought: logic, the use of numbers, meditative yoga, the

---

[1] 'Hindu' comes from the Persian, meaning inhabitants of the Indus river area.

[2] The most important section of the Mahabarata, one of the two gigantic epics of Hindu literature.

practice of right action (*karma*), *vedanta* or appreciation of the illusions of reality, and the understanding that man suffers for the wrongs he commits. Truth is also approached by recognizing two fourfold aspects of life. The first divides life into four chronological stages: childhood and youth, when one is educated by one's elders; adulthood, when one marries and raises a family; middle age, when (the children having left home) one is free to devote one's energies to the services of society; and old age, when one prepares for the time of shedding the physical husk. The second aspect is recognition of one's role in society in one of four basic classes which correspond to parts of the body of Brahma the Creator: the Brahmin (mouth) class of priests who minister to the spiritual needs of society; the Kshatryas (arms) class of priests and warriors for administration and defence; the Vaisyas (thighs) class of farmers, craftsmen and tradesmen who provide food, clothing and shelter and other material needs; and the Sudras (feet) class of labourers who do the physical work. Such classes were not to be hereditary; individuals could, in theory, move from one to the other as they developed. Truth, as envisaged in Hindu scriptures, includes an appreciation (virtually unique until modern times) of the vastness of the universe both in space and time, and a breadth and tolerance of ideas which strikes a sympathetic chord in modern minds. One aspect of Hindu tolerance is the belief that God may manifest himself as an *avatar* (or prophet) many times in history, but that all religions that result are essentially one. Krishna is recorded in the Bhagavad Gita as having said: 'Whatever God a man worship, it is I who answer his prayer.' As in other religions, there is the promise of a golden age in the future.

The second theme of Hindu teachings, the injunction to live a harmless life, is a positive rather than a negative, and means doing what will benefit oneself, other persons, and indeed nature as well. The teachings in support of this theme put emphasis on the family, the exalted position of women, cleanliness, charity, a ban on alcohol, and kindness to animals (which has as a corollary a vegetarian diet).

These pure teachings, conducive to a wise and contented society, were overlaid virtually since the beginning of recorded history with a vast array of practices and rituals which corrupted the religion and greatly reduced its spiritual power. Hinduism incorporated into its structure a whole pantheon of gods and goddesses, so that in practice it became for the majority a polytheistic religion.[3] At various times

[3] The three aspects of God no longer include Brahma, who has been replaced by the mother goddess Shakhti. In some manifestations the latter is portrayed as the evil goddess Kali, in whose worship certain groups broke all religious taboos concerning the consumption of meat and alcohol and indulged in illicit sexual practices; an extreme group, the Thugs, raised funds through highway robbery and murder by strangulation.

and places it reverted to the practice of blood sacrifice. The teachings concerning responsibility for one's actions developed into a belief in the transmigration of souls and reincarnation. The position of women was greatly reduced by such practices as child marriage, polygamy, a ban on widows remarrying (even when the marriage was not consummated), and suttee – the immolation of the widow on the funeral pyre of her husband. Extreme and useless asceticism was encouraged, while an exaggerated respect for nature resulted in a lack of equilibrium – for instance, the cow being considered of more value than humanity. The early emphasis on cleanliness seems to have been largely forgotten. Worst of all has been the growth of a rigid and all-pervasive caste system which has condemned a large part of the population (the Untouchables, who are outside the system) to a permanently inferior position in society.

There have been several attempts to reform Hinduism and take it back to its original purity. From the fifteenth to eighteenth centuries AD various religious leaders laid stress on the oneness of God and the brotherhood of man, and deplored the excesses of ritual and the caste system. Hinduism has produced many saints, of whom the most renowned in modern times was Mahatma Gandhi (1869–1948) who spoke out vigorously for the Untouchables, and who as he lay dying raised his hand to bless his assassin. Governments, most notably that of the Republic of India, have taken action (with, it must be said, varying degrees of success) to ban the worst corruptions such as thuggery, suttee, child marriage, polygamy and the ban on the remarriage of widows.

These reform movements have on occasion led to the establishment of separate sects and even a separate religion. The first of which we have record is Jainism, founded around 600 BC by Vardhamana who was given the title Mahavira (Great Hero) and who lived in the area now known as Patna. The Jains in particular abhorred the blood sacrifices of the Vedic traditions, and Jainism's main purpose became to teach man the highest perfections according to the three principles of right knowledge, right faith, and right conduct. Later it was to split in two, one group putting extreme emphasis on the assertion that there could be no salvation for women. Today about two million strong, Jainism is very tolerant of other religions and makes no attempt to spread its own teachings. Vastly more important in the perspective of history was the reform movement led by Gautama Buddha which began in the same era as Jainism.

CHAPTER 5

Buddhism and the Mauryan Empire

SIDDHATTHA GAUTAMA (563–483 BC), born the son of a king in the area that is now Nepal, knew all the material pleasures of life from an early age. Coming to manhood, He became dissatisfied with this way of life and left his home to investigate the philosophies of the time, including asceticism, but found none that brought Him peace. Then, at the age of thirty-five, the spiritual experience which he called 'enlightenment' came to him; out of it He developed the theme of the 'middle way' between extreme asceticism and extreme sensuality.

His teachings revolved around the 'Four Noble Truths':

1. That all life is suffering, like a disease of the body (*duhkha*);
2. That suffering comes from desire, greed, hatred and illusion about the true nature of life; and that such attitudes create suffering both for the self and for others;
3. The way to stop suffering is to eliminate desire and to cultivate the opposite virtues: generosity, love and clear insight. These will bring one to a state of spiritual health (Nirvana), a state that can be achieved by every man – whether rich, or poor and oppressed;
4. The way to achieve Nirvana is to follow the three-fold path of wisdom, meditation and morality. The three-fold path is then subdivided into a more specific eight-fold path, in which the first two elaborate on wisdom, the next three on meditation, and the last three on morality:

   1. Right view – an understanding of the Four Noble Truths;
   2. Right thought – the freeing of the soul from thoughts of lust, ill will, cruelty and untruthfulness;
   3. Right effort – the struggle to replace such evil thoughts with good thoughts;
   4. Right mindfulness – vigilant attention to every state of the body, emotion and mind;
   5. Right concentration – deep meditation on the purpose of life;
   6. Right speech – no lying, tale-bearing, harsh language and vain talk;

7. Right action – support of the family and no killing, stealing, sexual misconduct or use of alcohol;
8. Right livelihood – earning one's living without causing harm to others.

Buddha denied the authority of the Vedic scriptures; in particular he did not accept the elaborate ritual, the caste system and the hereditary priesthood which had become characteristics of Hindu practice in his time. The records of His teachings rarely make direct reference to a God, but close perusal shows that (contrary to the opinion of many) there is an underlying assumption of belief in God, and it has been suggested that reticence on this subject may have been designed to make a clear distinction between this religion of ethics and the corrupt superstitions of the prevailing religion, so as to prevent the former being eventually subsumed by the latter.

During His lifetime there gathered around Buddha a group of disciples who after His death began to carry the new Faith to all parts of the Indian subcontinent. The religion reached a peak of glory under King Asoka the Great (274–237 BC). Arguably the noblest monarch in all history, Asoka was the third of the Mauryan dynasty and his dominions, with their capital at Patna in the Indus Valley, embraced Afghanistan and the whole of the Indian subcontinent, including the extreme southern tip.[1] He became a Buddhist early in his reign after the shock of bloody battle, and thereafter he declined to participate in further military conquest. He promulgated a universal law for the government of his kingdom which stressed the dignity of man, religious toleration and non-violence – and he even abolished the royal hunt. He provided a whole range of services for his people, including large-scale irrigation schemes and trunk roads (shaded by specially planted banyan trees and equipped with rest houses every few miles). He called a council of the leading Buddhist authorities to bring together and codify the teachings of Buddha. There was an active programme for promulgating the Faith, which included the conversion of most of the people of Ceylon. Buddhism later advanced into South-East Asia, China and Japan, and for a period of several hundred years in the first millennium AD it was the most widespread religion in the world.

Soon after the death of Asoka the Mauryan Empire began to crack and eventually to fall apart, whilst simultaneously there was a Brahmin reaction against Buddhism. Mighty empires were to succeed each other in the subcontinent over the centuries: the

---

[1] It is estimated that the Mauryan Empire had a population of over 25 million, more than one-sixth of the total world population of the time. McEvedy and Jones, (*Atlas of World Population History*, p. 126.)

Kushans (first and second centuries AD), the Gupta (fourth and fifth centuries AD), the Moghuls (sixteenth and seventeenth centuries), the British (nineteenth century) but none reached the full extent of the Mauryan Empire or the relative peace and prosperity which it brought. Buddhism itself, which eventually lost its hold on India between AD 500 and 1200 as a result of the revival of Hinduism and the rise of Islam, became divided into a number of sects, acquired its own layers of rituals and man-made practices, and lost a great deal of its original spiritual fire. It still has a hidden strength which it shares with other great religions: the expectation of the return in the spirit of its Founder and the establishment of a universal peace:

I am not the first Buddha who came upon the earth, nor shall I be the last. In due time another Buddha will arise in the world, a Holy One, a supremely enlightened One, endowed with wisdom in conduct, auspicious, knowing the universe, an incomparable leader of men, a master of angels and mortals. He will reveal to you the same eternal truths which I have taught you. He will preach his religion, glorious in its origin, glorious at the climax and glorious at the goal, in the spirit and in the letter. He will proclaim a religious life wholly perfect and pure such as I now proclaim.[2]

---

[2] Carus and Nyanatiloka, *Buddha: His Life and Teachings*, p. 201.

CHAPTER 6

Confucianism and the Middle Kingdom

So FAR the discussion has revolved around civilizations associated with three of the world's great river systems: the Nile, the Tigris–Euphrates, and the Indus. This chapter is concerned with a fourth: the remarkable society which grew up in China around the Yellow and Yangtze rivers. The first significant attempt to bring together a number of small states into a large one was made around 1700 BC by the Shang dynasty which ruled some 40,000 square miles (a little smaller than England). This regime was based on slavery; torture and human sacrifice were rife. But it also presided over a society which created a 5,000-character pictograph script, a calendar, a decimal system; which made glass, silk cloth, jade ornaments and diamond drills; and which had a standard currency. In the eleventh century BC a new Chou dynasty came to prominence; it was to rule until the fifth century BC, and counted amongst its achievements the creation of large-scale canal systems and irrigation schemes. The power of the Chou, however, was weak almost from the beginning and deteriorated steadily until in the last four centuries its rule was virtually nominal; the general situation was one of division, violence and anarchy. It was during this period that thinkers debated on how peace and prosperity could be restored. One 'legalist' school argued that the ruler should be given unlimited authority to establish the law and to maintain it by force if necessary, and that profit to society should be a measure of success. Two other schools of thought, Taoism and Confucianism, disputed the 'legalist' view.

The Taoist philosophy was founded by Lao Tze, who is thought to have been born around 600 BC and to have been a librarian at the court of the Chou. The reasoning of Lao Tze, which is summarized in the eighty-one chapters of his 6,000-word book, the *Way*, was that a peaceful society could be established if men submitted to the rhythms of life and nature, and let events take their natural course. Men should act with absolute sincerity, be content and humble, not try to get ahead in the world, and avoid extravagance and boastfulness. They should be concerned to do good for all humanity. Government should be kept to a minimum and be based on a policy of *laissez-faire*. The Taoist philosophy was for centuries a major influence in Chinese culture and dominated government thinking until around the fourth century AD. It modified the development of Buddhism in the Far East; it was from this combination that there grew the contemplative school of Zen Buddhism.

In many ways the philosophy of Confucius was the direct opposite of the generally quietist approach of Taoism. Confucius (551–479 BC) was probably descended from impoverished nobility. In his youth he was poor and earned his living by keeping accounts. Self-taught, by the time he reached old age he was considered to be the most educated man in the country. Like others he was deeply concerned about the prevailing state of anarchy and violence. He believed that order could be achieved only by establishing a new standard of personal integrity, and then by persons of such integrity becoming the agents of government. He travelled throughout the land gathering around him a band of students as he went. His style was non-authoritarian and undogmatic, and his method of teaching was to ask questions.

His philosophy, known as 'The Way of Jan' (humility or love), sees mankind as one large family and is aimed at establishing harmony and peace at all levels of society: the individual, the family and the state, but using a more activist approach than that of Lao Tze. Each individual has the right, responsibility and duty to make his own decisions. In approaching these decisions he should have integrity and sincerity. His attitude to others should be one of love and understanding. 'Virtue is to love men: wisdom is to understand them.' It should reflect service and proper respect or propriety:

The truly virtuous man desiring to be established himself, seeks to establish others; desiring success for himself, he strives to help others succeed.

Confucius saw the family as the bridge between the individual and society; here the child could experience love and learn to love those around him. He emphasized the mutual support of members of the family and in particular the duty of children to be obedient and to look after their parents in old age. He saw the state as a cooperative enterprise: the object of government was not the pleasure of the ruler but the well-being of the subjects. If the state failed in its responsibilities the people had the ultimate right to overthrow it. The state should be well-ordered, and administered by disinterested, well-educated men capable of making good laws. Ministers and other agents of government should be chosen on the basis of merit by competitive examination, without discrimination of race, class, religion or sex. Recognition should be given to the hierarchy of rank. Government, wherever possible, should rule by example rather than by force; it should not indulge in useless wars and it should minimize taxes and punishment – torture should be abolished. A major function of the state was to educate the people and to provide schools for every community.

Confucius was a deeply religious man. His teachings assume the existence of a Supreme Being and a spiritual afterlife, and he was concerned to keep religion free of superstition and excessive ritual. However, his teachings are mainly concerned with the practical problems of establishing peace on earth and he has never been considered a religious teacher or a prophet.

The Confucian teachings were later summarized under eight steps by his pupil, Tzeng Tsu (505–436 BC),[1] in a book called the *Great Learning*:

1. investigation of things;
2. extension of knowledge;
3. sincerity of the will;
4. rectifying the mind;
5. cultivating the personal life;
6. regulating the family;
7. ordering the state;
8. bringing peace to the world.

Though Confucius never achieved recognition by the state in his own lifetime, and in that sense died a disappointed man, his ideas did gradually gain acceptance. When China was eventually united under the Han dynasty Confucianism was declared the official state philosophy (136 BC); since then Confucianism has remained a dominant force in Chinese civilization. The Han dynasty itself established for some 400 years (202 BC–AD 221)[2] an empire which rivalled Rome in size and prestige. Amongst its achievements were the establishment of a professional civil service whose staff had passed a standard examination, a nationwide education system, a standard script, the invention of paper, the unification of the laws, standard weights and measures, the first Chinese dictionary, annals recording the history of the country, the construction of roads of standard width and carts and chariots of standard size, and a great wall to protect the Empire from the barbarians of the north. The regime was tolerant of differing religions and did not resist the

---

[1] Also quoted as 483–402 BC.

[2] The first Emperor of China was Shi Huang Ti (221 BC) of the Chin dynasty, but that dynasty lasted only twenty years and was succeeded by the long-lasting Hans.

coming of Buddhism.

For some three hundred years after the fall of the Han there was an interregnum, but without the same violence and anarchy that had prevailed during the time of Confucius. At the end of this period the country was united again under the Sia (AD 589–618) and then the T'ang (AD 618–906) dynasties; the Empire, now the largest and most powerful in the world, became known to its subjects as the Middle Kingdom. The period was distinguished by the excellence of its central administration, a rise in levels of cultural sophistication and wealth, the building of the Grand Canal between the two great river systems and a continued tradition of tolerance for all religious groups including Buddhists, Zoroastrians, Manichaeans and Nestorian Christians. The Empire went from strength to strength under the Siang dynasty (AD 960–1279) who presided over the building of the largest and best-laid-out cities in the world at the time, complete with wide streets, public baths, public lighting and fire protection; the construction of the best ships, equipped with the magnetic compass, watertight compartments and balanced rudders; and an excellent medical system which included the development of a technique for inoculation against smallpox.

But though the Empire was to remain powerful for many centuries, the peaks of glory were past. The Mongol emperors (AD 1280–1368), invaders from the north, were never entirely secure and had to rely on foreigners to help govern an increasingly restive society. There was a period of brilliance under the Ming dynasty (AD 1368–1644) but it is significant that though they were ahead of the Europeans in organizing fleets to cross the Indian Ocean to East Africa they never followed up on their success. During the time of the Manchu dynasty (AD 1644–1912) the Empire fell into decline under pressure from a rapidly growing and restless population which the government was increasingly unable to feed, and from the now more advanced Europeans, competing for trade and colonies. A growing series of popular rebellions, plots and coups ended with the collapse of the Empire in 1912, to be followed by thirty-six years of division and anarchy until the country was again united by Mao Tse Tung.

Just as much of the brilliance of the Chinese civilization can be credited to Confucianism, so too can its fall be related to the weaknesses of the system as practised in later centuries. Confucianism declined into a rigid and ritualistic hierarchical system, unable to adapt quickly to change. The education system became one of learning by rote and was, despite the original intent, limited to a small minority of the population. The educated élite, who were supposed to run the country for the benefit of all citizens, did less and less as the centuries went by for the vast majority of the population – the poor farmers and peasantry. Another deficiency, by no means the least important, was that the philosophy put emphasis almost solely on worldly matters, a characteristic which ultimately undermined its capacity to arouse enthusiasm and motivate action. This deficiency was never to be completely removed by the multiple variations of Taoism or by the coming of Buddhism.

CHAPTER 7

Greece and the Rational Philosophers

THE spotlight now switches westward to Greece, like Israel a relatively small society when compared to the great empires of Egypt, Mesopotamia, Iran, India, and China. Like Israel too, its special contributions to the heritage of the just society were its ideas and experience: accountability of government and the theme of freedom and democracy. It is perhaps no coincidence that later in history these themes were to be further developed in other small-scale societies, such as Switzerland in the Middle Ages and the Netherlands in the sixteenth century, before beginning to flourish in the eighteenth and nineteenth centuries in the larger countries such as Great Britain, France and the United States.

The earliest known Greek civilization was the Minoan, centred in Crete (though with subsidiary colonies on the mainland) from about 1900 to about 1400 BC. These were not rich agricultural lands and the Minoans, like the Greek societies which succeeded them, acquired a certain toughness from the struggle to survive through the cultivation of marginal land (they were the first to develop the vine and the olive) and through sea trade. A second Greek civilization was that of the Mycenaeans during the fifteenth and fourteenth centuries BC. It arose from a mixing of the original inhabitants of the peninsula with invading barbarians from the north, spread all around the Aegean coast and islands, and established the city of Troy in modern-day Turkey. The third Greek civilization developed after another wave of invasions from the north by the Doric and Ionian peoples. This society gradually crystallized in the seventh century BC into a series of small city states of which the most important, in the perspective of history, were to be Sparta and Athens. Both these states were to make significant contributions to the heritage of the just society.

Sparta had two outstanding virtues. Its people put great emphasis on physical and mental fitness and self-discipline, and thus became amongst the best soldiers in the world. Their discipline and skills made it possible for them to execute complex manœuvres in the field, enabling them to defeat armies far larger than their own. (Though it was the Spartans who became a byword for this characteristic, physical fitness had been cultivated by all the Greek states as far back as 776 BC when the annual competition of the Olympic Games first began.) The second Spartan virtue was their simple, communal style of living and the absence in their city of many normal material temptations. It is of interest that they had an iron coinage and that for a long period their wars were purely for self-defence and they did not attempt to set up colonies as did Athens and other states.

The attractive qualities of the Spartans were balanced by two major weaknesses. First, their society rested to a large extent on the exploitation of a lower class of near-slaves (helots) and their society tended to be tense and harshly militaristic as a consequence of the perpetual fear of a violent uprising. Second (and perhaps not unconnected with the first), Sparta was, by sharp contrast with Athens, a closed-minded society ruled by a council of old men which did not respond well to discussion of ideas nor, in the long run, to changing conditions.

In its earliest days Athens was ruled by a king but the monarchy was soon replaced, as in several other Greek states, by a council of hereditary aristocracy (the Eupatridae) which took over most of the ownership of the land. Popular discontent with this arrangement led to the dominance in the sixth century of a series of tyrants who in turn were eventually replaced by a new system of representative government designed by Cleisthenes. One of the leaders of the opposition to the tyrants, Cleisthenes is considered the founder of Athenian democracy (c. 500 BC). Under the new constitution a direct participation[1] assembly (ecclesia) was established for the first time, based on ten districts which cut across the old divisive tribal lines, and on wide participation including resident aliens and emancipated slaves. The ten districts each had fifty representatives on a Council of five hundred (bouje) which prepared the agenda of the assembly and supervised the magistrates. Being somewhat unwieldy in size, the council operated by delegating day-to-day affairs to an Executive Committee of fifty whose membership was rotated between the ten delegations. The assembly also elected a court of nine magistrates, each one of whom was responsible for a specialized function of the state. To provide a means of removing future tyrants without violence, the device of ostracism was introduced.

The new system gave considerable power to the assembly and encouraged genuine debate on issues, which resulted in decisions

[1] i.e. as distinct from a representative assembly.

being made on the merits of an argument rather than on the basis of the interests and individuals involved. Certainly, the system was much more advanced than in the other cities, where there were also assemblies but with restricted membership and very limited powers. It was during the period of early Athenian democracy that Greek civilization reached its peak; it was at this time that the various cities united in defence against invasion by the Persians and successfully defeated them at the battles of Marathon (490 BC), Thermopylae (480 BC) and Salamis (480 BC).[2]

Democratic Athens, like Sparta, suffered many weaknesses, as the great philosophers were to point out. Taken together, they amounted to an 'Achilles' heel'. From the perspective of the twentieth century, some of these were that: (i) it practised slavery like every other society of the time (though it should be added that the institution was implemented less harshly than in many later societies, and was certainly not to be compared with the racially-based slavery of the United States in the eighteenth and nineteenth centuries); (ii) women were treated as second-class citizens unworthy of education, membership of the assembly, inheritance or equal rights in divorce; and (iii) though in theory the assembly was open to attendance by all free men, in fact only about one-eighth of those eligible ever attended. More obvious weaknesses to contemporaries were greed and lack of perspective in the democracy, which led to corruption; the establishment of overseas colonies; and attempts to dominate the other Greek cities. The latter characteristic resulted in a disastrous campaign to capture the Sicilian city of Syracuse (415–413 BC). In the bitterness that followed, democratic Athens executed its most distinguished citizen, the religious and highly-principled Socrates, on charges of atheism and corruption of youth.

In the fourth century, the city democracies fell under the domination of the Macedonian monarchy, remembered principally for the extraordinary military victories of Alexander the Great (356–323 BC). In several respects Alexander's empire was both ephemeral (it broke up immediately after his death) and barbaric (Persians remember Alexander for burning their books and so wiping out much of their cultural heritage, and for the wanton destruction of their capital, Persepolis, while in a drunken rage). However, on the positive side, it can be noted that as a result of Alexander's campaigns there was an intensification of the process of cross-fertilization of the great cultures of Greece and the Middle East, and for several hundred

---

[2] It should be added that the Persian–Greek wars were prompted by Greek support of Greek cities in the Persian Empire which had risen in revolt, rather than by straightforward aggression on the part of the Persians.

years the Greek language became a useful 'lingua franca' for most of the world west of India. These developments have undoubtedly contributed in the long run to the richness of the world's cultural heritage.

Though Athens's experiences with democracy were a major contribution to the growth of the idea of the just society, undoubtedly more influential in the wider perspective was its intellectual life, unprecedented in its depth and scope. It vastly strengthened man's appreciation of rational thought as a means for the advancement of civilization and protection against superstition and prejudice. It brought into sharp focus the complexity and beauty of the universe and the humanity of man. Of special significance were the great tragic poets, Aeschylus (525–452 BC), Sophocles (496–405 BC) and Euripides (480–406 BC), who, building on the literary traditions of Homer's *Iliad* and *Odyssey*, illuminated the depth of human character and in particular showed how pride and self can bring even the greatest men to disaster. Aristophanes (450–358 BC) in his comedies added a new dimension with universal implications to the discussion of public affairs by inviting laughter at various aspects of the political and social life of the city. The fifth-century historians Herodotus and Thucydides in their respective annals of the Persian wars and the disastrous Peloponnesian civil war, set new standards for historical scholarship and intellectual objectivity for the world to follow, and a new dimension to the understanding of society. There were also the great scientists, mathematicians, and engineers: Euclid, Archimedes, Eratosthenes (who worked out the size of the earth) and Hero (inventor of the first steam engine), whose use of observation and logic so enlarged man's understanding of the natural world. One who stands out in the present context was Hippocrates (400–377 BC) who gathered together most of the medical knowledge of the time and contributed to man's ethical life the famous oath which bears his name:

. . . The regimen I adopt shall be for the benefit of my patients according to my ability and judgment, and not for their hurt or for any wrong . . . What so ever things I see or hear concerning the life of men, in my attendance on the sick or even apart therefrom, which ought not to be noised abroad, I will keep silence thereon, counting such things to be sacred secrets.

But towering above the rest were the philosophers: Socrates (470–399 BC), Plato (428–348 BC) and Aristotle (384–322 BC). In his youth Socrates had been a soldier, like others of his class. Unlike many of them, and despite his interest in public affairs, he did not become involved in politics, although many politicians sought his advice. He cared nothing for material possessions, spending most of his later years teaching in the streets and squares of Athens, wearing the same clothes year after year. He was both a mystic and a logician, a man of humour and modesty who tried to raise the ethical standards of Athens by rational argument and personal example. He believed that the care of the soul came before that of the physical body and argued the case for an absolute morality. He was a strong patriot, but believed that it was the state's duty to put first the development in its citizens of their good qualities rather than their immediate material desires. He pointed out two major defects in Athenian democracy. First, it did not require that its leaders be educated in moral philosophy. Second, in consultation it tended to give equal weight to all opinions and there was no way of distinguishing those that were moral (and therefore in the real interest of the citizenry) from those that were not.

Plato, though not a pupil of Socrates, was a strong supporter of his general point of view. He too cared deeply about affairs of state, but was disillusioned with politics itself and generally avoided it, except for giving advice to the rulers of Syracuse. Most of his life was spent working for the Academy he founded, the centre of Athens's intellectual life in the fourth century BC. In discussing the various types of government, he rejected the military model because it is inclined to take action for its own sake, rather than thinking through the consequences; he rejected the aristocratic model because it merely looked after the interests of the rich and powerful; and he rejected the democratic model because of its irresponsibility and tendency to be intolerant (an example being the persecution of Socrates). He concluded that the best form of government was an aristocratic one based on merit. His ideal state, which he described in the *Republic*, would have rulers who had been given a thorough training in all branches of education. He believed that justice would prevail when every person in society carried out the function for which he was best suited. There should be a minimum of private property. He was so preoccupied with the need for order that, perhaps strangely for a thinker, he advocated communal censorship.

Aristotle was in his youth a pupil of Plato at the Academy, and in his middle age he was the tutor of Alexander before he became Emperor. In his *Ethics* he stressed the golden mean, moderation between asceticism and sensuality, and pointed to the value of good habit and meditation. In his *Politics* he touched on nearly all the lasting issues that pertain to social organisation. He argued forcibly that government is there only to serve the interests of the people; like all organisations and individuals it must be subject to the law, which is sovereign. Rulers are accountable to the people. He thought the city state the best form of government.

There were many other schools of philosophy at the time. There were, for example, Diogenes (412–323 BC) and the Cynics, whose reactions to the problems of the time were essentially negative: unbridled criticism and begging as a way to keep body and soul together. More interesting was the philosophy of Zeno (342–278 BC) and the Stoics who advocated acceptance of life with equanimity, and the practice of virtue for its own sake. One interesting aspect of the Stoic philosophy was that in recognizing the equality of all men it condemned the institution of slavery. Certain Stoic philosophical ideas were later to resurface in Christianity; the movement was also viewed with favour by many Romans, including the noblest Emperor of them all, Marcus Aurelius.

CHAPTER 8

Pax Romana

THE thousand-and-more-year history of Rome has had an impact on western civilization equal only to that of Greece and Christianity. In the evolution of the idea of the just society several aspects of this history are of significance: the experience of participatory government (especially during the early and middle years of the Republic), the great revolts against slavery, and the practical example of a near-universal state: the Pax Romana offering widespread citizenship, tolerance of different cultures and eventually a consolidated body of law. There is also a repetition of the lesson of what happens to society when it forgets morality and yields to greed and luxury, and when it fails to establish an orderly system of succession in government.

Rome was originally a colony of the Etruscans, and ruled by a king advised by a senate. This last was composed of the most powerful members of society and elected by an assembly of the people. Rome was essentially an agricultural society, most of its citizens being peasants. All citizens of property were obliged to perform military service. Tradition has it that the monarchy was overthrown in 509 BC and replaced by a republic headed by two magistrates (later to be called consuls). These were elected by the Senate for annual terms. No man could be elected consul unless he was a patrician and had previously held public office; the latter requirement tended to provide for good administration and was to be a consistent feature of Roman civilization for hundreds of years.

Rome prospered under the consuls; over the centuries it gradually expanded and became an empire, a development which resulted, however, in a growing gap between rich and poor and a consequent undermining of the basic institutions. This became particularly evident in the Punic wars against Carthage in the third century BC. Senators and generals grew rich from empire and booty so that they were able to buy up most of the land. Peasants became even more impoverished by long military service and the devastation caused by the invasion of Hannibal (218–201 BC). As a result, they moved to the city: a faceless proletariat with little real stake in society. Their votes could be easily purchased by the rich who kept them pacified with the demoralizing policy of 'bread and circuses': the bread subsidized and the circuses brutal.

Attempts to reverse these developments and to re-establish a more balanced society included a requirement that at least one of the consuls should be of plebeian background (366 BC), a law that the assembly should have the ultimate power, and the establishment of a system of peoples' tribunes whose function was to represent the interests of the poor and who had themselves certain powers of legislation and veto. The nearest the reform movement came to success was in the years before 100 BC when the Gracchus brothers[1] became tribunes. Taking their office seriously, they proposed land reform to reduce extremes of wealth and poverty, greater limits on the power of the Senate (which represented the interests of the powerful), and an extension of citizenship to all other Italians and Latin peoples of the Republic. A revolt of the Latin peoples led to acceptance of the latter programme but otherwise the reforms proposed were not implemented and the brothers were driven from office. As a result, Roman society became even more corrupt, riddled with gangsterism and ruled by a series of harsh military dictators – Marius, Sulla, Pompey and Caesar – who generally upheld the position of the rich but who did not hesitate to play on the hopes of the proletariat when it suited their purpose. Order was eventually restored with the replacement of the Republic with an Empire founded by Caesar Augustus who reigned from 31 BC to AD 17.

One of the ugliest features of the later Republican periods was the growing institution of slavery. Slavery was common to all societies of the ancient world, so much so that it was virtually accepted as a fact of life even by the moral philosophers of Greece and China and the religious leaders of early Judaism, Christianity and later Islam. In Roman law it was recognized that 'slavery is an institution of the law of nations whereby a man is, contrary to nature, subjected to the ownership of another'.

Slavery grew to such an extent that by the end of the Republic it is estimated that half the population were slaves.[2] One reason for this development was that a long succession of military victories had created a newly rich class whose vast land holdings could be most efficiently cultivated if manned by a large number of slaves.

---

[1] Tiberius Sempronius Gracchus (168–133 BC), Tribune in 133 BC; and Gaius Sempronius Gracchus (159–121 BC), Tribune in 123 and 122.

[2] Barratt (ed.), *World Christian Encyclopaedia*, p. 23.

Conveniently, military victories supplied the slaves that were
needed. Slaves were used for a great variety of functions, including
secretarial services, domestic chores, farming, mining, and gladiator
combat in the circuses. The conditions of those working in the mines
and in chain gangs on the large estates were particularly degrading
and resulted in two major slave revolts in 132 (in Sicily) and 104–
100 BC. The practice of having slave gladiators fight each other to
the death in the circus to amuse the crowds was a particularly unpleasant feature of an ugly institution and it was this that led to the
third and most significant slave revolt (73–71 BC) which started at
a gladiatorial training in Capua. Its leader was Spartacus, an able,
noble and humane man, who only wished for the freedom of the
slaves and meant no harm to the Romans. The gladiators were soon
joined by thousands of slaves from the surrounding area of Southern
Italy. The Roman leaders, fearing revolution and economic loss,
reacted fiercely but the slaves, inspired by their fight for freedom,
were able to defeat two Roman armies sent against them. They then
moved north to the Alps where they hoped to disperse and find a new
life for themselves. However, when it came to the time of decision,
the slaves refused to leave Italy, and Spartacus was obliged to lead
them south again in the hope that they could escape to Sicily. They
were finally stopped and defeated by eight legions led by Lucius
Crassus whose vengeance was extraordinary in its ferocity even by
the standards of the time. As an example to all other slaves, the road
from Rome to Appia by the sea was lined with six thousand crosses
on which were nailed the survivors of that last battle. The oppressors
had won, but in the long run it was clear that as a result of this gallant
rising the consciousness of mankind would never be the same again:
sooner or later it would have to be recognized that no stable or just
society could exist with such an institution. The cry of freedom has
echoed down the centuries and in our own time the importance of that
event was symbolized when the left wing of the German Social
Democratic party at the end of World War I adopted the name 'Sparta-
cist'. There was a certain poetic justice nearly twenty years after the
rising was crushed when in the battle of Carrhae (53 BC) the Parthians
inflicted on an army led by the infamous Lucius Crassus the most
severe defeat the Romans had been subjected to since the time of
Hannibal.

The Roman Empire paid lip service at first to many of the
representative institutions of the Republic, but as time went on their
power became less and less. But the Empire itself contributed to the
story of the development of the just society through many of its
most well-known features. An army of twenty-eight legions (about

300,000 men), a competent bureaucracy, a navy and a good system of roads were the basis of Pax Romana: an era of peace and law in the Mediterranean basin and its surrounding areas during a period of some 600 years, including 400 years under the Empire.[3] So long as the peoples of the Empire were law-abiding and paid their taxes, the government was tolerant of differing cultures, making, for instance, special concessions to the Jews, who in deference to their religion were not required as others were to worship the Emperor – though as noted earlier, this particular concession was not enough to win Jewish loyalty. The rights pertaining to citizenship which implied a degree of equality were gradually extended and in AD 212 the Emperor Caracalla finally gave them to all free subjects of the Empire.

The rule of law was taken seriously despite the turmoil which occurred all too frequently at times of succession to the rank of Emperor. Thus the Emperor Justinian (AD 527–565), who temporarily brought back Rome and the western half of the Mediterranean into the Empire after they had been lost to barbarians, made a great effort to have the law consolidated and codified. One major consequence of that effort was the strengthening of the concept of law in Western civilization, obviously a positive step forward in the direction of a just society, despite tendencies towards authoritarianism and patriarchy.

There were, of course, deep flaws in the system. The initial tradition of public service, the strong social ethic, and the sense of equality had long since died; society became more and more hollow, and willing to let barbarians do all the more unpleasant work. Rome itself became like a cancer on the Empire sucking in vast supplies, imposing heavy taxes for its support and giving very little in return. Agriculture, the economic base of society, declined; so did the army because of increasing neglect of the employment conditions of soldiers. Though the Empire was to linger on in name into the Middle Ages, the real end was symbolized by the sacking of Rome by Alaric the Goth in AD 410 (the first time this had happened since the attacks of the Gauls in 387 BC) and again by the Vandals in AD 455 when destruction was undertaken for its own sake.

---

[3] It is estimated that by AD 200 when the world population was about 190 million, some 46 million (24.2 percent) were living in the Roman Empire. This number was exceeded only by the 50–60 million in the contemporary Han Empire of China. (McEvedy and Jones, *Atlas of World Population History*, pp. 21, 126.)

CHAPTER 9

Christianity: The Concept of Brotherhood

IN TRACING the historical development of the idea of the just society, it is now chronologically appropriate to consider the contribution of Christianity. Having roots in both Judaism and the Roman Empire, this religion has, during the course of nearly 2,000 years, spread to just about every corner of the world and it is credited with at least the nominal adherence of about one third of the world's population. (See Table 1.) It is numerically the largest religious community in the history of the world. That being so, it is unlikely that the reader will be unfamiliar with the main facts concerning its history and teachings. Nevertheless, it is important to record here some of those facts because not to do so would be to leave a large gap in the story of the evolution of the concept of the just society. Clearly Christianity has had an enormous impact – particularly in the West – on the ethics of society over an extended period of time; it has been a major source, both direct and indirect, of many of the movements in modern times for political, social, and economic reform.

Jesus of Nazareth is believed to have been born about 4 BC in Bethlehem and to have been a descendant of King David. He had an active ministry of about three years, following baptism by His cousin, John the Baptist, a prophet who criticized the existing state of morality and foretold the coming of One greater than himself. In His talks, Jesus said that He had not come to abolish existing religion but to reform and complete it. His theme was a renewal of the Covenant between God and man, which came to be symbolized in the Last Supper. He called on men to love God, to develop their spiritual qualities and to be prepared to accept persecution rather than deny their Faith. He pointed out that man could not develop his spiritual qualities if he was preoccupied with material things. Outward form is not enough; there is a need for the heart to be pure and free of hatred and lust. A spiritual person should not swear to prove himself, nor should he make a great show of his religion (an implied criticism of the religious hierarchy), nor should he thrust it on those who are not interested. To love God is to love all men (including those previously considered to be enemies) because all are the children of God. We should treat others as we would that they treat us, be slow to judge, be merciful and forgiving, return good for bad, and act as peacemakers. The poor in particular should be our concern. Marriage is a spiritual union and divorce should only be undertaken if a party is in adultery.

Jesus called Himself the Son of God – God's representative on earth; He was seen as the prophesied 'Anointed One' (the 'Messiah' in Hebrew, 'Christos' in Greek) who would renew the spirit of man. He was also known as the Son of David; but it was made very clear in the episode of His forty days in the wilderness that He was not a secular king come to lead the Jews to freedom from the Romans. His kind and gentle personality and the power of His teaching attracted many to His cause, but as always with a Messenger of God there was strong opposition, especially on the part of the priesthood who also saw His claim to independent authority as a threat to their own, and who resented His charges of hypocrisy. Jesus did not shrink from His destiny and went up to Jerusalem, where, following trials by the Jewish religious council and the Roman civil authority, He was crucified. Before He died He promised His followers that He would return in the spirit – for He had yet much to tell them. He warned them to beware of false prophets who would appear as 'wolves in sheep's clothing' and told them they would know the true Prophet by the 'fruit' of His presence and teachings.

The crucifixion at first devastated His followers but then inspired them to continue, and at the instigation of Paul of Tarsus the teachings of Jesus were taken beyond the Jewish community to the wider world outside. The opportunities were great, for many were disillusioned with the beliefs and practices of the time, including the barbarism of Roman 'circus civilization', and were searching for something new. The Pax Romana itself, which ensured relatively safe travel over a vast area and which was united by a single language, made it easier to spread the new teachings.

At first Christianity was rivalled by other popular religions such as that of Isis (originally an Egyptian mother-goddess cult) and Mithraism (which apparently had originated in the old Vedic religion and had been picked up by Roman soldiers when serving in the wars against Persia). Though Mithraism in particular had a relatively advanced ethical system, in the long run it could not compete with Christianity because the latter had the advantage of being mono-theistic, of having a real Founder, not a myth, and of having heroic martyrs who in the face of persecution, first by the Jewish priests (St.

Stephen, the first martyr) and then by the Roman state, were prepared to die rather than deny their faith. As a practical matter, the nascent community was much strengthened because it involved women as well as men in its activities. Nevertheless, growth was slow at first and it was not until the year 200 that it became an officially recognized religion for the first time – in the city of Edessa. The first independent state to become officially Christian was the kingdom of Armenia in AD 287. Even by AD 300 only one-tenth of the population of the Empire was Christian – and they were nearly all in the towns. Soon after, however, the Emperor Constantine made Christianity the official religion of the Empire and it began to spread more quickly so that by AD 500 it is estimated that it had been embraced by over 20 percent of the world's population. By AD 1000 most of Europe, including England, Ireland, Germany, Poland, Scandinavia and Russia as well as the Mediterranean and Ethiopia had to a greater or lesser extent become Christian. There were also outposts in Asia: in Iran, India and even China.

This was a time of glory for the Christian Faith. Christianity proved a source of spiritual strength in the face of the terrible experience of seeing Roman civilization gradually collapse under attack from barbarian invaders. In *The City of God* Augustine (354–430) wrote that what was important was the inner spiritual world, not the physical world, pointing out that when man failed to follow the teachings of God then 'the Mandate of Heaven' might be withdrawn. During this period the Church became the centre of learning in the West, particularly the monks – virtually the only members of society who were literate. Though the Church was to be corrupted by materialism, there were always to be influential groups such as St. Francis (1181–1226) and the Franciscans who set an example of detachment and who devoted their lives to the service of the poor.

Almost from the beginning the message of Jesus was clouded by superstition and division, as has been the case with other religions.[1] It is one sign of the power of these religions that they succeeded nevertheless in making immensely significant contributions to the spiritual advancement of society. From the time of St. Paul onwards, non-Christian ideas (particularly Greek ones) were incorporated into the theological teachings of the Christian churches and it was from such outside sources that there developed the theory that Jesus was God incarnate. Disputes soon began concerning the details of such

---

[1] Even such basic documents as the four gospels of the New Testament (the earliest apparently written more than thirty years after the Crucifixion) give accounts of Jesus's life and teachings which are contradictory in some respects; this might not have mattered in 'ordinary' histories, but in Holy Writ it was to prove problematic.

theories. At first there was a laudable attempt to settle them through consultation between the leading figures at a general church council – a democratic practice dating back to the earliest meetings of the Apostles in Jerusalem. A council in 172 ruled against the gnostic view that the physical world is totally evil and therefore Jesus could not have been human. A much more important council was held in Nicaea in 325 with the support of the Emperor Constantine, which ruled against the view of Arius (260–336) that Jesus was superior to man but inferior to God, and supported the view of Athanasius that He was begotten, not made, by God, and therefore He *was* the Creator. Further rounds in this controversy were settled at the council of Constantinople (381) which rejected the Monophysite theory[2] and reaffirmed that Jesus was 'perfect in deity and perfect in humanity'. The latter decision was not accepted by the Coptic, Syrian, Nestorian and Armenian churches and in leaving the main body of the Church they created the first of what ultimately were to be many hundreds of divisions of the Faith. Another controversy which came to a head in the eighth and ninth centuries concerned the role of images (ikons) in worship: were these symbols or did they have their own *spiritual* significance? This particular controversy contributed to an even more important split of the Church – between the West under the Roman Pope, and the Eastern 'orthodox' churches which had originally accepted the primacy of Rome but in the event would not accept its right to interfere in their affairs. This division was several hundred years in the making before becoming formalized in the eleventh century.

Christianity differed from the non-prophetic religions of the time in its concern for the 'salvation' of the individual and its non-involvement with the state. Consequently it gave little guidance about public affairs except to say: 'Render unto Caesar that which is Caesar's.' Its greatest successes in politics came about when it played the role of objective moral standard-bearer, as in 390 when St. Ambrose (340–397), Bishop of Milan, forced the Emperor Theodosius to do penance for his massacre of the Thessalonians.

However, over the centuries the role of the church as moral standard-bearer in politics gradually deteriorated into crude power struggles with the secular authorities. One fundamental theme was who controlled the clergy. Thus Thomas-à-Becket (1118–1170), Archbishop of Canterbury, resisted the English King Henry II (1133–1189) at the cost of his life when the latter tried to make the clergy subject to the law of the state. Another aspect of this theme

---

[2] The Monophysites argued that Jesus had one, essentially divine, nature, not two natures divine and human.

was who should appoint bishops: the Pope or the local monarch. For the Church, at least theoretically, the point was to maintain the spiritual quality of its leading officers; for the state it was a question of control over wealth and influence. This issue was to come up time and again in European history. An early example was when the reforming Pope Gregory VII (1025–1085) tried to force Henry IV of Germany to submit to him at the dramatic meeting at Canossa in 1077.[3] This particular struggle also had more fundamental implications, for the Pope was in effect asserting a spiritual right to supervise, to nominate and if necessary depose the Emperor of the Holy Roman Empire, an institution which had been founded in AD 800 by Charlemagne (742–814) to be, as its title implied, a new universal Christian state.[4] It is still possible to detect a moral dimension to these types of struggle. However, there was no such dimension when the Papacy became involved in political intrigue and open warfare simply to expand its temporal dominion. The seeds of this particular corruption were planted in the eighth century when Pepin, King of the Franks, donated conquered lands in central Italy to the Papacy. These seeds came to full fruition in the fifteenth century at the time of the early Renaissance Popes.

As the centuries went by the moral leadership of the church institutions declined, especially after the rise of Islam. This was symbolized in the Crusades campaign to recapture and hold Jerusalem for Christianity, an attempt which continued without success for some two hundred years. Jerusalem had been lost to Christianity in the seventh century, at first temporarily to the Persians and then to Islam. The Caliphs had been conciliatory, recognizing the special interests of Christianity in Jerusalem, and all was well until the eleventh century when the Seljuk Turks conquered the area and began to interfere with the passage of pilgrims. Though nominally a spiritual enterprise, the Crusades rapidly deteriorated into a power struggle amongst the various European warlords, and the contrast between the barbarous Christians as compared with the civilized Muslims was shown up when the former captured Jerusalem in 1099 during the first Crusade and put all its 70,000 inhabitants to the sword, whilst the recapture of Jerusalem by the Muslims in 1187 under Saladin was carried out with minimum bloodshed and with courtesy towards all concerned. Perhaps even more ugly was the Fourth (of eight) Crusade which resulted in the

[3] Henry, in a weak political situation in Germany, crossed the Alps in the middle of winter and waited for three days in the snow for the Pope to withdraw his edict of excommunication. It was all a game, and the struggle was to continue for many more years.

[4] A hope never realised, although the Holy Roman Empire was to linger on for a thousand years before being finally terminated by Napoleon in 1806.

sack of Constantinople (1204), capital of Byzantium, the ancient Christian power in the East, in settlement of old religious and political scores.

The Crusades reflected the growing intolerance of the Church and its willingness to use its power to crush those whom it regarded as heretics. Soon after becoming the official religion of the Roman Empire, Christian leaders began to persecute Jews in the Empire and so began that anti-semitic aspect of western civilization which has lasted nearly two millenniums and which was clearly one of the most important factors making possible the Holocaust of the Jews in Hitler's Nazi empire. Nothing could have been further from the teachings of Jesus. However, up until the eleventh century persecution of those with different religious views was relatively mild compared with later practices and most church leaders agreed with the statement of Bernard of Clairvaux (1090–1153) that:

Faith must be the result of conviction and should not be imposed by force. Heretics are to be overcome by arguments, not by arms.

In the twelfth century came the Inquisition and a standard death penalty for heresy. It was used at first against deviant Christians in the crusade against the Albigensians in the south of France but later, particularly in Spain, it was used against Jews, Muslims and even converts to Christianity from these religions (Marranos and Moriscos). In the thirteenth century the Pope authorized the Inquisition to use torture.

But it was the material corruption of the church which caused most indignation, and led to the second major split of Christendom: the Reformation. On the one hand were the bishops of the Church with their ostentatious wealth, and on the other the priests of the people, poverty-stricken and ignorant. Attempts to remedy the situation by imposing celibacy on all the clergy had little effect. By the late Middle Ages by far the worst offenders were the Popes themselves: members of Italy's patrician families, little concerned with spiritual matters and almost totally devoted to their roles as powerful territorial princes. The papacy lost its moral authority; it fell under the domination of France during the period (1305–1375) when its seat was transferred to Avignon in the south of France, and for another forty years (1378–1417) it was split by the Great Schism when rival popes held office simultaneously.

Amongst the earliest critics of the corruptions of the Church was John Wycliffe (1330–1384) who denounced the practices of pluralism (holding of more than one office simultaneously) and non-residence, interference by the church in secular affairs, and all church teachings not based directly on the Scriptures. Another was John Huss (1370–1415), Dean of Prague University, who objected to the sale of indulgences (the practice of selling the churches' forgiveness of sins as revealed in confession), and who in consequence was burnt at the stake. The stand of John Huss was taken up by the Lollards, a group which questioned other practices of the Church including confession itself, the celibacy of the priesthood, the theory of transubstantiation (the physical presence of Jesus in the rites of communion) and even such fundamental issues as the basis of the Pope's authority and the practice of warfare amongst Christians. A third was Girolamo Savonarola (1452–1498), a Florentine monk who before he was burnt at the stake for his outspokenness vigorously attacked the extreme materialism of Pope Alexander VI (1492–1503), one of the notorious Borgia family.

These rumblings were the preamble to the Reformation itself. It began when Martin Luther (1483–1546) nailed his 95 theses to the door of All Saints Church in Wittenburg on 31 October 1517. Luther had been particularly shocked by the brazenness of a 'Jubilee' campaign to raise money (for the building of the new and gigantic St. Peter's Cathedral in Rome) through the sale of indulgences, which he fiercely denounced, along with celibacy and the use of relics. He saw the Scriptures as the Word of God, and as the only religious authority, and believed therefore that they should be made available to all the people through translation from the Latin to the vernacular (he himself was responsible for the translation of the Bible into German – as significant a step in the development of the German language as the King James Bible was to be for the English). In religious matters, Luther taught the Church had no authority over the individual who must be answerable only to his own conscience. In political matters he was more conservative; for instance, he did not give support to the peasants of Germany when they rose up against their oppressors in 1524.

Luther's rebellion (he was excommunicated in 1521) opened a veritable floodgate of criticism of the Church. Amongst the moderates was Huldreich Zwingli (1484–1531) who preached in Switzerland a position generally similar to that of Luther. More radical were the Anabaptists who advocated adult baptism (after the example of Jesus), communal property, and non-violence. Extremists in this group included a group led by John of Leyden, the polygamous dictator of Munster, until savagely suppressed, and the Fifth Monarchy Men[5] of the English Revolution in the seventeenth

---

[5] The 'five monarchies' were those of Babylonia, Persia, Greece, Rome and Jesus.

century. Far more influential in the long run was John Calvin (1509–1564), who like Luther stressed individual responsibility for one's own spiritual development. A special aspect of his view was that man could not bribe his way to heaven with good works or deeds (he was taking the argument against indulgences to the extreme position); what was important was having faith, a matter which was predestined. He believed that a priest's main function was to preach: to draw the attention of the populace to what they should be doing and what they were doing wrong. He also saw the state as having an active role in protecting the moral wellbeing of its citizens. His followers were often portrayed as Puritans: sombre, over-conscious of the temptations of the flesh, intolerant and humourless. This was, of course, less than fair. Calvinists have become known for their honesty and for an ethic of hard work, and as a group they have contributed much to the modern view that government should be elected by and accountable to the people.

The Reformation undoubtedly served to blow fresh air through the institutions of the declining Christian religion and arguably to give it a new lease of life. Its emphasis on individual responsibility for spiritual development and the importance of the Scriptures was an attempt to return to the roots of Christianity, though the focus was not as much on Jesus and His teachings as it might have been, and as a result of exaggerated literal interpretation the spiritual point was often missed. Superstition and ritual were challenged, though again much survived the reformers, including the whole idea of the incarnation of God. To a degree, even the Catholic Church accepted the need for reform, and was stimulated by the reformers to hasten its own Counter-Reformation. As a result bishops were given greater power to supervise activities in their dioceses, there was a tightening up of discipline in the monasteries, and rules were established that an individual could only hold one bishopric at a time and furthermore must be resident in that bishopric.

On the other hand, it can hardly be said that the Reformation rekindled the original spirit of love which came from Jesus. It was followed by one hundred years of religious wars that were amongst the most bloody in European history and the relative unity of western Christianity was shattered into a thousand fragments. There was, if anything, an increase in intolerance and self-righteousness (Luther was just as anti-semitic as the Papacy) and there was little or no interest in the condition of the poor. The motivation of many who joined the reform movement had less to do with the corruption of the Catholic Church than with material advantage, as in the case of Henry VIII of England and the establishment of the Anglican Church.

In the four centuries since the Reformation, Christianity has added much to its spiritual glory, though more through the activities of individuals and groups than through the established churches. Achievements have been particularly noteworthy in the social fields and in activities on behalf of the oppressed such as the anti-slavery movement and the protection of children, women and other manual workers from the worst excesses of the Industrial Revolution, as we shall see later. Leading parts in these activities were played by the Society of Friends (Quakers), the Unitarians, the Wesleyans and the Methodists. The churches, including the Catholic Church, also played a creditable part in moderating the worst aspects of European imperialism thrusting its way to all parts of the globe from the sixteenth to the nineteenth centuries, although again this was to be devalued to a degree by the cruel and intolerant approach to indigenous religions and cultures. In recent years Christians have played a prominent part in the human rights and peace movements, and at long last the Catholic Church has denounced anti-semiticism and stated publicly that the Jewish people have no responsibility for the Crucifixion of Jesus.

Yet it is undeniable that since the Reformation Christianity has continued to decline as a spiritual power. The Reformation wars exhausted Europe spiritually as well as physically, and resulted in a general distrust of religious enthusiasm. This over time turned into strong anti-religious feeling amongst many of the educated, who despised the churches for their superstition and opposition to science (notably in the cases of Galileo and Darwin), for their lack of unity, and for their general materialism and identification with the interests of the wealthier classes. There have more recently been well-meaning ecumenical movements, but attempts at re-establishing unity have been painfully slow and only successful when there is a general fear that otherwise there will be a drastic decline in the total number of believers.

CHAPTER 10

Islam and the Idea of Equality

FOLLOWING the sequence of history, it is time now to turn to Islam, a religion which raised the standard of civilization over the vast regions of the globe stretching from West Africa to the Pacific Islands in the East, from China and Russia in the North to East Africa in the South. It brought a new statement of religion easy for all to understand and appreciate; it strengthened ethical standards; it created a much greater sense of the equality of men; and, for the first time in the evolution of religion, gave guidelines on the adminis-tration of the state.

Islam (the word means submission to God's will) arose in the seventh century AD in Arabia, a vast land, mostly desert, measuring some 600 by 1,000 miles, situated to the east and west of the great river basins of the Nile, Euphrates and the Indus. The people of this land, a mixture of nomads, cultivators and traders, were grouped into a complex system of tightly knit tribes where kinship was the determining factor in a man's life. There were constant quarrels between the tribes; violence particularly in relation to blood feuds was endemic; and generally there was much brutality. Slavery was widespread and there was a low valuation of women – newly-born female babies were often buried alive to eliminate a perceived burden on the family. The chief city of the region, Mecca, was important both as a trading centre on the route between the Mediterranean and the Orient and as a holy place, for it was here that Abraham had built the Ka'ba (Cube) as a place of worship of the one true God. Though the Arabs recognized Abraham's God (Allah) as supreme, they had over the centuries added subsidiary cults of lesser deities and by the seventh century it was said that the city had shrines for some 360 gods. The shrines made of Mecca a centre for pilgrimage, a most profitable business for the inhabitants, and to encourage it agreement had been reached that there should be a four-month truce from inter-tribal quarrels each year.

Muhammad was born in Mecca in AD 570. He was either

posthumous or soon lost His father, 'Abdu'lláh, and at the age of six He lost his mother, Amínih, as well. He was then raised by His grandfather, the foremost chieftain of the city and a member of the Hashemite branch of the ruling Qurayshi clan. Two years later this grandfather died and Muhammad was taken in by His uncle, Abú Ṭálib, also a powerful figure in the city. As a child Muhammad tended sheep, but as He grew up He graduated to trade and travelled with caravans from one centre of trade to another. He became known for the purity of His life and was called Amín, the Trusted One. At the age of twenty-four (AD 594) He married a widow, Khadíja, who was sixteen years older than himself and a merchant for whom He had acted as agent. A daughter, Fáṭima, was the only child to survive from this marriage (which was apparently happy) and Muhammad did not take any other wife until after Khadíja's death twenty-five years later.

After his marriage Muhammad's life proceeded without incident for some sixteen years. Then in 610 during one of his periodic visits to Mount Hira where He liked to meditate and pray, He had a vision of the Archangel Gabriel, who commanded Him to arise and reform the religion of His land. At first He had grave doubts about Himself but was encouraged by His first followers, His wife and His nephew, 'Ali. In 613 He began to preach in the city against the idols and about the need for all to change their way of life in preparation for the Day of God. Gradually people began to respond to His teachings, but this caused increasing alarm amongst the rich and powerful who saw Him as a possible threat to their lucrative pilgrimage business, if not worse. They tried to dissuade Him, first with mockery, then bribery, but when these approaches failed they threatened violence to the point where in 615 He sent away many of His followers to other lands[1] for their own safety. For seven years the pressures on Muhammad gradually increased; major stages were His confinement to one sector of the city in 617 and the deaths in 619 (the Year of Mourning) of both His wife and His protecting uncle. Still He persisted, and His opponents finally resolved to kill Him (as a joint venture, so that there would be no subsequent blood feud). Just at that time Muhammad was invited by a delegation from Yathrib (later to be renamed Medina, the city of the Prophet), a small agricultural town some two hundred miles north of Mecca, to come to be their ruler. They had heard of His teaching of unity amongst all peoples and they hoped He would be able to end the constant strife in their own city between its various component groups. Muhammad

---

[1] Including the Christian kingdom of Abyssinia (Ethiopia).

agreed and in October 622 left Mecca in secret so as to avoid
assassination. It is said that 'Ali slept in Muhammad's place so as to
make those watching think Muhammad was still there. The move to
Medina marks the emergence of Muhammad as the formal head of a
state and of a reformed religion, and this is the reason the Islamic
calendar starts with this year of Emigration (Hijra) rather than with
the year when Muhammad received His first revelation, or the year
He first preached.

In Medina, Muhammad brought peace through conciliation and
compromise. He made a particular effort to include the Christians, a
relatively small group, and the Jews, who were more numerous.
Each group was given freedom to practise its own religion and some
of their customs were incorporated into Muhammad's own teachings, such as the Jewish practice of turning to Jerusalem when
praying. There was never complete agreement with the Christians,
especially over the stumbling-block of the Incarnation. Nor did the
Jews respond with much enthusiasm, and at times they were not
loyal. It is interesting in this context that Muhammad was later to
make Mecca, the site of the old religion, the point to which His
followers should turn when praying to God, rather than Jerusalem.

Fearing that He would return in force, Muhammad's enemies in
Mecca began a war of harassment to try and undermine His position.
Over a period of six years there were many skirmishes and three
direct attacks on Medina, all of which were defeated. Exhausted by
their effort, the Meccans responded to conciliatory offers from
Muhammad, and agreement was formalized in the treaty of
Hudaybiyya in AD 628. One of the treaty's provisions allowed the
Muslims to make pilgrimage to Mecca. Their moderate behaviour
and the continuation of the practice of pilgrimage attracted Meccans
to His Cause and in 630 the majority accepted Islam and recognized
Muhammad as their leader. Muhammad declared a general amnesty,
but had the idols of the city destroyed. During the final two years of
His life, before His death in 632, most of the tribes of Arabia came
over to His cause.

The two main sources of the teachings of Muhammad are the
Qur'án (the Book to be read) and the example of His life, actions and
sayings (the ḥadith). The Qur'án is a record of the revelations
received by Muhammad over a period of more than twenty-two
years, recorded at the time on whatever material was at hand (skins,
stones, bones, etc.). Divided into 114 surihs, the Qur'án was
completed by AD 650, less than twenty years after His passing, and
its content was confirmed by those who had known Him. It was the
most authentic record of the teachings of any Manifestation of God

made up to that time. The *hadith*, which in all comprise some 600,000 different traditions, are much less consistent in authenticity.

Muhammad's teachings revolve around the concepts of a single God of justice and mercy, each man's responsibility for his own actions, and the equality of all before God. The teachings are both simple and practical and are presented sometimes with a sense of humour, as in the admonition: 'Trust in God but tie your camel.' Four of the five obligations of the Faith relate to reinforcing man's understanding of his humble position before God: the reiteration of the profession of faith, the saying of prayers five times a day, observance of a fast from sunrise to sunset every day during the month of Ramadan, and pilgrimage once in a lifetime to the holy city of Mecca. In obedience to these teachings the proud Arab on his camel in the desert, lord of all he surveyed, would bow down and touch his forehead to the ground during the act of prayer.

The idea of the unity and equality of all had many facets of which one of the most important was the fifth obligation of the Faith to contribute alms for the benefit of the poor: 'wealth should not be allowed to circulate among the rich only' (Qur'án 11:7).

Another was the absence of prejudice on account of race: 'And among his signs are the creation of the Heavens and of the Earth, and your variety of tongues and colour. Herein truly are signs for all men' (30:21).

Muhammad enjoined his followers not to be cruel to others, and to be kind and forgiving:

molest not the harmless, spare the weakness of the female sex, injure not the infant . . . or those who are ill . . . abstain from demolishing the dwellings of the unresisting inhabitants; destroy not the means of their subsistence.[2]

He set an example in His own life when he forgave the killer of one of his daughters. Kindness should be extended to animals, while fellow human beings should be treated with the greatest courtesy and concern for their feelings. A Muslim might defend himself against an attacker but should not himself be the aggressor, nor should be be involved in blood feuds: 'Fight in the way of God against those who attack you but begin not hostilities, for God loveth not the transgressors' (2:186).

The principle of Holy War (*jihad*) was the right of the state to protect its citizens against corruption by pagan beliefs. More important, it was a reference to the need for individuals to struggle against their lower passions: 'The most excellent Jihad is that for the

---

[2] Ameer Ali, *The Spirit of Islam*, p. 180.

conquest of self.'[3] This principle was not to be interpreted as a right to impose Islam on others, which would be contrary to the principle of toleration: 'Let there be no compulsion in religion' (2:257).

During the early years of Islam this teaching was taken very seriously and it is of interest, in view of later interpretations, that it was more than three hundred years after Egypt became a part of the Muslim state before a majority of its citizens were Muslims. It is also noteworthy that Jews for centuries expressed a preference for living under Muslim rather than Christian rule. The Muslim state treated non-Muslims equally though differently insofar as they were exempt from military service in return for a moderate capitation tax (*jizyah*), and they were subject to a small income tax instead of the requirement to give alms for the poor.

Slavery was fundamental to contemporary society, and Muhammad did not require that it be abolished immediately, but it is clear that He intended that ultimately it should wither away. Manumission of slaves was strongly encouraged by: (i) His own example of freeing slaves; (ii) His statement that emancipation was a cardinal virtue; and (iii) the right given to slaves to purchase their own freedom. Furthermore, He taught that in the eyes of God a slave was equal to a free man. In accordance with this liberal view, slaves were not confined to menial jobs and indeed in the Muslim states slaves often rose to positions of great influence.

Similarly, Muhammad did not try to force equality of the sexes on a society which was clearly not ready for such a radical change in the practice of centuries. Nevertheless, many of His teachings tended towards raising the rights of women and respect accorded to them, so that during the early centuries of Islam there were better conditions for women than in any other culture or society of the time. Women were given the same property rights as their husbands and could inherit and dispose of their property. Muhammad said that women should be treated with respect, but in order to make that respect more likely in an unenlightened society he admonished women to make a special effort to be modest and said they 'should not make an exhibition of beauty'. The practice of polygamy by men may well have been a necessary protection for women in a still harsh society[4] and perhaps for this reason Muhammad gave permission for its continuance amongst His followers. However, they were not allowed to have more than four wives simultaneously and it was made clear that it was most desirable that the number be limited in

[3] Gail, *Six Lessons on Islám*, p. 21.

[4] The Arab world did not have convents, that useful device of medieval Christianity for the protection of women.

fact to one: 'Marry but two, or three, or four: and if ye still fear that ye shall not act equitably, then one only' (4:3).

In addition to high standards of sexual morality Muhammad also enjoined cleanliness and forbade the drinking of alcohol, gambling, usury and other forms of vice. Education was highly recommended: the great universities of the Muslim Empire would later become the pride of Islam.

There has been a great deal of prejudice and hostility towards Islam in the West, dating back to the wars of the Christian countries of Europe against the Islamic states during the Middle Ages. Much of this centred around an *ad hominem* attack on Muhammad Himself by Christendom, with a view to demonstrating that He was a 'false prophet'. It was argued that Muhammad's teachings were not original but that He stole them from the Bible and other sources; that He advocated the sword as a means of spreading His religion; and that in His teaching and in His practice (the fact that He had thirteen wives) He advocated the subjugation of women and encouraged sexual immorality. A review of His life and teachings make it clear that these charges were false. Many of His teachings, including those on religious toleration and the administration of the state were new. Had his religion been merely a reform movement rather than an independent revelation there could not have been a book with the power of the Qur'án, or a civilization as dynamic as that which ultimately emerged. Islam's success was due to the simplicity and power of its teachings in attracting adherents, not to the threat of the sword which in any case Muhammad had said should only be used in defence. As for the charge concerning women and personal lasciviousness, it is to be observed that Muhammad did not marry until He was twenty-four and then married a woman sixteen years his senior, and that he remained faithful to her and took no other wife until after her death. Then, the women He took to wife were often the widows of fallen comrades, who were taken in for their own protection, or they were political marriages to serve the interest of the state.

Just as Christianity was to be weakened soon after the death of Jesus by teachings added by His followers, notably the theory of incarnation, so too was Islam by the decisions taken by Muhammad's followers immediately after His passing (8 June 632) with regard to who was to succeed Him as leader of the new Faith. It is a tribute to the inspirational power of both religions that they were to achieve so much to raise the level of civilization despite these early divisive occurrences. Though Muhammad had apparently not left a written statement of who was to succeed Him, there is said to be record of at least two occasions when He made it clear that it should be 'Ali:

Whoever hath me as his master, hath 'Ali as his master . . . The greatest treasure is the Book of God . . . The other treasure is the line of my descendants.[5]

In any case, it must have been obvious that 'Ali, as nephew, adopted son, son-in-law and earliest and most distinguished of Muhammad's companions, had every right to be considered as first choice for the succession. Nevertheless, the leadership met together while 'Ali and Fátima were busy preparing for the funeral of Muhammad and decided that Abú Bakr, a Meccan and leader of prayers in Muhammad's absence, should be His successor. As part of this arrangement it was agreed that on Abú Bakr's death the leadership would then fall to 'Umar, one of Muhammad's earliest companions from Mecca who had been adopted by the Medinans as one of their own. 'Ali, though distinguished for his scholarship and military powers, was a man of humility and accepted the decision without argument. Nevertheless, the seeds of dissension had been sown.

At first all went well under the leadership of the two Caliphs Abú Bakr (632–634) and 'Umar (634–644). The new religion attracted many and so inspired its adherents that they were able to defeat in battle two of the most powerful states in the world: Persia, which was totally crushed, and the Byzantine Empire, which was reduced for the remaining eight hundred years of its existence to the status of a relatively minor power. During this period the forces of Islam swept through Palestine, Syria, Iraq, Persia and Egypt. True to the teachings of Muhammad, 'Umar entered Jerusalem in 638 in all humility and guaranteed the right of Christians to continue to visit it on pilgrimage.

Then the clouds began to gather. 'Umar was assassinated by a slave with a personal grievance and there was elected in his place 'Uthmán, a member of the Umayyad branch of the Qurayshi tribe which had been the main centre of opposition to Muhammad until His final triumph. Soon the new Caliph fell into the practice of filling all the high positions in the state with members of his own family; the resulting corruption brought forth an increasingly indignant reaction amongst the most sincere Muslims. 'Ali tried to advise the Caliph to change his ways and defended him against his opponents, but to no avail, and in 656 'Uthmán was killed. 'Ali was then elected Caliph, but by this time the damage had been done. The Umayyad family resented 'Ali's dismissal of many of them from office, and

[5] Quoted by Gail, *Six Lessons on Islám*, p. 29.

called for revenge. When 'Ali tried to conciliate the Umayyads he provoked the opposition of another group, the Kharijites, who thought 'Ali had betrayed Islam by having dealings with the Umayyads, and it was one of this party which assassinated him in 661.

'Ali's eldest son Hasan was elected to succeed him but soon abdicated in the face of the overwhelming opposition of Mu'áwiya (the Umayyad Governor of Syria and son of Abu Sufyán, the chief opponent of Muhammad) and of Hind (a woman who is recorded as having eaten the liver of a Muslim killed in one of the wars between Mecca and Medina). As Caliph, Mu'áwiya (661–680) arranged for the assassination of Hasan, a potential centre of opposition, and presided over a further advance of Islam across North Africa in the West, and into Afghanistan, India and Central Asia as far as Samaria in the East. On his death there was an attempt to restore 'Ali's family to the Caliphate. Husayn, 'Ali's second son, who was in Medina, was invited to Kufa, the principal town of Iraq, where he would be elected. The plan went awry, and the Kufans failed to give adequate support to Husayn when he was attacked by the Umayyad forces. Husayn and his family were killed at the battle of Karbila (10 October 680) in particularly gruesome circumstances, a traumatic event which has been marked each year since by the Shi'i branch of Islam in ceremonies of mourning and self-mortification. For Shi'is, the martyrdom of Husayn was a redemptive act.

The Umayyad party then seized the Caliphate and kept it in the family on the hereditary principle (thus undermining the original claim of the opponents of 'Ali to be the party of representative election), until they in their turn were deposed some seventy years later. These events irretrievably split Islam into its two main sects: the Sunni (the Way) and the Shi'i, the minority supportive of the Imamate and the claims of 'Ali's family. During this period the Islamic Empire continued to grow for a time in the West with the conquest of Spain, but its northern progress was finally halted in 732 by Charles Martel (688–741) at Poitiers in France. The regime, however, was not able to keep peace within its own dominions and there was a continuous series of revolts by Shi'is and Kharijites which increased in intensity during the forties of the eighth century.

Once the Umayyads were driven out, the new dynasty of the 'Abbasids (another branch of the descendants of Muhammad) seized and held the Caliphate for some three hundred and fifty years. There was a price, though: the loss of Spain and the western half of North Africa, which remained loyal to the one member of the Umayyad dynasty who survived this coup. The 'Abbasids took Islam to new heights of glory, particularly under the Caliphs Hárún ar-Rashíd (785–809), well known in the West from the stories in the *Thousand-and-One Nights*, and al-Ma'mún the Great (813–833). To gain support from non-Arabs (particularly the Persians) the capital was moved from Damascus in Syria to the new city of Baghdad in Iraq. Baghdad was to become world-famous for its House of Knowledge, its great university, its observatories, its arts and sciences, and the gathering together of the knowledge of the time through translation of works from Greek, Syriac, Persian, and Sanskrit. The teaching of Muhammad on religious toleration led Hárún ar-Rashíd to conclude an agreement with Charlemagne of France concerning the protection of Christian pilgrims travelling to Jerusalem.

Meanwhile, the direct line of 'Ali continued through nine more Imams[6] to make a total of twelve including 'Ali himself and his two sons, Hasan and Husayn, until the last one died in the year AD 878/ AH 260. During this period the Shi'i party, though maintaining the right of the Imams to spiritual leadership in Islam, was quietist in nature and did not attempt to overthrow the Caliphs. This policy did not bring the Imams much respite, for nearly all of them were murdered by one political group or another.

Though the 'Abbasids were at first relatively successful in holding the Empire together, major cracks in the edifice had become evident by the end of the ninth century and over the next two centuries it gradually fell apart and finally succumbed to the invading Turks at the end of the twelfth. Great Muslim empires were to arise again, but the dream of a universal Islamic empire bringing peace and justice was never to be achieved.[7] Yet the religion was to be immensely successful in raising the level of civilization and culture in the whole area occupied by the Empire, and it is significant that Islam has never retreated except from France and Spain and parts of the Balkans.

One of its brightest periods of success after the 'Abbasid Caliphate was in Egypt in the tenth to twelfth centuries: first under the Fatimids, a Shi'i branch who founded Cairo and the great university and mosque of al-Azhar; and then under Saladin, the model of nobility and courtesy whose fame spread even throughout Christendom. Two other distinguished manifestations of Islamic civilization at this time were in Persia, land of those great poets Sa'di and Hafiz, and in Spain with its great universities and cities. Later, after the periods of destruction following the Mongol invasions led by

---

[6] The title 'Imam' means 'spiritual leader' and is to be distinguished from 'Caliph', which means 'successor' with regard to both civil and religious affairs.

[7] Today it is estimated that about 15–17 percent of the world population is Muslim, a figure second only to the claim of about 33 percent for Christianity.

Genghis Khan (1162–1227) and Tamburlaine (1336–1405), there were further flashes of brilliance in the sixteenth and early seventeenth centuries: Turkey in the time of Sulayman the Great (1520–1566), who patronized the arts and added to the architectural heritage of the region; northern India in the time of Akbar the Great (1555–1605), who worked to reconcile his Muslim and Hindu subjects through toleration and who also encouraged those of Christian and Zoroastrian background;[8] and again in Persia under Abbas the Great (1587–1609), who made his capital Isfahan one of the most beautiful cities in the world and enforced law and order after centuries of anarchy and brigandage.

For many centuries Islam was successful in raising the level of civilization in areas where its influence was significant. Nevertheless, right from the beginning the community was flawed because of a major failure to abide by all the teachings of Muhammad, most obviously in its early divisions and its violence in affairs of state (a depressing parallel to Christianity where the most basic teachings of Jesus concerning violence were disobeyed by its leaders after it became a state religion). The decline was later to extend to all areas of life, as the initial inspiration and clarity of Muhammad's teachings was corrupted by a thousand and one interpretations and additions. By the beginning of the nineteenth century Islam had become associated with extreme intolerance of other religions,[9] and with anti-intellectualism and hostility to open discussion of ideas. It was also noted for its suppression of women – the practices of seclusion, trial marriage (prostitution by another name), elimination of any political or social rights, low priority to women's education, and a widespread belief that women do not even possess souls. In countries where Shi'i Islam dominated, most notably Iran, the lie had become a routine aspect of conversation, a habit which may have come from the practice of dissimulation when Shi'ism was a minority and under

[8] The long period of hostility between Islam and Hinduism in India led to the emergence of another religious movement – Sikhism. It was founded by Guru Nanak (1469–1539), the son of a Hindu revenue officer, who wished to unite Hinduism and Islam by taking parts from each religion – a parallel with Manichaeism which had tried to reconcile Zoroastrianism and Christianity. Sikhism emphasized monotheism, concern for the spiritual life, and the absence of a need for priests. Its social teachings are against the caste system, asceticism, drinking alcohol and smoking. Guru Nanak did not claim to be a Messenger of God and Sikhism is not, therefore, a separate religion such as Islam or Christianity. He was succeeded by a line of nine other gurus. The later ones were persecuted by the Muslim authorities after Akbar, and in self-defence the Sikhs became skilled in the military prowess for which they were later famed. Today, the group is noted for its high level of education, and skills in agriculture, business and trade. It has, however, lost its missionary zeal and is content to exist more or less as a hereditary religious movement.

[9] As in Christianity, even reformers such as the Wahhabis of nineteenth-century Arabia, determined to go back to the original teachings of the Faith, often resorted to harsh methods to impose their viewpoint and thereby defeated their own purpose.

persecution, but which by the nineteenth century had reached the point of tearing apart the basic fundamentals of civilization: a minimum of trust between all citizens. Torture and cruelty to man and beast in Muslim countries equalled the worst conditions in the world. Islam, once the light of the world, had become one of the most reactionary of forces, delaying rather than promoting the advancement of man. Nevertheless, like Christianity and the other great religions, Islam does give hope of a spiritual awakening – the coming of the Qa'im (the One who Arises), as expected by Shi'i Muslims, or the Mahdi (the Guided One, the Spirit of Jesus) as expected by Sunni Muslims.

CHAPTER 11

Three Revolutions

OUR attention now switches to the West. In the time known as the Age of Enlightenment, the sparks which sporadically have illumined the history of civilization suddenly caused three flames to burn brightly: revolutions in England, in North America and in France. These were to spread across the whole western world and in the nineteenth century to become a mighty blaze of ideas and movements for the creation of the just society.

The English Revolution

The first of the three revolutions took place in England. Its roots go back to the time of the Anglo-Saxons, if not further, but the first clearly identifiable major event in the story was the Magna Carta (Great Charter). John, King of England from 1199 to 1216, had made a series of attempts to extend his power by increasing his income through taxation of the revenues of his subjects (1207); by tightening up protection of the royal forests from poaching (1207–1209); by special measures of taxation against the Jews (1210); and by exploiting feudal privileges. Opposition to these measures amongst the barons of the kingdom was encouraged when the king's prestige was weakened in a quarrel with the Pope. After a period of fighting and manœuvring they finally forced the king to sign the Magna Carta on the field of Runnymede on 15 June 1215. The Magna Carta is of special interest, because as a result of the influence of the Church in the person of the Archbishop of Canterbury, Stephen Langton (d. 1228), it was broadened beyond the narrow interests of the barons to cover basic issues of liberty and the rule of law, affecting the lives of even the poorest in the land.

The Charter had a preamble and sixty-three clauses which put broad limitations on the arbitrary authority of the king and required him to rule in accordance with orderly legal principles. Perhaps the most significant and most well-known of the clauses were Nos. 39 and 40:

No freeman shall be taken or imprisoned, or disseised, or outlawed, or exiled, or in any way destroyed, nor will we go upon him, nor will we send upon him except by the lawful judgement of his peers or by the law of the land. (No. 39)

To no one will we sell, deny, or delay right of justice. (No. 40)

Other clauses protected the rights of tenants and subtenants, forbade unreasonable tolls on towns, barred the taking of property by royal officials without consent, regularized forest laws, and guaranteed the Church's right to run its own affairs, including the free election of its high officials. To make sure the law was carried out in an orderly fashion, provision was made for two of the King's justices to visit each county four times each year to hear cases, and for twenty-five barons to be guarantors of the Charter, with the right to appeal to the king if it was not observed.

King John soon broke his word and civil war was resumed until his death the following year. However, the regent during the minority of his successor, Henry III (King 1216–1272), accepted the Charter; and since then the governments of England have always, at a minimum, paid lip service to its basic principles. Later in the reign of Henry III there was another development of major significance in the gradual emergence of the concept of constitutional monarchy: the assembling of the first true parliament of England in 1265 at the instigation of Simon de Montfort. Though this was essentially only a ploy in a power struggle between baronial factions, it was, at a more profound level, a recognition of the principle that the 'people' should be consulted with regard to the governance of the country. This parliament differed from previous councils of the great barons (such councils of the barons were the precursors of the separate House of Lords) because it included elected representatives from each county (two knights) and from each town with a royal charter (two burghers).[1] Edward I, King from 1272 to 1307, took up the idea of parliament and established the practice of holding regular sessions. He found it a useful device for keeping himself informed of popular sentiment, for keeping a check on his own officials, especially in the provinces, and for helping him to develop the law in an orderly fashion for an increasingly complex society. At first Parliament often had an important judicial function, but as the years went by separate courts were established for this purpose and Parliament became

---

[1] Royal charters were usually given to seaports and fortified cities which had a special relationship to the King because of their usefulness to him in controlling the country. As Parliament became more important and as the monarchy became more sophisticated, more charters were given to cities which gave indication of being loyal to the King's interest.

specialized as a legislative body and in the voting of financial support
(i.e. taxes) for the king.[2]

Though the establishment of Parliament was a great step forward
on the path towards accountable government, it has to be remembered that until at least the nineteenth century, it represented almost
exclusively the interest of the nobility, the squirearchy and the rich
burghers of the cities. In the shires the vote was restricted to those
who had a freehold (i.e. owned their own property) with an annual
value of forty shillings or more. This effectively excluded most
peasants and villagers, who nearly all lived in rented property. The
suffrage in boroughs varied greatly according to local custom but
was usually narrow, and it was frequently possible for one family to
'own' a seat in a borough as well as in a shire, and in consequence it
was a fact that until the nineteenth century only a minority of
nominations for Parliament were contested.

The narrow representation of interest in Parliament contributed to
the frustration of the poorer classes, who finally rose up in the
Peasants' Rebellion of 1381 against the incompetent government of
Richard II (King 1377–1399). This was a spontaneous rising of
peasants and townspeople throughout the land against efforts to
tighten up the collection of a flat-rate poll tax which was particularly
burdensome on the poor. The revolt was not well coordinated and
was soon crushed; it is interesting that by contrast with the ferocious
suppression of similar risings on the continent around this time,
there was relatively little attempt at reprisal against those who had
rebelled, and though the rising made little immediate impact on the
conduct of government, there was a subtle long-term influence on
the collective memory of the country which was to contribute to the
development of the custom of fair play and justice for all people
regardless of wealth or influence.

During the period of the Tudor monarchs Henry VIII (King 1509–
1547) and Elizabeth I (Queen 1558–1603) and of the English
Reformation, the role of Parliament in the governance of the country
became significantly more important. In the dangerous game of
breaking with Rome and the traditions of centuries, and the taking of
wealth from the monasteries, Henry felt a need to have his actions
approved by Parliament and most of the major legal changes of the
period were in the form of Acts of Parliament rather than the less
authoritative ordinances of the King and his appointed advisory
council. So as not to create opportunities for opponents to appear in

---

[2] The House of Lords, however, still has a judicial function, essentially as a court of last appeal.

Parliament he made it a practice to have long parliaments (i.e. members held their seats for a long time without having to stand for re-election), though they would quite often not be in session. More weighty business and long period of office gradually attracted into parliamentary service more capable and eminent persons, who became increasingly knowledgeable in government and skilled in parliamentary practices, and who in addition acquired a strong sense of *esprit de corps*. As a result Parliament during the reign of Elizabeth, though still wary of the massive power of the monarchy, began to show increasing signs of independence, for instance, the unprecedented procedure of having private members introduce bills contrary to government policy on such an important issue as the abolition of bishoprics in the Anglican Church. Though Elizabeth was able to head off such proposals, the seeds of independence had been sown and were to spring to life during the reigns of the two succeeding Stuart monarchs, James I (King 1603–1625) and Charles I (King 1625–1649).

These two kings engaged in an increasingly bitter struggle with Parliament over the crucial issue of whether or not the government could tax the country without reference to Parliament, and over other important matters such as foreign alliances and the governance of the Anglican Church. They tried to persuade Parliament to vote taxation laws which would last for the duration of the reign, and the judiciary to declare that existing laws gave the right to raise taxes without further approval by Parliament. Charles went even further and tried to raise a compulsory loan from the citizenship, arbitrarily imprisoned many of those who refused to pay, and billeted soldiers in their homes. Matters came to a head with the third Parliament (1628) of his reign when a 'Petition of Rights' was presented to the government, which on the basis of principles going back to the Magna Carta condemned arbitrary taxation and imprisonment and the practice of martial law during times of peace. Charles reacted by dissolving Parliament and for twelve years he struggled to rule the country without its assistance.

This period came to an end when Scotland rebelled against the imposition of bishops on their Church, and Charles was obliged to recall Parliament in order to raise the extra funds needed to pay an enlarged army to put down the rebellion. The Short Parliament, April–May 1640 (so-called because it was soon dissolved) refused to help the King until he had redressed their grievances. The King could not escape his quandary and the next year Parliament was recalled. The new 'Long Parliament' was now in a much stronger position because the King's manœuvres had lost him the trust of the majority of his subjects and had revealed his ultimate dependence on Parliament. A united Parliament now insisted on a 'Triennial Act' which required the King to call a Parliament at least every three years and made it illegal for him to dissolve Parliament or to raise taxes without its consent. In the 'Grand Remonstrance' of November 1641, Parliament went further and demanded that henceforth ministers of the crown be approved by Parliament and that reform of the church be undertaken by Parliament in consultation with an assembly of religious experts. The King refused to accede to these demands, tried to arrest the five most important leaders of Parliament and, when that failed, fled to York and there began to organize forces to crush Parliament. There followed seven years of civil war which ended with the King's defeat and his execution in January 1649.

During the next eleven years England, for the only time in its history, had a republican form of government: the Commonwealth, headed for most of the period by Oliver Cromwell (1599–1658), the dominant general on the parliamentary side. Cromwell and the army, heavily influenced by a militant Puritan ethic, engaged in several military adventures including a most brutal suppression of a rebellion in Ireland which is remembered to this day, and a series of oppressive actions in domestic affairs including censorship and the banning of popular entertainments (particularly on Sundays) together with the imposition of heavy new taxes. Parliamentary supervision of government was not tolerated and Cromwell engaged in several ploys to tame Parliament (including a purge of all but a small minority of the membership) before finally resorting to dissolution. Though the government ruled with a heavy hand, the flame of liberty shone brightly in these years as various groups developed new ideas about a just form of government. One of the most interesting was the Levellers, who in October 1647 published an 'Agreement of the People' which advocated: (i) universal suffrage in elections of members of parliament; (ii) religious toleration; (iii) equality before the law as an inalienable right of all Englishmen; and (iv) freedom from arbitrary imprisonment.

Though the monarchy was restored in 1661, the clock could not be turned back entirely. All concessions to Parliament made by Charles I before the Civil War were endorsed by the new King, Charles II, and at first the principle of religious toleration was accepted. However, within a few years the royalists became the majority in Parliament and pushed through measures to reduce the civil rights of Catholics, nonconformists and Jews. The polarization of the country which had occurred in the first half of the seventeenth century between Catholics and those who were sympathetic to them, on the one hand, and nonconformists on the other hand, now re-emerged. Matters came to explosion point early in the reign of James II, the younger brother of Charles II and King from 1685 to 1689. Contrary to the wishes of the majority in Parliament he refused to disband a large army after it had completed its task of crushing a rebellion led by the Duke of Monmouth; and he insisted on appointing a large number of Catholics as army officers. The final provocation was the birth of a son to James's Catholic Queen in 1688; this was interpreted as increasing the probability that the monarchy would succeed in restoring Catholicism as well as imposing despotism on the continental model. All parties in Parliament thereupon united in inviting the King's brother-in-law, the Protestant Prince William of Orange, to come to England and take the crown. In return William agreed to a series of limitations on the power of the crown, of which the most significant was the Bill of Rights of 1689.[3]

The Bill, which had thirteen articles, covered the following points: (i) all laws henceforth must be approved by Parliament; (ii) the government might not raise taxes without parliamentary consent; (iii) there might not be a standing army without parliamentary consent (the Mutiny Act of 1688 required an annual renewal of the oath of loyalty to the monarch); (iv) there were to be no punishments for presentation of petitions; (v) elections to Parliament were to be free; (vi) there were to be no restrictions on freedom of speech in Parliament; (vii) there were to be no cruel punishments or excessively heavy requirements for bail; (viii) juries were to be required for trials of criminal cases; and (ix) Parliament was to be called frequently: this principle was later strengthened by the Triennial Act of 1694 which established the rule that parliaments were to be elected every three years at a minimum.[4] The Bill of Rights was supplemented with several other laws including the Toleration Act of 1689 and the Act of Settlement of 1694 which excluded Catholics from the throne of England.

These new arrangements were not seen as revolutionary new laws, but rather as repairs of omissions and clarifications of obscurities in existing ones. They nevertheless formed the basis for freedom from arbitrary government, reduced the aura of 'divine right' which had for centuries hedged the idea of monarchy about, and eventually created a new form of government – constitutional monarchy.

[3] Such limitations were hardly an affront to William who, coming from the Netherlands, was familiar with the idea of restrictions on the power of the chief executive and head of state.

[4] In 1716 the rule was changed to seven years on account of the emergency presented by the first Stuart Rebellion. This formula in turn was changed to five years in 1911.

Though it was a constitution with a tradition which went back at least as far as the Magna Carta, the 1689 settlement was undoubtedly a major step forward in the development of the idea of just government, and therefore it rightly merits its traditional title of the 'Glorious Revolution'.

A broad rationale for the 'revolution' and the new-style constitutional monarchy was provided by John Locke (1632–1704) who returned to England with William of Orange after being in exile for his liberal views. Like Thomas Hobbes (1586–1679) he saw the state as a social contract between citizens, whereby they gave up the freedom which exists in the state of nature in return for certain services to be provided by the state. Hobbes had concluded, however, that the state should have absolute power if it is to keep the peace and serve the interest of all, because people are naturally unruly and if given freedom fall into anarchy. Locke countered that Hobbes's ideal state would bring the 'peace of the dungeon', and because he had a less pessimistic view of human nature he came to a different conclusion. In *Two Treatises on Government*, published in 1690, he argued that citizens have a right to the preservation of life and property, to freedom of thought, speech and worship, and what they give up to the state is the right to judge and punish others. In short, the essential function of government is defence of the realm and maintenance of law and order. If a government fails to serve the public good, it forfeits its right to power and authority.

The American Revolution

The issues which had sparked the English revolution – taxation to be approved by representatives of the people, and freedom from oppression – were to reappear in North America in the following century and prompt the second of our three revolutions. The North American colonies in their early years had, for a series of reasons, acquired a culture of personal independence and a critical attitude towards government. First, many of those who came to North America were in effect fleeing from religious oppression in Europe and were determined never again to allow any government to unnecessarily impose on them. Second, the pioneer setting inevitably made people self-reliant and independent in their outlook. Third, a great distance from the homeland made direct every-day rule by the central government impractical and as a result the colonists were given, if only by default, quite a lot of freedom to manage their own affairs.[5]

[5] As formalized in the charters of many of the colonies, which included provision for elected representative assemblies to advise and consult with the appointed governor on local matters.

In New England the town meeting became an established institution which nurtured the democratic practice of consultation in public affairs. Occasionally the London government would institute laws such as the protectionist Navigation Acts (1653) and the Molasses Act (1733)[6] without consultation with the colonies, although these laws were potentially of great importance to them, but trouble was averted by lax administration and the turning of a blind eye to widespread evasion of the law – a practice which may have seemed prudent in the short run but which undoubtedly made disobedience to government acceptable to a large part of the population.

A turning-point came in the aftermath of the Seven Years War (1756–1763) which France with had as one result the removal of French power from North America. The war had been costly for all the powers concerned, including England, and the British government believed that the American colonialists, who had benefited from the British victory, should contribute to the cost and that they should also pay for a standing army in North America enlarged, supposedly, to protect against Indian raids and against a possible revolt by French colonialists in Canada. In 1764 Parliament passed the Stamp Act which placed a tax on all legal documents, licences and newspapers, and the government made an effort for the first time to seriously enforce the Molasses Act. When the right to impose the Stamp Tax was challenged, the British argued that there were precedents in taxes imposed in Ireland, the Isle of Man and Jersey, and they seemed to miss the wider point that they were denying to the colonialists the right of 'no taxation without representation' which they themselves had achieved in the Glorious Revolution. They refused an offer by the colonialists to raise the sum required through measures which state assemblies might enact, and they did not offer to allow the colonialists to be represented in Parliament. When the colonialists refused to pay the new tax, a new government in England had the Stamp Act repealed but, to make clear that this was a tactical retreat and not a surrender of principle, a Declaratory Act (1766) was approved which restated the British claim that the authority of Parliament applied equally to all parts of the Empire.

A second attempt at the end of the decade to impose taxes, including one on tea imports (partly to protect British traders against Dutch rivals) also ended in defeat for the British, but not before the colonialists had established a network of Committees of Corre-

[6] The Navigation Acts required that transportation of goods to and from Britain and the colonies be in British ships. The Molasses Act imposed a prohibitive duty on imports of molasses from foreign countries, e.g. French islands in the Caribbean.

spondence to coordinate opposition to the taxes – an ominous precedent for the next round. That occurred three years later when North's government had Parliament pass a new Tea Bill. The result was the famous Boston Tea Party of 1774 when a group of colonialists, thinly disguised as Indians, boarded a British merchantman and threw overboard its cargo of tea. This time the government was determined not to retreat; a military government was approved for Massachusetts, and troops were sent to occupy Boston and to close the port. The colonialists reacted by calling their own assembly outside Boston (in effect an embryo revolutionary government). This soon had the support of the first Continental Congress which had assembled in Philadelphia in the fall of 1774 and which included representatives from all the states except Georgia. The Congress demanded repeal of the coercive measures that had been imposed and questioned the authority of Parliament to tax the colonies. It declared that the British government was violating not only the charters of the colonies but also the natural rights of the American citizen to be consulted on his governance. A decision was taken to boycott all British goods until the situation was remedied.

In Parliament the wiser statesmen, including Lord Chatham (1708–1778) and Edmund Burke (1729–1797), aware of the essential good will towards England in the colonies, urged reconciliation, but the government, with the support of King George III, refused to change its position. The situation rapidly deteriorated; there were armed skirmishes between British troops and civilians, and in August 1775 the colonies were declared to be in a state of rebellion. Three months later a Prohibitory Act withdrew the King's protection – virtually a declaration of war.

A second Continental Congress assembled in 1776, and even such moderates as George Washington (1732–1799) saw that there was no alternative but to break the tie with England. On 4 July Congress approved the Declaration of Independence. The Declaration, which owed a great deal to the drafting skills of Thomas Jefferson (1743–1826), presented the American case in terms of natural rights and the theory of contract – the arguments of John Locke and the English Revolution of 1688:

We hold these truths to be self evident, that all men are created equal, that they are endowed by their Creator with certain inalienable Rights, that among these are Life, Liberty and the pursuit of Happiness. – That to secure these rights, Governments are instituted among Men, deriving their just powers from the consent of the governed. – That whenever any form of government becomes destructive of these ends, it is the Right of the People to alter or to abolish it, and to institute new Government laying its foundation on such principles and organizing its powers in such form, as to them shall seem most likely to effect their Safety and Happiness.

The statement went on to list the specific grievances which had made the Declaration necessary, including the suspension of state legislatures, the imposition of taxes without consent, and military occupation.

Eventually, with the help of the French, the American people were able to defeat the British armies and their independence was formally recognized in 1783 in the Treaty of Paris. During the Revolution many states took steps in the direction of a more egalitarian society, such as the banning of aristocratic titles, abolition of automatic primogeniture in inheritance of land, the separation of church and state (i.e. toleration of different religions), a reduction in the severity of punishments for criminals, and a greater role for the state in education, for it was anticipated that a democratic republic would not be able to function unless its citizens were literate and informed. Slavery was a crucial issue, pitting morality against the apparent economic interests of the owners. In the northern states where slavery was less important economically it was essentially abolished as an institution by 1800, after early examples in 1780 by Pennsylvania with its liberal Quaker tradition, and in 1783 by Massachusetts with an equally strong religious feeling. The horrors of the Atlantic slave trade affected even the southern states, and by 1800 virtually all the states of the union had passed laws against the importation of slaves from abroad. (The abolition of slavery is discussed in Chapter 12.)

At first the states were reluctant to surrender their new liberty to a central government. They were formally linked together by the Articles of Confederation in 1781 but these made little provision for a central executive (there were offices for a secretary for foreign affairs and for a superintendent of finance but no head of government as such) and Congress had very little authority to raise taxes or to regulate interstate commerce. The next few years showed that this arrangement was totally inadequate, and eventually a group of reformers led by James Madison (1751–1836) and Alexander Hamilton (1755–1804) persuaded Congress and the states to approve a new constitution.

That constitution, which came into effect in 1789, had seven articles. The first three dealt with the legislative, executive and judicial branches of the new federal government, which though greatly strengthened were kept separate from each other so as to prevent a repetition of the experience with an all-powerful centralized government. As a compromise between the interests of the large and the small states, it was agreed that in the lower house of the legislature (the House of Representatives) distribution of representatives would be according to population[7] and that in the upper house (the Senate) it would be on the basis of two per state. To provide for frequent accountability to the people the House of Representatives would be elected for two-year terms, and to provide for continuity the Senate would be elected for six-year terms, with one-third being elected on every two-year cycle. In theory all freemen had the vote, but the administration was left to the states, and as a result there were to be considerable variations from this principle until the second half of the twentieth century. The legislature was given wide powers over federal appropriations, taxation, other legislation and foreign policy, and, in addition, it had the authority to impeach any member of the three branches of government. The President, the head of the executive branch, was independent of Congress insofar as he was to be elected separately every four years by the states. However, he would be subject to close supervision, not only in terms of legislation, but also with regard to budgets, appointments of senior assistants, and the requirement for an annual 'state of the union' address. The federal judiciary, who were to be appointed by the President for life unless impeached for improper behaviour, had authority to rule on the acts of the other two branches, and of the states, as to whether they were in accordance with the Constitution. To safeguard against arbitrary rule, trials were to be by jury and the legislature was forbidden to suspend the law of *habeas corpus* unless there was an invasion or the public safety was otherwise declared to be in danger.

The fourth article of the Constitution dealt with the states and included clauses which declared that each would recognize the laws of the other, that citizens of one were citizens of all, that all would be republics, that new states could be formed in territories outside the existing states and that the federal government would guarantee the safety of all the states equally. The remaining three articles covered such issues as amendments to the Constitution which could only be accepted if ratified by at least two-thirds of the states in the union.

At first there was considerable criticism of the new constitution, a feeling that it did not provide enough safeguards for the liberties so hard won in the war of independence. Some two hundred and ten amendments were proposed by the states. These were consolidated into twelve, of which ten, to be known collectively as the Bill of

[7] Numbers were calculated on the basis of one for every free man, two-thirds for every slave, and none for indigenous Americans ('Indians').

Rights, were eventually approved by Congress and the states in 1791. These articles covered the right to free speech, peaceful assembly and petition; specified that trials must be in front of a jury; and banned state religion, quartering of soldiers, search without warrant, excessive bail or fines, and cruel and unnatural punishments.

Of course the revolution did not solve all the problems of the American people – far from it. Nevertheless, in the perspective of history the American Revolution can be seen as one of the most significant events in the development of the idea of the just society. What is important is not only the emphasis on democracy and government accountability to the people – as Abraham Lincoln was later to put it:

. . . government of the people, by the people, and for the people . . .

but also the magnificent precedent whereby a group of independent states voluntarily banded together to give up, for the common interest, large portions of their sovereignty.

The French Revolution

The French Revolution, like those in England and America, was the bursting into flame of social discontent which had been simmering for the best part of a century. One important cause was an unprecedented doubling of the population of France in the eighteenth century, putting great stress on the country's food supply and food prices and contributing in the last part of the century to the growth of widespread unemployment. The situation was aggravated by the political, social and economic privileges of the Church and a numerically large aristocracy.[8] Over a period of time the traditional deference to the aristocracy (going back to feudal times) was undermined not only by the blatant selfishness of the aristocrats themselves, but also by the rational ideas of the philosophers of the Enlightenment which became well known amongst the educated bourgeois.

The French philosophers of the eighteenth century, taking as their model the discoveries of the seventeenth-century scientists, argued that there must be social laws, like natural laws, which if followed would lead to a society where the great majority would be happy. Jean François Marie Arouet de Voltaire (1694–1778), one of the most influential, held that it was the duty of rulers and philosophers to find

[8] France had 250,000 aristocrats, a much larger proportion of the population (20 million) than the aristocracy in England.

these laws, to apply them, and to teach them to the general population. The sign of good government was the happiness and prosperity of those ruled, not military success and empire. He recognized that the aristocracy and the Church had a vested interest in opposing such a process, because clearly a society organized on rational principles would have no place for their unjustified privileges. He argued that such a project could only succeed if there was real freedom of thought and public discussion, unrestricted by tradition and the institutions of society. There must be religious toleration and the abolition of torture and the other cruel apparatus of the medieval legal system. Voltaire crusaded on this particular issue, often at high personal cost, as for instance in the 1762 case in which Jean Calas, a Protestant, was broken on the wheel because of accusations (later proved to be false) that he had murdered his son in order to prevent him converting to Catholicism.

Another of the most influential philosophers was Jean-Jacques Rousseau (1712–1778) who argued that the vast inequalities in wealth, and the system of hierarchy and privilege in government and society caused ordinary people to be passive and indifferent to their own interest. This in turn led to corruption and injustice. His solution was to divide society into small self-governing units and to insist on equality of all before the law. He recognized that such a society would only work if all citizens were well informed and had high ethical standards.

The philosophers, though very critical of society, were not necessarily revolutionaries. Indeed, some of their ideas were taken up by the so-called 'enlightened despots' of the period, of whom perhaps the most distinguished was Catherine the Great, Czarina of Russia 1762–1796, who took steps to abolish torture and otherwise humanize the law of her adopted country,[9] and who devoted much of her energy to developing its industry and system of education. The ideas of the philosophers did become revolutionary in France because the monarchy failed to follow the example of the enlightened despots and adapt to changing conditions.[10] Revolution became more probable with the experience of the American Revolution, brought to France by soldiers who had fought on the American side.

The immediate chain of events leading to the outbreak of revolution began soon after the end of the American War of Independence when the French government was struggling desperately

---

[9] She was German by birth.

[10] To be fair, some reforms were undertaken, particularly during the ministry of Jacques Necker, 1776–1781, such as the abolition of serfdom on the royal lands (but not elsewhere) and a reduction in the amount of torture permitted under the law. This was not enough.

to deal with a huge deficit caused by a series of long wars and an expensive style of life at the court on the one hand, and limited sources of income on the other – the latter largely because the aristocracy and Church were virtually exempt from taxation. At first the government tried the easy option of covering the deficit by borrowing, but it soon became obvious that this was not a policy that could be pursued for long. Eventually in 1787 the government summoned an assembly of the nobility to try and persuade them to agree to a tax on their lands, which as a concession they could administer themselves. The assembly refused to agree and instead demanded that the King call into session the Estates-General, which had not met since 1614, and which was an approximate equivalent of Parliament in England. Out of desperation, the government reluctantly agreed and also yielded to a demand that the third of these estates (houses), which represented the general population, should have 600 delegates instead of the normal 300. The number in each of the other two estates, which represented the nobility and the Church remained at 300. This was the first concession to the idea that the third estate might carry more weight than either of the other two, an idea which was strongly advocated in a pamphlet by the Abbé Emmanuel Joseph Sieyes (1748–1836) entitled *What is the Third Estate?*, widely read as a result of a general relaxation of the censorship of the press. The issue came to a head when the Estates-General finally met on 5 May 1789 at Versailles. After passionate debate the Third Estate, which to a large extent had been elected by universal male suffrage, took a decision (the famous Tennis Court oath) on 20 June that it would not disperse until France had been given a new constitution. The King again reluctantly agreed to the demand and instructed the two other estates to merge with it to form a National Constituent Assembly (27 June 1789).

The reformers in the new assembly were in a majority because the representatives of the former Third Estate were supported on many issues by some of the clergy and nobility. The first major act of reform occurred on 4 August 1789 when the assembly voted to abolish feudalism. Over the next year or two the details were worked out. These included a system for buying out feudal rights, the abolition of hereditary titles, the end of unequal taxation, recruitment on the basis of merit rather than class for all positions in the civil service and armed forces, and the termination of compulsory tithe payments to the church. On 27 August 1789 the assembly approved a Declaration of the Rights of Man, modelled on the United States declaration, which stated that all citizens had a right to liberty, equality before the law, property, personal security, and a voice in their government. To handle the financial problem of the government it was decided (partly because of resistance to the imposition of new taxes, and partly because of widespread hostility to the Church amongst the educated classes) that the vast lands of the Church should be taken over and sold off for the benefit of the state. This action created the new problem of what to do about the clergy and their financial support. It was decided that they should be paid a salary by the state, but that in return all clergy (including the bishops) should be elected to office; that they should swear an oath of allegiance to the state; and that they should abide by new rules against absenteeism and pluralism. This somewhat high-handed ruling prompted an inevitable denunciation by the Pope, which in turn caused the King – already fearful of the way events were unfolding – to try and flee the country. He was caught at Varennes on 20 June 1791 and brought back to Paris; his flight complicated the whole process of reaching agreement on the political institutions of the new constitution.

The 1791 constitution had as a preamble the Declaration of Rights, summarized in the revolutionary slogan 'Liberté, Egalité, Fraternité' – Liberty: the end of the absolute monarchy; Equality: the end of feudalism; and Fraternity: the state is the people or nation rather than a collection of vassals ruled by a monarch as a result of the accident of inheritance, marriage or conquest: hence Louis XVI was to be called King of the French instead of King of France. The last two principles took the idea of the just society further forward than either the English or American Revolutions which had been primarily concerned with only the first – liberty. The constitution guaranteed the right of petition, the right to emigrate, the abolition of extreme poverty through a new poor law and system of free education, and a rationalization and codification of the law. As in the United States, there was an emphasis on the separation of the legislative, executive and judicial branches of government. There would be one legislative assembly consisting of 745 deputies elected for fixed two-year terms. To guard against radicalism, the vote was restricted to men of property (about two-thirds of the adult male population). Furthermore, voting was a two-step process, with election first of primary assemblies which then elected representatives to the national assembly. In addition, constituencies were designed to minimise the influence of the big cities. As a gesture of detachment the members of the constituent assembly agreed to a self-denying ordinance which prevented them from being elected to the new legislative assembly. The powers of the executive, to be headed by the King, were to be severely restricted: he had no power to dismiss the assembly; his ministers could not sit in the assembly; he could delay but not veto legislation approved by the assembly; his control over the army and national guard was to be limited; and he himself was to be dependent on a civil list, i.e. his salary would be approved by the assembly. In local affairs the old provinces with their centrally appointed 'intendants' were abolished, and were to be replaced by a uniform hierarchy of departments (83), cantons and communes (44,000), each with its own elected assembly and executive. The judiciary were also to be elected independently of the other two branches of government.

As the Revolution progressed opposition grew. Aristocratic groups moved into surrounding countries and plotted the overthrow of the new regime. The revolutionary principle of national self-determination was put into practice when in September 1791 the people of Avignon broke their allegiance to the Pope, who had been the ruler of the city since the Middle Ages, and joined the new French nation. This caused considerable consternation amongst the monarchs of Europe, and they gave increasing support to the *emigré* opposition. In April 1792 war broke out, and for a period it seemed that the Great Powers of Europe would crush the Revolution. The situation was saved by a mass rising of the people to defend their Revolution, and in September the invading armies were stopped at the battle of Valmy. Invasion, however, brought fear as well as a sense of national solidarity, and it was this that was to corrupt and pervert the Revolution. The King and aristocracy were suspected of treason. In September some twelve hundred aristocrats and other unfortunates were massacred by a rampaging Paris mob. The King was deposed, arrested, put on trial, and in January 1793 executed. A new national convention was elected to draw up a new republican constitution.[11] However, the resulting '1793' constitution, despite its many progressive features such as direct election of the national assembly by universal male suffrage, and referendums for major issues, was put aside by the revolutionary leaders who felt a need for a centralized and powerful dictatorship to defend the Revolution against its enemies, internal and external. An all-powerful Committee of Public Safety managed to finally drive the foreign armies from French soil, but its policy of crushing with terror anyone with differing views eventually prompted opposition forces to unite and

[11] One of the deputies elected to the national convention was Thomas Paine (1737–1809), an Englishman of Quaker background, who had defended the American case in a pamphlet called *Common Sense* (1776), and the French Revolution in another pamphlet called *The Rights of Man* (1791–92) – the latter against the criticism of Edmund Burke. Paine, with his broad international concern for social, political and economic justice, and his desire for reform of religion, was one of the most powerful spokesmen for all that was best in the age of revolution. He offended extreme radicals by voting for the exile of Louis XVI to America rather than for execution.

overthrow it as soon as the foreign danger had receded. Many of the political reforms of the Revolution were rolled back, including ideas on the elimination of extremes of wealth and poverty, and democracy was replaced first by oligarchy and then by the military and absolute monarchy from 1804 to 1814 of Napoleon I (1769–1821).

Nevertheless, the Revolution had achieved much that was to last: the end of feudalism in France and elsewhere, a major step forward towards the idea of legal equality, as incorporated in the *Code Napoléon*,[12] and the promotion of the idea of national self-determination which in the next hundred and fifty years was to capture the imagination of millions. Ultimately, however, the main lesson to be learned from the Revolution – that reform imposed by force will in the end be largely self-defeating – was not appreciated, and the mistakes made in France in the last decade of the eighteenth century were fated to be repeated over and over again. Perhaps the worst perversion was the twisting of the idea of national determination into one of oppression of others rather than one of brotherhood and enrichment of the human experience.

---

[12] The *Code Napoléon* was a systematic compilation of French law incorporating reforms based in reason rather than custom. The review began during the early days of the Revolution but was not completed until 1804. Since then the Code has been adopted by a multitude of countries.

PART II

The Present Age

THE three revolutions of the eighteenth century were the prelude to a multitude of developments in the nineteenth and twentieth which would touch upon virtually every aspect of man's social life and lead to major advances in hopes and practices of a more just form of society. In the first instance, this movement had its centre in the West – that is, in Europe and other areas where European influence was strong, particularly the Americas and Australasia – and it was not until the twentieth century that the movement became generally significant in other parts of the world. It was associated with the gradual emergence of the West in the eighteenth and nineteenth centuries as the most vital region of the world, particularly in technology and military and political power. Previously, Europe had always been relatively less important from a political point of view than the great civilizations of the Middle East and Asia, except for the few hundred years when Rome had ruled the Mediterranean basin and rivalled the power of Persia, India and China.

The three sections of Part II discuss advances towards a more just society with regard to (a) political and social equality, (b) reduction in material poverty, and (c) moves towards greater international cooperation and the effort to reduce warfare between nations.

A
GREATER POLITICAL AND SOCIAL EQUALITY

THE following discussion focuses on three broad themes. The first concerns the abolition of slavery and serfdom. Clearly, any society upholding these practices, which put such extreme limits on the freedom of a major portion of the population, is not one of equality. Like all instruments of oppression, slavery and serfdom take freedom away not only from those who are the direct victims but also from the oppressors and those who tolerate the oppression, because they are always weighed down by a constant fear and a sense of guilt, whether acknowledged or not.

The second theme is the widespread emergence of the national state which has allowed peoples of a common background to live and express themselves in their own culture and language, free of alien rule. The patriotic spirit that has been associated with the national state does indeed make a major contribution to a sense of self-respect and equality between peoples so long as it remains positive and does not involve negative feelings towards other cultures. Unfortunately, the spread of the national state has been accompanied in a series of instances by much negative hate-filled nationalism, and in consequence the development of equality and freedom which should come with national self-determination has been slowed down and sometimes reversed.

The third of our broad themes is the development and spread of democracy, an idea involving on the one hand the right of all citizens to take part in public affairs and their own government, and on the other the duty of government to serve and to be accountable to its citizens and to abide by the rule of law. The advance of democracy has not been uniformly successful around the world, nor has it been free of major flaws in those countries where it has been adopted. (For a statistical assessment of democratic practice today in regions of the world, see Table 4 on p. 143.) Nevertheless, there can be little doubt that its development has created a situation in which actual and potential equality amongst the citizens of the world is far greater today than it was at the beginning of the modern age.

CHAPTER 12

The Abolition of Slavery and Serfdom

THE greatest moral triumph of the nineteenth century was the abolition of slavery as a major institution of civilization. As remarked earlier in the discussion of Ancient Rome, slavery had been a feature of nearly all societies since the beginning of recorded civilization. Most slaves were either captives from war, those who had been convicted by the law, or those sold into slavery to pay off debt. Conditions of slaves varied greatly from those employed in the household, who sometimes acquired an education and occasionally even high office in the service of the state, to those working in the fields and mines who suffered immense physical as well as spiritual hardship. In the West the fall of Rome saw a marked decline in slavery and its replacement by serfdom. Serfdom was also, of course, a most onerous condition but at least it was superior to slavery insofar as serfs had legal rights in return for their services, and lord as well as serf each had responsibilities to the other, unequal though they might be. Slavery still continued to exist in the Middle East during the time of Islam, but as observed earlier the institution was much less harsh in theory and practice than in other parts of the world because most slaves were part of the domestic household and because of Muhammad's teachings recommending manumission.

Slavery underwent a great revival with the opening up of the New World and the establishment of extensive contacts with Africa. The European invaders of the New World wanted cheap manpower to operate the silver mines and to raise crops that were labour-intensive and were most profitable when cultivated on a large plantation scale: tobacco, sugar, and towards the end of the eighteenth century, cotton. The imposition of slavery on the indigenous population was not a success because they soon died of demoralization and diseases caught from their conquerors. The problem was solved by the massive importation of slaves from Africa, where European traders were able to purchase the war captives of local potentates. Over three centuries (sixteenth, seventeenth and eighteenth) some 15 million slaves were transported from Africa, of whom it is estimated that some 3 million (20 percent) did not survive the terrible conditions of the transatlantic voyage. Though it was the Catholic powers Spain and Portugal which began the brutal process of colonization of the Americas, it was in the colonies of the Protestant powers, particularly England, where slave conditions were the most harsh. From the beginning the Roman Catholic church showed a much greater sense of responsibility for the souls of those subject to slavery and serfdom; for instance, slaves were encouraged to have church marriages, there was strong opposition to separation of slave families, and manumission of children of mixed free/slave relationships was advocated. Nevertheless, in the end the fight to abolish slavery rather than to ameliorate it was to be led by certain Protestant sects, most notably the Quakers,[1] and by followers of the French enlightenment and the English rationalists.[2] The main battlefields of the struggle against slavery were in the three revolutionary countries, Great Britain, France and the United States.

The British Empire

In Great Britain the movement against slavery first started to coalesce in the last quarter of the eighteenth century. The process began in 1772 with a legal decision obtained by a Quaker, Granville Sharp, in the 'Somerset' case in which it was ruled that slaves could not be held in the United Kingdom because this would be contrary to common law. The movement was given further impetus with the publication of an *Essay on Slavery and Commerce of the Human Species* (1781) by Thomas Clarkson (1760–1846) and with the formation of the Abolitionist Society (1787). The Society, which had a mainly Quaker membership to begin with, including Clarkson, gave support to William Wilberforce (1759–1833), a young Member of Parliament and friend of the Prime Minister, William Pitt the Younger, who laboured to win the votes of fellow MPs for his proposed anti-slavery legislation. To strengthen the prospect of success the group concentrated initially on the task of stopping the horrendous transatlantic trade in slaves, a large part of which was carried in British ships, rather than of trying to abolish the whole slave system all at once. At first there was some government

[1] George Fox (1624–1691), founder of the Quaker sect, had been highly critical of the institution of slavery. The repugnance felt by his followers intensified in the eighteenth century and in 1774 it was decided that any Quaker who continued to own slaves would be expelled from the sect. Two years later all Quakers in North America freed their slaves.

[2] One of the first rationalists to criticize slavery was John Locke (1632–1704) who described it in his *Treatise on Civil Government* as a violation of the natural rights of man.

sympathy for the movement, but after the Revolutionary War began in 1792 it was treated with increasing suspicion and began to be seen as one more radical idea which would undermine the strength of the Empire. It was not until 1807, after the formation of a more liberal administration headed by James Fox, that the movement was able to obtain approval of a Slave Trade Abolition Act which forbade both the carrying of slaves in British ships and the importation of slaves into the British colonies. The Act was given practical strength in 1811 with the passage of supplementary legislation which made slave trading a criminal offence and authorized searches by the Navy of suspicious British ships. When the Napoleonic Wars eventually ended in 1815, the British government tried to persuade other powers to cooperate in the suppression of the trade. Though unsuccessful in reaching this goal, the British were able nevertheless over a period of several years to negotiate bilateral agreements with Portugal, Spain and Brazil, and later with Prussia, Russia, France and the United States, by which each power was given the right of search of the others' vessels when there was reasonable suspicion that they were carrying slaves. In practice, because of the dominance of the British Navy at this time, the agreements in effect meant that it was to become the world's policeman against the slave trade.

After achieving the goal of significantly reducing the volume of international trade in slaves the movement then turned to the task of abolishing the holding of slaves in the British Empire. The movement was helped in the 1820s as fear of revolution began to give way to a more calm and rational discussion of issues and as news seeped into England of harshening conditions on the West Indian plantations where slave owners, deprived of their supply of fresh slaves, tried to extract more labour from those they already had. A new Anti-Slavery Society was formed in 1823 to give direction to reviving public interest. After ten years of struggle victory was finally achieved with the approval on 28 August 1833 of the Abolition of Slavery Act. Under the provisions of the Act slavery was to be abolished in seven years time; meanwhile slaves were to remain apprenticed to their owners with three-quarters of their time being provided free in return for food and lodging. The Act further provided that the owners were to be given full compensation. In practice the new Act created so much expectation on the plantations that it proved virtually impossible to postpone freedom for seven years, and in 1838 the slaves were finally set free two years ahead of schedule. Thus for the first time in history a major slave power renounced the institution as a matter of moral principle and actually put its word into practice. This was indeed a major event in the evolution of the just society.

The French Empire

Though Great Britain was the first major power in history to actually do away with a thriving slave system, it had been preceded in principle at least by one of the other two great revolutionary powers of the West: France. The French philosophers of the Enlightenment such as Montesquieu, Voltaire and Rousseau had vigorously denounced the institution. Thus Montesquieu wrote:

Slavery is just as much contrary to civil law as it is in opposition to natural law; what kind of civil statute could prevent a slave from escaping?

Only a year after the establishment of the Abolitionist Society in England, a group of Frenchmen including the Marquis de Condorcet (1743–1794), a philosopher and scientist, and the Marquis de Lafayette (1737–1834) founded the 'Société des Amis des Noirs' (1788) which took a more comprehensive position than its English counterpart by advocating the abolition not only of the slave trade but of slavery itself. The French Revolution with its themes of liberty, equality and fraternity was clearly incompatible with slavery, and on 4 February 1794 by the Decree of 16 Pluviôse An II, slavery was abolished throughout the French territories, and all peoples regardless of colour were declared equal.

Unfortunately, this magnificent declaration was not to be put into effect in the colonies, where revolutionary fervour was not so marked as in Paris, the excuse being the emergency conditions relating to the war with Britain and the other great powers (i.e. the same argument being used in England at that time to justify postponement of reform). This situation continued throughout both the revolutionary and Napoleonic periods. When the Bourbons were restored in 1814, it was clear that the government could not reverse the anti-slavery declaration of the Revolution, so the conservative regime contented itself with simply taking no action to enforce it. Changing public opinion, influenced by events in the British Empire, put pressure on the more liberal Orleanist regime (1830–1848) to take minimum measures to ameliorate the situation. Slaves were placed under the protection of the judiciary (i.e. summary punishment by the owner would no longer be legal); manumission was encouraged, and it was forbidden to forcibly break up slave families. Final action came with the 1848 revolution. The revolutionary government set up a commission headed by Victor Schoelcher to advise on the matter; in August 1848 it accepted the commission's report and for the second time slavery was declared abolished throughout the Empire. This time the law was enforced and slavery disappeared in the world's second largest empire – just ten years after abolition in the British Empire.

The United States of America

Immensely important as were these developments in the British and
French Empires, it was to be in the third of the revolutionary
countries, the United States of America, where the struggle was to
be the most dramatic. Slavery had first become significant in the
eighteenth century in the southern states on plantations growing
tobacco and cotton. The Declaration of Independence had stated that
'all men are created equal' but in the negotiations leading up to the
formation of the United States, the southern states resisted attempts
to include abolition of slavery in the Federal settlement and it was
agreed that this matter should be left to the individual states. All that

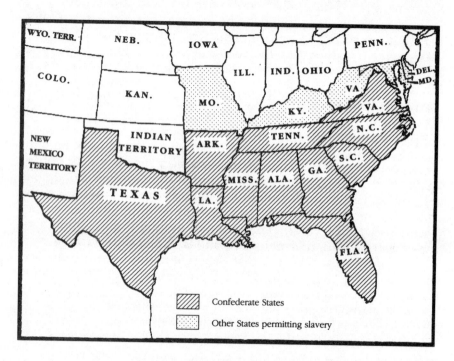

The Slave-holding States of the USA, 1860

could be agreed was that overseas slave trading would be abolished
within twenty years and this indeed was achieved on time with effect
from 1 January 1808 (i.e. at almost the same time as in the British
Empire). In addition, most of the northern states abolished slavery
within their own borders between 1777 and 1804. The North-West
Ordinance of 1787 also laid down that there would be no slavery in

new territories north of the Ohio River and of the Mason–Dixon line which linked the Ohio to the coast between Pennsylvania and Maryland.

These developments, which sharpened the differences between the northern and southern states, helped to make slavery a symbol of the gradually diverging interests of the two sections of the country which had come about as the North became the centre of industrialization whilst the South centred its economy on the great plantations. At first a balance of interests was achieved. The two regions had approximately equal-sized populations and therefore equal representation in Congress; also, there was an informal understanding that the balance would be maintained by making sure that new states joining the Union would be alternately slave and non-slave. But within a few decades the agreement was under stress because the North, with a population growing faster than the South, came to see slavery as disadvantageous to its interests. Northerners took particular objection to the Southern practice of counting slaves for the purpose of allocating congressional seats (distributed on the basis of population) and because of the importation of slaves to Missouri which was north of the unofficial demarcation line. The situation was temporarily patched up in the Missouri Compromise of 1820 whereby Missouri was allowed to join the union as a slave state in return for the creation of a new state of Maine which was non-slave, and agreement that there would be no slave territories henceforth north of the latitude 36:30.

Another proposal to ease the tension by sending liberated slaves to a new state, Liberia, in Africa failed to win the support of Congress and relations between South and North began to deteriorate again. In the South the Nat Turner slave rebellion of 1831 in Virginia served to increase fear and a defensive attitude. In the North there was a growing moral repugnance for the institution as a result of the work of the Quaker community in particular and widespread respect for Frederick Douglass (1817–1895), a distinguished anti-slavery orator and himself a former slave. Northerners were particularly outraged by the practice of Southern agents in pursuing slave fugitives into Northern states and taking them back by force. Abolitionists responded by organizing what was to become known as the 'underground railroad' to help fugitive slaves to escape to Canada, and they won widespread world sympathy for their cause with the publication in 1852 of Uncle Tom's Cabin by Harriet Elizabeth Beecher Stowe (1811–1896). Nevertheless, the Southerners insisted on the right to pursue slave fugitives across state lines, and in the so-called Compromise Agreement of 1850 the North was bullied into agreeing that the fugitive law should actually be strengthened in return for abolition of the slave trade in Washington, the nation's capital. Abolitionists were further incensed by the infamous Dred Scott decision of the Supreme Court in 1857 which ruled (a) that negroes were not citizens of the United States, (b) that a slave who fled to a Northern state was still subject to the law of the state where he came from, and (c) that a slave was the property of his owner who could not be deprived of that property without due process.

Matters finally started to come to a head in 1858 with the election campaign for one of the Illinois seats in the US Senate which prompted the famous Lincoln–Douglas debates. Stephen Douglas (1813–1861) took a compromise position, arguing that though Congress could not force slavery on states that were opposed to it, it could not, on the other hand, prevent states from having it if that was the popular will. Abraham Lincoln (1809–1865) would not accept such a compromise: 'We think it [slavery] is a moral, a social and a political wrong'; and he made it clear that he thought slavery should not be permitted to expand to any new territories and that eventually it would have to be abolished. The campaign thrust Lincoln forward as the leading anti-slavery politician and in the 1860 presidential election he was chosen to be the candidate of the Republican Party of the North. His victory in that election over Douglas, the candidate of the Northern Democrats, and over Breckinridge of the Southern Democrats, prompted high passions on both sides of the issue. In the North, John Brown, a fanatical abolitionist, led a small band in attacking and capturing a Union military depot at Harper's Ferry, Virginia, with a view to encouraging a major slave revolt. In the South, South Carolina decided in December 1860 to secede from the Union – even before Lincoln had taken office. Other states soon followed and in March of 1861 they joined together to form a Southern Confederacy. What faint hopes still remained for another compromise were dashed in April 1861 when the Southerners besieged and captured the Union base at Fort Sumter.

Though the ensuing bloody civil war (over 600,000 soldiers were to die in the four-year conflict) was formally about preservation of the Union and state's rights, the issue in the last analysis was slavery. However, President Lincoln chose to handle the issue with caution, and it was not until the war had been raging for over a year that he made a proclamation (22 September 1862), that all slaves were to be freed in the rebel states unless they surrendered by 1 January 1863. As the South refused to surrender by the deadline, a formal Emancipation Declaration was issued effective from that date. As a result, when the war finally ended some 16 months later, a total of some 4 million slaves gained their freedom. Their rights were formerly incorporated into the US Constitution by means of the 13th Amendment which was ratified by the states on 18 December 1865. Two more constitutional Amendments, the 14th and the 15th, gave Federal guarantee of their personal and property rights and the right to vote. This victory for justice was unfortunately to be profoundly weakened by subsequent failure to combat deep racial prejudice (a subject which will be taken up later in the next chapter), particularly in the South, and for another hundred years black Americans were to be deprived in practice of many of their civil rights and to be horribly oppressed politically, socially and economically. Nevertheless, a beginning had been made: there could be no return to a civilization based on slavery.

The Abolition of Slavery in Other Countries

Though events in England, France and the United States were the most significant in the story of the abolition of slavery around the world, the record would not be complete without some reference to what happened in other important slave-holding countries and to further developments in the field of international cooperation in the suppression of the slave trade. Generally, the former Spanish colonies of South America abolished slavery soon after they began the struggle for independence, e.g. Buenos Aires in 1813, Colombia in 1821, and Mexico in 1829. The Netherlands abolished the institution in 1863, the same year as the United States, and Spain, Portugal, and Brazil followed in the 1870s and 1880s. Later in the century, as the European imperial powers extended their influence in the Middle East and Asia, slavery was also abolished in Egypt, the Ottoman Empire, Thailand and China. In some of these countries, of course, practice followed quite a long way behind the law; nevertheless, the change in the law itself was of the utmost significance because of the break it represented with several thousand years of acceptance.

There still remained Africa. Though the great imperial powers at the end of the nineteenth century were primarily concerned with carving out colonies for themselves in that continent, their collective consciences could not be entirely put aside. At the Congress of Berlin in 1885 the assembled powers agreed that they would cooperate to suppress the slave trade in the Congo. Five years later they approved the General Act of Brussels which was to be the fundamental charter for international cooperation for the suppression of slavery throughout the world. This act was important because (a) it was accepted by virtually all the independent states of the world of the day, and (b) it established a permanent international organization to monitor information on slavery with offices in Zanzibar and Brussels. It also made provision for such practical aspects as (c) establishment of military posts and patrols in areas where slavery still existed, (d) a declaration by all that slave owning was a criminal offence, and (e) assistance for slaves who were liberated.

The General Act of Brussels has been followed by supplementary international agreements under the auspices of the League of Nations, e.g. the International Slavery Convention (1926) and the permanent advisory committee of experts on slavery (1932), and of the United Nations, e.g. Article 4 of the Declaration of Human Rights (1948) which includes the statement:

No one shall be held in slavery: slavery and the slave trade shall be prohibited in all its forms; no one shall be held in servitude.

Under the League an important precedent was set when Ethiopia and Liberia were denied membership until they agreed to take action to eliminate slavery within their areas of sovereignty. Today, all nations assert that they are against slavery, although there are still some isolated instances in practice of its continued existence: debt bondage arrangements in certain third world countries, for example, and forced labour camps maintained by some authoritarian regimes.[3] These practices are increasingly criticized and it would seem reasonable to expect that these last bastions of one of the most unjust institutions of civilization will also soon crumble away.

The Abolition of Serfdom

The virtual elimination of slavery throughout the world in modern times has been paralleled by a similar decline in serfdom, which has existed widely for centuries and affected millions of people. In theory at least this practice was not as damaging to the human spirit as slavery because serfs had certain rights such as the retention of some of their produce and protection by their lords from attack from outside. On the other hand, the oppression was still very heavy: they were obliged to stay on the land where they were born, to work free for their lord and hand over most of their produce, and often to be subject to his will with regard to marriage and inheritance.

---

[3] One of the worst and most widespread types of slavery still in existence is child bondage. The International Labour Organization estimates there are some 200 million children around the world who have been sold into domestic service by poverty-stricken parents. One example of this practice reported recently in the media is in Colombo, Sri Lanka, where it is estimated there are some 40,000 children in bondage.

As noted earlier, the institution had been largely abolished in much of Western and Eastern Europe during the eighteenth century as a result partly of the reforms of the enlightened despots and partly of the French Revolution. At the end of the Napoleonic wars the one remaining major European power which still had serfdom was Russia, where more than 40 million people were subject to this form of semi-slavery. As the nineteenth century progressed the Czars' advisors became increasingly persuaded that the system would have to change, if only because it was so clearly inefficient and was holding back the economic development of Russia as compared with rival powers in Europe – as seemed to be clearly demonstrated in the humiliating experience of the Crimean War. Furthermore, the serfs themselves were no longer passive, perhaps hearing echoes of freedom from the West, and the country was periodically rent by rebellion. In 1842 a preliminary step in the direction of reform was taken when a law of voluntary accords was introduced which encouraged serf owners to enter into agreements with their serfs to eliminate personal serfdom in return for annual fixed payments. It was soon recognized that this was a totally unsatisfactory arrangement and when Alexander II (1818–1881) became Czar in 1855 he set up a special commission to advise on the whole issue. As a result of the commission's report, the Czar approved on 3 March 1861 a law which abolished serfdom throughout his Empire.

Under the new law each former serf would receive a plot of land for which he could make a fixed payment to the landowner. Such payments would be financed by a government loan which had to be paid off over 45 years (eventually completed in 1905) and which was the collective responsibility of each village rather than of the individual peasant. This arrangement clearly made it very difficult for a long time for a former serf to leave the land, because of the pressure on him from his village to pay his full share of the collective debt to the government. Nor did it lead to a significant improvement in the appalling standard of living of most of the peasantry, at least in the short term, and the deep division between them and the landowners was to remain and to become a central factor in the Revolution of 1917. Nevertheless, there is no question that in the perspective of the evolution of the just society, the emancipation of the Russian serfs was a major event, occurring, interestingly enough, just two years before the Emancipation Declaration of President Lincoln.

CHAPTER 13

National Self-Determination and the Building of Nations

A SECOND major political movement of modern times, and one of untold importance in the development of the just society, has been nation building: the process of self-determination for peoples with a common cultural heritage. Since the beginning of civilization most states have been built around centres of power which did not co-incide with language and cultural boundaries; states either dominated peoples of many different backgrounds, or consisted of only part of a language or cultural group. On the one hand there were the great empires of Babylon, Persia, Rome, India and China, and later the Hapsburgs and the Ottomans, and on the other the city states of Greece, Northern Italy and the Baltic. In the course of centuries, empires would expand and recede and peoples would find them-selves subjects first of one state and then of another; their sense of belonging was based on submission to military power and law, or loyalty to a ruling family. The spirit of patriotism, a feeling of oneness and solidarity with all the peoples of the same culture and history, was rarely strong or encouraged by political institutions. There were early exceptions to this pattern, notably in the case of the Jewish people, as mentioned earlier, who tried to maintain their own culture in the face of Greek influence and Roman military might, and who after the Dispersal always dreamed of the day when Israel would be re-established.

This situation gradually began to change in Europe as traditional empires and absolute monarchies gave way to constitutional forms of government which created a minimum sense of participation by ordinary people in their own government and of some identification with the state. This process was given an immense push forward by the French Revolution which promoted the idea that France was not just a territory, but a people – as emphasized by the change of title from King Louis XVI of France to Emperor Napoleon of the French.

Since the French Revolution, the process of nation building has gone through three distinct phases: the hundred years up until the outbreak of the Great War; the interwar period; and the post–Second World War period. In this chapter each of these phases will be briefly reviewed in turn.

The Nineteenth Century

In the first phase much of the activity was in Europe and was largely associated with the early stages of the disintegration of two of the great autocratic monarchies: the Hapsburgs and the Ottomans. These were reluctant to surrender power to their subject peoples who desired self–determination, and in consequence the process of nation building in these areas was accompanied by a considerable amount of violence, a precedent which set the pattern for much of what was to follow in the twentieth century.

A second main area of progress towards nation building in this period was in those lands outside Europe which had received large numbers of European migrants and had been formed into colonies by the mother countries. These developments took place mostly in South America, where nations were formed out of the Spanish and Portuguese Empires, and in the largest of the white colonies of the British Empire in North America, Australasia and South Africa.

Europe

In Europe the largest nation to achieve self–determination and unity was Germany. For centuries the peoples of Germany had been part of the so-called Holy Roman Empire, a ramshackle institution embracing some three hundred sovereign states of varying size and power, loosely presided over by the Hapsburg Emperor of Austria.[1] The Holy Roman Empire was easily knocked aside by France under the leadership of Napoleon, and for a while the German people were all but subjects of that country. The growing middle class, already attracted by the principles of patriotism associated with the French Revolution, concluded that their future well-being depended on establishing a united German nation. This view, however, was not shared by the two biggest continental powers, the autocratic empires of Russia and Austria, which perceived such a union to be threatening to their own interest and maybe even to their survival. They therefore ensured that in the peace arrangements of 1815 only a minimum gesture towards German unity was made: a confederation

---

[1] A contemporary once aptly remarked that it was neither Holy, nor Roman, nor an Empire.

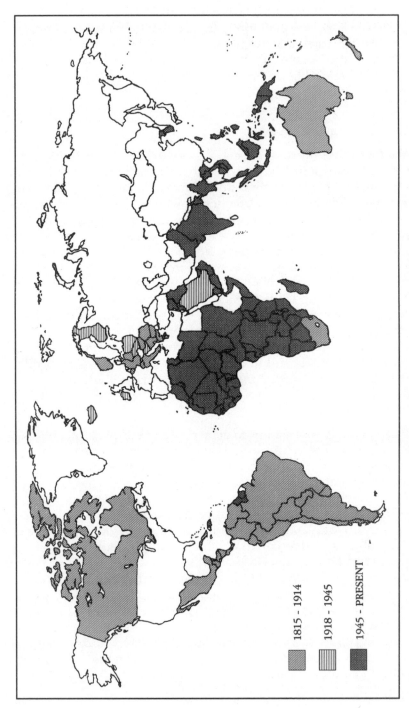

Achievement of national independence in the nineteenth and twentieth centuries

1815 - 1914

1918 - 1945

1945 - PRESENT

still divided into a number of virtually sovereign states (now reduced to 35) with an all-German Diet (or Parliament) limited to advisory functions, which had its seat in Frankfurt-on-Main. The Diet consisted of delegates nominated by the governments of the states, and was presided over by an Austrian representative.

Prussia, however, as the second power in Germany, was ever ready to try and strengthen its position *vis-à-vis* Austria, and in pursuit of that goal it initiated a gradual, low-key, programme of bilateral tariff treaties with the other states of Germany. This policy was so successful that by 1844 Germany had become, almost surreptitiously, united into a single customs union (*Zollverein*) to which all the states belonged – except Austria. In 1848 German middle-class patriots, encouraged by the outbreak of revolutions that year in France and Austria, which had caused disarray amongst the forces of reaction, organized the election by the peoples of Germany of a new constituent assembly. This was to be the first step towards a politically united Germany. The dream was shattered, however, because the delegates could not agree as to whom they should offer the throne of Germany: the King of Prussia or the Emperor of Austria. The Prussian King, Frederick William IV (1840–1861), after a period of dithering opted to support Austria against the assembly rather than risk war with Austria or become behoven to a democratic body.

In the long run the Prussian monarchy came to recognize that a Germany united under Prussian leadership was the only way to escape Austrian tutelage. The most influential political personality of the time, Prince Otto von Bismarck (1815–1898), who became chief minister of Prussia in 1863. Bismarck carried out a complex series of foreign policy manœuvres over a period of nearly two decades. A first step was to persuade Austria–Hungary to join Prussia in driving the Danes out of the German-speaking provinces of Schleswig-Holstein. A second was to cultivate good relations with the Czar and to make an alliance with Italy, who desired to take Venice from Austria–Hungary. The third was to provoke Austria–Hungary into a quarrel over the administration of Schleswig-Holstein, which gave an excuse for Prussia to declare war. In the subsequent Seven Weeks War of 1866 Austria–Hungary was defeated and forced to withdraw from Germany. Prussia then took the opportunity to annex Hanover, Hesse, Nassau and Frankfurt, and to dissolve the confederation and replace it with a North German confederation which she completely dominated. The southern German states were allowed to form their own separate confederation but were persuaded to make a strong military alliance with Prussia as a precaution against possible

attack by France. The final round of unification came when
Bismarck managed to exploit a diplomatic storm in a teacup to force
a war on Napoleon III and his rickety Second French Empire.
Military victory in the war of 1870–71 led to the annexation of
Alsace-Lorraine (which had a mixed French and German population)
and the formation of the German Empire (the Second Reich) with
William of Prussia as Emperor.

At last the German people had their own united state. The
arrangement, however, was far from ideal. First, its boundaries did
not embrace all Germans (most particularly those still in the Austro–
Hungarian Empire) and at the same time did include many non-
Germans, particularly Poles, some of whose lands had fallen to
Prussia in the three-way partition with Austria and Russia at the end
of the eighteenth century. These deficiencies, together with the fact
that unity had been achieved through an imposed policy of 'blood
and iron' rather than through the free will of the people, were to
become sources of conflict in the future – and of much misery for
Europe and the world as a whole.

Another people who were able to obtain national self-determination in the nineteenth century in central Europe, despite the initial
opposition of the Hapsburgs, were the Hungarians, the most
numerous of the subject peoples of the Empire after the Germans.
When, more than a century before, the Hapsburgs annexed Hungary
to their dominions after defeating the Turks they had allowed the
Hungarians to have their own Diet (Parliament) but this was made
up almost entirely of great landed magnates and the nobility. There
was little in the way of either self-government or sharing in the
administration of the Empire. The first significant concession to
Hungarian patriotic feeling in the nineteenth century was made in the
thirties when the Emperor agreed that the official language in
Hungary should be Magyar rather than Latin. That was as far as he
would go, however, and he refused the Ten Points Manifesto
requesting local autonomy which had been drawn up by Francis
Deak (1803–1876). In consequence, when the 1848 revolutions broke
out the more radical nationalists led by Louis Kossuth (1802–1894)
had much popular support and they took the opportunity to establish
an independent Hungarian Republic. Within a year the Republic was
brutally crushed by the Austrian army supported by the soldiers of
Czar Nicholas of Russia, and the old centralized Hapsburg system
was once again forced on the peoples of middle Europe. But the
growing weakness of the Hapsburgs in the face of the struggle with
Prussia in Germany and the general unrest amongst peoples of the
Empire, desirous of national self-determination, persuaded the

Emperor to make a compromise with the Hungarians (1867) whereby the Hapsburg Empire was divided into two, with the Germans dominant in one part and the Hungarians in the other. The two halves had in common the Emperor, a foreign ministry, an army and navy (in which the language was German), and a treasury. The Hungarians were united in one state, but as in the new state of Germany the seeds of conflict were hidden within it because victory had been obtained at the price of the continued subjugation of other peoples, such as Czechs, Slovaks, and Romanians, living in the territory of what was defined as Hungary. The Magyars, like so many other peoples struggling for independence, failed to see a connection between freedom for themselves and freedom for their neighbours.

The peoples of Italy, like those of Germany, had suffered the humiliation of occupation by Napoleon I, and at the same time had been inspired by the patriotic principles of the French Revolution. Again, as in Germany, the collapse of the Napoleonic Empire in 1814–1815 led to the restoration of the old patchwork of independent states. There were nine of these, all under the watchful eye of the Hapsburgs who also occupied large sections of Northern Italy, including Venice and Milan. Patriotic feeling was strong, but the Italians could do little against the might of the Hapsburg Empire. Some looked to the liberal kingdom of Piedmont, the most solid of the Italian states, to take the lead in uniting Italy despite Austria. Others followed Giuseppe Mazzini (1805–1872) who plotted to achieve unity through revolution, but each of his attempts ended in abysmal failure. The 1848 revolutionary risings in France, Germany and Hungary were echoed in Italy too. Liberal regimes were established in the Papacy and Naples, and Venice declared itself a Republic. National unity seemed at last to be at hand. But these hopes were soon dashed, as in Germany and Hungary. Marshall Radetsky put down a rising in Milan, Venice was retaken, and by July 1849 the Pope had had his power fully restored.

In the next round the heroes were to be Camillo Benso di Cavour (1810–1861) and Giuseppe Garibaldi (1807–1882). Cavour, who in the 1840s had founded the newspaper *Il Risorgimento* to promote support for Italian independence and unity, became Prime Minister of Piedmont in 1851 and immediately set about the task of winning the diplomatic support of the Great Powers (Austria, England, France and Russia) for these goals. In 1855–1856 Piedmont joined France and England against Russia in the Crimean War, although Piedmont had no direct quarrel with Russia. In 1858 Cavour made a secret treaty with Napoleon III whereby the latter undertook to give

Piedmont support in a war against Austria, provided that a respectable excuse could be found. The objective of the war would be to facilitate the establishment of a federation of four Italian states under the presidency of the Pope. In return France was to be given Savoy and Nice (then part of Piedmont). The war with Austria duly occurred in April 1859 but after two bloody battles at Magenta and Solferino, Napoleon, sickened by the reality of war and fearful of Prussian intervention on the side of Austria, chose to arrange an immediate armistice rather than press on until Austria conceded all that had been promised to Piedmont. As a result, Piedmont was awarded Lombardy but the region of Veneto was returned to Austria. This disappointing result was soon improved by Garibaldi, who landed in Sicily with a small band of his 'redshirts' and with the enthusiastic support of the local population overthrew the Bourbon King of the Two Sicilies and advanced on Rome. The freed territories were handed over to Piedmont whose parliament on 17 March 1861 declared the establishment of the Kingdom of Italy. The Italian people were at last united, but with the two important exceptions of those in the Veneto – still under the heel of the Hapsburgs – and those in the Papal States. The latter were under the protection of Napoleon III who feared that otherwise he would lose the support of the Catholic Church in France.

This unsatisfactory situation did not last long. Within ten years these territories were to be united with the Kingdom of Italy. In 1866 the Veneto was ceded by the Austrians to Italy as a reward for supporting Prussia in the Seven Years War. In 1870 Napoleon III was obliged to withdraw from Rome in order to concentrate his whole army in the war against Prussia of that year, and soon afterwards the Romans voted overwhelmingly in a plebiscite to be united with their fellow Italians under King Victor Emmanuel.

These successes for national movements in opposition to the Hapsburg Empire were matched by similar successes in the Ottoman Empire, which by the nineteenth century was even weaker and in a more advanced state of decay. There were indeed good reasons for it to be known as the 'sick man of Europe'. The first nation to break away from the Ottoman Empire was Greece whose independent spirit had been encouraged by Russia since the time of Catherine the Great because of common adherence to the Orthodox Church. Greek patriots were also inspired by the French Revolution and had the support of romantic idealists in the West who recalled the glories of Ancient Greece. In 1821 there was a popular rising in Moldavia and the Morea which led to the expulsion of the Turkish rulers. The following year a representative assembly declared the independence of Greece and established a liberal constitution for the new state. In 1823 the Turks tried but failed to reoccupy the lost territory. Refusing to accept defeat, they called upon Ibrahim Pasha of Egypt, who was nominally a subject of the Ottoman Empire, to bring in his powerful forces to crush the Greeks. Greek appeals for help were heeded in England, France, and Russia despite the conflicting interests of these countries, and despite warnings from Austria that the Great Powers should, in their own interest, oppose all revolutionary and nationalist movements. After destruction of the Egyptian fleet at the battle of Naverino in 1827 the Turks agreed to negotiate, and at the London Conference of 1830 the Great Powers gave official recognition to Greek independence.

The Greek example was soon to be followed by three other peoples subject to the Ottomans: the Serbs, the Romanians and the Bulgarians. As a result of successful revolts in Serbia in 1815–1817 the Turks recognized a local leader, Milosh Obrenovich, as Prince of Serbia, as this seemed to be the only practical way of keeping some sort of presence in this most northerly of their possessions. In 1829 at the treaty of Adrianople formal recognition was given to Serbian autonomy. Sensitivity on the part of Austria, which also had Serb subjects, delayed formal acceptance by the Great Powers of complete independence for Serbia until the Treaty of Berlin in 1878. As anticipated by Austria, the Serbs were not satisfied and nationalist feelings continued to smoulder for decades to come, bursting into conflagration in 1914 with the assassination by a Serb nationalist of the heir to the Hapsburg throne.

Revolts in the mid-nineteenth century in the provinces of Wallachia and Moldavia, heartland of the Romanian people, led to recognition of local autonomy for them at the Treaty of Paris in 1858. Full independence for Romania was granted by the Great Powers twenty years later at the Treaty of Berlin, but in return Romania was required to cede Bessarabia (part of Moldavia) to Russia.

The Bulgarian people first rose up in revolt in 1876 but were brutally suppressed in what were to be known as the Bulgarian atrocities, a matter given great publicity in Great Britain by William Gladstone (1809–1898) in attacking the pro-Ottoman foreign policy of Benjamin Disraeli (1804–1881), then Prime Minister. As a result of the Treaty of Berlin, Bulgaria was recognized as a principality of the Turkish Empire with right to local autonomy. Eight years later the principality was doubled in size to include East Rumelia, a development which meant that most Bulgarians were within the boundaries of their own principality. In 1908 Prince Ferdinand, the ruler of the principality, declared that Bulgaria should be an independent kingdom, a claim which was accepted the following year by the two most interested parties, Austria–Hungary and the Ottoman.

Despite this progress, the Balkan situation remained very unstable because the new states did not embrace all of their own peoples, some of whom were still in the Hapsburg Empire as noted above, while others were still under the yoke of the Ottoman. In 1911 Greece, Serbia and Bulgaria allied against the Ottoman, the weaker of the two oppressors of their peoples, in the hope of driving them entirely out of the Balkan peninsula. They would have succeeded but for the intervention of both Austria–Hungary and Russia which rushed to limit the power of Serbia and Bulgaria respectively. Frustrated, the allies quarrelled amongst themselves and in 1913 Greece and Serbia (with the help of Romania) fought the Second Balkan War against Bulgaria. The resulting settlement was based on military occupation with little effort being made to reconcile the different national interests involved, so leaving a source of discontent for the future.

Though the movement towards national self-determination in Europe in the nineteenth century was most dramatic in the central, southern, and eastern regions of the continent, the story would be incomplete without mention of the independence achieved in the north by the Norwegian people and in the west by the Belgians. In the early Middle Ages Norway had been a great power in its own right, but had later (15th century) become a dependency of Denmark as a result of dynastic arrangements. In 1814 the Allies against France agreed that Norway should be handed over to Sweden as a reward to its King Bernadotte, who was a former marshal of Napoleon, for switching to the allied side in the final stages of the Napoleonic wars. Though in many ways there were close cultural links between all three of the core Scandinavian countries, such high-handed action did not meet with much enthusiasm in Norway. For a time the Norwegians were pacified because Norway was treated as a free, independent, and indivisible kingdom with its own separate parliament, united with Sweden only through common fealty to the Swedish crown. During the nineteenth century, however, even these minor impediments to full sovereignty began to irk the Norwegians, who became increasingly conscious of their own separate identity as a result of a great cultural renaissance. Demands for their own national flag and a separate consular service to look after their growing overseas trading interests were refused by the Swedes. The inevitable happened. In 1905 the Norwegian Parliament (*Storting*) declared the union with Sweden dissolved, an action which was ratified by a popular plebiscite within three months and accepted by the Swedish parliament a short time afterwards. Six years later the independence of Norway was symbolically drawn to the attention of the world through the magnificent achievement of the Norwegian Roald Amundsen (1872–1928), the first man to reach the Antarctic Pole.

The Belgian people had their own special story. When the northern Dutch embraced Protestantism and broke away from the Hapsburg Empire in the seventeenth and eighteenth centuries, the people of the southern lowlands, partly Flemish (Dutch) and partly Walloon (French), remained Catholic and within the Empire. As a result they evolved their own special culture and feeling of identity. After the Napoleonic wars the Great Powers decided that their lands should be joined with the Netherlands, an arrangement which the British hoped would make Belgium (considered the best place for launching an invasion of England from the Continent) more secure against possible occupation by France or any of the other Great Powers. The Belgians not unnaturally soon became restless with the imposed arrangement and had grievances because Dutch was the official language of the whole country, Protestantism was given special favours, and there was under-representation of Belgium in the joint parliament (the Belgians at that time outnumbered the Dutch almost two to one but were only given half the seats in Parliament).

The French Revolution of July 1830 prompted Belgian nationalists to take matters into their own hands, and on 30 November 1830 they made a unilateral declaration of independence. The Dutch government refused to acknowledge it and for nine years the issue was in dispute. Eventually, however, the Dutch were forced to concede defeat because unexpectedly they did not have the support of Great Britain, which decided to recognize the reality of the situation and to settle for Belgian independence if it was guaranteed by all the Great Powers. This was agreed, and the Belgians were able to elect as their own King, Leopold of Saxe-Coburg (1790–1865), the uncle of Queen Victoria, who did much to help build up a tradition of constitutionalism and a healthy economy – an achievement which has stood Belgium in good stead during times of trial such as the recent period of tension between the Flemish and the Walloons.

European Colonies

Having briefly touched on the story of movements for national independence in Europe in the nineteenth century, the focus of attention needs now to be switched to parallel developments in some of the major overseas colonies of the European empires. Following the bid for independence in the late eighteenth century of the thirteen British colonies of North America, it was in Latin America where the movement for national independence outside Europe was first successful in the nineteenth century. After the colonization of South and Central America in the sixteenth century the Spanish monarchy chose to rule through a very centralized system giving the local population – even those of Spanish descent (Creoles), not to speak of mixed blood citizens (Mestivos) and native Indians – very little say in public affairs except to a certain degree in municipal government. Interest in self-government had already begun by 1808 when Napoleon invaded Spain in order to complete a system for denying England trade access to the European continent – which he hoped would force England to sue for peace. Napoleon deposed the Bourbon King, Ferdinand VII, and replaced him with his own brother, Joseph. The Spanish colonies refused to give allegiance to Joseph, who could not enforce his rule over them because contact was cut off by the British Navy. Upon overthrow of the Napoleonic Empire in 1814 the Bourbon monarchy was restored in Spain, and for a short while the restoration forces were able to subdue the South American colonies. But within a decade (1816–1825) the peoples of the whole area, under the leadership of José de San Martin (1778– 1850), Simon Bolivar (1783–1830), and Bernardo O'Higgins (1776– 1842), had risen up and defeated the Spanish forces and declared independence. Not a little help was given to this process by the British, who hoped that an independent continent would provide new markets for their industrial goods. A separate movement beginning in 1821 brought independence to Mexico and Central America.

Early dreams of a united Latin American republic soon evaporated partly because of the sheer difficulty of communication over such a vast area and partly because of clashes of interest between the different regions. Soon the main component regions of South America broke away from the centre to become separate nations: Argentina, Chile, Bolivia, Peru, New Grenada (Colombia) and Venezuela. Similarly, in Central America several of the small provinces broke away from Mexico to become the independent states of Guatemala, El Salvador, Honduras, Nicaragua and Costa Rica. Perhaps because of lack of prior experience in public administration and because of vast social and economic differences between Creoles, Mestivos, Indians and imported Africans, few of the new nations were able to maintain stable and democratic government and most were to undergo extensive periods of rule by military dictators, a condition which has been maintained well into the twentieth century.

The movement towards independence of the Spanish American colonies was paralleled by similar events in those ruled by Portugal. When Napoleon invaded the Iberian Peninsula in 1808, the Regent, Prince John, fled to Brazil and established his court there. After the overthrow of Napoleon, John, King since 1816, stayed in Brazil and ruled from there with the help of a regent in Portugal. In 1820 the regency in Portugal was overthrown and the King was obliged to return. The King's son, Dom Pedro (1789–1834), was left as regent in Brazil. Brazilians affected by the general movement towards independence in Spanish America persuaded Dom Pedro to act as their leader. The Portuguese offered some concessions but made it clear that Brazil should be a subordinate of Portugal within the Empire. In 1822 the regent declared Brazilian independence and became its constitutional monarch. Little resistance was offered by the Portuguese due to the organization by Lord Cochrane (1775–1860) of an efficient protective Brazilian navy. By contrast with the failure to maintain unity in the former Spanish territories, the whole of Brazil remained loyal to the new administration except for the province of Uruguay which opted for separate nationhood in 1828; and so Brazil became the largest and most powerful of the South American states, equal perhaps to New Spain (Mexico) itself.

The movement towards autonomy and self-determination affected not only the declining empires of Spain and Portugal, but also the most vigorous of the imperial powers in the nineteenth century: Great Britain. By the beginning of the twentieth century there was increasing talk of the Empire evolving into a commonwealth of autonomous nations united by one sovereign and by a common heritage and interest. The first nations of the new Commonwealth other than the 'mother country' were Canada, Australia, New Zealand and South Africa: all countries where white Europeans were in a dominant position. It would be many more years before commonwealth status would be granted to territories in India, Africa, and the oceans where indigenous populations predominated.

At the beginning of the nineteenth century Canada was divided into three separate colonies, each of which was essentially ruled by its own governor appointed from London, who was supported by a legislative council which he in turn had appointed. The British government not only controlled the appointment of the governor but it had also the right to review and approve local legislation. There were in addition elected assemblies at the local community level but these had little power. In many ways the arrangements were similar to those which had prevailed in the thirteen colonies before the 1776 Revolution. A rebellion in 1837 prompted the British government to send Lord Durham (1792–1840) to Canada to make a report on what changes should be made to conciliate the colonists. In 1839 he recommended that the three colonies should be united and given responsible government, with London retaining authority only over defence, foreign affairs, regulation of foreign trade, disposition of land, and changes in the Constitution. The British government responded in 1840 with an Act of Union which incorporated most of the Durham proposals, with the major exception that the legislative assembly continued to be appointed; it was not changed into an elective, representative body until 1856. The new arrangement was a compromise which could not last indefinitely, and in 1867 in response to a changing situation, including a greatly strengthened United States after the conclusion of the Civil War, the British parliament approved the British North America Act which established Canada as an independent dominion of the Empire with control over virtually all its own affairs including foreign policy and defence. The Act established a federal form of government with a two-house parliament, together with legislative assemblies for each of the four provinces: Ontario, Quebec, New Brunswick and Nova Scotia.

A similar pattern of development occurred in Australia and New Zealand. In Australia the legislative council of New South Wales, the first colony, was initially (1823) appointed by the governor and it was not until 1843 that it was agreed that two-thirds of the council should be elected representatives. The next step forward was the Australian Colonial Government Act of 1850 which in effect gave the Australian colonies autonomy with regard to local affairs. The final major step was the Commonwealth of Australia Act of 1901 (the first formal use of the term Commonwealth) which united the six states of Australia into a federal dominion with responsibility for foreign affairs, defence, trade, the currency and immigration, all of which had previously been reserved for the Imperial government. Like Canada, Australia was now essentially a sovereign nation with ties to Great Britain which were purely voluntary and based on sentiment. In the case of New Zealand, the British government had been reluctant to take any responsibility for its government and had claimed sovereignty only in order to maintain law and order and to forestall possible occupation by other colonial powers. The first constitution of 1852 made provision for the usual paternalistic arrangement of a nominated council. In 1856, six years after

Australia, New Zealand was granted a system of responsible government, i.e. control over its own domestic affairs. In 1870 British troops were withdrawn. Finally, in 1907, New Zealand won dominion status with full control over its foreign as well as domestic affairs.

The pattern of events in South Africa was more complicated because of clashes between Dutch settlers and the British, and because of the problem of relations between a minority white population and a majority of indigenous black Africans. The original Dutch Cape Colony was awarded to Britain as part of the peace settlement at the end of the Napoleonic Wars. However, within a few years most of the Dutch (Boer) farmers were disenchanted with British attempts to regulate their way of life and with immigration of new British settlers. In 1837 the Boer farmers made the Great Trek out of Cape Colony to the north and east where they formed new communities called Transvaal and Orange Free State. The British conceded control of local affairs to Cape Colony in 1872 and to Natal in 1892, but found it increasingly difficult to accept the independence of the two Boer republics especially after the discovery in the Transvaal of diamonds (1867) and gold (1882). Furthermore, there was a fear that the Boers would block the British drive northward to fulfil an ambition to join up with British colonies in East Africa and eventually with British-dominated Sudan and Egypt, i.e. to have an empire stretching right across Africa from Cape Town on the south coast to the Mediterranean coast in the north.

Chopping and changing policy, Britain drifted into war with the Boers in 1899 and after a long and bloody conflict eventually subdued the two republics. A few years after their victory the British recognized that military occupation was not going to be a workable long-term solution. In 1910 South Africa was given dominion status with a unitary form of government,[2] rather than the federal system adopted for Canada and Australia, in the hope that this would facilitate moderation of Boer policies by the English population of Cape Colony and Natal. The new dominion had two official languages: Dutch and English. The fundamental weakness of the constitution was that it failed to provide any protection for the interests of the majority non-white population, a weakness which was to have dire consequences in future years.

---

[2] The federal system of government, pioneered in modern times by the USA, shares power with regard to domestic matters between the constituent states or provinces on the one hand and the nation's federal government on the other. Such an arrangement would have given the Boers in Transvaal and Orange Free State more independence than a unitary system.

Between the Wars

Though the nineteenth century had seen an unprecedented advance in the number of peoples enjoying national independence and unity, especially in Europe and the Americas, the vast majority of the world's population in 1914 still lived under alien rule. The First World War gave encouragement to the movements for self-determination, particularly in those parts of Europe still not free, not only because it shook the existing international order to its foundations but also because the Great Powers, in order to justify the huge sacrifices that were made during the war, felt obliged to set out some broad general principles on how the world would be organized when peace came – including the principle of national self-determination. It might be added that though the Allies took the initiative in proclaiming national self-determination as the future basis of international relations (idealism apart, it generally served the Allied interest, insofar as it tended to weaken the resolution of Austro-Hungary and the Ottoman in particular), the Central Powers were on occasion supportive of the idea also, when it suited their purpose. Thus they were willing to re-establish Poland as an autonomous state – so long as she gave support to their foreign policy. The Allied presentation was initially laid down in President Wilson's Fourteen Points (which actually named certain nations that should be given independence) and most of these principles and plans were later incorporated into the Peace Treaties and the League of Nations Covenant.

With defeat, the Austro-Hungarian Empire broke up into its two component parts, Austria and Hungary. Then the northern section of the Empire, occupied mainly by Slav peoples (Czechs, Ruthenes, and Slovaks), joined together to form the new state of Czechoslovakia. The Czechs, whose homeland Bohemia had been an independent state for many centuries in the Middle Ages, were fortunate to have the distinguished leadership of Thomas Masaryk (1850–1937) and Eduard Beneš (1884–1948). It was perhaps for this reason that Czechoslovakia, despite the obvious obstacles to viability of its geography – a long and thin territory difficult to defend – and of a mixed population including a large minority of Germans, was nevertheless able for a while at least to establish one of the most stable and democratic governments in Europe. The strength of the nation was later shown when it re-emerged after the Second World War despite dismantlement by the Nazis in 1938 and 1939 following the Munich Agreement.

In the south of the former Empire, Bosnia and Herzgovina were joined to Serbia to complete the process of unification of the southern Slavs begun in the nineteenth century. The expanded nation initially took the name Kingdom of the Serbs, Croats and Slovenes, but was renamed Yugoslavia in 1929 to signify evolution from a loose confederation to a more tightly knit union.

The largest nation to win independence in Eastern Europe after the First World War was Poland. The Poles had been a major power in the Middle Ages and later it was one of their kings, John Sobieski (1629–1696), who had saved Vienna from the besieging Ottoman Sultan in 1583. But extreme emphasis on individual liberty amongst the nobles and a general lack of unity, together with a land which was militarily hard to defend, led to the partition of the country by its three powerful neighbours – Prussia, Austria and Russia – at the end of the eighteenth century. In Russia, where the largest number of Poles resided, there were two major revolts in 1830–31 and 1863–64 with the goal of national independence but both were brutally crushed by the Russian army and the Polish patriots were obliged to wait for the collapse of all three of the oppressing states in 1917–1918 before they could obtain their freedom. The new state was essentially carved out of the old Russian Empire but did manage to embrace most of Polish lands previously ruled by Austria–Hungary (Galicia) and by Germany. The latter arrangement involved a corridor to the Baltic which cut off East Prussia from the rest of Germany and provided a grievance which Hitler exploited in order to provoke war in 1939.

Four other nations were able to gain independence as a result of the collapse of the Russian Empire: Finland, Lithuania, Latvia and Estonia. All these peoples had distinct cultural traditions, but except for Lithuania none of them had ever previously been independent; they had been subject throughout history to other powers such as Sweden, Prussia and Russia. The Bolshevik government in Russia, like the earlier provisional government, accepted, albeit grudgingly, the declaration of independence by the Finns, but tried hard to subjugate the three Baltic states, mainly because of their strategic importance in relation to the Baltic Sea and Germany. However, the Bolshevik's power was greatly weakened by the long civil war which followed their revolution and they were not strong enough to reimpose Russian authority in this area. Accordingly the independence of the three nations was recognized in 1920. This only lasted for some twenty years and came to an end following the Nazi–Soviet Pact of 1939 which included provision for Russia to have a free hand in reoccupying these states, an option which was taken up without much ceremony almost immediately.

The interwar period also saw the achievement of independence (1922) by the Irish people after centuries of dominance by the British, who feared to have an independent country on their back doorstep which might combine with continental enemies against them. The relationship had been an unhappy one and there was a long bloody history of rebellion and suppression. The struggle became more complicated and bitter after England and Scotland became Protestant during the Reformation whilst Ireland remained Catholic. There are long memories both of the brutal regime of Oliver Cromwell with his self-righteous disdain for Catholic 'idol worshippers', and of defeat of the Catholic James II's Irish supporters by the 'Orange' Protestant army of William III. The last shreds of Irish independence were removed by the 1801 Act of Union of Great Britain and Ireland which followed an unsuccessful rising of the United Irishmen supported by French revolutionaries. The Act abolished the separate Irish parliament and instead additional seats were provided for Irish representatives in the parliament at Westminster. The process of rebellion and suppression continued and finally, in response, towards the end of the century a growing number of the English including William Gladstone himself were persuaded that there was no prospect of peace until the Irish people were given autonomy or Home Rule. This view was fiercely resisted, especially by the Protestants of Northern Ireland who feared that they in turn would be oppressed if they were to be a minority in a reactionary Catholic state. When independence did at last come the problem had not been resolved and Northern Ireland was excluded from the new state – an arrangement which has led to much resentment and hatred that has continued to this day.

After World War II

To complete this brief review of the modern movement towards national self-determination, our attention must now be shifted to the third phase which began after the end of the Second World War. Whereas the central focus in the first two phases had been Europe and its 'white' colonies, the main thrust in the third phase has been the emergence of new nations out of the non-white sectors of the colonial empires, which took place essentially over a thirty-year period from 1945 to 1975.[3] The dissolution of the great colonial empires, which happened at an unprecedented speed, was due to a

---

[3] The last European country to achieve independence was Iceland which was under the rule of Denmark until 1944, though it had had control over its own domestic affairs since 1918.

series of factors. One was the gradual loss by the European nations of their reputation for military prowess – a process which began with the defeat of Russia by Japan in the war of 1905 and came to a climax with the stunning victories of Japan over all the European powers represented in the Pacific in 1942. This loss of prestige gave additional courage to those challenging the empires and demanding freedom. A second factor was the huge loss of wealth and power suffered by the colonial countries during the Second World War, which made it difficult for them to re-assert and maintain their military presence in the post-war period. A third factor was the education of many of the upper and middle classes of the colonial countries at the universities of Western countries where they were encouraged to take up modern ideas of democracy, national self-determination and socialism. Yet another element contributing to the dissolution of the empires was the fact that a growing number of people in the metropolitan countries were becoming doubtful about the legitimacy of their rule over other peoples in the light of their own democratic and constitutional principles. There was also a growing feeling that they themselves as well as the peoples in the colonies would benefit socially and economically if the colonies were to be given independence.

India

By far the most important development in the post-war period in the process of decolonization was the achievement of independence by the world's two most populous countries: India and China. The modern movement for independence in India can be traced back at least to the founding of the National Congress Party in 1886, which gradually, by working at the local level, built up interest in the idea of self-government. The British, for their part, after the loss of the American colonies in the eighteenth century saw India as the cornerstone of the Empire: the jewel in the crown – a concept exemplified by Queen Victoria adopting the title Empress of India (1877). There was a strong desire to keep hold of this valuable asset. On the other hand, there was also a growing acceptance of the idea, already mentioned, of conceding self-government to the colonies at least with regard to most domestic issues. A sense of racial superiority, however, made the British hesitate much longer with non-European colonies than with those where whites were in a dominant position. When the British government took over formal responsibility for the Indian territories from the East Indian Company in 1858 after the disaster of the Indian Mutiny, the structure of government gave virtually all power to English expatriates with only minor influence for Indians in the advisory legislative council – and even they were nominated by the government.

In the next fifty years or so, and partly in response to actual and anticipated Indian pressure, the British took some steps to involve Indians further in the administration of their country, particularly at state or provincial level. An important milestone in this period was the Indian Councils Act of 1909 which made provision for the appointment of Indians to the Indian Council in England and to the Viceroy's Executive Council in India, as well as for direct election of the majority of Indian representatives on local legislative councils: at the same time these were given greater powers. During the First World War some 1.4 million Indians volunteered for military and ancillary service with the British forces, and this reinforced the sense that Indians should be taken into greater partnership in the administration of their country. The Government of India Act of 1919 made provision for an enlarged Council of State with 60 members of which 34 were to be Indians, and for a central legislative council of 140 of which 100 would be elected Indian representatives. It also allowed Indians to become ministers in provincial governments.

By comparison with developments in the 'white' parts of the Empire at this time and in the light of the principles of the Fourteen Points, these reforms were clearly very modest and it is hardly surprising that they were not acceptable to the growing movement for self-government. The situation was aggravated by heavy-handed acts of repression of popular expressions of displeasure, including the terrible massacre at Amritsar (1919) when soldiers under the control of General Dyer fired on an unarmed assembly, killing 379 and wounding 1,200 more.

The movement for Indian self-government had many distinguished leaders but the one who most captured the imagination, love and reverence of the Indian people was Mahatma Gandhi (1869–1948), undoubtedly one of the most noble men of this century, whose influence for the spiritual advancement of society around the world has been indeed very great. Prior to involvement in the struggle for Indian independence, Gandhi (who was trained as a lawyer) had spent many years in South Africa working to alleviate the conditions of the Indian community and suffering like other non-Europeans under a racially discriminating legal, economic and social system. During this period he had read widely; not only the scriptures of Hinduism but also those of the other great religions: Islam, Buddhism, and Christianity, as well as the writings of leading contemporary philosophers such as Tolstoy, Kropotkin and Ruskin. From these wide-ranging studies he evolved his own philosophy of the need to stop exploitation in society. By the end of the First World War he was already revered throughout India as the 'Mahatma' (great soul), and he had established an ashram (or community) where he urged his followers to concentrate on truthfulness, non-violence, celibacy, fearlessness and self-control, and to help their fellow countrymen, particularly the Untouchables, by using local languages, wearing only hand-spun and hand-woven cloth, and generally by buying only Indian-made goods. Gandhi insisted that the movement for self-government be non-violent and use such alternative methods of persuasion as boycotting British goods, non-cooperation with the government, and, when necessary, civil disobedience to unjust laws. It was not easy to apply such high principles in a continent with such a diverse and vast population, and on several occasions Gandhi felt obliged to call a temporary halt to the campaign when violence broke out. All things considered, the campaigning was remarkably less violent than might have been expected, or than has been the case in many other countries during their struggles for independence.

The British responded with the traditional mixture of modest concessions, repression, and encouragement of division between the various communities (particularly between the Hindus and the Muslims). Repression became increasingly difficult after Gandhi adopted the tactic in the 1930s of fasting when put in prison, because it was feared he might die, become a martyr, and thereby trigger massive disorders. A series of efforts were made to negotiate a compromise settlement, including a round table conference in England which Gandhi attended. In England he received much public sympathy, even from the cotton workers of Lancashire despite the fact that they had lost jobs as a result of Gandhi's boycott movement. These efforts culminated in the Government of India Act of 1935 which gave Indians the possibility of much greater influence in domestic affairs at the central level and effective control of government at the provincial level. The only functions over which the Governor-General retained absolute control were foreign affairs, defence, and matters affecting the Christian Church. Though the Congress party did not regard these concessions as going far enough, they did serve to reduce tension, especially when Congress candidates, having won most seats on local councils, were able to form their own local governments and terminate political imprisonments and restrictions on civil liberties.

Indian dissatisfaction with the compromise arrangement was reinforced when the government of India declared war on Germany in

1939 without so much as a prior notification, let alone consultation, of the Indian leaders. The latter, although anti-Nazi almost to a man, reacted sharply with a demand for full dominion status immediately as price for supporting the war effort. Promises made by Stafford Cripps (1889–1952), a leader of the Labour Party speaking on behalf of the British wartime coalition government, that dominion status would be granted immediately the war was over, were rejected and a 'Quit India' campaign began. For a while the Congress party was once again suppressed, but in 1945 the situation improved when the Labour Party, pledged to a policy of independence for India, won the first post-war British general election. Within a short time all the portfolios of the India Cabinet were in the hands of Indians.

The main issue then boiled down to how to devise a constitution for the whole of India in the light of Muslim insistence on their right to set up their own separate nation of Pakistan. Almost from the beginning of the movement for self-government, the Muslims had had reservations concerning the plans of Congress for independence because they saw no attempt to really protect their interests in a predominantly Hindu India. Gandhi understood their fears and tried to calm them, going so far as to suggest that the first prime minister of an independent India should be a Muslim. However, their fears increased with time and by 1946 there was nothing that either Gandhi or the British could do to make them abandon their goal for a separate Muslim nation. The intermingling of Hindu and Muslim communities throughout the subcontinent created immense diffi-culties in dividing it up into two nations when independence finally came on 15 August 1947. The consequence was that the joy of freedom was badly marred by the misery involved when some seventeen million people, Hindus as well as Muslims, felt obliged to flee from one state to the other – an event during which it is estimated over half a million persons lost their lives. Less than six months after independence had been achieved Gandhi himself was assassinated by a Hindu fanatic as he was on his way to prayers.

China

Unlike India and most other countries of Asia and Africa, China was never formally occupied by an outside power, but during the decline of the Manchu Empire in the nineteenth century the colonial powers, including Japan as well as the Europeans, occupied the main Chinese ports, divided up the country into spheres of economic influence, took over control of customs as security for loans, and imposed extra-territorial law for their citizens in China. These were indeed humiliating events for a civilization which for centuries had seen itself as the Middle Kingdom, and the rest of the world as peripheral and inferior. Full of hatred but weak and degenerate, the Manchus tried to strike back in the murderous Boxer rebellion of 1900 but this was crushed by the colonial powers, working for once in concert, and further humiliating conditions were imposed including the razing of certain important fortifications, and an indemnity in gold to be paid over 40 years with a value then equal to US$739 million.

This was the lowest depth of Chinese degradation and thereafter things gradually began to improve. Thus in 1907 England agreed to reduce opium exports from India (forced on China in the middle of the nineteenth century in one of the most disgraceful episodes in British history)[4] and the following year the United States (which generally was the most considerate of the imperial powers in China)[5] remitted its share of the Boxer indemnity. In 1911 the Manchu Empire was finally overthrown and a republic proclaimed. Hopes for a Chinese renaissance, however, were premature because of civil wars between the republican or nationalist party and the various old-style warlords, and then between the nationalists and the communists.

Though China remained weak, most of the colonial powers began to treat her with a little more respect. At the Washington Conference of 1922 the Great Powers formally recognized Chinese independence, the German concessions were cancelled and the British agreed to terminate their lease on the port of Wei-Hai-Wei. In 1924 the Soviet Union gave up Tientsin and Hankow and cancelled its share of the Boxer indemnity. Within six years nearly all the colonial countries surrendered their extra-territorial legal privileges. The one nation which took a much harsher line was Japan, which being arrogant after its victory over the Chinese in 1894 and the Russians in 1905, tried to take advantage of the Chinese civil wars to annex Manchuria (1931) and then the eastern provinces of China itself (1937). Terrible as was the Japanese invasion, it did serve at last to stir up the deepest feelings of patriotism amongst the Chinese and for a time the nationalists and the communists worked together to defeat the common enemy. As the foreign war grew to a close, however, the civil war was resumed, but this time the communists had the advantage not only in military terms but because they had won the support of an increasing proportion of the population on account of

[4] This agreement was the beginning of a process, advocated by the United States in particular, which eventually led to a Hague international agreement in 1912 to control world traffic in drugs.

[5] Germany was probably the most arrogant. It was the Kaiser who coined the term 'Yellow Peril'. The Chinese had a much greater right from actual experience to talk about a 'White Peril'.

their demonstrated concern for the well-being of the poor, especially the peasantry, an absence of corruption, and a strong patriotism. The nationalist armies were totally defeated and in 1949 a Peoples' Republic was declared. At long last the country was united again under one government and able to give a reality to national independence and self-determination.

The End of the Colonial Empires

In the following twenty years or so, one hundred new states were to be formed out of the former colonial empires. Generally, the United States (whose principal colonial concern was the Philippines) and Great Britain were the most successful in handing over power peacefully and in establishing an orderly administration for the successor national states. The British policy of responding quickly to calls for independence originated with the Labour Party but was soon embraced by the Conservatives as well, and it was a Conservative leader, Prime Minister Harold Macmillan (1894–1987), who coined the famous phrase 'wind of change'. In some instances the process did not move fast enough, especially when there was a local white community resisting change, and in such cases nationalist leaders were imprisoned for a time – as in India – and in three cases – Kenya, Cyprus and Aden – an armed struggle ensued. Generally, however, from a historical perspective the process of decolonization in the British Empire was quite remarkable for the minimum amount of violence and bloodshed, and for the continuation after independence of good will between the mother country and most of the new nations. The relatively small Italian Empire in North and East Africa was also broken up without much violence mainly because Italy was on the losing side during the Second World War and was given no choice in the peace settlement but to surrender her overseas possessions.[6] The same was true of Japan, which was obliged to give up her Empire in China, Korea and the Pacific as well as lands conquered in the first part of the Second World War.

France was much more resistant to demands for independence in the early post-war period, partly because she saw the colonies as integral parts of France with representation in the national parliament. The result was a series of long-drawn-out guerrilla wars, especially in Indo-China and Algeria. Unable to resist the tide of history, France eventually withdrew from these areas after two dramatic crises and then in quick succession also agreed to independence for the vast territories in West Africa. Similarly, the

[6] The third country on the losing side in World War II, Germany, had already been deprived of her colonies at the end of the previous war.

Call #

te special International
to **Saddam Hussein.**" The
ig. Mr. Namig is the
e Iraqi officers and civilians
g the Iraqi dictator. The
ardroom of Henkel Hall on
Call the Marsh Institute at

Topics Forum
, **Dr. Cal Allen**
Tisinger (right),
Religion and
ardroom of Henkel Hall
h Institute at 540-665-

Netherlands, Belgium and Portugal were also slow to accept calls for independence by their subject peoples and each to a greater or lesser extent resisted the movement with force. Indonesia, one of the largest nations in the world, eventually won independence from the Netherlands after intervention by the United Nations. The United Nations also played an important role in helping to stabilize the new state of Zaïre, formerly the Belgian Congo, after it was virtually abandoned by Belgium in 1960. The principal Portuguese colonies did not achieve independence until 1975, and then only after a revolution in Portugal itself against a long-standing conservative dictatorship.

* * *

In the process of nation building during this period several problems have emerged. One has been the proliferation of so called 'micro-states', mostly small islands in the Caribbean and in the Atlantic, Indian and Pacific Oceans, which are barely viable as sovereign political and economic units and which are certainly very vulnerable to outside predators (e.g. the attempted coups by international brigands against at least two island nations in the Indian and Pacific Oceans in recent years). Such micro-states have a particularly strong incentive to group together in regional federations and to push for the strengthening of international institutions so that they can have real protection.

Another problem has been that some of the new states, especially in Africa, have inherited artificial frontiers which reflect the convenience of the European colonial powers when they were carving up the continent for their own benefit and which have created anomalies whereby tribes which have real social meaning have been split between different states. When the new states were established their leaders failed to consult together to rationalize their mutual boundaries because they feared that once adjustments started there would be no end to them and the inevitable result would be anarchy. The problem might have been alleviated if the movement for a Pan-African federation had come to fruition, but the opportunity for such a union seems to have been lost, at least for the immediate future.

Yet another problem has been that some of the new states have embraced a mix of differing cultural groups, and in some instances the minorities involved have become dissatisfied and have demanded either some degree of autonomy or outright independence as a separate nation – and the more militant have resorted to force in order to impose their will, e.g. the Sikhs in India, the Tamils in Sri Lanka, the Kurds in Turkey, Iraq and Iran, the Muslims in the

Philippines, peoples of Timor and Papua in Indonesia, Christians in the Sudan, Ibis in Nigeria, and Turks in Cyprus.[7]

Even more explosive has been the failure of some new nations to resolve territorial disputes with their neighbours, of which the most important examples from the point of view of the wider world community have been those between India and Pakistan (three major wars since 1948) and between Israel and the Arab countries (five major wars since 1948). Some of these conflicts have become stalemates and the aggrieved parties, out of frustration, have resorted to a new brand of international terrorism which puts emphasis on high-profile attacks on, for instance, international travel so as to obtain maximum publicity (though surely not sympathy) for their cause.

Though much remains to be done before all the peoples of the world enjoy the cultural self-determination which they feel they need in order to have self-fulfilment and respect, it is nevertheless clear that the main era of nation building is now over. This period has coincided with an age in which the first steps have been taken towards the establishment of new international institutions to coordinate the activities of the whole world community – the logical and inevitable next step in the history of civilization. The two developments have an important relationship because it is clear that a system of national states is a much firmer foundation on which to build a new world order than the system of states based on the dynastic right and conquest which existed before. The patriotic feelings engendered in each of some one hundred and seventy national states is one of the more important and practical safeguards against a future world government ever declining into dictatorship.

---

[7] There are minority groups desirous of national self-expression within the borders of old-established states as well, e.g. the Basques in Spain, the Bretons and Corsicans in France, Irish Catholics in Northern Ireland, Tibetans in China, and various cultural groups in the Soviet Union.

CHAPTER 14

Democracy and the Rule of Law

CLOSELY linked with the movement for national independence and cultural self-determination, and equally significant to the development of the just society, has been the evolution and spread of the principles and practice of accountable and participatory government: democracy. As has been noted in the first part of this book, there was a long history prior to the nineteenth and twentieth centuries of representative assemblies at local and national levels in many parts of the world, and indeed the very word 'democracy' goes back to the practices of Ancient Greece. Nevertheless, most such assemblies had very limited power and were for the most part representative of only a small section of the population. The three revolutions of the eighteenth century pointed the way to new standards. Gradually but steadily, from that time onwards, it became the accepted view that the only legitimate form of government was one freely chosen by all the people to whom it had to be fully accountable. Governments in power on the basis of force, tradition, inheritance, or claims of divine appointment found it increasingly difficult to win acceptance of their moral authority from those they ruled.

In its most primitive form, democracy means direct participation of all citizens in the process of government decision-making, at a general meeting of all citizens or by means of the referendum. The former approach has been practised in small communities at various times, e.g. in tribes, some Swiss cantons[1] and in New England townships, but clearly this is not a practical option for communities with mass populations spread over vast areas, even with the help of modern technology such as television. The referendum, though a useful device for popular participation in government, also has very severe practical limitations: it has to be confined to a small number of issues, otherwise the citizens would be overwhelmed, and there is also the problem of ensuring that the citizens are given full and

[1] The general meeting is still practised in the Swiss canton of Appenzell.

objective information on which to make a decision – it is only too easy for a referendum to be manipulated through the use of slanted phraseology.[2]

Thus a main avenue to democracy in practice is for citizens to elect a representative assembly to oversee the interests of the community. A key requirement of such an approach, if the representatives are indeed to look after the interest of the whole community rather than just a part of it, is that they be elected by all the people. It is one sign of progress towards a just society that this simple concept is now almost universally acknowledged, because for long all sorts of sophisticated arguments were used to justify limiting the electorate, especially so as to exclude women and the poor. For example, it would be argued that the poor, being ill educated and illiterate, would not have an informed opinion of the issues and could easily be swayed by demagogues who would then have the power to effect their own selfish policies which would not be in the interest of society as a whole.[3] Furthermore, it was argued, as the poor had little property they had little vested interest in the well-being of the state and therefore should not have a say in its management. Of course, behind these apparently rational arguments was a selfish motivation on the part of those who propagated them. An objective assessment could only conclude that the poor had as much need as anyone of the protection of the state (which after all is its first function) and indeed because of their very weakness they had more need than others of the assistance of the state in order to help them gain equal opportunity to develop their potential.

In order to ensure that universal suffrage is not diverted from the goal of establishing a true representation of the people, there are at least three subsidiary requirements. The first is secret balloting to minimize the possibility of intimidation – a practice which was for long resisted on the seductive but false premise that any citizen should have the courage to stand up and state his view, which is all very well for those who are in a comfortable position but is unrealistic when there is extreme inequality in society.[4]

[2] Important occasions when the referendum has been used in the last fifty years include: 1946 in France with regard to a new constitution; 1946 in Italy with regard to continuation of the monarchy; 1950 in Belgium with regard to the return of King Leopold III; 1975 in the UK with regard to entry into the Common Market; and 1986 in Switzerland when the Swiss people voted against their government's proposal to join the United Nations.

[3] These types of argument are still used on occasion, e.g. in Brazil to disfranchise some 220,000 Indians.

[4] Some have gone further and argued that because the poor generally have the lowest incidence of voting, their interest would be protected only if voting were made compulsory. Thus Australia enacted legislation in 1924 to make voting compulsory but this precedent has not been widely followed in other democracies. (Data on voting patterns in leading constitutional nations is shown in Table 2).

A second requirement is that all citizens have equal voting rights. This excludes, for instance, the common practice in many countries, when universal suffrage was first introduced, of giving citizens of property more than one vote. It also means that all electoral districts should have approximately the same number of citizens, so as to ensure an equal weighting for each vote cast. There are many also who argue that it requires a system of proportional representation, because the simple 'winner takes all' approach means that the citizens who have voted for the losing candidates are not fairly represented in parliament. Thus in the United Kingdom a third party with, say, 15–20 percent of the total vote is lucky to win even half a dozen seats out of more than 600 in the House of Commons (i.e. 1 percent) if their support happens to be spread evenly across the country; the problem is less evident if support is concentrated in certain geographic areas, as in the case of Scottish nationalists.[5] However, critics of proportional representation, whilst generally conceding that it is more democratic than the 'winner takes all' approach, argue that it often leads to weak and unstable coalition governments (as has happened in the Weimar Republic, the Fourth Republic in France, and in republican Italy). Furthermore, coalition governments on a routine basis diffuse sense of responsibility and blur issues for the electorate; they can also give excessive power to small minorities especially when there is a near balance between the other parties. Such critics argue that on the other hand the 'winner takes all' approach forces minority groups to band together in two or three parties which can provide strong government and at the same time give opportunity for minority views to be heard during internal consultation. In practice there have been good as well as bad experiences with proportional representation, which suggest that perceived problems are really caused by other problems, not proportional representation as such.

A third subsidiary requirement, if an elected assembly is to be truly representative of the people, is that membership be open to any adult elector, other than a convicted criminal, and that representatives be paid a reasonable salary, so as not to exclude those who are poor and do not have independent means.

One sign of democracy, then, is the election of a truly representative assembly to supervise the government. Another sign is that the

[5] There are two main systems to ensure proportional representation. The first is the single transferable vote in multi-member constituencies which makes allowance for each elector's alternative choice. The second is the list system which gives representation to a party in proportion to total votes received. Proportional representation systems have been introduced in such countries as Germany, France, Italy, those in Scandinavia, the Netherlands, Belgium, Ireland, Greece and Australia.

THE SEARCH FOR A JUST SOCIETY

TABLE 2

PARTICIPATION IN DEMOCRACY

Percentage of Adult Population Voting in National Elections in Selected Countries
Status in 1970s

Percentage Group	AMERICAS	ASIA	EUROPE	OCEANIA
90% & over			97.0 Italy 93.0 Netherlands 90.8 Sweden	90.0 Australia
80–89%	85.3 Jamaica	89.4 Israel 88.9 Iceland	89.9 Austria 88.3 Denmark 87.6 Belgium 87.2 Germany 85.7 Ireland 85.3 Finland 80.8 Greece	88.6 New Zealand
70–79%		75.3 Japan 71.1 Sri Lanka	79.6 Spain 78.7 Norway 75.4 UK	
60–69%	67.6 Canada	66.6 India	66.2 France	63.2 Fiji
50–59%	54.0 USA			
40–49%		41.0 Malaysia	42.7 Switzerland	

Source: C. Lewis Taylor and David A. Jodice, *World Handbook of Political and Social Indicators*, Yale University Press, 1983.

government is genuinely accountable to that assembly and to the community at large. The government should make periodic reports of its plans and activities which should be open to question and audit. In addition, it is a normal practice for the assembly to have authority to approve all devices for raising revenues to defray the cost of government, particularly taxation, and that the executive be subject to limitations on length of office unless it wins re-election either directly from the citizens or indirectly from their representative assemblies.

Other requirements if a democracy is to be effective are freedom of speech; an independent, responsible and informative news media; the rule of law (i.e. the opposite of arbitrary rule and meaning, in effect, that the government is subject to law like all private individuals and bodies); and careful control over the power of wealth in the government process so that it does not divert government from the general interest to its particular interest by such means as bribery and corruption, uneven election campaign expenditures, and unfair advantage in obtaining public positions.

There is no single model of the democratic state; differing historical circumstances have radically affected the structure and spirit of democracy in each country, as is clear, for instance, with the three original revolutionary countries of the modern era, Great Britain, the United States and France.

In Great Britain the formal centrepiece of democracy is Parliament, which for centuries struggled with the monarchy to win executive accountability especially with regard to public finances and the rule of law (the so-called Westminster System). Manifestations of this central role of Parliament include the extraordinary emphasis put on parliamentary privilege and the virtually total practice of appointing only Members of Parliament (both houses) to the cabinet of the executive government. However, in recent decades the development of a highly disciplined political party system and a vast expansion in the size of government has led many to the view that it is the executive, including the top levels of the civil service, which is really dominant, notwithstanding such parliamentary institutions as Question Time and the annual audit of government by the Public Accounts Committee.

In the United States there is, as noted earlier, major emphasis on division of power between the executive, legislature and judiciary;[6] on strict limitations to federal government power *vis-à-vis* the component states; and on individual liberty; – all essentially on account of disillusionment in the eighteenth century with the authoritarian style of rule of the British government and parliament. In practice the division of power among the institutions representing popular sovereignty has given opportunity for undue influence by powerful special interests (especially big business) to the detriment of the general good. Furthermore, the reality of individual liberty has been quite different from theory, e.g. in the case of slaves, the poor, and radicals during the McCarthy era.

As noted later in this chapter, the French experience with democratic institutions has been quite volatile. Nevertheless, it is possible to detect a generally consistent theme running from the

---

[6] By contrast with Great Britain, the people elect the Executive and Legislature separately and the President's cabinet does not include members of Congress.

Jacobins to General de Gaulle which puts value on a strong central government to carry out 'the will of the people' – an idea demonstrated in the institution of an élite top civil service and in the practice of having key officials of local government (the departments) appointed from Paris. This represents, in fact, a democratic adaptation of a centralizing tradition going back at least to Richelieu and Louis XIII.

This view that democratic government should be strong so that it can effectively carry out the will of the people has been taken to an extreme in communist nations. In such countries, which frequently take the title 'people's democracy', lip service is paid to such democratic institutions as universal suffrage and national representative assemblies, but the reality has been a tight dictatorship of self-appointed representatives of the proletariat. In the case of the Soviet Union, there is an obvious connection with the autocratic style of the Czars.

Other important models of democracy are to be found in Switzerland and in Scandinavia. The Swiss system gives a major role to the cantons, relatively human-sized communities where the ordinary citizen can feel that he (and now she) can play a real part in the process of government. The Scandinavian countries have a parliamentary system similar to that of Great Britain in terms of historical roots and structure but with the added quality of greater emphasis on protection of the individual through such techniques as the ombudsman (see p. 140), early guarantees of freedom for the media, and sophisticated programmes to minimize poverty.

Two general aspects of the democratic experience deserve special mention: (i) the question of the head of state in a democratic nation, and (ii) the structure of the legislative branch. In some countries such as the USA, the chief executive of the government is also the head of state. (This is in a sense an adaptation of the monarchical tradition.) Other countries see such an arrangement as a potential threat to national unity and prefer to have a head of state separate from the executive and above party politics – a presidential figurehead or a constitutional monarch. The latter arrangement has been possible when an original executive monarchy has gracefully retreated before the rise of democracy, as in Great Britain, Scandinavia, the Low Countries, and Japan. A constitutional monarchy has an advantage over a republican presidency in that it generally brings a much greater sense of continuity and tradition – powerful forces for binding together a national community. A recent example of the real value of constitutional monarchy has been the active role of King Carlos of Spain in helping his country go through a potentially difficult period when moving from dictatorship to democracy. Of course, for constitutional monarchy to be truly successful, royalty has to behave in a way which is acceptable to the vast majority of the nation and in particular should not become associated with special unearned privilege, i.e. with the rich or a hereditary aristocracy.

With regard to the legislative branch of government, the almost universal experience has been that a two-assembly or bicameral system is preferable to a single assembly because it gives better protection against hasty and ill-thought-out legislation. Only in situations of revolutionary crisis has there been a strong sense that a second assembly is an unnecessary brake on the desire of the people for speedy reform and change. However, as with constitutional monarchy, the bicameral system depends for success on the upper house acting in a sensible manner and in not abusing its power. Ultimately, it is the spirit of a people, much more than institutional technicalities which largely determine how successful a democracy will be.

In the remaining part of this chapter it is proposed to make a brief review of the evolution of democratic or constitutional government in modern times. The review will be subdivided according to the three periods which were used in Chapter 13 in analysing the emergence of the world system of national states: the hundred years up until 1914, the interwar period, and the period since the Second World War. In the first period the approach will be one of briefly reviewing developments in individual countries so as to give examples of the interrelationship of the various features of democracy. The focus, as mentioned earlier, will be on Europe and its extensions overseas, with prime emphasis on the three revolutionary countries and the other large nations. There will be also brief comment on some of the smaller nations, especially those which took a leading role in the development of some aspects of democracy. After tracing events in the countries which were in the vanguard of democracy in the nineteenth century, the treatment of the two later periods will be a broad brush approach to major trends around the world during the twentieth century. The subject is multifaceted, and for the purposes of clarity it is perhaps most convenient to give separate treatment to two subjects because of their special importance. These subjects are the emancipation of women and the Fourth Estate – the news media; they are discussed at the end of the chapter.

Constitutionalism in the Nineteenth Century

Great Britain

By the end of the eighteenth century, England had many of the basic characteristics of an open society and responsible government, essentially as a result of the 'Glorious Revolution' one hundred years before. There were, however, major blemishes. The most obvious was a limited and biased system for electing Members of Parliament which was grossly to the advantage of the aristocracy and landed gentry at the expense of an increasingly prosperous and active middle class in the towns, not to speak of the poorer classes both in the countryside and in the new industrial cities. A closely related matter was the exclusion from public office, including membership of Parliament, of Roman Catholics (the majority of the population in Ireland), Jews and nonconformist Protestants. In addition, the central and local administrations were incredibly inefficient, not least because they were staffed with persons appointed according to a political spoils system rather than according to merit, and, in the case of local government, because of the absence of a comprehensive and uniform structure necessary for handling the new and complex needs of an industrial society.

For about thirty years after the beginning of the French Wars, British governments were extremely nervous of reform, fearing that it would encourage revolution, and the prevailing policy was to suppress all public discussion of the matter. However, by the early 1820s such fears were beginning to subside and more level-headed views began to emerge, which accepted that reform was necessary if Britain's proud tradition of political stability was to be maintained. The first reforms reduced the restrictions on religious minority groups which had been maintained by the Toleration Act of 1689. The principal pieces of legislation were the Tests and Corporation Act of 1829 which benefited nonconformists, and the Roman Catholic Relief Act of 1829 which allowed Catholics to be both Members of Parliament (MPs) and ministers of the Crown. These measures were but a prelude to the legislation, rightly known as the Great Reform Act of 1832, which was as important for the precedent it set for future reform to meet changing circumstances as for the actual improvements which it made at the time. The Act more than doubled the size of the electorate (from about 200,000 to more than 400,000 out of a total population of about 24 million) by extending suffrage on a uniform basis to much of the middle class in the towns[7]

[7] Occupiers of houses with an annual rent of £10 or more.

and to some of the better-off farmers in the counties.[8] Very important also was the abolition of 50 rotten boroughs (boroughs where there were very few voters and which in effect were in the ownership of a local landowner) and the creation of 42 new boroughs to increase the representation of towns in Parliament. A companion Municipal Reform Act (1835) created a uniform and comprehensive local government authority for the towns which consisted of a town council elected by the rate-payers (i.e. owners of property).

Though these reforms were a major step forward, they did not satisfy many who looked to the principles of the three Revolutions, particularly that of France, as a guideline for representative government. In the late 1830s and the 1840s the Chartist Movement won widespread support for its six-point programme: (1) universal male suffrage; (2) equal electoral districts; (3) removal of property qualifications for MPs; (4) pay for MPs; (5) a secret ballot; and (6) annual elections for the House of Commons. Though the Chartist Movement failed in its immediate campaign and soon collapsed, the principles which it had enumerated were not forgotten; over a period of time all of them except the last were to be adopted and put into effect.

By the 1860s there was general agreement that the franchise had to be widened further. Eventually action was taken by the government of Benjamin Disraeli with the Second Reform Act of 1867[9] which more than doubled the electorate (to about 2 million) by extending suffrage to virtually all skilled workmen in the towns[10] and to all the middle classes in the counties.[11] In addition another 45 seats were transferred to the towns to make for a more equitable distribution. Soon afterwards the movement towards more effective representative government was strengthened by the Civil Service Reform Act of 1870 which made it a requirement that all new entrants to the Civil Service pass a standard competitive public examination,[12] and by the Secret Ballot Act of 1872.[13]

[8] £50 leaseholders, as well as the previously qualified 40-shilling freeholders.

[9] Most of the English constitutional reforms of the nineteenth century were sponsored by parties of the centre and left. However, it is worth remarking that the Second Reform Act was the policy of a Conservative government which began the enlightened tradition of 'Tory democracy'.

[10] All householders and all lodgers paying an annual rent of £10 or more.

[11] £5 leaseholders and £12 householders.

[12] This Act represented the second phase of a process begun with an Act in 1855 which had established a supervisory Civil Service Commission, set up a system for standard grading of all civil service posts, and which in addition required departments to hold examinations for all new entrants.

[13] The first parliament in the world to be elected by secret ballot was that in Victoria, Australia in 1856.

Though the Second Reform Act had been preceded by a national debate second only in extent to that preceding the Great Reform Act, it was soon clear that its terms were not going to satisfy the country for long, because it still only allowed somewhat less than one-eighth of the adult population (a quarter of the male adult population) to participate in the electoral process. In 1885 the Third Reform Act effectively took the country over the threshold of democracy by expanding the electorate to include all male heads of households and excluding, amongst male adults, only domestic servants, sons living at home, and the homeless. As a result the electorate rose to about 5 million, or some three-quarters of the adult male population. Closely associated with the Reform Act were two other important measures: the Corrupt Practices Act of 1883 which put a ceiling on the amount that could be expended on constituency elections, thereby making for greater equality between rich and poor candidates, and the Redistribution Act of 1885 which virtually completed the process of redistributing constituencies so that all voters more or less had equal weight.[14]

During this period, too, steps were taken to further reduce religious and other handicaps in the public realm: in 1858 an Act abolished property qualifications for MPs and removed the bar on Jews becoming MPs;[15] in 1886 after years of dispute, Charles Bradlaugh (1833–1891), an agnostic, was allowed to take his seat in the House of Commons on the basis of a simple affirmation of loyalty rather than being required to swear on the Bible. Attention was then switched to further reform of local government. In 1888 and 1894 the logic of house suffrage was extended from the town boroughs, which had had it since 1834, to the countryside through the establishment of a new system of elected county and parish councils. A final spate of reform came just before the First World War with the Parliament Act of 1910 and an Act of 1911 to provide pay (originally £400 a year) for MPs. It was laid down in the 1910 Act that henceforth the House of Lords would (a) not be able to veto money bills approved by the House of Commons; and (b) other legislation approved by the House of Commons could not be refused more than three times or delayed for a total of more than two years.

In summary, reform of the British constitution in the nineteenth century was slow and laborious. However, in some respects this evolutionary process had the virtue that reform could be more

[14] There continued to be minor exceptions, until as late as 1948, which for instance allowed men an additional vote on account of their business property in certain circumstances.

[15] Benjamin Disraeli was descended from a distinguished Jewish family but he and his siblings had been baptised Christians as children and accordingly he had been able to take a seat in Parliament in 1837. The family of Karl Marx had made a similar conversion in the same era.

readily accepted and that virtually all sections of society could adjust to it, with the consequence that by 1914 the British political system, for all its blemishes (and there were still quite a few, not least being the exclusion of women from the electoral rolls) was one of the most solidly democratic in the world at that time. In succeeding years the British 'Westminster' constitutional model was to be copied more than any other system by newly-emerging countries after the disintegration of the great colonial empires.

The United States of America

By contrast with the steady progress towards accountable and democratic government in the United Kingdom, the story of the United States in this respect in the nineteenth century is a little disappointing. This is partly because at the beginning of the century the United States had a much more advanced constitution than the United Kingdom and therefore presumably had less far to go. In fact, what happened was that the United States barely advanced at all and in some respects, because the spirit of the constitution was constantly undermined almost from the beginning, it is hard to say that the government was more accountable or democratic in 1914 than it was in 1800. Thus, though theoretically universal manhood suffrage was implicit in the constitution, actual control of the electoral lists was left to the states which often in the interest of powerful groups took steps to restrict suffrage on the basis of religious and literacy tests, property qualifications, and payment of poll taxes.[16] Rapid expansion of the economy led to the emergence of 'robber baron' capitalists who did not scruple to corrupt the electoral process for their own selfish purposes. Massive immigration of millions who did not initially speak English and were vulnerable to pressure made possible the 'Tammany Hall' city machine, whereby politicians were able to buy their way into power and stay there by judicial rewards in the shape of public jobs[17] and social security for those who voted for them. Having said this, it should be acknowledged that the country had one immense achievement to its credit in the nineteenth century, and that was the abolition of slavery and the passage of the 13th Amendment to the constitution, as discussed earlier. Furthermore, although the system was often corrupt and less than fully democratic, it did operate in a

[16] For example, the introduction of a two-dollar flat poll tax in Mississippi in 1876 reduced the electorate from 80 to 17 percent of the adult population over a period of twenty-five years.

[17] The worst excesses of corruption in the Federal civil service were stopped by the 1884 Act of Congress which required most positions to be filled by candidates who had passed a competitive written examination.

remarkably open fashion, and freedom of speech and debate was certainly as strong in the United States as anywhere in the world.[18] Ultimately this was to pay off in the early years of the twentieth century when progressive governments were elected which implemented a range of social and economic reform to be discussed later.

France

The French experience in the nineteenth century was different from that of both Britain and the United States insofar as it went through quite extreme phases of progress, reaction and progress again. As noted in the first part of this book, the French Revolution at its apex had provided the highly democratic '1793' constitution, incorporating such features as universal male suffrage and provision for referendum. However, the 1793 constitution was put aside during the emergency of invasion by other great powers – the Austrians and the Prussians – and was destined never to be implemented. Napoleon's Empire, which replaced the Republic, had several progressive features: the law was rationalized by the Code Napoléon (see p. 79 above), the uniform system of local government instituted during the Revolution was confirmed and strengthened, and public positions, at least in theory, were to be filled according to merit ('careers open to all the talents') rather than by the rank and privilege of the old regime. Despite all this the Empire was a dictatorship. Elected assemblies were useful for giving the Empire a veneer of popular legitimacy but there was to be no nonsense about giving them real power. There was certainly no provision for free discussion of public matters and the press was tightly controlled. Carried away with hubris, Napoleon (1769–1821) used his immense talents to destroy himself and to ruin half Europe.

The restored Bourbon monarchy of 1815 had a constitution, modelled to a large extent on that of England, which provided for a parliament with an upper chamber of hereditary peers and a lower chamber elected on the basis of a very restricted property qualification. Initially the press was given relatively wide freedom but this was soon withdrawn at the instigation of Prince Metternich (1773–1859), the chief minister of Austria, 1819–1848, who orchestrated the policies of the Great Powers in the direction of suppression of independent or popular expression, out of well-justified fear that if permitted press freedom would cause another revolution. The 1830 Revolution and the establishment of the Orleans Monarchy initially

---

[18] One innovation was the referendum. Parallel with Switzerland, several of the states pioneered the use of the referendum for key policy issues, e.g. amendments to the constitution.

led to more liberalization, including restoration of freedom of the press and broadening of the electorate by reducing the property qualification from 300 francs to 200 francs (the new law gave an electorate of 160,000 out of a total population of 31 million, i.e. about 1 in 200, compared with 1 in 30 in Great Britain after the Great Reform Act of 1832). After an initial 'honeymoon' period, however, the Orleanist government tended to step back into a defensive, reactionary policy, instead of adjusting to changing circumstances – in sharp contrast with British government policy after 1830.

The result was the predictable third French Revolution of 1848 which established the Second French Republic. A freshly elected constituent assembly drew up a new constitution which harked back to that of 1793 and which included provision for a single chamber parliament, to be elected by universal manhood suffrage, and for a president to be elected directly, also by universal manhood suffrage. However, disputes between the various revolutionary factions were exploited by Napoleon's ambitious nephew, Louis Napoleon (1808–1873), who was able thereby to win election as president and then to organize a *coup d'état* as a prelude to establishing the Second Empire. The new constitution, like that of the First Empire, was severely autocratic. The government reserved for itself the right to make laws and the only limit conceded was to an appointed senate which could review laws for their constitutionality and to an elected legislative assembly which could accept or reject laws proposed by the government but which could not propose laws itself. The legislative assembly continued to be elected theoretically by universal manhood suffrage (this principle could no longer be pushed aside), but even this was qualified by a requirement for three years residence in one place which disenfranchised large numbers of industrial workers who migrated frequently in search of jobs. Furthermore, the Parliament was only in session for three months a year and it was not permitted to publish its debates. It was not until the last decade of the Empire (1860–1870) that the constitution was liberalized as Louis Napoleon tried to win broader-based support for his increasingly unpopular regime. The legislative assembly was given more powers and the press greater freedom.

With the establishment of the Third Republic after the Franco-Prussian war of 1870–71 France at last was to have a constitution which fulfilled the promise of 1793 and provided for an open and accountable system of government. The constitution of 1875 made provision for a chamber of deputies elected by universal manhood suffrage which had considerable powers, similar to those enjoyed by the British House of Commons and the US House of Representatives. There was also a Senate which was elected by the Chamber of Deputies, some for lifetime office, others for nine-year terms. The President was elected by both Chambers for a seven-year term. The Third French Republic, like other constitutional systems, had many flaws, which were to become particularly evident during the interwar period when there was a series of highly unstable governments at a time when France had to face the power and aggression of Nazi Germany. Nevertheless, at the time when it was introduced, the constitution was undoubtedly one of the most progressive in the world and gave promise for the future.

Germany

Following the end of the Napoleonic war Prince Metternich was able without much difficulty to persuade the rulers of the German states to stamp out Western liberal ideas about constitutional and accountable government. Occasional rumblings in the universities, and new constitutions in Brunswick, Saxony, Hanover and Hesse Cassel, inspired by the French Revolution, were put down by such devices as the Carlsbad decrees of 1819 which instituted a strict monitoring of the universities and publications, and the Six Articles of 1832 which required every German sovereign to strictly limit the powers of representative assemblies. The revolutions of 1848 gave promise of a new day with the establishment of the Frankfurt all-German constituent assembly and a constituent assembly in Prussia, both elected by universal manhood suffrage, with secret ballot and equal single-member constituencies. But after the collapse of the revolutionary movement in 1849 the Frankfurt assembly was replaced by a revived Diet which was made up of representatives nominated by the governments of the member states. In Prussia the constitution was brutally amended: universal male suffrage was kept but the electoral roll was divided into three classes according to ability to pay taxes, with the result that two-thirds of the assembly were elected by only 17 percent of the male adult population. Furthermore, the assembly's power was considerably reduced by the rule that ministers were responsible to the King, not to Parliament, and they had the right to issue ordinances with the full force of law when the assembly was not in session. This very limited form of representative government was to remain in effect in Prussia until 1918.

The general practice for federal affairs as Germany became united was a little better, though still behind that prevailing in the three large Western democracies: Britain, the United States and France. The constitution of the North German Confederation of 1867, which was later extended to cover the whole of the German Empire when it was established in 1871, made provision for a bicameral parliament with the lower house (*Reichstag*) elected by universal manhood suffrage in secret ballot, single-member constituencies and equal weighting of votes. On the negative side, the powers of the Reichstag were strictly limited. The constitution, for instance, could only be amended by a two-thirds vote in the upper house (*Bundestag*), where representatives were appointed by the governments of the member states, and control over the purse strings of government – always a key indication of the real power of representative assemblies – was narrow, e.g. military expenditures were approved in seven-year blocks. Though popular political parties such as the Social Democrats were to win large numbers of seats in the Reichstag, they were relatively powerless to control the Imperial government which remained autocratic and militaristic in style. Perhaps the most successful constitutional development in Germany in the nineteenth century was the decision in 1873 to give municipalities autonomy and free them from the provincial 'land' governments which were dominated by the great landowners. Within a few years Germany's cities were leading the world in the quality of their local government and the services they provided.

The Hapsburg Empire

Before 1848 there was little in the way of representative assemblies in the government structure of the Hapsburg Empire except for the Hungarian Diet, which, however, was in the hands of the great land magnates (the Upper House) and the landed gentry (the Lower House). During the 1848 revolution the Hungarian Diet was liberalized by the 'March Laws' to allow for popular representation, responsible government, greater freedom for the press and equality before the law. A new democratic Reichstag met in Vienna and passed laws completing the emancipation of the serfs in the Hapsburg dominions, but it had achieved little else before it was dissolved in 1849 by Prince Schwarzenberg (1800–1852) who had succeeded Metternich as chief minister of the Empire.

Autocratic rule was re-established for more than a decade throughout the Hapsburg Empire, but defeats in the war with France (1859) and Prussia (1866) badly shook the government and it found it prudent to try and win greater public support by changing to a more liberal policy. The Compromise of 1867 which established the Dual Monarchy of Austro-Hungary resulted in the restoration of the Diet in Hungary, and a new bicameral parliament in Vienna for the remaining Hapsburg territories, each being dominated by the middle classes: Magyars in the one and Germans in the other. After some fifty years the government finally gave in to demands for universal manhood suffrage (1907) for elections to the Reichstag. Within a few years the Reichstag changed from being almost totally an assembly of German representatives to one which reflected the national and cultural diversity of the Empire. This development, however, which in other circumstances might have been fruitful, led to great disunity and the government, unable to win the support of the majority, reverted to rule by decree. In Hungary, the Magyars refused to allow universal suffrage because they were now a minority in their own bailiwick and accordingly they made an agreement with the Imperial government whereby they undertook complete cooperation in return for maintenance of a restricted electoral status quo.

Italy

Experience in Italy followed much the same pattern as in Germany and the Hapsburg Empire. There was virtually nothing in the way of constitutional government in the nine Italian states prior to 1848. During that year of revolutions, liberal constitutions were enacted in Piedmont, the Papacy and the Kingdom of the Two Sicilies, but the latter two did not survive the reaction of 1849. The constitution of Piedmont was modelled on that of Great Britain with a senate whose life members were appointed by the King, and a chamber of deputies with members elected on the basis of a limited property suffrage. Ministers of the crown were responsible to Parliament. When Italy was united in 1861 the Piedmont constitution was extended to the rest of the country. In 1881 the electorate was more than tripled by reduction of a tax–paying requirement from 40 lire per annum to 10 lire and by lowering of the voting age from 25 to 21 years. Virtual manhood suffrage was finally enacted in reforms instituted in 1912 which also included for the first time provision for salaries for members of Parliament.

Russia

The one remaining great power of Europe was Russia. It was here that there was the strongest resistance to any form of constitutional government. The Czar was the 'Little Father' of his people and knew what was best for them. Others, of course, did not see it that way and the failure of the government to consult the people and take account of their various interests inevitably led to frustration and violence which in turn provoked counter-violence. During the nineteenth century the only significant step towards representative government was at the local level, with the introduction in 1864 of the Zemsto Law which established local government boards in the countryside, on which sat representatives of the nobility, townsmen and the peasantry; and in 1870 with a law to reform municipal government in the cities, which gave the cities self-rule under councils elected by the propertied classes.

In 1905 the Czar finally gave way to demands for a national assembly when, following defeat in the war with Japan, popular unrest reached such a pitch that it was clear that traditional policies of repression would not keep public order; there was even a distinct possibility that the monarchy would be overthrown. First offers of a very limited franchise and restricted powers for the national assembly did not win popular support and the Czar was obliged to make further concessions which were listed in the October Manifesto. It was conceded that the national assembly (*Duma*) should be elected, in effect, by universal manhood suffrage, and that it should have real legislative powers. But before the first Duma was able to meet (May 1906), the Czar backtracked and promulgated the 'Fundamental Laws', which included the statements that: (i) he was in complete charge of the executive, the armed forces and foreign policy; (ii) he could legislate by decree when the Duma was not in session; (iii) only he could change the constitution; (iv) the Duma would have to share legislative power with an appointed Imperial Council; and finally (v) the budgetary power of the Duma was to be very limited. The Duma refused to accept these limitations and the Czar ordered its dissolution.

A similar impasse developed after an election for the second Duma in 1907. The government then issued a new electoral edict which gave much greater representation to the propertied classes and it was on the basis of this law that more conservative Dumas, which were cooperative with the government, were elected in 1907 and again in 1912. The Czar had moved some way towards the limited constitutions of the other imperial powers of Central Europe, Germany and Austro-Hungary, but it was all too little and too late: the government did not have a solid popular base and the tradition of violent opposition was firmly established.

Other Countries

In the smaller countries of Western Europe and in some of the major British colonies the process towards constitutional government was sometimes ahead of even the most progressive larger countries, as is indicated by the basic dates shown in Table 3.

TABLE 3

DATE OF ACHIEVING KEY CHARACTERISTICS OF CONSTITUTIONALISM IN SELECTED COUNTRIES

Country	Representative Assembly	Accountable Government	Universal Manhood Suffrage	Votes Equal Weight	Press Freedom	Referendum	Ombudsman
Denmark	1831–34	1834	1914–15		1848		
Sweden	1864	1864	1907	1907	1766		1809
Norway	1814	1814	1898		1815		1963
Netherlands	1814	1848	1917	1917			
Belgium	1830	1830	1893	1919			
Switzerland	1848	1848	1848	1848	1828–33	1831	
Canada	1856	1847–54	1920[1]				3
Australia	1843	1850	1901[2]			1901	1977
New Zealand	1852	1856	1889				1962

[1] This was the formal date. In practice the franchise had been wide since colonial times because it was based on property qualifications which were easy to acquire.
[2] In practice this did not include the Aborigines who were not formally enfranchised for the purposes of federal elections until 1967.
[3] Canada has ombudsman offices at the provincial level, the first being established in 1967 in Alberta.

Generally speaking, advances towards democracy in these countries tended to be bunched together at certain key points in history, e.g. about 1815 immediately after the Napoleonic wars, about 1830 and 1848 at times when revolutions emanating from France swept across Europe, and in the early years of the twentieth century when governments were obliged to respond to the demands of growing movements of radicalism and socialism. Achievements in the nineteenth century laid solid foundations for open societies which have continued to the present day in all these smaller countries, a development which has made a contribution to the progress of world civilization in aggregate perhaps as important as that made by the larger countries. Thus several of them in recent years have conducted their foreign policy in a way which shows unusual international responsibility and global perspective.

The constitutional movement had periodic flickers in the Iberian peninsula, the Balkans and Latin America. In the case of Spain the '1812' constitution, at least on paper, was one of the most advanced of the day. However, in these countries the people had little practical experience of the art of consultation and the give and take of sectarian interest for the benefit of the whole community, because they had for so long been subject to autocratic and often brutal rule. In consequence, when constitutional government was tried there were always powerful groups which were not prepared to play by the rules and they tried to obtain their ends by corruption of the spirit and the letter of law, and by outright violence. In the Iberian peninsula and in most of South America there were frequent bouts of civil war and corrupt dictatorships, and by the end of the century constitutional practice was hardly better than a hundred years earlier. The situation was somewhat similar in the Balkans, but with the added complication of clashes of interest between various national and cultural groups which could not find a way to accommodate each other's desire for self-expression. The only positive comment that can be made is that there was a sense in the collective consciousness that ultimately the countries would and should progress towards real democracy.

Constitutionalism between the Wars

In the interwar period the main area of interest in the development of democracy continued to be Europe, just as it was for the evolution of the practice of national self-determination. Initially, despite all the upheaval and tensions in society which came in the train of the Great War, democracy seemed to be on the upsurge. In the defeated countries democratic republics replaced autocratic and militaristic regimes in both Germany and Austria. In addition, all the new states in Eastern Europe had to a greater or lesser extent liberal constitutions and there was reason for hoping that they would evolve into strong centres of democracy and the rule of law. Czechoslovakia was particularly noteworthy for the equitable character of its system and the law-abiding way it was administered. In the West, newly independent Ireland managed to establish and maintain a constitutional form of government despite several years of civil war.

The chief disappointment was, of course, Russia where an embryo democracy had emerged in March 1917 after the fall of the grossly incompetent and unsavoury Czarist regime. The new democracy did not have time to establish itself before it was overthrown in a *coup d'état* organized by the Bolsheviks a few months later. The Bolsheviks, although deeply committed to improving the lot of the poor, had little time for democracy because they believed that only a professional and highly organized revolutionary group could ever defeat the Czarist regime and establish a just society. The struggle against the Czarist secret police over two decades or more with its continuous game of infiltration, spying, betrayal, plot and counter-plot, had inevitably made the party conspiratorial, not to say paranoid, which all contributed to the emotional commitment to the use of force when necessary and disregard for the niceties of 'bourgeois' democracy.

The totalitarian aspect of Bolshevism was strengthened even more in the life-and-death struggle of the Civil War, 1918–1920, which involved opposition not only from anti-Bolshevik Russians but also from interventionist armies sent by the Allied powers. The final factor was Stalin's series of five-year plans to industrialize Russia as rapidly as possible and on a massive scale, which was partly motivated by a desire to strengthen military defence against possible foreign attack. The programme required immense sacrifice on the part of the people, a sacrifice that could only be extracted at the point of the gun, not through the ballot box – or so it was assumed. The cumulative effect was that, contrary to the hopes of the early Marxists, the first Marxist government was to become the most totalitarian and oppressive in the world. Even discussion at the highest level of the party, which at least had always been quite lively during the time of Lenin, was utterly stifled as all bowed in terror to the will of Stalin, the Great Leader.

The advance of constitutional government in Europe in the twenties soon gave way to darker forces. Within a few years many had come to believe that democratic institutions were ineffective in dealing with the central issues of the time: inflation, unemployment, social unrest, and, all too soon, national security, and they began to heed the siren call of brutal men with simple answers and appeals to prejudice. In 1923 Benito Mussolini, a former socialist, and his Fascist bully boys took over the tottering constitutional system in Italy and within a few years had established a modern autocratic state which was seen as a model by reactionary groups around the world. Nine years later Adolf Hitler and the National Socialists were able to capture the levers of power in Germany after a long campaign in which democratic procedures were consistently exploited and abused. A major contributory factor to the Nazi victory was the failure of the democratic and progressive parties to unite to defend constitutional government. Soon the democratic institutions of the Weimar Republic were replaced by a regime more thoroughly evil than had ever been seen before in an advanced culture.

These two fascist powers then gave assistance to General Franco, who after a bitter civil war of three years overthrew the Spanish Republic, an embryo democracy which had come into being in the early thirties but which from the beginning had been fatally wounded by deep divisions and by extreme and imprudent policies. Meanwhile, in the new states of Central and Eastern Europe, constitutional safeguards were being suspended and autocratic rulers were taking over, partly out of frustration at failure to resolve deep internal conflicts, and partly because it was believed that this was the best way to achieve maximum strength in defence against attack from outside by Germany, Italy or Russia. The last to fall was Czechoslovakia, not from internal action but from the failure of Western democracies and the League of Nations to give support against the predatory plans of Nazi Germany.

Constitutionalism after the Second World War

The rallying cry of the Allies in the Second World War was democracy and social justice against the evils of extreme nationalism, militarism, racism and dictatorship, and with victory the tide once again turned in favour of constitutional government. In the first place, the Allies imposed democratic institutions in the defeated countries – Germany (the west), Italy, Austria and Japan. The German and Japanese constitutions even forbade the re-establishment of the armed forces, though these provisions were soon put aside in practice, especially in Germany, because of the superpower confrontation. Remarkably, despite the occasional crisis, the new institutions have flourished and these countries have joined the old-established democracies as bastions of constitutionalism and up-holders of the rule of law.

A second forward wave in the advance of democracy in the post-Second World War period has been associated with the successor states to the colonial empires, particularly that of Great Britain. Of special significance was the establishment and survival of democratic institutions in India, which today can claim to be the largest functioning democracy in the world. This is indeed a remarkable achievement, considering the deep divisions in Indian society and the immense problems associated with extreme poverty and lack of education amongst the masses. Success in India can be attributed to a variety of factors. The first has been a strong British influence with regard to respect for the rule of law. This grows out of a long relationship in which the British had gradually, perhaps grudgingly sometimes, built up a solid tradition of constitutional institutions: executive, judicial, legislative, and military. The second has been the education of a large part of the Indian middle class in the democratic principles of the West. A third factor, and without doubt just as important as these Western influences, has been the humane and spiritual teachings of Hindu culture.

The transplanting of European-style constitutions to other former colonial territories has not always been as successful as in India, partly because the system was shallow-rooted and not in accordance with local custom, and partly because the new nations were often left with an insufficient number of well-trained administrators. In addition there were deep splits in society on account of tribal rivalries and fierce struggles to grab what few resources were available in order to survive. The consequence has been a great disappointment for the high hopes held at the time of independence. Many of the new countries are now ruled by military dictatorships of varying degrees of stability and harshness, whilst others, though still formally paying lip service to the rhetoric of democracy, in fact have autocratic governments which pay scant attention to the niceties of the constitution or the rule of law.

There have been three other major worldwide developments in the advance of constitutional government in the post-war period. The first of these has been the steady refinement of institutions in the established democracies to make them more open societies: the final establishment of universal suffrage in national and local elections, including equal treatment of women, greater equality in the value of each vote (i.e. a reduction in gerrymandering of electoral districts), greater freedom of the press, and the impact of regional and international conventions regarding human rights. One special device pioneered by Sweden as early as the beginning of the nineteenth century has been the focus of increasing interest: the institution of an ombudsman to investigate complaints from ordinary citizens of unfair treatment by the bureaucracy – now much larger than ever before because of the requirements of the welfare state – and which it is impractical to leave to overworked legislative assemblies.[19] Another device has been the passage of freedom-of-information legislation – this time with the United States in the lead – which has the potential for reducing unnecessary secrecy in government that all too frequently has more to do with incompetence or skullduggery than with national security or the needs for personal confidentiality.[20]

Perhaps the most important development in the established

[19] The office of ombudsman, or something akin to it, has been introduced in the Scandinavian countries, New Zealand, Australia, Japan, Israel, United Kingdom, and in some of the states or provinces of the United States and Canada.

[20] Other countries with freedom-of-information legislation include Australia, France and those in Scandinavia.

democracies since the Second World War has been the passage of civil rights legislation in the United States which has radically changed the face of public life in that country and at the same time had positive effects in other countries too. The failure of the United States in the decades after the Civil War to enforce legislation designed to bring the black people to equality with the rest of society was the greatest blot on democracy in that country for a hundred years and provoked bitter cynicism. The campaign to purify the system owed a great deal to a large number of whites (amongst whom the Jews played a disproportionately distinguished role) and blacks alike. From the ranks of the latter emerged a great spiritual leader, Martin Luther King (1929–1968), who was awarded the Nobel Peace Prize for his civil rights work before he was shot down, like his mentor Mahatma Gandhi, by a hate-filled fanatic. The executive branch was reluctant to move fast and it was left to the judiciary to start the chariot of justice moving with the Brown *versus* Board of Education ruling of 1954 which outlawed segregation in public schools. Under pressure from the civil rights movement with its 'Freedom Rides' and the great demonstration in Washington DC in August 1963 when Martin Luther King made his famous 'I have a dream' address, the executive branch finally started to take the initiative. Several Civil Rights and Voter Registration Acts were put into effect in 1964 and 1965 which at last put an end to all the devices for denying blacks equal political and social rights, especially in the Southern states. These developments in the United States received worldwide publicity and contributed not a little to a reduction in racism in several other countries as well.

Another major worldwide development has been the decline of right-wing military governments in recent years in Latin America, Europe and Asia. Experience has conclusively shown that despite their claims to efficiency and ability to get things done, military regimes are not apt at handling the complex issues of modern society. As noted earlier, constitutional government (with a few exceptions) did not take firm root in Latin America in the nineteenth century, and most countries went through a repetitive cycle of semi-anarchy when the experiment was in progress, followed by military coups justified on the grounds of unity and public order.[21] Recent events give hope that this unrewarding cycle may be coming to an end. In Argentina a military regime, particularly brutal and indiscriminate in crushing a semi-violent radical movement which

[21] One of the exceptions of special interest in this context is Costa Rica which after a civil war in 1948–49 took the decision, maintained ever since, to abolish its armed forces so as to make future *coups d'état* more difficult. Like most Latin American countries, Costa Rica has no real need for military forces as there is little real military threat from outside.

had been angered by the continued existence of extremes of wealth and poverty in this comparatively well-off country, abdicated in favour of a new democratic government. Of the remaining large states of Latin America, Brazil has seen similar developments to those in Argentina, and Mexico, suffering from immense problems of poverty, is showing signs of decentralizing a system of government which has since a revolution in the early part of the century at least paid lip service to the principles of democracy, even if the practice has been less than perfect. In Europe there has been heartening progress in recent years. In Spain and Portugal two long-lasting dictatorships have been replaced by constitutional governments which seem to be establishing firm roots after initially dangerous periods when the possibility of a reversion to authoritarian regimes in both countries seemed a distinct possibility. At the other end of Southern Europe, both Greece and Turkey, after post-war periods of military governments, have moved or are moving towards constitutionalism and the rule of law. It is encouraging that these changes, which have completed the process of making democratic all the north, west and south regions of Europe, have been given support by the activities and rules of regional institutions, particularly the European Community. Finally, reference should be made to recent events in East Asia – South Korea, the Philippines, Thailand and Burma – which seem to indicate a similar trend towards more individual freedom and more accountable government in that region also.

The third post-war development of significance in this context relates to the socialist-bloc countries. Immediately after the war, prospects for democracy and the rule of law in these countries looked grim indeed, following the military occupation of Eastern Europe by Stalin and the imposition there of an iron discipline similar to that in Russia. This was a policy, no doubt, based not only on political ideology but on perceived security priorities and a determination to build up a protective barrier against any possible future invasion from the West. (Since 1800 there have been three major invasions, each of which cost Russia millions of lives.) However, over time things have begun to change: Stalin died and the worst aspects of his regime of terror were abolished after Premier Khrushchev's famous speech at the Twentieth Congress of the Russian Communist Party in 1956. There were several popular revolts in East Germany, Hungary, Poland and Czechoslovakia demanding 'socialism with a human face', and though each was crushed by force it was becoming increasingly evident that changing conditions were making it necessary for the authorities to relax their monolithic control and thereby provide opportunities for a freer, more open society – based perhaps on the democratic principles of the 1936 Soviet Constitution (ironically enacted at the height of Stalin's terror). Changing conditions included: (i) the absence of great international crises which alone might have rationalized extreme emergency measures in the past; (ii) an increasingly sophisticated economy which was becoming too complicated to be run efficiently on a highly centralized basis, even with the aid of computers; (iii) a more educated citizenry which was no longer content to have the party give them detailed supervision and direction in the running of their lives; (iv) the spread of democratic and human rights ideas from the West, despite the 'iron curtain' and other devices for controlling information and the movement of peoples; and (iv) a sense, amongst a growing number, of lack of spiritual fulfilment in a totally materialistic society.

These trends have come to the attention of the world with the dramatic changes in tone and style of the Soviet government since Mikhail Gorbachev became General Secretary of the Soviet Communist Party in 1985, and began vigorously to promote policies

TABLE 4

NUMBERS OF DEMOCRATIC AND NON-DEMOCRATIC NATIONS

System	Number of Nations & States						Percentage of Total	
	AFRICA	AMERICAS	ASIA	EUROPE	OCEANIA	TOTAL	COUNTRIES	POPULATION
Multi-party Democracies	3	18	9	16	3	49	41.2	43.5
One-party States	25	3	19	9	–	56	47.0	50.1
Military Governments	9	3	2	–	–	14	11.8	6.4
Total	37	24	30	25	3	119	100.0	100.0
not surveyed[1]	14	11	9	8	9	51	–	–
Grand Total	51	35	39	33	12	170	100.0	100.0

[1] Most of the nations not surveyed have less than 1 million population.

Source: Charles Humana, World Human Rights Guide, Pan Books, 1987; Sunday Telegraph, 30 October 1988.

of *glasnost* (openness) and *perestroika* (restructuring). These develop-ments in Russia and Eastern Europe have been paralleled by similar events in China, where in recent years the leaders of the country, after decades of authoritarianism and repression which reached a peak during the Cultural Revolution of the 1960s, have opted for more decentralization and a more open society.

In the broader sense it is possible since the end of the Second World War to detect, despite occasional hiccups, a general conver-gence of ideas and ways of life between the capitalist democracies and the Eastern bloc. On the one hand, Communist countries have taken action to gradually decentralize and allow more individual freedom to their citizens, a development which is in accord with a main interest of Western democracy. On the other hand, the Western democracies have taken major steps to reduce economic inequalities in their territories, a development which brings them closer to some of the key values of the Communist bloc.

This positive picture of the evolution of political institutions around the world needs to be kept in perspective, of course. Depending on definition, the majority of the governments of the member countries of the United Nations, containing the majority of the world's population, are still essentially authoritarian and can be offhand in the application of the rule of law and in respect of human rights. (For an analysis of democracy and observation of human rights by the nations of the world today see Table 4 and the map on p. 389.) The established democracies still have major flaws: corruption is still widespread and nearly always there is a short-term perspective and an emphasis on sectarian interest rather than the interest of the whole community. Nevertheless, much progress has been made, and it is clear that democratic institutions, though imperfect, are an advance in the right direction, and represent a higher stage in the process towards a just society than the systems which preceded them. It is therefore important that the governments and peoples of the world see their development as being in the common interest. Like national and cultural self-determination, the widespread prac-tice of the rule of law and principles of democracy at the national community level makes more likely the prospect of a democratic world federation which in the last resort is the only effective instrument for ensuring a lasting peace around the world.

The Emancipation of Women

This discussion of the rise of constitutionalism and democracy in the modern era has excluded two facets of the subject because their special importance would seem to justify separate treatment. The first is the movement for women to have equal rights in society with men, and in particular to make a full contribution to the conduct of public affairs. This subject is of special importance not only because of the obvious point that women represent about half of the population, but more profoundly because feminine qualities are required just as much as masculine qualities in the development of a balanced and just society.

Universal and durable peace cannot be attained without the full and equal participation of women in international relations, particularly in decision-making concerning peace . . .

It is evident that women all over the world have manifested their love for peace and their wish to play a greater role in international co-operation, amity and peace among different nations. All obstacles at national and international levels in the way of women's participation in promoting international peace and co-operation should be removed as soon as possible.[22]

This view is confirmed by the general record in recent times which shows that women, despite all the handicaps imposed on them by society, have constantly played leading roles in nearly all progressive movements, most notably the anti-slavery, temperance and collectivist movements of the nineteenth century, and the human rights, environmental and peace movements of the twentieth.

Women's voting record (in the USA) shows that they are more likely to favour stronger environmental protection regulation, gun control, abolition of the death penalty, and are more likely to vote against weapons build ups (Seager and Olson, *Women in the World*, p. 115).

Christabel Pankhurst (1880–1958) wrote on 7 August 1914, three days after the outbreak of the Great War:

Had women been equal partners with men from the beginning, human civilization would have been totally different from what it is. The whole manner of humanity would have been at a point other than we have reached at this moment of terrible calamity.

There are men who have a glimmering idea of something better, but only by the help of women could civilization have been made other than cruel, predatory, destructive. Only by the help of women as citizens can the World be saved after the holocaust is ended . . .[23]

---

[22] *The Nairobi Forward-Looking Strategies for the Advancement of Women*, paragraphs 235 and 237 adopted by consensus of 157 countries in July 1985 and by the UN General Assembly in December the same year.

[23] Quoted by Humphries, *A Radical Reader*, p. 602.

Since the beginning of civilization women have been considered as inferior beings in virtually all societies. This has limited not only the prospects for women themselves in reaching their full potential, but the quality of society as a whole. The handicaps imposed on women, not any innate inferiority, resulted in only a few women rising to prominence in public affairs, the arts or sciences, and those who did, such as Boadicea, Elizabeth I of England or Catherine the Great of Russia, were constrained to act more or less like men. One major exception has been in the field of religion, where women have often been amongst the most notable of the immediate followers of the founder of their religion and where numerous women saints have contributed to the development of a female perspective to society.[24] The founders of the great religions all upheld the position of women in emphasising the spiritual equality of men and women in the eyes of God. Some went further. Muhammad, for instance, gave specific instructions for the protection of women. Yet religion in decline has been one of the greatest barriers to the emancipation of women, as is once again being demonstrated by those Muslim fundamentalists who are to-day busy reversing gains already achieved.[25] In the Christian world the Catholic Church, which for so long insisted that women should be essentially confined to the kitchen, nursery and bedroom, has been one of the main opponents of the emancipation of women in the West, and it is noteworthy that generally Catholic countries have lagged behind in giving women the vote. Of the three great revolutionary powers (which have all to a greater or lesser extent been in the vanguard of progressive movements) the women's movement had relatively little success in Catholic France, as compared with Protestant Britain and the United States. It should be added that the Protestant record is not all positive, for there is still a strong fundamentalist tradition which identifies women with Eve, the temptress of man, who must be strictly regulated if the moral fibre of society is to be maintained!

The West has taken the lead in the emancipation of women in

[24] The barriers began to come down in western society very fast in the nineteenth century. Not only was there the extraordinary role of women in progressive political and social movements as mentioned in several chapters of this book but also a flowering of female talent in several fields of artistic and scientific endeavour. Most noticeable was the success in the field of letters: in Britain, Jane Austen (1775–1865), Charlotte Brontë (1816–1855), Emily Brontë (1818–1848), Elizabeth Gaskell (1810–1865), and Mary Ann Evans, working under the male pen name George Eliot (1819–1880); in France, Madame de Staël (1766–1817) and George Sand (1804–1876); and in the United States, Emily Dickinson (1830–1886).

[25] Thus it is reported that leading Islamic fundamentalists have made such public comments as: 'The average size of a man's brain is larger than a woman's . . . women cannot compete with men in the rational sciences and problems of pure logic . . . a woman is completely in the service of her husband . . . abstaining from housework is a dreadful torture for a woman.' (*Washington Post*, 21 December 1988)

modern times, as it has in most other progressive movements. In the nineteenth century progress was exceedingly slow compared with improvements in other areas of society, and a sense of frustration built up which finally burst forth in the Suffrage Movement in the decade or so before the Great War. The two World Wars helped women to advance considerably, but by the 1960s it was apparent that progress was not as comprehensive as had been hoped. Hence the women's movement was reborn, to press for the full emancipation of women at all levels (and eventually on the world stage) and for society to acquire a better balance between masculine and feminine points of view in the way it functions.

In England the first statement about the emancipation of women is usually identified as *A Vindication of the Rights of Women* (1791) by Mary Wollstonecroft (1759–1797), inspired at least in part by the general principles of equality being advocated by the French revolutionaries. The publication did not arouse much public interest and for over fifty years very little happened, though women's emancipation was championed by the Chartists and by such political figures as Joseph Hume (1777–1855), Richard Cobden (1804–1865), John Bright (1811–1889), and Benjamin Disraeli. Things began to change during the excited discussion of the Second Reform Bill, when a Woman's Suffrage Committee was formed in Manchester (1865) with Elizabeth Wolsteneholme Elmy as honorary secretary. Soon afterwards a London Suffrage Committee was established to give support to John Stuart Mill (1806–1873) who worked hard to have the Reform Bill amended to apply equally to men and women, and who later presented the case for emancipation in *The Subjection of Women* (1869). Opposition was very strong, and included not only William Gladstone, a liberal in so many other matters, but Queen Victoria herself, and so the early apparent successes in amending the 1867 Bill (and later that of 1884) were reversed. In the next twenty years or so women had to be content with a series of relatively minor improvements such as the Married Women's Property Act of 1870, which gave married women the right to own property and to make contracts in the same way as spinsters and widows.[26] Unmarried women also won the right to vote in elections for municipal boroughs (1882) and county councils (1888), and all women, married

[26] A major regressive step of this period, however, was the Naturalization Act (1870) which deprived British women of their citizenship when they married foreigners, though the same did not happen to men. This Act was not repealed until 1948. This unequal practice is still common and is a concern of the United Nations. In 1957 the UN General Assembly adopted a Convention on the nationality of women, but less than half the member countries have ratified it at the time of writing.

and unmarried alike, were able to vote for parish councils (1894).[27]
At the same time the cause was beginning to win the support of
several powerful advocates in the House of Commons including
James Keir Hardie (1856–1915), Philip Snowden (1864–1937), and
George Lansbury (1859–1940), all from the newly-formed Indepen-
dent Labour Party. During this period the struggle for women's
rights was coordinated by the National Union of Women's Suffrage
Societies under the presidency of Millicent Garnett Fawcett (1847–
1929). However, in the first decade of the twentieth century the pace
was increasingly set by more radical advocates, most notably the
Women's Social and Political Union which had been founded in
Manchester in 1903 by Emmeline Pankhurst (1888–1928), widow of
Richard Pankhurst, one of the most indefatigable campaigners for
women's rights in the House of Commons. Stimulus was given to
militant and eventually to violent action in 1905 when Christabel
Pankhurst (one of Emmeline's daughters) and Annie Kenney were
manhandled and then thrown into the street after they had raised
questions at a public meeting in Manchester for Edward Grey, one of
the leaders of the Liberal Party. The militant campaign over the next
few years, which culminated in the tragic death of Emily Davidson
after she threw herself in front of the horses in the Derby Race of
1913, was dramatic indeed and won some public sympathy on
account of the brutal countermeasures of the government. On the
other hand, the campaign did not result in any specific reforms
before the outbreak of the Great War. The situation was turned
around by large numbers of women volunteering to work in the
factories during that epic struggle. Men of all political persuasions
were impressed and there was little opposition to inclusion in the
1918 Electoral Reform Act of provision for equal suffrage for
married women, women graduates and all other women over the age
of thirty, or to an Act to permit women to be elected to the House of
Commons. Ten years later, in 1928, the process was completed
when all women aged twenty-one or over were able to vote, so
putting them on the same footing as men.

The timetable of events in the United States was to be remarkably
similar to that in Britain. There, in the first half of the century,
women had played a leading role in the anti-slavery movement but
had not organized to promote their own interest until women
delegates were excluded from an Anti-Slavery Convention in

---

[27] The differences in treatment of married and unmarried women came about because, for a
time, supporters of women's emancipation were split between the more conservative who did
not see a need for married women to have the vote and the more liberal who treated all women
alike. This split had been overcome by 1894.

London in 1840. The first action of the women concerned, including Elizabeth Cady Stanton (1814–1902) and Lucretia Mott (1793–1880), was to call for a convention to discuss women's rights, which met at Seneca Falls in July 1848.[28] This was followed by a much larger convention in Worcester in 1850. One of the participants in this conference was Susan B. Anthony (1820–1906), who together with Elizabeth Stanton was to be a vital mainstay of the movement for the next fifty years.

At first the highest priority was given to winning the right to vote for state legislatures. An early attempt (1867) in the promising state of Kentucky, where women had been able to vote for school boards as early as 1861, was defeated. Next, attempts to have the 14th and 15th Amendments to the Federal Constitution (which enfranchised newly liberated slaves) apply to women as well as to men were blocked even by male supporters of women's rights because they feared that such a move would impede passage of the Amendments. Soon afterwards, in 1869, a new National Women's Suffrage Association was formed to campaign for a sixteenth amendment which would enfranchise women. This was to be a long hard struggle and, as in Britain, American women had to make do with victories on a more modest scale for many decades. The first of these was in the recently formed Territory of Wyoming, where in 1869 a group of women led by Esther Maines were able to manœuvre local politicians into giving them the right to vote for representatives in the territorial legislature. It is believed that this was the first time anywhere that women had won the legal right to vote for a legislative assembly. In the next fifty years women managed to obtain concessions here and there in the complex voting system of the United States, including, early on, voting rights in the party primary elections in Arkansas and Texas. By 1918 women had won the right to vote for 15 state legislatures as a result of voter referenda.[29]

As in Britain, it was the war effort of women which tipped the scales with regard to Federal elections, and in June 1919 Congress submitted to the states proposals for a nineteenth amendment to the constitution[30] which read, 'the right of citizens of the United States to vote shall not be denied or abridged by the United States or by any

---

[28] By coincidence in the same month (see below, p. 451) there was held in Persia the first conference of the new Bábí-Bahá'í Faith at which the distinguished Persian poetess Tahirih spoke out vigorously about equal rights for women as taught by the new Faith, an event without precedent in that part of the world or indeed in any other.

[29] By this time there were 48 states in the union.

[30] The Sixteenth Amendment authorized federal taxation (1913, see Chapter 18); the Seventeenth dealt with vacancies in the Senate (1913); and the Eighteenth brought about prohibition (1919, see Chapter 19).

state on account of sex'. The proposal was finally ratified by the required two-thirds of the states on 20 June 1920.

Suffrage for women in the large states of continental Europe came in two stages. In Russia and Germany, as with Britain and the United States, it was associated with the traumatic events of the Great War. The revolutionary government in Russia authorized votes for women in 1917. Similarly in Germany women obtained the vote under the terms of the Weimar Republic constitution of 1919 which replaced that of the defeated Second Empire. It should be added that in Germany the benefits of votes for women were to be longer in coming than in many other countries, and for decades more the reality was that women were still very much treated as inferiors, especially during the regime of the National Socialists. Long traditions were hard to break in that country, and it has been speculated with good reason that there was a close link between the extreme militarism and heavy-handed bureaucracy of the Second Empire and the complete absence of women's influence on public affairs.

In France and Italy, the two great powers with a long Catholic tradition, the vote for women was not obtained until after the Second World War. In France it came partly as a reaction to the policies of the collaborationist regime of Marshal Pétain which (like its ally, National Socialist Germany) had decreed in Bismarckian tradition that women be more or less confined to the nursery, kitchen and church. French women first voted in the October 1945 elections for a new constituent assembly and their right was confirmed in the constitution of the subsequent Fourth Republic. In Italy it was a similar story. Women were given the vote in the 1946 republican Constitution, after having been under the heel for nearly twenty-five years of Mussolini and his paternalistic Fascist regime.

The campaigns for women's suffrage in England and the United States were echoed in several smaller countries where opposition was less deeply entrenched and where in consequence victory was achieved at an earlier date. The New Zealand Liberal government of John Seddon (1845–1906) can claim the distinction of being the first to give women the right to vote in national elections (1893) – some twenty-five years ahead of Britain and the United States. Other countries where women's suffrage was enacted before World War I include Australia (South Australia 1894; Western Australia 1899; the Commonwealth government 1901); Finland, which was part of the Russian Empire at the time, 1906; and Norway 1913. After the Great War and more particularly after the Second World War, women's suffrage was to come into effect in the majority of countries which had elections for national governments, including the largest nations: Brazil 1932, Indonesia 1945, Japan 1947, China 1947, India 1949, and Pakistan 1956.[31] The campaign for women's suffrage won a major triumph when the principle was adopted by the United Nations. A United Nations Convention of 1952 states that 'women shall be entitled to vote in all elections on equal terms with men, without any distinction'.

The achievement of equal suffrage for women has been slowly followed by a greater role for women in political affairs. By the 1980s there were about a dozen countries (mostly Socialist or Scandinavian) where women constituted 20 percent or more of the membership of legislative assemblies,[32] and about half a dozen where 20 percent of the cabinet were women (almost all Scandinavian countries).[33] In the United States Jeanette Rankin (1880–1973) was the first woman to be elected to Congress in 1916. In Britain the first woman Member of Parliament was Nancy Astor (1879–1964), who was elected in 1919 immediately after women acquired the vote and the right to sit in the House of Commons. The first woman cabinet minister in the world came to office in Finland in 1926. The first women ministers in large countries were Margaret Grace Bondfield (1873–1953), Minister of Labour in the British Labour government of 1929, and Frances Perkins (1882–1965), Secretary of Labour in the 1933 Cabinet of President Roosevelt. The first woman to be a prime minister was Mrs Sirimavo Bandaranaike (1916–) of Sri Lanka, who came to office in 1960. She was followed in quick succession in 1966 by Mrs Indira Gandhi (1917–1984) of India, in 1969 by Mrs Golda Meir (1898–1978) of Israel, in 1979 by Mrs Margaret Thatcher (1925–) of the United Kingdom, and in 1987 by Dr Gro Harlem Bruntland (1939–) of Norway. One of the most successful applications of the feminist point of view was achieved by Mrs Eleanor Roosevelt (1884–1962) in her capacity as chairman of the United Nations Commission on the Universal Declaration of

[31] It is interesting that one of the last countries to implement women's suffrage was Switzerland (1971), which like France was for so long a leader in adopting other features of a democratic form of government. Giving women the vote at the federal level did not necessarily imply suffrage at the cantonal level in Switzerland's decentralized democratic system; the canton of Appenzell still held out against it until 1989. It is interesting that this is also one of the last cantons where voting is still done by the simplest method – a show of hands.

There are now only a few countries left, such as Kuwait and Bhutan, where men have the vote and women do not. There are also a few other countries, mostly in the Arabian peninsula where there is neither male nor female suffrage because there are no elected executives or legislative assemblies.

[32] As of the time of writing some 43 percent of Norwegian Labour party MPs are women, as are 57 percent of Green (environmental) party MPs in the German Reichstag.

[33] Eight of the eighteen cabinet members in the Norwegian government at the time of writing are women.

Human Rights, an achievement which in the perspective of history may rank higher than any of the achievements of her distinguished husband.

Twenty years after the Second World War it was clear that women had largely won the battle of the ballot box and that women, albeit very slowly, were beginning to have some influence in public affairs even though they still fill only a small minority of elected offices. But deeper analysis showed that society in virtually every country around the world was still male-dominated, that women were treated generally as inferiors, and that society was barely touched by feminine values[34] – even the welfare state (see Chapter 18) was managed in a relatively harsh and cold fashion. A growing awareness of these deficiencies in society came about in the sixties, first in the United States and then in other industrial countries, as a side consequence of the turmoil created by the battles over civil rights and the doubts about the war of Vietnam.

Within a short time a new and outspoken women's movement had emerged which was heard around the world. There is no question that the new movement had many flaws which weakened its effectiveness, not the least of which was that it was affected by the shallow values of the consumer society (see Chapter 19) with its crass materialism and basic selfishness (more concern for rights than for duties). Sometimes the movement was uncharacteristically aggressive in its attitude towards men, and in its concern to even the balance in society between men and women it undermined the vital role of women in raising children and making a warm home for the family. There was angry discussion and for a time obsession with such controversial and non-essential issues as the right of abortion and lesbianism. Not surprisingly this all aroused much opposition not only among men, but among many women too, who felt that their deepest beliefs were being casually brushed aside. In the United States an attempt to obtain approval for a broad-based Equal Rights Amendment (ERA) to the Constitution was defeated. For ordinary men and women there was much tension as they floundered here and there, trying to adjust to a new type of relationship. The number of people needing psychiatric care, already at a high level on account of the pressures of a competitive and materialistic society (see Chapter 19), increased substantially. Divorce rates shot up (in the United States the point was reached where one in two marriages was likely to end in divorce). Some considered this to be progress, as it represented an end to the façade of unhappy marriages in which as

---

[34] Virtually 100 percent of the media in industrial countries was owned and controlled by men.

often as not the woman had been the chief sufferer. Gradually, however, it became evident that this trend was not all to the advantage of women: laxer attitudes typically encouraged middle-aged men to divorce their wives for younger women, and statistics showed that despite efforts to make for fairer financial settlements, divorce usually meant a significant drop in women's material standard of living – and of their children. Families with women as head of the household were identified as those most likely to be in poverty.

Yet the modern women's movement can rightly claim to have benefited society in many ways. There can be little doubt that women in Western nations, perhaps in the world as a whole, are treated better today than they were thirty or even twenty years ago both within the family and in the wider society. There is a greater knowledge about women's concerns and a greater sensitivity to them. Two extreme examples have been (i) gradually changing attitudes towards rape and a greater willingness to acknowledge that the woman is a victim rather than the instigator; and (ii) a recognition that there is a great deal of physical violence against women within the family (it is estimated, for instance, that in the USA 2 million women are beaten each year and that in Canada one in ten women has been assaulted by a man). The first shelters for battered women were established in Britain and Canada in 1972 and such facilities are now available (if sparsely) in a multitude of other countries too. Feminine values have unquestionably led to a gradual humanizing and softening up of bureaucracy, both public and private, with more attention being paid to the needs and concerns of the ordinary individual, including the lower-paid employee. It may well be too that the rise of feminism is partly responsible for the noticeable muting of aggressive 'macho' or 'military' talk on both the domestic and the international stages of public affairs. One aspect of a rising consciousness of feminine values has been a willingness to reduce sexism in language, although when taken to extremes this can become little more than a silly point-scoring exercise and may divert attention from more substantive issues.

Of considerable importance has been the impact of the women's movement on various aspects of the economy. In education, for instance, most industrial societies had achieved equal enrolments between boys and girls in primary and secondary education by the Second World War, but in tertiary education women still lagged far behind. In the nineteenth century women had been excluded from most established universities and colleges and were confined to an inadequate number of new women's colleges. In the last twenty or thirty years this situation has been largely corrected in most Western countries, and women are now free to enter any university and any department within those universities. In many countries such as the United States, Russia, Canada, Argentina and Brazil, the number of women enrolled in tertiary education is the same as for men, and in virtually all Western countries women's enrolment is no less than 50 percent of men's enrolment, a significant advance over the situation even as late as the immediate post-Second World War situation.

Similarly in employment a new generation of women has been able to break out of the old ghettos of generally low-paid jobs: factory workers, agricultural labourers, office clerks, primary school teachers and nurses,[35] and now women are a significant proportion of new entrants into the professions such as medicine and the law. A recent survey reported in *The Economist* (14 March 1987) showed that in the United States, for instance, management positions in business held by women have increased over the last twenty years from less than 20 percent to well over 30 percent. But current data also show that only 2 percent of senior positions in North America and Western Europe are held by women. Some progress too has been made on the important issue of equal pay for equal work, and equal pay legislation has been enacted in several countries. Unfortunately such basic justice is opposed by many employers and unions alike on account of a variety of hollow arguments, and it is clear from the following table that much remains to be done:

TABLE 5

WOMEN'S PAY AS A PERCENTAGE OF MEN'S PAY FOR THE SAME WORK
1980s Data

Percentage Group	Countries
80% and over	Burma, Denmark, Hungary, Italy, Norway, Sri Lanka.
70–79%	Australia, Austria, Belgium, Finland, France, Germany, Israel, Kenya, Netherlands, Portugal, Tanzania, USSR.
60–69%	Canada, Czechoslovakia, Egypt, Ireland, Switzerland, Thailand, UK, USA, Venezuela.
50–59%	Japan, Korea, Peru.

Source: Joni Seager and Pam Olson, *Women in the World: An International Atlas*, Pan Books, 1986.

[35] Important jobs which should be far better paid but which have been exploited largely because they were mostly taken up by women.

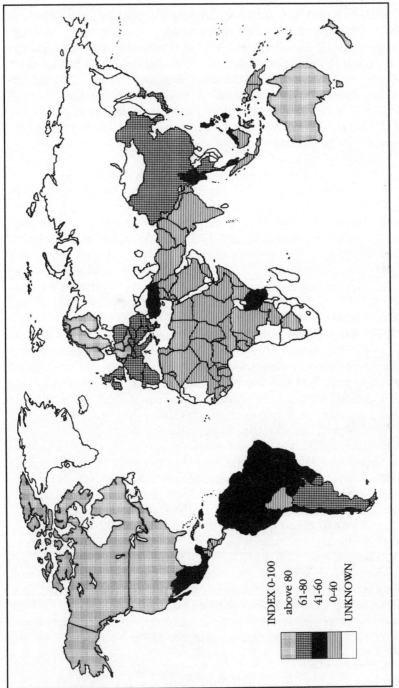

The overall status of women in the 1980's
(Constitutional provisions for women's rights and equality: general issues;
marriage and the family; and employment)

Source: Joni Seager and Ann Olson, *Women in the world*, Pan Books, 1986

INDEX 0-100

above 80

61-80

41-60

0-40

UNKNOWN

Though education and jobs are the key to economic equality for women in the long run, several other economic issues have been of immediate importance. Progress has been made in inheritance and property control (an issue touched on earlier in this chapter and which had been largely resolved in most Western countries by World War II), bank credit, and social welfare. In connection with the last of these, there has been a recognition in recent years that the state should make an effort to get family allowances into the hands of the wife/mother so as to ensure that it is indeed used for the benefit of the family.

When the women's movement was first revived in the 1960s there was common feeling in Third World countries, overwhelmed by the problems of extreme poverty, that for them it was an irrelevancy. Since then the work of women in United Nations programmes and activities such as the International Women's Decade (1976–1985)[36] has raised consciousness of the vital role that women can and must play in social and economic development. Third World women are often the primary breadwinners, particularly in agriculture, and always at the centre of the health issues which are critical to successful development programmes.

To fulfil their development role women need education, yet surveys show that in nearly all Third World countries women have a lower degree of literacy than men, and that the enrolment of girls in primary and secondary schools is less than 50 percent of that of boys. Today in eleven countries, all Muslim, the ratio is 35 percent or less. However, greater consciousness of this issue has led to a major effort, notably in Saudi Arabia, to remedy the situation.

Those engaged in development work recognize that if women are to fulfil their vital role in this activity they must have independent access to finance and credit. Lack of such access has been the prevailing situation in the Third World just as until very recently it has been in the industrial countries. In the last few years there have been several initiatives to meet this need, including Women's World Banking which has operations in all five continents, the Grameen Bank in Bangladesh, and the Women's Bank organized in India by the Self-Employed Women's Association. Experience to date suggests that women take their financial obligations very seriously and tend to be better than average credit risks.

Important as is the need to raise the standard of education of women in Third World countries and for them to have access to

[36] The focus of the proclamation of the Decade for Women was, significantly, 'Equality, Development and Peace'. The proclamation followed the World Conference of the International Women's Year, held in Mexico City in 1975.

finance, these factors are only part of a much more fundamental problem: the changing of social attitudes which have for millennia put a low value on women. Such attitudes have all sorts of damaging effects. Statistics show, for instance, that though girls are biologically stronger than boys, they nevertheless have a higher death rate than boys in many countries (e.g. Bangladesh, Egypt, India, Pakistan, Peru, Korea and others). In many African countries young girls are subject to a barbarous rite of circumcision which is physically dangerous and mentally damaging. It is estimated that 84 million women alive today have been mutilated in this fashion. In many countries in Asia and Africa the practice continues of marrying girls off at an early age (child brides) so as to reduce the financial burden on their families, even though the result is likely to be health difficulties for the children involved. In India there is an apparent practice amongst the poor in some cities of families ganging together to murder brides who have not brought the dowry promised, or so that the man can take another wife. In other countries there is a massive business in prostitution of young girls of poor families to cater for the demands of well-off men from the industrial countries. The story can go on. What is important is that much of this information has come to light partly as a result of the work of the women's movement, and this is the first and most important step towards improving the situation.

The News Media: The Fourth Estate

If collective or participatory government is to function efficiently there is a need for objective information on public issues to be readily available through the news media to all those concerned. In the first place that means information for those directly involved in government, including the legislature as well as the executive branches. But in the wider perspective it also means information for the general public, so that the public is able to make sound decisions when voting in elections or, when applicable, in referendums. It is of course important that the information be objective and not subject to slanted presentation or bias by those with a vested interest – a very difficult requirement to meet in a society where moral principles are not given the highest priority. One conclusion that seems inescapable in this context is that the news media should not be controlled by the government, which clearly has one of the greatest incentives to manipulate news to its own advantage if given the opportunity. Another requirement is that the media should be split up into competing units to avoid the possibility of control by one source, whether private or public. The news media has been described as an essential fourth estate of government after the executive, legislative, and judiciary, and is therefore included in this discussion of the development of democracy in modern times. It merits special treatment, however, simply because to be true to its function it has to be separate from the formal government structure.

The first instrument of the news media to be developed was the newspaper. Newspapers of sorts had started in Europe as early as the sixteenth century, having being made feasible by the invention of the printing press[37] and prompted to a large extent by the passionate debate stirred up by the Protestant Reformation. Sometimes the newspapers were government-owned and when they were not the government would nevertheless go to considerable lengths, through censorship,[38] to control the news reported in the papers. At first newspapers were in effect occasional pamphlets on particular subjects, but by the seventeenth century there were examples of newspapers being issued at regular intervals with information on an increasing range of public affairs.

The weekly *News* published first in 1621 in London is generally identified as the first English newspaper. A few decades later after the abolition of the infamous and censorious Star Chamber in 1641, England had several weekly newspapers but the virulent standard of debate in them, typical of those turbulent times, prompted Oliver Cromwell to restore censorship soon after he came to power, and this arrangement was maintained by the Restoration monarchy. It was not until the Revolution of 1689 that press censorship was first relaxed, and then formally abolished in 1693. There then followed the first golden age of the British news media when there flourished such papers as the *Review*, founded in 1704 by Daniel Defoe (1660–1731), the *Tatler* (1709) edited by Richard Steele (1672–1729), and the *Spectator* (1711) edited by Joseph Addison (1672–1719). In practice, though, it was to be a long time before the principle of a free press was accepted as an essential institution of constitutional government. It only came when government had a strong sense of being accountable to the public and was confident that the majority of the press would use its power with responsibility.

[37] 1440 is generally accepted as the date of Johann Gutenberg's printing press.

[38] The arguments for censorship are similar to those for confidentiality with regard to government documents: national security, efficiency, personal confidentiality. These are surely all legitimate concerns, but too often they are used as a cover to stifle legitimate public inquiry and criticism, which is a necessary part of keeping government responsible and honest. That aspect of censorship which relates to the question of public morals, i.e. the publication of material grossly offensive to public taste such as blasphemy and pornography, is a somewhat different and perhaps more difficult issue which need not concern us in this context.

During the eighteenth century the British press was hampered by various actions on the part of government including imposition of a tax on each newspaper copy sold, which over the years was gradually increased. This meant that the price of newspapers was kept artificially high and that, of course, severely limited the readership. Furthermore, for several decades (1728–1771) newspapers were actually prohibited from reporting the proceedings of the House of Commons. Restrictions were particularly harsh in the last decade of the century and in the first two decades of the nineteenth century, when there was fear that the revolutionary spirit of France would infect the British population. It is remarkable that during this period there was published for a number of years the first genuinely popular newspaper, the *Political Register*, edited by William Cobbett (1763–1835), which had a circulation of some 50,000 copies per week.[39] Cobbett successfully argued that, appearances to the contrary, the *Register* was not a newspaper and so he avoided the 4d. stamp duty per copy and was thus able to keep its sale price down to 2d. per copy.

As the fear of revolution died away and reform ideas became more respectable, steps were taken to reduce government interference. In 1855 the stamp duty, by then scorned as a 'tax on knowledge', was finally abolished and six years later the tax on newsprint was also eliminated. These changes helped to once more make for a flourishing press. The annual number of newspaper copies, which had been about 11 million in 1767, reached 39 million by 1836 and 122 million by 1854. A large number of high-quality publications became available, covering the whole spectrum of political discussion in both London and the provinces. They included such daily newspapers as *The Times*, the *Morning Post*, the *Daily Telegraph*, the *Morning Chronicle*, the *Standard*, the *Manchester Guardian*, and the *Scotsman*. Some of the greatest editors of the time who set the highest standards for journalism were Thomas Barnes and John Thadeus Delane, editors of *The Times*, 1817–1841 and 1841–1877 respectively; C.P. Scott, editor of the *Manchester Guardian*, 1872–1929; and Walter Bagehot, editor of the weekly *Economist*, 1860–1877.

Wide as the circulation had become in comparison to the past, the readership was still for the most part confined to the upper and middle classes and it was not until the end of the century that the true popular newspapers, with a circulation in excess of 1 million per day, were first published.[40] A circulation of 1 million copies per day was

[39] Before the *Political Register* the largest circulation for a newspaper had been about 7,000.

[40] The popular newspapers were founded soon after the Education Acts of the 1870s and 1880s (see Chapter 18) started to produce a generally more literate public.

first achieved in 1900 by the *Daily Mail*, founded only four years earlier. But the new popular press, whose character was captured by the title of the first one (*Titbits*), failed for the most part to reach the standards required to contribute to the evolution of accountable and participatory government, and in this important respect it did not follow the honourable example of the *Political Register*. All too frequently the tone was jingoistic (i.e. my country, right or wrong, and a good thump for any other country standing in the way) and frivolous, with little attempt to encourage people to start thinking about what was the best interest of the country, let alone the best interest of the world as a whole.

Despite the miserable quality of the popular newspapers, the British press was possibly the best in the world during the nineteenth century and early twentieth century, taken as a whole. Nevertheless, there were many other countries where good newspapers flourished and helped to build up the practice of participatory government. In the United States, freedom of the press had been guaranteed by the first Amendment to the Constitution which stated:

Congress shall make no law . . . abridging the freedom of speech, or of the press.

Unfortunately, in the early years of the Republic scurrilous attacks in the press on public officers and fears of disloyalty (when there was a possibility of a war with revolutionary France) prompted the passage of the Aliens and Sedition Acts (1798–1801) under which several newspapers were persecuted. Later a more liberal attitude came to prevail, as embodied in the so-called 'Hamilton' doctrine which laid it down that statements in the press could be allowed without punishment if it could be shown in court that they had been made with good intention. During the nineteenth century the United States was the first country in the world to have a penny newspaper (the *New York Sun* in 1833). The American press was also distinctive because of the high quality *New York Times*, and the passionate campaign against slavery and in favour of the temperance movement in the pages of Horace Greeley's *New York Tribune*. But the popular press of the common people, as in England and epitomized in the so-called 'yellow journalism' introduced by William Randolph Hearst at the end of the century, did not live up to the responsibilities of the institution and was characterized by scare headlines, sensationalism and jingoism.

In France, government intervention and control over the press had a long history going back to the early seventeenth century, and even the Revolution failed to change the situation significantly. It was not until the establishment of the Third Republic in 1871 that the press was given freedom over an extended period of time. One aspect of government control having a lasting effect which could be seen in a positive as well as negative light was a requirement of the 1850 *Loi Tinguay* that all newspaper articles be signed by the author. Despite these generally constraining conditions, France was to produce some distinguished newspapers which were equal to the best in the world, notably *L'Eclair* and *Le Matin* – a tradition which has continued into the present day with such papers as *Le Monde* and *Le Figaro*.

Similarly in Germany, where some of the earliest journals had been published, there were to be some of the best newspapers in the world in the nineteenth century, such as the *Allegemeine Zeitung*. This was despite heavy-handed control and censorship by the government throughout the whole period, including the last quarter of the century when there was supposedly guaranteed freedom of the press. The strong independent tradition of a quality press has survived into the post-war period despite temporary eclipse during the time of the National Socialist regime.

Other countries which had a distinguished record in the nineteenth century and beyond, with regard to the development of a healthy press in defence of a free and participatory democracy, were Sweden, which passed the first law giving formal protection to freedom of the press (1766), and Switzerland, which after adoption of the democratic constitution of 1848 became home to a range of high-quality newspapers with a strong foreign as well as domestic readership, e.g. the *Neue Zürcher Zeitung*, the *Gazette de Lausanne* and the *Journal de Genève*.

In the twentieth century the news media has been subject to a large number of important changes in the context of this discussion, of which the most significant have been the invention of radio and later of television.[41] Both these new media systems have the great advantage over newspapers of not requiring literacy on the part of the audience in order to be understood, and with the design and production of cheap receivers it has become possible to reach millions of people, particularly in the Third World, who have never read newspapers. These systems have also had their own drawbacks. Inevitably they required more regulation than newspapers because of the need for central allocation of a limited number of wave bands, and this has given opportunity for considerable government control. In many countries radio and television is a government monopoly and is government financed, and the news service is doctored to suit

---

[41] Another new media was of course the cinema, but movie newsreels were never significant as a means of informing the public of current affairs: they were always short, shallow and biased, and in any case suffered the handicap of lacking timeliness.

the convenience of the government. In other countries, of which the most spectacular example is the United States, radio and television is in private hands and largely financed by commercial advertisements. This has tended to make the news coverage, along with other material, shallow, parochial and at the level of the lowest common denominator. This trend could change, however, as commercial stations seek out special interest markets, some with high levels of education.

One institution which stands out and fits neither of these patterns is the British Broadcasting Corporation (founded in 1927), which was for several decades a monopoly under the direction of an independent Board and a secretary-general. Sir John Reith (1889–1971), secretary-general from 1927 to 1938, was determined to set a standard which would uplift the audience both intellectually and spiritually. The BBC established a reputation, especially during World War II, for objective news reporting and as a result it won a large international as well as domestic audience. It is perhaps not unreasonable to describe the BBC international news as an embryo world service – as distinct from the biased overseas broadcasts of most other great powers at the time. The high general standards of the BBC of that period have for the most part survived to the present day despite occasional attempts at government interference after the BBC started to become a little more assertive and critical in its reporting during the radical sixties. The success of the BBC has aroused interest outside Britain and in several Commonwealth countries the model has been copied to a greater or lesser extent, with a consequent standard of broadcasting well above the norm.

Deplorable as has been the standard in many countries, note should be made of the very useful service that was rendered by commercial TV services in the United States when covering the war in Vietnam – the first war in history to be shown live on TV on a daily basis. The graphic pictures of the horrors of that campaign, appearing on the screen in every home across the country every night, made clear to the ordinary person as never before the sheer absurdity of war. This time the usual patriotic propaganda could not cover up the reality.

Though the electronic news media are now of immense importance, they have not replaced the printed newspaper entirely, as was once expected, because the latter are still able to present better in-depth and detailed information in the least amount of the audience's time; in recent decades the world's press has continued to flourish. In the context of this discussion one important trend has been the emergence of good quality papers in a growing number of countries

TABLE 6

INDICATORS OF MEDIA DISTRIBUTION PER THOUSAND POPULATION
1980 Data

Region	Radio Receivers[1]	TV Receivers[2]	Daily Newspaper Circulation[3]
Africa	73	15.3	14
Asia	107	53	72
Americas, North	1,970	619	258
Americas, South	302	107	95
Arab States	153	52	33
Europe	455	311	310
Oceania	867	297	272
World	339	152	134

[1] 88.4% of total in 12 countries: USA, USSR, Japan, UK, France, Brazil, India, West Germany, Canada, Moscow, Australia and South Korea in descending order. Total number of receivers: 1,179 million.

[2] 76.8% of total in 10 countries: USA, USSR, Japan, UK, Italy, West Germany, France, Brazil, Canada and Spain in descending order. Total number in receivers: 527 million.

[3] 66.2% of total in 10 countries: USSR, Japan, USA, UK, West Germany, India, France, East Germany, South Korea and Italy in descending order. Total number of copies: 453 million.

Source: George Thomas Kurian, *New Book of World Rankings*, Facts on File Publications, 1984.

outside the traditional 'European' circle, most notably in such countries as Japan and India. Another has been the development, greatly assisted by modern technology, of newspapers which are available on a worldwide basis – the beginning, as with the BBC, of a true world news media of which typical examples are the *International Herald Tribune* and the *Economist*. Nevertheless, the bias and parochialism of the majority of the press causes concern not least in Third World countries where many believe that the powerful Western news services do not provide a fair picture of events in their countries. This has led to an attempt to assert more control over the news media, including the laying down of rules of behaviour by UNESCO, an attempt which has been strongly resisted by the media ever on its guard against intervention for ulterior reasons. In the last resort this is a spiritual matter for all concerned: it is about objectivity, preservation of the principle of freedom of inquiry, and a focus not on selfish parochial interests, but rather on a profound vision of the welfare of all the peoples of the world.

B
REDUCING MATERIAL POVERTY

THE second main theme of Part II is progress in the modern age towards eliminating poverty. Some basic information on economic differences between nations, and within nations, is given in Tables 7 and 20 (p. 000. Important as are the political and social freedoms to the establishment of conditions in which all people can be free to develop their individual potential and to live a full and fruitful life, they are not sufficient in themselves: if people are crushed by extreme poverty they have neither the time, nor the energy, nor the education to look to anything but the immediate and all-demanding task of physical survival.

Living at the margin of subsistence, threatened almost daily with disaster from famine, war or disease, has been the lot of the vast majority of humankind throughout history. The possibility of significantly changing this state of affairs came with the Industrial Revolution. The Revolution gave society the means for a vast increase in total wealth. It began in England in the eighteenth century with increasing use of water power to drive machinery, mostly in cotton spinning mills, and with the construction of a modern communication system of canals and metalled roads. But the critical development was the invention of the steam engine[1] and its use for a growing number of industrial applications, for instance in the mines for winding machinery and for pumping water, in the spinning and weaving of cloth, in the metallurgy and pottery industries, and in new systems of transportation: the railway and the steamship.

As the potential of the Industrial Revolution came to be realised, many men and women abandoned the passive philosophy which had largely prevailed until that time, whereby poverty and gross inequalities were seen as inevitable, and they began to think how society might be changed so as to abolish poverty and to achieve greater economic equality. The impetus to action was strengthened by the way the Industrial Revolution was manifested: crowded houses, poor sanitary facilities and smoke pollution in the new

[1] In a series of developments, it is generally recognized that the key invention was that of James Watt in 1769.

TABLE 7

EXTREMES OF WEALTH AND POVERTY WITHIN NATIONS
Mostly 1970s Data

The table below shows average income for the top 10 percent of the population as a factor of average income for the lowest 40 percent; i.e. a factor of 10 means a household in the top percent has an average income 10 times as large as the income of a household in the lowest 40 percent.

Factor grouping	Number of Nations & States						Percentage of Total
	AFRICA	AMERICAS	ASIA	EUROPE	OCEANIA	TOTAL	COUNTRIES
2.5–4.9	0	0	1	8	1	10	14.9
5.0–9.9	4	6	7	7	1	25	37.3
10.0–14.9	4	7	5	1	0	17	25.4
15.0–19.9	2	1	0	0	0	3	4.5
20.0–24.9	4	2	0	0	0	6	8.9
25.0–29.9	2	2	0	0	0	4	6.0
30.0 & above	0	1	1	0	0	2	3.0
Total	**16**	**19**	**14**	**16**	**2**	**67**	**100.0**
Not surveyed	35	16	25	17	10	103	
Grand Total	**51**	**35**	**39**	**33**	**12**	**170**	

General Note: Though the survey is limited it is sufficient to show that poorer countries generally have the greatest internal extremes of wealth. The figures for the leading OECD countries are: USA, 7.0; Japan, 5.2; Germany, 7.2; France, 8.6; UK, 5.0; Italy, 7.9; and Canada, 5.9 – all well below 10.0. The lowest differentials are in the socialist countries of Eastern Europe, Scandinavia and Australia. The highest extremes are in Brazil, Ecuador, Gabon, Honduras, Iraq and Zimbabwe.

Source: C. Lewis Taylor and David A. Jodice, *World Handbook of Political and Social Indicators*, Yale University Press, 1983.

industrial cities, long hours and harsh working conditions in the factories, and a sharp contrast between the material wealth of the capitalists and the low wages of the factory workers which suggested undue exploitation (though it is now generally acknowledged that the standard of living of the factory workers was an improvement over what they had when they had been labourers in the countryside).

Those struggling to eliminate poverty followed five broad avenues: trade unions, cooperatives, socialism, the welfare state, and the consumer society. Generally, those engaged in these movements worked hand in hand with the progressive movements concerned with political equality, civil liberties and the rule of law, which have already been reviewed, but there were many who were so indignant at the extent of poverty in the midst of wealth that they were prepared to brush aside such 'bourgeois' niceties in favour of revolutionary violence if these in any way delayed progress towards economic justice. The resulting split in the progressive movement, which became most marked in the twentieth century, has undoubtedly slowed down the march towards a just society.

Of the five avenues taken towards a more economically just society it will be noted that the first four are collective in nature and to a greater or lesser extent involve redistribution of wealth, i.e. the reduction of extreme wealth as well as extreme poverty. The supporters of the fifth approach claim that it is different: it concentrates on making the economy bigger so that there will be more for everyone, and consequently poverty can be eliminated without any deliberate redistribution of wealth. Of the four 'collectivist' approaches, trade unionism and socialism have tended to be more confrontational than the other two in challenging the richer segment of society, and in consequence have been most resisted, sometimes to the point of violence. There has been little direct opposition to the cooperative movement, and in the twentieth century most sections of society have come to accept the main features of the welfare state – though very recently this consensus has started to crumble under the pressure of concern that it has undermined the competitive spirit, and also because of the perhaps more important demographic trend in the industrial countries which is likely to lead to a significant increase in the cost of the welfare state that will have to be borne by a shrinking proportion of the population.

CHAPTER 15

Trade Unions

ONE of the first methods to emerge in the last two centuries for tackling the question of poverty was the trade union. Trade unions are a self-help movement of working people who have banded together to defend and improve their working conditions and their general economic, social and political status in society. In pursuit of this goal they have been engaged at various times in a wide range of activities. The provision of social services for members, such as contributory insurance schemes to protect against unemployment, sickness, old age and the financial consequences of death, was the earliest such activity; later most of these services were taken over by the welfare state (see Chapter 18). But perhaps the most important activity and certainly the one most readily identified with the trade union is the function of negotiating with an employer about wage levels, benefits and other conditions of work. Such negotiations may be with a single plant or company or with a whole industry or even with the state itself – either because the state is the employer or because it has an interest on behalf of the general public in seeing that a satisfactory settlement is reached. A union may be negotiating on behalf of a select group, e.g. a particular craft, or on behalf of all employees. Its initial strength as a negotiator is that it does represent its members, in most cases, on the basis of democratic election. If necessary, it has at its call various methods of sanction to support its case, ranging from appeals for public sympathy (for the worker as underdog in negotiating with the rich owner), to threats of working to rule, working on a go-slow routine, withdrawal of labour, sit-ins and violence against either property or employer.

A third activity of trade unions has been to act in the political sphere to improve general conditions in society on behalf of its members, e.g. to persuade the people and parliament to have universal suffrage in elections, or to provide social services. Such activities may take the form of direct action such as public demonstrations or general strikes against public services, or they may be indirect, for instance in providing financial and voting support to political parties (usually socialist) who are committed to policies which it is believed will benefit members. Unions in nearly all countries have been involved in politics, but it is perhaps in the poorest countries, where the opportunity to make gains through conventional pressure on employers are least, that commitment to politics has been the greatest.

While unions limited their activities to social services they were not opposed from outside, but when they started to negotiate with employers and to become involved in politics, opposition – particularly from the state and employers – could be harsh. In authoritarian countries governments are naturally loath to tolerate within their territory an independent power centre with the potential to oppose their rule and it is not surprising that unions in such countries are normally persecuted or made toothless. Bismarck, for instance, made trade unions illegal from 1875 until he was removed from power in 1890 and his policy was continued in a watered-down form until the end of the Second German Empire. In Fascist and Communist states unions are normally taken over and become agents of the state, providing various social services and diverting attention from areas of conflict.

But opposition to unions has not been confined to authoritarian regimes. In England, where the union became a reality somewhat earlier than elsewhere because that is where the Industrial Revolution started, the governments at the end of the eighteenth century and during the early years of the nineteenth took legal action to severely restrict their activities. The Unlawful Oaths Act of 1797 made illegal a normally innocent way of binding workers together in face of threats from the employer; the Combination Acts of 1800 reinforced the general interpretation of the common law at the time which made collective action against an employer illegal; and the Six Acts of 1820 made illegal public meetings and demonstrations. As late as 1834 a small group of agricultural trade unionists (later known as the Tolpuddle Martyrs) were sentenced to be transported to Australia for supposedly administering illegal oaths. Conditions were no better in revolutionary France where the Loi Chapelier (1791) made unions illegal; this law was not effectively repealed until 1884. In the United States hostility to unions was to be long and fierce, and to last well into the twentieth century. It was a common practice for local authorities in the United States to issue legal injunctions in the public interest against strikes, and employers were given support when they used strike breakers, 'yellow dog' contracts (forbidding a hired worker to join a union), and *agents provocateurs* to counter union activities.

But after a while public attitudes towards unions started to change in England, and later in continental Europe too. Fears of revolution, initially strong in the years after the end of the Napoleonic Wars, began to recede; and the majority of unions were seen to be led by respectable, even conservative, men. Over a period of three-quarters of a century or so England set an example in liberalizing the law so that unions could be effective in negotiating terms of employment for their members. Thus in 1824 and 1825 Acts of Parliament specifically stated that unions were not illegal as such and that they could bargain with employers on wages and conditions of work provided that there was no violence or prospect thereof. Though these Acts were a great improvement, they did leave some questions open. These were mostly settled in the 1870s with further legislation which limited trade union liability for civil damages (1873) and which explicitly legalized peaceful picketing (1875) and declared legal anything done by a union which would be legal if done by an individual. Some doubt was thrown on the position of unions by the Taft case of 1903 in which the railway union was successfully sued for damages arising from loss of profit in a strike. This situation was corrected by the Trade Disputes Act of 1906 which reinforced union protection against liability for loss of business from a strike. During the next thirty years there was considerable controversy about the more political issue of trade unions collecting funds for political parties, i.e. the Labour Party. The Trade Unions Act of 1913 made it legal for unions to collect political funds automatically from members unless they opted out of the scheme; this right was reversed in 1927 after the General Strike of the previous year, and then restored in 1946 by the Labour Government of that time. Most recently, government legislation has been passed to ensure greater democracy in the administration of unions and to curb some of the more extreme tactics such as semi-professional 'flying pickets'.

The British example was generally followed in most Western 'open society' countries by the turn of the century, although it was not until the time of the New Deal that the legal position of unions in the United States became thoroughly protected: the National Industry Recovery Act of 1933 gave workers 'the right to organize and bargain collectively through representation of their own choosing' and 'free from the interference, restraint or coercion of employers of labor'; the National Labor Relations Act (1935) listed various unfair practices of employers against unions which henceforth would be illegal and which were to be monitored by a new National Labor Relations Board.[1]

In the early years of the nineteenth century union activity was confined largely to Great Britain and the United States. In both countries unions were mostly engaged in providing their members with social services, though in the United States local unions would sometimes negotiate with employers or the local town council about conditions of work. Some over-ambitious plans for national strikes in support of improved working conditions came to naught in the 1830s and 40s in both countries, mainly because of inadequate organization. During the middle years of the century, in reaction to these failures the emphasis with regard to negotiating with employers was very much on small craft unions whose members were relatively well off and therefore (i) somewhat cautious and (ii) able to contribute to the establishment of large reserves of funds to make threats of strike credible. No further attempt was made to create an all-embracing trade union organization in Britain until the craft unions were firmly established. Even then there was considerable caution and the arrangement was limited to a loose confederation – the Trade Union Congress (TUC) – to coordinate activities (1868).

As knowledge about the appalling working conditions of many workers became more widespread during the last quarter of the century, public opinion became much more favourable to unions, especially in Britain. John Stuart Mill wrote as early as 1868:

Readers of other classes will see with surprize, not only how great a portion of the truth the unions have on their side, but how much less frequent and condemnable even their errors appear when seen under the aspect in which it is only natural that the working classes should themselves regard them.

There was much public support and sympathy for the strike of the London match girls in 1888 because their extremely unhealthy working conditions were known. There was similar support the next year for the London dockers in their strike to maintain a wage of sixpence per hour (the dockers' tanner) as the public came to understand the hardship and uncertainty of casual labour arrangements. Much sympathy went out to the dockers' leader, Ben Tillett (1860–1943), when he spoke to the dockers and tried to raise their heads in dignity as he asked them:

to behave as human beings – not to beat their wives, not to fight one another savagely, not to drink themselves stupid at the first opportunity.

[1] The Taft Hartly Act of 1947 supposedly added to the symmetry by listing union practices which were considered unfair and which henceforth were to be illegal also.

Little by little the union movement began to expand and to become a powerful force in Europe, North America and Australasia in the period immediately before the Great War. In Great Britain new mass unions were formed for non-craft workers such as the agricultural labourers, dockers, miners, and railway workers. The expanded movement was soon strong enough to field its own candidates for Parliament; they were organized into an Independent Labour Representation Group that later became part of a new Labour Party in which the trade unions have continued to wield considerable influence. In the United States union power greatly increased with the founding of general 'umbrella' organizations such as the Knights of Labor (1880) and the American Federation of Labor (1886), the latter under the leadership of Samuel Gompers (1850–1924), originally of the Garment Workers Union. On the European continent the unions, which came into being with the coming of industry, grew rapidly in the last quarter of the nineteenth century. It was here that unions were able to organize the first effective general strikes in history – in Belgium (1893 and 1902) and in Sweden (1902 and 1909) – in support of such political goals as universal manhood suffrage. In Australasia the unions, also going from strength to strength in this period, were successful in winning the eight-hour day, a legal minimum wage, and the first arbitration councils (1894 in New Zealand; 1904 in Australasia).

All, however, was not plain sailing, and during the interwar period the trade union movement in all countries continued to encounter difficulties. Its power was particularly affected by the trade cycle. When there was full employment unions were able to attract membership and as a result to win many of their goals, but when the business cycle brought recession and unemployment, membership and effectiveness tended to fall drastically, as indicated by the following statistics on the ups and down of union membership in the USA and UK between the World Wars:

	USA	UK
1920	5.0	8.3
1933	3.0	4.4
1940	9.0	6.3

Figures given in millions

In Britain the General Strike of 1926 coordinated by the Trade Union Congress in support of the coal miners collapsed within a week. In the USA the unions were forced into the most ferocious struggles to defend the wages and working conditions of their members, particularly in the coal mines, the steel industry and the auto industry – struggles which brought back memories of the brutal days of the 1870s and 80s, the Molly Maguires in Pennsylvania and the Haymarket bomb explosion in Chicago. Hard conditions also brought division, and on the European continent the unions became increasingly divided along political and religious lines – radicals (later communists), liberals, Catholics and Protestants – a development which in the long run greatly reduced their effectiveness.

Nevertheless, as trade unions became a part of the established industrial scene they were slowly accepted as an essential pillar of democracy throughout the western nations. This was true during the First World War and even more so during the Second World War when they cooperated in keeping up production of munitions, so that even Winston Churchill (1879–1965), never hitherto a friend of the unions, described them as 'an estate of the realm'. One important symbol of acceptance was the establishment of the International Labour Organization in 1919 as a result of the Versailles Peace Treaty (see Chapter 22). Another was the inclusion of trade union leaders in the highest councils of government, most notably Ernest Bevin (1884–1951), General Secretary of the powerful Transport and General Workers' Union. Ernest Bevin became Minister of Labour (1940–1945) and then Foreign Secretary (1945–1951) in the cabinets of Winston Churchill and Clement Attlee (1883–1967).

After the Second World War the Allies actively encouraged the re-establishment of unions in the defeated countries and in the multitude of newly independent countries which emerged after decolonization. Thus, twenty years after the end of the Second World War, the trade union movement around the world was stronger and more accepted than ever before. Mostly they used their power for the normal day-to-day routine of negotiation with employers but occasionally they would take an important political stand as in the 1968 General Strike in France against the government of General De Gaulle.

Since that high mark of influence, however, union power has started to slip.[2] This has happened partly because of a growing incidence of unemployment in the industrial countries. Also, there has been a marked shift in those economies from the basic heavy industries[3] where unions have for long been strong, to service and

[2] In the United States, for instance, trade union membership has dropped from a peak of about 33 percent of the workforce in 1955 to less than 19 percent in 1985–86. Current proportions in other advanced industrial countries are about 50 percent in the UK, about 45 percent in Italy, about 40 percent in Germany, about 30 percent in Japan and about 20 percent in France. On the other hand high figures (60–80 percent) still prevail in Scandinavia. The average for all the OECD countries is about 40 percent.

[3] Even as early as 1977 the industrial workers were less than 50 percent of the total work force in all advanced industrial countries. In Germany the figure was 48 percent, in the UK 43 percent, in France 41 percent, in Japan 37 percent and in the USA 33 percent. Since then the figures have declined further. (Taylor and Jodice, *World Handbook of Political and Social Indicators*.)

white-collar occupations where unions have generally never won as much support.[4]

Though unions are subject today to a great deal of popular criticism, it should be acknowledged in all fairness that they have played a useful role in the development of the idea of the just society. In the first place, they were amongst the first institutions in the nineteenth century to give a sense of self-respect and dignity to the ordinary working man and to arouse the sympathy of the general public for the condition of the poor. There seems to be little doubt that they contributed considerably to the raising of the standard of living of the worst paid and to the elimination of the worse aspects of working conditions in the mines, on ships, and at the docks. The union has become one of the pillars of democracy, contributing to the process of enforcing government accountability and in certain countries making it more difficult for the military or other power groups to carry out successful coups. There have been many instances, too, where unions have played a prominent role in forwarding equitable principles in societies even where they were not the immediate or obvious beneficiaries, for example the support of racial equality in the United States by the Automobile Workers' Union under Walter Reuther (1907–1970), and action in favour of environment protection by construction unions in Australia.

On the other hand, there has been a great deal to justify public criticism and disenchantment. Contrary to original expectations, unions have rarely represented a majority of the working population in any country even at the peak of their success, and quite often they have acted for selfish interests against the general good of society as a whole. Unions often fail to look after the interest of the long-term unemployed (who are usually not members) and will sacrifice the interest of future generations of workers in favour of present members of the union, e.g. the present practice of two-tier wage systems which give lower rates to new employees. Some will demand disproportionately high wages for a minimum of work, without regard to the probable long-term impact on employment levels or the possibility that the result will be continued inflation which hurts all. All too often, trade unions are associated with restrictive practices which supposedly keep open more jobs, at least in the short run, but which in the longer term lead to inefficiency, lack of competitiveness, high prices and ultimately unemployment.[5]

[4] With the notable exception of government employees.

[5] However, sometimes trade unions will favour technical innovation because it leads to greater productivity per worker, and therefore higher wages (as noted in Daniel and Pinter, *Workplace Industrial Relations and Technical Change*).

There is also an ethical question involved when unions, as has often been the case in recent years, deliberately hurt the general public in order to put pressure on the employer and/or the government to concede their demands. This is quite different from the original theory of a straightforward struggle with the employer, and seems to have little to do with the concept of worker solidarity. There are times also when unions can be criticized for being undemocratic (manipulation of internal elections of officers), corrupt and criminally violent.

Weighing all the experience and arguments, there seems to be still a good case for the trade union movement in the medium term as a necessary pillar of democracy against the possibility of authoritarian government, and within democracy as a necessary balance against exploitation by possibly ruthless managers or owners of capital (for instance, in the case of stock market takeovers when the new owner cares only about making a quick profit). However, in the long run the need for trade unions should decline as society moves away from confrontational methods of economic management to a more advanced and efficient system of full consultation and cooperation between all the parties concerned: capital, labour, government and consumer. This issue will be discussed in Chapter 29.

Chapter 16

Cooperative Themes

The Cooperative Movement

ANOTHER approach which emerged in the nineteenth century to the problem of eliminating extremes of wealth and poverty was the cooperative movement. Like the trade union movement it involved ordinary people banding together to raise their own standard of living, but the approach was different. Rather than confrontation with the capitalist to force him to give workers a greater share of a firm's income as reward for their input, the cooperatives sought to by-pass the capitalist altogether by establishing their own business which they would own themselves. The essence of the idea was that a large group of workers, each contributing a small amount of capital, would then have sufficient to set up a business for which they would all work, not so much in terms of the traditional fixed wage, but more in terms of a sharing of the profits. In the producer cooperative the workers would band together to buy supplies cheaply in bulk, there would be common ownership of equipment needed for production, and common marketing in order to obtain the highest price for their product. A variation on the cooperative model, which so far has generally proved more successful than the producer cooperative, has been the consumer cooperative in which ordinary people band together to buy what they need in bulk and at the cheapest price and then share the profits of the operation in proportion to the amount each of them buys from the cooperative.

Again, it was in England that the cooperative idea was first developed and put into practice. The main early influential figure in the movement was Robert Owen (1776–1858), a highly successful cotton manufacturer, who at his model factory in Lanark demonstrated that when employees are given good working conditions and treated generously the result is much improved productivity and greater profit. Robert Owen committed his life to the struggle of reducing the appalling conditions associated with industrialization and became a leading figure not only in the cooperative movement but also in the development of trade unions and of the socialist view that the state should be actively involved in eliminating poverty. During the 1820s the cooperative movement spread around the country and by the end of the decade there were some 300 societies in existence. However, the movement was dealt a heavy blow by the recession of the 1830s. It was also hampered by Owen's pre-occupation with a system of pricing goods according to the amount of labour it had taken to produce them, an approach which not only failed to take account of distinctions between different types of labour, but, more important, the demand side of a commercial transaction as well as the supply side. Nevertheless, the movement had some successes, notably under the direction of Dr William Kay in Brighton where cooperative movements had used profits to build houses and schools for the local community.

A major revival of the idea on a practical level was undertaken by a group of weavers in Rochdale, Lancashire, who in 1844 formed a society named 'The Rochdale Society of Equitable Pioneers'. The society differed from earlier cooperatives, which had been largely producer cooperatives, because its main concern was in selling goods to its members – a consumer cooperative. The new venture was an instant success and its charter was to become a model for cooperation around the world. The charter had six basic principles: (i) membership would be open and voluntary; (ii) there would be no discrimination against any groups or individuals; (iii) members would contribute to the capital of the society and at the same time would be its customers; (iv) the society would be democratically controlled, with management elected by the membership on the basis of equal votes; (v) emphasis would be placed on honesty in weighing and measuring goods for sale, a major attraction for that time; and (vi) surpluses from the operation would be distributed as dividends at the end of the year to members in proportion to the amount of purchases they had made. It was this last feature which made the cooperative particularly attractive to its members.

The idea soon spread and a growing number of other societies were established on the same model. The movement was streng-thened by new legislation sponsored in particular by a group of Christian Socialists including Charles Kingsley (1819–1875) and Thomas Hughes (1822–1896), which permitted cooperatives to hold shares in each other's enterprises. One important result was the formation in 1863 of the Cooperative Wholesale Society, which was a federal body for local cooperative societies and served to coordinate their production and the distribution at a low price of the goods they needed. The movement continued to grow over the next few decades and by the middle of the twentieth century it had become the largest consumer organization in the country.

The cooperative idea was by no means confined to the British Isles. There had been a cooperative producer movement in the United States in the early part of the nineteenth century, but like that in England it had fallen apart under the stress of the business cycle. Later in the century the principle was once again tried when the National Grange, an organization of American farmers, set up cooperative ventures for joint purchase of supplies, sharing of production costs, and marketing. In the latter half of the nineteenth century the movement spread to France, Germany, Switzerland, Scandinavia, Australia and New Zealand and was adapted to a vast range of activities including banking (credit unions or building societies), medical and life insurance, group health, rural electricity, housing ownership and student assistance.

One interesting example of the cooperative movement in the twentieth century has been the kibbutz system in Israel, where Jewish immigrants banded together in their new country to form farms which produced most of their own requirements and which became, in effect, strong self-supporting fortresses to defend the new state against outside attack. The kibbutz, inspired for the most part by the European socialist cooperative traditions, have a system of great economic equality between the members and a rotating system of management. They have now lasted for three generations and are still thriving, replacing those who leave (about 50 percent of the children in each generation) with new members attracted by the communal life style.

Another highly successful cooperative scheme in recent times has been in the town of Mondragon in the Basque region of northern Spain. The first cooperative in Mondragon was established in 1956, mainly as the result of the dedication and work of a local Roman Catholic priest. Some twenty years later the town had 82 cooperatives engaged in manufacturing, agriculture, banking and social services; together these employed 14,000 people out of a total population of 30,000. A typical cooperative in Mondragon is run by an assembly of all the workers who each have one vote. The assembly appoints a supervisory board which meets monthly and appoints the senior managers. Each group of 200 workers is represented on a social council which channels ideas and suggestions between management and workers on such matters as working norms and conditions. Generally, a cooperative in Mondragon will put 45 percent of its profits into a reserve for investment, 10 percent will be used for community education and welfare projects, and 45 percent will be paid to workers in proportion to earnings. Earnings differentials do not exceed 3 : 1. Thus the wage index for an unskilled worker is 1, for a foreman 1.6, for middle executives 2, and for top management 2.5 to 3. This means that many executives earn only a fraction of what they might elsewhere. Nevertheless, few leave because there is a strong sense of idealism and loyalty to the community and an appreciation of the dynamism and scope for innovation offered by the cooperatives. The high rate of investment makes for up-to-date equipment and therefore a strong competitive position. It also makes it possible for cooperatives to expand and provide employment for others. If a worker's job should become redundant, the cooperatives will pay for him to be retrained for another job. As might be expected, there is a long waiting list of those wanting to join the cooperatives. Normally a new employee has one year of probation and is then permitted to buy one share in the enterprise; this is usually paid for with a low-interest loan from the cooperative. When an employee leaves the cooperative he is paid the current market value of his share. Out of self-interest, workers themselves enforce a clearly defined disciplinary code against selfish behaviour. Strikes are extremely rare, and in 1974 when a small group of workers at one cooperative did go on strike, the workers' general assembly voted overwhelmingly for their dismissal.

Despite these successes and the lack of any real opposition from any section of the political spectrum, the cooperative movement has not won as much popular support as might have been expected, and certainly not as much as trade unions or the socialist movement. It is not altogether clear why this is so, though some argue that the movement tends to be less flexible than the standard entrepreneurial company ever anxious to adapt in order to win new markets. Whatever the reason, the lack of widespread popular support for the cooperative idea is a pity, for the cooperative has the advantage over the normal owner/employee arrangement of a greater potential for commitment on the part of all involved, whilst avoiding the monopolistic bureaucracy of state-run public enterprises. It would seem, therefore, that there is a case for reviewing further the cooperative idea, for it has not by any means reached its full potential as a device for ensuring greater economic equity.

Profit Sharing

In addition to the mainstream movement, there have been several other variations on the theme of cooperation as a means of eliminating extremes of wealth and poverty. One of these has been the profit sharing system, whereby workers are given a share in the profits of the company they are employed by, as well as their normal wages. Sometimes the profit sharing is an extra cash payment at the end of the year, sometimes it is the award of shares in the company which may or may not be available for immediate sale, and which may or may not be associated with workers' representation on the Board of Directors. The system is intended to do away with the old 'them' and 'us' relationship in the hope that it will encourage the worker to identify more with the interests of the company and work hard for his own benefit as well. The normal expectation is that a higher proportion of the earnings of the company will accrue to the employees and that therefore it contributes to a reduction in the extremes of poverty and wealth in society.

The first identified profit sharing scheme in modern times was started in 1820 by the French National Insurance Company. Other early schemes in France included that of E.J. Le Claire, a Paris home-decorating company, in 1842 and that of the well-known Paris shop Bon Marché, which began somewhat later. The earliest example recorded in England was that of Henry Biggs, Son & Co. Ltd., a Yorkshire colliery company set up in 1869. During the last quarter of the nineteenth century an increasing number of such schemes were started in Britain, and the example was soon taken up in many other countries: Scandinavia, the Low Countries, Switzerland, Germany, South America, Australia, New Zealand, and later India. The concept was only rarely practised in the United States until the Second World War when the government gave some encouragement through changes in tax regulations. Until recently some of the largest companies with profit sharing schemes have been ICI, Marks & Spencers, Rowntree, and W.H. Lever in Great Britain, and American Motors and Sears Roebuck in the United States. In the last decade the European Community and Germany in particular have taken steps to encourage more democratic management of private companies, arrangements which have included provision not only for workers' representation on boards of directors but also for profit sharing schemes. In Britain and the USA there appears to be growing interest in the profit sharing model known as the Employee Share Ownership Plan (ESOP). In a typical ESOP a trust is set up to buy a slice of a company's equity, sometimes as much as 50 percent or even more, from the existing owners. The trust will borrow to pay for the shares which are then held on behalf of the workforce. Normally workers can only sell their shares when they leave the company.

For long, however, the profit sharing idea has been greeted with considerable scepticism, and consequently it is still not practised by the majority of companies. Some employers argue that profit is a reward for the risk that the entrepreneur has in investing his capital in a company and that it is not just for that profit to be shared with the wage earner. This is perhaps not quite fair, because a worker too has an important stake in a company – his job would be at risk if the company were not to thrive. It is also argued that the system does not really strengthen worker loyalty, as is shown by the fact that workers will often sell shares in their company at the first opportunity. Furthermore, it is argued, it is usually difficult in practice to relate profit to reward for the hard work of an individual. Instead, profit is largely a result of outside forces such as demand and the trade cycle which have nothing to do with the input of the workers. The unions, too, have been suspicious, because profit sharing clearly weakens the sense of 'them' and 'us' which is the easiest and least demanding relationship for negotiation. They argue (i) that profit sharing is often associated with reductions in regular wage levels, thus pushing more of the risk of the enterprise onto the worker, and (ii) that such schemes sometimes collapse during times of recession and therefore cannot be relied upon to keep up the standard of living of the worker. Others have responded to such arguments by pointing out that the flexibility in labour costs associated with profit sharing tends to stabilise levels of employment and thus reduces the incidence of unemployment during a recession. On balance, the arguments in favour of profit sharing appear to be much stronger than those against; it has strong attraction both from the point of view of ethics and from straightforward economic self-interest.[1]

Anarchism

A more radical variation on the theme of cooperation was that of the anarchists, who took up the theme of the eighteenth-century philosophers and argued that man was essentially good and was only corrupted by the state. The state was there only to defend property, and if the army, police and prisons were abolished, life would be less evil. The conclusion was that the state should be abolished and replaced by cooperatives which could be grouped into voluntary associations when there was a need for services and functions beyond the capability of an individual cooperative.

[1] Profit sharing is in a sense part of the much wider subject of the property-owning democracy. Other aspects of this wider issue are mentioned later in this book in connection with trends towards popular houseownership and large-scale distribution of shares – especially after the sale of state enterprises.

As an idealistic alternative to the typically oppressive and warlike autocracy of the nineteenth century, anarchism had great appeal to many of the intelligentsia and won the support of such distinguished thinkers of the time as William Godwin (1756–1836) in England, Charles Fourier (1772–1837) in France, Henri Thoreau (1817–1862) in the United States, and Prince Kropotkin (1842–1921) and Leo Tolstoy (1828–1910) in Russia. Not surprisingly, such ideas were not welcome to conventional politicians, and anarchists, like many socialists, were fiercely persecuted especially by the more autocratic regimes of Central and Eastern Europe. Saint-like people such as Prince Kropotkin spent years in prison for their writings, and Tolstoy himself was only saved from the worst rigours of persecution because of his worldwide prestige.

Many anarchists became embittered by this experience and advocated direct and violent action to do away with the oppressive state. They differed from the more extreme socialists and from the syndicalists (see below) who had similar views on the need to overthrow the existing political system, insofar as they encouraged individual action rather than mass action such as a general strike or an armed uprising. The anarchists hoped that a campaign of terror and assassination of prominent public figures would create so much fear, popular pressure and dissent that the political system would collapse.[2] Perhaps the best-known advocate of this point of view was Michael Bakunin (1814–1876). During the last quarter of the nineteenth century and the first decade of the twentieth the movement was responsible for a considerable number of assassinations of public figures, including four heads of state and an Empress Consort: Alexander II of Russia (1881), President Carnot of France (1894), Empress Elizabeth of Austro-Hungary (1898), King Humbert I of Italy (1900) and President McKinley (1901). This strategy achieved little save to blacken the name of a movement which might otherwise have been able to make a useful contribution to the humanising of society.

Anarchism as a movement lingered on for a few more decades but its very philosophy prevented it from becoming very united and in a climactic struggle with the communists during the Spanish Civil War the last significant anarchist party was vanquished and the movement disappeared as a major political force. The anarchist movement, though attractive in theory, had always been fatally weakened not only by disunity but by a fundamentally unrealistic approach to the achievement of its goals.

[2] Socialist opposition to such strategy led to the expulsion of the anarchists from the Second Workers' International in 1896.

Syndicalism

Yet another radical variation on the cooperative theme was the syndicalist movement, which might be described as a marriage of anarchism and trade unionism. Like anarchism, syndicalism evolved from a non-violent philosophy into advocacy of the violent overthrow of the state. It originated in the theories of Pierre Joseph Proudhon (1809–1865), a typesetter from a southern French peasant family who saw the accumulation of capital in private hands as a source of exploitation, summed up in his expression: 'What is property? Property is theft.'

Proudhon believed that only a few possessions are necessary for each individual's independence and for his moral and social dignity. He argued that the workers in each industry should set up their own producer cooperatives, which should be linked together in a voluntary federal system that would replace the state. He warned workers to avoid involvement in political processes, where they would always be out-manœuvred by the more sophisticated bourgeois. Proudhon was himself against violent revolution, which he believed would inevitably give power to evil men. But the harshness of the system and frustration had the same effect on the movement as on anarchism, and made violence attractive, especially the weapon of the general strike which was rationalized and given romantic appeal in the writings of George Sorel (1847–1923), notably in his *Reflections on Violence* (1908).

For a time in the years immediately before the Great War these ideas captured the imagination of many trade unionists, particularly in France, Italy, Spain, South America, the United States, and even for a short period in Britain. One of the more dramatic and highly committed syndicalist unions was the International Workers of the World (known as the 'Wobblies') founded in the United States in 1905. As could only be expected of that country, the reaction was immediate and violent, and a campaign of persecution of the 'Wobblies' reached a climax with the 'kangaroo' trial and execution of one of its leaders, Joe Hill, in 1915 in Salt Lake City on trumped-up charges of murder. In subsequent years the movement lost its appeal and has left little trace. Yet like anarchism itself it did in its day contribute to the raising of consciousness of the evils of extremes of wealth and poverty in the world, and at the same time demonstrated from its own failures that the solution does not rest in violence.

CHAPTER 17

Socialism

THE third approach in the nineteenth and twentieth centuries to the problems of poverty and the extremes of economic inequality has been socialism. Socialism differs from the two other approaches discussed so far – trade unions and cooperatives – in that it sees the state as the major instrument of reform. The socialist approach embraces a comprehensive programme which includes several broad policies. Perhaps the most distinctive is the view that to achieve the goal of greater economic equality it is necessary for the 'commanding heights' of the economy (production, distribution and financing functions) to be owned and managed by the state.[1] Closely linked with this idea is the concept of state planning of the economy so as to make sure that a country's resources are used to produce what is most needed and to facilitate full employment. In addition, great emphasis is put on a collection of policies to provide for some of the main basic needs of the population (safe and reasonable working conditions, minimum income, universal basic education, decent housing and health protection services, etc.) which are generally considered to be characteristic features of the 'welfare state'. As these 'welfare' policies have been advocated by others besides socialists, and since they are of great significance to this review they are discussed separately in the next chapter. The socialist movement has also been noted in general for its international outlook and the idea that the poor of the world should become united in their own interest.

Like the trade union movement, socialism has from the beginning been hampered by internal tensions between those who wished to achieve their ends through peaceful, constitutional and democratic means and those who have advocated force: general strikes,

[1] Greater economic equality is not the only motivation of state enterprises. Another is the need to encourage industries considered vital to the security or economic well-being of a nation. This was the main goal of Colbert in seventeenth-century France, and the kings of Prussia in the eighteenth century. Even *laissez-faire* England established a national post office in the nineteenth century and the state-owned British Broadcasting Corporation in the twentieth.

revolutions, and other similar means. The democratic socialists could argue – at least in the nineteenth century – that the poor are the majority in every country and (assuming universal suffrage) should therefore be able to win elections and become a major influence on government. The revolutionary socialists would argue that the rich will always manipulate democracy to protect their own interests, that the democratic process takes too long to handle the urgent problems of poverty, and that in any case the poor are often so ignorant that they do not understand their own best interest. Generally speaking, and in the long run, the democratic socialists have flourished where democratic institutions are functioning well and where they have had a real opportunity to achieve their programme, and the revolutionary socialists have been strong where there is an autocratic regime and the only hope seems to be revolution. These different approaches to socialism came to a head immediately after the Great War and the Bolshevik victory in Russia. As a result there was a formal split in the movement which was symbolized by the formation of two international socialist organizations representing the revolutionaries and democrats respectively. This development further undermined the sense of international solidarity already gravely weakened by the pull of nationalism in 1914. Within a short time the democratic socialists were to see themselves as having far more in common with other democratic parties than with revolutionary or totalitarian socialists.

The idea of state intervention in society to make for greater economic equality has a long history: it goes back at least to Plato's *Republic*. In modern form it essentially has its roots in the French Revolution of 1789 with its themes of liberty, equality, and fraternity, and it was indeed in France where the socialist theory as such was first developed. Of course, most of the emphasis in the French Revolution was on political and social equality, but there was one small group, in particular, known as the 'Company of Equals' and led by Gracchus Babeuf (1760–1797), which took the theme of equality to its logical conclusion and applied it to economic as well as to political and social conditions. Babeuf advocated public ownership of land and industry and argued that all men should be able to enjoy equally the produce of nature; that all should work; that all have a right to education; and that extremes of wealth and poverty should be abolished in the interest of general human happiness. He believed that such a socialist society could only be achieved through a revolution led by a small, ruthless group who would wield dictatorial power until the poor had been educated to manage the affairs of society for themselves. The group put its theories into practice by attempting a *coup d'état* in 1796 but was easily defeated by the government of the Directorate; Babeuf and the others were executed.

Another early French socialist thinker was the aristocrat St. Simon (1760–1825), who reacted in horror against the violent excesses of the French Revolution and believed that socialism would evolve naturally, worldwide, as an inevitable result of advances in technology. His central theme was that the means of production should be owned and managed in a scientific and businesslike manner by the productive classes, and that there should be no place in society for parasitic non-producers, i.e. the old aristocracy. He did not advocate equality, but rather a just reward according to the quantity and quality of service rendered to the state. The state had an obligation to provide work for all, and all had an obligation to work for the common good. Much of St. Simon's philosophy was attractive to the middle class in France and several of his followers were later to become leading figures of the Second Empire (1851–1870).

A third important socialist pioneer thinker in France was Louis Blanc (1811–1882) who, like St. Simon, wanted the state to provide work for all the unemployed. He advocated the establishment of national workshops to be managed collectively by the workers, and is the man who coined the phrase, 'From each according to his abilities, to each according to his needs.' He became a member of the provisional republican government after the Revolution of February 1848, but his attempts to establish national workshops were frustrated by other more conservative members of the government who accused him of setting up 'make-work' relief projects which would be a useless burden on the taxpayer.

The fourth of the early French socialist thinkers was Louis Auguste Blanqui (1805–1881) who, like Babeuf, believed in the necessity for a secret society of professional revolutionaries and a 'dictatorship of the proletariat' (a phrase which he coined) in order to achieve a socialist state. In the 1830s his views became known through his newspaper *L'Homme Libre*. After a failed coup against the Orleanist monarchy in 1839 he was put in prison where he remained most of the rest of his life, for all regimes, monarchical and republican alike in nineteenth-century France, feared his revolutionary ideas.

Though modern socialism has its roots in France, it was in Germany, a country with a well-established tradition of state direction of all aspects of society, where the idea was to be placed in the framework of a powerful and comprehensive theory of society and history which subsequently caught the imagination and support of millions around the world. This approach was developed largely by Karl Marx (1819–1883) with the assistance of Friedrich Engels (1820–1895).[2] Marx was deeply critical of the writings of the early French socialists which he dismissed as sentimental and impractical. His aim was to make socialism seem highly scientific, in accordance with the tide of history and inevitable, an approach which would give confidence to the socialist movement and undermine the resolution of its opponents.

Marx's philosophy, developed between 1845 and 1883, began with the idea that history is about man's struggle to free himself from the bondage of nature so that he can rise to his full mental and physical potential. One of man's inventions to achieve this goal has been the division of labour which, by having each concentrate on doing what he is best at, increases the efficiency of society as a whole and thereby creates wealth over and above that which is necessary just to survive. However, the division of labour leads inevitably to inequality and then to exploitation of the weaker by the more powerful. History becomes a series of struggles between the exploiters and the exploited (the majority), each struggle ending with the exploited, driven by desperation, overthrowing their oppressors and thus fulfilling Marx's theory of dialectical materialism. According to this theory, there is a dialectical process whereby the struggle between the oppressor (representing a thesis) is eventually overthrown by the oppressed (anti-thesis) and as a result a new force emerges (synthesis). Marx identified several main stages in history in accordance with this theme: primitive society; slave-based society; feudalism; and capitalism. He contended, though, that the outcome of the struggle between the capitalist and the worker would be different from the pattern of the past and would not lead to a further round of exploitation, because once the worker was victorious all property would be communal and there would not be a new exploiter class.

The capitalist system bore within itself the seeds of its own destruction because its main driving force, competition, forced the capitalist to beat down the wages of the workers to the point where, in order to survive, they would be obliged to counter-attack and defeat him. Competition also led to the elimination of the weaker capitalists over time so that in the end there would be just a few very powerful capitalists left wielding monopoly power against the rest of society, which would have sunk into the ranks of the working class.

These underlying laws of society, Marx argued, have been

[2] The most well known works of Marx are The Manifesto of the Communist Party (1848) and the first volume of Capital (1867). Engels is particularly remembered for Anti-Dühring: Socialism Utopian and Scientific (1878).

obscured by superficial ideas such as religion, which distracts attention from the misery of the poor in this world by promises of happiness in the next; nationalism, which divides the working classes of the world so that the oppressors can more easily hold them down; and the concept of the great leader, who in fact is only a tool of the ruling class. All culture is a reflection of class interest, and therefore morality is relative, not absolute. It is the duty of the enlightened person to tear aside these superficial veils and to demonstrate to the workers what is the reality of their exploitation and encourage them to take action in their own interest.

The workers should form their own party to fight for their interest alone. Such a 'socialist' party could make temporary alliances with reforming parties of other classes for tactical advantage in a particular situation, but should never compromise on the ultimate goal of overthrowing the capitalist system by whatever means available, democratic or revolutionary. Violence is unfortunate but is justified by the end result. A successful revolution might leave pockets of resistance, made up of disgruntled former property owners, and it might be therefore necessary to have a transitional period during which there would be a workers' dictatorship (after Babeuf and Blanqui) to protect the socialist system of state ownership of all productive property, before the ultimate goal of communism would be established. In the state of communism all goods and services produced would be free to those who needed them, and all would voluntarily contribute to the general wealth of the community according to his or her ability.

In the last quarter of the nineteenth century socialist parties were formed in the more powerful industrial countries (Germany, 1864; United States, 1877; France, 1880; Great Britain, 1884; Italy, 1892; Russia, 1901) and in a multitude of smaller countries, mainly in Europe (Denmark, 1879; Spain, 1879; Belgium, 1885; the Netherlands, 1894) and Australasia (Australia, 1893; New Zealand, 1910), and soon they began to win mass support from the working classes. By 1914 there was a socialist party in just about every country in the world which had some experience of the Industrial Revolution.

The first large-scale socialist party in Germany was the German Working Men's Association founded by Ferdinand La Salle (1825–1864) in 1864. In subsequent years the association was joined by a group of Marxists led by William Liebknecht (1826–1920) and August Bebel (1840–1913). Though the party was influenced by much of Marx's philosophy, it voted at its Congress of Gotha in 1875 to adopt an essentially evolutionary approach in cooperation with the existing state. A few years later, in 1891, at a Congress held in Erfurt it adopted a programme somewhat closer to the view of Marx, including statements about the inevitable conflict between capitalists and workers, but it did not go so far as to advocate revolution. Indeed, as the party (now the Social Democratic Party) grew in number – by 1912 it had become the largest single party in the Germany Reichstag and had the largest membership of any socialist party in the world[3] – it became even more clearly an evolutionary party with a typical German inclination in favour of law and order, a position which it was able to maintain without serious difficulty being caused by its left wing. Partly as a result, the party representatives in the Reichstag could not bring themselves to vote against the war in 1914, so ending any hope of international workers' solidarity in favour of peace (see Chapter 20).

In France, the experience was somewhat different. The first beginnings of a mass socialist party in France occurred in 1871 when the Commune of Paris rose up against the national government in the aftermath of the French defeat by the Prussians. The Commune, however, had little opportunity to put into practice socialist ideas, for it was totally preoccupied with defending itself against suppression by the national government. Within a few months it had been utterly crushed and many of its leaders executed or imprisoned. In 1880 the Parti Ouvrier Français was formed but failed to win much popular support because it was soon torn into rival factions representing the evolutionary and revolutionary viewpoints. It did have one early success when one of its leaders, Alexandre Millerand (1859–1943), became a minister in the radical cabinet of 1899 – apart from Louis Blanc, he was the first socialist to achieve ministerial rank anywhere. Later, in the last few years before the Great War, the various factions were reunited under the charismatic leadership of Jean Jaurès (1859–1914), and the party began to win popular support and to show signs that it might ultimately achieve power by constitutional means.

In Great Britain socialism was late in winning popular interest because progressive thinking was generally suspicious of the state and, as noted earlier, there was rather more interest initially in trade unions and cooperatives as means of achieving greater economic equality. It is true that Thomas Spence (1750–1814) and Robert Owen himself had written in favour of socialist-type measures, but these writings had not aroused much attention, whilst the Chartist Movement, though embracing some socialist principles, had been essentially radical in terms of political and social rather than

[3] That year it won 4.25 million votes (35 percent of the total) and 110 seats.

economic issues. The climate began to change in the 1880s with the formation of a small Social Democratic Federation by a Marxist journalist, H.M. Hyndman (1842–1921), and of the Fabian society by a group of left-wing intelligentsia. The Fabians believed that the best way of rationalizing society in the interest of greater equality was to infiltrate their ideas into existing political institutions, particularly, to start with, at the municipal level. Later the trade unions (as noted already), lacking confidence in Liberal Party policies on trade union and welfare measures for the poor, decided to put up their own candidates for Parliament. The first to be elected was Keir Hardie in 1892. The labour and socialist groups formed an alliance, and by the beginning of the Great War the resulting Independent Labour Party was the third most numerous party in the House of Commons. Yet, as its name implied, it was still at this stage more of a party representing the trade unions and cooperatives than a formal socialist party dedicated to state takeover of the economy along the lines of the classic continental model; and it was influenced more by the thinking of radical nonconformist Christians than by the Marxists.

In Russia the autocratic system of the Czar made it all but inevitable that any socialist group would be revolutionary, because there seemed to be no way that such a programme could be achieved by peaceful means. The Russian Social Democratic Party was founded in 1898, but for many years it was overshadowed by the much larger Socialist Revolutionary Party (formally founded in 1901 but with antecedents going back to the 1870s) which had as its main concern land reform in favour of the peasantry rather than classical socialist concern for industry and the industrial workers. At the second congress of the Social Democratic Party, which was held in Brussels and London in 1903 (the party was, of course, in exile and not able to operate openly in Russia), the majority (Bolsheviks) adopted the proposals of Lenin (1879–1924), particularly with regard to the nature of the party. Lenin believed the party should be essentially a group of professional revolutionaries dedicated to the overthrow of the Czarist regime. He argued that it should be secretive in all its actions and built on a 'top down' directed module cell system, so as to limit the chance of penetration and exposure by the fifth column of the Czarist secret police. The minority (Mensheviks) had wanted a large, open membership and they were willing to collaborate with bourgeois radical parties to achieve their socialist goals. Lenin's victory at this critical meeting was of great importance in moulding the character of an important section of the socialist movement in the coming decades of the twentieth century.

A final comment on the world socialist movement prior to the Great War is to note that the United States, despite the prevailing hostility to collective state action to achieve greater economic equality, was the location of one of the earliest socialist parties in the world: the US Socialist Labor Party, founded in 1877. The party drew much of its support from workers who had migrated from the industrial cities of Europe. In 1901 the popular labour leader Eugene Debs (1855–1926) became the leader of the American socialists and in the 1912 presidential election he received over one million votes (6 percent of the total).

The Great War was a watershed for the socialist movement (as it was for society at large) because it marked the beginning of a period when socialist parties began to have power on a routine basis.[4] The most significant development was the conquest of Russia by the Bolsheviks after the Revolution in October 1917. In 1914 few would have forecast that Russia would be the first socialist country, partly because it was relatively backward, and partly because of the obvious growing power of socialist movements in the main industrial countries, particularly Germany. But the Bolsheviks were able to take advantage of the breakdown of the Czarist administration after three years of disasters in the Great War, the relative disorganization of the other political parties, and the support of the German High Command (which rightly saw the Bolsheviks as the best means of taking Russia out of the War). Though they never won a majority of votes in a free election of all the Russian people, there was no doubt that the Bolsheviks' policies of instant peace regardless of the immediate cost, and of an immediate distribution of land to the peasantry, brought them a great deal of popular support. They were nevertheless obliged to fight a ferocious civil war and to fend off foreign intervention for several years in order to stay in power.

In the initial period of the civil war under a regime of 'war communism', the party confiscated all productive facilities and supplies in order to conduct the war – a very brutal and primitive form of communism. This policy was extremely unpopular, especially amongst the peasantry, and led to a revolt at Kronstadt in 1921 by sailors who had previously been amongst the most loyal supporters of the Revolution. To defuse the situation Lenin introduced a New Economic Policy which gave more economic freedom to both peasants and small businessmen.

[4] Labour representatives had been part of a coalition in New Zealand as early as 1890 and over a period of twenty years that coalition won worldwide fame for its reforms. The Australian Labour Party joined a coalition government at the Commonwealth (federal) level for the first time in 1904 and in 1910 it formed the first fully independent Labour government in the world, which lasted until 1917.

This policy came to an end in 1928 with the introduction of the first of Stalin's Five Year Plans, which, as mentioned in Chapter 14, involved a high degree of centralization of the economy, great sacrifices on the part of the peasantry, and the re-establishment of terror as an instrument of state policy. Amongst other consequences of the Stalinist era was a further split in the socialist movement, this time within the revolutionary wing between those led by Joseph Stalin (1879–1953) who wished to concentrate on building up socialism in Russia itself ('socialism in one country') and those led by another powerful figure of the Revolution, Leo Trotsky (1879–1940), who believed that socialism could only succeed if revolutions were carried into other countries as well, so that the capitalists would have no base from which to counter-attack.

In the rest of the world the successes of the socialist movement in the interwar period were limited. The German Social Democratic Party did hold power briefly at the end of the Great War, thereby earning the odium of having agreed to the Versailles Treaty (a false charge as it was clearly the responsibility of the German High Command for having lost the war). Thereafter it was crippled by a split into democratic and revolutionary factions, a split which ultimately made it possible for Hitler to take over the government of the country. In Austria the democratic socialists had some initial success in the city of Vienna where they provided many fine public facilities for the citizens, but their lack of cooperation with the other parties eventually led to their destruction at the hands of the dictator, Engelbert Dolfuss (1892–1934) in 1934 – three years before the Nazis marched in from Germany.

In Great Britain in 1918 the Labour Party finally adopted a fully fledged socialist programme, including the principle of the state taking over the commanding heights of industry. It twice formed governments (in 1924 and 1929–31) but was not able to carry out the new programme to any degree because it did not have a majority in the House of Commons and therefore had to depend on the Liberal Party for support. The second Labour government collapsed in ignominy because the leadership was unable to come up with an alternative to conservative orthodoxy in handling the huge problems of the Great Depression, and as a result it became associated with massive unemployment, wage reductions, and cuts in social welfare programmes which created much bitterness amongst rank-and-file supporters.

In France, the hard-won unity achieved by Jean Jaurès began to disintegrate after his assassination in 1914 (for advocating peace) and for many years the movement was crippled by a division between the revolutionary communists (the majority) and the democratic socialists. The two wings of the movement did come together briefly in 1936–1937, and after winning some 60 percent of the popular vote in a general election they formed a Popular Front[5] which carried out a real socialist programme, not only with regard to 'welfare state' type policies but also the nationalization of the Bank of France and the armaments industry. The coalition, though, fell apart after a short time mainly because it could not make up its mind on how to deal with Hitler's Germany and the other fascist powers.

Socialist parties also came to power at various times in several of the smaller European countries: Denmark (1924), Norway (1927), Belgium (1925), and Sweden (1920–1926; 1932–1934) but always in coalition with other parties so that their activities were largely restricted to 'welfare state' type programmes which were broad-based in appeal. In no case was there any extensive state takeover of ownership of industry. The Swedish socialist party won acclaim for its success with its welfare state programme and for reducing unemployment from 150,000 in 1932 to 10,000 in 1937.[6] The socialists were also part of the new government formed in Spain after the 1936 general election, but before any programme could be carried out the country was overwhelmed by civil war.

It was in the first decade after the Second World War that the socialist movement gained unprecedented successes around the world. There were at least three reasons for this development. The first was the military power of Soviet Russia after her victory over Germany, which allowed her to impose friendly (i.e. communist) regimes in neighbouring countries, particularly in Eastern Europe. The second was a strong desire in the countries which had been ravaged by the war for a new beginning after all the pain which had been endured through two world wars and a great depression: a more just and equitable society. The third was the decolonization of large areas of the world and the coming to power in the newly-emergent successor states of an élite strongly influenced by socialist parties in the West and East which had a long record of supporting their struggles for independence.

Revolutionary socialism or communism relied on Russian bayonets to achieve power in six countries in Eastern Europe, but there

[5] Popular Front alliances were encouraged by Soviet Russia in the 1930s out of fear of further fascist advances and after having learnt from the failure of the German communists and socialists to unite to stop Hitler taking power.

[6] This success has been repeated in recent years through a systematic approach to government-assisted job mobility and job retraining, with a special focus on the long-term unemployed. As a result Sweden has had a much lower unemployment rate (currently 2.7 percent) than most other industrial countries. (*The Economist*, 7 March 1987)

were in addition a host of countries – including most notably Yugoslavia, China, Vietnam and Cuba – where power was achieved by armed rebellion with the backing of the majority of the population. Often this was because the party was identified with patriotism, not so much because of any real popular interest in socialist practice. The communist-bloc countries gave considerable support to revolutionary movements elsewhere, and though this might be justified and applauded on the basis of international solidarity of working peoples around the world, it soon came to be seen as another rather cynical weapon in the *real politik* struggle between the two superpowers, the Soviet Union and the United States; as a result it brought the revolutionary socialist movement into disrepute – a development already started in reaction to the violence and perversion of idealism at the hands of Stalin.

Until the death of Stalin in 1953 the communist world gave the impression of monolithic unity and extreme centralization. There-after fissures began to appear. Already Yugoslavia, which alone amongst the Eastern European countries had a communist govern-ment not imposed from outside by Russia, had chosen to follow an independent path with regard both to foreign policy and to the internal organization of the socialist state: there was a much greater degree of decentralization than in the Soviet model. China, poten-tially another superpower, and proud of its own record of revolution on the backs of the peasantry rather than industrial workers (of whom there were relatively few, contrary to the standard Marxist–Lenin model), also chose to pursue a separate line from that of the Soviet Union.[7] Even in Eastern Europe, where Russia was all-powerful, there were popular stirrings, not against socialism as such, but in favour of greater national independence and democracy, as mentioned in Chapter 14. A similar change, too, began to take place in the communist parties of Western Europe, which not only resented the blatant manipulation of their interests for the benefit of Soviet Russia during the Stalin era, but which had come to realize that they would never achieve power by revolution and that their only chance was to use democratic methods (the so-called Euro-communist alternative).

In the last few years the trend away from the Stalin model of monolithic centralism in revolutionary socialist countries has gathered momentum, most dramatically in the two most influential socialist countries, China and the Soviet Union. There the initiative has been

[7] An interesting initiative taken by China was one to prevent bureaucracy from becoming rigid and anti-progressive, a problem made familiar from over 2,000 years of history. The attempted solution – the Cultural Revolution – was a disaster because of the immense disruption caused, not least to the vital education system.

taken to decentralize the economy and to introduce market pricing in place of pricing dictated by the state bureaucracy, to give state corporations greater control over their own activities and to make them more accountable (for instance, they can go bankrupt) and to encourage private enterprise, especially in agriculture where state socialism has been a notorious failure. Even the most dogmatic socialists in these countries have started to realize that something drastic has to be done to arouse initiative if the economies of the revolutionary socialist states are not to fall even further behind those of the capitalist countries (the boast of Nikita Khrushchev that the economy of the Soviet Union would overtake that of the United States within a few decades, which was made in the late fifties, has long since been forgotten). This policy of economic decentralization, named restructuring or 'perestroika' by Mikhail Gorbachev, is associated with liberalization of the political structure or glasnost (see Chapter 14) and with a growing recognition of converging interests of all nations in the field of international relations (see Chapter 23).

Amongst the democratic socialists it was the British Labour Party which was to have the most dramatic initial success after the Second World War with its sweeping victory in the 1945 general election. In the next few years it carried out one of the most comprehensive socialist programmes ever attempted in a non-communist country. It included a series of measures such as the National Health Service and the National Insurance Act that all but completed the welfare state in Britain; and it brought about the nationalization of several of the 'commanding heights' of the economy: the railways, coal, gas, electricity and steel. In contrast with the practice in communist countries, nationalization in Britain involved payment of compensation to the former owners; but it grew increasingly unpopular both because it became associated with shortages (due to the ravages of war, to a great extent) and poor service, and because employees were not coopted into management and so remained sullen, if not hostile, in their attitudes to the state, their new employer. As a result of this experience the British Labour Party has since essentially dropped plans for further extension of state ownership, and has settled for elimination of poverty by further development of its other traditional programmes.[8]

Such an approach has been followed by virtually all other democratic socialist parties in the industrial countries, including Germany, the Scandinavian countries, and Australia and New Zealand, where the socialists have been in power quite frequently. One exception was

---

[8] It should be added, of course, that the left wing of the party has not been reconciled to this development.

the socialist government which came to power in France in 1981 (for the first time since the Popular Front of 1936–1937) and which implemented a modest programme to socialize parts of the economy including the commercial banks.[9]

It should be noted also that socialist governments in industrial democracies have been generally less committed to overall planning of the economy than either the communist countries with their five-year plans or the Third World countries with their development plans. There seem to be many reasons for this, including the rather short perspective of democratic parties of all types which rarely lift their eyes beyond the next election. Because the democratic socialist parties have become so moderate when they achieve power their victory in an election does not attract the attention, or alarm, of others that it once did, though there are exceptions – for instance, the violent reaction of the right to the election of Salvador Allende (1908–1973) to the presidency of Chile in 1970.

Attempts to introduce socialism in Third World countries, of which perhaps the most well-known case has been Tanzania where it was planned to build a new African system based on the village, have generally not been a success, not least because of the absence of a well-trained bureaucracy necessary to the running of a state-centred economy. In fact, most Third World countries calling themselves socialist have not so far carried out real socialist policies; words have far exceeded deeds.

In recent years the socialist movement around the world seems to have lost much of the élan which brought it so much success in the first part of this century. This can be attributed, no doubt, partly to the coming of new generations of leaders who have not experienced the passion of the early struggles, and partly to the disrepute brought on the revolutionary wing by Stalin and other socialist dictators. Another problem for the socialists has been that the advanced economies of the world appear to be gradually moving into a post-industrial age where the working class, supposedly the main supporters (and beneficiaries) of a socialist programme, are dwindling in number and are certainly no longer a majority in any of the leading industrial countries. Another factor is that with the erection of the welfare state in the majority of industrial countries much of the basic programme of the socialist party has been achieved already. The main issue in recent years has been how to manage such a system efficiently, especially in view of the rising costs caused by demographic changes in the population balance between those who pay for the system and

[9] The French socialist party has since modified its position and it now is similar to that prevailing in most other Western socialist parties.

those who are its beneficiaries (the very young and the aged). These issues are discussed further in Chapter 18.

More fundamental, perhaps, have been growing doubts based on experience in First, Second, and Third World countries about the efficiency of state-run enterprises, and the widespread view that more competition is necessary in order to ensure a healthier economy for the benefit of all. Nevertheless, public enterprise can still be the most efficient and effective arrangement in certain sections of the economy, but only if all the employees of such enterprises have an intense patriotic pride in providing the very best possible service to the community. Socialism has undoubtedly made a major contribution in the past to a more equitable and just society, and the question now is whether it still has a major role to play or whether it will be replaced by movements more adapted to problems of the present and future.[10]

[10] In response to this challenge there appears to be a shifting in socialist philosophy, some manifestations of which have been already mentioned, towards one where equality of opportunity is given more weight than equality of outcome. In pursuit of this changed goal there is a tendency to give greater weight to such issues as: (i) systematic elimination of discrimination (to the point of countering the results of past discrimination with temporary regimes of reverse discrimination); (ii) equality of opportunity in basic education; (iii) wider distribution of inherited wealth (e.g. tax the recipient of wealth, not the donor); (iv) removing all unjustifiable forms of economic monopoly; (v) open government; (vi) changing the role of the state in the economy from one of administering busy-body rules to one of setting broad goals (a concept associated particularly with the Austrian economist Friedrich von Hayek). As some British Fabians have put it: socialists must stop being the 'stupid party' which cannot win elections, and regain the intellectual and moral initiative.

CHAPTER 18

The Welfare State

THE term 'welfare state' covers a wide range of interventions by the state in the economy to achieve the elimination of poverty.[1] The concept has, of course, been a major element in the socialist programme, but it has also been advocated and implemented in varying degrees by parties from all sides of the political spectrum. In consequence, the theme of social welfare, while an integral part of the state apparatus of those countries with communist governments, has also been adopted by a majority of non-communist countries as well, and in an especially comprehensive manner by those that are industrially advanced.

There have been five broad stages in the evolution of the concept of the welfare state and its implementation. The first was during the first half of the nineteenth century when there was acceptance, albeit reluctant, that state intervention was necessary to remedy some of the worst side effects of the Industrial Revolution, especially with regard to unemployment and public health. Emphasis was placed on efficiency and on minimizing the level of intervention and cost to the state. The prevailing view of poverty was that it was essentially self-inflicted and that applicants for welfare should be discouraged by making it demeaning and unattractive except for those in extreme need. The second stage was the second half of the nineteenth century up until the Great War, a period when there was a growing sympathy with the poor and a greater willingness to acknowledge a need for state intervention in the economy for the benefit of all. The third stage was the interwar period when there was a feeling that the heroes of the war, including the young men of the working class, should be rewarded for their sacrifices, a feeling no doubt spurred on by the thought that if this was not done, there was a real danger of

---

[1] The term was coined by Alfred Zimmern in the 1930s and was intended as a contrast with the 'warfare state' of fascism. Several decades previously Bismarck, an early practitioner of welfare-type policies, had associated the term 'welfare' with the state in his remark: 'the policy of the state must be one which would cultivate the idea among the propertyless classes . . . that the state is not only an institution of necessity but also one of welfare bringing recognizable and direct advantages.'

communist revolution. During this time the basic elements of the welfare state were applied in just about all industrial countries, especially after the Great Depression. Benefits were made available to a higher proportion of the population, particularly with regard to unemployment, and for less limited periods. In the fourth stage, which followed the Second World War, there were two main developments: (i) completion of fully comprehensive 'cradle to grave' systems in all democratic industrial countries and countries where communist regimes had come to power; and (ii) implementation of some elements of the welfare system in most of the newly independent Third World countries, although few if any of them could afford the fully comprehensive model. Thus recent data, as shown in Table 13 on p. 00, indicate that as a percentage of gross domestic product less developed countries spend on welfare state programmes only about 40 percent of the amount spent by an industrial country.

The fifth and most recent stage in the evolution of the welfare state started to form in the late 1970s and early 80s. It represents a major rethinking of the whole concept in the light of high and rising costs and a perception of failure to achieve its goal of eliminating poverty. Though the new thinking is basically motivated by concern to restrain the rise in costs and even to reduce them, it also reflects a return to the old view that in the long run it is not healthy for society when people feel they are entitled to something for nothing. There is concern that the system as designed saps initiative and self-motivation, creates long-term dependency, and in fact perpetuates poverty. The new thinking focuses on such themes as targeting the welfare state to those who are truly in need as well as encouraging independence and self-respect through such policies as selling off public housing to the occupants and requiring the able-bodied on welfare to work (workfare) and to methodically seek jobs and undergo retraining.

The core of the welfare state is a group of policies designed to protect the income levels of the poorest members of society so that they have sufficient means to obtain necessary food, clothing and shelter. By 'necessary' is not meant the minimum to actually survive but rather the vaguer concept of what is reasonable and acceptable to a civilized society. Thus, as the standard of living in society rises so too will the minimum level considered necessary for the poorest members. Around this main core are several supplementary themes which are often associated with the welfare state, such as the provision of public health facilities and decent housing; protection against excessively harsh conditions of employment; a system of universal education; an approach to punishment of crime which puts emphasis on rehabilitation rather than vengeance; and a fair sharing of the tax burden required to finance public services.

Income Maintenance

Three broad concepts have emerged with regard to the core theme of minimum income. The first is a need to protect the poor at critical points in the normal life cycle when they are particularly vulnerable to extreme economic hardship: when so sick or disabled as not to be able to work; when orphaned or widowed; and in old age.[2] The second is the need to protect the able-bodied when unemployed. This normally means providing support until such time as a job is found, but it can also mean the creation of additional jobs provided either by the state or by a private sector which has expanded in response to state policies aimed at boosting the economy. It has been a constant feature of the capitalist system, whatever its virtues, that it frequently is not able to provide employment for everyone despite the fact that there are always large numbers who are in need of the goods and services which it provides. The third concept is one of ensuring that a person working has a wage on which he or she can live. This might imply a statutory minimum wage or such techniques as subsidization of the prices of critical basic items such as a staple food or housing.

All the great religions have called upon the rich to look after the poor; their teachings have been put into practice both through individual charity and through the services to the poor provided by religious institutions. Thus in Europe throughout the Middle Ages the Christian churches and monasteries carried the main burden of caring for those who were in dire poverty. However, by the sixteenth century this system was beginning to break down for a variety of reasons, particularly in Great Britain where the Reformation had deprived the Church of its monasteries and much of its wealth, and where the enclosure of common land and the conversion of arable land to pasture for sheep was creating unemployment in the countryside. The public authorities felt increasingly the need to take up the burden of responsibility for the poor, initially as much from fear of brigandage and the spread of disease as from any sense of social conscience.

A major step in England towards acceptance of public responsibility for the poor was the Poor Law Act of 1601 which gave general authority to justices of the peace to levy a poor rate on all households

[2] This approach often also includes protection in case of maternity or when an individual has to support dependents who are unable to work for themselves.

in order to provide assistance for the indigent aged, to help apprentice orphaned children, and to provide work for the able-bodied unemployed. The major problem was always the matter of the unemployed. Local authorities were often unable to provide work for all of their unemployed and were obliged to make payments to them nevertheless. The authorities were in constant fear that if they gave too much support they would not only encourage idleness (why work for a living if plenty is provided free?), but in addition they would attract the unemployed from other areas. In response to the latter problem an Act of 1662 gave local authorities power to send unemployed persons back to the parish where they had been born.

By the end of the eighteenth century there was mounting criticism of the system because of its growing cost. It has been estimated that the cost of administering the Poor Law at this time reached as high as one-sixth of all public expenditure. One of the reasons for the high cost was the increased resort to a practice first implemented in 1795 by the Speenhamland justices of the peace, whereby the wages of the poorest workers were supplemented out of Poor Law funds. This not only put a burden on the public purse but obviously encouraged employers to reduce wages.

Opponents of the Poor Law system had several arguments. First, there was a strong puritanical view that it was immoral to give something for nothing and that the unemployed could find work if they really tried. Second, the followers of Adam Smith (1723–1790) argued that the state's intervention in the market economy should be minimized in the interest of efficiency and prosperity for all. Followers of the Reverend Thomas Malthus (1766–1834) went further and argued that charity was self-defeating (a strange position for a clergyman!) because it hindered natural laws for limiting the size of population, and that as a result the population would grow faster than the food supply and eventually lead to famine: the same result as if no action had been taken in the first place. The more positive Utilitarian school of Jeremy Bentham (1748–1832) saw the Poor Law as one more public institution in need of reform with a view to obtaining at minimum cost the goal, on the one hand, of not allowing citizens to die from want and, on the other hand, of not giving any encouragement to idleness.

Increasingly strident criticism led eventually to the Poor Law Reform Act of 1834. This act encouraged local authorities to band together in 'unions' which would be financially strong enough to support a workhouse where the indigent could be housed and given 'make work'. The workhouses were to be administered by an elected

Board of Guardians. The authors of the Act intended that a network of new workhouses would make it possible to do away with 'outdoor' relief, i.e. payments to people living at home instead of in the workhouse. Conditions in the union workhouses were to be extremely spartan so that residence would be less attractive than even the lowest paid job in the area.

The new Poor Law guardians in many instances carried out their mission of deterrence with great enthusiasm. A public outcry arose in Andover, Hampshire, in the 1840s, where conditions in the workhouse were made so hard that they actually resulted in local wages being reduced. The indigent preferred to accept any wage offered, no matter how low, rather than have to live in the workhouse. From this point onwards an increasing number of people drew attention to the condition of the poor and demanded more humane treatment. Charles Dickens (1812–1870), whose novel *Oliver Twist* described conditions in a typical workhouse after the Reform Act of 1834, Charles Kingsley (1819–1875), Elizabeth Gaskell and other writers gave widespread publicity to the plight of the poor. Liberal utilitarians argued that the abysmal condition of the poor could not be reconciled with their guiding principle for society of 'the greatest happiness for the greatest number' and joined with evangelical Christians in campaigning for reform, together with trade unionists, cooperative societies, and socialists. Scientific studies of the condition of the poor culminating in *Life and Labour of the People of London* (1889) by Charles Booth (1840–1916), *Study of Town Life* (1901) by Seebohm Tree, and a Royal Commission on Inquiry into the Poor Law (1905) all gave substance to the protests.

In face of this campaign and a generally more sympathetic public opinion, there was some amelioration of conditions in workhouses in the last decade of the century: toys and books were allowed in workhouses for the first time (1891); then snuff and tobacco (1892); afternoon teas (1894); and outdoor relief for the aged 'of good character'. Furthermore, the view was gradually gaining ground that charity itself was demeaning[3] and that the poor should be given a 'right' to protection. Such a right would exist if the charity system was replaced by one based on a contributory insurance system.

The idea of insurance for the lower classes was not new. Working men, especially the skilled, had long insured themselves voluntarily through friendly societies and trade unions in order to provide for the cost of burial, for widows, and for periods of sickness. There had even been isolated instances of state sponsored compulsory schemes

[3] One aspect of confinement to the workhouse was loss of civil rights, including the right to vote – a practice which was not changed until 1918.

of insurance for certain groups of working men, e.g. in England an Act of Parliament in 1757 had laid it down that coal heavers working on the Thames River should have compulsory deductions made from their wages to cover the cost of sick periods and of old age; and a few decades later the US federal government had made provision for US seamen to be protected against disability. Social insurance had attractions for both the left and right in the political arena: for the former because it gave the insured person a right to protection and was therefore not demeaning; and for the latter because of implied self-responsibility.

The first country to actually put into practice a comprehensive scheme of social insurance, however, was not Great Britain but Germany, at the instigation of its Chancellor, Otto von Bismarck, to whom credit should be given for this progressive initiative even if his motivation was largely to steal the thunder of the 'socialists' and win the support of the working class for his government. The scheme had its roots both in the tradition of voluntary self-help (guild and factory sick clubs, benefits societies and others) as well as the long practice of Prussian governments intervening strongly to guide social and economic developments. In 1883 legislation was implemented whereby certain classes of industrial workers were required to enrol in a contributory sickness insurance scheme. The following year a state insurance scheme was instituted which gave financial assistance in case of incapacitating industrial accidents, and this was followed in 1889 with an old age and invalid contributory insurance scheme. Initially, these programmes provided only very modest benefits and did not apply to the whole population. Nevertheless, they represented a model for the world which once established could easily be improved (as indeed happened in the next twenty years), to give an advanced comprehensive system for the whole country. The German example was soon emulated in other countries such as Austro-Hungary, Denmark, Switzerland, New Zealand and Australia.

The governments of Great Britain were slow to follow, and initially limited their interest to provision of protection for workers who were incapacitated by injuries at work. Theoretically a worker injured at work could sue his employer under common law. But to take an employer to court required financial resources and time which were just not available to the average worker. To remedy this handicap an 'Employers' Liability Act' came into force in 1880 which made the employer liable to pay compensation in accidents where there was evidence of gross negligence on his part. In practice this Act was not effective because it was always easy for the lawyers of employers to create the impression that an accident had been caused by the worker's own carelessness. This weakness was eliminated by the passage in 1897 of Joseph Chamberlain's (1836–1914) Workers' Compensation Act which dropped all reference to who was at fault in an accident, and made compensation to the injured worker a right. The main group of reforms came with the Liberal Government of 1906–1914 which emulated Bismarck's programme by initiating legislation for old age pensions insurance (1908) and for employees' health insurance (1911). Breaking new ground, the Liberal administration also took some pioneering steps to tackle the problems of unemployment, first by establishing a system of employment exchanges (1909) to help unemployed workers find jobs, and, second, by creating an unemployment insurance scheme. The latter scheme only provided insurance for a limited period of unemployment, as it was assumed that most unemployment was caused by the trade cycle and would therefore be quite short in duration. Workers were sternly warned that benefits would not be paid to those who were voluntarily out of work, for instance as a result of a strike. Another innovation of the time was the Trades Board Act of 1909 which established the principle of a legal minimum wage for the first time in the case of certain types of sweated labour occupations, where employees working at home had been paid a very low wage based on a piece-rate system rather than by the hour.

In the period between the wars there were four important developments in Western countries in the evolution of the principle of income maintenance by the state for those in need. The first was the broadening of programmes approved before the Great War to include a larger proportion of the population and to make the benefits more generous.[4] This was of particular importance with regard to unemployment benefits because in the post-war period levels of unemployment in many countries were persistently higher than earlier and rose to unprecedented heights after the financial crash of 1929. In Britain, for instance, unemployment insurance was extended to cover all industrial workers and the number of weeks of unemployment to be covered was lengthened beyond the fifteen a year originally covenanted. Nevertheless, many unemployed were out of work so long that they exhausted even the extended insurance benefit and had to fall back on the Poor Law. This caused great bitterness, although it should be mentioned that by this time outdoor

[4] Mention also should be made of a new type of social security benefit, the family allowance, first introduced in New Zealand in 1926. This type of policy, which no doubt is partly motivated by national concerns for maintenance of population size, was later adopted by many countries, especially in Europe.

relief was standard and recipients were not required to reside in the workhouse. In response the Poor Law system was abolished in 1934 and replaced with a nation-wide unemployment assistance scheme which at least assured uniformity of treatment throughout the country, although it was still administered by local authorities and still continued the hated 'means test'.

The second development between the wars was the spread of the basic elements of the welfare state, including most particularly provision for unemployment insurance, to virtually every Western country. Amongst the last to fall into line were the two revolutionary countries, France and the United States. In France action had been taken to provide worker's compensation protection as early as 1898, but it was not until 1930 that the country had a national insurance scheme to cover sickness, old age and burial costs. In the United States, the old nineteenth-century spirit of self-reliance, strengthened by the cult of the frontier, prompted a long rearguard action against public welfare policies. In their place had evolved a vast network of charity organizations with coordinating committees in each city; in 1874 they held their first national conference. These organizations provided such services as shelters for the homeless, legal aid, baby clinics, free milk for children, visiting nurses, playgrounds and parks. Admirable as was the work of the charity organizations it was always weakened by being less than comprehensive; too frail to handle crises such as occurred during major business recessions; and always in the back of the mind was the sense that the recipients were being demeaned. The first steps towards recognition of public responsibility at the federal level were taken during the presidency of Theodore Roosevelt (1858–1919), who called a White House Conference in 1907 to look into the problem of dependent children, and who sponsored in 1908 a workmen's compensation act. Individual states were also beginning to take some responsibility, culminating in the decision by Wisconsin to provide public unemployment insurance in 1932. However, it was not until the New Deal Program of President Franklin Roosevelt (1882–1945) in the mid-1930s that a basic framework for a national welfare state was established. One of the key elements in the New Deal was the Social Security Act of 1935 which made provision for a contributory old age pension scheme, unemployment insurance, and special assistance for the handicapped, dependent mothers and the blind. As originally enacted the social security scheme only applied to a limited section of the population, but various amendments were approved in the next three decades which gradually extended coverage to virtually the whole population of the country.[5] The New Deal also included a Fair Labor Standards Act (1938) which for the first time made mandatory a minimum wage – at that time $0.25 per hour.

The third and fourth developments between the wars with regard to public programmes for maintaining income levels were also largely associated with the New Deal. The first of these was a major effort by the federal government to create additional employment opportunities to offset the massive unemployment caused by the Great Depression. This programme included the Civilian Conservation Corps, which established work camps for young people to carry out needed public service projects throughout the Union, and which over a ten-year period provided work for over 3 million; the Federal Emergency Relief Administration, the Public Works Administration, the Works Progress Administration and the National Youth Administration. Of course, the idea of government-created jobs for the unemployed was not new at that time – it can be traced back at least to the national workshops of Louis Blanc in 1848. Nevertheless, the New Deal was on an unprecedented scale for the capitalist world.

The fourth of our list of developments in the interwar period was the use of the state subsidy, particularly for agriculture, to help business survive the Depression. A series of programmes was enacted to give assistance to farmers who had for long been a special concern of most countries, partly because of the need for self-sufficiency in food in case of war, and partly because of a respect for the virtues and strengths of the country life as compared with that of the city and a desire to encourage people to stay on the land. Some programmes paid farmers to take land out of cultivation and others made provision for government-financed stockpiling of surpluses, the overall intent being to reduce supply and thereby help to increase prices and the income of the farming community.

In the period since the Second World War there have been several more important developments. The first of these has been the final establishment of a truly comprehensive income maintenance system for the whole population, from cradle to grave. The pioneer model system was created in Great Britain by the Labour Government (1945–1951) headed by Clement Attlee. The existing system was greatly strengthened by such legislation as the National Health Act (1946), the National Insurance Act (1946) and the National Assistance Act (1948). As a result a comprehensive national health scheme

---

[5] Nevertheless, recent reports showing that only one-third of those unemployed in the USA received unemployment benefits suggest that the system is not as comprehensive as most systems in Europe.

was established which provided free services for all. Previous health insurance schemes had only covered employed persons, not their dependents; furthermore, they had not covered dentistry or eye care. The scheme was made available to all, the rich as well as the poor, in the intention of (a) ensuring a high-quality service – experience had shown that services confined to the poor tended to be of low quality; and (b) removing the perceived stigma of going to the government for medical care. The National Insurance Act and the National Assistance Act established uniform benefits for all types of insurance, based on calculated need, and by centralizing administration at national level made it easier to disburse benefits with both a more flexible approach and a more mild version of the offensive means test.

The British example was followed in spirit, even if the technical details were often different, by most other industrial countries. Again it was the United States which tended to lag behind, particularly with regard to health care. The 'Great Society' programme of President Lyndon Johnson (1908–1973) did make provision for a fairly comprehensive medical insurance plan for the aged (Medicare) and for the indigent (Medicaid), but the legislation still left certain segments of the population exposed,[6] and even those who were covered could be liable for massive medical bills in certain circumstances because of limits on insurance coverage. Furthermore, by providing a special plan for the poor it was inevitable that they would be treated in effect as second-class citizens by contrast with the poor in Europe. Proposals for a truly comprehensive national health plan were continually blocked by arguments to the effect that the cost would be enormous – although there was evidence that the existing insurance approach seems to encourage cost escalation, and the comprehensive European systems cost less as a percentage of gross domestic product than that of the United States. It should be added that the Great Society legislation did include one innovative approach to income maintenance which has been highly successful, namely the Food Stamp programme which allows the poor to obtain basic foodstuffs at concessional prices. Though these programmes have been helpful, the problem of poverty remains in this, the richest country in the world. Current studies show that nearly 14 percent of the population is still below the poverty line, including 22 percent of children.

The second important post-war development has been a much greater commitment to the principle that the state has a responsibility

<hr>

[6] It is true that the majority of these have private insurance but that varies greatly in the protection provided.

to ensure maximum employment, to be achieved largely through the workings of the new Keynesian approach to the economy. The principle was even incorporated into the United Nations Universal Declaration of Human Rights (see Appendix 4). In the United States a centrepiece of the Fair Deal legislation of President Truman (1884–1972) was the Maximum Employment Act of 1946 which set up a Council of Economic Advisers to help develop policies which would encourage the private sector of the economy to maximize employment opportunities. Later, the Great Society programme of President Johnson included several pieces of legislation aimed principally at helping disadvantaged minority groups and the young to obtain employment: the Equal Opportunity Act (1964) which established the Job Corps, Neighborhood Youth Corps, Community Action Programs and Operation Head Start. Similarly in Great Britain the Labour government (1974–1976) headed by Harold Wilson (1916–), sponsored an Employment Protection Act in 1974 and much effort was expended on encouraging industry and commerce to move to regions of the country which were not thriving: the North, Scotland, Northern Ireland and Wales. The European Community also developed massive programmes for the international transfer of funds to help maintain employment in backward areas and to maintain the income levels of farmers in particular.

Most recently, as mentioned earlier, there has been a gradual shift in thinking about the welfare state, including that aspect concerned with income maintenance. There is concern particularly about unemployment benefits and young people coming straight out of school on to the 'dole', so acquiring a habit of dependency without ever having had the self-discipline associated with earning a living. One response has been the workfare schemes being introduced in some parts of the United States. The most successful approach, however, has been training schemes such as those pioneered in Sweden. The main difficulty is that in the short run such schemes increase public expenditures at a time when reduction of such expenditures is becoming a high priority goal in many countries (see p. 241 on cost sharing). Another approach which is finding favour is to be more flexible in the administration of minimum wage laws so that young people in particular can be placed in jobs which would not otherwise be economic.

So far the focus has been essentially on Western industrial countries where the income maintenance aspect of the welfare state has been most comprehensive. It should be added that similar programmes, often even more watertight, have been introduced in socialist countries, especially those in eastern Europe. Such countries had the additional device in dealing with the unemployment issue that workers could be directed to jobs and, until recently at least, it was always maintained that in these countries there was not any unemployment. In addition, the majority of Third World countries now claim to have some social security provision in effect for their citizens.

One feature of the welfare state of a large number of Third World countries which can be identified as the third major development in the post-war period has been the widespread use of subsidies to keep down the price of staple foods so as to help the poor, especially in the cities. The idea of keeping down the price of basic goods was not new, for instance, rents in many public housing schemes of industrial countries have been kept below economic levels for years (see below, p. 217) and there have been temporary rationing schemes, especially during wartime, aimed at controlling the price of food and clothing, as well as rent control schemes for private housing. Nevertheless, it seems reasonable to identify the food subsidy as a new factor in the post-war period if only because of its widespread long-term use at immense cost to states which have only limited resources to carry out their functions. In recent years there has been an attempt to gradually reduce food subsidy programmes in the Third World because it is now recognized that they have badly skewed their economies. In particular, farmers have been discouraged from maximizing production, and countries previously self-sufficient in food have become dependent on imports which they can ill afford. This is a difficult problem, for clearly poor people living on the edge of subsistence are going to resist significant price rises for essential food items unless they are compensated in some other form.

Public Health

One of the most important aspects of the welfare state, after income maintenance, has been a concern for the physical and mental health of the community. This has been expressed in three broad fields: (i) preventive means to protect the health of the community; (ii) curative measures to assist those who are sick; and (iii) provision of financial measures to make sure that the sick are not constrained from seeking medical help because of lack of financial resources. This last field has already been briefly discussed in the preceding paragraphs describing concern of the welfare state with maintenance of minimum income levels for all citizens. It will be recalled that some of the highlights in the evolution of that issue in providing financial protection in case of sickness were Bismarck's contributory sickness insurance scheme of 1883, the Asquith government's employees' health insurance scheme of 1911, the Attlee government's National Health and National Insurance Acts of 1946, and President Johnson's Medicare and Medicaid legislation of the 1960s. The following paragraphs discuss briefly some of the highlights in the evolution of the other two fields of public health pertaining to the welfare state: preventive measures and means to help care for those who fall sick.

There is a long history of public preventive measures to protect the health of a community. Several of the ancient civilizations, including Greece and Rome, took great care to provide their cities with clean water and to dispose of sewage. This practice was not followed in the European 'dark ages' and for well over a millennium after the fall of the Roman Empire the cities of Europe literally wallowed in their own filth. Another long-standing practice was for municipalities to quarantine peoples at times of disease epidemics and to monitor sale of certain foods to minimize adulteration. It was not until modern times that the national state began to take action on a systematic and comprehensive basis. Such action was provoked by the rapid urbanization of the population associated with the Industrial Revolution in Europe and North America[7] which brought with it a significant intensification of the unhealthy conditions that already existed in most pre-industrial cities. Haphazard housing construction, overcrowding, and poor public utilities were all conditions likely to lead to outbreaks of bubonic plague carried by rats, typhus carried by lice, and typhoid spread by poor plumbing, not to speak of cholera which periodically swept across Europe in the first half of the nineteenth century. The city poor suffered the most (for instance, the death rate for labourers in an English city in the first part of the nineteenth century was three times higher than for a country squire), but the whole population was affected to a greater or lesser extent.

A campaign to take action to remedy the situation was led by many in Great Britain who had been influenced by the Utilitarian philosophy of Jeremy Bentham. Their view was that such action was a legitimate function of government in providing efficient and effective service to the community. A lead was taken by Edwin Chadwick (1800–1890), one of the Poor Law Commissioners, who published in 1842 a report on *The Sanitary Condition of the Labouring Population*. Following the recommendations of that report Parliament approved in 1848 the first Public Health Act, which has been described as 'a landmark in world public health'. The Act established

[7] The proportion of the European and North American population living in cities of 25,000 people or more (the United Nations definition of an urban environment) increased from about 5 percent in 1800 to some 75 percent in 1970. In the world as a whole the increase was from about 3 percent to 30 percent.

locally elected boards of health which were given powers to appoint local medical officers, to establish local sanitary codes and to impose local taxation in order to pay for such utilities as water supply, draining, and cleaning of public places. The operation of the Act was to be supervised by a national Board of Health which was modelled on the Poor Law Commission. The role of government in the preventive health field was streamlined considerably by the legislation of the Disraeli government of 1874–1880, which included another Public Health Act (1875) that made certain sanitary standards mandatory nation-wide, and a Food and Drug Act (1875) which gave powers to public officials to monitor foods and medicines to make sure they were safe for consumption.

Similar preventive measures were taken elsewhere in Europe and North America. At the beginning of the nineteenth century, for example, compulsory vaccinations were introduced in Germany, and Denmark established a system of free treatment for venereal disease. In the middle of the century France pioneered the concept of the infant consultation centre. In the United States municipal health boards were established as early as 1798 in Baltimore, 1815 in Charleston, 1818 in Philadelphia, and 1866 in New York. In 1870 a supervisory Federal Public Health Service was formed and in the next forty years health boards were established in all the states. Powers were given to the Federal government to monitor drugs in 1848 and foodstuffs in 1890. A dramatic highlight in the evolution of such monitoring programmes by the state was the publication in 1906 of *Jungle* by Upton Sinclair (1878–1968) which drew attention to the filthy condition of meat-packing plants in the United States and which prompted subsequent legislation for the public supervision of this industry.

In Russia after the Bolshevik Revolution use was made of some 70,000 soviets (workers' committees) at the street and local community level to supervise local sanitary conditions. Major steps were also taken in the last several decades of the British Empire to instal public health and sanitary utilities in a large number of cities and towns – one of the more positive aspects of imperialism.

In recent decades, as health authorities have become more firmly established they have taken on a growing range of additional preventive responsibilities, including public education programmes, diagnostic and preventive care for mothers and children,[8] licensing

[8] Some important initiatives in this field in the early twentieth century were Acts to provide meals for children at school in Britain and for state registration of midwives in Britain, Scandinavia and the Netherlands, and the establishment of a children's bureau in the United States which had the function of investigating and reporting on the condition of children throughout the country.

of new drugs and food mixtures, collection and analysis of basic health statistics, and large-scale research programmes, for instance into the causes of cancer and possible remedies. Since the Second World War a major effort has been made to improve public health in Third World countries in the face of immense difficulties with regard to extreme poverty and huge populations. The World Health Organization (see Chapter 23) has played an important role in international assistance for drawing up, for instance, national health plans and establishing model health units, and as the century draws to a close is implementing a programme entitled 'Health for All by the Year 2000'.

Until modern times institutions for helping the sick have normally been provided by religious or philanthropic bodies, though occasionally a monarch would endow a state hospital. Doctors would operate individually and on a private basis. Gradually in the nineteenth and twentieth centuries, as government intervention on behalf of public

TABLE 8

NUMBER OF PHYSICIANS PER MILLION OF POPULATION
1975 Data

Physicians per million	Number of Nations & States						Percentage of Total	
	AFRICA	AMERICAS	ASIA	EUROPE	OCEANIA	TOTAL	COUNTRIES	POPULATION
1000 & more	1	4	6	27	1	39	28.9	33.5
500–999	0	12	5	1	0	18	13.3	10.2
200–499	5	10	10	0	1	26	19.3	32.4
100–199	5	1	4	0	0	10	7.4	3.4
50–99	20	1	4	0	0	25	18.5	14.8
less than 50	14	0	3	0	0	17	12.6	5.7
Total	45	28	32	28	2	135	100.0	100.0
Not surveyed	6	7	7	5	10	35[1]		
Grand Total	51	35	39	33	12	170		

[1] The most important countries not covered by the survey are China, Taiwan, Australia and Algeria.

General Note: The highest rates are often in the socialist countries. The USSR for instance has 2,877 compared with 1,692 in the USA. The very lowest countries (below 20) are Niger, (18), Upper Volta, (18), Equatorial Guinea (16) and Ethiopia (12).

Source: C. Lewis Taylor and David A. Jodice, World Handbook of Political and Social Indicators, Yale University Press, 1983.

health increased, there were a growing number of 'care' institutions run by public authorities. In the United States, for example, many of the states in the nineteenth century established medical facilities for the mentally handicapped. At the same time considerable advances were being made in the provision of hospital care. By the middle of the century most European countries were beginning to build state hospitals, and these institutions became vastly more effective with the acceptance of the Pasteur theory of pathogenic bacteria and the Joseph Lister anti-sepsis principle. A major influence in this field was Florence Nightingale (1820–1910), who first made her name in the Crimean War when she bullied the incompetent British military authorities into providing more hygienic and humanitarian care for the war-wounded. Subsequently she played a leading role in extending the same principles into British civilian hospitals and in the training of a professional corps of nurses – practices which were so well received that they were copied worldwide within a short period of time. The general improvement in hospital standards was also strengthened by the Red Cross organization after its founding in 1863 (see Chapter 20), as it developed its own centres for handling disasters and other emergency situations. By the last quarter of the twentieth century it has been estimated that some 95 percent of all hospitals in the world are owned and managed by public authorities, the main exception being the United States where there is still a large proportion of hospital care provided by the private sector of the economy. To a greater or lesser degree doctors have been drawn into state health systems essentially through arrangements for state health insurance, with control ranging from direct state employment in socialist countries, to a middle position under the British Health scheme in which payment is made on the basis of number of registered patients, and to a still relatively free arrangement in the United States in which doctors set their own fees.

The improvements in the general health of the community (especially in the industrial countries and amongst the poorer classes) which can be attributed to these activities, and the general advance in the standard of living, have been quite remarkable. Thus since 1870 the incidence of a whole range of killer diseases have become increasingly rare: such childhood diseases as measles, scarlet fever and whooping cough, and such general diseases as cholera, smallpox, typhoid, diphtheria and tuberculosis. As a result there has been a dramatic decline in the annual death rate, especially in industrial countries, e.g. in Europe from 35 per 1,000 in 1880 to 18 per 1,000 in 1950.

Though much has been achieved there is clearly much that remains

THE SEARCH FOR A JUST SOCIETY

TABLE 9

A. LIFE EXPECTANCY AT BIRTH
1982 Data

Life expectancy at birth in years	Number of Nations & States						Percentage of Total	
	AFRICA	AMERICAS	ASIA	EUROPE	OCEANIA	TOTAL	COUNTRIES	POPULATION
70 & above	1	12	7	28	2	50	31.3	20.2
60–69	7	19	15	1	3	45	28.1	41.8
50–59	18	4	7	0	4	33	20.6	31.4
40–49	20	0	6	0	0	26	16.3	5.9
39 & below	5	0	1	0	0	6	3.7	0.7
Total in survey	**51**	**35**	**36**	**29**	**9**	**160**	**100.0**	**100.0**
Not surveyed	0	0	3	4	3	10		
Grand Total	**51**	**35**	**39**	**33**	**12**	**170**		

Source: World Bank Atlas, 1985.

B. MORTALITY RATES FOR CHILDREN UNDER AGE 5
1987 Data

Rate per 1000 live births	Number of Nations & States						Percentage of Total
	AFRICA	AMERICAS	ASIA	EUROPE	OCEANIA	TOTAL	COUNTRIES
More than 300	–	–	1	–	–	1	1.0
251–300	7	–	–	–	–	7	5.4
201–250	9	–	2	–	–	11	8.5
151–200	12	2	7	–	–	21	16.2
101–150	11	3	3	–	–	17	13.1
51–100	3	8	11	–	1	23	17.7
16–50	1	6	6	4	–	17	13.1
25 or less	–	6	4	21	2	33	25.4
Total surveyed	**43**	**25**	**34**	**25**	**3**	**130**	**100.0**

Source: OECD Annual Report on development cooperation, 1988.

to be done. By far the biggest task is to raise the general standard of health in Third World countries which remains deplorably low, as shown by such basic indicators of social health as life expectancy and infant mortality tables (see Table 9). There are also some very broad issues of a universal kind. Some of these spring from the very success of medicine in the last fifty years with regard to the development of new drugs (particularly penicillin in 1944, and other antibiotics) and advanced diagnostic and surgical techniques. These scientific wonders have undoubtedly contributed to a general improvement in the health of the community, though such improvements have not been as significant as those which resulted from reform of sanitation and other preventive care arrangements. But the extensive, perhaps indiscriminate, use of drugs is raising fears of the emergence of drug-resistant diseases, and indeed already there is concern that hospitals may themselves become dangerous because of a high risk of infection.[9] Furthermore, many of the new diagnostic and surgical techniques are very expensive, while their effect is often just to prolong life for a short period and at a low-quality level. This all forces questions about social priorities when it comes to allocating scarce resources. Another problem has been that health authorities have been perhaps too preoccupied with the virtues of new drugs and technologies at the expense of preventive care, and this has led to major errors of judgement. One well-known case was the government approval of the drug thalidomide in the 1960s for use by pregnant women. Another has been the failure until recently to take a strong line against smoking, even though it has been known for years that this was one of the main causes of cancer.

Housing

Housing for the poor throughout history has generally been miserable, both in the countryside and in the city. Yet it was not until the development of big industrial towns in Europe and North America that housing became a major concern of government, under pressure from groups such as the Utilitarians, the new Christian evangelists, and later organisations representing the poor themselves. When farm labourers moved into the new industrial towns to work in the factories they were not able to build their own houses because of the unavailability of necessary materials, and extreme poverty forced them to crowd together in whatever accommodation they

[9] Another example of indiscriminate use of drugs is the practice of using them as a preventive device for maintaining the health of cattle destined for slaughter. It is estimated that this practice accounts for 50 percent of all antibiotics used each year in the USA. Thus a few years ago 18 people in Michigan became seriously ill and one died from a strain of salmonella that had become resistant to antibiotics because of their overuse in animals. (*The Economist*, 14 March 1987.)

could rent. Not surprisingly these structures were very poor and unhealthy. In England, for instance, a significant number of working-class homes in the new towns were built in long terraces, back to back, so that only one of the four outside walls of a house would be open to the air. The walls of such dwellings were frequently damp, windows were few and small, the floors were bare earth, heating arrangements were inadequate and potentially a fire hazard, and few if any had their own water supply, baths or toilets.[10] In the cities of America much of the accommodation was in high-rise apartment blocks where accommodation was equally crowded and unhealthy. In coal-mining areas houses were owned by the coal-mine operators who took pains not only to exploit their employees but to let them know that anyone showing independence of spirit would be evicted.

Initial public intervention to eliminate the worst housing conditions was aimed at (a) establishing regulations which set minimum housing standards; and (b) improvement of existing housing and where existing housing was beyond rehabilitation, its clearance and replacement with new housing. In Great Britain during the nineteenth century there were a series of Acts of Parliament, starting with the Shaftesbury Acts of 1851, and including the Cross Artisan and Labourers' Dwelling Act of 1875, which were intended to achieve these ends. However, the clearance and replacement provisions of this legislation was not very effective and by 1914 had only resulted in the clearance of some 14,000 slum houses. This was mainly because the provisions gave powers to local authorities which were optional rather than mandatory. Generally, local government in Great Britain in the nineteenth century had to be pushed to take constructive initiatives as its main philosophy was one of economy, not to say parsimony (though there were notable exceptions such as Birmingham when Joseph Chamberlain (1836–1914) was Mayor during the 1870s). More success was achieved with building codes and their impact on the quality of new working-class houses, and by 1914 the general standard of accommodation was far higher than it had been 60–70 years earlier. This was also partly attributable to a rising standard of living in the towns, to increased public interest, and to private initiatives such as the system of women housing managers organized from the 1860s onwards by Octavia Hill (1838–1912) with the strong support of John Ruskin (1819–1900). The women housing managers helped create a more positive attitude to housing than had existed when the harsh rent collector was the main

---

[10] For instance, an 1843 survey of working-class housing in Manchester found there was on average 1 toilet for every 212 people.

intermediary between the landlord and the tenant. The system was so successful that later it was copied in many other countries.

Serious large-scale clearance of slums in Great Britain did not take place until the Greenwood Housing Act of 1930 which included a five year plan, later extended, for systematic clearance and replacement. By 1939 some 400,000 slums had been cleared as a result of this Act. The process was resumed in the 1950s after the worst housing shortages caused by bombing in the Second World War had been eliminated, so that by the late 1960s most of the slums of the mid-nineteenth century had been cleared. The United States was much slower to take action, though the city of New York took some serious initiatives to regulate housing conditions in the early years of the twentieth century, after publication in 1890 of the book *How the Other Half Lives* by Jacob Riis (1849–1914).[11] It was not until enactment of a series of urban renewal programmes after the Second World War that the Federal government took active steps to encourage large-scale clearance and replacement of slum areas.

A second approach to the easing of the housing problems of the poor was to impose rent controls. An early example of such legislation was the Rent and Mortgage Interest Reductions Act implemented in Great Britain in 1915, at a time when housing shortages were developing due to diversion of resources to the war effort. Similar legislation was enforced during the Second World War and continues in reduced form to the present day. Though such policies may be helpful in the short term, there is a large body of opinion which argues that they are counter-productive in the long run. This is because they discourage further private investment in property for rent, which would otherwise keep down rental prices in the market place. Moreover, such policies discourage spending on maintenance of existing rental property.

The feeling of a debt of gratitude to the returning soldiers after the First World War and the slogan that there should be provision of 'homes fit for heroes' led to the development of a third approach to the problem of housing for the less well-off: large-scale programmes for construction of publicly-owned property for rent. In Great Britain the first major initiative in this direction was the Addison Housing and Planning Act of 1919 which included provision for payment of central government subsidies to local authorities who would build houses for rent. Of the 4 million new houses built in Britain between the Wars some 1.5 million were constructed by local authorities under this Act and subsequent legislation. Similar large-

11 The impact of this book was greatly increased by the use for the first time of line drawings based on photographs.

scale programmes were undertaken on the European continent, including the much admired apartments built by the socialist municipal government of Vienna in the 1920s, which were subsequently severely damaged during the civil war of 1934. Much of the new housing on the continent differed from that in England because it consisted of apartments rather than individual housing units, and because it was financed on a cooperative basis rather than through the local government – this was particularly true in Scandinavia, the Low Countries, Switzerland and Germany. In the United States, the New Deal programme of President Franklin Roosevelt included provision for public housing, but this was slowed down by a Supreme Court ruling against the constitutionality of direct investment in housing by the Federal government.

After the Second World War there were even more massive public housing programmes in continental Europe, Great Britain, and, especially after the Housing and Urban Development Act of 1965, in the United States. In the latter two countries the programmes included much greater provision for high-rise apartments than before, a concept taken from the French architect Le Corbusier (1887–1965). He argued that the high-rise concept made for more pleasant living because it economized on land which could then be landscaped and used for parks. Though all the public housing was a big advance when compared with nineteenth-century accommodation (especially with regard to interior facilities), there were major mistakes in both concept and details of design, especially in Britain and the USA. Much of the problem has been attributed to authorities failing to consult with ordinary people about their views on what was needed: a classic example of the paternalistic attitude that the experts know best. In some cases vast estates were built without adequate public facilities such as shopping and public entertainment areas. In the case of high-rise apartments there was insufficient attention to privacy and security, which made them most unsuitable for family use in particular. To the widespread lack of pride and commitment which prevailed on many public housing estates in Anglo-Saxon countries was added the dominance, not to say terrorism, by violent young men often under the influence of alcohol and other drugs. Soon the estates were to become modern-day slums and in some cases the deterioration was so bad that local authorities (e.g. in Liverpool and St Louis) were obliged to 'solve' the problem by demolishing buildings which were barely a decade or two old.

The failure of much of the public housing programme in the Anglo-Saxon countries has coincided with a period of general disillusionment with 'big government', and this has helped to strengthen a trend already growing towards a fourth approach to the provision of adequate housing for the whole community: the encouragement of occupant ownership. Thus in the last decade a great many publicly-owned houses have been offered for sale to the tenants. It is believed that owner occupiers tend to take a much greater pride in their housing, to feel that they have a much greater stake in the well-being of society, and that therefore they will act with greater social responsibility. Public policies to encourage the spread of occupant ownership have centred around three broad themes: (i) to make housing loans more easily available; (ii) to ease methods of repayment of loans through amortization and low interest rates; and (iii) to provide tax exemptions on account of such interest. Such policies have been practised at least since the beginning of the twentieth century. For instance, in Britain there was the Small Dwellings Acquisition Act of 1894, which gave local authorities power to offer loans to citizens wishing to buy a house. A major milestone in the worldwide development of such policies was the New Deal programme of President Roosevelt which included legislation: (i) for emergency financial support to savings and loans associations (such institutions had been in existence since early in the nineteenth century); (ii) for the buying out of loans which could not be repaid and their renegotiation on an extended amortization basis with low interest; and (iii) for public insurance of small deposits in savings and loans associations so as to encourage an ample supply of funds for financing housing loans. Another important highlight of such policies in the United States was the Severance Readjustment Act of 1945 which guaranteed loans with no initial down payment by the borrower if he was a returning serviceman. As a result of these policies and a continuing rise in living standards in the industrial countries there has been a significant increase during the last eighty years or so in the proportion of housing which is owned by the occupiers. For instance, during this period in Great Britain, the United States, Australia, and some other countries the proportion of owner-occupied houses has risen from one-third, or less, to well over two-thirds of the total housing stock.

Yet another important aspect of improving housing conditions is advance planning (especially when large-scale construction is undertaken) by both the public and private sectors, with regard to such matters as location, internal layout of estates, public facilities, relationship to industry and commerce, utilities, and architectural aesthetics. There is a long record of city planning going back to the ancient civilizations, but much of this was primarily concerned with the layout of roads (usually for military purposes), the designation of districts for certain occupations (a type of zoning), and above all the construction of public buildings designed to enhance the prestige of the state. In the nineteenth century many new towns were laid out in the United States, as it advanced westwards, on a basic gridiron pattern of streets but with little concern about housing as such. Similarly, when states have planned new cities as capitals they have tended to emphasize prestigious state buildings and perspectives rather than the convenience of ordinary citizens.[12] Some of the earliest planning of towns for the benefit of all their citizens was undertaken in Great Britain by philanthropists such as Robert Owen in New Lanark at the beginning of the nineteenth century, Titus Salt in a new village for mill workers near Bradford from 1853 to 1876, and, at the end of the century, George Cadbury (1839–1922) at Bournville (began 1895), W.H. Lever (1851–1925) at Port Sunlight (began 1888), and J. Rowntree at New Earswick. Public interest in towns planned for all citizens was given considerable impetus by the 'city beautiful' presentation at the Columbian Exhibition in Chicago in 1893.

But the most important development was the founding of the garden city movement by Ebenezer Howard (1850–1928), whose ideas were outlined in his book *Tomorrow: A Peaceful Path to Real Reform* (1898). His basic theme was that new and self-supporting towns of about 30,000 population should be built in the countryside to counter the attraction of the big city and so lead to a more even balance in the population distribution. The garden city should be surrounded by a green belt of parks and open space, should have low-density housing (no more than 12 houses per acre), and should provide for balanced and integrated areas for residence, commerce and industry. The purchase of relatively cheap land in the country-side would make it possible for such projects to offer low-cost housing and at the same time be financially viable. The general soundness of the garden city principles has been demonstrated by two examples which have been constructed north of London: Letchworth (began in 1903) and Welwyn (began in 1921).

The idea of town planning gradually became the policy of government. In Great Britain there was a pioneering Town and Country Planning Act in 1908 and various pieces of legislation in the interwar period, including steps to try and stop ribbon development (building along arterial roads). In the period immediately after the

[12] One example of a new capital city which has been designed to benefit ordinary citizens as well as the government is Canberra, Australia. Here attention has been paid to such factors as contour planning, separation of highways from residential areas, provision of shopping centres in every district, footpaths, tree-lined streets, public parks and a good public transportation system.

Second World War there were two ambitious Acts: (i) the Town and Country Planning Act of 1946 which provided, among other things, for a nation-wide plan as well as development of regional and local plans, and for the public rather than large landowners to benefit from capital appreciation of property on account of development,[13] and (ii) the New Towns Act for the building of fifteen new towns. In the United States the first municipal planning commissions were established in 1907 (Hartford) and 1908 (Chicago), and in the latter year there was held the first national planning conference. In 1916 New York set a precedent, followed later by the majority of local authorities in the United States, with the introduction of zoning to regulate the location of various types of construction. In both countries there have been a considerable number of examples of well-planned development e.g. in Great Britain the interwar towns of Speke (Liverpool) and Wythenshawe (Manchester), both built by local authorities, and in the United States the towns of Levittstown (New Jersey), Columbia (Maryland), and Reston (Virginia), all built by the private sector. Similar developments have taken place in a number of other countries. Though many of the ideas of the garden city were adopted in these projects, few if any, apart from the original two mentioned earlier followed the total concept and in practice most were suburbs or satellites of existing towns rather than self-supporting communities deep in the countryside. Moreover, the new towns represented but a small proportion of total construction, and as a result many opportunities for a significant upgrading of housing for the general population have been lost. This has been particularly true in the United States where 'developers' have squandered national resources around big cities, building hundreds of square miles of ugly, featureless suburbs, with poor utilities and other public facilities, and with virtually no restraint by so-called local 'planning' authorities. At the same time, inner cities have been allowed to deteriorate and become ghettos for minority non-white populations all over America and Western Europe.

To summarize, there is no question that there has been a major improvement in the general standard of housing in all the rich industrial countries over the last hundred years or so. Nevertheless, there are still significant deficiencies and much remains to be done to achieve desirable minimum standards for all. Great as are these challenges, however, they are dwarfed by those of the cities of the Third World where the world's biggest housing problems are to be found. Since the Second World War there has been a massive

---

13 The latter provision was later repealed because, it was argued, it discouraged development.

migration to the cities in nearly all Third World countries[14] reminiscent of that of the nineteenth century in the West. As a result, within a short space of time cities such as Calcutta, Rio de Janeiro, Mexico City and several others have outgrown even the largest and most established of the great cities in the industrial countries. Poverty-stricken, and with little or no assistance from governments (which have few resources to help anyway) the new immigrants have had to make their own shelters as best they can – building shanty towns out of scraps of boxes, drums, tyres and other materials. The best that some authorities have been able to do has been to install some minimum utilities including power and clean water. All this has prompted another approach to improving the housing of the poor and that is the sponsoring of self-help schemes, which in essence involve the provision of key building materials and some basic instruction and then letting the people build their own accommodation. Successful schemes of this type have been carried out in rich and poor countries alike: Ghana, Greece, India, Israel, Sweden and the Soviet Union. One interesting feature of Soviet programmes has been that those building their own houses were paid a regular wage during the period of construction.

Conditions of Work

An offshoot of the public health and housing issues is the protection of the health of the citizen in the workplace. State intervention to protect employees at their place of work from dangerous and onerous conditions first emerged as an important issue in England at the beginning of the nineteenth century. Of course, the working conditions of the poor had often been deplorable before this time in all parts of the world. The Industrial Revolution, however, brought new burdens for the worker which were normally not associated with an agricultural economy, in particular very long working hours for seven days a week and all the year round, and an unremitting pace of work set by the power machinery in the factory. An additional factor was the widespread employment in the new factories of women and children who had to work just as hard as the men. Women and children were particularly useful on account of their nimbleness, their ability to go in places where men, being larger, could not go (in mines, for instance), and the fact that they could be paid lower wages.[15]

[14] One of the few countries to take active steps to discourage such migration has been Malawi.

[15] This is not to argue that agricultural workers – men, women and children – did not work hard also, but their work tended to be seasonal. For instance, there was a peak of activity

These conditions soon attracted the attention of the same groups of people (including those who were members of new evangelical churches) as were campaigning against the slave trade. When it first started the factory reform movement was primarily concerned with the working conditions of women and children, but interest was soon widened to the broader issues of the health and safety of all workers. Between 1802 and 1891 a series of factory acts laid down a minimum age for hiring a child (originally nine but raised to eleven in 1891), set limits on the number of hours per day and week which women and young people under age eighteen could be made to work, and made mandatory time off during the day for meals and for the schooling of children. Early factory legislation was not particularly effective because there was no machinery for enforcement. This was remedied by the 1833 Factory Act which included provision for the appointment of four full-time inspectors to visit factories. A key role in obtaining the approval of Parliament for this Act and several others was played by Anthony Ashley Cooper, 7th Earl of Shaftesbury (1801–1885), a philanthropist and evangelical Christian.

At first the Factory Acts were limited in application to cotton and other textile factories where there was a particularly high ratio of women and children employed, but later they were extended to cover other occupations including engineering and agriculture. The extremely dangerous conditions in the coal-mining industry required special attention, not only with regard to the employment of women and children (a matter addressed in Lord Shaftesbury's Mines Act of 1842) but also in relation to minimum general safety regulations which were first mandated by the Coal Mines Regulation Act of 1860. To ensure compliance this Act, like the Factory Act of 1833, made provision for special inspectors.

Another important step along the road to state-imposed safety regulations in industry was the Merchant Shipping Act of 1876, which was finally approved after much hard work by the Radical MP Samuel Plimsoll (1824–1898), who like Lord Shaftesbury was fiercely opposed by powerful vested interests. The main purpose of this Act was to prevent dangerous overloading of ships (what Plimsoll called 'coffin ships') by requiring that each ship have a hull line (the Plimsoll line) which would sink below the water level if the ship was loaded beyond its maximum safety capacity. Once again the Act was to be enforced by a specially recruited group of inspectors.

In the last few decades before the Great War much of the attention

during the harvest, and in Europe the year was sprinkled with a liberal number of saints' holy days when work was largely suspended.

was switched to setting a maximum number of regular working hours for all employees, men as well as women and children (overtime, of course, could be worked for extra pay at higher rates). In the 1890s several Acts of Parliament pertaining to naval dockyards and other government establishments, and the Coal Mines Act of 1908, all established a maximum eight-hour working day which over the years has become the standard not only in Great Britain but in much of the Western world.

The example set in Great Britain was followed in many other countries, notably Germany, Austro-Hungary, Sweden, Australia and New Zealand by the end of the nineteenth century, and by the 1930s most Western countries had laws limiting the employment of women and children in factories. As with other welfare legislation, two advanced countries which tended to lag behind were France and the United States.[16] Conditions in France were substantially improved as a result of the legislation of the Popular Front government (1936–1937) which included provision for two weeks of paid vacation per annum for all workers as well as the forty-hour week. Similarly in the United States there were considerable improvements in the last years before the Second World War.

Initiatives taken by national governments have been supported and encouraged by the International Labour Organization since its formation in 1919 (see Chapter 22). However, prevailing levels of poverty and limited government ability to carry out regular and comprehensive inspections has meant in practice that conditions in many Third World countries are still at an appallingly low level. In the advanced industrial countries standards are now fairly reasonable though there are always new dangers arising from the advance of technology which require alertness on the part of the state, the trade unions and the workers themselves – for instance, in recent years asbestos, fine cotton in the air of garment factories, and even lighting and ventilation in office buildings.

Universal Education

An important dimension of the welfare state is a system of education available to all equally. In the widest sense the purpose of education is to contribute to the development of all the faculties of a human being: physical, mental and spiritual. Until modern times most societies have not seen the state as responsible for providing education for its citizens, the notable exceptions being Greece and

---

[16] The United States was, however, one of the first countries to lay down safety regulations for railways (1887).

China. In some societies (for instance Rome) education was left to the initiative of parents who would hire tutors for their children, a practice which clearly meant that education was generally restricted to the better-off classes. In other societies religious institutions, with their special interest in the moral and ethical upbringing of children, played a vital role. This was particularly true of Christianity and Islam, each of which in its own distinctive way provided a public system of education ranging from the primary to the tertiary (university) levels. Though religious institutions never provided a universal system which reached all children, there is little doubt that the coverage provided, for instance, in Europe by the Christian churches in their prime was far greater than had been provided under the Roman system. Thus in England it is estimated that there were some 400 grammar schools in the year 1400 for a population of about 2.5 million.

By the eighteenth century, though, the greatest achievements of both Christianity and Islam in the field of education were long over and the effectiveness of education was seriously hampered by division and rivalry between the various sects and by conservative and unimaginative administrations in the universities. In Europe the inadequacy of the system began to cause concern because it was recognized that in modern conditions a state without an educated population is at a serious disadvantage both in terms of military expertise and in the creation of wealth. Concern for education was strengthened by the realization that the new ideas of democracy and universal suffrage would not function properly if the majority was illiterate and therefore badly handicapped when trying to make informed decisions. An illiterate electorate was prone to manipulation by charlatans and might produce worse governments than restricted electorates. An additional factor was the realization that education was a vital element in giving people skills with which to increase their earning power and was therefore an important device for eliminating poverty. The conclusion was inescapable: an education system capable of meeting all these needs required the active participation of the state.

One of the first states to start playing an active role in education was Prussia, whose rulers recognized that if their ambitions for Great Power status in Europe were to be realized the small size of their domains and population would have to be offset by exceptional skills: a disciplined and well-trained army supported by an educated populace. As early as 1717, Frederick William I (1688–1740) had given orders that all children were to attend schools when these were available. Later edicts laid down that schools should be established to fill gaps in the network and that in principle (if not in practice) elementary education would be compulsory. The drive to establish an effective education system to strengthen the state was given impetus by the humiliating defeats inflicted on Prussia by Napoleon in the early years of the nineteenth century. In response to advice given by Johann Gottlieb Fichte (1762–1814) and Wilhelm von Humboldt (1767–1835), the central government established (i) a new ministry of instruction to supervise and develop state education; (ii) a new system of secondary schools, to prepare boys for the university and the professions; and (iii) a new university at Berlin. A standard examination system was established to encourage schools to achieve high levels of excellence. The system was later expanded to include apprenticeship programmes managed jointly by schools and industry, which did much to provide Germany with one of the most highly skilled labour forces in the world. Nevertheless, under the monarchy the emphasis on education as a device primarily for strengthening the state did not lead to equal opportunity for all. Thus it was not until the Weimar Republic (1919–1934) that all children were guaranteed even a full primary education, and not until the Federal Republic (post-1945) that secondary and tertiary education became available to a large proportion of the population. Today, however, Germany has one of the highest ratios in the world of young people staying on at school until age 18–19 and then going on to university (about 22 per cent of school-leavers go to university).[17] The German system has for long been seen as a model by the rest of Europe and in fact many surrounding countries have continued to this day to follow the German example.

As might have been expected, France in the 1789 Revolution initially took a very democratic stance on the issue of public education and the 1791 Constitution made provision for free primary education for all. In practice, however, for most of the nineteenth century France followed the Prussian example of being more interested in creating a well-educated elite for the benefit of the state rather than a universal system of benefit for all. Napoleon established a University of France, a government department of education, and a large number of state secondary schools (lycées) but he left primary schools to the churches and communes. A tradition of providing superb training for an élite chosen to direct institutions both of the state and of the private sector was established which continues to the present day, and which arouses the admiration of the rest of the world. In the 1830s François Guizot (1787–1874), the Minister of

---

[17] It has to be added that Germany presently has an above-average drop-out rate at universities.

Education of the liberal Orleanist monarchy, took steps to fill some of the gaps left by Napoleon, and made it mandatory for each town or commune to have a primary school and each department a teacher training college. But it was not until the 1880s that under the vigorous direction of Jules Ferry (1832–1893) primary education became free and compulsory and thereby available to all, including girls (who hitherto, as in Germany and other countries, had been mostly neglected). Development of a universal system was hampered, however, by a long-running battle between the Roman Catholic Church and the secular leaders of the Republic for the control of the education system, a feud which still continues in a muted form even today.

The United States can claim to have been in the forefront of public education along with Prussia, but its approach was much more egalitarian because there was an early appreciation of the connection between education and effective democracy. Thus in the mid-seventeenth century the state of Massachusetts had made it compulsory for local communities to provide elementary schooling for children; this practice was soon followed by many of the other states. In the nineteenth century New York was the first state to appoint school inspectors. Soon afterwards the first public high schools were established because fees for the private academies, which had grown up in the eighteenth century, were too high for the majority of people. In the 1860s a series of new public universities, to supplement private universities, came into being, financed by Federal grants of free lands in the West. By the end of the century most states had made attendance at schools both free and compulsory, and girls were treated on the same basis as boys. In recent decades the United States has been distinguished by the high proportion of young people (approximately one-third) who attend tertiary education institutions,[18] a characteristic of the American education system which evolved from establishment of the state universities in the nineteenth century. The trend was given significant impetus by the GI Bill of Rights of 1944 which helped many war veterans go to university[19] and the Higher Education Act of 1965 which followed a general alarm about the education system after the Soviet Union beat the United States in placing the first man in space. Creditable as is the education record of the United States, the present public education system undoubtedly is gravely weakened by several major flaws

[18] In the twenty-year period 1964–1984, the number of students obtaining BA degrees increased from 460,000 to 986,000 per annum.

[19] Out of 15 million servicemen who were demobilized, 2 million went on to college and 6 million to technical colleges.

including (i) low standards in the public schools[20] partly attributable to a breakdown in the maintenance of discipline and respect for teachers, and (ii) a continuing lag in the proportion of certain minority groups, notably Blacks (9 percent) and Indians (1.5 percent) in attending tertiary institutions. The state school system has also been weakened by its reluctance to provide an ethical education out of fear of offending any of the multiplicity of religious groups in the country. The latter deficiency has been highlighted in a recent popular book by Allan Bloom entitled *The Closing of the American Mind* (1987) which has the sub-title 'How higher education has failed democracy and impoverished the souls of todays students'. Mr. Bloom says:

The kinds of questions children ask: 'Is there a God? Is there freedom? Is there punishment for evil deeds? Is there certain knowledge? What is a good society?' were once also the questions addressed by science and philosophy. But now the grown ups are too busy at work, and the children are left in a day care center called the humanities, in which the discussions have no echo in the adult world.

The United States is rivalled by the Soviet Union and other European socialist countries with regard to egalitarianism in education. Prior to the Revolution the Czars had gradually created a reasonably good system of education for the Russian upper classes, but it has been the Communist regime which has made education, including adult education, available to all. The system, which now includes some three million students at the tertiary level, is recognized as having produced one of the most highly educated societies in the world, especially in technology. It is remarkable that given such an advantage the Russian economy has failed in recent years to keep abreast of technological advances in the economies of the Western capitalist countries. One of the outstanding features of the Soviet education system is a large network of public libraries which is credited by the *Encyclopaedia Britannica* with being 'a powerful help in raising educational standards, abolishing widespread illiteracy and furthering scientific advancement'. Lenin (who like Marx spent a lot of time in libraries) was a strong advocate of their usefulness and in 1913 had written:

. . . the pride and glory of a public library [system should be] . . . in its ability to allow the widest possible circulation of books among the people, in how many new readers libraries have had, in how quickly a demand for a given book may be satisfied, in how many books are distributed to a given

---

[20] As indicated by the fact that 40 percent of entrants to tertiary institutions now need remedial education for reading and writing skills.

house, in how many children are drawn to reading and using a library.[21]

Britain and the Commonwealth countries which follow the British model have generally not been in the front ranks of nations making innovations in the field of education with regard to producing either a highly-skilled élite or a well-educated democracy, though the quality of education for a small minority at universities and in secondary schools has generally been recognized to be high, and certainly Britain has contributed a disproportionate number of achievements in both the arts and sciences (particularly theoretical) for the benefit of mankind. As in several other Christian countries, religious sectarianism was an issue which hampered progress. Thus as early as 1807 Samuel Whitbread had introduced into the House of Commons a bill which provided for the establishment of elementary parochial, i.e. public, schools throughout the country, but the bill was defeated because it did not give the Church of England absolute control over them. The field was then left largely to the Church of England which worked through the National Society for Promoting the Education of the People (established in 1811) and to the non-conformists who worked through their own British and Foreign School Society (established in 1808). The issue of state support for education was not raised again until the 1830s when the government undertook an annual programme of small building grants for religious schools. Over time it became clear that this was not enough. A report by the Newcastle Commission in 1861 showed that British education was not working well when compared with systems on the European continent, both in terms of the numbers being educated and the quality of education provided. Slowly steps were taken to make some improvements. An Education Act of 1870 empowered local authorities to set up public schools which could compete with but not replace religious schools. Ten years later primary education was made compulsory and another eleven years later still it was made free. Another significant piece of legislation gave women the specific right to enter English universities (1875), an important step in the long-drawn-out process of eliminating discrimination between the sexes with regard to education.

Meanwhile there was growing concern about secondary education, which was private and expensive and therefore excluded

[21] Great Britain and the United States also had distinctive records in provision of public libraries. In Great Britain Public Library Acts in 1850 and 1919 encouraged the provision of library services by local authorities, and by 1926 it is estimated that some 96 percent of the public had access to such facilities. Highlights in the commitment to public libraries in the United States include the establishment of the first municipal library in Boston in 1852 and inclusion in the constitution of the State of Michigan (1837) of specific reference to public library services.

most children from poorer backgrounds. An Education Act of 1902 gave local authorities specific power to establish public secondary schools, and as a result the number of secondary school pupils doubled within ten years although the number still remained relatively small. This was because the minimum school-leaving age was at the low level of 12, and because the new secondary schools, though cheaper than private schools, still charged an attendance fee. The Act introduced for the first time nation-wide examinations to establish uniform standards of achievement. Further legislation in the interwar period raised the minimum age level for leaving school to 15, and an expanded scholarship programme made it easier for poor children to attend secondary schools. In addition a new system of state grants to universities was started. Major improvements came after the Second World War starting with the Butler Education Act of 1944 which (i) established a new Ministry of Education to direct the system; (ii) brought together all education facilities from primary to tertiary levels into one education system; (iii) abolished fees for grammar schools; and (iv) set up a new system of secondary technical schools for those who were not able to obtain places in the grammar schools. In subsequent years fourteen new universities were opened and grammar and technical schools were merged into one system because it was argued that the former dual secondary school system was perpetuating class divisions in society. This latter reform, however, was bitterly resisted by many who felt that it would lead to a lowering of standards. Despite the advances that have been made, the system of education in Great Britain is open to the criticism that it is still essentially élitist, especially at the tertiary level (only about 8 percent of school-leavers go to university and another 6 percent to polytechnics) and that it is failing as compared, for instance, with the systems in Germany, Japan, Russia and the United States to provide the technical skills which are needed in an advanced post-industrial society.

One approach to the question of how to improve standards which has attracted attention in recent years in Great Britain as well as the United States is the application of the principle of competition, for example by allowing parents to have education vouchers for their children which they may use at a school of their choosing. This is one aspect of a general interest in privatizing much of the public sector of the economy, and is discussed further in the section on cost sharing.

An important highlight in the field of education in the period since the Second World War has been the active role of the United Nations, and particularly the UN Education, Scientific and Cultural

Organization (UNESCO) in encouraging universal education in the Third World countries. The Declaration of Human Rights (see Appendix 4) sets the minimum standard desirable: that all children are entitled to a free education at least at the primary level, and this should be compulsory. Lack of resources is one of several major factors delaying the achievement of such a standard. India, for instance, has so far not fully implemented a long-standing goal to provide free and compulsory education for all children between ages 6 and 14. As a result the rate of illiteracy – that most elementary indicator of lack of education – is still extremely high in a significant number of countries with some averaging over 50 percent of the population, including over 80 percent of women. (For basic world data on primary school attendance and adult literacy rates see Table 10.) At the time of writing UNESCO is cooperating with other international agencies to develop a high priority plan to eliminate illiteracy by the year 2000.

Crime and Punishment

Dostoevsky, who had first-hand experience at the receiving end of the Russian criminal system, is reported to have said that the quality or humanity of a society can be judged by the way it treats its criminals. In line with that thought has been the trend in the last two centuries throughout the world, but with Western countries generally in the lead, towards a more humanitarian approach to the problem of punishment of crime, a development which has been an important subsidiary aspect of the welfare state.

Throughout history the majority of societies have been extremely severe in their treatment of criminals, with frequent use (even for relatively minor crimes) of the death sentence, mutilation and slavery. It is true that in some societies, generally those which had a relatively small population in relation to the territory occupied (such as some European tribes in the Dark Ages) there was a tendency to prefer fines and family compensation payments. These, however, were the minority. In many societies frequent use was also made of torture. This, for example, became a common practice in Europe in the Middle Ages to combat heresy. On the other hand, most societies did not put much emphasis on the extensive use of prisons, presumably because they are a relatively expensive device for punishment. As in every other aspect of social life, the criminal system tended to bear down on the poorer sections of the community in particular, not only because poverty and ignorance could provoke crime out of desperation, but because the richer, by

TABLE 10

LEVELS OF EDUCATION

Percentage	Number of Nations & States						Percentage of Total	
	AFRICA	AMERICAS	ASIA	EUROPE	OCEANIA	TOTAL	COUNTRIES	POPULATION
A. Adult Literacy Rates, 1970s[1]								
80–100	0	16	5	24	3	48	35.6	52.3
60–79	2	8	7	3	0	20	14.8	13.2
40–59	11	3	5	0	0	19	14.1	4.6
20–39	14	1	9	0	1	25	18.5	24.9
0–19	20	0	3	0	0	23	17.0	5.0
Total	**47**	**28**	**24**	**27**	**4**	**135**	**100.0**	**100.0**
Not surveyed	4	7	10	6	8	35		
Grand Total	**51**	**35**	**39**	**33**	**12**	**170**		
B. Primary School Enrolment, 1982								
80–100	23	32	26	27	4	112	73.2	72.2
60–79	9	3	6	0	2	20	13.0	22.1
40–59	6	0	2	0	0	8	5.3	4.1
20–39	10	0	3	0	0	13	8.5	1.6
Total	**48**	**35**	**37**	**27**	**6**	**153**	**100.0**	**100.0**
Not surveyed	3	0	2	6	6	17		
Grand Total	**51**	**35**	**39**	**33**	**12**	**170**		
C. Graduates as a Percentage of Population, 1980								
5 & over	0	5	5	11	2	23		
1–4.9	7	19	12	15	3	56		
less than 1	14	6	5	0	0	25		
Total	**21**	**30**	**22**	**26**	**5**	**104**		
Not surveyed	30	5	17	7	7	66		
Grand Total	**51**	**35**	**39**	**33**	**12**	**170**		

[1] 'Adults' mean people aged 15 and over. 'Literacy' means ability to both read and write.

Sources: A: C. Lewis Taylor and David A. Jodice, *World Handbook of Political and Social Indicators*, Yale University Press, 1983. B: *World Bank Atlas*, 1985. C: G.T. Kurian, *New Book of World Rankings*, Facts on File Publications, 1984.

means of clever lawyers or connections with the power structure, were often able to escape punishment for crimes altogether or at least to have their punishment greatly reduced.

In eighteenth-century Europe the death sentence was still widely used,[22] as was flogging and the pillory, and could be applied to young children as well as adults. On the positive side there was decreasing use of mutilation and torture (no doubt because the religious passions of the Middle Ages had been all but exhausted).[23] Instead there was a growing resort to imprisonment, frequently in appalling conditions and sometimes in remote locations (to which criminals were transported). The criminal punishment system was still extremely harsh and attracted the critical comment both of the philosophers of the Enlightenment, particularly Voltaire[24] and Montesquieu, who believed it undermined civilization, and of the English utilitarian philosophers who criticized it for being ineffective in reducing crime and for being wasteful.

One of the most influential early thinkers on the subject of crime was an Italian, Cesare Bonesana Beccaria (1738–1794), whose *Essay on Crime and Punishment* was translated into twenty-two languages. His main points were that there should be proportionality between the punishment and the crime; that prevention is a more important goal than punishment; and that the certainty of being caught is far more use than excessive severity of punishment.[25] Another early and

[22] For instance, between 1660 and 1819 there were in England 187 new statutes involving capital punishment, mostly to protect property. (By contrast, attempted murder was considered a misdemeanour until as late as 1803.) Perhaps the most notorious legislation was the Walthorn Black Act of 1722 which made possible capital sentences on account of some 200 different offences, including poaching. This particular Act was approved after a minor agrarian revolt.

[23] Torture was formally abolished in England by the Bill of Rights of 1689. It was abolished in Prussia between 1740 and 1754, in the Holy Roman Empire in 1776, in France in 1789, and in Russia in 1801. It was also forbidden by the American Constitution of 1788 and by the United Nations Universal Declaration of Human Rights. Torture is still widely used by authoritarian governments to eliminate opposition (brainwashing) and to obtain confessions to crimes against the state. Military forces often use it to obtain critical military information especially in guerrilla warfare. In all cases, however, the authorities will try to keep it secret, thus admitting that they are acting in an unacceptable and uncivilized way.

[24] As noted in Chapter 10, Voltaire had played a major personal role in stopping the practice of torture in France as a result of his campaign to publicize the case of a Huguenot broken on the wheel in 1769 for heresy.

[25] It was generally believed, for instance, in eighteenth-century England that the juries would often find a defendant not guilty rather than be responsible for his execution for a relatively minor crime. It was well-known, for instance, that stolen goods would be often valued at no more than 39 shillings so as to avoid the death sentence that came with theft of property with a valuation of 40 shillings or more. There was much resort also to pardon by the Crown to avoid carrying out a large proportion of death sentences. For instance, Robert Hughes in *The Fatal Shore* gives the following figures for capital convictions in the London and Middlesex region at the turn of the century:

	Capital Convictions	Actual Executions	Executions as % of Convictions
1789–1798	770	191	24.8
1799–1808	804	126	15.7

influential reformer was Jeremy Bentham (1748–1832) who in *An Introduction to the Principles of Morals and Legislation* argued that the two main principles in life are those of pain and pleasure and that 'punishment causes pain and therefore is evil, and ought only to be administered so far as it promises to exclude some greater evil'.

As the reform movement gathered force some general principles began to emerge about the purpose of punishing crime, with an underlying view of man as a rational being and humanitarianism as a quality of an advanced civilization. There was general condemnation of the old emotional motive of revenge and its consequences in terms of extreme cruelty and punishment far in excess of the crime committed. Instead there was growing support for the more rational motivation that the punishment of crime should be to protect society either by removing a criminal from society permanently, i.e. by execution, or for a sufficient time for him to learn to change his way of life, i.e. by imprisonment. Punishment should be a deterrent not only to a future crime by the person already caught and sentenced, but also to others who might be contemplating crime. Deterrence came more from the certainty of being caught than it did from the harshness of the punishment if caught. This meant having an efficient police force. Another theme that was increasingly adopted by reformers was that a criminal was seen not as an outcast of society, but rather as a human being who could be rehabilitated if treated positively. This theme was associated with the idea that a criminal is not a completely free agent but is a product of his environment and that the desperation and soul-crushing effects of poverty or limitations of mental capacity should be taken into account when setting the level of punishment.

The most fundamental of reforms and the one which ultimately was to be most controversial was the abolition of the death sentence. There were two broad stages. The first was to reduce the number of crimes for which the punishment could be used by eliminating those where the punishment was clearly excessive in relation to the crime. At this stage capital punishment would be limited to those crimes which involved the taking of life: murder, and such variations on direct murder as arson, high treason, and, in some countries, possession of drugs. The second stage was the abolition of capital punishment altogether. The first stage was generally achieved, at least in the Western world, in the nineteenth century without too much opposition. Typical was the experience in England, where as a result mainly of the initiative of Samuel Romilly (1757–1818) who was the Solicitor-General in the famous Ministry of All the Talents of 1806, there was a repeal of an Elizabethan statute requiring the

death sentence for pickpocketing and of another law which mandated transportation for stealing clothes laid out for bleaching, and
for soldiers caught begging without a permit. This initiative was
followed by further reforms so that the number of different types of
crime which could result in capital punishment was reduced from
some 500 in 1800 to 15 by 1834 and 4 by 1861.

At the same time there was a reaction against public executions.
Theoretically the public execution made sense as a device for
deterrence from crime, but in practice the public, from all reports of
the time, treated such occasions as public entertainment and so the
reality was that public executions involved the state in pandering to
the coarser and more barbaric aspect of humanity. New York was
the first state in the United States to ban public executions. Great
Britain banned them in 1868 and most Western countries followed
suit in the next few decades.

Reductions in the number of crimes which could be punished by
death were accompanied by the elimination of some of the harsher
physical punishments such as the pillory, flogging, the treadmill and
transportation. There was a major outcry in the United States against
flogging in the Navy around 1850 as a result of the revelations of
what it was like in practice in *Two Years Before the Mast* by Richard
Dana (1815–1882). In Britain flogging as a punishment in the
military forces was abolished in 1870. However, it was not until the
Criminal Justice Act of 1948 that corporal punishment was finally
stopped in British prisons. Transportation as a device for getting rid
of criminals was largely practised by Great Britain and France, each
of which had large overseas empires containing places remote and
unpleasant enough to satisfy even the most draconian judge. The
British stopped transportation to the colonies in the 1840s (mainly
Australia at that time) but France continued the practice of sending
its criminals to Devil's Island in French Guinea until the beginning of
the Second World War.

The arguments concerning a total abolition of capital punishment
have been long-running and passionate, especially it seems in the
Anglo-Saxon countries. Some of the main arguments used by those
in favour of abolition are as follows. First, it is basically immoral,
barbaric, and repugnant for the state to take the life in cold blood of
one of its citizens – an argument which perhaps loses some of its
weight when it is conceded that the state may take life in defence of
the realm or in maintaining internal order. More convincing is the
argument that all statistical and objective studies have shown that the
presence or absence of capital punishment has no effect on the levels
of crime (and murder in particular), and it can be argued therefore

that it is not a deterrent. Abolitionists also point out that there have been quite a few instances where the wrong person has been executed for a crime. In such cases if the punishment had been imprisonment, for instance, compensation of sorts could have been given but that is not possible once an execution has taken place. Another powerful argument is that in many countries there is evidence of lack of equity in the use of the death sentence: thus in the United States there is a much higher incidence of execution of black murderers than of white murderers. It is further argued that there is no clear-cut relationship between murder and capital punishment. Some crimes attract particular public anger, crimes such as mass murder, murder associated with torture, rape or robbery, murder of policemen, and treason, whereas others do not, such as what the French have reputably always forgiven: *crime passionel*. In other words, the issue of whether a man lives or dies can get somewhat blurred at the edges. The arguments of those in favour of capital punishment tend to be perhaps more emotional: an instinctive feeling, despite all the statistics, that capital punishment really does deter and frustration when a murderer who has committed a particularly horrible crime literally seems to 'get away with murder'. The case is perhaps more rational when it fastens on the lack of symmetry in not taking a life for a life, which seems to be a basic principle of justice, at least for the most outrageous crimes. Supporters of capital punishment, of course, argue that the answer to the occasional mistake in sentencing the wrong person is to improve the quality of investigation, rather than abandon the principle of 'an eye for an eye'.

Whatever the merits of the arguments on either side, the general trend has been a victory for the abolitionists. Already in the nineteenth century there were several countries which abolished capital punishment totally (e.g. the Netherlands in 1870, Costa Rica in 1880, and Brazil in 1891) and by the third quarter of the twentieth century it had been abolished in the majority of the countries in the world, especially in Europe and the Americas.[26] Two of the last countries to hold out against the trend were Great Britain, which finally abolished capital punishment in 1964, and the United States, which still has the institution in 37 of the 50 states although there was a decade when it was not used because it had been declared unconstitutional by the Supreme Court, mainly on grounds of lack of equity in administration.[27] Ways have now been found around that

[26] Of course, there are many countries with authoritarian governments which do not hesitate to eliminate political opponents on charges of treason.

[27] Interestingly enough, the United States was ahead of most of the rest of the world at the beginning of the nineteenth century. To start with, the colonies only ever had 12 crimes which carried the death penalty. This number was soon reduced drastically in the early part of the

ruling and executions have been resumed; but the incidence is at a much lower rate than it was before the matter became a major issue in the 1960s.[28]

A second main trend in reform over the last two hundred years, after the abolition of capital punishment and the related matters of corporal punishment and transportation, has been to take special account of those who cannot be held fully responsible for their actions either because of mental incapacity or tenderness of age. In the United States, for instance, Dorothy Lynde Dix (1802–1887) undertook a vigorous and ultimately successful campaign to de-criminalize the treatment of the insane and as a result of a vigorous lobbying campaign in the 1830s she was able to persuade all the states east of the Rockies to remove the insane from prisons and to house them in a new system of state mental hospitals. In England the McNaghten rules were introduced in 1843 for murder cases, whereby a person could be declared insane and therefore not subject to the full force of the law when it could be demonstrated that at the time of committing the act

the party accused was labouring under such a defect of reason, from disease of the mind, as not to know the nature and quality of the act he was doing, or if he did know it, that he did not know it was wrong.

Two years later, following the precedent of the work of Dorothy Dix, the British Parliament approved the Lunacy Act which recognized that the insane are not social outcasts to be treated like criminals but sick people who need medical care. Special protection for children took somewhat longer, at least in Great Britain, and it was not until 1908 that separate courts were established to handle cases in which the defendant was a child. A few years later, largely at the instigation of Sir Evelyn Riggles Brix, Chairman of the Prison Commission at that time, regulations were adopted whereby children under the age of 14 could no longer be detained in prison and those between 14 and 16 only in very restricted circumstances. All young people sentenced to imprisonment were to be kept separate from adults in a new system of Borstal detention centres.

A third major trend of reform has been to humanize the prison system and to make the sentencing system more flexible so as to take account of the circumstances of each case, especially with regard for the possibility of rehabilitation. Two of the early reformers in this

nineteenth century as many individual states followed the example of Pennsylvania which restricted its use to murder as early as 1794.

[28] In terms of the numbers of legal executions per year the USA is well behind the two world leaders, China and Iran. (*The Economist*, 2 May 1987.) Other countries which still maintain capital punishment at the time of writing include the USSR, South Africa, India and Belgium.

field were British: John Howard (1726–1790) and Elizabeth Fry (1780–1845). As a result of the work of John Howard, Parliament passed two Acts which (i) mandated the freeing of prisoners at the end of their sentences to stop the practice of prisoners who fell into debt to their warders being detained almost indefinitely;[29] and (ii) made Justices of the Peace responsible for ensuring that prisoners were kept in good health. Howard's book *The State of Prisons in England and Wales*, published in 1777, led to an Act of Parliament two years later which mandated the building of new prisons which would provide for solitary confinement, regular labour, and religious instruction – features which were considered an improvement over the sheer anarchy of existing prisons. Years later, in 1835, a Prison Commission was established to make sure that all British prisons observed minimum standards. The work of Elizabeth Fry was largely in separating female and male prisoners,[30] with the female prisoners having their own female warders; classifying criminals according to the degree of seriousness of the crime committed; and the provision of useful employment for prisoners. Both John Howard and Elizabeth Fry had considerable influence on the European continent as well as in Great Britain. Though there was a marked improvement in the prison system in Great Britain during the nineteenth century in terms of a less harsh discipline, standards of accommodation, and equity of treatment,[31] it was in the United States, with its vast size and diversity, where there was most opportunity for progressive experiments and the application of new ideas with regard to rehabilitation of prisoners. Some of the most important innovations made in the United States have been the introduction of parole for good behaviour, 'no bar' prisons with many of the comforts of living at home, periodic conjugal rights, education and job training, sport, pet animals and birds, probation instead of imprisonment, counselling, group therapy, and others.

Two other developments which had the potential to make the criminal law system work more effectively were the establishment of modern civilian police forces and the protection of the legal rights of prisoners. The first modern civilian police force was that established in England following the Metropolitan Police Act of 1829. This professional police force, which replaced a ramshackle system of

[29] Many prisons at the time were managed by private bodies, including aristocrats and members of the Church.

[30] In the eighteenth century there was no segregation in prisons on account of age, sex, or gravity of crime.

[31] Especially after a series of Prison Acts in the 1830s led to the building of more prisons, reducing overcrowding and generally raising the standard of prison accommodation. This programme was started after the decision to discontinue transportation.

nightwatchmen, hue-and-cry appeals for public assistance in catch-
ing criminals, and the periodic calling out of the militia in times of
public unrest, was originally established in London but the model
was soon adopted by local authorities in the provinces. The new
British police forces, known affectionately as 'Peelers' or 'Bobbies',
after Sir Robert Peel (1788–1850), Home Secretary at the time of the
Act, had two characteristics which made them particularly effective.
First, the individual policeman was given his own 'beat' or
neighbourhood to supervise so that he would get to know all the
local people and win their trust as a protector, even as a friend
(except perhaps in the worst slum areas), in sharp contrast with the
usual image of the policeman as an oppressor engaged in corruption
and in occasional military-type sweeps through working-class areas.
The second feature of the new force, which reinforced the sense that
the policeman was not an oppressor, was that he did not carry
firearms, a practice which, unfortunately, has not been widely
copied.

Regarding legal rights, the majority of countries with welfare state
programmes now make provision for free lawyers to assist poor
defendants. The Supreme Court of the United States has taken
particular care, because of past unfair practices at the time of arrest,
to ensure that steps are taken at that time to protect an accused person
from self-incrimination.

Though much has been achieved, there is still generally great
discontent with the criminal system in most countries. One
complaint is that reform has not led to a reduction in crime – on the
contrary, almost uniformly it seems to increase every year for a whole
range of reasons, not least of which is a general breakdown of respect
for authority and a reduced sense of social responsibility (see the
commentary on the consumer society in Chapter 19 and Table 11).
The proportion of cases where a crime actually leads to someone
being punished is very low, to the point where for some relatively
minor types of crime the police barely bother to go through the
motions of investigating. There is a widespread perception that
criminals are being treated better than victims[32] and this has led to
campaigns, on the one hand, for harsher treatment for the criminal
such as mandatory sentences for certain types of crime, and on the
other hand, programmes of compensation for the victims. There is
general recognition, even amongst professionals, that rehabilitation

[32] This perception is strengthened by such factors as routine plea bargaining in exchange for
information (a practice used widely in the USA in particular), apparently erratic relationships
between the punishment and the seriousness of a crime, and widely publicized paroling of
violent criminals after a relatively short term in prison.

TABLE II

CHANGES IN VOLUME OF VIOLENT CRIME IN OECD COUNTRIES, 1950–1970

Data shows 1970 in relation to 1950 per 100,000 population

$1950 = 1.00$

Country[1]	Murder	Rape	Assault
Australia	3.98[2]	20.00	12.57
Austria	1.08	.84	1.02
Belgium	1.03[2]	1.05	NA
Denmark	.53	.44	5.89
Finland	.42	1.76	NA
France	.32	.22	1.27
Germany	1.94[2]	1.33	1.21
Ireland	2.38	2.94	4.86
Italy	.61	NA	.23
Japan	.56[2]	NA	1.02
Netherlands	1.96[2]	2.56	.64
New Zealand	.43	.76	2.82
Norway	1.28	1.29	1.24
Portugal	.47[2]	NA	.45
Spain	46[2]	3.00	.70
Sweden	3.20	1.53	1.88
UK	1.59	2.53	8.59
USA	1.71	3.25	2.70

[1] Data not available for Canada, Greece, Iceland, Luxembourg, Switzerland and Turkey.
[2] Homicides, a somewhat broader term than murder.

Source: Dane Archer and Rosemary Gartner, Violence and Crime and Cross-National Perspective, Yale University Press, 1984.

schemes are often both very expensive and not noticeably effective.[33]

Despite the public perception of light treatment for criminals, it is nevertheless true that in many countries prison conditions are so bad (because of overcrowding, unhealthy facilities, and a complete breakdown in discipline to the point where warders are in effect content to guard the perimeters and all but allow the prison to be run by the criminals themselves) that a stay in prison has become a

[33] The rate of recidivism for male prisoners in the USA is 69 percent. Undoubtedly there are strong cultural factors at play here. Thus, the rate of recidivism in the People's Republic of China is only 4.7 percent, a difference which is attributed to different social attitudes to crime, a greater sense of community responsibility and a system of values which does not reward the criminal – a contrast, for instance, with the social prestige of the successful drug pusher with his flashy car and clothes in a typical American slum or urban public school. Another cultural factor is gender. Far fewer women than men are involved in crime, and studies show that their crimes often arise from romantic attachments to male criminals (85 percent in one study) and that their crimes are generally non-violent.

nightmare which in some respects may be more horrific than even in the eighteenth century. Part of the reason for this is that the public, though often willing to pay for dramatic increases in the number of policemen, is less willing to pay for an expanded judiciary to speed up cases, and still less to pay for improvements in the prison system – after all, the political power of prisoners in any system, autocratic or democratic, is not great. Some improvements could no doubt be made if more money were spent on the system, if greater distinctions were made between crimes which require imprisonment (generally those that involve violence) and those which should be treated by other methods. But in the long run there is a need to tackle the root causes of crime: to eliminate extremes of poverty and, even more important, to establish high moral standards at all levels of society, including a sense of personal responsibility, whatever the personal circumstances, for the well-being of society.

Cost Sharing

A final subsidiary aspect of the welfare state is the concept of equity in sharing of the tax burden. Until modern times states raised most of the income they needed to carry on their business from such sources as profits from state-owned mines, rents for the use of state-owned land, payments from satellite states, war booty, and forced loans. As the cost of managing the state increased, owing not least to more expensive methods of war especially after the introduction of gunpowder and firearms, these sources of income had to be increasingly supplemented with a wide range of taxes. Some of these, such as the poll or head tax and taxes on property, were imposed directly on individuals, while others were indirect, such as excise duties on domestic sales, for example the salt tax in France, and customs duties on foreign imports, particularly high-value items such as wines and spirits. Often the administration of such taxes was handed over to 'tax farmers', private individuals who were required to pay a certain sum to the state each year on the basis of a rough evaluation of the area in question, and in return the tax farmer was given authority to collect taxes in the area, with no questions asked if he should (as was inevitable) make a huge profit on the arrangement. Another common practice was to exempt certain groups from the obligation to pay taxes – usually the most powerful and rich such as the aristocracy and upper clergy, just those in fact who were best able to afford payment of taxation and whose exemption put an additional heavy burden on the poor. Imposition of taxes by the state has always been a very sensitive issue, and discontent over such matters played a large part, as has been noted already, in the events leading up to the Magna Carta, the revolt of the English Parliament in the 1640s, the American War of Independence, and the French Revolution.

By the beginning of the nineteenth century many of the worst abuses of the tax systems in Europe and North America had been eliminated. Nevertheless, they were still essentially regressive: there was a proportionately greater burden on the less well-off than on the rich. Thus a typical indirect tax on trade in a basic commodity such as food weighed more on the poor because the poor spent a higher proportion of their income on such basics than did the rich. The main instrument for remedying the regressive features of taxation was an income tax which could be either proportional in its impact (a flat percentage of income) or progressive (the percent tax would actually increase on additional amounts of income). It was not, however, in the desire to increase equity that income taxes were introduced, but rather because: (i) the gradual evolution of the banking system and administrative practices made the collection of an income tax practicable for the first time; (ii) the expense of various wars made it essential, at least temporarily, to exploit this potentially rich new source of income for the state; and (iii) the widespread movement towards free trade (see below, p. 290) made it imperative that a new source of income be found to replace that formerly derived from customs and excise duties.

The first income tax system in the world is generally believed to have been that imposed by the Pitt government in Great Britain in 1799 to help pay for the war against revolutionary France. The tax was quickly rescinded after the Peace of Amiens in 1803, but was reintroduced again when war was renewed and remained in effect until 1816. The tax was not heavy (the basic rate was 10 percent of income) but it was progressive, insofar as the poor sectors of the population were exempt while the richest paid a marginal rate which was higher than the standard. In 1842 the Peel government reintroduced an income tax (3 percent) to offset loss of income on account of reductions in tariffs as a result of the policy of making Britain a free trade country. Thereafter the income tax in Britain was maintained continuously but always at a relatively low level even in time of war (6 percent during the Crimean War and slightly more during the Boer War) until the Great War of 1914.

Towards the end of the nineteenth century the idea that the well-off could and should bear a higher proportion of the cost of the state was increasingly advocated by progressive movements, although the extreme position of the American journalist and economist, Henry George (1839–1897), who campaigned for a single tax to be levied on private land only,[34] was not adopted by any party which achieved power. In 1891 the British income tax was supplemented by the so-called 'Harcourt' death duty, a small tax on large estates (a precedent which, as might be expected, has since been greatly expanded). In 1907 the Liberal government introduced measures to tax unearned income (generally believed to accrue disproportionately to the better-off) more heavily than earned income. Two years later the radical budget of David Lloyd George (1863–1945), which provoked a constitutional crisis with the House of Lords, introduced several other progressive tax features: a 'supertax' on incomes in excess of £5,000, a tax on unearned land values, and special deductions from taxes for families with children.

The example set by Great Britain was followed by many countries on the continent: income taxes were introduced, for instance, in Belgium in 1828, in Austro-Hungary in 1849, in Italy in 1864, and in Germany in 1894. By 1918 most of the countries in Northern Europe, North America, and the 'white' British Commonwealth had income tax systems which were a major source of income for the central government. France, ever conservative in such matters, was one of the last major countries to have such a system; it became effective there in 1914. Even the United States, where the record of state moderation of extremes of wealth and poverty was generally well behind that in Europe, had a system by 1913. An income tax system had originally been introduced in the United States in 1862 to help pay for the Civil War and had continued for ten years before the original legislation lapsed. A modest attempt to revive the system in 1894 (a proposed tax of 2 percent) to help offset lost income due to cautious reductions in tariffs, was declared unconstitutional by the courts, and the matter was dropped until the passage of the 16th Amendment to the Constitution made income tax officially legal. The government of President Woodrow Wilson (1856–1924) followed the British example and introduced a progressive system with a standard rate of one percent for individuals with incomes of $3,000 or more (for married couples with incomes of $4,000 or more), to which was added a surcharge which gradually raised the total marginal tax rate to 6 percent on incomes in excess of $20,000.

Since the Great War income taxes have become increasingly burdensome in all industrial countries, mainly because of the grow-

---

[34] First suggested in his book *Progress and Poverty* which was published in 1879.

ing expenses of the state for defence and for welfare programmes.[35] For instance, the standard rate in the UK rose to 30 percent in World War I, and by World War II had reached 50 percent with a highest marginal rate of 97 percent. Even today, in times of so-called 'peace', it is not unusual for a modern industrial welfare state to have a standard rate of 30–40 percent and a highest marginal rate in excess of 60 percent.[36] In addition, an increasing proportion of the population is required to pay income tax, including ordinary working–class people, especially after the introduction of tax withholdings from each weekly pay cheque (PAYE) from the Second World War onwards.

Experts have begun to complain that the heavy burden of the income tax is having two undesirable effects. First, it has become a disincentive to hard work and high productivity because those who work hard are especially penalized by the high marginal rates. It results in their keeping only a small proportion of the extra money they earn by putting special effort into their work. Second, it encourages people to look for ways to avoid paying tax either by illegally withholding information about the size of their income, or by excessive use of legal loopholes in the system. Loopholes or special exemptions were originally intended by legislators to serve a useful social purpose, for example to encourage desired investment with a view to increased productivity, or to help particularly worthy and hard-pressed citizens. All too soon, however, such exemptions were being used purely for selfish interests and they had virtually no benefit to the community as a whole. Since it is the rich who generally benefit from tax dodging and tax loopholes, the net effect has been to cancel out much of the progressive redistributive effect originally intended.

With growing discontent, there has been a flurry of effort in the last few years to try and solve these problems. One broad approach has been directed towards reform of the tax system itself. Some have advocated a simplification of the system by elimination of loopholes,

---

[35] Some indication of the growth in government expenditure in the last two hundred years in the average industrial economy is given by the following figures for Great Britain of government expenditure as a percentage of Gross National Product:

1790   12.0
1890   8.0
1932   29.0
1951   40.2
1984   54.7

Source: C.V. Brown and P.M. Jackson, Public Sector Economics (Oxford: Blackwell, 1986), p.139.

[36] The highest marginal rate in the world at the time of writing is 84 percent which applies in Japan on taxable incomes over $520,000 p.a. More onerous is the 80 percent marginal tax applied in Sweden on the much lower ceiling of $46,000 p.a.

but admirable as this idea may be it is very difficult to apply consistently because of fierce defence of the loopholes by the powerful vested interests which benefit from them. If it were carried out, however, such an approach has the advantage that the additional income which would accrue from closing loopholes would allow a general lowering of rates. Such an approach also makes the tax system more neutral in its impact on the economy including the removal of incentives such as tax shelters which make for inefficient use of resources. One of the best examples of such a policy is that carried out in New Zealand in the second half of the 1980s.

Another tax reform theme has been to reduce the progressive nature of income tax systems, i.e. in the direction of a flat percentage tax, on the grounds that it is the higher marginal rates of tax which are the real disincentives to productivity.[37] It would also do away with the 'ratchet' effect of progressive taxation which automatically occurs in times of inflation unless the tax system is indexed to the rate of inflation. This reform is defended against the charge that it is regressive on the grounds that the original purpose of progressive taxation was to benefit those who were genuinely poor, but today, at least in the advanced industrial nations, most working families can afford luxuries and there is consequently less need to give them a tax privilege.[38] Linked to this approach is one of shifting the tax burdens away from income taxes back to those that are indirect, particularly sales taxes (most notably in recent years the value added tax (VAT) system which has been adopted in the European Community and elsewhere). An indication of the relative importance of direct and indirect taxes in paying for government expenditures in a world perspective is given in Table 12. Yet another tax reform idea is to replace 'income' tax with a similar 'consumer' or 'expenditure' tax system in which that part of an individual's annual income which is saved would not be taxed. The purpose of such a tax would be to

[37] Some instances of significant reductions in the highest marginal rate of income tax over the last decade are as follows:

	From	To
United States	70%	33%
United Kingdom	83%	40%
Australia	65%	49%
New Zealand	66%	33%
Canada	43%	29%

[38] An interesting side aspect of this theme has been the proposal in the UK to reintroduce a 'poll' tax (i.e. a flat tax per person/household) for the financing of local government. The purpose is to strengthen a sense of responsibility in spending programmes, which is considered necessary by some because of expensive programmes being undertaken by several local councils elected by a majority who do not pay rates. However, at the time of writing there is fierce opposition to this concept, both because of its regressive nature and its complexity of administration.

TABLE 12

SOURCES OF CENTRAL GOVERNMENT REVENUES
As a percentage of total revenues

Area	Individual & Profit Tax	Social Security Taxes	Tax on Domestic Goods & Services	Tax on International Trade	Non-tax Revenue	Total
World[1]	33.19	28.12	20.40	4.35	13.16	100.0
Industrial countries	36.68	33.67	17.17	1.24	10.02	100.0
Developing countries	22.15	8.99	30.64	14.18	23.09	100.0
USA	49.90	33.31	5.38	1.34	11.12	100.0
France	17.58	44.04	29.40	0.03	6.01	100.0
Germany	16.95	55.04	21.98	0.02	6.46	100.0
UK	38.62	17.69	28.51	0.04	12.94	100.0
New Zealand	63.57[2]	–	20.43	4.02	10.59	100.0

[1] World data does not cover all countries. In particular data is not available for Socialist countries.

[2] This is the highest figure quoted by the source.

Source: Government Finance Statistics 1985, published by the International Monetary Fund.

encourage savings and investment and therefore, it is hoped, create greater productivity and wealth for society as a whole.[39]

The other main approach to the burden of taxation is to tackle the other side of the income–expenditure equation and to reduce public expenditure (see Table 13). Those advocating this approach have generally placed much emphasis on efficiency and effectiveness in government and, in particular, a welfare state more sharply focused on those who are in genuine need. They also argue for reduced government intervention and regulation of the private sector as well as the elimination of subsidies for state-owned industries and services. The latter objective, it is often now argued, should be achieved by selling off enterprises to the private sector, where it is hoped they will be better managed and where there may even be a

[39] The USA is an obvious candidate for such a change. Fifteen years ago Americans saved 9.2 percent of after-tax income; in 1987 the rate was 3.2 percent, one of the lowest in the world, this despite the fact that US per capita income in real terms is probably still the highest. Several countries in South East Asia with much lower per capita incomes have saving rates of around 30 percent and not surprisingly their economies are growing rapidly. An expenditure tax encouraging greater savings might also contribute to lower inflation (by reducing consumer demand and increasing the efficiency of supply) and lower interest rates. The latter result would in turn help reduce domestic public debt as well as the international debt of Third World countries.

TABLE 13

GOVERNMENT EXPENDITURE AS A PERCENTAGE OF GROSS DOMESTIC PRODUCT
1982 and 1983 Data

Area	Welfare State				Defence	Other	Total
	EDUCATION	HEALTH	SOCIAL SECURITY & HOUSING	SUBTOTAL			
World[1]	4.85	4.92	13.36	23.13	4.03	15.37	42.53
Industrial Countries	5.05	5.42	14.81	25.28	4.41	16.01	45.70
Developing Countries	3.56	1.77	5.53	10.86	2.75	18.69	32.30
USA	5.32	4.66	10.85	20.43	6.24	12.48	39.15
France	4.48	6.49	22.80	33.77	3.19	13.80	50.76
Germany	4.23	8.13	21.07	33.43	2.90	12.95	49.28
UK	NA	NA	NA	NA	5.23	NA	49.26
Netherlands	NA	NA	NA	NA	3.16	NA	61.67

[1] World data does not cover all countries. In particular date is not available for Socialist countries.

Source: Government Finance Statistics 1985, published by the International Monetary Fund.

spirit of competition (not likely, however, in the many cases where the privatised enterprise still has a monopoly or near-monopoly position in the market).[40] These policies, it is hoped, would have the effect of significantly reducing the public sector of the economy below the present world average level, excluding the communist countries, of 42.5 percent of the total gross domestic product, which some consider too high for the economic health of a country in the long run.

However, all these efforts to reduce public expenditure run into severe difficulties because of several broad factors. First, tense international relations have provoked heavy spending on war preparation (see Table 14 for data on real increases in defence expenditure, 1976–

[40] An interesting side effect of privatization of the public sector in Great Britain has been the conscious effort to use the occasion to encourage a significant increase in the percentage of the population which own shares, so as to strengthen direct popular interest in the profitability and efficiency of enterprises and the economy in general. Another important aspect of privatization when it involves encouragement of competition is its connection with the philosophy that a market economy is not only more efficient but that it is an essential feature of democracy. The citizen should be free to make economic choices for himself rather than have them dictated to him by state monopoly.

TABLE 14

DEFENCE EXPENDITURES AS A PERCENTAGE OF GDP/GNP
1984 Data

Percentage of GDP/GNP	Number of Nations & States					
	AFRICA	AMERICAS	ASIA	EUROPE	OCEANIA	TOTAL
Less than 1	2	5	–	1	–	8
1–1.99	4	8	6	6	3	27
2–2.99	16	6	1	5	1	29
3–3.99	2	1	2	9	–	14
4–4.99	3	2	1	3	–	9
5–5.99	4	–	4	2	–	10
6–6.99	–	1	2	–	–	3
7–7.99	1	2	2	2	–	7
8–8.99	2	1	2	–	–	5
9–9.99	2	1	–	–	–	3
10 & over	3	1	13	1	–	18
Total	**39**	**28**	**33**	**29**	**4**	**133**
Not surveyed	12	7	6	4	8	37
Grand Total	**51**	**35**	**39**	**33**	**12**	**170**

Countries spending more than 10% of GDP/GNP on defence are:
Africa: Angola (16.9); Ethiopia (11.4); Somalia (11.3).
Americas: Nicaragua (11.7).
Asia: Iran (12.3); Iraq (51.1); Israel (24.4); Jordan (13.4); North Korea (10.2);
                 Lebanon (19.2); Mongolia (11.5); Oman (24.2); Qatar (13.1); Saudi Arabia
                 (20.9); Syria (15.1); North Yemen (17.8); South Yemen (16.3).
Europe: USSR (13–15).

Sources: The Military Balance, 1986/87, International Institute for Strategic Studies, 1986; and *The Economist,* 6 June 1987, with regard to USSR.

1985), a process which is aggravated by the increasing expense of technology which multiplies the cost of each generation of weapons several-fold.[41] Second, welfare programme costs are difficult to cut in aggregate because of high levels of unemployment, an ageing population which increases the number of welfare state pensioners and decreases the number of working contributors, and a middle-

[41] For instance, the British Spitfire fighter aeroplane cost £5,000 in 1939 or £98,000 at today's prices. Its current equivalent, the air defence version of the Tornado, costs about £17 million, i.e. it is 172 times more expensive than the Spitfire in real terms after allowing for inflation.

[42] Two obvious examples are deduction of mortgage interest payments from taxable income, and the subsidization of rail fares.

Stele, 18th century BC. Musée du Louvre

Stele, Manchu dynasty

1. Hammurabi
A god presents the laws to the King.

2. Confucius

Engraving by Daumont

Socrate Fondateur de la
Philosophie morale chez les Grecs
mourut l'an du monde 3572
agé de 72 ans

3. Socrates

Houdon. Institut et Musée Voltaire. Photograph by François Martin

4. *Jean-François Marie Arouet de Voltaire*
(1694–1778)

Hulton Picture Company

5. *Thomas Paine*
(1737–1809)

Hulton Picture Company. Engraving by P. Vanderbancke

6. *John Locke*
(1632–1704)

Hulton Picture Company

7. *'Mad Tom – or the Man of Rights'*
Caricature of Thomas Paine, published by
W. Locke, 1791.

8. *Abraham Lincoln reading the Emancipation Declaration to his cabinet September 1862.*

9. *Frederick Douglass (1817–1895). Born a slave, he became the most influential Black leader of his time.*

10. *Harriet Beecher Stowe (1811–1896) Her book* Uncle Tom's Cabin *(1852) won sympathy for the anti-slavery movement.*

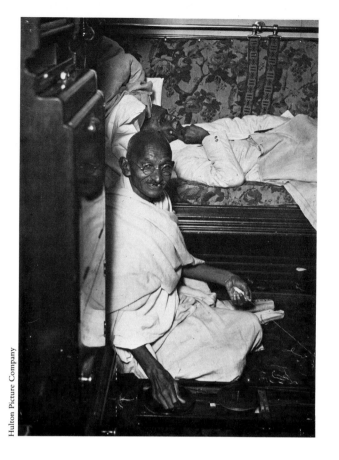

Hulton Picture Company

11. Mahatma Gandhi on board ship on his way to Britain in 1931 to meet government leaders about Indian self-determination. Gandhi is weaving.

12. Martin Luther King (1929–1968). Inspired by Gandhi's example of non-violence, as well as by Christian ethics, he became the moral and spiritual leader of the 1960s civil rights movement in the United States, and was awarded the Nobel Peace Prize in 1964. Both Gandhi and King were assassinated.

13. Elizabeth Cady Stanton
(1814–1902)
One of the organizers of the
first convention on women's rights
Seneca Falls, 1848.

14. Suffrage cartoon by
Blanche Ames Ames.

15. *Nineteenth-century reformers*
*Top left: Octavia Hill (1838–1912). Her system of women housing managers
in England was copied in many other countries. Top right: Anthony Ashley
Cooper, 7th Earl of Shaftesbury (1801–1885), whose name is associated
with Acts of Parliament to improve housing for the working classes, and
with the amelioration of working conditions in factories and mines.
Bottom left: Robert Owen (1776–1858), the successful English industrialist
who became a leading figure in the struggle to improve working conditions
through cooperatives and trade unions. Bottom right: Frances Willard
(1839–1898), who played a leading role in the United States in
movements for the abolition of slavery, for women's suffrage, trade unions,
temperance, prison reform and improving the lot of the poor.*

16. *Jean-Henri Dunant (1828–1910).*
Founder of the Red Cross Committee.
He was awarded the first Nobel Peace Prize
in 1901.

Red Cross Museum, Geneva

17. *Jean Jaurès (1859–1914),*
socialist and leader of the
Parti Ouvrier Français until
his assassination in 1914
for advocating peace.

Hulton Picture Company

18. Jane Addams (far right), (1860–1935). One of the foremost American women in the early twentieth century, she was active in campaigns to help the poor and promote the civil rights of Blacks and women. She wrote New Ideas on Peace *(1907) and later became chairman of both the International Congress of Women and the Women's International League for Peace and Freedom (see opposite page). She won the Nobel Peace Prize in 1931.*

19. Eleanor Roosevelt (1884–1962), chairman of the UN *Commission on Human Rights, and instrumental in drafting the Universal Declaration of Human Rights, 'one of the great milestones of the modern age'.*

20. Thomas Woodrow Wilson (1856–1924) 28th President of the United States, his Fourteen Points became the basis for the League of Nations Charter.

21. The first session of the Council of the League of Nations,
16 January 1920 at the Quai d'Orsay in Paris.

22. Women's International League for Peace and Freedom
presenting proposals to the League of Nations.

United Nations

23. Signing the UN Charter at the San Francisco Conference, 1945.
Delegates of fifty nations met and hammered out the Charter of the
United Nations and the Statute of the new International Court of
Justice. The Charter was passed unanimously and signed by all the
representatives. This picture shows John Sofianopoulos, delegate of
Greece, signing the Charter in the presence of other representatives
of his country.

United Nations

24. The United Nations Security Council.
An early meeting in March 1946.

United Nations

25. The International Court of Justice.
A hearing in 1962 at The Hague on the obligations of
member states.

United Nations

26. The United Nations Secretariat, New York 1985, a representative group.
They include linguists, economists, editors, social scientists,
legal experts, librarians, journalists, statisticians, broadcasters,
administrators and experts in all the varied fields of United Nations
activity. They are supported by stenographers, clerks, maintenance
personnel, and security officers. The head of this multi-national
staff is the Secretary-General.

27. *The International Bahá'í Convention. Delegates meet every five years to elect the Universal House of Justice and to consult on their goals and current activities in helping to bring about a just society. All ethnic, religious, cultural and social groups are represented – a true cross-section of humanity.*

28. *'Abdu'l-Bahá (1844–1921), son of Bahá'u'lláh, Founder of the Bahá'í Faith. His life, in its outstanding spiritual qualities and years of service to mankind, is the example Bahá'ís try to follow.*

class electorate which is unwilling, in any case, to have its particular benefits reduced.[42] Third, though there is undoubtedly scope for reducing excessive regulation which stifles the economy for no good reason, there are signs of a need in some areas for enhanced monitoring of the economy in the public interest particularly with regard, for example, to the impact of technology on the environment. Finally, there is the increasing burden in many countries of a large debt built up because of a failure in the past to match expenditure with income, a development aggravated by historically high real interest rates.[43]

After many decades of expansion of the public sector when concern for the efficient and effective use of resources was not always given a high priority, the recent movement to halt and even reverse that trend is potentially in the public interest. In the broadest sense wasteful use of resources by the public sector contributes to a slowing down of the process of abolishing poverty and this is particularly important when typically the public sector represents nearly half of an economy.

Nevertheless, imposing arbitrary ceilings on government expenditures is not by itself going to lead to greater efficiency. That requires close examination of the main public goals of society, their ranking in order of priority, and objective assessment of the most efficient and effective means of achieving them either through the public or private sectors. Experience suggests that the private sector (including cooperatives) is generally more efficient than the public sector, especially when there is real competition. Accordingly it is argued that the state should limit its direct economic activity to those functions which are naturally monopolistic and where the spur of competition is unlikely. This would help free the state for its main economic function which should be the setting of broad goals, for instance for the elimination of poverty and the protection of the environment. Clearly this approach of making the state more efficient should apply to all aspects of government, not just that of the welfare state. For instance, there is a profound need, rarely acknowledged, to see whether spending more and more on armaments is the best way to maintain national security, or whether a shift of some resources to improving international peacekeeping organizations might not be more cost effective.

A related problem with the 'axeman' approach to government (i.e. the setting of arbitrary ceilings on expenditures) is that it is likely to lead to unfairness unless there is a conscious effort to balance gains and losses between broad economic classes. Thus in the United

---

[43] In 1978 non-socialist countries were spending 6.2 percent of gross domestic product on interest on government debt. By 1984 this figure had increased to 11.3 percent.

States the process has coincided with a widening of the gap between rich and poor:

Wealth and poverty in the United States continue to go up. The wealthiest 20 percent of Americans received 44 percent of aggregate income in 1987, up from 40 percent 20 years ago. The poorest 20 percent of Americans received 4.6 percent, down from 5.5 percent in 1967.[44]

In addition deep cuts in taxation without equal cuts in expenditures have resulted in a huge increase in the US national debt: a way of shifting the cost of this generation's standard of living on to the backs of future generations.

[44] 'The American Agenda: a bipartisan report prepared by former Presidents Ford and Carter for President-elect Bush' (*Washington Post*, 23 November, 1988).

CHAPTER 19

The Consumer Society

Pluses and Minuses

IN the last few decades a growing number of people have argued that the capitalist system itself will eliminate the worst aspects of poverty by increasing the total wealth available, some of which will 'trickle down' to the poorest. The image of the Industrial Revolution is of smoke-enshrouded towns, where the workers were crowded together in back-to-back jerry-built houses; of long hours of labour; and of harsh business cycles which periodically caused large numbers to be unemployed for considerable periods of time. It is not surprising that such images should make the Marxist theory of the inevitable destruction of capitalism and its replacement with socialism seem both necessary and plausible. Nevertheless, there was always another side to the picture: however bad the conditions were in the industrial cities, they were generally better than in the countryside and it was the prospect of higher wages in industry which drew the poor from the land, rather than the absence of jobs in the countryside.

In the first stages of industrialization much of the benefit does seem to have gone to the middle class, but by 1914, and certainly by 1939, the working classes of the industrial cities were living in much better houses than ever before, with a growing number equipped with electricity and/or gas, running water, their own bathrooms and flushing toilets, and, as noted earlier, a growing proportion of the population were owner-occupiers. Free trade, the development of vast new agricultural lands, particularly in the Americas and Australasia, and technological innovation including the refrigerator steamship, all combined to provide a much improved diet for all classes of people at relatively cheap prices. These factors, together with improvements in medical care and the public health infrastructure described above in discussing the welfare state, contributed to an unprecedented increase in average life expectancy and in other indications of physical well-being such as average height and weight.

Thus life expectancy, which in Europe and North America in 1800 had been about 35–40 years, had virtually doubled to 70-plus years by 1960. (See Table 9, p. 214.) In addition, the poor were gradually able to clothe themselves better; one indication of this change, which is not as frivolous as it may sound at first, is that working–class men and women started to wear the same style and fashions as the better-off for the first time in history. No longer were children in working-class districts seen to be without shoes and socks any more than to be afflicted with rickets, both familiar sights of earlier years. This upward trend in basic material well-being was of course jolted by the two World Wars and the Great Depression, but these were only temporary setbacks, more than offset by four decades of prosperity in the post-Second World War era.

The post-World War Two period has also seen a general improvement in the material quality of life in the industrial countries going far beyond the provision of the basic necessities of life: adequate shelter, food, medical care and clothing. These developments have justified the coming of the expression 'consumer society'. Prime Minister Macmillan (1894–1987) caught the point in the fifties with his famous comment: 'You've never had it so good.' One aspect of this improvement in the material quality of life has been the widespread distribution to all classes of society of new labour-saving devices for use in the home, as well as in the workplace, which have considerably reduced much of the old drudgery of daily life, especially for women. Some of the main items in this classification have been electric vacuum cleaners, clothes washing machines and dryers, dishwashing machines, refrigerators and freezers, nylon carpets, drip-dry clothing, telephones and the cheap motor car. Another aspect of improvements in the material standard of living has been the mass production of a growing range of goods and services for leisure: mass sports events, cheap holidays,[1] transistor radios, movies, television, record players, video cassettes and home computers. Essentially falling into the same category has been the development of new contraceptive devices, especially the Pill, which within a decade of its development in the early sixties has come into widespread use throughout Western society. The Pill has provided a more 'aesthetic' and easy method for family planning than any available before, and has been credited with being a major step in the liberation of women from the fear of unwanted pregnancies.

---

[1] A hundred years ago all that an average worker could expect in the way of vacation was an occasional outing at the weekend. Now he is able to take off weeks to go to resorts in his own country or, as a result of the coming of the cheap air package tour, to foreign parts as well.

The consumer society is essentially a development of Western capitalism. Its glitter has hypnotized the whole world, especially the young, and the governments of socialist countries and Third World countries alike have been obliged to bend and allow entry of the consumer society and its goods in order to keep their people reasonably contented, even though the consequence might be frivolous items taking precedence over those that are basic and essential. Though the consumer society has been a progressive factor in our age, in many respects it has been obtained at a high price indeed. This is not the place for a full critique of the consumer society, but it is perhaps appropriate to mention two of its negative consequences – hedonism and the destruction of the natural environment – because these in turn have prompted two subsidiary progressive movements which need to be mentioned in this story of the search for the just society.

The very expression 'consumer society' suggests a lack of balance. On the one hand it is associated with a decline in interest in spiritual values and ethics, a process already in full swing on account of the decline of religion in the last two centuries and the massive social disruption caused by great wars and revolutions. On the other hand, the consumer society gives emphasis to unrestrained and immediate gratification of all physical desires. Some of the manifestations of this extreme hedonism associated with the consumer society are as follows.

The first is a compulsive urge to collect material things not because they are needed but for the sake of the activity itself and perhaps as a game of competition with others. Shopping has become the main entertainment in the United States – leader of the consumer society nations – and is an all-year-round occupation, seven days a week, and with some shops open twenty-four hours per day. The shopping mall is the new centre of the community, indeed of life itself.

Another manifestation of hedonism is the high priority given to ease and comfort. Ride in a motor car rather than walk or bike. Watch sports all day long on the TV rather than go out into the field to be an active player. Watch others rather than create oneself. The result is a physically unfit society despite its richness, and a lazy one – not the stuff from which great civilizations have emerged in the past.

A third and dramatic example of the hedonism of the consumer society in full bloom is the cult of sexual freedom, made vastly more practical as a result of the Pill, in which old 'killjoy' constraints are thrown aside in favour of sex as a consumer service to be enjoyed on every possible occasion. To avoid boredom there has to be variety: group sex, homosexuality, and more. This all undermines the profound theme that sex is primarily intended for the procreation of children and is also an expression of love for the marriage partner and therefore a bonding for the family cell. One result of the permissive society is a vast increase in the number of divorces. This process is encouraged by the hedonistic attitude that life is too short to be wasted struggling to overcome the difficulties of married life.

Another dramatic example of the hedonism of the consumer society is the widespread use of alcohol and other drugs for purposes of stimulation and entertainment. A few years ago a prominent Californian academic was given all the publicity he needed to spread the seductive view that drugs are mind-expanding and an essential experience of life. Alcohol in particular is given great respectability.[2] Advertisements and social attitudes make it clear that it is essential for normal social intercourse, that in the case of men it is considered a proof of masculinity; it is even associated with sport – an extraordinary example of the power of commercial advertising! Any opposition is dismissed as at best killjoy and at worst unpatriotic. After all, alcohol is part of the national cultures of our time: beer in Germany, Britain and Australia; wine in France and Italy; vodka in Russia; and the martini or cocktail in the United States. The medical profession prostitutes itself by producing studies which reassure everyone that alcohol is all right, indeed health-giving, if taken in moderate quantities!

The reverse side of these tendencies to self-indulgence is a declining interest in public services (which cost taxes), a combination aptly described by the American economist John Kenneth Galbraith (1908–) as 'private affluence and public squalor'. A preference for motor cars and televison over public transport, clean streets, well-maintained parks, and, of course, help for the poor. There is resistence to any authority which puts any kind of limitation on self-indulgence. The breakdown in respect for authority – the state, the family, the school, or the police – has a whole series of complex causes, not the least of which has been the failure of these institutions to advance with the times. Nevertheless, the trend has been reinforced by the values of the consumer society, as can be seen from the very frivolousness of much of the content and expression of the opposition. Wrecked public telephone booths, obscene graffiti on public buildings and trash in the streets symbolize this aspect of our society. The values of the consumer society inevitably have contributed to the continuing worldwide growth in crime. Such values undermine constraint and encourage instant gratification even

[2] In consequence consumption tends to increase. For example, consumption per capita has more than doubled in the USA and the UK in the last fifty years.

when one does not have the funds for purchase – maybe a 'pop' record or the day's fix for the drug addict. Even those who are uneasy with the emptiness of their life and are vaguely aware of a need for a spiritual dimension all too often look for a solution which is easy and demands nothing of them: astrology for the superstitious, or consumer religious sects which provide comfort, glitter and miracles for money, or which identify groups in society (usually progressive or racial minority groups) as scapegoats to be blamed and hated for all that is wrong.

Hedonism is one negative feature of the consumer society. Another is the related destruction of the natural environment. This involves, first, the consumption of scarce resources – land, fresh water, minerals and forests – at a rate never before achieved in history and often for relatively frivolous needs: the building of vacation houses in the woods or where there is sun but no natural renewable supply of fresh water, the spreading suburbs serviced by more and more roads, and worst of all perhaps, the continued replacement of throwaway items ranging from the motor car to the beer can, to the book-sized newspaper. A second aspect of this destruction is pollution – poisoning – of all elements of the environment: air, water and land. Thus the air is poisoned by fumes from millions of private automobiles and from coal-fired power plants producing all the energy demanded by a consumer society; the rivers and lakes are poisoned by chemical factories including those making plastic, the symbol of the consumer society; and the land by farmers using chemical fertilizers to produce luxury foods far beyond the requirements of a healthy diet. This process is worse in the industrial societies simply because the population is richer and consumes more than those in poorer countries (it is estimated that American citizens on average consume twelve times more resources per person than do citizens of Third World countries). Disposing of a massive and growing volume of garbage, which is often dangerous as well as unpleasant, is becoming a major social and economic problem of the consumer society as highlighted in such recent stories as hospital refuse, including old syringe needles, being washed up on the resort beaches of New Jersey, and the shipping of dangerous waste from Italy to Africa after payment of bribes to the right people.

Though the problem is most obvious in the industrial countries, the rest of the world also presents a real threat to the environment as well because it wishes to emulate the industrial countries and is in a hurry to do so. Anyone who has visited any big city in a Third World country like New Delhi or Mexico City will know that the pollution can be as bad as in London, New York, or Los Angeles.

The problem is compounded by the sheer numbers – after all the Western capitalist nations as a whole represent only about 25 percent of the world's population. This is an issue made worse by the rapid growth in population of Third World countries (see Table 26 on p. 000).

These negative side-effects of the consumer society – hedonism and the destruction of the natural environment – have provoked two broad progressive forces which are discussed in the following paragraphs: the temperance and related movements, and the environmental protection movement.

The Temperance Movement and Similar Causes

Nearly all cultures have developed and made use of alcohol. Here are a few examples:

Country	Beverage	Source Crop
China	Tchar	Rice and millet
England	Mead	Honey
India	Toddy	Rice and molasses
Ireland/Scotland	Beer	Oats and barley
Italy/France/Spain	Wine	Grapes
Japan	Sake	Rice

The purpose of alcohol is usually to provide relaxation but sometimes it is also used as a medicine. The general attitude is that the benefit of alcohol in helping people (mostly men until recently) to let off steam and escape from reality for a while is greater than the costs that arise when over-indulgence leads to drunkenness. Those costs that are so casually dismissed are high indeed. Drunkenness leads not only to loss of self-control and degradation of the human spirit for the individual concerned, but hurt for those around him, especially the children who suffer the bad example from one who is often the head of the family, as well as violence, verbal abuse, and deprivation of scarce resources which are desperately needed for the basic necessities of life. It is not surprising, therefore, that nearly all the great religions have at a minimum urged extreme moderation in the use of alcohol and in several cases, as noted in Part I, have condemned its use entirely. Of course the amount of drunkenness and its side-effects have varied. Some societies – the Jews, the Japanese, and the Mediterranean peoples for example – have been more successful than others, such as the peoples of northern Europe, in exercising limits on the use of alcohol. Most of the former relied on family pressure and the regular use of wine with daily meals to discourage excessive consumption. On the other hand, the colder climes of northern Europe and the long depressing winter nights seemed to provoke an additional need for the warming effect (always temporary, of course) of alcohol.

A series of factors combined to make alcohol an increasing scourge of society in the eighteenth and nineteenth centuries in northern Europe and North America. First, distilled alcohols such as whiskey, gin, vodka and rum, which had a much higher alcohol content than older alcoholic beverages such as wines and beers, became cheaper than ever before and thus more readily available to the mass of the population. It is an irony of history that distillation techniques had been originally developed in the Middle Ages by monks and others in response to perceived medical needs. Second, the growth of large new industrial cities with their horrific living conditions for the poorer sections of society and their increased opportunities for evasion of family control led to much greater use of spirits by poor as well as rich, by women as well as men. Stories of gin-swilling, poverty-stricken women, for example, are common in the literature of the time.[3] Third, in the United States there was the additional stimulus of the hardships of the frontier where men were for a period more than usually free from the refinements of regular society. In addition there were the great pressures on immigrant families arriving in a strange and harsh land where living conditions for the first generations were hard indeed. It is not surprising that statistics show that between 1860, when US consumption was already high, and 1880 the average amount of spirit taken per head of population doubled.

It was against such a background that the modern temperance movement began. The leaders of the movement were often associated with the churches, particularly the new evangelical sects of the eighteenth and nineteenth centuries, including the Methodists and Congregationalists. They were generally progressive in their outlook, and often – like Frances Willard (1839–1898), for instance – associated with other progressive movements of the time such as those for the abolition of slavery, women's suffrage, trade unions, prison reform, and the improvement of the social and economic conditions of the poor (including the immigrants in the case of the United States). The strength of the movement came from a revitalized interest in religion, and from support from women of all classes of society because all too frequently they and their children were the main victims of alcoholism. In addition there was the

[3] In 1750 it is estimated that in London there was one gin shop for every 120 inhabitants. There was a saying that you could get drunk for a penny and dead drunk for twopence. The scene was immortalized in Hogarth's famous picture 'Gin Tavern'.

general feeling amongst the leaders of progressive movements of the time that a better society would only come with self-help, self-discipline and self-respect, and that such qualities were undermined by alcohol. The obstacles were immense, particularly the deep-felt need by so many for alcohol as at least a temporary release from the harshness of life. This was encouraged, sometimes surreptitiously, sometimes openly, by the manufacturers and their associates who profited from the trade, and often by those in power who saw alcohol as a means of diverting the attention of the underprivileged from the injustices of society: *pace* Karl Marx, false religion was not the only 'opium of the people'.

In its early days the temperance movement put emphasis on voluntary abstinence from spirits, rather than from all alcoholic beverages. The first temperance organizations to be recorded in history's roll of honour included the Temperance Society of Saratoga in New York (1808), the Massachusetts Society for the Suppression of Intemperance (1813), an association in Skibbereen, Ireland (1818), and the American Society for Propagation of Temperance (1826). Similar movements began in Norway and Sweden in the 1830s. A most dramatic movement was organized in Ireland by the charismatic Reverend Theobald Mathews (1790–1856) from Cork in the period 1838–1842, which resulted in the collection of 4.6 million pledges of abstinence, and a decline over a three-year period in the consumption of spirits in Ireland from 10.8 million gallons to 5.3 million.

As the temperance movement grew in strength it widened its concern from spirits alone to all alcohol consumption (as did, for example, the American Society for the Propagation of Temperance in 1836), and extended its activities from simple voluntary abstinence into politics, with a view to persuading governments to pass laws against the sale of alcohol. There were some early successes in the political arena. In 1838 Massachusetts made it a requirement within the state that spirits be sold in minimum quantities of 15 gallons. This practice was intended to make it more difficult for the individual to obtain alcohol, and was subsequently adopted by twelve other states. For a short time in the eighteen-forties New York actually banned the sale of liquor. Many, however, were not satisfied with these victories and felt that real progress would only be achieved if there were a political party especially dedicated to the issue – hence the formation in 1869 of the National Prohibition Party which fielded its own candidates for political office.[4] On the other hand, many others, perhaps more realistic, preferred to put their energies into a National Women's Christian Temperance Union

(1874) led by Frances Willard which had the more modest goal of supporting any political candidate willing to help with temperance legislation.[5] During the 1880s and 1890s some five states of the American Union passed prohibition legislation. In the next two decades or so the campaign became more intense as several progressive groups, including the Progressive Party and the Populist Party, joined with the Anti-Saloon League (formed in 1895) in their opposition to the vast number of drinking saloons in every city and town across the country[6] which had become centres not only of drunkenness but also of political corruption and prostitution.[7] Gradually the number of 'dry' states grew until by 1919, immediately prior to federal prohibition, there were thirty-three, some 63 percent of the population of the forty-eight states. The federal government gave support in 1913 by means of the Webb–Kenyon Act which forbade the transportation of intoxicating liquor into dry states. When the United States joined in the Great War in 1917, prohibition was imposed nation-wide as a temporary measure to strengthen the nation's war effort. Public support for prohibition was now at a peak and resulted the next year in the passage through Congress of the 18th Amendment to the Constitution which, effective 16 January 1920, forbade the manufacture, sale or transportation of intoxicating liquor throughout the Union.

The drama of the temperance movement was somewhat more subdued elsewhere. In England, for example, there was very little legislation on the matter. Some initiative had first been taken in 1751 with the Gin Acts which made it a requirement that any sale of gin be licensed by the local authorities.[8] After that there was no more significant legislation until 1872 when Gladstone's Liberal ministry took modest steps to limit the hours of business of public houses and made it possible for police to enter them without prior warning. It has been asserted that this legislation, which also put limits on the adulteration of beer by the manufacturers, contributed to the defeat of the Liberals in 1874 because of the success of publicans in arousing

---

[4] The National Prohibition Party was progressive in several other respects, e.g. in support of women's suffrage.

[5] Frances Willard later, in 1883, founded the World Women's Temperance Association which eventually had branches in some 50 countries.

[6] It was calculated that by 1900 in the big cities there was a saloon for every 200 inhabitants (men, women and children).

[7] One of the most colourful opponents of alcohol was Carrie Nation (1846–1911), six foot tall and weighing 180 lbs, who would burst into saloons with her famous hatchet which she would use to smash up the place and chase out customers.

[8] Landed gentry had been reluctant to curb gin sales as it was made from corn and its widespread use helped keep up the price of this crop.

opposition amongst their clientèle. In 1904 the Conservative government (1902–1909) of Arthur Balfour (1848–1930) took further modest steps to control alcohol consumption by reducing the number of public houses that could be licensed. It was not until the Great War that more serious legislation was approved, prompted by the need to improve productivity amongst munition workers. This legislation (which has been in effect ever since that time) set limits on hours of opening and thereby helped reduce the general consumption of alcohol. Though this was indeed a melancholy record, England did at least have the distinction of hosting the first World Prohibition Conference which was held in London in 1909. In addition branches were established of the American-founded Alcoholics Anonymous Society[9] which has done so much to motivate alcoholics to fight their own affliction, and of Bands of Hope which from the middle of the nineteenth century worked to encourage the young to break with the custom of their elders and to be life-long abstainers.

Unfortunately, the success of the temperance movement in the United States in 1919 proved to be less solid than appeared at the time. The movement had not persuaded enough of the population of the absurdity of alcohol, and it soon became evident that a large number of people in a democratic society cannot be forced to abandon a deep set custom by the law alone. The 18th Amendment was increasingly evaded, and the pushing underground of the alcoholic trade made it, even more than before, a breeding ground for crime and corruption. Progressive people began to have doubts about the law and its impact on civil liberties, and in any case became more and more preoccupied, especially after 1929, with other issues such as mass unemployment during the Great Depression. Soon the only enthusiastic supporters of the law were the minority of religious fundamentalists who were willing to use force on a reluctant population. Thus it came about that repeal of the 18th Amendment was one of the first acts of Franklin Roosevelt after he became President in 1933.[10]

The collapse of the temperance movement was a tragedy for all humanity. Yet the forces of reason and progress in this area have not been totally overwhelmed. Thus some of the more responsible members of the medical profession have demonstrated that even small amounts of alcohol consumed regularly will damage the brain

[9] Founded in 1935 by Bill Wilson, a Wall Street stockbroker, and Robert Smith, a medical doctor.

[10] The only other Western country to legislate prohibition was Finland (1919–1931), where the law was aimed at spirits rather than all alcohol. In addition many areas of India have been declared 'dry', as have most Muslim countries.

and thus have countered part of the harm done by their self-serving colleagues.[11] Those concerned about the condition of the American Indians have recognized how disastrous alcohol has been for these peoples who have turned to it to salve the pain of self-doubt induced by the white man and his power. Others are concerned about the use of alcohol (and drugs) in a world of high technology following an increasing number of cases where individuals in charge of civil airliners and other transport systems, nuclear power stations, and military weapons, have been at least temporarily intoxicated, to the danger of large numbers of their fellow citizens as well as themselves.[12] Others point to the high social and economic costs in general.[13] Societies are being formed (especially by women in the United States and elsewhere) to campaign about the number of persons killed in traffic accidents caused by inebriated drivers.[14] Physical fitness groups are defying social convention and eliminating alcohol from their diets and every now and again a prominent statesman will stand up and speak out despite the general conspiracy of silence on the subject – as did, for instance, the milk-drinking Prime Minister of France, Pierre Mendès-France (1907–) in the 1950s.

By contrast with the general cowardice of governments on the subject of temperance, there have at least been some gestures of

[11] Recent studies using cat scans have shown that use of alcohol leads to a shrinkage of the brain. Tests have also shown that the use of alcohol leads to significant loss of memory and reduced ability to plan and organize. It also affects adversely the liver, heart and the nerves, blood pressure, and unborn infants. The World Health Organization states that alcohol is the third biggest killer, after cancer and heart disease.

[12] An article in the *Economist* (18 April 1987) strongly criticised the prevailing alcohol culture and ended with the following statement: 'Alcohol causes 100 times more premature deaths than hard drugs. Consumption (in Great Britain) has increased steadily since the 1950s, particularly among the young. Alcohol may act as a 'gateway' to other drugs, including heroin. And whereas heroin and cocaine abusers damage only themselves, heavy drinkers damage others – in car accidents or football hooliganism, for example . . . Society's amused tolerance of alcohol abuse makes it harder to persuade other drug abusers of their dangerous folly.'

[13] A recent article in *Marxism Today* (August 1988) reported that studies in the UK showed that alcohol was associated with ¼ of all admissions to hospital; ⅘ of suicides; around 40,000 premature deaths per year; ⅓ of road deaths; ⅓ of divorce cases; ⅘ of family cases involving violence; ½ of all murder and rape cases; and ½ of all burglaries. The article adds that 95 percent of the British adult population will take alcohol on occasion, and that contrary to conventional thinking, it is the moderate drinkers, not the heavy drinkers, who cause most alcohol-related problems, simply because they are the vast majority. Data for the USA is similar: alcohol is connected with 10,000 murders per annum, 24,000 out of 44,000 road fatalities, etc. It is estimated that 3 out of 10 adolescents routinely get drunk and that 40 percent of the population are directly affected adversely by alcohol. On the bright side, the USA has a remarkably high proportion of abstainers – 30 percent of the population – a reminder that the temperance movement was not a complete failure.

[14] e.g. the MADD organization – Mothers Against Drunken Driving. Recent statistics show that states in the USA which have raised the minimum age for drinking from 18 to 21 have had significant reductions in road accidents.

concern about the spreading use of other drugs. Governments of the United States and other countries have made a considerable effort to interrupt the drug traffic both domestic and international. Several countries punish drug pushing with death. Others have tried to control it by providing drugs or substitutes for registered addicts.[15] The purpose of the latter approach is to prevent the price of drugs increasing, because when that happens criminals become more involved and producer countries, now particularly in South America and South East Asia, earn so much from it that they have little incentive to cooperate in crushing the drug culture. The problem is, as was true in the time of prohibition, that a large part of the population is out of sympathy with the government campaign and it is extremely unlikely that much impact will be made on the traffic until there is a major change in values.[16] Many will not be convinced until there is consistency of policy with regard to alcohol and drugs, because otherwise there is a perception that what is involved is selectivity by vested interests rather than moral principle.

Alcohol and other drugs are far and away the most damaging items physically consumed by individuals because they affect the mind and the spirit as well as the body, and because they can have a negative impact far beyond the immediate consumer. With regard to lesser issues the picture of physical consumption is more encouraging. Thus in recent years, particularly in Western industrial societies, there has been considerable success in reducing the use of tobacco and in encouraging a more healthy diet and the taking of more exercise.

Though the powerful tobacco industry has fought a long rearguard action, most governments have at long last recognized the connection between smoking and cancer (especially cancer of the lungs) and have insisted not only on clear warnings being placed on cigarette cartons (not a very effective measure in itself) but on reduced advertising on television, especially at times when there is likely to be a young audience, and on the banning of smoking in an increasing number of public areas. Though some young people, especially young women, still identify smoking with proof of adulthood and independence, there is evidence that society as a whole is slowly coming to see smoking for what it is: a dirty, dangerous, and anti-social habit.[17]

[15] A variation on this soft approach is to legalize drugs, or at least those types which are considered least harmful, e.g. marijuana.

[16] Recent calculations are that Americans alone spend $60 billion each year on cocaine, not to speak of other drugs (quoted in the TV programme 60 Minutes as broadcast by the Australian Broadcasting Corporation on 5 June 1987).

[17] A deplorable exception to this general trend is an apparent increase in smoking in South East Asia and Japan, encouraged by tobacco companies after seeing their markets shrink elsewhere.

The issue of healthy diet and the need for exercise has become important because the consumer society has encouraged over-eating and discouraged physical movement. Characteristic are, on the one hand, the consumption of relatively unhealthy foods such as fatty meat (from animals fast-grown on a hormone-spiked diet), fast foods and excessive amounts of sugar and salt; and, on the other hand, less incentive to exercise either at work (labour-saving devices), in travel (the car) or at leisure (TV and video, etc.). Campaigns in favour of a healthier diet (less red meat, sugar and salt; more vegetables, fruits, nuts and white meat such as fish and chicken) and more exercise (yoga, aerobics, hiking and jogging) have gradually won much support. A growing number of shops, restaurants and 'fitness centres' cater to these tastes, although a healthier diet is generally more expensive, and hence not taken up very much by the poor, and exercise requires a lot of effort. Clearly the campaign has been successful to some extent because of the general interest in keeping young, particularly with regard to physical appearance, which is one of the key attributes of the consumer society.

Protection of the Environment

Man's activity throughout history has always had a disruptive impact on the natural environment. Until modern times the damage was relatively minor, with a few notable exceptions such as the early destruction of good quality agricultural lands in Spain, Sicily, Palestine and Egypt as a result of bad practices, including over-grazing by sheep and goats. During the nineteenth century the rapid growth in population in Western countries, and the Industrial Revolution, resulted in depredations of nature on a scale not previously experienced. This process has continued at a frightening pace into the twentieth century (see Table 15).

In England, as in many other countries, there had been a long tradition of protecting game from poachers so that the ruling classes could enjoy more hunting. In the nineteenth century the idea of conservation was broadened into a less selfish concern for the welfare of society as a whole, not just for the privileged. In particular there was a growing interest in the protection of places of great natural beauty. An appreciation of nature had been stimulated at the beginning of the century by the Romantic movement and especially by the poetry of William Wordsworth (1770–1850) who lived in the English Lake District. Later in the century there was also the interest of American writers and artists such as the poet Walt Whitman (1819–1892). One of the first landmark victories in the struggle to

TABLE 15

CHANGES IN THE EARTH'S PHYSICAL CONDITION

Indicator	*Reading*
Forest Cover	Tropical forests shrinking by 11 million hectares per year; 31 million hectares in industrial countries damaged, apparently by air pollution or acid rain.
Topsoil on Cropland	An estimated 26 billion tons lost annually in excess of new soil formation.
Desert Area	Some 6 million hectares of new desert formed annually by land mismanagement.
Lakes	Thousands of lakes in the industrial north now biologically dead; thousands more dying.
Fresh Water	Underground water tables falling in parts of Africa, China, India, and North America as demand for water rises above aquifer recharge rates.
Species Diversity	Extinctions of plant and animal species together now estimated at several thousand per year; one fifth of all species may disappear over next 20 years.
Groundwater Quality	Some 50 pesticides contaminate groundwater in 32 American states; some 2,500 US toxic waste sites need cleanup; extent of toxic contamination worldwide unknown.
Climate	Mean temperature projected to rise between 1.5 and 4.5 degrees Celsius between now and 2050.
Sea Level	Projected to rise between 1.4 metres (4.7 feet) and 2.2 metres (7.1 feet) by 2100.
Ozone Layer in Upper Atmosphere	Growing 'hole' in the earth's ozone layer over Antarctica each spring suggests a gradual global depletion could be starting.

Source: Lester R. Brown and others, *State of the World 1988*, World Watch Institute, Washington DC.

protect the English countryside was the defeat in Parliament in 1887 of a proposal to build a railway line from Ambleside to Keswick in the Lake District. The leader of this struggle was Octavia Hill, inspired to action by John Ruskin. A few years later, in 1895, Parliament was prevailed upon to approve the National Trust Act to protect initially the Lake District and later other beauty spots from unregulated development. It also provided for easy access to the area for hikers and other holiday-makers, which was later to prove a great, if unforeseeable, boon to young Northerners out of work during the Great Depression. Pioneer work in the protection of nature was also carried out by the Royal Society for the Protection of Birds, founded in 1889 by a duchess and the wife of a Manchester solicitor.

It was in the United States, where rapid colonization of the frontier was leading to large-scale depredation of natural resources, that conservation first became a major political issue. As compared with more settled communities in Europe, there was a rather cavalier approach to land management in the United States because the apparently limitless amounts available encouraged the idea that when one piece of land was exhausted more could always be found by moving on, westwards. This tradition of lack of respect and responsibility for the environment is still strong even today in some important sectors of American society. The most immediate cause of concern was the highly visible and massive destruction of the country's forests which was brought to the attention of the nation at a meeting in 1873 of the American Association for the Advancement of Science. Other bodies such as the Audubon Society pointed out the need to protect the habitats of wild animals, birds and flora if they were not to become extinct. Despite outcries by experts and public alike the federal and state governments were as slow to take any action to protect the environment as they were to protect the poor. In the early years there were a few isolated initiatives, such as the declaration by the State of California in 1864 that the Yosemite Valley and Mariporan where grew the Sequoia Gigantea would be a state park[18] and the establishment by President Grant in 1872 of the first National Park at Yellowstone, site of a great variety of natural life and of the world's largest geyser. In 1881 Chicago became the first city in the world to issue a smoke-controlling ordinance. Ten years later the Forest Reserves Act gave the President authority to set aside forest areas for conservation for the future.

The pace of action was greatly speeded up under the presidency (1901–1908) of Theodore Roosevelt (1858–1919) who had a personal interest in the subject arising from his great love of the outdoors. His actions in support of conservation are seen by many as the greatest and most long-lasting of the achievements of his administration. One of his first decisions on assuming office was to take advantage of the 1891 Forest Reserve Act to increase the area of forest set aside for conservation from 45 million acres to 280 million.[19] To supervise the Act a new Forestry Service was established in the Department of Agriculture, headed first by Gifford Pinchot (1865–1946), a distin-

[18] The area became a National Park in 1906. A major role in creating the national parks was played by the naturalist John Muir (1838–1914).

[19] Today there are 155 national forests in the USA covering 191 million acres.

guished conservationist. In 1902 the President was given authority under the Reclamation Act to build dams, both to control rivers so as to prevent periodic flooding, and to provide irrigation waters and electrical power. Making use of his powers under the Antiquities Act of 1906, he established five national parks, four national game reserves and fifty-one wild bird refuges. In 1907 his administration sponsored a first National Conservation Conference which brought together the most distinguished group of citizens in the history of the nation up to that time and included cabinet members, Supreme Court Justices and state governors, as well as highly experienced technical experts, to discuss a whole range of conservationist issues such as forests, waterways, minerals, soil erosion and irrigation. As a result of that Conference national conservation commissions were established in each state of the union, as was a National Conservation Association chaired by the then President of Harvard University. In addition, a National Commission was appointed (with Gifford Pinchot as chairman) to make a detailed and comprehensive inventory of the natural resources of the nation.

After Theodore Roosevelt's presidency there was little conservationist activity in the United States until that of Franklin Roosevelt in the 1930s. As noted earlier, Franklin Roosevelt, who shared some of the interest of his uncle in nature and the open air, introduced New Deal measures which simultaneously served the purpose of providing employment opportunities during the Great Depression and of protecting the nation's natural resources, e.g. the Civilian Conservation Corps, the Tennessee Valley scheme, and the Soil Erosion Act.

Environmental issues during the next twenty-five years or so tended to be pushed on one side as the world focused its attention first on the Second World War and thereafter on the process of reconstruction of the war-torn countries and the economic development of those of the Third World. During that time the world economy expanded rapidly with little regard for the impact on the environment except for a few isolated instances such as the anti-smoke ordinances for British cities, which, incidentally, brought to an end the infamous London fogs. Then the alarm bells began to ring furiously. The first brought to the fore the issue of serious pollution of the environment, as a result of Rachel Carson's (1907–1964) book *The Silent Spring*, published in 1962. Next, through the prompting of the United Nations and such individuals and groups as E.F. Schumacher, Dennis Meadows, J.W. Forrester[20] and the Club of

---

[20] These three individuals respectively published the following influential books on the issue in the early 1970s: *Small is Beautiful, The Limits to Growth* and *World Dynamics*.

Rome, came the issue of an alarming rate of consumption world-wide of basic non-renewable resources.

This time the alarm resulted in action, partly because governments were still willing to intervene at any point of the economy where there was a problem, in line with the philosophy of the New Deal and the Second World War. There was a scurry of activity, especially in the industrial countries of the West. A little later they were followed to some extent by socialist and Third World countries, after the initial suspicion had been overcome that the alarm was some sort of plot to hold back development. On this issue the United States was amongst the leaders, perhaps because it had hitherto been one of the most profligate users not only of other countries' resources but of its own as well. An environmental agency was established and legislation enacted to protect the quality of fresh water and the air, and to clean up waste expelled from both public and private enterprises around the country. States were coerced into imposing low maximum speed limits on the roads, a quite remarkable achievement considering the vast distances in the United States and the national obsession with the motor car. Indeed, the Federal government went further and forced the auto industry, hitherto one of the most reactionary and selfish powers in the country, to make cars more fuel-efficient and less polluting.[21]

In England, a relatively small country with a high population/land ratio, noise was added to the list of pollutions to be reduced by state action. In Germany a new political party, the Greens, was formed to campaign directly at the hustings to protect the environment in this highly-populated country which had a large industry and a political establishment unwilling to risk any unemployment on account of environmental issues. Sometimes the Greens were eccentric and violent, which did not help their cause. Nevertheless, they have had immense provocation from incredibly selfish people including those who insist on driving at very high speeds (a driver was recently stopped at 280 kilometres per hour) though it is wellknown that such speeds make car exhaust lethal for the country's great forests which are part of the national heritage. Europe has generally been slow to follow the American example given in the mid-1970s of switching to lead-free petrol (lead being one of the most dangerous pollutants in the air) and it was not until the second half of the 1980s that governments, for example in Germany and Switzerland, began to take the matter seriously.

During this period it was also recognized that environmental

21 Unfortunately, there are signs that government resolution on these issues is now beginning to waver, no doubt partly because of a fall in the price of oil in the 1980s.

issues were international in scope, as one nation's pollution or depredation of resources could and would have a serious impact on other nations. In Europe the nations made international agreements to control pollution of the Rhone and Rhine river systems and of the North Sea and the Mediterranean. The UN Education, Scientific and Cultural Organization (UNESCO) gave support to member nations, including Third World countries, so that they would protect areas which were considered to be in the class of world heritage. After witnessing the pioneering examples of the USA and Britain, Third World countries came to recognize the value of protecting certain wild habitats not just for their own sake, but because this would promote tourism and so bring in valued foreign exchange. Capping the whole worldwide effort was coordination and publicity organized through the agency of the United Nations, which held world conferences of experts to discuss and make recommendations with regard to the growing world population and the multiplicity of factors endangering the environment. At one of those conferences, held in 1974, it was agreed that there was a need for a permanent UN Environment Programme to continually monitor environmental issues, and such an agency was established that year in Nairobi, Kenya.

Several recent developments have reinforced understanding of how serious is the environmental issue for the future welfare of humanity. One such is the growing understanding of the effect of fluorides (used in airconditioners, spray cans etc.) and other pollutants in thinning out the ozone layer which encompasses the earth. The ozone layer serves to protect the earth from the sun's ultra-violet rays, and one consequence of its depletion is a real risk of a massive increase in the incidence of skin cancer. Recognition of how imminent this risk has become has prompted an unprecedented international convention signed in Montreal in 1987 which requires the signatory nations to set targets for elimination of the damaging agents from their economies over a period of years.

A second major environmental issue which has come to general public attention recently is the so-called 'greenhouse' effect or the heating up of the earth as a result of the massive use of fossil fuels which dump carbons into the atmosphere, and the simultaneous destruction of the earth's forests which act to render the carbon harmless. There are clear implications involved regarding use of energy by the nations of the world: finding alternatives to fossil fuels (coal, oil, gas) such as nuclear power (which carries its own immense risks especially with regard to safe disposal of large amounts of dangerous waste), or renewable power sources (biomass, the wind, ocean waves, the light and heat of the sun); aiming for greater efficiency in use of energy (smaller cars, car-pooling, better insulations);[22] and, most fundamental of all, lower demands for energy which might come from a world society more focused on services, e.g. education, than on accumulation of material possessions – the two-house, three/four car family unit.

A third environmental issue is the concern that world food production, and especially grain production (wheat, rice, corn) which represents well over half the caloric intake of humanity, is no longer growing as fast as the increase in the world's population. The methods used in the last three decades or so to rapidly increase production – chemical fertilizers, improved varieties of plants, irrigation schemes, use of marginal lands – are all beginning to show lower rates of return and alternative means of significantly increasing production are not in sight. As a result, world annual per capita production of grains which grew from 246 kilos in 1950 to 345 kilos in 1984, has since fallen to 300 kilos.[23] The situation may well be aggravated by the greenhouse phenomenon. The implications with regard to population growth are starkly evident.

A fourth serious environmental issue which is now coming increasingly into focus is the massive destruction in recent decades of species of life on earth as a result of insensitive and unbridled human activity. This is not just a matter of sentiment about the possible loss forever of intelligent or beautiful mammals – whales, jungle cats, birds with specialized habitats, or exotic flowers, important as that might be; rather the significance is to do with the restraints which would be imposed on humanity's development and ability to respond successfully to changing conditions, which will come about with the loss of species (see Table 16). One imaginative and practical response to this danger is a proposal of the World Wide Fund for Nature (World Wildlife Fund) that there be a concentration on protecting species in the seven countries (Brazil, Colombia, Mexico, Zaïre, Madagascar, Indonesia, and Australia) in which are to be found the greatest variety of species. About 54 percent of all known species in the world are located in these seven 'mega diverse' countries.[24] The WWF argues with good reason that the 'M7' should have the same sort of recognition with regard to their importance for

[22] Much has already been achieved. Between 1973 and 1987 the GNP of the 24 OECD countries increased by 40 percent but energy use increased by 6 percent only – a clear sign of the positive impact of the two oil crises of the seventies.

[23] For further information see Lester R. Brown, 'The Growing Grain Gap', in *World Watch*, Sept/Oct 1988.

[24] 40 percent of mammals including 79 percent of primates; 60 percent of birds; and 50 percent of plants.

the well-being of all human society as do the industrial countries of the Group of Seven (USA, Japan, Germany, France, UK, Italy, and Canada).

TABLE 16

KNOWN AND ESTIMATED DIVERSITY OF LIFE ON EARTH

Form of Life	Known Species	Estimated Total Species
Insects and Other Invertebrates	989,761	30 million insect species, extrapolated from surveys in forest canopy in Panama; most believed unique to tropical forests.
Vascular Plants	248,400	At least 10–15 percent of all plants are believed undiscovered.
Fungi and Algae	73,900	Not available.
Microorganisms	36,600	Not available.
Fishes	19,056	21,000, assuming that 10 percent of fish remain undiscovered; the Amazon and Orinoco Rivers alone may account for 2,000 additional species.
Birds	9,040	Known species probably account for 98 percent of all birds.
Reptiles and Amphibians	8,962	Known species of reptiles, amphibians and
Mammals	4,000	mammals probably constitute over 95 percent of total diversity.
Misc. Chordates[1]	1,273	Not available.
Total	**1,390,992**	10 million species considered a conservative count; if insect estimates are accurate, the total exceeds 30 million.

[1] Animals with a dorsal nerve cord but lacking a bony spine.

Source: Lester R. Brown and others, State of the World 1988, World Watch Institute, Washington DC.

C
FROM WAR TO PEACE

So FAR, discussion of the just society in the modern era has focused on the domestic themes of accountable government and equal economic opportunity for all. A third and equally vital theme concerns relations between nations: the development of international cooperation and arrangements for the peaceful settlement of disputes. Until modern times the world was divided into a myriad of local and regional communities each with its own separate history which touched or overlapped with those of other communities in only a minimum or spasmodic way. Thus a farmer living in Cheshire, England, would have had only occasional contact even with the local city of Chester, still less with London, the capital of his country, and hardly at all with any of the cities of his own continent, Europe, outside of England. In the last two centuries all that has changed greatly; relations between communities both domestically and internationally have become intense and are now a major factor in the day-to-day life of ordinary people.

Several developments have contributed to this change. The process was started by the voyages of discovery undertaken by European sailors from the fifteenth to the nineteenth centuries which brought the main heartland of Europe and Western Asia into contact with the Americas, with South and Central Africa, with Eastern Asia including Japan, and with Australasia and the Pacific islands, all of which had before that time been self-contained civilizations with little or no contact with other areas. By the nineteenth century contact between the five inhabited continents and within each of them were becoming stronger and more regular as a result of the development of faster and cheaper means of transport and communications: the metalled road and the stage coach, the canal and barge, the railway engine, the fast sailship, the steamship and the telegraph. This process has been greatly reinforced in the twentieth century with even more effective systems: the motor car, the jet airliner, the telephone, radio, television, electronics and the communications satellite. As a result, nations have become more unified internally in all aspects of life: political, social and economic, and the clear hard divisions between nations have started to melt and soften. A mundane example is afforded by a quick glance at the origins of goods on display in any grocery store or supermarket in any country around the world. In a very real sense, what happens in one nation of the world, or in one region, may now have an immense impact on the daily life of ordinary people living on the other side of the world in a way that was rarely true before the modern age. This has meant that in order to try and influence and protect conditions of life in their homeland, citizens have increasingly had to turn to cooperation with their neighbours. David Thomson, the English historian, comments: 'Such an effect is the creation of only the last two centuries of modern history: only they constitute truly "world" history.'[1]

This phenomenon has become of critical importance in military affairs where the development of increasingly destructive weapons in the last two hundred years (improved artillery, the machine gun, the aeroplane, gas and chemical weapons, and, above all, the nuclear bomb) have put continuation of the very existence of nations at risk. Thus international cooperation and peaceful conduct of relations between nations is the vital third dimension of the just society. Failure with regard to this would threaten all else that has been achieved. On the other hand, progress with regard to the other two dimensions has increased the chances of success in establishing peace between nations. The three dimensions, accountable government, elimination of poverty within the nations, and peace between nations, are mutually supportive and vital to the just society.

Before the nineteenth century there were two main institutional forces which tended to promote the establishment of peace between peoples. The first was religion. All the great religions taught the brotherhood of man and the benefits of cooperation between peoples. At the peak of their influence and maximum spiritual power each of the great religions has indeed reduced the incidence of warfare and tempered its worst effects, for instance by obtaining agreement to certain laws of war. This is not to deny that religions in decline have often become themselves the cause of some of the most bloody strife in history.

The second institutional force was the large empire. The rulers of Egypt, Babylonia, Persia, China, India and Rome had all imposed peace by force over wide areas. Though many would benefit from such an imposed peace, empires were inevitably vulnerable because subject peoples would always be looking for ways to escape from exploitation and to win their freedom. Furthermore, empires have always had to be on their guard against outsiders anxious to steal

---

[1] *World History*, p. 2.

some of the prosperity the armed peace had brought within their domains.

The best experiences of the great religions and the great empires have created an image in the mind of man of what might be achieved: the dream of a future universal peace. In the West after the decline of the Holy Roman Empire and the Catholic Church at the time of the Reformation[2] there were many thinkers who meditated in various ways on the question of how institutions might come into being which would be conducive to the establishment of peace and universal order. They include Desiderius Erasmus (1466–1536), Hugo Grotius (1583–1645), the Quaker William Penn (1644–1718), John Bellers, also a Quaker (1654–1725), the Abbé Charles de St Pierre (1658–1743), Jean-Jacques Rousseau (1712–1778), Immanuel Kant (1724–1804), and Jeremy Bentham (1748–1831). Some of the basic principles associated with the establishment of world peace originated with these early thinkers. Thus Hugo Grotius in *Three Books on the Laws of War and Peace* (1625) identified three peaceful alternatives to war as ways of settling international disputes: international conferences; arbitration; and the ancient practice of 'lot'. He also suggested that if all these alternatives failed, it would be better to decide an issue on the basis of single combat rather than war – an idea which gives food for thought! William Penn wrote of the need for an international legislature. John Bellers mentioned the need for an international standing army to enforce peace. The Abbé de St Pierre in his *Project for the Perpetual Peace of Europe* (1713) argued for inspection and verification systems with regard to armaments, and for punishment of sovereigns and their ministers if they should wage aggressive war – ideas which were warmly endorsed by Jean-Jacques Rousseau. In his work *On Perpetual Peace* (1795) Immanuel Kant spoke of the need to: (i) declare war illegal; (ii) abolish national armies; and (iii) protect basic human rights. Jeremy Bentham's *Principles of International Law*, written at about the same time, made mention of the need for a World Court and for independence to be given to colonial territories.

It was against this background that the modern age has witnessed efforts to organize international cooperation on a regular basis, in growing recognition that in the long run the only permanent solution would be some form of world federation. Such attempts have twice proved inadequate and mankind has suffered tragic

[2] The era of the international regime of equal and completely sovereign states is generally dated to 1648 and to the Treaty of Westphalia which finally settled the religious wars that had torn Europe apart for more than a hundred years after the Reformation. The Treaty acknowledged that the Pope no longer had the moral authority to be the supreme arbiter amongst Christian nations.

conflict on a world scale. Nevertheless, these efforts have not been a waste of time. Such experiences are of use in developing new methods for the future. The highlights of these experiences are the subject of this section.

As has been the practice earlier in this book, it is perhaps useful to describe these highlights in terms of three broad periods of time: (i) the nineteenth century up until the Great War; (ii) the interwar period; and (iii) the period since the end of the Second World War. Each of these periods coincides with the lifetime of a basic international institution of cooperation: the Congress System, the League of Nations and the United Nations. In the first period, and to a lesser extent in the second, the focus is again largely on Europe and North America as these regions included most of the powerful nations of that time, and it was there that much of the interest in and discussion of ideas on international cooperation took place.

CHAPTER 20

The Congress System
1815–1914

Congresses and the Hague Conferences

IN 1815, after more than twenty years of more or less continuous large-scale warfare in which some four million people were killed, the French bid to make Europe into one empire was finally defeated by the other Great Powers – Austria, Prussia, Russia and Great Britain – acting in unison. There was a strong feeling amongst those in power that after so much bloodshed there should be a special effort to make arrangements which would be conducive to a lasting peace – an emotional response which was to be repeated in 1919 and 1945 after two more horrifying wars. It was envisaged that all the Great Powers of Europe should meet together periodically at international congresses to discuss joint action on issues of mutual concern. There was even some preliminary discussion of the possibility of a European peace-keeping army which would be commanded initially by Wellington. International congresses as such were not new: over the previous two hundred years there had been international congresses at the end of each major war: at Westphalia in 1648, at Utrecht in 1713, and at Paris in 1763. What was new was the idea of meeting regularly to avoid conflict rather than just to reach agreement on a peace settlement after a war had essentially already resolved an issue of power relationships.

After an initial Congress in Vienna in 1814–1815 which settled the terms of peace with France, there were four subsequent Congresses: at Aix-La-Chapelle (1818), Troppau (1820), Laibach (1821) and Verona (1822). The Congress of Aix-La-Chapelle has been identified as 'the first ever held by the Great Powers of Europe to regulate international differences in times of peace'.[1] But there was a problem. The three continental empires, Prussia, Russia and Austria, prodded along by Prince Metternich of Austria, were deeply

[1] C.K. Webster, *The Foreign Policy of Castlereagh*, p. 121.

committed to a policy of maintaining the status quo established after the defeat of France, and in particular to the defence of absolute monarchy. As a sign of their solidarity on the issue, the three powers had formed what was known as the 'Holy Alliance'.[2] Though initially in partial sympathy, Great Britain, even with a Conservative government, could not long support an arrangement which in practice meant the suppression of all movements that were in favour of constitutional government and national self-determination. There was initial agreement (at Aix-La-Chapelle) on preserving peace on the basis of the Vienna Treaty, but the proposal of Czar Alexander (1777–1825) for a universal guarantee of all its features was not accepted by Britain. Furthermore, Britain refused to give support to the continental powers when they took action to crush democratic rebellions in Sicily and Spain which the Holy Alliance declared to be illegal, and later Britain joined the United States in warning the continental powers not to try and interfere with movements of national independence in Latin America. The continental powers retaliated by refusing support for British efforts to suppress the slave trade. Thereafter, the Congress System was a dead letter in the formal sense at least, and there could no longer be any pretence that the Holy Alliance represented the views of all the Great Powers.[3] Though the system, while it lasted, did represent a significant advance over 'the empire' in terms of the evolution of methods of maintaining world peace, it continued to have one of the key flaws of the empire: lack of flexibility in accommodating the interests of all peoples. Peace could not last long when it was based on the interests of a select minority group and was maintained by force alone.

Though the formal Congress System lasted for only a few years, its spirit did not die out; it continued to be significant in international relations in Europe for the rest of the century. Thus the system has been described by Alfred Zimmern, the noted authority on international law, as 'a tradition under which peace between the Great Powers was a habit and a general war unthinkable'.[4] For forty years (1815–1854) there were no major armed conflicts between the Great Powers of Europe. Later, when major conflicts involving several

---

[2] The Holy Alliance was actually a continuation of the wartime alliances which had existed off and on since 1791 when the monarchs of the Great Powers first became alarmed by the French Revolution and its democratic principles.

[3] Small powers counted for little at international conferences; it was not until 1907 that the Great Powers grudgingly accepted that in international law all sovereign states should be treated equally. The original Congress powers were Russia, Austria, Prussia and Great Britain, to which was soon added Restoration France. The system was later expanded to include Piedmont (Italy) in 1856, Japan in 1902, and the United States in 1906.

[4] Zimmern, *The League of Nations and the Rule of Law*, p. 78.

Great Powers did occur, European congresses were called to settle the main issues: in 1856 after the Crimean War, in 1878 to resolve the Eastern question, and in 1884 to agree on a partition of Africa. The last such congress was held in London in 1912–13 in connection with the Balkan Wars. Because these meetings were less committed to the status quo than the original congresses, they had, in principle, the support of liberal opinion as well as conservative. Thus William Gladstone, for instance, spoke frequently of the need for cooperation between nations to achieve goals desired by all:

Common action means common objects; and the only objects for which you can unite together the powers of Europe are objects connected with the common good of them all.[5]

As the nineteenth century progressed there was a growing recognition that the system of *ad hoc* international congresses was not enough and that other measures were needed to reduce the risk of war and to ameliorate the circumstances of war if it should occur. Governments, however, were reluctant to consider measures which might impinge significantly on national sovereignty. The discussions about the additional measures needed revolved around three main subjects. The first was the development of a system of international law, an idea promoted in particular by the International Institute of Law after its formation in 1875. Little consideration was given to the provision of machinery for enforcing international law but it was hoped that the Institute's very existence would exert a moral, and in the long run a practical, pressure which governments would find hard to brush aside. The second subject was how to facilitate the arbitration of disputes between nations. The third was disarmament, which was advocated because it would reduce the temptation for heavily armed nations to make war whilst they had a temporary military advantage, and of course because it would reduce tax burdens.

The first initiative in the evolution of the ideas discussed above came about not from a government, but from an individual, Jean-Henri Dunant (1828–1910), a Swiss citizen who had witnessed the bloody battle of Solferino fought between France and Austria in Northern Italy in 1859. Appalled by the casual lack of care for the wounded in that battle, he gathered together a group of fellow Swiss who in 1863 established a Red Cross Committee to lobby nations to provide better treatment for those wounded in battle, friend and foe alike.[6] The committee was highly successful and the following year

[5] A.J.P. Taylor, *The Trouble Makers*, p. 85.

[6] Dunant was also one of the founders of the Young Men's Christian Association.

an international congress approved a Red Cross Convention.[7]

Thereafter much of the initiative for discussion of ways to reduce the risk of war and its accompanying horrors was to come from Russia.[8] Thus in 1874 Czar Alexander II, already distinguished as the 'Liberator' of the serfs of Russia, called for a second meeting of representatives of the Great Powers to discuss the laws of war. Little came of that proposal, however, and it was not until 1899 that such a meeting came about as a result of the initiative of his grandson, Nicholas II (1868–1918). Nicholas was encouraged to make this proposal by his minister, Sergei De Witte (1849–1915) who was engaged in promoting the economic development of Russia.[9] De Witte believed such development would be hampered by the heavy cost of armaments, specifically at that time a major military programme to replace artillery equipment.[10] Thus the agenda of the meeting held at the Hague in 1899 included disarmament as well as the rules of war and arbitration of disputes between nations.

In the light of history the Hague Conference is of great importance. It has been described as 'the first general international conference concerned with building a world system based on law and order'.[11] Contemporaries sensed that this was a special time: 'People felt in awe at the turn of the century, as if the hand of God was turning a page in human fate.'[12]

The meeting, which lasted from 15 May to 24 June, was attended by 108 representatives of 26 nations, including small and medium nations as well as the Great Powers, and, interestingly, by private bodies and individuals concerned about international relations, such

---

[7] The Convention was subsequently extended by treaties in 1907 to assist all wounded at sea as well as on the battlefield, in 1929 to humanize conditions for prisoners of war, and in 1949 to provide some protection for civilians in time of war. Today the International Red Cross Committee is supported by national committees in just about every country of the world. The organization has expanded its activities to assistance in time of peace, as well as war, and has won the confidence of nearly all countries as a result of its non-political character. In response to local feelings it readily agreed to national organizations in Muslim countries being called the 'Red Crescent', and in Iran the 'Red Lion'. It now has some 170 million members organized in 102 national societies.

[8] It is interesting to note in the context of present-day politics that both Russia and the United States of America have a long record, going back at least to the beginning of the nineteenth century, of initiatives to promote world peace. Perhaps this gives some hope for the future.

[9] De Witte may have been influenced in turn by a six-volume work published in Russia at this time, *The Future of War*. The author, Ivan Bloch, propounded the view that armaments necessarily exhausted a nation.

[10] There were many other motives, not least fear that the growing socialist movement would win credit with the public as the 'peace' party.

[11] Riggs and Plano, *The United Nations*, p. 6.

[12] Tuchman, *The Proud Tower*, p. 267.

as W.T. Stead, the radical British journalist.[13] Of the three main items on the agenda, disarmament proved to be the most intractable. There was no agreement of any sort on this issue mainly because of a German refusal to discuss specific limitations.[14] With regard to the second major issue, the rules of war, there was some limited success in that there was agreement to ban: (i) the firing of projectiles from balloons; (ii) the use of asphyxiating gases; and (iii) the use of expanding bullets. It was with regard to the third main agenda item, the arbitration of disputes between nations, that there was most success. The participants agreed to a Convention on Pacific Settlement of International Disputes which incorporated three approaches to the problem.

The first was to encourage the use of good offices of third party nations for mediation between two countries in dispute. This was a recognition that a war between two nations could no longer be considered a private affair, but was rather a concern for the community of all nations. Signatory nations agreed to the principle of third party mediation, albeit with very heavy qualifications and the use of such 'weasel' expressions as 'when convenient'.

The second approach was to establish the practice of international commissions of inquiry in case of disputes. An early example of the successful use of this technique occurred in 1904 in connection with the so-called 'Dogger Bank' incident in which the Russian Baltic fleet, sailing through the North Sea on its way to the war with Japan, fired on and sank some British fishing vessels which had been mistaken for Japanese torpedo boats. As a result of the inquiry Russia agreed to pay compensation for the error.[15]

The third approach to peaceful settlement of international disputes incorporated in the Hague Convention was to establish an orderly

---

[13] Stead was correspondent for the *Manchester Guardian*. Other prominent individuals attending the conference included Baroness von Suttners, author of *Lay Down Your Arms*; Benjamin Trueblood, secretary of the American Peace Society; Charles Rich, secretary of the French Peace Society; and Mme Selenka, bearer of a peace petition signed by women from eighteen countries.

[14] In view of the dismal track record of disarmament discussions since that time, it is perhaps worth remembering that a successful precedent for international disarmament had been established as early as 1817 in the Rush-Bagehot agreement between the United States and Great Britain to disarm along the US–Canadian border – an agreement which has been maintained ever since.

[15] An attempt to strengthen this approach through a system of bilateral treaties of agreement not to go to war before there had been an international commission of inquiry and a 12-month 'cooling off' period was subsequently made by the US Secretary of State, William Jennings Bryan (1860–1935), but little progress had been made before the whole matter became moot with the outbreak of the Great War.

system for arbitration of disputes. Arbitration between nations has a long history and was used, for example, by the city states of ancient Greece. One of the first examples of its use in modern times was the Jay Treaty between Great Britain and the United States whereby a mixed commission was established to resolve all border disputes left over from the War of Independence – a task which was successfully completed by 1804. During the course of the nineteenth century the technique came into increasing use especially by the constitutional powers, Great Britain, the United States and France.[16] Most of the cases arbitrated during this period concerned minor issues, but there was one major one in particular, the 'Alabama' case of 1863–1870, in which Great Britain (under William Gladstone's leadership) agreed to pay the United States $15 million damages on account of the depredations of a Confederate warship built in England during the American Civil War.[17]

The concrete result of the arbitration approach to international disputes was agreement to establish a Permanent Court of Arbitration at The Hague in the Netherlands. In a sense this institution was misnamed, for it was neither permanent nor truly a Court, and use of it was not compulsory – each nation was at liberty to decide, on an *ad hoc* basis, whether to go to the Court in a dispute, and the Court could only act when both parties had taken such a decision. The Court consisted of a panel of some 150–200 jurists, selected by signatory parties on the basis of four per country, from which disputing parties could choose judges for their case. The Court was provided with a small secretariat (initially a staff of five, all Dutch nationals) to maintain archives, to record proceedings, and to draw up a record of existing international laws and practices. As might well have been expected in these circumstances, the Court's activities as such have not been very significant. It has handled only some two dozen cases in its whole history, and all these have concerned minor issues. Nevertheless, it has some importance because it is a precedent – a first, and therefore significant, step, however small, towards the eventual concept of a World Court with comprehensive and compulsory jurisdiction.

A second Hague Conference was held in 1907. Though still not

[16] Alfred Zimmern quotes the following statistics on numbers of such cases for the period 1794–1914 with respect to the Great Powers:

UK	71	Germany	15
USA	69	Russia	3
France	33	Austria-Hungary	2
Italy	19	Japan	2

[17] The arbitration panel for this case consisted of one representative each from Great Britain, the United States, Brazil, Italy and Switzerland.

truly a world body, this second Conference was broader based than that held in 1899, when attendant states had been nearly all European. This time there were 256 delegates representing 44 states, including a large bloc from Latin America. The agenda was similar to that in 1899, but much of the initiative for the Conference came not from Russia but from the new Liberal government of Great Britain, which was concerned about certain aspects of the Dogger Bank case and, more important, the growing naval armaments race with Germany. With regard to the rules of war there was agreement that unfortified coastal towns and ports should not be subject to naval bombardment and that creditor nations should not take military action against other nations in arrears with debt until such time as the case had been arbitrated and the debtor nations had subsequently refused to abide by the decision of the arbitration court. Once again proposals to limit armaments were rejected, though Great Britain made the gesture of eliminating one of its planned Dreadnought battleships from its 1907 naval building programme.

There were two aspects to the issue of arbitration. The first concerned the specialized matter of naval blockade in wartime. There was an initial agreement concerning naval blockades, signed by 39 nations, whereby an International Prize Court would be established which would arbitrate issues relating to seizure of property on the high seas, specifically that belonging to non-belligerents. The proposal was that the judgements of such a court should be compulsory. This was unprecedented, and prompted the remark that the court would be the 'first truly organized international court in the history of the world'.[18] However, before the treaty could be ratified there was a perceived need to codify naval law with regard to blockade and related matters. Unfortunately, proposals made by the Liberal government in Great Britain were defeated in the House of Lords and the whole pack of cards fell down.

The other aspect of the arbitration issue was an initiative taken by Elihu Root (1845–1937), US Secretary of State in the administration of President Theodore Roosevelt, to strengthen the power of the permanent court by (i) replacing the unwieldy panel of jurists with a small standing group of judges; and (ii) making the use of the Court compulsory in all international disputes. This initiative was not accepted by the majority of nations attending the Conference. There was an agreement, however, to have a third meeting in 1915 (i.e. on an eight-year cycle) but this was never held because of the Great War. After that the Hague series of conferences was essentially replaced by the League of Nations.

[18] Ferenz, A Common Sense Guide to World Peace, p. 10.

The Growth of International Cooperation

In addition to these direct attempts by governments to reduce and limit armed conflict between nations there were six other important developments in this period which contributed to the growth of international cooperation and the evolution of a sense of the community of nations. These were (i) the establishment of technical organizations for improving the coordination of day-to-day international facilities which are essentially non-political; (ii) the creation of intra-regional organizations; (iii) the peace movement; (iv) various initiatives by non-government bodies to work across the borders of sovereign states; (v) popular cross-frontier solidarity; and (vi) free trade.

International technical organizations

Communication was the most important area where nations first felt a need for international cooperation in technical matters. The earliest examples of such cooperation were regional in scope. In 1804 France and her German neighbours formed a Central Rhine Commission to regulate river traffic, to maintain navigational facilities, and to adjudicate disputes concerning its rules. A similar 'European Danube Commission' was established in 1856. The principle of international technical cooperation with a wider scope than a geographic region was first applied in connection with the newly invented telegraph and reorganized national postal services. In 1865 an international convention was held to discuss telegraph services. The outcome was the establishment of the International Telegraph Union (ITU) whose function was to help with the standardization of equipment and international charges.

However, the telegraph was still then very much a tool of government, with military implications, and in the final analysis there was not a desire for real international cooperation. In consequence the ITU was given little power or responsibility.[19] This was to remain the situation for many decades, and it was not until 1934 that the organization was both strengthened and broadened in scope and became the International Telecommunications Union.

Much more success was achieved in the coordination of the mail of letters and parcels, which was seen as more of a general public service. In the middle years of the century there had been major

---

[19] Similar problems were encountered when the wireless was invented. A first international conference to coordinate national wireless policies in 1903 was a complete failure; one held in 1906 had only limited success, such as agreement on transmission of certain types of calls, including, most notably, distress calls from ships at sea.

improvements in the internal mail systems of several countries;[20] but some of the benefits of such improvements were lost when the mail crossed national borders because international mail was subject to excessive charges and was handled in a generally haphazard manner. A meeting in Paris in 1863 at the initiative of the United States came to nothing, but in 1874 a much more successful conference was held in Berne, largely as a result of proposals drawn up by the German representative, Dr Von Stephens, with the strong support of the Swiss. The conference agreed to the establishment of a General Postal Union (renamed the Universal Postal Union in 1878) and to the standardization and simplification of procedures for international mail. The new Union had an original membership of 22 nations; it was directed by a Congress which met every five years and which could make decisions by majority vote. It was given a small secretariat, initially with a staff of nine (mostly Swiss nationals) to monitor and assist with the resolution of technical difficulties. The UPU was a pioneer international institution in several ways: it was the first really successful permanent international body for governments (as distinct from private organizations discussed later), the first with an international secretariat, the first to have decision-making by majority vote, and the first to have compulsory arbitration. The UPU has survived to the present day as the second oldest (after the ITU) of the international agencies of the United Nations system, with a present membership of 168 nations and territories.

A few other small public international bodies were established before 1914, including permanent offices in Brussels and Zanzibar to monitor information on slavery, set up in accord with the General Act of Brussels (1890) as mentioned earlier. Another was the International Institute of Agriculture (a precursor of today's Food and Agricultural Organization) which was created in 1905 at the initiative of King Victor Emmanuel III (1869–1947) of Italy. Its principal function was to gather information on market trends for agricultural produce to help farm communities plan their production. Another international organization of this period was the International Office of Public Health which was established in Paris in 1909 to coordinate quarantine measures and the international standardization of drugs. A very specialized area where cooperation

[20] Sir Roland Hill (1795–1879) had generally simplified the British postal service in 1840 by introducing the standard penny post for ordinary letters to replace a complex system of charges based on distance. In Germany a single mail service had been introduced even before the country was unified and this had been linked with the Austrian system in 1850. Switzerland and the United States had also made improvements to their national systems.

was also attempted was regulation of international trade in sugar and sugar beet. The problem arose from over-production, stimulated in part by subsidies given by governments wanting to be self-sufficient in this commodity which was an important element in nineteenth-century European diets. Conferences were held in 1864 and 1877 with a view to reducing export subsidies and in 1902 a permanent international sugar commission was established in Brussels to co-ordinate such matters. The system eventually collapsed in 1920 when Great Britain, the biggest player in the game, opted for a protectionist policy: Imperial Preference.[21]

Intra-regional organizations

The second subsidiary development which strengthened the idea of the community of nations was the intra-regional organization. The first true regional organization was the Pan-American Union. A first American Congress had been called in 1826 at Panama by Simon Bolivar with a view to setting up a permanent offensive and defensive alliance to protect the nations of America. The United States, the most powerful nation on the continent, failed to attend the conference and the proposed convention was never ratified. Over the next sixty years there were several more American congresses but none of them led to commitments for regional mutual security nor did they win the interest of the United States. They did, however, lead to some success with regard to lesser technical matters of regional interest, such as agreement on various aspects of commercial law within the hemisphere. The first Pan-American Conference (covering the full continent including the north) was held in Washington DC in 1889. The conference agreed on procedures for future arbitration between member countries and established a small secretariat of regional staff. Subsequent conferences have been held regularly every five years or so, and have served to some degree to strengthen the sense of solidarity between nations of the continent, despite the perennial problem of a lack of power balance between the United States and the other nations.

The Peace Movement

The actions taken by governments in the nineteenth century to reduce the risk of war and to begin international cooperation in various fields might have been even slower to develop had it not been for the pressure of a gradually evolving but increasingly vocal

---

[21] Imperial Preference meant that Britain would import sugar from the colonies without tariffs, but sugar imports from foreign nations would be subject to tariffs.

peace movement. This is the third of the subsidiary developments under discussion here. As mentioned earlier (p. 273), a number of thinkers in previous centuries had written of the need to set up international institutions to reduce the incidence of war between nations, but it was not until the nineteenth century that there developed an international peace movement as such.

The earliest identified peace movements were various 'friends of peace' societies in Great Britain and New England (mainly with a Quaker influence) which expressed public revulsion against the carnage of the Napoleonic wars. The first of these groups was the New York Peace Society founded in 1815. For a period in the 1830s Jean-Jacques Sellon, a radical reformer, managed a Société de La Paix from Geneva. The first non-governmental international peace conferences were held in London in 1843, mostly attended by Americans and British, and in Brussels in 1848, attended by a rather wider range of participants. The growing number of wars and the increasing power of weapons in the last third of the nineteenth century prompted a greater interest in peace. In 1867 the first permanent international peace organizations were established: 'La Ligue Internationale et Permanent de la Paix', founded in Paris by the French lawyer and economist, Fréderic Passy (1822–1912); and the more radical 'Ligue Internationale de la Paix et de la Liberté' which had its base in Geneva. The latter organization, which counted among its members such persons as the radical French writer Victor Hugo (1802–1885) and the Italian patriot Giuseppe Garibaldi, held the view that real peace could only be obtained if peoples were given national self-determination, if there was universal application of democracy, if public education was made available to the masses, and if basic human rights were observed by all governments. These views brought into the open a polarization of the peace movement between the pacifist, pure and simple, and those who believed peace had to be based on justice and who in certain circumstances might favour a 'just' war rather than peace.

In the next few years several new non-governmental organizations were established which stressed the importance of international law and constitutional government in the peace process: in 1874 the International Institute of Law (as noted earlier) founded by a Belgian journalist, Gustave Rolin Jacquemyns; in 1885 the International Arbitration League, founded by the British Trade Unionist and MP, William Cremer (1828–1908); in 1888 'La Paix par le Droit', an organization of Parisian students; and in 1889 the International Parliamentary Union, founded largely on the basis of a partnership between Frederic Passy and William Cremer. Another significant organization was the Bureau International de la Paix which was set up in Berne in 1891 at the initiative of Frederick Bajer, a Danish MP and journalist, to follow up on the work of an International Peace Congress held in 1889. The Bureau was the first permanent international centre to coordinate worldwide peace activities, to provide information on peace issues and to act as a clearing house for ideas about peace. It was described as 'the living soul of the great body of peacemakers all over the world'. The Bureau was fortunate to have as directors in the years before the First World War two distinguished Swiss, Elie Ducammon (1833–1906) and Charles Albert Gobat (? – 1914), whose work gave the organization the strength and prestige that have helped it to survive into the present day. The peace movement was given much publicity by several writers, of whom perhaps the most well-known were the Austrian Baroness, Bertha von Suttner (1843–1914); an American social reformer, Jane Addams (1860–1935); and the Englishman, Norman Angell (1874–1967). The first of these published in 1889 *Lay Down Your Arms*, an appeal to human reason on the issue of international relations. This book was considered one of the most influential of the nineteenth century, being compared by Leo Tolstoy, for example, with *Uncle Tom's Cabin*. Jane Addams, a supporter of President Theodore Roosevelt, wrote *New Ideas of Peace*, published in 1907 to coincide with the Second Hague Conference.[22] Norman Angell was the author of *The Great Illusion* (1910), which pointed out that in modern conditions war pays neither the victor nor the vanquished, an assertion which was supported with reviews of the end results of several recent wars including the Franco-Prussian War of 1870–71.

As a result of all this activity, the peace movement managed to obtain a popular hearing and quite a lot of support, and by the early years of the twentieth century there were branches and societies in support of peace in most countries in Europe and North America, with outposts in Latin America, Australia and Japan.

Before finishing this brief review of the peace movement prior to the Great War, mention should be made of the Nobel organization, founded in 1901 in accordance with the will of the Swedish millionaire inventor of dynamite and other explosive devices, Alfred Bernard Nobel (1833–1896). The main function of the organization was to award annual prizes for the world's greatest achievements in the arts and sciences. The most significant of these prizes, in terms of encouraging a sense of world unity, was the one awarded to the

---

[22] Jane Addams was active in support of campaigns to help the poor, and to promote the civil rights of blacks and women. She was later chairman of both the International Congress of Women and the Women's International League of Peace and Freedom.

person or organization deemed to have made the greatest contribution to world peace. The very first peace prize (1901) was awarded to Jean-Henri Dunant, founder of the Red Cross; since then the honour has been given to that organization no less than three times: in 1917, 1944, and 1963. A remarkable number of the early recipients of the prize were individuals and organizations associated with the peace movement who have been mentioned above: 1901, Frederic Passy; 1902, Elie Ducammon and Charles Albert Gobat; 1903, William Cremer; 1905, Bertha von Suttner; 1908, Frederick Bajer; 1910, the Bureau International de la Paix; and 1933, Norman Angell. A list of all the Nobel Prize winners up to 1985 is shown in Appendix 3.

Non-governmental International Organizations

A multitude of other non-governmental international organizations in the nineteenth century were strengthening the sense of world community. Alfred Zimmern quotes a figure of 257 non-governmental international conferences being held by such organizations between 1864 and 1914.[23] Three of the most significant of these were the International Workers' Congress (founded in 1864), the International Chamber of Commerce (1869), and the International Cooperative Alliance (1895). An exceptional indirect contribution to the cause of peace was made by Ludovic Zamenhof (1859–1917), who, from his own experience as a Jew living in Poland near the frontier with Russia, had seen how language barriers can exacerbate national and racial antagonisms. In response he devised a new international language, Esperanto (meaning a person who hopes), which is much easier to learn than national languages. The new language, which was first publicised in 1889, soon began to win favour and in 1905 a committee of supporters was formed, which in 1908 became an Esperanto association, with headquarters in Rotterdam. In the next few decades many Universal Esperanto Congresses were held and millions drawn from over eighty countries learnt this potential world language.

Popular Cross-frontier Solidarity

The growth of a world system of politics and economics in the nineteenth century and a sense of solidarity with fellow human beings in other countries was not confined to formal organizations; it was often experienced by the masses of the people. This phenomenon can perhaps be linked to teachings of the brotherhood of man coming from the great religions. One of the most impressive and effective

23 The League of Nations and the Rule of Law, p. 36.

examples was, of course, the campaign for the abolition of the slave trade and then of slavery itself, discussed earlier. Another was the growing sympathy, especially in the liberal constitutional countries, with the aspirations of peoples in other lands (especially in Europe and the Americas) for national self-determination. Revolutionary France, for instance, felt a certain solidarity with the Italians, Germans and Poles, subject peoples of the three autocratic empires of Central and Eastern Europe, although this feeling became somewhat subdued when Napoleon I came to power and established his Empire on the backs of many who were not French. One of the most dramatic movements to assist in the independence of another people was that waged on behalf of the Greeks in the 1820s, particularly by members of the British upper and middle classes who had been educated to appreciate the glories of Ancient Greece. An outstanding figure in their cause was the English romantic poet Lord Byron (1788–1824), who ultimately gave his life for it. At the same time sympathy was being given (though perhaps with more obviously self-interested motives) to those struggling for independence in Latin America. During the revolutions of 1848 there was much fellow-feeling in England for Hungarians in their fight for freedom from the Austrian Empire. This was shown by the popular reception in London of Louis Kossuth and the wild demonstrations against the Austrian General Haynau during his visit to London because of his brutal suppression of the Hungarian freedom fighters. The next decade saw popular support in both England and France for the Italian patriots, particularly Giuseppe Garibaldi and Giuseppe Mazzini in their fight to unite Italy and free it from the domination of the Hapsburgs. In the 1860s initial assistance to the US Confederates by the British government and various business interests was drowned by a groundswell of popular support for the North, because it was perceived to be fighting for the abolition of slavery. In the seventies, one of the most emotional events of British politics over the whole century was the campaign led by William Gladstone in opposition to Benjamin Disraeli's *real-politik* policy of support for the Ottoman Empire in its struggle with the Russians, because the Turkish rulers had massacred some 12,000 Bulgarians. At the end of the century there was widespread reaction both in Great Britain and on the European continent against the Boer War and the British government's effort to stifle Boer independence – an issue that became confusing because of the obnoxious behaviour of the Boers in relation to the black peoples of southern Africa.

Another manifestation of cross-frontier goodwill was an under-lying wish on the part of the liberal and radical wing of the political spectrum for some sort of grand alliance of democratic countries. The idea was that such an alliance should somehow exert its power in the interest of world law and order based on the freedom of all peoples. One of the earliest advocates of this point of view was Thomas Paine, who at the beginning of the nineteenth century was pressing for an alliance of the three great revolutionary powers: England, the United States and France. Thomas Paine was also a strong supporter of the view, common amongst radicals in the nineteenth century, that the main problem of mankind is the sovereign state, whose interest often does not coincide with the interest of the ordinary men and women who are its citizens.

Man is not the enemy of man, but through the medium of a false government.[24]

Variations on the theme of a grand alliance of liberal powers were constantly debated by the left throughout the century. One of the difficulties, of course, was defining 'liberal' in this context, and views tended to change with circumstances. Thus there were those at the end of the century who objected to the 'balance of power' alliance between the Western constitutional powers France and England with that most reactionary of powers Czarist Russia, against what were considered to be the relatively advanced empires of Central Europe, Germany and Austro-Hungary, which by that time had functioning national parliaments, universal suffrage, and large radical and socialist parties. The issue had been even more complicated at the time of the Bulgarian atrocities when liberals had to make a choice between the blood-thirsty Ottoman on the one hand and Czarist Russia on the other. The latter at least had the merit of supporting the freedom of the Slav peoples of the Balkans.

Another variation on the theme of international solidarity on the basis of political ideology was the socialist belief in the natural unity of the world's industrial workers against the exploiting capitalist, a view epitomized in the famous phrase of Karl Marx:

Workers of the world unite; you have only your chains to lose.[25]

This belief was given some form by the Socialist International (1864) – the International Workers' Congress referred to earlier.[26] Unfor-

[24] *Rights of Man*, p. 78. There is a clear link here to some of the ideas of the French Enlightenment.

[25] *Communist Manifesto* (1848).

[26] The First International died in 1874 as a result of internal disputes in which Karl Marx himself played a major role. A 'Second' International was formed in 1889 but this too collapsed in 1914 with the failure of the movement to stop the Great War. After World War I the International split in two: the Third International representing the communist wing, and the Fourth International representing the non-communist socialists.

tunately, this sense of solidarity did not prove strong enough to resist the power of nationalism in time of crisis. In 1914 the German Social Democratic Party, then the most powerful socialist party in the world, was the first to break ranks and vote for the government's military plans instead of supporting a nation-wide general strike in conjunction with national general strikes in other countries which together might have paralysed the war preparations of all the belligerent governments.[27]

The Free Trade Movement

One more powerful force in the nineteenth century made an important contribution to the breaking down of barriers between states and thereby helped on the process of 'one world' thinking. This was the Free Trade movement, whose strongest base was in England with the initial lead being taken largely by the cotton manufacturers of Manchester. The first moves in England towards free trade had been taken as early as 1784 by the government of William Pitt the Younger (1759–1806), but the main thrust did not come until after the end of the French wars. Beginning with measures taken in 1823 by William Huskinson (1770–1830), then President of the Board of Trade, to reduce import duties on a range of items including silk and wool, the climax came in the 1840s when tariffs were lowered on 750 articles (1843) and the Corn Laws were abolished (1846), together with the Navigation Laws (1849). The most controversial item in this programme was the abolition of the Corn Laws, which for many years had protected the British farmer against foreign competition (at least that was the intent). Opponents of the Corn Laws argued with some force that the Laws increased the price of bread and thereby hurt the poor, and that at the same time they made it necessary for the manufacturers to pay higher wages and therefore harmed their competitive position in the world market. A series of bad harvests at the beginning of the 1840s (known as the 'hungry forties'), which were responsible for the great famine in Ireland, so pushed up the price of corn that the majority came to see the fears of the farmer about foreign competition as a relatively minor matter. The Free Trade programme in Britain was further refined in the next twenty years and included a special bilateral agreement with France (1860) to reduce mutual trade barriers. By 1874 all that remained of the old protective system were a few 'revenue' duties on such items as beer, spirits and tobacco. The

---

[27] To be fair to the German Social Democrats, it should be added that their fear was of an invasion by the Czar with his huge armies of illiterate peasants, who were believed to be unfamiliar with the concept of the solidarity of the working peoples of the world.

British example was followed to some extent on the continent of Europe, especially in Germany where tariffs were progressively reduced between states under the Zollverein agreements.

The Free Trade movement had its roots in the writing of Adam Smith (1723–1790) who had criticised the prevailing mercantilist practices of the eighteenth century. These emphasised the manipulation of trade barriers to promote exports, limit imports, and build up a large bullion reserve (which mercantilists believed to be the true indication of a state's economic power). Adam Smith answered that just as individuals within a country prospered when they specialised in tasks at which they were the most efficient, so too did each state. Accordingly, restraints on international trade should be removed so that the peoples of each nation would be free, for the benefit of all, to buy the goods they needed at the cheapest price available on the open world market, and to sell the goods and services they had produced at the highest price they could obtain. Though the English cotton manufacturers and their supporters clearly saw their own self-interest in free trade, and the policy was in accordance with the view of the new middle classes that government activity should be reduced to a minimum, it was also true that there was a general ethical dimension to the creed. This was a strong conviction that free trade was genuinely in the interest of all countries, not just of England. Thus Richard Cobden (1804–1865), one of the great leaders of the movement, put it as follows:

The progress of freedom depends more upon the maintenance of peace, the spread of commerce and the diffusion of education, than upon the labours of cabinets and foreign affairs.[28]

The Free Trade movement reached its peak in the 1870s. Thereafter there was a growing demand in nearly every country for protection (i) for farmers facing increasing competition from a flood of cheap food from the United States after the Civil War, and from other new lands in Australia and South America; and (ii) for fledgling industries (especially those perceived to be important for military reasons) against the competition of manufactured exports from Britain. One of the most extreme of the protectionist countries was the United States. Alone among the Great Powers, Britain maintained the principle of free trade until the Great War despite the rapid decline of British farming in the last quarter of the century and a strong movement in favour of Empire Free Trade or Imperial Preference (i.e. with trade barriers against the rest of the world).[29]

[28] Don Pacifico Debate, 1850. See A.J.P. Taylor, The Trouble Makers, p. 53.

[29] Several small nations with economies dependent on overseas trade followed the British example, e.g. Belgium, Denmark, the Netherlands, and Switzerland.

Though there is general agreement that free trade has stimulated international commerce and has thereby contributed to an overall rise in the standard of living, there have also been some very harsh consequences for certain occupations, provinces, and countries which have been buffeted by changes in technology and swings in trade patterns. For peoples so affected it could hardly be argued that free trade has brought them any nearer to the 'just society'. It seems clear that the full benefits of free trade will only be gained when there is a world government with the resources and authority to give transitional assistance to peoples adversely affected, so that the cost of adjustment can be borne by all, not just the unfortunate ones who are initially thrown out of work.

CHAPTER 21

The Forces for War

THESE nineteenth-century trends towards a greater sense of the brotherhood of man, international cooperation and peaceful settlement of disputes between states – the Congress system, the Hague Conventions, international technical organizations, regional organizations, peace movements, international non-governmental bodies, international solidarity of progressive forces, and free trade – were paralleled by some very powerful forces which drove society in the opposite direction. The following paragraphs touch briefly on three of the most significant of these: nationalism, imperialism, and militarism.

Nationalism

Pride of patriots in their national culture and an associated yearning for self-determination can both be reconciled with the general welfare of mankind. But patriotism can be degraded, if there is not care and sensitivity, into a negative force of excessive nationalism involving contempt, hatred and violence against peoples of other cultures. This was to happen frequently in nineteenth-century Europe as the desire for national self-determination gathered force.

The worst clashes came where peoples of different nations were living in mixed societies and it was therefore not practical to draw boundaries embracing peoples of only one nation or culture. In an ideal and mature situation such a mix would be seen as of mutual benefit, because it would allow all peoples to broaden their cultural experience of the arts and literature, philosophy, dress, food and entertainment. In practice, national differences often coincided with class and occupation divisions; these exacerbated cultural distinctions. In several Eastern European areas there were strong minorities of Germans and Jews in the cities, surrounded by a sea of Slav peoples in the countryside; in Hungary the landowners were usually Magyars (Hungarian) while the peasants were drawn from a variety of Slav backgrounds. In other areas national differences would be sharpened by differences of religion: Muslim, Catholic, Protestant,

Orthodox. A typical quarrel would be about the official language of government, because the chosen language would obviously give great advantage to those for whom it was the mother tongue.

The frequent result of these divisions was that when a nation threw off its chains and achieved independence, almost its first action would be to oppress in its turn the minorities in its territory. The Balkans and neighbouring areas were certainly one of the most deplorable examples of this phenomenon, and it is hardly surprising that in the first years of the twentieth century this region was to be the tinder-box of Europe.

The evils of nationalism were by no means confined to Eastern Europe. Immensely dangerous, too, was its contribution to the relationship between France and Germany. In the name of nationalism Alsace-Lorraine (with a mixed French–German population) was taken from France for the New German Empire after its victory in the war of 1870. This action intensified the feeling of bitterness and fear between the French and German peoples, sowing the seeds of two more dreadful wars before there was a final reconciliation of exhaustion.

Nationalism, with its associated emotions of fear and cultural prejudice, was easy for demagogues to promote amongst populations with little education, and was to become the most powerful of the political ideas which at the critical point could overwhelm progressive ideas conducive to peace and international solidarity. This was to happen in the German Reichstag in 1914. Many of the leaders of the nineteenth century threw away the opportunity to lead their people to a larger vision of the future, and instead used their influence to promote national privilege and prejudice. They have a lot to answer for at the bar of history.

Imperialism

The second of the major trends in international relations mitigating against the development of a just society was imperialism. Empires have existed, of course, since the beginning of history. Some brought peace to large areas for long periods of time, though often at the cost of the exploitation of subject peoples and the crushing of local cultures. There were, however, several features of nineteenth-century imperialism which made it quite distinctive from past experience and more negative in its impact.

The first of these was its worldwide scope, involving to a greater or lesser extent the subjugation of nearly all the peoples of the world outside Europe and the Americas.[1] The British took pride in the fact

[1] Japan being the most important exception. Some countries such as China remained nominally independent, but in practice they too were subject to the colonial powers.

that their Empire ringed the world and described it as the Empire 'on which the sun never set'. It was in fact the largest, encompassing about one quarter of the world's population.

Strangely enough, the British Empire had happened almost by accident. It began in the sixteenth century with explorers searching for trade in other lands, particularly for goods which were not available at home such as silks, precious gems and spices. Trading posts were established where sources were found. To protect their trading posts the British felt compelled to meddle in local politics. One thing led to another, and the result was often warfare, overlordship and straightforward occupation (as in India). Another driving force was the desire to provide for surplus population at home by settling people on farmlands in the new territories. These were usually stolen from the sparsely-spread indigenous peoples who were not equipped with the European's modern technology of war (as in the Americas, Australia and Africa). Widely scattered colonies and trading posts led in turn to the need for additional military settlements to protect them: perhaps buffer states (as with the North-West frontier of India) or islands around the world which lay on strategic lines of communication and could be used as ports and fortresses for the protecting navy. Similar motivations were behind the great overseas empires of the other European nations – France, Spain, the Netherlands, Germany and others. Only Russia seemed to be different: virtually all of its Empire was contiguous to the Russian heartland and its creation involved additional motivation such as security barriers and access to ice-free ports.

The second distinguishing feature of nineteenth-century imperialism was the practice of using the colonies as markets for the industrial goods of the mother country and of forcing them to pay with agricultural produce and other raw materials at low prices. For a time there were quite a few British, at least, who questioned the assumption that foreign trade required the maintenance of an expensive empire. They were quite happy to see the American colonies take their independence and for self-government to be given to other colonies such as Canada. But as the century progressed, competition in selling industrial products became increasingly fierce and the possession of colonial markets where such products could be sold on advantageous terms became more and more attractive. In consequence there was another round of empire-building, notably in Africa, China, South East Asia and the Pacific. The possibility of a major clash in the rush to colonize Africa was reduced by a Congress in Berlin in 1884 when the main details of the division of the 'pie' were agreed. To make the most of the arrangement, the colonial powers discouraged industrial development in the colonies in favour of agricultural growth and the development in the colonies in favour of agricultural growth and the development of mining. This policy of exploitation made the colonies dependent on the West to such an extent that even today, when the former colonies are now formally independent nations, they are still to a large degree economically dependent on the former imperial powers.

The third distinctive feature of imperialism in the nineteenth century was racism. All the main colonial states were European or North American:[2] England, France, Spain, Portugal, the Netherlands, Belgium, Russia, Germany, Italy and the United States. In the early days of colonialism the Europeans had treated local people with respect, both those whose civilizations had previously been more advanced than the European (e.g. India) and those whose societies were more simple (e.g. the Indians of North America in the seventeenth century). But by the nineteenth century the Europeans had come to see themselves as a separate and superior race destined to rule the world (the white man's burden), partly because of their obvious military, administrative, and commercial strength, and partly because of the fashionable philosophy of social Darwinism which concluded that some races were inherently superior to others. This sense of racial superiority was reinforced by the disdain of Christian missionaries for the native religions of the colonies. Nearly all these native religions had fallen into decay and were rife with superstition and meaningless ritual; but this was true to a great extent of Christianity too. The idea of racial superiority justified the exclusion of native peoples from holding office at important levels of administration in their own countries, and their social ostracization. Terrible as was the economic exploitation of colonial peoples in many lands, far more disastrous was the blow given to the collective self-respect of an entire people when they were continually told by the whites that their culture was worthless. Loss of self-esteem led whole peoples into alcoholism and self-destruction. There is some irony in the fact that at a time when Europeans were busy encouraging the idea of national self-determination in their own continent they were suppressing the same spirit in the rest of the world.

Of course, imperialism had a positive side too. The great empires, notably that of Great Britain, did bring peace (Pax Britannica) and law and order to large areas of the world. Good administration and a general respect for constitutional procedures[3] (the latter less universal

[2] Except for Japan, which had joined the ranks of the imperial powers by the end of the century.

[3] Not, however, that the colonial powers necessarily had respect for constitutional states if to do so would require some self-restraint. Russia and Great Britain had no scruples about dividing up Persia into zones of influence even after the autocratic Shah had been overthrown and a constituent assembly properly elected in 1909.

than the former) were brought to places where previously there had been decadent and corrupt autocratic regimes or near anarchy. The British navy played a major role in the suppression of the slave trade and piracy. Railways, roads, irrigation schemes, hospitals, schools, and much else undoubtedly brought benefits to the colonies, although it should be added that such largesse was by no means universal. Impressive as were these achievements of the colonial powers, there seems little question that for the recipients the price was far too high and that in the balance colonialism in the nineteenth century was a most divisive experience for humanity.

Militarism

By the eighteenth century the European powers had refined warfare to a point where it was conducted almost like a chess game. Relatively small armies of mostly professional soldiers manœuvred according to accepted rituals that limited the impact of war on ordinary people, even for those unfortunate enough to be in the direct paths of opposing armies. A dramatic change in the rules occurred when the French revolutionary government called up the people in a *levée en masse* to repulse the armies of the other Great Powers of Europe which had been sent to crush the Revolution. The age of the mass army had arrived.

From that point on the great continental Powers felt obliged to maintain large armies of conscripts numbering up to a million or more, even in peace time.[4] In addition, when conscripts had completed their period of service with the colours they were obliged to be enrolled in the reserves for many years and to be ready for mobilization in times of crisis – a mobilization which would increase the size of the army manyfold. In other words, nearly all men in society were involved with the army for a large part of their lives.

To keep up enthusiasm there was a culture of glorification of things military. Officers and men alike were given splendid uniforms of great variety, not very practical for the battlefield but ideal for attracting the admiration of womenfolk at social functions. Such fashions were universal, even in England and in small countries. Military brass bands played in the parks and even small children were dressed up in naval uniform. Religion made a contribution by cluttering up churches with memorials to the military prowess of the nation. The point was reached where many, at all levels of society, could envisage war as an exciting and spiritually uplifting experi-

---

[4] Great Britain, with the English Channel to protect, preferred to spend its money on maintaining the largest navy in the world.

ence, by sharp contrast with the drabness of everyday life in peacetime, especially in the smoke-filled industrial city. War meant glory and should be quick and easy – the latter idea strengthened by nationalist prejudices which encouraged the view that others were inferior.

The leader of the pack was Prussia, a name which by the nineteenth century had become almost synonymous with military power. It was associated with the Teutonic knights of the Middle Ages who had conquered the Slav peoples to the East, with Frederick the Great and his disciplined Pomeranian grenadiers, and with the reformed army of Roon and Scharnhorst which had been organized after defeat by Napoleon. Prussia indeed epitomized the military spirit with its goose-step parades and Bismarck's talk of 'blood and iron'. The Second German Empire, with Prussia at its centre, was not only the state with the most exaggerated military spirit but also – as already noted – the one where women were totally subjugated in public life. Nowhere could their influence be detected. No wonder Princess Victoria, wife of the Crown Prince and daughter of Queen Victoria, felt suffocated in Berlin as compared with London.

Austro-Hungary and Russia were not far behind Germany in their militarism, if only because their armies were vital not only to the protection of their own border but to the deterrence of popular uprisings at home. Even in those Great Powers which were civilian and constitutional – England and France – the popular spirit was frequently affected by militarism, as indicated by the expressions 'chauvinism' and 'jingoism'.[5]

There were, of course, counter views. Thus Switzerland, tired of centuries of warfare and soldiering, had actually incorporated the principle of neutrality into its constitution after restoration of independence in 1815.[6] In England amongst the educated there was scepticism about standing armies, which had once been associated with oppressive government. There were always dissenters to prick the balloon of military bombast; as, for instance, when Charles James Fox (1749–1806) responded to the call of William Pitt the Younger for a renewal of the war with France in 1803:

When I hear all these fine and eloquent philosophies, I cannot help

---

[5] The latter phrase derived from the music-hall song popular at the time of a crisis with Russia in 1877–1878:

We don't want to fight, yet by jingo if we do,
We've got the ships, we've got the men, we've got the money too!

[6] Instead of a large standing army Switzerland opted for a well-trained citizen army in reserve (including the daring practice of letting citizens keep their army rifles at home) which can be called up quickly in a national emergency. Many today are attracted to this Swiss model army because it provides good security without being a threat to other nations.

recollecting what fruits such speeches have generally produced, and dreading the devastation and carnage which usually attend them.[7]

Such protests were continually made by peace movements which (as noted earlier) had emerged in many countries by the beginning of the twentieth century. Yet these protestors were all very much in the minority, lonely voices drowned by brass bands, parades, the clatter of horses' hooves, and marching boots.

In the end the positive gains of the nineteenth century in the direction of international cooperation and the peaceful settlement of disputes between nations were overwhelmed, at least temporarily, by these negative forces. The period came to an end with the greatest war the world had ever witnessed up to that time. The chain of events leading to the Great War in 1914 can be traced as far back as the break-up of the formal Congress system in the 1820s. After that event there was always the possibility of war involving two or three of the Great Powers: in 1854–1856 with England and France against Russia, in 1859 with France against Austria, in 1866 with Prussia against Austria, and in 1870–1871 with Prussia against France. But so long as the three great empires of Central and Eastern Europe remained together in their Holy Alliance (which they did until 1890 despite some dithering at times, notably in 1854 and 1866) the risk of a major conflagration was minimized. Under Bismarck's leadership Germany made a great effort to maintain this alliance so that France, if contemplating revenge after the Franco–Prussian war and the loss of Alsace-Lorraine, would be isolated on the continent and therefore unlikely to risk another war with Germany.

But with Bismarck's departure from office in 1890 the alliance began to fall apart once and for all. Austro-Hungary felt immensely threatened by Russia's support for Slav peoples seeking independence in the Balkans and neighbouring areas, and was ultimately ready to risk all to resist that threat. Simultaneously, Germany felt a long-term threat from Russia with its vast population, especially after she began to industrialize seriously in the 1890s. Within a short time these two Central Powers froze Russia out of the alliance. The result was predictable. A new alliance between France and Russia was formed which threatened Germany on two fronts; that alliance was later joined by England, more alarmed by German naval ambitions and industrial competition than by the old threat of a Russian advance on Constantinople and the lifeline to India.

The new alliances created two hostile blocs of powers in Europe of about equal strength, in place of a Congress of all (or most of) the

7 *Speeches*, vol. VI, p. 527.

Great Powers. This situation was made more dangerous by the prevailing militaristic climate, because any international crisis was likely to be intensified by demands of the military leaders that they be allowed to call up the reserves in order to forestall an overwhelming attack by an enemy quicker off the mark with mobilization. An additional twist was given by the German military leadership's paranoid fear of a war on two fronts. Their solution was to destroy the enemy on one front as quickly as possible so that they could then concentrate all their forces on the other. Fearing that, like Napoleon, they would be bogged down in the vast expanses of Russia if they were to attack that country first, their conclusion was that the first strike must be against France. However, since France had built up a line of defensive fortification along her frontier with Germany after the Franco-German War of 1870–1871, the only way to obtain a quick victory would be to march through Belgium in a vast wheeling movement. The consequence of such a strategy would be to confirm all Britain's fears of Germany, because Belgium was the best place from which to launch an invasion of England from the continent. In short, by the beginning of the twentieth century Europe had become like a powder keg. It only needed a spark to set it off.

In July 1914 the spark was struck. Serb nationalists assassinated Archduke Ferdinand, heir to the Austro-Hungarian throne, in Sarajevo, a provincial city of the Hapsburg Empire. Austro-Hungary issued a harsh ultimatum to Serbia demanding compensation. British offers of mediation under the Hague system were brushed aside. Russia, feeling obliged to defend a fellow Slav nation, began to make preparations for mobilization. Germany, in support of its ally, issued an ultimatum to Russia demanding an end to mobilization, and then without waiting for a reply decided to attack France in the hope of a knockout blow before Russia was ready to give assistance. The invasion of Belgium prompted an ultimatum to Germany from England. The Great War had begun. Before it ended, ten million soldiers would be killed and another ten million civilians would have died from the side effects of the war.[8]

---

[8] Including the great influenza epidemic of 1918–1919. The Great War resulted in more deaths than any war in history to that date, though not as many as the 40 million attributed to the depredations of Genghis Khan in the thirteenth century. The worst modern war in Europe prior to 1914 was the Thirty Years which ended in 1648, and during which some eight million people are estimated to have lost their lives.

CHAPTER 22

The League of Nations
1918–1939

The First World War

ONCE the war had started it acquired a momentum which swept all before it. Germany failed to inflict a decisive defeat on France in 1914 and was then faced with the prospect, long dreaded, of an extended and probably unwinnable war on two fronts. On the other hand, Allied counterstrokes in 1915 and 1916 also failed miserably and at great cost. Both sides by then having suffered huge losses were faced with an impasse, and the rational policy in terms of 'real politik' would have been to negotiate a ceasefire. But governments on both sides felt that the sacrifice already made of millions killed and wounded as a result of their policies could only be justified if the final result was a victory – and so they carried on. The ultimate degradation of this policy was its reduction to a strategy of bleeding the other side white: a war of attrition to see which side would absorb the greater loss. This theory reached a peak with the dreadful battle of Verdun in 1916 when over a million soldiers died in the most appalling conditions.

Though the majority were hypnotised by the horror of it all and were unable to take action to bring the madness to an end, there were nevertheless some individuals and groups here and there who protested and began to struggle for peace. Though the Socialist International had failed in 1914, there were soon courageous attempts by socialists to counter war hysteria. Meetings were held in Copenhagen (January 1915) by socialists from neutral countries, in London (February 1915) by socialists from Allied countries, and in Vienna (April 1915) by socialists from the Central Powers. Greater initiative was taken by socialists further to the left who managed to organize a meeting at Zimmerwald in Switzerland in September 1915 with representatives drawn from states on both sides. The theme of this meeting was the need for an immediate peace based on the principle of no annexations and no indemnities, i.e. essentially the *status quo ante bellum*. Unfortunately, this meeting and a subsequent one held in April 1916 were undermined by attempts on the part of Bolshevik participants to exploit the war for their own revolutionary ends.

More promising were the efforts of President Woodrow Wilson of the United States to mediate from a position of neutrality. In 1916 his representative, Colonel House, was sent to Europe to talk to both sides. Bethman Hollweg (1856–1921), the German Chancellor, was interested enough in these talks to fight off the demands of the German High Command for an all-out campaign of unrestricted submarine warfare which, if implemented, would clearly turn the United States against Germany.[1] To obtain a basis for serious negotiation, President Wilson proposed in December 1916 that each side state explicitly what were its war aims, and when this failed to win response he proposed a 'peace without victory'. This effort was brought to naught by a German declaration at the end of January 1917 that it intended after all to pursue a policy of unrestricted submarine warfare, and by the publication in March 1917 of the Zimmerman telegram which showed that Germany and Mexico were discussing the possibility of joint military action against the United States. The next month the United States came into the war on the side of the Allies.

Throughout 1917 there were several other attempts to get the peace process started. In March, Charles I (1887–1922), who had just succeeded Franz Joseph (1830–1916) as Emperor of Austro-Hungary, made secret soundings to the Allies about the possibility of a separate peace, but this petered out in the face of harsh demands by Italy, one of the Allies since 1915. In July there was a remarkable 'peace resolution' approved by the German Reichstag at the initiative of the socialists. Based on the concept of 'no territorial annexations', the resolution was taken over by the government which modified it so much that there was no chance that it would be acceptable to the Allies. A month later an initiative of the Pope for peace on the basis of no territorial annexations was rebuffed by France and Britain, as was a similar proposal from Lord Lansdowne (1845–1827), a former Conservative Foreign Secretary, made in a letter to *The Times* in November 1917.

---

[1] Though there was some sympathy for France and Britain in the US, there was a genuine reluctance to get involved in old-world disputes so long as they did not threaten US interests. There was, too, some resentment of the British naval blockade of Germany which affected US trade and shipping. Another factor was the substantial number of Germans in the US population. Finally, the presence of Czarist Russia on the Allied side weakened any idea that the Allies represented democracy fighting against autocracy.

At the end of 1917 the Bolsheviks, who had seized power in Russia, decided to make peace with the Central Powers regardless of cost, both for ideological reasons (they saw the war as a quarrel between the ruling classes of Europe) and because as a practical matter the Russian army had collapsed[2] and the people were no longer willing to fight. Peace with Russia gave new hope to the German High Command that they might be able to win the war after all, if they could concentrate their forces in the West and organize a massive blow before the United States had transported a large number of its soldiers across the Atlantic. For a time in the summer of 1918 it seemed that the Germans would win the gamble. Then suddenly the effort began to crumble. More and more Americans began to arrive, and morale in Austro-Hungary and Germany amongst both civilians and soldiers, all of whom had been subject to immense stress for four years, began to falter. The German High Command, seeing no choice, encouraged the government to open negotiations with the Allies, although in a rather cowardly fashion it refused to be involved itself, thus hoping to save face.

The Fourteen Points

The Germans wanted to make President Wilson's Fourteen Points the basis for negotiations. First published in January 1918, the Fourteen Points were much wider than previous peace proposals insofar as they went beyond the immediate issue of stopping the war and provided some general principles for the formalising of the lasting peace Wilson hoped would emerge. They had two main themes. First, in future the basis of the states of the world should be national self-determination: all nations should ultimately be given independence if that was their wish (points 6–13). In practice this theme would be especially costly to the Central Powers because among other things it would mean the break-up of the Austro-Hungarian and Ottoman Empires into their component nations, and an independent Poland carved out of the territories of the German Empire as well as out of Austro-Hungary and Russia. But the theme was not entirely one-sided: it also embodied the principle that colonies should be administered for the benefit of their inhabitants, not for the benefit of the colonial powers (point 5), and clearly this would imply sacrifice on the part of Britain, France, and other colonial powers amongst the Allies.

The second theme of the statement was the elaboration of certain

[2] Earlier in the year there had been a large-scale mutiny in the French army also, but this had been kept a secret by the authorities and eventually had been ruthlessly crushed.

general principles for the conduct of international relations which would be conducive to international peace and justice. These included:

- The formation of a general association of nations under specific covenants for the purpose of affording mutual guarantees of political independence and territorial integrity to great and small alike (point 14);

- open covenants openly arrived at, i.e. the abolition of secret treaties which were perceived by many to have had a major role in dragging nations into war without full public discussion of the alternatives (point 1);

- a reduction in the armaments of all nations (point 4);

- freedom of the seas in both peace and war (point 2), including specifically the passage of the Dardanelles (point 12);

- the removal of trade barriers between nations (point 3).

The Fourteen Points were clearly a radical break with conventional 'real politik' which with its secret diplomacy, its militarism, and its lack of principle had brought so much death and destruction. They had great popular appeal because they promised something worthwhile, for which all mankind would be thankful, in return for the great sacrifices that had been made. In the last months of the war the Allies adopted the Fourteen Points as their statement of war aims. This contributed to a significant change in the perceived character of the struggle. For most of the war the issues had been essentially about which power or power blocs would dominate Europe. With replacement on the Allied side of Czarist Russia by the United States, and with the adoption of the Fourteen Points as the main war aims of the Allies, the conflict had been converted into one in which constitutional governments embracing principles of international law were resisting autocratic military regimes still operating in accordance with the law of the jungle. This shift, important as it was, should not be exaggerated. Clearly the Allies still had many *real politik* motivations, some hidden from public view, and it was these which were to pervert the peace process and make war once again a probability. There had, too, been a gradual evolution of constitutional forces in both Germany and Austro-Hungary. When the monarchies were swept away in disgrace after the failure of their aggressive policies, it was these progressive forces which stepped into the breach and began the process of negotiating with the Allies.

Tragically, as victory became imminent in the last months of the war the Allied statesmen allowed themselves to be swayed by feelings of great bitterness, in particular against Germany which was held to be totally responsible for the war. Instead of responding magnanimously to the communications from the new democratic government in Germany they chose to make drastic changes to their terms. One was a demand that Germany pay reparations to the Allies to compensate them for the losses they had incurred during the war. Another was that the British reserved the right to use a naval blockade and would not therefore subscribe to the full application of the principle of the freedom of the seas at all times. The German government never formally reacted to these drastic changes and all that could be said is that they were accepted by default when the German High Command agreed to an armistice to begin on 11 November 1918.

The Versailles Treaty

Drawing up a peace treaty after such a vast war involving so many nations was clearly a mammoth undertaking. In the end the process had to be divided up into four separate treaties with each of the Central Powers (Germany, Austria-Hungary, Bulgaria[3] and Turkey[4]) of which by far the most important was the Treaty of Versailles between the Allies and Germany. The Versailles Treaty contained 440 articles covering six broad topics: (i) the establishment of a League of Nations, and various ancillary issues relating to the future conduct of international relations; (ii) national self-determination in the territories occupied by Germany; (iii) disposition of the German colonies; (iv) the disarming of Germany; (v) reparations; and (vi) prosecution of German 'war criminals'. There is no question that with regard to all six topics the approach was punitive and discriminatory against Germany and therefore quite contrary to the spirit of the Fourteen Points. Even membership of the League of Nations (see below) was initially denied to Germany.

With regard to disposition of territory, it was perfectly reasonable that German troops should be required to evacuate Belgium, that Alsace-Lorraine should be returned to France (taken after the war of 1870), and that Poland should be created from those territories where the Polish people were a majority. It was less clear that the Saar should be placed under the mandate of the League of Nations for fifteen years or that East Prussia should be cut off from the rest of Germany by

[3] Bulgaria had come into the war in 1915 on the side of the Central Powers in the hope of being awarded Macedonia, then a part of Serbia. Bulgaria, however, is a Slav nation and the war against fellow Slavs had not been popular and was essentially undertaken by a pro-German monarchy with shallow roots in the country.

[4] Turkey was in the war from the beginning, fighting the traditional enemy: Russia and the Slavs of the Balkans.

a Polish corridor to the Baltic Sea. All told, the Treaty deprived Germany of six million of her population (of which the majority were German) together with much of her iron ore and coal reserves. German colonies were not given independence but rather were placed under the mandate of the League of Nations, which in turn divided them up amongst the Allied colonial powers for administration on its behalf.

The disarmament arrangements were even more one-sided, because the Allies gave no undertaking with regard to their own forces (though in practice they undertook massive demobilization soon after the end of the war), whereas very strict limits were placed on the German armed forces. The army was restricted to 100,000 officers and men, conscription was to be abolished along with the General Staff, and arms manufacturing capability was to be drastically reduced; the navy was to be reduced to 16,500 men and there were to be no dreadnoughts or other warships over 10,000 tons, or any submarines; the air force was to be completely abolished; and the Rhineland border between France and Germany was to be completely demilitarized and occupied by the Allies for fifteen years.

Even more humiliating for Germany was the imposition of reparations (the amounts were to be worked out after the treaty was signed), although it should be remembered in fairness that (a) Germany herself had imposed a heavy indemnity on France after the Franco-Prussian war of 1870–1871, and (b) in practice the reparation burden turned out to be far less than anticipated. In the twelve years during which reparation payments were made (the National Socialists stopped such payments as soon as they came to power in 1932) Germany borrowed from abroad almost as much as it paid out in reparations.[5]

Perhaps the ultimate humiliation was a demand that one hundred of Germany's wartime leaders, including the Kaiser, should be put on trial as war criminals. In theory this was the beginning of a progressive idea which would contribute to the strengthening of the concept of international law; it was to be developed further after World War II at the Nuremberg Trials (see Chapter 23). However, in 1919 there were obvious overtones of bias. Were there no war criminals on the Allied side? Had the Allies themselves abided by the Hague Conventions? The subject inspired a great deal of hysteria and a campaign demanding the hanging of the Kaiser. Eventually the matter was allowed to peter out when the Dutch, who had been

[5] Between 1919 and 1931 Germany paid 36.1 billion gold marks in reparations and borrowed the equivalent of 33 billion.

neutral in the war and had given the ex-Kaiser refuge, refused to hand him over to the Allies. Quietly it was agreed that the trials of the other 'war criminals' should be conducted by the Germans themselves, and this was clearly a formula for inaction.

When the Allies had thrashed out amongst themselves a treaty which they could all accept, they summoned the German representatives, who were then told to sign on the dotted line in just the sort of way that might have been expected for the vanquished if the Germans had been the victors. On 28 June 1919, after a period of agonizing, the German democratic government signed because they could see no other option.[6] The German army was in total disarray and the country was on its knees after suffering the effects of a continuation of the wartime blockade over the winter of 1918–1919. Thus the democracies of the West threw away an unusual opportunity, made possible by the sacrifice of twenty million dead, to build a new world order based on a just settlement. Twenty years later the world was to suffer as never before for their shortsightedness.

The League Covenant

In the perspective of history the peace treaties at the end of the Great War were a tragedy for mankind. Yet all was not totally lost. Those parts of the Versailles Treaty which related to the establishment of the League of Nations provided a priceless legacy for succeeding generations and contributed to the realization of mankind's age-old hopes of cooperation and peaceful settlement of disputes. For years before the War the Great Powers had been arguing in a desultory fashion about the development of international law and international institutions. Progress was extremely slow and what had been achieved by 1914 was far too limited to have any noticeable effect in restraining them from violent conflict. It was the shock of the Great War which finally pushed the nations of the world into taking the

6 Over the next year the remaining four treaties were signed with the other former members of the Central Power bloc. The Treaty of St Germain (10 September 1919) with Austria imposed reparations (which were never paid); handed over a large number of German-speaking citizens to the new state of Czechoslovakia; and forbade a union between Germany and Austria. The Treaty of Trianon with Hungary (4 June 1920) also imposed an indemnity, reduced the army to 35,000, and transferred 10.6 million people (including 3 million Magyars) and their lands to neighbouring countries. The Treaty of Nevilly with Bulgaria (27 November 1919) was also punitive though on a lesser scale. Finally, the Treaty of Sèvres (10 August 1920) dissolved the old Ottoman Empire and carved up the Arab territories into League of Nations mandates to be administered by England and France, established a new Armenian republic, and further handed over territories to Greece. Greece tried to take more than it had been awarded and in the ensuing fighting the Turks reasserted themselves by crushing the Armenian Republic and driving the Greeks out of Smyrna and off the Turkish mainland.

giant step forward represented by the establishment of the League of Nations.

The League Covenant of 1919 did not suddenly appear out of the blue. It developed from the interplay of at least three broad factors over several years. The first of these was the experience of intense international cooperation which was forced on the Allies by the extreme exigencies of the war itself. Thus, by 1917 the Allies in the West had appointed a Supreme War Council consisting of two representatives from each nation, and, unprecedented in history, a generalissimo, Marshal Foch (1851–1929), to command all the Allied armies. In addition there was increasing cooperation in the planning and distribution of scarce economic resources and shipping, through some twenty-two inter-Allied committees coordinated by a powerful inter-allied Maritime Transport Council. The latter organ which was supported by a four-man secretariat, had eight members, two from each Allied power, and by the end of the war it controlled some 90 percent of shipping on the high seas. The emergency situation forced the Council to act for the general good rather than waste time bickering about narrow advantage for one ally or another. The second factor bearing on the League was past experience with such institutions as the Congress system and the Hague Convention. The third factor was a debate carried on during the war about what new international measures should be taken to make sure that the disaster of the Great War would never be repeated. The debate drew to a considerable extent on the ideas of the various pre-War peace movements discussed earlier.

The wartime debates took place in private as well as public circles. Five broad approaches were discussed: (i) an improved system of international consultation through a broadened and regular Congress system; (ii) the idea that all nations should guarantee each other's territorial integrity and independence – an approach which had its roots in the Monroe Doctrine of the early nineteenth century when the United States had in effect guaranteed to intervene if European powers tried to occupy the territory of independent countries in the Americas; (iii) the Hague system of mediation, inquiry and arbitration; (iv) strengthening of the application of the old domestic police system of 'hue and cry' to the international scene, whereby all nations would band together to restrain any aggressor nation; and (v) the idea of a multi-faceted permanent international body which would promote coordination of services in a whole range of social and economic areas as well as the political area – a thought encouraged by the success of the Universal Postal Union.

One of the most influential private groups was that in the United

States headed by ex-President Taft (1857–1930) and President Lowell (1856–1943) of Harvard University which advocated *A League to Enforce the Peace*. This was essentially a development of the 'Hague' and legalistic approach with provision, among other things, for compulsory arbitration by a World Court, a Council of Conciliation for dealing with political (as opposed to legal) disputes, a cooling-off period (as in the Bryan scheme), and periodic international conferences to update international law. In England a second group, the Fabians, tended to favour a gradualist approach to making international relations more orderly, and put emphasis on an improved political Congress system rather than the legal Hague system. They wanted Congresses to be held regularly and to be supported by a permanent secretariat. Their most immediate concern was the need to coordinate food supplies immediately the war ended in order to avoid widespread famine. Another approach was that of Lord Parker who in a speech in the House of Lords in March 1918 first raised the concept of 'hue and cry' which he saw as the key to maintenance of peace. On the other hand, the greatly respected Field Marshal Smuts (1870–1950) of South Africa presented in 1918 *The League of Nations: A Practical Suggestion* in which there was more emphasis on a permanent league with economic and social functions as well as political. Interestingly, in the light of subsequent developments, he advocated decision-making in an international assembly on the basis of a two-thirds majority. As a military man he was much interested in the issue of disarmament and saw as the key point the need for universal abolition of conscription.

There were interesting differences in the priorities of each of the Allied Great Powers. The British, like the Fabians, with long experience of the Congress system and its flexibility, liked the political approach. They wanted a two-tier international assembly system with an upper tier of the Great Powers meeting regularly once a year and a second-tier assembly with representatives of all nations meeting once every four or five years. They saw a need for a permanent secretariat. They also were interested in the concept of 'hue and cry' against a nation declared by the upper council to be an aggressor, and in an organization which provided a wide range of economic and social coordination services. The French preference as enunciated by the French representative, Leon Bourgeois (1851–1925),[7] was for a Hague-style legal system focused just on keeping the peace on the basis of existing international law, including most

[7] Leon Bourgeois, who won the Nobel Peace Prize in 1920, had long been an advocate of means to improve international relations and had been associated with both the Hague Conferences.

specifically the 1919 peace treaties. Italy also had a preference for a legalistic 'Peace through Justice' approach but differed from the French insofar as they wanted provision for the law to be subject to review on a regular basis to bring it into line with 'natural justice', particularly with regard to distribution of economic resources. The United States government, with its tradition of the Monroe Doctrine, leaned towards emphasis on mutual guarantees of territorial integrity and independence, as well as the legalistic approach of President Taft. President Wilson himself had an interest in disarmament and a policy of nationalizing all armaments manufacturers so as to control the international trade in arms. He also had an initial inclination to confine the League to countries with responsible (i.e. constitutional) governments, and it was only later that a no-restriction policy was adopted. Finally there was Japan, with a strong position only on the issue of racism and a desire to have a statement against racial discrimination incorporated into the eventual peace document. Japan was, of course, the only non-white Great Power involved in the peace negotiations and had been unhappy about racially discriminatory immigration policies in the United States and the British Empire.

In the hectic months following the German armistice President Wilson, to his great credit, worked hardest to make a League of Nations a practical reality, whilst France and Great Britain, in particular, put much of their effort into winning their points in other aspects of the Versailles settlement – with, as noted, disastrous long-term results. Nevertheless, the document that finally emerged contained elements of all five approaches to the problem: (i) it was an improved Congress system for international consultation; (ii) it contained elements of the Monroe Doctrine idea of international territorial guarantees; (iii) it made provision for mediation, inquiry and arbitration as in the Hague system; (iv) it incorporated the concept of 'hue and cry' against an aggressor; and (v) it made provision for economic and social services between nations. The resulting organization was certainly not a super-state federation or even a confederation, rather it was what Professor Zimmern has called a voluntary cooperative to encourage the replacement of old-style 'power politics' with 'responsibility politics'. The League concept had such popular appeal throughout the West that there was little real argument in the preparation of the League Covenant, and within two months of a draft being presented to the conference delegates in February 1919 it was approved and incorporated into the Versailles Treaty.

The Covenant of the League of Nations incorporated eight basic principles:

(1) That every member would recognize the integrity and independence of every other member;

(2) That war was a threat to all and was automatically a subject for deliberation by the League;

(3) That all members bound themselves to submit all disputes to peaceful arbitration and that in no case would they go to war for at least three months after there had been a reasonable time to settle the issue peacefully;

(4) That all nations would take common action against any state making war in violation of the Covenant and bind themselves to come to the assistance of any member which was subject to aggression. Sanctions initially would be economic but if this should fail to restrain the aggressor, then military action could be taken, together with expulsion from the League;

(5) That members should reduce their armaments to the minimum necessary for security (bearing in mind the collective security mentioned above);

(6) That all members would conduct diplomacy in the open and would not make secret agreements: any existing secret agreements would be automatically abrogated;

(7) That former colonies of the defeated powers would be the responsibility of the League but would be administered on its behalf by nominated countries until such colonies were ready for independence;

(8) That members agreed to cooperate for the common good in a wide range of economic and social fields such as international transportation, postage, other communications and commerce, international health matters, conditions of labour, and the suppression of the international traffic in slavery.

One serious omission from the principles was a statement on the equality of all races, an omission criticized bitterly by Japan, and one which clearly showed that Westerners were still befogged by nineteenth-century imperial and social Darwin-type views which made them insensitive to the feelings of others. William Hughes, the Australian statesman, with the support of other representatives of the

British Empire, was the driving force behind this disgraceful episode.

The organizational structure of the League consisted of four main bodies: an Assembly, a Council, a Secretariat, and a Permanent Court. Each member country was represented in the Assembly and each had one vote.[8] A resolution in the Assembly could become a decision only if it received unanimous approval (however, abstentions were permissible). The main practical function of the Assembly was to be a forum where the approximate voice of the peoples of the world could be heard.

The Council was more of an executive body charged in particular with questions of international security. The initial intent was that it would have nine members, five (i.e. the majority) being the Great Powers (the United States, Britain, France, Italy and Japan)[9] and four others elected on a rotating basis by the Assembly. Things did not work out that way. The United States never did join the League (see below) and the number of elected representatives was raised to six in 1922, to nine in 1926, to ten in 1933, and to eleven in 1936, thus putting the Great Powers very much in a minority. This was perhaps not as significant in reality as it seems on paper because great powers have a way of being very persuasive. Nevertheless, it did mean that the Great Powers would often meet together informally outside the Council and thereby lowered the prestige of the League.

At first there was some vagueness about the functions and structure of the Secretariat. This is surprising in view of the importance of this arm of an international organization – an importance that stems from its central role in continuity, as a source of information and potentially at least as a central point of contact between members. Some consideration was given to the creation of a post at the top of the Secretariat which would have considerable political powers (the title of Chancellor was even mooted) and to the appointment of someone with established political weight such as Thomas Masaryk (1850–1937) of Czechoslovakia, Jan Smuts of South Africa, Maurice Hankey (1877–1963) of Great Britain, or Eleutherios Venizelos (1864–1936) of Greece. Wilson even toyed with the possibility of taking the position himself. Such ideas, however, were associated with a much stronger League than many nations were prepared to accept and there was soon agreement that

---

[8] The League originally had 41 members (16 European, 16 American, and 9 from Asia, Africa and the Pacific). This number gradually increased to an average of between 55 and 60. All told, 63 countries were members at some point during its twenty years of active life.

[9] The other two Great Powers, Germany and Russia, did not become members of the League until 1926 and 1934 respectively.

the position should be essentially one for an administrator to serve the needs of the Council and Assembly rather than an independent world statesman. Accordingly, the person chosen for the post was Sir Eric Drummond,[10] a senior civil servant in the British Foreign Office. As Secretary-General from 1919 to 1933, Eric Drummond set the low-key style of the international civil servant which has been essentially followed ever since both within the League and the United Nations. He tried very hard to recruit a staff (which eventually numbered between 600 and 700) on the basis of merit and a loyalty to the League and the world interest rather than to the country of origin. This was an uphill task because many of the member nations wanted to have their own 'representatives' on the staff, especially at the senior levels (a perennial problem in nearly all international organizations) and concessions had to be made which tended to undermine morale. Later, especially in the 1930s, there were criticisms that the Secretariat did not have the moral backbone to stand up for the common interest. Nevertheless, the creation of the Secretariat, for all its faults, was one of the great achievements of the League:

The creation of a secretariat international alike in its structure, its spirit, and its personnel was without doubt one of the most important events in the history of international politics – important not only in itself but as the indisputable proof of possibilities which had hitherto been confidently denied.[11]

The fourth organ of the League, the Permanent Court of Justice, was a fulfilment of the plans originally discussed at The Hague in 1907 and rejected at that time. It was a considerable improvement over the Permanent Court of Arbitration because it made international arbitration more regular, uniform and professional. The Court consisted of eleven judges and four deputies elected by the Assembly and the Council, and each held office for nine years on a staggered basis (a similar practice to that used in elections for the United States Senate) so that every three years one-third of the Court would be replaced. The judges were not nominated by the country of their nationality, so as to minimise partisan pressure on them. If the Court should include a judge from a country which was involved in a case being considered by the Court, then the other country involved could request that the Court include a judge of its choice also. The

[10] Sir Eric Drummond (1876–1951) was a Scottish aristocrat and had been private secretary to such statesmen as Asquith, Grey and Balfour. He had struck up friendships with Colonel House and President Wilson whilst taking part in the negotiations for the creation of the League.

[11] Walters, *A History of the League of Nations*.

Court made a point of being flexible in its procedures, drawing on both the Anglo-Saxon adversary system and the French investigative approach. Compulsory arbitration was still resisted, especially by the British, and jurisdiction of the Court only extended to those member countries who accepted it voluntarily. Furthermore, member countries who so volunteered were permitted to limit their acceptance to particular types of dispute. Judgements could only be given when both parties had given prior agreement to acceptance. Some 47 states volunteered to accept the rulings of the Court, of which 29 put restrictions on the area of jurisdiction they would accept. From 1922 onwards the Court met annually and at that time issued its judgements and opinions on cases brought before it during the year.

There were several ancillary organizations associated with the League, of which the most important was the International Labour Organization (articles 387–427 of the Treaty of Versailles) which was in effect an expansion of the pre-War International Association of Labour Organizations. Trade Unions had played a crucial role in producing munitions for the Allied armies, and the governments felt under obligation to respond to union demands for special provision in the post-War international arrangements for the protection of working people in all countries. The articles of agreement of the ILO were drafted by a committee of distinguished labour leaders, including Samuel Gompers (1850–1924) from the United States, George Barnes (1859–1940) from Great Britain, and Albert Thomas (1878–1932) from France. The latter was to be president of the ILO from 1920 to 1932. The purpose of the organization was to secure and maintain fair and humane conditions of labour for men, women, and children both in their own countries and in all countries to which their commercial and industrial relations extended. In pursuit of this goal, the ILO could undertake any of the following activities:

(i) propose international treaties for governments to sign;

(ii) make recommendations to governments about specific practices;

(iii) provide technical assistance and act as a channel for cooperation;

(iv) investigate complaints;

(v) provide information, including statistics, and give publicity to its activities.

The governing body of the ILO consisted of 24 members, of whom 12 were nominated by member governments (8 of these seats were reserved for representatives of the largest industrial countries), 6 were elected by employers, and 6 by workers' organizations. The number of members was later increased to 32 but the same ratio (2:1:1) between governments, employers and workers was maintained. All members of the League were automatically members of the ILO.

Other international bodies associated with the League included a Permanent Mandates Commission to supervise the administration provided by the mandated powers in the former German colonies; a minorities committee; an economic and finances organization; an organization for communications and transport; and various facilities for cooperation in the fields of health, intellectual property, the protection of women, child welfare, refugee issues and the suppression of international drug traffic and slavery. Somewhat separate was an international clearing house for information on criminal matters (Interpol) which was set up in 1923 at the initiative of the Austrian government.

International cooperation between governments was supported by a growing number of voluntary non-governmental international organizations which it is estimated had grown to between 400 and 500 by the end of the twenties and which between them held something like 100 international conferences per year.

A survey of international society would show it to be composed not only of the intercourse of each state with every other state, but of the collaboration of doctors, statisticians, trade unionists, hotel keepers, boy scouts, chambers of commerce, parliamentarians, and innumerable specialists drawn from almost every country of the world into an association not as nationals of their countries but as representatives of a special occupation or interest.[12]

Successes and Failures

In the last half-century the League of Nations has been severely criticized because its existence did not prevent the Second World War. This criticism has obscured the fact that the League was, despite all its flaws, a giant step forward on the road towards a just society, and in the perspective of history its creation must be seen as one of the great milestones in the evolution of civilization. The Covenant of the League set forth, more clearly than ever before, agreed fundamental principles of international relations on such matters as the peaceful settlement of disputes, collective security, reduction of armaments, open diplomacy, and cooperation in

[12] S.H. Bailey, *The Framework of International Society* (1932), quoted in Thompson, *World History*, p. 29.

economic and social fields. It provided a regular forum, backed by an international civil service, for discussion and resolution of these issues. It was the 'first attempt to establish a permanent international organization of a general political nature with machinery functioning on a continuing basis'.[13] Perhaps above all it contributed to the raising of the consciousness amongst all peoples that ultimately they were world citizens, not just members of their own nations. The League had many tangible successes too, especially in its early years, which demonstrated that an international organization could indeed function effectively when the majority of its members wished it to do so.

One area of success was to contribute to the settlement of international disputes. Examples include the settlement of an early dispute between Germany and Poland over the border in Silesia, another between Sweden and Finland over the Åland Islands, dangerous differences between Greece and Bulgaria, a quarrel between Italy and Greece which enabled even Mussolini to step back without losing face, assistance to Austria in overcoming a major financial crisis (an arrangement which became a model for financial rescue plans in other countries and for the Dawes Plan to rearrange reparations payments), and acceptance of some twenty-three judgements and twenty-seven advisory opinions given by the Court of Justice between 1921 and 1945. Even as late as 1934, when the League was beginning to fall apart, it was able to successfully mediate a dispute between Colombia and Peru, and so prevent a war which was deemed otherwise to have been inevitable.

A second area of success was in generally contributing to a sense of security which for a decade at least encouraged the peoples of the world to stop assuming that war was an inevitable fact of life, and to act accordingly. A key development in this context was the Locarno Pact of 1925 which at the initiative of Gustav Streseman (1878– 1929),[14] foreign minister of Germany, 1923–1929, gave an international guarantee of the Franco–German border, supported by France, Germany, Britain and Italy.[15] Another important event was the 1928 Pact of Paris (better known as the Kellogg Pact) by which signatory nations 'renounced war as an instrument of national policy'. This pact was initially inspired by an 'outlaw war' movement in the

[13] Riggs and Plano, *The United Nations*, p. 8.

[14] Gustav Streseman won the Nobel Peace Prize for this work in 1926, as did the other two principal participants, Austen Chamberlain (1863–1937) and Aristide Briand.

[15] The heart of the treaty was an assurance to France that England would come to her assistance in the event of another German attack. This went a long way to allaying fears in France that in the future she might have to fight alone against a Germany perhaps even more powerful than in 1914.

United States.[16] Aristide Briand (1862–1932), foreign minister of France, proposed a bilateral treaty to the United States along these lines, to which Frank Kellogg (1856–1937)[17] the US Secretary of State, replied that such a treaty should be multilateral and open to all nations to sign. The response was quite remarkable: voluntary signature by 65 nations – virtually all those independent at that time. It has been fashionable to sneer at this pact because there was no means of enforcing it and its terms have been broken many times since by signatory nations. In the short run such criticism has some validity, but in the longer term it can be seen as one more step in the process of discouraging war because increasingly nations do not like to be seen acting illegally in front of the world news media and world opinion. Constitutional governments with their basic respect for the rule of law are clearly more susceptible to the moral pressure involved, but even authoritarian governments, more used to acting in an arbitrary fashion, can be made to feel uncomfortable when acting illegally on the world stage.

There are two other activities in the field of international security where the League had some success and set a precedent for the future. One was the temporary establishment of the first world police force in connection with a plebiscite held in the Saar in 1935 to determine if the people of that region wished to be reunited with Germany. The plebiscite was in accordance with the terms of the Treaty of Versailles. Whilst it was being held the region was patrolled by an international peace-keeping force of 3,300 soldiers from the United Kingdom, Italy, the Netherlands and Sweden. The force successfully kept law and order during this time of tension.

The promotion of disarmament was the second activity. A major milestone in the history of international relations was the first multilateral disarmament agreement signed at the Washington Naval Conference of 1921. Though this was a separate agreement between the five major naval powers of the time, it was clearly in accordance with the Covenant of the League and inspired by its principles. Under the terms of the agreement ratios were set for the number and total tonnage of battleships (the most powerful type of warship of that era) to be maintained by the great naval powers over the next fifteen years: 15 with a total tonnage of 525,000 each for Britain and the United States; 9 with a total tonnage of 315,000 for Japan; and 5 each with a total tonnage of 175,000 for France and Italy. Limitations

[16] Started by S.O. Levenson, a Chicago lawyer, and Charles Clayton Morrison, editor of the *Christian Centre*.

[17] Another winner of the Nobel Peace Prize (1929) and later a member of the Permanent Court of Justice (1930–1935).

were also set for the maximum tonnage and calibre of guns for major classes of warships: 35,000 tons and 16-inch guns for battleships, 27,000 tons and 8-inch guns for aircraft carriers (a new type of warship), and 10,000 tons and 8-inch guns for cruisers. In addition undertakings were given not to further improve existing naval bases in the Pacific and to put a limitation on the number of submarines. This treaty represented a genuine reduction in the number of modern ships (the United States, for instance, agreed to scrap 11 battleships which were under construction), as well as those of an older vintage (Britain scrapped some 20 pre-Jutland ships in accordance with the treaty). Later attempts to extend the treaty to limit the number of other types of warship ran into difficulty,[18] but in 1930 a London Treaty was signed by the three nations with the most powerful fleets (United States, Great Britain and Japan) whereby it was agreed that replacement battleships should not be constructed for another five years. In 1936 the United States, Great Britain and France agreed on further limitations on the size of replacement warships, but this agreement soon had to be abandoned in view of the naval rearmament programmes of the Axis powers.

Meanwhile in 1926 the League itself had established a Preparatory Commission to draw up a draft general document on disarmament for consideration by member countries. Participants included representatives from several important non-League nations: Germany (which became a member that same year), the United States and Russia. The bargaining was hard, but by the end of 1930 the Commission had agreed on some useful broad principles. These included budget ceilings for defence expenditures, limitations on the number of years' service for conscripts, a limitation on the manpower in land, sea and air forces, a renunciation of chemical and bacterial warfare (a protocol on this subject was signed at Geneva in 1925), and provision for a permanent disarmament commission to monitor adherence to the agreements.

By 1932 the League was at last ready to begin to move from agreed broad themes to discussion of detailed principles and goals, and their implementation. A formal Disarmament Conference was convened. The chairman was Arthur Henderson (1863–1935), who had devoted a large part of his later life to the issue of international peace.[19] In the early stages of the Conference, which was attended by representatives of 64 nations, agreement was reached on the principles that

[18] The British, for instance, had far more cruisers than any other nation and were not prepared to reduce the number which they felt necessary for the protection of the sea lanes of their worldwide Empire.

[19] Arthur Henderson won the Nobel Peace Prize in 1934.

there should be limits on the number of aircraft in each air force, that no power should carry out air attacks against civilians, that there should be limits on the maximum calibre of artillery and size of tanks, and that chemical warfare should be outlawed.

From that point onwards, however, the Conference ran into major difficulties which the participants were never able to overcome. These paralleled growing tensions in the whole field of international relations. In pursuit of the idea that military forces should be purely defensive, there arose disagreement over the definition of defensive weapons. More serious was the rejection of a proposal of Ramsay MacDonald (1866–1937), the British Prime Minister, that the Conference follow up on agreed principles and set specific limits on the armed forces of each country. France proposed as an alternative that there should be a five-year freeze at current levels for all military forces, a proposal which provided a perfect excuse for indignation on the part of Germany, where Adolf Hitler and the National Socialists had recently come to power, because this was obviously a formula for keeping Germany in an inferior position. The Germans walked out of the Disarmament Conference, then withdrew from the League itself, and finally began a massive rearmament programme. Britain, looking to her own short-term interests, broke ranks with the other participants and negotiated a separate bilateral naval treaty with Germany which recognized the latter's right to build warships in excess of the number authorized by the Treaty of Versailles. Multilateral disarmament was dead. The frantic rearmament programme in Germany forced the democracies to rearm too, although there was initially great reluctance and much opposition from peace movements of the time.[20]

Much has been written to explain the decline and fall of the League during the 1930s. What is clear, at least, is that one of the key factors was the rebirth of militarism in three out of the seven great powers of the world: Germany, Italy and Japan. This development can be attributed partly to the immense social and economic strains set in motion by the disruptions caused by the Great War, of which the

[20] Whether the peace movements of the period, which in the author's view often lacked the vision and wisdom of the early peace leaders of the nineteenth century, actually contributed to the security of the world is a moot question. They were caught in the classic dilemma of most peace movements: that they can be effective in democracies but not in countries with authoritarian regimes, and it is precisely the latter which have a tendency to become aggressive. These regimes, it can be argued, are actually encouraged to be even more aggressive when democracies are militarily weak. Thus a peace movement could be said to make war more likely rather than less. The peace movements of the time did rightly stress the importance of the League as a potential instrument of peace but did not follow the logic that if the League was to enforce the peace against militaristic great powers, the League's own supporting powers would have to provide it with enough military might to ensure victory in case of conflict – otherwise there would be no deterrence.

most devastating was the Great Depression itself.[21] The militaristic regimes in each of these three countries prescribed military glory and expansion in order to achieve national self-respect and overcome the pessimism associated with the Depression; they despised the democracies as ineffective in dealing with economic problems and spineless in looking after national self-interest. In addition the Nazi regime in Germany made a great deal of noise about the insulting inequalities of the Versailles Treaty, which they maintained had been signed on behalf of Germany by democratic traitors, and they made a point of challenging the Treaty, including the League itself, at every opportunity. It is conceivable, however, that the bully-boy tactics of the three great militarist powers could have been stopped dead if the four remaining Great Powers (Britain, France, USA and Russia) had united in upholding the League's principles of collective security, especially as it was clear that they would have had the support of most of the smaller powers – a support which might have been of considerable significance in applying economic and even military sanctions. The failure to take such action was therefore the second key factor in the fall of the League.

The possibility of collective action by the four powers had, of course, been greatly weakened right from the birth of the League by the decision of the United States not to join the organization which its President had played such a distinguished role in creating. Originally, support for the League had been widespread in the United States but by the end of 1919 grave doubts had come to the fore because of fears of a permanent entanglement in European affairs and of the cost to US overseas trade if the United States should be obliged to apply economic sanctions against some country in accordance with a League directive. The United States Constitution requires that all foreign treaties, including the Versailles Peace Treaty which provided for the establishment of the League, be approved by two-thirds of the Senate. Votes in November 1919 and again in March 1920 went against the Treaty and the United States retreated into isolation. In a sense it is remarkable that the League was formed at all after this devastating rebuff by its original sponsor and creator.

The possibility of collective security was still further weakened by the mutual hostility between the Western powers and Russia after the Communist Revolution in the latter. The Western powers for their

[21] The Great Depression also dealt a massive blow to League attempts to coordinate international trade policies for the benefit of all. A World Economic Conference in 1933 was a complete failure because national governments, alarmed at mass unemployment, opted for extreme protectionism in the hope of creating more jobs at home – a self-defeating policy which in the long run hurt everyone and greatly aggravated the Depression.

part feared that the new regime planned to stir up revolution amongst their peoples, whilst Russia was deeply suspicious of the Western powers, not only on account of ideological theory but because Western armies had actually invaded Russia during the Revolution in order to suppress it. Russia was not admitted into the League until 1934 and even then was treated with intense suspicion.

Collective security in practice therefore depended on Britain and France. Two great powers upholding collective security against three powerful aggressors was clearly a risky option, even when support might be obtained from a host of smaller countries; and both had good reason to fear that such action might actually drag them into another great war of uncertain outcome, rather than deter war. So much would depend on trust of other nations and close cooperation in an entirely new international environment. After all, collective security (as distinct from *real politik* alliances) had never been tried before in history. On the other hand, both these democracies had emotional and intellectual reasons for supporting the principle of collective security. The tragic result of these contending pressures was the worst sort of dithering and compromises which served to antagonize the aggressors but not to deter them. In the end, democratic France and Britain drifted into war to defend a dictatorship for reasons of *real politik* after having first betrayed a democracy and the principles of world law and order. To make things worse, the place and timing of the conflict put them at maximum military and diplomatic disadvantage. Once on the slippery slope of compromise and unprincipled diplomacy, events seemed to lead inevitably towards disaster.

As compared with these two major factors accounting for the fall of the League – the rise of militarism in three of the seven Great Powers of the world, and the failure of the other four to collectively resist that aggression – the other flaws in the League which are sometimes discussed seem peripheral and of doubtful validity. Thus, though it is true that it was unfortunate that the League was so closely identified with the Treaty of Versailles which eventually emerged as an old-style settlement of past scores instead of a forward-looking charter for a post-war world, it has to be noted that Germany, the main grievant country, was quite able to work with the League in a constructive manner while she was a democracy. The fact that votes in the Assembly had to be unanimous did not cripple the decision-making process, because on most occasions dissenting countries were content to abstain rather than to cast a negative 'veto' vote. Finally, the fact that the League did not have its own standing police force was not of critical importance. In the long run such a world police force will be of vital importance for the maintenance of world peace, but in the early days of international cooperation collective security could have been maintained quite adequately with national armies acting together on behalf of the League.

The Collapse of the League

The first major test of the League came in 1931 when Japan invaded Chinese Manchuria.[22] This was a clear-cut case of aggression against a League member, but France and Britain hesitated to oppose a former ally. They feared that economic sanctions might not be effective if non-League countries in the Pacific (such as the United States and Russia) did not comply with a League directive[23] and that the result would be merely to antagonize Japan. This was of particular concern because both countries had possessions in the Pacific to be defended if Japan should retaliate. The result was a useless compromise. A committee headed by Lord Lytton reported that sanctions were not appropriate because Japan had set up a puppet state in Manchuria called Manchukuo (with the last Emperor of China as titular head) and was therefore not formally in occupation of Chinese territory! Nevertheless, the Commission recommended that the territory be reunited with China. This compromise did not put pressure on Japan to comply: it merely made her hostile to the League and she left the organization in 1933.

A second major defeat for the League occurred in connection with the Italian invasion of Ethiopia in October 1935, which was again a clear-cut case of war against a member of the League. At first it seemed that the Western powers had learnt from the Manchurian case and the League decided to impose economic sanctions against Italy until she withdrew her armies from Ethiopia. This was the first time in history that the nations of the world had applied collective sanctions against an aggressor as a matter of principle. In November a ban was imposed by 50 participating nations on all imports from Italy and on exports to Italy of arms and various raw materials, as well as financial credit.[24] By the end of the year sanctions were clearly beginning to cause difficulties for Italy, and it seemed that if plans for an embargo on oil exports to Italy were imposed she might well have to capitulate. At that point the resolution of France and

---

[22] Ironically, Japan to this date had been one of the most supportive members of the League.

[23] The situation was complicated by the Great Depression and fears that economic sanctions would make it worse.

[24] Britain, however, did not use her power to block passage of Italian troops through the Suez Canal, an act which would have stopped the invasion immediately.

Britain faltered as they contemplated the possibility that their action might drive Italy into the arms of Hitlerite Germany. Talks were started with Italy without consultation with the other members of the League and as a result the proposed oil embargo was abandoned. By July 1936 the whole economic sanctions programme had collapsed. Once again Britain and France had the worst of both worlds. Italy kept her ill-gotten possessions and at the same time was so antagonized that the following year she too left the League and became an ally of the other two militaristic aggressor nations which had already left: Japan and Germany. The Axis pact of the three aggressors was in effect an anti-League alliance.

The *coup de grâce* for the League was finally delivered by Nazi Germany, ever anxious to destroy this instrument of the 'weak' and of the hated Versailles Treaty. After having walked out of the Disarmament Conference in 1932 and having embarked on his vast arms programme, Hitler next marched his troops into the Rhineland – which had been demilitarized under the terms of the Versailles Treaty. The British and French, by now full of self-doubt concerning the Treaty, made virtually no protest. The following year, 1937, Austria was invaded with the assistance of local Nazis and was absorbed into the German Reich – again in violation of the specific terms of the 1919 Peace Treaties. Yet again there was little protest from the Western democracies or from the League itself. In 1938 Hitler turned his attention to Czechoslovakia, a solid democracy and the most successful of the new nations to emerge from the ruins of the old Austro-Hungarian empire. The excuse was the minority of German-speaking Austrians who had lived in Czechoslovakia quite contentedly until Hitler's toughs started to stir up emotions. Czechoslovakia initially resisted German bullying (she had a strong army and frontier fortifications backed up by a powerful arms industry inherited from the old empire) with the hope that the Western democracies would rally around. The Soviet Union, in the League since 1936 and now thoroughly alarmed by German militarism, offered to join France and Britain in guaranteeing Czechoslovakia. But once again the Western powers lost their nerve and rejected the Russian offer. At a hastily convened conference in Munich, the Western powers, encouraged by Mussolini, virtually ordered Czechoslovakia to hand over key areas where large numbers of Germans lived. They were not going to risk their skins for some unknown people in Central Europe. This was the reality behind Neville Chamberlain's (1869–1940) cry 'Peace in our Time'. Munich was indeed a black event in the evolution of the 'just society'.

A few months later Hitler occupied the rump of Czechoslovakia to maintain 'law and order'. This crude insult to the West at long last provoked cries of indignation. When Hitler began his next round of aggression by threatening Poland with regard to the German population in that country, the Western Allies immediately rushed forward and offered Poland a protective alliance. This was not of much practical military value to Poland, on the other side of Europe, unless it was to be linked with support from the Soviet Union. Such support was indeed offered but rejected by Poland which feared Russia almost as much as Germany, whilst the Allies dithered between prejudice and common sense. The opportunity was lost. The Soviet Union, fearing that time was running out, decided to make a direct deal with Hitler to protect herself even though this contradicted everything that the Soviet Union claimed to stand for. The Nazi-Soviet Pact in the summer of 1939 had at its core an agreement to divide Poland between them. After that the Allied threat seemed feeble in the extreme and Hitler could reasonably gamble on the Allies backing off once Poland had been overrun. After all, this was what the track record of the last few years seemed to suggest. On 4 August German armies rolled across the Polish frontier and the Second World War began.

During these last fateful years the League was effectively by-passed in critical international negotiations. Then suddenly it was in the news again to endure a final ignominy. At the end of 1939 Russia invaded Finland as part of its strategy of erecting a barrier of occupied lands between itself and Nazi Germany. Finland appealed to the League for assistance. The Allies were now clearly not in a position to take on Russia as well as Germany. All they could do was to expel Russia from the League and make a few noises of protest. The League was now effectively dead, though its formal existence was not to be terminated until 1946.

CHAPTER 23

The Creation of the United Nations

The Second World War

THE new war was at first limited in scope. Only three major powers were involved, compared with five in 1914; and after the devastating German blitzkrieg against Poland in the first six weeks there was relatively little fighting for several months. In this period of 'phoney war' it seemed that people's worst fears might not be fulfilled after all. There might even be hope of peace; after all, Poland was already defeated and there was little prospect that France and Britain would be able to force Germany to retreat, let alone win a decisive victory over her. But this picture was soon to be radically changed by the dynamics of Fascist policy: once embarked on a campaign of aggression there was no stopping until all the other Great Powers had been forced to acknowledge their dominance. They had to strike quickly whilst they still held the advantage stemming from the delay in the rearmament programmes of the democracies and the disarray in the Soviet forces after the vast purges of party and military officers which Stalin had carried out in the late thirties.

By the end of 1941 all the remaining Great Powers had been caught up in the maelstrom. Soon the struggle had become the most gigantic in history, covering not only Europe but the islands of the Pacific, South-East Asia, parts of Africa, and nearly all the oceans and seas of the world. It was to involve some fifty-seven nations, the vast majority of those independent at that time. Death and destruction were even greater than in the First World War, reflecting not only the wider geographic area involved but also a longer period of fighting (six years instead of four), more destructive weapons (particularly the aeroplane), and, worst of all, ideologies which cultivated hatred and nihilism. It is estimated that some 15 million military personnel were killed (of whom about half were members of the Soviet armed forces) and that possibly as many as three times that number of civilians lost their lives, including some six million Jews murdered by the Nazis. Millions of others were wounded, imprisoned, forced into hard labour, driven from their homes. Numerous cities, towns and villages were destroyed. The war ended with the dropping of atomic bombs on two Japanese cities, so ushering in the nuclear age.

As in the previous struggle, the war was to begin with essentially about German domination of Europe. Again it was the United States which played a leading role in changing the tone and encouraging the view that the Allies were fighting the militaristic dictators in the interests of justice and a lasting peace. This was a theme developed from the nobler side of United States history, that exemplified by Jefferson, Lincoln and Wilson. The mistakes made after the Great War must be avoided. This alone would make sense of the great sacrifices that had to be made. Soon there was a clear ideological content to the war: in the broadest sense it was a struggle between democracy and dictatorship. The issue was made explicit on the Allied side in August 1941 when President Roosevelt and Prime Minister Churchill drew up an eight-point statement of the goals of their two nations: the Atlantic Charter. The Charter stated that neither the United States nor Great Britain sought aggrandisement or territorial changes not approved by the peoples concerned; that they believed that all nations, including those which had been occupied during the war, had a right to self-determination and to choose the form of government under which they lived; that there should be worldwide economic collaboration with a view to raising the standard of living of all peoples; that the use of force between nations should be abandoned and a peace established which would give security to all peoples within the bounds of their own frontiers and on the high seas. The Charter clearly had echoes of President Wilson's Fourteen Points though it was much less specific in content.

The more intense ideological tone of the struggle prompted a major difference from the Great War in how the war was to be conducted. At a conference in December 1941–January 1942 the American and British governments agreed that they would not negotiate a separate peace, and at the Casablanca Conference of January 1943 they declared that their goal was the 'unconditional surrender' of Germany, Italy and Japan. In the First World War there had always been the possibility of a negotiated peace; in the Second that option was deliberately closed off.[1] This policy was later

[1] There was little interest in a negotiated peace on the Axis side either at least after 1939. Rudolf Hess, the deputy leader of the Nazi Party, did fly to Scotland in May 1941 apparently with a view to negotiating a separate peace with Britain. This eccentric gesture was apparently undertaken without the approval of Hitler and was probably motivated by a desire to ease the German position before the attack on Russia. The possibility of a negotiated peace was taken seriously, however, by the underground opposition. Operating in the most difficult conditions they made a final desperate effort when they attempted to assassinate Hitler on 20 July 1944. They hoped to set up a new government which would be acceptable to the Allies and would

criticized by some who argued that it made the war longer than might otherwise have been necessary. However, the Western powers undoubtedly took this position so as to give assurance to the Soviet Union that there would be no double-dealing at her expense. In addition, the record of law-breaking by the dictators showed that they could not possibly be trusted and that the only solution was to have them totally removed from power. This policy was made easier because there was little opposition from the left, the main traditional bastion of peace movements in the past, because of a deep-felt ideological repugnance for fascist philosophy, particularly after the Nazi assault on the Soviet Union in the summer of 1941.

The Nuremberg Trials

Closely related to the theme of unconditional surrender was the evolution of the idea that after the war there should be a trial of those responsible on the Axis side for 'crimes against humanity and against peace'. There was, of course, the risk that the Allies would be accused of merely taking revenge against their enemies and dressing it up as justice, and there was the unfortunate precedent from the Great War of the failure to carry through the war criminal trials. This time the brutality of the Axis powers was quite unprecedented for so-called civilized countries. There could be no doubt that the deliberate policy of attacking neighbouring countries without warning, of ruthless use of slave labour, and murder of civilian hostages in prosecution of the war, and, above all, the practice of genocide against various cultural groups (including most notably the Jews) which led to the deaths of some 11 million people, were all acts contrary to either formal international conventions or generally accepted standards of civilization. To allow such acts to go unpunished would be a far worse precedent than that of the conqueror imposing his justice on the conquered. The case for bringing war criminals to trial was most clearly made in a US State Department memorandum as follows:

In troubled times, progress towards an effective rule of law in the international community is slow indeed. Inertia rests more heavily upon the society of nations than upon any other society. Now we stand at one of those rare moments when the thought and institutions and habits of the world have been stricken by the impact of world war on the lives of countless millions. Such occasions rarely come and quickly pass. We are put

then be able to negotiate an end to the war. Those involved – soldiers, Christians, socialists, and businessmen – were amongst the most noble and brave of their nation. They failed, and Hitler wreaked a terrible vengeance on them.

under heavy responsibility to see that our behaviour during this unsettled period will direct the world's thought toward a firmer enforcement of the laws of international conduct, so as to make war less attractive to those who have governments and the destinies of peoples in their power.[2]

A major initiative to hold a war crimes trial was taken by US Supreme Court Justice Robert Jackson (1892–1958), whose recommendation was approved by President Roosevelt and the other Allied leaders. Chief Justice Jackson argued that:

The commonsense of mankind demands that the law shall not stop with the punishment of petty crimes by little people.[3]

In late 1945 twenty-four of the highest Nazi leaders who had survived the war were put on trial in front of a four-power International Military Tribunal in Nuremberg, site of the largest mass demonstrations of the Nazi Party in its days of triumph.[4] The defendants faced three charges:

1. crimes against peace, i.e. waging wars of aggression;

2. war crimes, i.e. violating the laws and customs of war;

3. crimes against humanity, i.e. extermination, enslavement, and other inhumane acts conducted against a civilian population.

The charges arose from the political, military and administrative policies and procedures of the Nazi government, and those on trial were former members of the cabinet, the military, and the secret police. The procedures of the trial were a blend of Anglo-Saxon practices (with the accused testifying and being subject to cross-examination) and of continental practices (with the accused making a statement not under oath and not subject to cross-examination). The trial was conducted with dignity and judicial propriety (contrasting sharply, for instance, with Hitler's kangaroo trial of those involved in the 20 July 1944 plot), and in view of the crimes involved the sentences were not extreme: 11 were sentenced to death,[5] 11 to varying terms of imprisonment, and 2 were acquitted. The main trial was supplemented by 12 other trials of 153 other major war criminals of whom 14 were sentenced to death. A similar trial was held later in Japan and there were in addition a large number of national trials spread over several years. Some of the national trials did not always

[2] US Department of State Publication no. 3080, pp. 42–54.

[3] Ferenz, *A Common Sense Guide to World Peace*, p. 16.

[4] The trial lasted from November 1945 to September 1946.

[5] Including Hermann Goering who committed suicide the night before he was due to be executed.

observe the highest standards of fairness and objectivity, and it has been pointed out that the Soviet Union, one of the four prosecuting nations at Nuremberg, had itself perpetrated crimes similar to some of those of the Nazis and yet none of those involved were ever put on trial as equity would demand. Nevertheless, in the perspective of history, there is surely little doubt that these trials, taken as a whole, represented a major step forward in the evolution of the idea of the just society. As Telford Taylor put it in his report on the Nuremberg War Crimes Trials:

Nuremberg is a historical and moral fact with which from now on every government must reckon in its internal and external policies.[6]

The Organization of the United Nations

In tandem with the policy of unconditional surrender went a deep concern to ensure that this was the war to end all wars. Though much of the discussion between the Allies during the war centred on immediate military strategy and on the medium-term issues of territorial settlements in Eastern Europe (to satisfy the wish of the Soviet Union for a protective barrier of subject nations against a possible revival of German militarism), considerable attention was also given to the longer-term problem of how to make arrangements for a lasting peace. Winston Churchill was a strong advocate of the idea that a permanent international organization, including as a minimum all the Great Powers, was the only effective means of providing security for all nations. The United States government shared this view. Of course, there was consciousness of the fact that victorious alliances had soon fallen apart after the great conflicts in the past, notably in 1815 and 1918, and of the particular failure of the League of Nations. Yet there was hope that the lessons of the past had been learned and that this time it would be different. These views were endorsed by the Soviet government at a conference in Moscow in 1943 (though it should be added that the Soviet Union never demonstrated great enthusiasm for the United Nations project, perhaps for the ideological reason that communist states should not work to save capitalist governments but more likely because of a deep mistrust of Western motives). Churchill's initiative was taken up by US Secretary of State Cordell Hull (1871–1955), whose State Department prepared a draft Charter for a new United Nations to replace the League.[7] This was discussed and approved by

6 International Conciliation No. 450, April 1949, p. 352.

7 Cordell Hull received the Nobel Peace Prize in 1945 for his work in connection with the founding of the United Nations.

representatives of the Big Four at Dumbarton Oaks, Washington DC, between August and October 1944. The Charter was then presented to a gathering of the representatives of all the Allied nations assembled in San Francisco in April 1945. It was duly signed by representatives of 51 nations on 26 June and became effective on 24 October 1945.[8]

The Charter of the United Nations consists of a preamble and one hundred and eleven articles organized into nineteen chapters covering the following subjects: (i) purposes and principles of the organization; (ii) membership; (iii) a general statement on the organs of the UN; (iv) the General Assembly; (v) the Security Council; (vi) pacific settlement of disputes; (vii) action with respect to threats to the peace, breaches of the peace and acts of aggression; (viii) regional arrangements; (ix) international economic and social cooperation; (x) the Economic and Social Council; (xi) a declaration regarding non-self-governing territories; (xii) the international trusteeship system; (xiii) the Trusteeship Council; (xiv) the International Court of Justice; (xv) the Secretariat; (xvi) miscellaneous provisions including legal privileges and immunities of the organization and its employees; (xvii) transitional arrangements; (xviii) amendments; and (xix) ratification and signature.[9]

The purposes of the United Nations are spelt out in Article 1 of the Charter as follows:

1. to maintain international peace and security, and to that end to take effective collective measures for the prevention and removal of threats to the peace, and for the suppression of acts of aggression or other breaches of the peace, and to bring about by peaceful means, and in conformity with the principles of justice and international law, adjustment or settlement of international disputes or situations which might lead to a breach of the peace;

2. to develop friendly relations among nations based on respect for the principle of equal rights and self-determination of peoples, and to take other appropriate measures to strengthen universal peace;

3. to achieve international cooperation in solving international problems of an economic, social, cultural or humanitarian character, and in promoting and encouraging respect for human rights and for fundamental freedoms for all without distinction as to race, sex, language or religion; and

---

[8] The treaty was approved by the US Senate on 25 July with a vote of 89 to 2. By 27 December the treaty had been formally ratified by all 51 participating governments.

[9] The Charter has been amended twice, in 1963 and 1971, to increase the number of nations represented on the Security Council and the Economic and Social Council.

4. to be a centre for harmonizing the actions of nations in the attainment of these common ends.

The United Nations was given an administrative structure made up of six separate organs (see Table 17) similar to those of the League, though in some instances they are more fully developed. These are:

1. *The General Assembly.* All member countries of the UN are to be represented in the Assembly.[10] Each member has one vote, and decisions are made on the basis of a two-thirds majority present and voting in the case of important questions such as those pertaining to international peace and security, and on the basis of a simple majority for all other matters. The Assembly may investigate, discuss and make recommendations with regard to any matter within the scope of the Charter, except that it is not to make recommendations pertaining to peace and security issues currently under consideration by the Security Council unless the Council has asked it to do so. The Assembly has specific responsibility for admitting new members and expelling members from the organization, for approving the organization's budget, and for electing non-permanent members of the Security Council, members of the Economic and Social Council, and members of the Trusteeship Council, and for appointing the Secretary-General of the United Nations.

2. *The Security Council.* The Council has five permanent members who were the great powers on the Allied side in the Second World War (USA, USSR, UK, France and China) and which coincidently now happen to be the world's first nuclear powers. In addition there are seats for temporary members, who are rotated every two years and are elected by the General Assembly. Originally there were six such seats but the number was raised to ten in 1963. The articles state that in electing the non-permanent members due regard should be paid by the Assembly:

in the first instance to the contribution of the members of the United Nations to the maintenance of international peace and security and to the other purposes of the organization, and also to equitable geographical distribution. (Article 23)

In practice the last factor has been given the most importance with an agreed distribution between geographic areas as follows (since 1963): 5 from Africa and Asia; 1 from East Europe; 2 from Latin America;

[10] UN membership has grown from 51 in 1945 to 159 today. Both figures include 3 for the Soviet Union (the USSR, the Byelorussian SSR and the Ukraine SSR). States which are not members include Taiwan, Switzerland and the two Koreas. (See Table 28 on p. 388.)

THE SEARCH FOR A JUST SOCIETY

TABLE 17

THE UNITED NATIONS SYSTEM

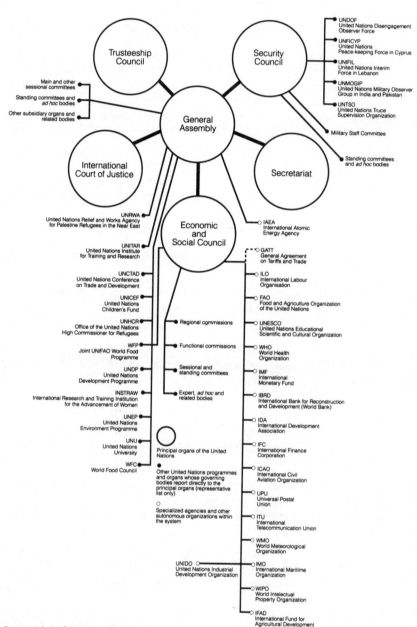

Source: United Nations Publication.

and 2 from Western Europe and elsewhere. Each member of the Council has one vote. Decisions of the Security Council on procedural matters are made by an affirmative vote of nine members (since 1965) and for all other matters also an affirmative vote of nine members with the additional provision that the nine include the concurring vote of the permanent members. In effect the latter requirement gives veto power to each of the permanent members.

The council has been given special responsibility for maintaining peace and security. It has power to investigate any dispute between nations to see if there is a danger to international peace and security, and to make recommendations for provisional arrangements, without prejudice to the final outcome, in order to prevent the situation being further aggravated. If the parties involved fail to respond, the Security Council may call upon all member states of the UN to apply sanctions, including:

complete or partial interruption of economic relations and of rail, sea, air, postal telegraphic, radio and other means of communication and the severance of diplomatic relations. (Article 41)

If these measures prove inadequate it might take such military action to restore peace and security as necessary including:

demonstrations, blockades and other operations by air, sea and land . . .(Article 82)

In order to make military action possible it was planned to make agreements as soon as possible with member countries as to what armed forces each would hold available for use on call by the Council, with regard to numbers and types of forces, degree of readiness, and general location, together with the nature of other facilities to be provided. The Security Council was to be advised on military affairs by a Military Staff Committee consisting of the Chiefs of Staff of the permanent members of the Council. Because a direct relationship was seen between these functions and (i) membership of the UN, and (ii) the person of the Secretary-General, the Council also votes on the issue of election and expulsion of members and on the appointment of the Secretary-General.

3. *The Economic and Social Council* (ECOSOC). This Council originally had 18 members but the number was raised to 27 in 1963 and then to 54 in 1971. All are elected by the General Assembly for three-year terms. The Great Powers did not insist on permanent membership of ECOSOC for themselves because its decisions are not binding and its powers are very general as compared with the powers of the specialized agencies. In practice, however, the main

industrial countries have been consistently elected to the Council. Each member has one vote and decisions are taken by a simple majority. The main functions of the Council are to formulate general principles with regard to economic and social matters, then to draw up general programmes of action, to make recommendations to the Assembly, and to coordinate the activities of the specialized agencies.

4. *The Trusteeship Council.* The membership of this Council consists of those nations which administered former colonies of Germany and Italy on behalf of the United Nations,[11] other permanent members of the Security Council, and as many other non-administering members (elected by the Assembly for three-year terms) as are necessary to ensure an equal number of administering and non-administering members in the total membership of the Council. Each member of the Council has one vote, and again decisions are made by a simple majority. The purpose of the Council is to watch over the administration of the Trust Territories by the countries given this responsibility. The Council has not had a very important role because much of the responsibility has remained with the General Assembly and because within a decade or two nearly all the territories in question had been given independence. The one important exception is South-West Africa, now known as Namibia, which is still controlled by South Africa.[12]

5. *The International Court of Justice.* The structure and functions of the Court are very similar to those of the Permanent Court of the League of Nations. It consists of 15 judges who are elected by the combined vote of the General Assembly and the Security Council for nine-year terms, with three changing every three years. With a view to minimizing a possible perception of partisanship, judges are not to be nominated by their own nation, no two judges may be of the same nation, and in cases when a judge is from one of the countries seeking arbitration then the other has a right to nominate a judge to the case. The function of the Court is to settle disputes between nations which voluntarily submit cases to it for its review and to give legal advice to the General Assembly. Like the Permanent Court it does not have power of compulsory arbitration.[13] The main differ-

[11] Several of the administered territories were former mandates of the League of Nations.

[12] The UN terminated the mandate in 1966. A recent agreement will give Namibia independence in the last half of 1989. The one UN trusteeship still remaining is that for the South Pacific islands (Micronesia) which is administered by the USA.

[13] As of 1986 only 46 nations out of the total UN membership of 159 had agreed to accept compulsory jurisdiction of the Court and many of these have attached reservations to their acceptance which deprive it of much of its meaning. Neither the USA nor the USSR are amongst the 46.

ence is that the Court's statute is an integral part of the UN charter rather than separate, as was the case of the League and the Permanent Court,[14] so that in consequence membership of the UN automatically requires recognition of the Court. This procedure was intended to put emphasis on the Court's role in maintaining peace. It should be added that access to the Court is not limited to members of the UN; thus Switzerland, Liechtenstein and San Marino have volunteered to take part in its activity. However, access is not permitted to private groups and individuals.

6. *The Secretary-General and the Secretariat.* The Secretary-General is elected for five-year terms by the General Assembly and the Security Council. He is the chief administrative officer of the United Nations and has the same functions as did the League Secretary, with the additional right 'to bring a dispute or situation to the attention of the Security Council'. He is the secretary of the Assembly itself and all three of its Councils. His supporting staff are in effect the international civil service who are to be recruited on the basis of efficiency, competence and integrity, but with due regard within these parameters for as wide a geographic distribution as possible. In practice, of course, the Secretariat has had the same problems as the League in the allocation of position by nation rather than on the basis of merit. A list of all the Secretaries-General of both the League and the United Nations is shown in Table 18.

TABLE 18

SECRETARIES-GENERAL OF THE LEAGUE OF NATIONS AND
THE UNITED NATIONS

Period of Service	Secretary-General		
League of Nations			
1920–1933	Sir Eric Drummond	1876–1951	UK
1933–1940	Joseph Avenol	1879–1952	France
1940–1947	Sean Lester	1888–1959	Ireland
United Nations			
1946–1953	Trgvie Lie	1896–1968	Norway
1953–1961	Dag Hammarskjöld	1905–1961	Sweden
1961–1971	U Thant	1961–1974	Burma
1972–1981	Kurt Waldheim	1918–	Austria
1981–	Javier Peres de Cuellar	1920–	Peru

[14] The League and the Permanent Court were established on the basis of separate sections of the Treaty of Versailles.

7. *Autonomous Agencies and other bodies.* The central organs of the United Nations are supported by 18 (originally 12) specialized agencies and autonomous organizations as well as by a number of subsidiary bodies managing specific programmes. There are also several coordinating regional commissions. The specialized agencies each have their own independent governing organs, secretariats and budgets. The autonomous organizations were created by the UN General Assembly and their degree of independence is less. Furthermore, in several instances they are partly dependent on voluntary contributions as well as public support for the financing of their activities.

Several of these agencies were hold-overs from the time of the League of Nations, e.g. the ILO, UPU, and the International Telecommunications Union (ITU). Others were new organizations which took over, and expanded, functions which had been carried out on a smaller and narrower scale by the League.

One of these was the Food and Agricultural Organization (FAO), founded in October 1945. Cooperation in this field went back to the pre-World War I International Institute of Agriculture. In the years immediately prior to the Second World War the League itself had also begun to take an active role in this field and had been involved in such activities as studies of nutrition and the concerns of consumers as well as producers. The new FAO had a much broader mandate than either the IIA or the League, not only because its interest was worldwide instead of being directed primarily to Europe, but because of its long-term concern about food supplies in relation to a growing world population.

Another organization in the same category is the World Health Organization (WHO), established in 1948, which evolved from the pre-World War I International Office of Public Health and its successor, the Health Office of the League (founded in 1923). The new organization had as its purpose the promotion of 'the highest possible level of health of all peoples'; by health was meant 'a state of complete physical, mental and social well-being'. Its mission was defined as:

(a) to act as a world centre of information and research on health matters;

(b) to coordinate measures for the control and eradication of epidemics and endemic diseases;

(c) to strengthen and expand the public health administration of member countries by means of surveys, technical assistance, pilot projects, etc.

A third specialized agency was founded to take over from a League office responsibility for promoting intellectual cooperation between nations. This agency, the UN Education, Scientific, and Cultural Organization (UNESCO), which was set up in Paris in 1947, has a constitution whose preamble states:

Since wars begin in the minds of men, it is in the minds of men that the defense of peace must be constructed . . . peace must be founded upon the intellectual and moral solidarity of mankind.

Apart from the issue of peace and international security, the subject which attracted the most concern in planning for the post-war world was the need to greatly expand the somewhat limited activities of the League in international economic cooperation. There were two main concerns. The first was a strong desire to avoid a repetition of the Great Depression of the 1930s. During that period nations, as already noted, had tried to reduce unemployment by encouraging exports and minimizing imports through such devices as subsidies on exports, tariffs and quotas on imports, and competitive devaluations and manipulation of their currencies in relation to other currencies. The cumulative effect of many countries pursuing such policies was a drastic reduction in the total volume of world trade, and thus an aggravation of the Depression which made conditions worse for all involved. The second concern was the need for the reconstruction of devastated economies after the end of the war and then the need to develop the economies of the less advanced parts of the world. Clearly these vast functions could not be undertaken by one international economic agency. Instead it was considered necessary to divide the main functions into three, each to be managed by a separate agency.

The first was to be an international trade organization which would supervise the dismantling of trade barriers between nations with an ultimate goal of genuine world free trade. This ambitious project at first seemed to have general support, but the US State Department, its main advocate, failed to persuade the US Senate that it was in the US interest – there was the usual fear of 'unfair' competition from countries which paid their workers low wages. Instead it was agreed to settle for a much more modest arrangement based on the grouping together of a series of bilateral trade concessions, which was known as the General Agreement on Tariffs and Trade (GATT). This was not a formal international treaty and therefore did not need to have the approval of the US Senate.

There was much more agreement on the monetary side of the world economy, and in 1946 the International Monetary Fund was established with the function of supervising the stabilization of exchange rates[15] and the elimination of exchange restrictions, processes which it was hoped would contribute to an expansion of international trade. The new institution was given a large fund based, in effect, on membership fees, which was to be used to provide short-term monetary assistance to countries suffering a temporary balance of payments deficit as a result of adjusting their policies to comply with requirements of the Fund.

The third of the core economic organizations planned was the International Bank for Reconstruction and Development (later known as the World Bank), which was also established in 1946 and which as its title implied was to channel international assistance for reconstruction of war-torn economies, and development of those which were least advanced. Later the World Bank established two specialized agencies: in 1956 the International Finance Corporation (IFC) to stimulate private investment in development; and in 1960 the International Development Agency to provide loans at concessional terms for the (50) economically most poor countries.

These agencies were circled by several others which had functions related to economic and social matters: the UN Reconstruction and Rehabilitation Agency (UNRRA), established in 1943 to give immediate assistance in the wake of the war, and which was later (1948) replaced by the UN International Children's Fund (UNICEF); the International Civil Aviation Agency (ICAO), founded in 1947; the World Meteorological Organization (WMO) and the UN High Commission for Refugees, both established in 1950. As the UN evolved over the next forty years more agencies and commissions were created, including the International Atomic Energy Agency (IAEA) in 1957, the UN Conference on Trade and Development (UNCTAD) in 1964, the UN Environment Programme (UNEP) and the World Food Council in 1974, the UN Centre for Human Settlements (HABITAT) and the UN University in 1975.

The Declaration of Human Rights

An important aspect of the United Nations Charter was an emphasis on the need to uphold human rights. The experience of the Second World War showed that governments which abused human rights were likely to be those which were aggressive in their relations with other countries. It was clear, too, that populations deprived of basic

[15] All national currencies were to have a fixed value in relation to the US dollar which in turn had a fixed value in terms of gold ($35 per ounce). This was known as the par value system. Changes could only be made with the prior approval of the IMF.

human rights would have a tendency to dissatisfaction, and continued oppression would eventually lead to a disturbance of the peace which could very well drag in outside powers in sympathy with the oppressed. Above all it was recognized that the main purpose of the UN (i.e. the peace and security of the world) had no meaning unless it embraced the physical, mental, and spiritual development of all humanity, and clearly that could not be the case when basic human rights were being abused.

The issue was first raised in the UN Declaration of 1942 which had included reference to the four freedoms: freedom of speech and expression; freedom of worship; freedom from want; and freedom from fear. The Charter of the UN gave emphasis to the subject in a sentence right at the beginning of the second paragraph of the preamble:

to reaffirm faith in fundamental human rights, in the dignity and worth of the human person, in the equal rights of men and women . . .

This was further reinforced in the statement of the purposes and principles of the UN which, as already noted, included the phrase:

promoting and encouraging respect for human rights and for fundamental freedoms for all without distinction as to race, sex, language or religion.

It was recognized that these very general principles could only be made effective if they were supported with a detailed statement of what precisely was covered by the term 'human rights', and ultimately if there were specific legally binding covenants, ratified by member countries. To this end, in February 1946 the Economic and Social Council (ECOSOC) established a Commission on Human Rights to study the issue. As noted earlier, the distinguished chairperson of the Commission was Eleanor Roosevelt (1884–1962).

At first there was a difference of opinion between the UK (Labour government) which wanted the Commission to prepare a Bill of Rights Covenant for ratification by members, and the US which, fearing difficulties with approval of such a treaty by a conservative US Senate, had a preference for a simple Declaration. A compromise was agreed whereby the Commission would prepare both a declaration and a series of separate covenants on implementation of the declaration.[16] A declaration was, of course, much easier to prepare, and, after clearance by ECOSOC, was sent to the General Assembly where it was approved without dissent on 10 December 1948

---

[16] Obviously, in studying the question the Commission had very much in mind the great declarations of the past: the Magna Carta, the United States Bill of Rights, and the French Declaration of the Rights of Man.

(however, the Soviet Union and Saudi Arabia did abstain). The full text of the Declaration is shown in Appendix 4. It can be truly said that this was one of the great milestones of the modern age on the way to the just society.[17]

The Declaration covers essentially two groups of rights. The first group included all the important traditional political and civil rights typically incorporated into national democratic constitutions and legal systems such as: equality before the law; protection against arbitrary arrest; the right to a fair trial and freedom from *ex post facto* criminal law; the right to own property; freedom of thought, conscience and religion; freedom of opinion and expression; and freedom of peaceful assembly and association. The second group, which were economic and social and reflected the special concerns of social democracy, included: the right to work and to choose one's work freely, the right to earn equal pay for equal work, and the right to education. All rights in both groups were to apply without distinction of race, colour, sex, language, religion, political or other opinion, natural or social origin, property, birth, or other status.

It was to be another eighteen years before final agreement could be reached on covenants which would legally oblige signatory governments to actually put the Declaration into practice in their own countries. Separate covenants were prepared for each of the two broad groups of rights. The Covenant on Civil and Political Rights states that signatory nations will undertake to enforce these rights immediately within their territories. The wording of this Covenant differs slightly from the Declaration insofar as it does not specifically mention the right to own property or to asylum; on the other hand, it has much stronger reference to the rights of all peoples to self-determination and to the rights of ethnic, religious, and linguistic minorities to enjoy their own culture, to profess and practise their own religion and to use their own language. The Covenant makes provision for a Human Rights Commission of 43 members[18] elected by contracting parties, which would consider complaints of violation of the Covenant (if agreed by the accused nation) and exercise its good offices to conciliate the parties involved. A protocol which could be signed separately from the Covenant gives individual citizens (as distinct from member countries) the right to bring grievances to the attention of the Commission. The second Covenant, covering economic and social rights (of which some might be beyond the capacity of a nation to implement immediately) is more

[17] Each year on 10 December, Human Rights Day is observed around the world. The other international day which is generally observed is United Nations Day on 24 October.

[18] To be advised by an eighteen-strong Committee of Experts.

flexible in terms of undertakings given and only requires signatory nations to give periodic reports showing that they are progressing towards the stated goals. The Covenants and optional Protocol, which were adopted by the General Assembly in 1966, came into force in 1976 after ratification by a minimum of 25 nations. So far about 90 countries out of the 159 membership have ratified the Covenants and about 40 the Protocol.

Within the general theme of human rights three particular aspects have attracted special attention and are considered to require supplementary comment. The first is genocide, defined as acts designed to destroy in whole or in part a national, ethnic, racial or religious group. The holocaust of the Jews was such a shock to the civilized world that in December 1948 the United Nations approved, with no dissenting vote, a Genocide Convention which provided for the prevention and punishment not only of the actual act of genocide, but of conspiracy and incitement to commit genocide, as well as attempts at and complicity in genocide. The Convention has now been ratified by the majority of member nations (about 100), though it was only in 1985 that the United States Senate, for long fearful that ratifying the Convention would invite foreign intervention in domestic affairs, finally gave its approval.

The second area of particular concern has been racial discrimination, a matter raised largely at the initiative of Third World countries, though with the support of Communist and some Western countries. This resulted in a Universal Declaration against Racial Discrimination in 1963 and a Convention in 1965 which, among other things, allows individuals to complain directly to the United Nations about violations. The Convention has now been ratified by more than 120 members.

The third special area of concern has been to reduce the incidence of discrimination against women. To provide leadership on the issue the UN Commission on the Status of Women was established in 1946. The work of the Commission resulted in adoption by the General Assembly of a Declaration on Elimination of Discrimination against Women (1967) and a legally binding Convention (1979). The Commission has also drawn attention to the vital role that women should play in development and peace activities, and has won wide publicity for women's issues by organizing two major international conferences (1975 and 1985) and by declaring an International Women's Year (1975) and a UN Decade for Women (1975–1985). The goal is 'to achieve a just society in which dignity, opportunity and power are not the monopoly of one sex'.

Other UN Conventions which relate to the area of human rights include those against torture, slavery, slave traffic, apartheid, discrimination in education and in employment, and that in favour of the right of workers to organize trade unions.

The United Nations Compared with the League of Nations

The founders of the United Nations were very conscious of the failings of the League and consequently concerned to avoid past mistakes when the new world organization was founded. How far were they successful and in what way can it be said that the United Nations is an improvement over the League? There are at least three major improvements.

The first is that the United Nations has become a true world organization representing virtually all the nations of the world (particularly after the influx of newly independent member nations in the 1960s). The Congress system during the nineteenth century was almost exclusively a European organization, although it had started to broaden membership and interest in the decade or so before the Great War. The League was certainly more widely representative than the Congress/Hague system, but even so it did not have members from the large parts of Africa, Asia, the Pacific and the Caribbean which were still under colonial rule, and its prime focus of attention tended still to be Europe. As a result of this new characteristic of universality, the UN General Assembly can be seen at least as a potential – if not yet an actual – forum for all the peoples of the world. One very important aspect of this universality has been that the United Nations, unlike the League, has had the membership of all the great powers, so strengthening its credibility. From the beginning membership has included the two superpowers, the United States and Russia, as well as France, Great Britain and India. The former Axis great powers, Italy, Japan and Germany, were at first excluded but later granted membership respectively in 1955, 1956 and 1974 (both West and East Germany simultaneously). China was temporarily excluded after the establishment of a Communist government in 1949 but became a member again in 1971.

The second important improvement over the League is the much greater weight given to economic and social cooperation, in which the activity is broadened not only in range but in depth – that is, from mainly exchanges of information and coordination of national policies to an international activist approach to the elimination of poverty, including the multilateral transfer of financial and technical assistance. This approach is connected with the recognition that ultimately peace can only be achieved by removing the underlying causes of conflict.

Springing from this same theme is the third improvement, which is the much greater emphasis given to the need to defend the basic human rights of all peoples and to the development of instruments to encourage improvements in conditions. Human rights as such had not been a major concern of the League (e.g. the failure to act on the race issue, as mentioned earlier). The League had in effect limited its activities in this field to certain requirements in the treatment of minorities in the former lands of the defeated Central Powers, or in lands which had changed hands as a result of the war – an unequal approach which caused resentment, especially in Eastern Europe.

In addition to these broad improvements as compared with the League, there are a series of minor technical advances in the organization itself, though some are perhaps more theoretical than real. Thus it has been considered an improvement that sanctions are no longer automatic but require the decision of the Security Council. In practice, of course, the League did not impose automatic sanctions either but depended on the decisions of the Council, as in the Ethiopian case. One minor improvement of this sort in making decisions more effective and real has been the confinement of veto power in the Security Council to the five permanent members – whereas in the League all members of the Council (temporary as well as permanent) had veto power. In the two leading economic organizations, the IMF and World Bank, voting on the ruling bodies (Boards of Governors and Executive Directors) is weighted according to financial contribution so as to encourage the support of the rich countries which otherwise might not have had confidence in the way their assets or donations were being used. This might not be very democratic, but it is a recognition of the importance of power in making things work in this early stage of internationalism. (It could be argued on the other hand that the one-nation-one-vote system in the General Assembly is also undemocratic, because it equates a country with a tiny population – such as Grenada – with one with a vast population such as India or China.)

A second organizational improvement claimed for the UN is the establishment of a separate Economic and Social Council to coordinate the organization's many specialized agencies in that field. In the League the Council itself was responsible for supervising such activities along with matters relating to peace and security. This did not prove effective, and in 1939 the League's Bruce Commission recommended that the two functions be separated – a recommendation which was followed by the founders of the UN.

A third organizational improvement (which has been noted earlier) was the increased authority given to the Secretary–General to take the initiative to bring to the attention of the Security Council any matter which he judges is a threat to the peace and security of the community of nations.

Yet another improvement which was claimed for the United Nations in 1945 was that it put more emphasis on removing the causes of conflict than in trying to solve problems by attacking such symptoms as arms races. In practice there has been little difference between the League and the United Nations on this matter, and certainly in recent years much of the focus of attention in the peace-keeping area has been on disarmament negotiations.

What, then, are the main characteristics of the United Nations? The first is obvious. Notwithstanding its strength as compared with the League it is still a 'cooperative' of sovereign states. It is still very far from being a world federation, even in embryo.[19] Its legal powers are extremely limited. The General Assembly has no powers to legislate for the world, to raise taxes or to interfere in the internal affairs of member countries, and it does not have its own police force for maintaining law and order between nations. It is true that the Security Council can make decisions with regard to peace and security matters, and that such decisions are indeed binding, but they require the approval of all five permanent members of the Council. The International Court can make legally binding judgements but only when member countries have agreed in advance to submit to its arbitration. There are certain legally binding covenants, such as those in the field of human rights, but again each covenant is only effective if specifically agreed in advance by the nation concerned, and in any case there is no effective instrument for enforcement.

A second general characteristic of the organization is that it goes beyond the minimalist approach to government advocated by *laissez-faire* liberals of the nineteenth century which essentially argues that government should be confined to defence, diplomacy, and law and order (a philosophy which, as noted earlier in the chapter on the welfare state, is having something of a revival at the time of writing). The minimalist approach was clearly still dominant when the League of Nations was founded in 1919. The United Nations, with its much greater emphasis on public intervention on a wide range of economic and social affairs, would seem to reflect the

[19] The UN Charter begins with the words, 'We, the peoples of the United Nations . . .', which might give the impression that the organization was indeed to be a government of the peoples of the world. This misleading introduction is soon corrected in the rest of the statement which consistently talks of the governments of the member nations, not the peoples. This is, of course, all confirmed by the very title of the organization.

philosophy of social democracy and the New Deal which flourished in the democracies in the years before the UN was founded and which were particularly strong in the heady days immediately before the end of the war.

A third characteristic of the UN is its decentralization. Clearly the General Assembly is intended to be the central organ, as it represents all the nations of the world, but its terms of reference are severely limited and other bodies have been given responsibility for important functions. Very obvious is the Security Council's role in peace and international security matters. Perhaps even more obvious is the independence of the multitude of specialized economic and social agencies, each with its own governing body, which are coordinated by ECOSOC but only in a very general fashion. This was partly a historical accident: several of the agencies were already in existence in fully fledged or embryo form before the UN came into being, with powers which they were not going to willingly surrender. No doubt it is also a matter of efficiency and convenience not to have the General Assembly interfere in matters where there are special interests, for instance at the ILO where there is representation for labour and employers' organizations as well as for governments; or in the principal economic institutions (IMF and the World Bank) where the donor countries will not allow outside control of the disposition of their contributions. Perhaps in addition there has been a prudent concern not to create an overly-centralized world organization which might become too powerful and authoritarian even as a 'cooperative'. Of course, decentralization has brought the usual penalties of overlapping programmes, duplication, and gaps in service, but though serious enough these deficiencies are as nothing compared with the waste of some one hundred and sixty national governments seeking their own national solutions to international problems – the immense sums spent on defence, for example, equal to about 5 percent of the world's annual production (see Table 14, p. 248).

CHAPTER 24

International Relations since World War II

The Background to the Work of the United Nations

BEFORE discussing the activities of the United Nations over the last forty years or so it would seem useful to identify some of the key external factors which have affected them. In particular, it is perhaps useful to briefly review relationships between member countries and the United Nations, and, more fundamentally, between themselves. This is because the United Nations, being a cooperative organization with little independent authority of its own, is necessarily deeply affected by such factors.

There are at least six broad trends in international relationships in the last four decades that would appear to have had an important bearing on the work of the United Nations. The first of these, which began to come into focus even as the United Nations was being formed, was the polarization of the world between West and East, between capitalism and communism – the so-called Cold War. The second trend, which started to take shape a decade or two later, was another division of the world's nations into two groups, this time on a North–South axis, between the nations of the 'First' or democratic-capitalist world (and to a degree, the 'Second' or communist world) on the one hand, and the 'Third World' of economically poor countries on the other, most of which were former colonies of the capitalist countries. This new division had the effect, at least partially, of blurring the hard edges of the confrontation between the West and East. A third general aspect of international relations, which had significance for the United Nations, relates to the impact of the post-war settlement, in the broadest sense, at the regional level. In some regions this caused a series of conflicts; in others it led to cooperation. As a result of all three of these factors, there was a changing balance in the relative power and influence of the most important nations of the world and this can be identified as a fourth trend of significance to the United Nations and its work. The fifth trend which should be mentioned in this context is a group of factors, mostly associated with the advancement of science and technology, which have together gradually turned the world into a global village where the activities of one nation increasingly affect the well-being of all other nations: the village neighbours. Finally, there has been the impact of a growing number of voluntary non-governmental organizations with a global perspective which have taken the initiative to encourage government at every level to give more attention to the collective long-term interest of all of humanity. Each of these six factors bearing on the work of the United Nations is discussed briefly in turn in the following paragraphs.

The Cold War

The clash between West and East has been centred largely around the rivalry of the two superpowers of the post-war scene, the United States and Russia. A traveller from outer space might at first be surprised at the intensity of the rivalry. In the past most wars have been between states which are contiguous with one another or nearly so. The United States and Russia, except at the Bering Strait, are thousands of miles from each other, on different continents and separated by two oceans. Furthermore, militarily, one is a traditional naval power, and the other a land power. The situation, of course, is not that simple. Powerful states typically like to protect themselves with a belt of friendly smaller states. The United States has always had a special concern about the whole American continent (expressed, for instance, in the Monroe Doctrine), and in modern times has extended that concern to the opposite rims of the two oceans which provide protection to East and West: Europe on the east side of the Atlantic and East Asia on the west side of the Pacific. Similarly, Russia has for centuries striven to extend its influence in Europe in the West, in South Asia along its southern border, and in East Asia. Thus, though the two superpowers are geographically widely separated, their two 'protective' belts of interest do touch, perhaps overlap, at two points: Europe and East Asia. Coincidentally, these two regions, notably Europe in the early post-war decades, are among the richest and most developed in the whole world and therefore of vital significance. It is not a coincidence that much of the tension between the superpowers has occurred in these protective zones and in Europe and East Asia in particular.[1]

[1] In recent years there has also been tension between the two sides about the Persian Gulf region, i.e. the southern flank of the Soviet Union, because of the growing importance of the region in supplying the non-communist world with oil. Talk of the Gulf being the jugular vein of the West is reminiscent of similar fears in nineteenth-century Britain that Russia was poised in this region to cut its communications with its empire in India.

The potential for conflict in the situation described above has no doubt been sharpened by the very fact that the United States and Russia emerged from the Second World War as by far the most powerful states on earth. It is argued, with good reason, that this situation alone would in most circumstances – though not all – lead to rivalry as to which would dominate the world – to be 'number one' as American politicians often put it.

Another unfortunate factor of the times that added to the tension was the experience of both nations of sudden attack, without warning, by another powerful nation – a truly life-threatening experience. On 23 June 1941 Nazi Germany, a nominal ally, had launched a full-scale attack on Russia and almost defeated her. The cost was perhaps as high as 20 million lives. On 7 December 1941, the 'Day of Infamy', Japan had launched its attack on Pearl Harbour and almost destroyed the American Pacific fleet. These traumatic events have sunk deep into the thinking of the governments and peoples of both the United States and Russia. Fear of surprise attack has been a dominant theme in their attitudes to one another. This was to be significantly reinforced when both nations had nuclear weapons and still more when they acquired huge fleets of ballistic missiles to deliver them to each other's territory at extreme short notice.

Important as all these factors are, it is a fourth which added a special ingredient of hatred, bitterness, and mistrust, namely the ideological dimension: the struggle to mould the whole world into one system – democratic capitalism on the one hand or egalitarian communism on the other. The West was very conscious of the Marxist willingness to use violence to overthrow governments in order to create a communist society, and in particular the threat that established communist governments would give political and military assistance to such efforts. In Eastern Europe after the defeat of the Axis, Russia maintained a large military presence after the West had demobilized, and this was seen as a clear threat to Western Europe.[2] Communist parties in non-communist countries were apparently manipulated to work in the interest of Soviet Russia rather than the interest of their own country. In the East, communist North Korea sent its armies to conquer its southern neighbour. The communist countries also had deep fears of the capitalist nations. Marxist theory predicted that capitalists would not accept communism but would plot counter-revolution. This had been confirmed when Western armies invaded Russia during the civil war of 1918–

---

[2] After the war the Soviet Union reduced its armed forces from about 12 million to about 5 million. The United States cut its forces from about 14 million to 1.4 million.

1920 with the objective of crushing the Revolution. During the 1950s American politicians spoke openly about rolling back the communist advance and periodically the United States would threaten to take advantage of its superiority in nuclear weapons.[3]

In reflecting on all these factors for conflict between the super-powers, it is perhaps a matter of surprise that a third world war has not occurred. There are no doubt many reasons. One is that both nations are, in the last analysis, extremely fearful of such a conflict: remembrance of the two world wars and knowledge of the horrific consequences of a nuclear war have acted as a powerful restraining factor. Each side for the most part learned to limit risks by (a) gener-ally avoiding provocation of the other in the most sensitive areas (the Cuban missile crisis being the most obvious exception to the rule), and by (b) conducting the military aspects of the duel through surrogates. Neither side had the willingness which existed in Germany in 1914 and 1939 to risk all to achieve the goal of world dominance:

. . . two powers have finally realized that while each has the capacity to destroy the other, neither is able to unilaterally control it.

Instead of a direct and major military confrontation, each preferred a more subtle and long-term approach, using a mixture of political, economic and social weapons as well as military to achieve their ends and to work with perceived forces of history. The main risk, there-fore, was not so much a coldly calculated plan to destroy the other side in a massive military strike, as one arising out of fear, an accident, misunderstanding, or miscalculation in a situation where there was virtually no time to correct a mistake.

During the post-war era it is possible to identify three broad peaks and three troughs in the degree of tension existing between the Western and Eastern blocs. The immediate post-war period (1945–1955) was one of extreme tension typified by such events as the Berlin Airlift (1948), the *coup d'état* in Czechoslovakia (1948), the communist insurgency in Greece (1949), the explosion of Russia's first nuclear bomb (1949), and the invasion of South Korea (1950). On both sides there were bouts of intense hysteria, e.g. the McCarthy Senate hearings in the United States[4] and charges of a doctors' plot against Stalin in Russia. The West created a series of regional military alliances, beginning with the North Atlantic Treaty

---

[3] Just as the USA would argue that nuclear weapons were necessary to offset the Russian superiority in conventional forces in Europe, the Russians could use the mirror-argument that their large army in Europe was to balance the nuclear threat from the West.

[4] The main source of alarm was discovery that Russia had been able to obtain secret information about US nuclear weapons through use of a network of spies.

Organization (NATO) in 1949, to oppose the Soviet Union and its European allies, and the latter responded with a mirror-image organization of their own.

Tension between the two blocs eased in the second half of the fifties following the death of Stalin, whose harsh, paranoic and monolithic regime had seemed particularly ominous to Western eyes, and the end of the Korean war. There was talk of peaceful rather than military competition. Soon, however, tensions were to reach a second post-war peak which extended into the early years of the sixties. Such tensions arose from fears on both sides: signs of widespread discontent in East Europe which led to the creation of the Berlin Wall (1961); revolution in America's own backyard (Cuba, 1958), and the apparent superiority of Russian technology in developing the first orbital space vehicle (Sputnik) and associated rockets, as well as extraordinary 'doomsday' bombs. A climax was reached with the Cuban missile crisis (October 1962) when for several days the whole world contemplated the imminent possibility of a nuclear holocaust.

That shock seemed to have had a sobering effect on both sides. Certainly in the next fifteen years tensions were reduced and there was even talk that the Cold War might be over. The collapse of the Russian–Chinese alliance blurred the hard edges of the distinction between the communist and capitalist worlds; a conservative government in the USA could contemplate a real political detente with Maoist China and put aside, almost overnight, the decade-long hysteria about the 'loss of China'. The new atmosphere made possible the first serious discussions about arms control since 1945. All was not wine and roses, however. The United States allowed itself to be drawn into a war on the Asian continent, propping up a corrupt, post-colonial regime against communist nationalists in Vietnam. Western governments lost a great deal of credibility when it became known that their intelligence services had also been engaged in unprincipled covert operations, which sometimes included the undermining of democratically elected governments. Soon it was apparent that the Soviet Union was taking advantage of the situation. She seemed to be gaining influence (and military bases) all around the world: Asia, Africa, and Latin America. There was the perception that she was growing relatively stronger in military terms[5] as the United States wasted its assets in Vietnam and then withdrew into itself after defeat. Matters came to a head with the Soviet invasion of Afghanistan in 1979 with the purpose of propping up an

---

[5] Of significance was not just the steady build-up of nuclear forces but expansion of conventional forces including, for the first time, a global navy.

unpopular communist government which had recently achieved power by sleight of hand. The third period of tension had begun. A new government in the United States was elected with a popular mandate to 'stand tall': to engage in a massive rearmament programme and to confront communism on every front. For a time hot rhetoric seemed to indicate a return to the worst days of the Cold War during the Stalinist era (see Table 19).

Then quite unexpectedly and suddenly, tensions began to ease for a third time with the coming to power in Russia of a new generation of leaders conscious that the real long-term power of Russia – its economy – was declining dangerously by comparison with those of the capitalist countries. Already there were signs that Russia was slipping to the number three spot in economic terms with the steady rise of the Japanese economy. There were signs of worse to come: Russia could not afford to waste 15–20 percent of its GNP on military affairs and to support dependent communist governments and revolutionary groups all around the world. Furthermore, if the economy was to grow, it would have to adapt to the efficiency-inducing rigours of the marketplace, which meant in turn that there would have to be room for initiative and freedom. Coincidently, these developments occurred at a time when the Soviet military leaders could afford to feel more confident than in the past because they had at last achieved an approximate parity with the USA in nuclear weapons. Accordingly, Russia offered an olive branch to the West:

Since an alliance between a socialist country and capitalist states proved possible in the past, when the threat of fascism arose, does this not suggest a lesson for the present, for today's world which faces the threat of nuclear catastrophe and the need to ensure safe nuclear power production and overcome the danger to the environment?[6]

Easier terms with regard to mutual arms reduction were proposed and significant unilateral reductions were undertaken; arrangements were made to help reduce conflicts around the world, most significantly in Afghanistan, and there was a relaxation of restrictions on human rights and emigration. Though suspicious at first, the West began to respond. Europe, and to a lesser extent the United States, were also becoming conscious that ever-increasing arms expenditures were a serious drag on their economies too (70 percent of the federal budget for research in the USA goes to the military). The Chernobyl accident and the nuclear cloud theory reinforced

6 From a speech of Mikhail Gorbachev in November 1987, quoted in *World Watch*, July/August 1988.

sense that a nuclear war is simply not winnable. The opportunities for establishing safer arrangements for the world on a permanent basis seemed greater than at any time since 1945, perhaps since 1918.

The North–South Conflict

The second key theme of post-war international relations has been the emergence of a division between the North and the South. After a decade of Cold War, many countries not directly involved began to realize that the situation was resulting in the neglect of their interests.

TABLE 19

NUCLEAR WEAPONS OF THE SUPERPOWERS

A. Growth of US and Soviet Strategic Nuclear Missile and Bomber Forces, 1945–85

	1945	1950	1955	1960	1965	1970	1975	1980	1985
Warheads									
USA									
Missiles				68	1,050	1,800	6,100	7,300	7,900
Bombs and ALCMs	2	450	4,750	6,000	4,500	2,200	2,400	2,800	3,300
Total	**2**	**450**	**4,750**	**6,068**	**5,550**	**4,000**	**8,500**	**10,100**	**11,200**
USSR									
Missiles				some	225	1,600	2,500	5,500	9,300
Bombs and ALCMs			20	300	375	200	300	500	600
Total			**20**	**300**	**600**	**1,800**	**2,800**	**6,000**	**9,900**
Delivery systems									
USA									
Bombers		some	400	600	600	550	400	340	263
ICBMs				20	850	1,054	1,054	1,050	1,028
SLBMs				48	400	656	656	656	648
ALCMs									1,080
USSR									
Bombers			some	150	250	145	135	156	160
ICBMs				some	200	1,300	1,527	1,398	1,398
SLBMs				15	25	300	784	1,028	924
ALCMs									200

B. Nuclear Warheads of the Two Superpowers, 1985

	USA	USSR
(A) Strategic (see above)	11,200	9,900
(B) Intermediate Range	236	1,435
(C) Tactical		
Artillery shells	2,400	900
Anti-submarine warheads	2,000	600
Anti-ship cruise missile warheads	0	1,000
Battlefield ballistic missile warheads	300	1,600
Anti-aircraft missile warheads	200	300
Anti-ballistic missile warheads	0	32
Anti-demolition mines	600	some
Non-strategic bombs	4,000	4,000
Subtotal	9,500	8,432
Total	**20,936**	**19,707**

In addition there are believed to be considerable reserve stocks giving all told a total of about 50,000 for the two superpowers together.

Source: Robert McNamara, *Blundering into Disaster*, Pantheon Books, 1987.

The Bandung Conference of 1955 attended by Asian countries was the first sign of a collective desire to work for an independent line. Much more explicit and global was the formation of the Non-Aligned Movement at a conference in Belgrade in 1961 sponsored by Marshal Tito, a pioneer rebel against the Cold War alignments.

In the late fifties and early sixties, the Third World bloc became much more numerous as it was joined by the new nations that had won independence from the colonial powers. In 1964 the expanded bloc formed a committee, known as the G-77,[7] to coordinate promotion of their mutual interests. Those interests fell into two broad categories: political and economic. Politically there was a strong desire to remove all vestiges of colonialism and outside intervention in their affairs. One example of this was support of the Arab nations against Israel, because the latter was seen as essentially an outpost of the West in the Third World. Another was to focus human rights discussions on racism and in particular opposition to the white-imposed apartheid regime in South Africa. The main economic concern was to reduce the vast difference in the wealth

[7] There were originally 77 countries in the group, but since then it has grown to include nearly 130 countries. In response the industrial nations formed their own caucus, the G-7 (USA, Japan, West Germany, France, UK, Italy and Canada).

between the industrial and Third World countries, and especially to eliminate the grinding poverty which was the lot of the majority of the peoples of the Third World. Many argued that this poverty had been aggravated by the exploitation of the colonial powers and recompense was demanded in the shape of substantial transfers of financial and technical assistance, as well as a restructuring of the world trading system so as to make it fairer for the less developed countries. A major problem with the trading system was a tendency for the relative prices of primary commodities to decline, a trend which was extremely damaging to the Third World countries whose exports were largely in this category.[8]

Though the West responded with some sympathy to the concerns of the Third World with regard to economic development, as will be

TABLE 20

RICH AND POOR NATIONS OF THE WORLD
GNP per capita, 1983

Wealth Category[1] in US dollars	Number of Nations & States						Percentage of Total	
	AFRICA	AMERICAS	ASIA	EUROPE	OCEANIA	TOTAL	COUNTRIES	POPULATION
5500 & above	1	3	13	19	3	35[2]	20.6	15.6
1635–5499	5	11	9	13	0	37[3]	21.8	20.7
401–1634	17	20	8	1	9	56[4]	32.9	13.5
400 & less	28	1	9	0	0	42[5]	24.7	50.2
Total	**51**	**35**	**39**	**33**	**12**	**170[6]**	**100.0**	**100.0**

[1] World Bank categories as used in the World Bank Atlas, 1985.
[2] Essentially Western Europe, North America, Japan, Australia and New Zealand, together with rich oil-producing nations in other parts of the world. Twenty-four of the thirty-five have per capital wealth of US$10,000 or more.
[3] Includes USSR (population of 272 million) and Brazil (population of 130 million).
[4] Includes Indonesia (156 million) and Nigeria (94 million).
[5] Includes Bangladesh (95 million), China (1022 million), India (733 million) and Pakistan (90 million).
[6] All the independent states of the world except for the Vatican. The figure does not include about 40 overseas territories and islands, most of which are very small. The most important are Hong Kong (5.3 million), Macao (0.3 million) and Namibia (1.1 million).

Sources: World Bank Atlas, 1985; and 'The World in Figures', The Economist, 1976.

[8] More than half of Third World countries are still dependent on only one or two products for more than half their export earnings. Another quarter depend on four products or fewer. (Report in The Washington Post, 19 February 1989).

discussed later, there continued to be a great deal of dissatisfaction. Then an opportunity seemed to occur for the Third World, or at least part of it, to take matters into its own hands. Rapid expansion of Western economies over two decades and increasing preference for oil as the main fuel had gradually made them more and more dependent on the Third World, particularly countries in the Middle East, for supply of this vital commodity. Following defeat in the fourth Israeli–Arab war in 1973, the Arab nations, which were the majority in the newly-created international oil cartel, the Organization of Petroleum Exporting Countries (OPEC), were able to organize a quadrupling of world oil prices – an accomplishment followed in 1979 with a further doubling of prices.

There were several results. The first was a major shift in the distribution of the world's income in favour of the OPEC countries. A second was increased inflation and a slow-down in the growth of the world economy which caused hardship for all countries, developing as well as industrial. A third was a major effort on the part of the industrial countries to develop alternative energy sources and to improve energy efficiency. As a result, a decade later the OPEC was to lose control over the international oil market and the price of oil fell by nearly two-thirds. A fourth result was the imposition of an additional financial burden on most Third World countries. In the first place this arose from the higher cost of imported oil. More serious in the long run was the growth of a huge international debt, now amounting to $1.3 trillion, for developing countries. This came about because much of the new wealth in the oil-exporting countries could not be invested at home and because they did not have the necessary skills to invest abroad. In consequence much of the money ended up in the banks of industrial countries. The banks found that the biggest demand for money was in the Third World countries, and there was competitive pressure to make loans accordingly, without the usual careful assessments. As might have been expected, poor use was made of the loans. For instance, in the case of Brazil, one of the biggest borrowers, it is estimated that less than a quarter of the funds were invested in productivity capacity. The rest were consumed by fees of middle men (ending up in Swiss bank accounts), military hardware, and prestigious public works. The payment of interest on these non-productive loans came to resemble a gigantic deflationary external tax on the economies of many nations, a situation made worse because interest rates (which were not fixed) increased in the early eighties primarily in response to large public sector and external account deficits in the United States.

When the crisis first broke in 1982 there was concern that the commercial banks would go bankrupt if, as seemed likely, countries failed to repay not only the principal, but the interest as well. This might, at least, have given the debtor countries some leverage. However, within a few years it became apparent that the banks had been able to build up sufficient reserves and to sell enough debt at a discount to largely safeguard their own position. The burden of the debt was then well and truly on the shoulders of the Third World – and, as always, it was the poor who were hurt most. Contrary to global needs, repayments of interest and principal far exceeded further loans to Third World countries and there began a net outflow of capital to the industrial countries (see Table 21). Development projects stopped, public expenditure on education and health was drastically reduced, unemployment was rampant. The per capita standard of living in several countries dropped over 5–6 years by as much as 40 percent. The UN Children's Fund (UNICEF) reported that the number of infants dying for lack of basic medical care in Third World countries had increased by 400,000 per annum. In this desperate situation the Third World countries were obliged to tone

TABLE 21

NET TRANSFER OF RESOURCES TO ALL
DEVELOPING COUNTRIES

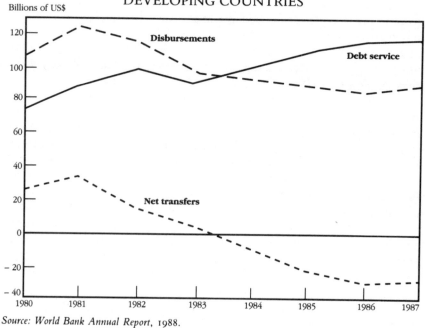

Source: *World Bank Annual Report*, 1988.

down the rhetoric of the North–South conflict and to get down to the pragmatic business of negotiating practical schemes of relief with the industrial countries. Thus, by the end of the 1980s, on the surface at least, there was a softening of relations along both axes of international relationships – North–South as well as West–East.

Regional Developments

During the last forty years the world has witnessed some 150 armed conflicts which have cost the lives of some 20 million people. Though a few of these were directly linked to the Cold War, e.g. Korea, and to the struggle for independence from the colonial empires (India, China, Indonesia, Kenya, Cyprus, Algeria, and others), the vast majority were concerned primarily with local disputes.[9] These struggles fall into two main groups: those between nations, and civil wars within nations. The wars between nations were generally about territory. The most important have been those between Israel and her Arab neighbours (five wars), between India and Pakistan (three wars), between India and China, China and Russia, Russia and Vietnam, Great Britain and Argentina, Iran and Iraq. Civil wars have been rampant in Latin America, Africa, and Asia. They have often involved outside intervention by the Great Powers or neighbouring countries. Most civil wars have fallen into one or more of the following three groups: national/tribal/cultural rebellion in the name of independence from an oppressive or indifferent majority; left-wing rebellion against corrupt and grossly unfair economic systems which result in terrible poverty for large sections of the populations, and most recently, efforts by international drug criminals to dominate nations in their own anti-social interest. In the vast majority of cases one or both sides in the conflict, lacking wealth, has resorted to use of so-called 'poor man's' tactics – hit and run warfare and terrorism. A special problem for the world community has been the widespread resort to international terrorism in order to attract attention to grievances – hijacking and bombing of airlines, attacks on airports, and others. Another more recent problem of regional conflicts has been the acquisition by a number of countries of the 'poor man's' nuclear bomb – chemical weapons and ballistic missiles for their delivery.

There has been a positive side to regional developments as well as negative, particularly with regard to the development of cooperative

[9] It is true, though, that some of the local disputes became subsumed to some extent by the Cold War (e.g. those involving left-wing guerrilla rebellions) and by the North–South conflict (e.g. the Israeli-Arab wars and the struggles in Southern Africa).

institutions. This is clearly a very important factor in establishing peace, because, historically, most clashes between countries have been between those that are physically close to one another with concerns about contiguous territory, surrounding seas, and cross-country movements of culture. There is always the risk that regional organizations will become inward-looking and hostile to the rest of the world, but in practice the positive aspects have tended to outweigh the negative. Certainly the United Nations Charter made a point of encouraging regional organizations (Articles 52–54) and was itself instrumental in establishing a series of regional commissions to coordinate the activities of its various agencies at that level.

Regional institutions, which have been established since the end of World War II independently of the United Nations, include the League of Arab States (1945), the Council of Europe, the European Community (1957), the Organization of African States (1963), the Association of South-East Asian Nations (1967), and the Caribbean Community (1973). Perhaps the most significant of the new regional organizations has been the European Community which has several subsidiary organs with real authority to which member countries have surrendered a degree of sovereignty even in their domestic affairs, for instance the European Court and the European Human Rights Commission. Of special interest is the European Parliament, which is in the process of evolving from an appointed consultative body into the world's first multinational elected legislative assembly – a precedent for a future world assembly. The very existence of the Community, which plans to have internal free trade by 1992, makes it very unlikely that there will ever again be a repetition of the frequent wars between members which have marred their history for centuries. Another useful European organization has been the Organization for European Economic Cooperation (OEEC) which was originally founded in connection with programmes for post-war reconstruction. In 1961 it was broadened to include non-European nations and to pursue the added objectives of promotion and coordination of international aid. The expanded organization was renamed the Organization of Economic Cooperation and Development (OECD). It presently has a membership of 19 European and 5 non-European countries.

Just as regional organizations help to promote peaceful relationships between nations, so too do those with common cultural ties, such as the British Commonwealth. Though the Commonwealth has little formal machinery for coordination of the activities of its members, it does serve as a useful channel, despite strong disagreements on certain matters, for strengthening understanding and empathy between nations in all parts of the world and with a wide diversity of size and economic wealth.[10]

Changes in the Balance of Influence between Nations

Without question, the character and work of the United Nations is deeply affected by the relative influence of the member countries. The democratic and constitutional nature of the institution clearly reflects the dominant influence of the western democratic capitalist nations, and in particular the United States, at the time of its formation.

The process of influencing international relations is undoubtedly complex and embraces a range of factors. Of course, military power and economic strength (meaning total wealth either on the basis of a large population or high per capita income, or both) are the constant underlying bases of influence – the ability to intimidate or resist intimidation, to provide or withhold material reward. In the long run, military power is closely related to a strong economic base, but in the short term at least it can be an independent factor if, for instance, associated with a willingness to make exceptional sacrifice (e.g. those two powerful military nations of modern times, Israel and Vietnam, are both relatively small and not wealthy). Other factors which can have an important bearing on national influence include cultural ties, e.g. the influence of France in French-speaking regions of the world, and language, e.g. the advantage the Anglo-Saxon nations have as a result of English becoming the commercial language of the world. Influence can also be strengthened by sheer national self-confidence and unity (e.g. the USA under President Reagan), skill in diplomacy (e.g. the Soviet Union under Mr. Gorbachev), and projection of an image or idea with wide appeal (e.g. President Kennedy and democracy, or Iran and the protection of Islam against Western materialism). Conversely, influence is lost when a nation is divided, full of self doubt, or shown to be acting in a disreputable manner (e.g. the worldwide revulsion against the covert operations of the Great Powers). Not to be forgotten is the respect and influence earned by those countries which give priority in their foreign policy to moral principle and to concern for the well-being of all peoples (e.g. the Scandinavian countries, Switzerland, Canada, Costa Rica, and others).

When the United Nations was formed, three of the pre-war Great

---

[10] Similar relationships of common interest and culture have developed over time between countries formerly in the empires of the other European powers – notably those of France and Spain.

Powers (Germany, Italy, and Japan) were without influence because of their total defeat during the war. Five nations were nominally Great Powers, but two of these (China and France) were almost as devastated by the war as the defeated nations themselves. Great Britain, too, was totally exhausted by the effort of fighting two world wars within a decade or two, and after several years she was forced to acknowledge that she was no longer in the first rank of powers. Russia had suffered most of all, but she had the advantage of exceptional size in terms of land and populations, all of which made possible maintenance of the largest army in the world. This gave Russia power and influence second only to the United States, the other superpower, which had not only a strong military arm but a huge and dominant economy.

The extreme pre-eminence of the two superpowers was to some extent linked to the weakness of the other large nations as a result of the war, and it was therefore likely to be temporary. As the other nations recovered from the war and rebuilt their economies the relative influence of the two superpowers was bound to be reduced. By the 1960s Europe had recovered and was to acquire, collectively, an economic power in the same league as the superpowers. By the 1970s the same was true of Japan. In the next decade, several newly industrialized nations in East Asia were to become important economic centres also. At the same time other countries, though less prosperous, were beginning to have more influence, especially in regional matters, simply because of their great size and population, e.g. China, India, Indonesia, Brazil, and Mexico. For periods, other nations would have unusual influence because of special circumstances, e.g. Saudi Arabia during the period of high-priced oil, or Iran after its 1979 revolution when she took leadership of the Islamic world in opposing Western culture.

While the influence of other nations was increasing the two superpowers found that there were severe limitations to their power, particularly that based on brute military strength. Both nations suffered humiliating military defeats (Vietnam, Afghanistan) when they tried to impose their will on smaller nations determined to have national independence. Possession of thousands of nuclear weapons proved to be less of an asset than originally assumed because in practice they could not be used and this became obvious to all. Even economic strength was less influential than in the early post-war period not only because of the rise of other economies but because both nations adopted policies of reducing overseas economic assistance.

Thus, by the end of the 1980s the original situation in which the

United Nations was largely influenced by power blocs led by the two superpowers was changing to one in which there were multiple centres of influence. There was growing recognition that even the most powerful could not 'go it alone' but would increasingly have to cooperate on the basis of something approaching equity in order for each to maintain its own security and well-being.

Global Village

The fifth trend in the relationships between nations which has bearing on the evolution of the United Nations system has been a series of technological developments which, cumulatively, are making the world into a global village where every nation is affected by and dependent on the activities of neighbour nations.

The first such development to come about was the invention of the atomic bomb. By coincidence this occurred in the same year, 1945, as the United Nations came into being.[11] It was recognized almost immediately that the new weapon was so powerful that it had the potential of destroying civilization. Nevertheless, for several decades national leaders seemed to act on the assumption that it was possible to win a nuclear war if one side was sufficiently superior in such weapons. The West talked of a nuclear deterrent to offset the Russian superiority in conventional forces in Europe and at various times (e.g. 1951, 1954, 1962, 1969, and 1973) one nuclear power or another would threaten to use these weapons to achieve its political ends.

Then a series of developments started to cool down the rhetoric. The first was the achievement of nuclear parity between the superpowers which made it more obvious than ever that even a successful surprise attack would not save a first user of nuclear weapons from massive retaliation. The second was the accident at the Soviet nuclear power plant at Chernobyl in 1985, which vividly illustrated in practical terms what would be the consequence of even a few nuclear bomb explosions. Thirdly, a series of studies showed that governments for over forty years had consistently under-estimated the devastating effect of nuclear war and that in fact even a limited nuclear war would probably create a 'nuclear winter', a cloud of dust which would encircle the earth and block out all sunlight for an extended period of time – thus killing off most life.[12] It was becoming clear that a nuclear war could not be won – any power

[11] The first explosion of an atomic device occurred on 15 July 1945, one month after 51 nations approved the creation of the UN; the first military use of this weapon was on 6 August 1945 at Hiroshima.

[12] The theory developed from studies of large explosions on other planets.

starting one would in effect commit suicide by shooting itself with its own weapons (leaving aside the effect of counter-bombardment). This theory served to reinforce the point that the issue is vital to all nations, whether or not they are likely to be direct participants in a nuclear war. The situation is given even more urgency when it is recognized that unless drastic action is taken there is a certainty that the number of countries with nuclear weapons will steadily increase, thus multiplying severalfold the risk of a nuclear war.

Though the nuclear bomb is still by far the most destructive weapon, it is certainly not the only one capable of killing masses of people in one blow. Thus, in recent years chemical and biological weapons have been improved to the point where they have a reasonable degree of reliability; they are cheap and can be easily hidden. Already several nations have such weapons together with the means to deliver them. The record of some of these nations suggests there would not be much hesitation in using them if it was thought that a military advantage would be gained thereby.

The second group of developments making for a global village is the massive threat to the natural environment brought about by a growing world population and the practices of industry, commerce, and agriculture. As discussed earlier, the air, water, and land are all being polluted and poisoned on a massive scale, and limited or fragile resources are being rapidly destroyed or exhausted. Most recently has been concern about the possible thinning of the ozone layer which protects life on earth from the radiation of the sun's rays, and about the heating up of the earth's atmosphere – the greenhouse effect – all as a result of man's activities. At best, the degradation of the natural environment will drastically lower the quality of life for ourselves and succeeding generations; at worst, it is a threat to life itself. The problems are so widespread (the greenhouse effect results from man's worldwide activities) that it is virtually impossible for even the most powerful governments, acting alone, to provide solutions. The situation calls for cooperation and commitment on the part of all nations.

The third trend making for a global village has been a group of factors which are steadily pushing national economies towards integration into a single world economy. A major role in this process has undoubtedly been the quantum improvement in communication systems since the end of the Second World War, e.g. the jet airliner and the application of electronics in such devices as radio, television, telephone, computer, and the artificial earth satellite. The jet airliner has facilitated multifold increases in the amount of international travel for both business and pleasure. One significant consequence of the microchip, the computer and the earth satellite is that national and regional financial markets (the heart of a modern economy) for currencies, commodities, and corporate shares are increasingly affecting each other and in some cases it is not an exaggeration to speak of the existence of a global market open twenty-four hours a day. Another facet of improved communications has been the tendency for English to become more than ever the standard world language – a consequence of the pre-eminence in world commerce of two Anglo-Saxon countries, first Great Britain, and then the United States.

Another factor which is moving the world towards a single economy has been the growth in number, size, and influence of transnational and global corporations.[13] Such corporations have evolved and expanded to take advantage of national variations in the cost of labour and raw materials; to achieve economies of scale which are not available within a national market; and to avoid national trade barriers (e.g. the building of factories in Europe and the United States by Japanese car manufacturers). This process has been strengthened by a huge increase in the volume of international trade in oil. This has come about because of the growth in the economies of the world as a whole; the popularity of the motor car; a general preference for oil over other fuels for power stations and industry; and the fact that the United States has joined Europe and East Asia as well as other parts of the world in being a net importer of oil after depletion of its own reserves. Not unconnected with the rise of the transnational and global corporations has been the development of a vast range of cheap and attractive consumer products such as soft drinks, cigarettes, automobiles, television, radio and records which are standardized worldwide. The point is driven home by the universally recognized advertisement such as the red and white sign for Coca Cola. The demands of the consumer and the advantages of trading in a world market have become irresistible. In the last few decades, the proportion of gross national product related to overseas trade has increased dramatically in nearly all countries (see Table 22). Even the Soviet bloc which for long largely isolated itself from the world trading system is now taking significant steps to become a part of it.

Though the move towards a global economy is generally perceived to be advantageous in aggregate, it can have brutal consequences for particular interests in the short and medium term. Cheaper labour in poorer countries and more efficient methods can lead to the

[13] A transnational corporation is essentially based in one country with branches elsewhere. Control of the corporation is in the hand of nationals of the base country. In global corporations, management and staff are recruited on the basis of merit and there is less concern to identify with a particular country.

TABLE 22

GROWTH IN WORLD PRODUCTION AND INTERNATIONAL
TRADE, 1780–1985
Average Annual Percentage Real Growth

Period	Number of Years	World Industrial Production	International Trade
1780–1820	40	2.6	1.4
1820–1840	20	2.9	2.8
1840–1860	20	3.5	4.8
1860–1870	10	2.9	5.5
1870–1900	30	3.7	3.2
1900–1913	13	4.2	3.8
Subtotal 1820–1913	93	3.5	3.8
1913–1929	26	2.7	0.3
1929–1938	9	2.0	−1.2
1938–1948	10	4.1	0.0
Subtotal 1913–1948	55	2.3	−0.1
1948–1970	22	5.6	7.3
1970–1985	15	3.2	6.1
Subtotal 1948–1985	37	4.6	6.8
Total 1780–1985	**205**	**3.5**	**3.2**

Sources: W.W. Rostow, *The World Economy, History and Prospect*, University of Texas Press, 1978; *International Financial Statistics Yearbook for 1980*, IFS, Washington DC.

undercutting of whole industries in other countries, e.g. the elimination of much of the ship-building industry of Northern Europe and North America as a result of competition from Japan and Korea. Such events naturally lead to calls for protection of home markets in order to maintain employment. Perhaps even more powerful have been lobbies in Western Europe and Japan to protect farmers from the competition of cheap agricultural imports. The farm lobbies are powerful partly because of such factors as favourable distribution of parliamentary seats, and partly because of national security concerns to be self-sufficient in food and a sense that the farmer epitomizes the best values in society. Though protectionism in many instances is understandable, it is generally accepted that the net result will be a slowing down in the growth of total world wealth. In particular, as always seems to be the case, those penalized the most by protectionism are the poor countries, already hampered by over-dependence on export of a few commodities, of which many have a long-term tendency to fall in value in relation to industrial goods and services. There is an overwhelming case for cooperation, as observed in Chapter 20, to make sure that all benefit from the emergence of a world economy and that the burden of transition not be borne by the poorest.

Initiatives by Voluntary Organizations

As noted in previous chapters, voluntary organizations have played a major role with regard to every aspect of the evolution of the just society, not least in the field of international relations and the struggle to establish world peace. Most obvious was the vital role of voluntary organizations and private individuals in supporting President Wilson in the creation of the League of Nations. The importance of voluntary organizations comes from their dedication and interest in specific issues and the fact that for the most part they can be free of some of the constraints of governments, which are often overly concerned not to antagonize vested private interests whose support they need. Voluntary organizations raise consciousness, provide ideas, build up a constituency for these ideas, and then encourage governments to put them into effect.

During the lifetime of the United Nations voluntary organizations and private individuals have played a role at least equal to that achieved in earlier periods in promoting global perspectives and the interests of the whole of humanity. The range of subjects has included peace and world government, human rights, population, the environment, food supplies, famine relief, and many other fields. The United Nations itself recognizes the importance of voluntary activity in supporting its own goals and Article 71 of the UN Charter states that 'suitable arrangements for consultation with non-government organizations (NGOs)' should be made, especially by the Economic and Social Council (ECOSOC).[14] The point was empha-

[14] The UN divides accredited NGOs into three categories: first, those with broad membership and interest in many activities; second, those with specialized competence in a limited range of subjects; and third, all others. There are about 30 in category I, 200 in category II, and over 400 in category III.

sized by the Secretary-General in his 1988 report to the General Assembly:

Non-governmental organizations play an invaluable role in this respect, especially in campaigns for disarmament and human rights: the future is bound to call for even greater dedication from them.

Perhaps a few supplementary comments might be added about the two areas of special interest identified in this quotation: peace and human rights. One observation that can be made about the peace movement is the variety of organizations involved, ranging from popular mass movements to corporate foundations, university departments, networks of professionals, concerned soldiers, and many others. The Swarthmore College (US) *Peace Collection* a few years ago listed 1,500 peace groups in some 50 nations. One peace group which deserves special mention because of the widespread respect it has won for professional objectivity is International Physicians for Prevention of Nuclear War. It was founded in 1980 by groups of physicians in both the USA and the USSR and now has a membership of 135,000 in 41 countries. It was awarded the Nobel Peace Prize in 1985. In addition there have been distinguished individuals who have spoken forcefully on the issues, including Albert Einstein, Bertrand Russell, and most recently such writers as Gwynne Dyer, Carl Sagan, and Jonathan Schell. The second point worth making is that despite all its achievements, the peace movement is not a truly broad-based constituency; it exists in only about one-third of the independent nations of the world. Occasionally it will marshal large and impressive demonstrations for peace, for instance that at the UN headquarters in New York on 17 June 1982, which was attended by some 750,000 people. Unfortunately, the peace movement is often associated with a confrontational style and lack of evenhandedness – many Westerners believe, for instance, that it is subversive and devoted to the interest of the communist bloc. There is a clear need for the peace movement to broaden its appeal and its worldwide constituency by being objective, conciliatory in style, and truly global in its outlook, so that it can become a really effective force for promoting the highest priority issue of the time: the abolition of war between nations.

World human rights has been an activity where voluntary organizations have been particularly effective. All too frequently governments will compromise on this issue in the name of politics and diplomacy and this tendency has at times even affected the work of the United Nations itself. The bright searchlight directed by the human rights movements into the darker corners of government activity has encouraged democracies and the United Nations to stand firm and to shame oppressors into reducing abuse of their fellow human beings. Two of the most successful organizations in this field have been the International Commission of Jurists and Amnesty International.[15]

[15] The latter was founded in 1961 to campaign worldwide on behalf of those imprisoned because of their political or religious beliefs, and to work for basic human rights, humane treatment of all prisoners, and the abolition of the death penalty. The organization now has about half a million supporters in 55 countries. In 1977 it was awarded the Nobel Peace Prize for its work on behalf of some 16,000 prisoners specifically identified.

CHAPTER 25

The United Nations at Work

Adjustment to Reality, 1945–1962

The first decade and a half of the life of the United Nations was one of a broad leadership by the United States and of adjustment of expectations in the light of the Cold War. The commitment of the United States to the United Nations was strong. It had been largely responsible for the drafting of the Charter, and it provided between 40 and 50 percent of the cost of the organization and its agencies as well as a large proportion of the Secretariat staff. Generally, the United States had the support of the majority of the UN membership – friends and allies in Western Europe, the Americas and East Asia – and therefore the organization's activities were usually in accord with US wishes.[1] Though the UN was unable to live up to the high hopes of 1945 because of the Cold War, it was generally supported in most non-communist countries by governments and ordinary citizens alike.[2]

The Soviet Union, being in a permanent minority, was less committed. What influence it had was largely negative, as symbolized by frequent use of the veto in the Security Council.[3] Soviet staff in the UN Secretariat were routinely rotated, thus discouraging loyalty to internationalism, and the Eastern bloc as a whole was often in arrears with contributions. The quarrel between Russia and the USA was most damaging to the UN because the system of collective security envisaged in the Charter

was based on the assumption that the grand alliance of the victors of the

[1] It has been calculated that in the period 1946–1960 the US was in agreement with about 70 percent of UN General Assembly roll calls. (Riggs and Plano, *The United Nations*, p. 86).

[2] This benign approach was shaken somewhat in the early fifties when right-wing groups in the USA claimed that the UN was an instrument of international communism, and the US began the practice of requiring all US employees of the UN to pass a national loyalty test.

[3] In the period 1946–1950 the Soviet Union used the veto 92 times; the other permanent members of the Security Council used it 7 times.

Second World War would continue and develop into their joint custodian-ship of world peace.[4]

As President Roosevelt said, the Great Powers are the world's policemen; when they quarrel, world law and order is clearly at risk.

The first way in which the division between the superpowers reduced the potential of the UN as a peace-keeping organization was with regard to its ability to apply military sanctions against an aggressor. It soon became apparent that there was deadlock in the Military Staff Committee about arrangements for earmarking of national armed forces for use by the UN during an emergency. In the light of this difficulty it is remarkable that on two occasions the UN was, nevertheless, able to take significant military action to halt aggression and restore law and order. The first occasion was in 1950 when the Security Council authorized a UN force[5] to block the invasion of South Korea by communist North Korea. Normally such authorization would have been subject to a Soviet veto, but a short time before the vote the Soviet representative had walked out of the Council in protest against exclusion of communist China from UN membership. The second occasion was in 1960 when the UN provided 20,000 troops in response to an appeal from newly independent Zaïre for assistance in restoring law and order and preventing the secession of Katanga, one of the richest provinces. Much of the initiative in this episode came from Dag Hammarskjöld, the Secretary-General. The Soviet Government, still suspicious of the UN, took strong exception because such action was seen as an effort to strengthen the role of the UN in international affairs. Accordingly, there was a campaign to limit the power of the Secretariat by having three senior positions (a *troika*) instead of one, with one being assigned to the West, one to the East, and one to neutral nations. This proposal did not win approval and was eventually dropped.

The second activity of the UN deeply affected by the division between the two superpowers was disarmament. Agreement to reduce the level of armaments possessed by the superpowers in particular was an obvious way of reducing tension and making resources available for reconstruction and development. An under-lying difficulty which remained constant for decades was the issue of verification of agreements. The West, learning from the pre-war experience when the fascist dictatorships had secretly broken

---

[4] Annual Report of the UN Secretary-General, September 1988.

[5] Twenty-two members made contributions to the UN force but most of these contributions were small and 90 percent of the total was provided by the USA and South Korea.

international treaties on disarmament, were unwilling to sign any agreement to reduce their armaments unless there was a reasonable way of checking that the Soviets would actually abide by their side of the bargain. There was consciousness that evasion of international treaties is much easier for authoritarian governments than for democratic governments operating in an open society. The Soviets, for their part, aware of their own military weaknesses, particularly with regard to nuclear weapons, were adamant that they would not permit capitalists to spy on their armed forces. Until this fundamental problem could be solved, much of the disarmament discussion lacked reality and was reduced to an exercise in propaganda.

The debate began in 1946 with the 'Baruch' plan whereby the US proposed the establishment of an International Atomic Energy Commission, which would supervise destruction of existing atomic weapons (the US alone had them at this time) and then carry out inspections to make sure that the ban on such weapons was being observed. The Soviet Union rejected the proposal because it seemed designed to give the US a monopoly of knowledge on how to make such weapons and because of the verification issue. Not to be outdone, the Soviet Union responded with proposals for either complete disarmament (in 1946, 1959 and 1960) or deep cuts in armed forces (in 1949 a uniform one-third cut in those of the Great Powers).

For years UN disarmament commissions struggled with the issue but to no avail. Then in 1961 it seemed that there was to be a breakthrough. Under the terms of the McCloy–Zonin agreement there was to be complete disarmament supervised by an international disarmament organization which would have 'unrestricted access, without veto, to all places, as necessary, for the purposes of effective verification'. There was even talk of an international police force. Then it became clear that Russia, though ready to allow destruction of its weapons to be supervised, was not prepared to permit a count of existing stockpiles. The United States considered this a fundamental flaw in the process and consequently the negotiations ended in failure.

The third area of UN activity hampered by the suspicions and enmity of the Cold War was in judicial arbitration of disputes – the work of the International Court of Justice (World Court). As noted earlier, neither superpower was willing to agree in advance to the compulsory jurisdiction of the Court in disputes to which they were a party, and clearly this set an unfortunate precedent for less powerful nations. They would turn to the Court only when it was convenient. As a result, the World Court, like the Permanent Court of the League of Nations, has tended to be under-used and in effect of marginal significance. Nevertheless, there have been some successes which should not be overlooked. Between 1946 and 1984 the Court issued 42 judgements in cases submitted to it and gave 18 opinions on questions of international law. Among the judgements were several dealing with disputes which were a potential threat to peace, e.g., the mining of two British destroyers in the Corfu Channel (UK v. Albania); the shooting down of an airliner over Bulgaria (USA and Israel v. Bulgaria); the Iceland fishing dispute (UK v. Iceland); the Aegean Sea shelf dispute (Greece v. Turkey); and the Teheran hostages case (USA v. Iran).

Though lack of unity amongst the Great Powers made it very difficult for the UN to play the role of policeman (military sanctions against aggressors) or of judge (compulsory arbitration), the organization was able to perform other less dramatic functions which were useful in reducing tensions and armed conflict between nations. Such functions included the traditional 'go-between' good offices role of a third party which could often save face for governments unable to deal directly with an opponent (a role usually played by the Secretary-General); Commissions of Inquiry; mediation and conciliation activities. In addition there also evolved a role in monitoring cease-fires and armistice lines by placement of an international peace-keeping force between the disputants.

A recent study of the work of the United Nations showed that in the period 1945–1960 48 disputes were referred to the United Nations, of which 14 were settled and 29 others were ameliorated with its assistance.[6] Some of the more well-known instances when the UN was able to mediate and/or monitor cease-fire agreements included the Dutch/Indonesian dispute of 1947, the Greek border issue of 1948, the Kashmir dispute between India and Pakistan of 1948, the Israel/Arab War of 1948, the Suez War of 1956, and the 1962 dispute between the Netherlands and Indonesia over West Irian. Several of these disputes were side effects of the process of decolonization, and it is generally recognized that one of the most useful roles that the UN was able to play in this period was in facilitating and speeding up a process which might have been more violent and destructive than it actually was. Special mention should also be made of the useful 'good offices' service of Secretary-General U Thant in helping the two superpowers to back off from the 1962 Cuban confrontation with a minimum loss of face for both sides.

One valuable subsidiary role of the UN associated with peace-

6 Riggs and Plano, p. 212.

keeping was that of assisting international refugees fleeing from persecution and conflict. Pioneer work had been performed by the League but the circumstances of recent decades have made it necessary for the UN to undertake much larger programmes in this field. Thus, in the years after the Second World War the UN helped resettle some 1.6 million refugees.

New Directions, 1962–1975

The character and the work of the United Nations in the sixties and first half of the seventies was different in several ways from that of the forties and fifties. This reflected two developments in international relations which were discussed earlier. The first was the reduction in tensions between the superpowers which generally prevailed during this period, especially after the 1962 Cuban missile crisis; and the second was the entry into the UN of a large number of new member countries, most of which were newly independent and economically underdeveloped.[7]

With regard to its peace-keeping mission, the United Nations had a somewhat lower profile than in the earlier period, reflecting perhaps a desire for consensus and consolidation after the controversial actions in Korea and the Congo. Small peace-keeping groups were used in Indonesia, the Yemen, along the Indo–Pakistan border and again between Israel and her neighbours. For the most part, however, the UN was not able to contribute much to the resolution of these conflicts, and it should be added that it was virtually excluded from any role at all with regard to several other significant conflicts, e.g. those in Vietnam, between China and Russia, and between China and India.

By contrast, the period did witness some precedent-setting, if modest, progress with regard to disarmament. The first significant achievements came in the late fifties with (i) the establishment of the International Atomic Energy Agency (1957), which was charged with both promoting peaceful use of this form of power and, at the same time, administering safeguards against diversion to military use; and (ii) the signing of the first post-war arms control agreement – the Antarctic Treaty (1959). After this initial advance, there was a pause of about five years which was then followed by a veritable flood of agreements, largely focused on nuclear arms, but not exclusively so,

[7] Between 1955 and 1975 the membership of the UN virtually doubled (from 76 to 144). Forty-two of the sixty-eight new members were African countries. As already noted, communist China also became a member after the USA dropped its opposition.

TABLE 23

GROWTH IN MEMBERSHIP OF THE UNITED NATIONS,
1945–1985

Year	Total Membership						Increase in Members in last 10 years
	AFRICA	AMERICAS	ASIA	EUROPE	OCEANIA	TOTAL	
1945	4	22	9	14	2	51	
1955	5	22	21	26	2	76	+25
1965	37	24	27	28	2	118	+42
1975	47	29	34	30	4	144	+26
1985	51	35	36	30	7	159	+15

and dealing with such issues as testing, non-proliferation and limitations on size of arsenals. The main agreements were as follows:

The Antarctic Treaty (1959) to internationalize and demilitarize this continent. This treaty was a model for subsequent treaties on outer space and the sea-bed.

The Moscow Limited Nuclear Test Ban Treaty (1963) to ban nuclear tests in the atmosphere, in outer space and under water. Over one hundred nations were parties to this agreement though two important nuclear powers, France and China, were not.[8]

Hotline Agreements (1963) whereby Moscow and Washington were linked together with emergency teletype communication systems with the purpose of avoiding accidental war on account of a failure of communications. The need for such a system became evident during the Cuban missile crisis when the two superpowers were obliged to communicate through regular commercial facilities. Similar links were later established between Moscow and London, and Moscow and Paris.

The Treaty of Tlatelolco for the Prohibition of Nuclear Weapons in Latin America (1967). This treaty was supplemented by two protocols whereby existing nuclear powers agreed to abide by the treaty which had been signed by 22 Latin American nations. The three Latin nations most likely to acquire nuclear weapons – Argentina, Brazil and Chile – did not sign the treaty.

The Outer Space Treaty (1967) to ban all military activity in outer space.

The Non-Proliferation Treaty (1968) to pledge non-dissemination of nuclear

[8] In the eighteen-year period 1945–63, there were 526 nuclear explosions in the earth's atmosphere of which all except 31 were carried out by the USA and the USSR. In the twenty-one-year period from 1963 (the date of the test ban treaty) until the end of 1984, there were another 967 nuclear explosions of which 63 were in the earth's atmosphere – all of the latter being carried out by France and China. (*Source*: Ball and Mack, *The Future of Arms Control*).

weapons by those nations (USA, USSR, UK, France and China)[9] already possessing them and non-acquisition by all others. The UK, USA and USSR gave a guarantee to non-nuclear nations that they would protect them against nuclear blackmail. Again, over one hundred nations are party to this treaty, but several nations are not, including two that are nuclear, France and China, as well as several that are near-nuclear: Israel, India, Pakistan, South Africa, Brazil and Argentina.

The Treaty to ban weapons of mass destruction on the sea-bed (1971) beyond the twelve-mile coastal zone. This agreement does not, however, make illegal the passage of weapons through the sea, i.e. on submarines or surface ships.

The Convention on prohibition of the development, production, stockpiling and distribution of bacteriological (biological) and toxic weapons (1971). This is a strengthening of the 1925 Geneva protocol which only banned the use of such weapons but said nothing about production. The Convention did not cover chemical weapons, which are considered much more practical and therefore more likely to be used.

The Strategic Arms Limitation Treaty I (1972) to limit each of the two superpowers to two anti-ballistic missile systems and to an equal number of missile delivery systems for a five-year period. Though SALT I and related treaties were formally bilateral arrangements between the superpowers, they were linked to the UN because they arose from undertakings given to other nations in connection with the Non-Proliferation Treaty.

The Strategic Arms Limitation Treaty II (1974) was to remedy the main deficiency in SALT I which was the absence of a limitation on the number of nuclear warheads that could be placed on missile delivery systems. SALT II set a ceiling for each superpower of 2,400 on the total number of delivery systems with a subceiling of 1,320 for systems with multiple warheads. The US Senate refused to ratify this agreement mainly on account of the invasion of Afghanistan, but in practice, both sides have apparently observed its terms.

The Threshold Test Ban Treaty (1974) and Peaceful Nuclear Explosions Treaty (1976) to set a limit of 150 kilo tons on the power of underground tests. Like SALT II these treaties were not ratified by the US Senate.

The Helsinki Final Act (1975) with regard to security and cooperation in Europe. Thirty-five nations agreed to recognize Europe's post-1945 frontiers and linked security to economic cooperation and human rights. Ten years later the Helsinki 'process' evolved to include such specific rules as prior notification of large-scale troop movements and the right to observe them at short notice (challenge inspections).

The Convention on the prohibition of military or any other hostile use of

---

[9] The USA became a nuclear power in 1945, the USSR in 1949, the UK in 1952, France in 1960 and China in 1964. Since then India has exploded a 'peaceful' nuclear device (1974). Some 50 nations have nuclear power reactors.

environmental modification techniques (1977). This does not cover chemical weapons, however.

Though the advances in the arms control field were significant, they were overshadowed in terms of importance in this period of the UN's history by the shift in emphasis in UN activities towards economic and social affairs, particularly international development. This shift reflected the prime interest of the new majority in the General Assembly. For more than a decade the rich industrial countries were willing to go along with the desires of the Third World countries, acting on the assumption that international development would be beneficial to all. Not only would it contribute to the expansion of Western economies but it seemed likely to ameliorate grievances about the maldistribution of world wealth and therefore reduce some of the more fundamental causes of war.

Many of the UN's economic and social institutions established in the forties, which had hitherto pursued quite modest programmes, began to expand. Soon some 80 percent of the budgets of the UN and its agencies were devoted to development and related activities. The General Assembly adopted resolutions whereby the sixties were declared to be the First Development Decade and a target was set that the industrial countries should annually contribute 1 percent of their GNP to international development (the aid could be bilateral or, preferably, multilateral). This target was never reached in aggregate (see Table 24) and when the seventies were declared to be the Second Development Decade the target was lowered to 0.7 percent of GNP.[10]

During this period the international agencies charged with promoting an open world economy (GATT and the IMF) achieved some useful things. These were important not only for the industrial countries but perhaps even more so for the less-developed countries whose economic advancement depended as much on being able to export their products at a reasonable price as on direct financial and technical assistance. With the assistance of GATT, the main trading nations have negotiated, all told, eight rounds of reductions in trade barriers since the end of the Second World War. As a result, tariffs on imports of the leading industrial nations, for example, have fallen from an average of 40 percent *ad valorem* to about 5 percent. In 1964 a complementary institution – the UN Conference on Trade and Development (UNCTAD) – was organized, largely at the instigation of the distinguished development economist Raul Prebisch, to

[10] Though failure to achieve the target was disappointing in contemporary terms, it should be acknowledged that the amount of assistance which was given was quite remarkable in the perspective of history.

TABLE 24

OFFICIAL DEVELOPMENT ASSISTANCE FOR SELECTED NATIONS, 1960–1986

Donor Country	ODA as percentage of GNP				Proportion through Multilateral Agencies
	1960	1970	1980	1986	
Group of Seven					
USA	0.53	0.32	0.27	0.21	0.04
Japan	0.24	0.23	0.32	0.30	0.09
Germany	0.31	0.32	0.43	0.41	0.07
France	1.35	0.66	0.64	0.50	0.08
UK	0.56	0.41	0.35	0.29	0.07
Italy	0.22	0.16	0.17	0.37	0.09
Canada	0.19	0.41	0.43	0.47	0.17
Other OECD					
Norway	0.11	0.32	0.85	1.13	0.46
Netherlands	0.31	0.61	1.03	0.99	0.24
Denmark	0.09	0.38	0.73	0.88	0.36
Sweden	0.05	0.38	0.79	0.87	0.28
Belgium	0.88	0.46	0.50	0.48	0.10
Australia	0.37	0.59	0.48	0.39	0.09
Average OECD	0.51	0.34	0.38	0.35	0.09
OPEC Countries					
Kuwait		6.19	3.52	2.91	
Saudi Arabia		5.57	4.87	4.67	
Average OPEC		4.04	1.47	0.60	
Socialist Countries					
USSR		0.15	0.25		
German Democratic Republic		0.13	0.20		
Average Socialist Countries		0.15	0.20		
Third World Donors					
China			0.09	0.09	
India			0.10	0.06	
Official UN Target	1.00	0.70	0.70	0.70	

Sources: International Development Association in Retrospect, Oxford University Press, 1982; *World Bank 1986 Annual Report; OECD 1988 Report on Development Cooperation.*

press for trade and related measures which would reduce the disadvantages experienced by Third World countries in the world trading system, e.g. removal of discriminatory measures on a non-reciprocal basis as, for instance, in the Lome Convention, which gave special access to the European Community for former colonies of its members. Another concern was to stabilize the often volatile prices of primary products of Third World nations.

For its part the IMF, after a period of transition, obtained the agreement of most of the important trading nations to the abolition of monetary exchange restrictions and to observance of rules against competitive manipulations of currency exchange rates. During this period it developed a systematic programme of consultations with member countries with regard to economic, monetary and fiscal policies, as they affected the balance of payments and the world economy, as well as a system of conditionality in return for short-term financial assistance to bridge temporary balance of payments difficulties. In 1969 agreement was reached to create the Special Drawing Right (the SDR), an international accounting device which would supplement members' international reserves and thereby remove excessive and potentially disruptive dependency on one trading currency, the US dollar. It was hoped that by strengthening international liquidity the new device would help the growth of world trade. Later, when the par value system of fixed relationships between currencies had to be abandoned (1971) and the international currency market became volatile, the SDR was to become increasingly recognized as a useful international measure of value.[11] There was a clear visionary dimension to the SDR as it was a step towards a single world currency which would eliminate altogether the risk of loss on exchange rates, a factor which tends to hinder the growth of international trade.

As previously noted, the core UN institution for direct multilateral development assistance was the World Bank. In its early years, the Bank had concentrated on loans for Europe and Asia to help with reconstruction after the Second World War. This activity was relatively modest and in Europe had been completely overshadowed by the much larger and highly successful US programme, Marshall Aid.[12] Most of the early projects financed by World Bank loans were industrial in nature: power stations, dams, railways, steel mills. During the sixties and seventies the Bank expanded rapidly to

[11] The valuation of the SDR is calculated on the basis of a mix of the five leading internationally traded currencies. The value is relatively stable because a fall in the value of one currency will be offset by the rise in the value of another.

[12] The size of Marshall Aid can be judged from the fact that it absorbed 2 percent of US GNP over several years. During the war the US had become used to providing assistance on this scale, e.g. Land Lease, UNRRA, etc. The offer of assistance under the programme was extended to the USSR and its Eastern Europe allies as well as to Western Europe, but this offer was refused because they feared that strings were attached. It is generally acknowledged that Marshall Aid was a major factor in helping Europe to speedily recover from the devastation of the war.

meet the needs of the new membership of former colonial countries and the range of its projects became more diverse. Special emphasis was given to agriculture and rural areas, so as to funnel aid directly to the poorest section of the population, to slow down migration to the urban slums, and to promote self-sufficiency in food production. Priority was also given to such long-term necessities of development as literacy and general education, as well as to schemes to limit population growth. Two satellite agencies were established: (i) to focus very concessionary assistance to the poorest countries (the International Development Agency); and (ii) to encourage more private investment in less-developed countries generally (the International Finance Corporation). The three World Bank organizations between them have loaned nearly $160 billion to over 100 countries in the forty-year period 1946–1986, with most of the assistance being provided in the last twenty years. The work of the World Bank has been supported by several regional development banks and such special programmes as the Colombo Plan (1950) in Asia and the Alliance for Progress (1961) in Latin America. The Inter-American Development Bank (IDB) established in 1961 has made loan commitments amounting to $20 billion, the African Development Bank (ADB) dating from 1964, $0.25 billion, and the Asian Development Bank (AsDB), founded in 1966, $10 billion.

Many other UN agencies which make contributions to economic and social development also experienced rapid growth during the sixties and seventies. In 1965 two relatively small programmes for technical assistance and encouragement of capital flow into developing countries were merged into a new and expanded UN Development Program. Provision of technical assistance and training is considered a vital element in the development process because nearly all the newly-independent nations were lacking in trained personnel to manage their economies. By the seventies the UNDP was providing several thousand experts a year to about 150 countries. Other agencies playing an important role in development included the Food and Agriculture Organization (FAO), the World Health Organization (WHO) and the UN Children's Fund (UNICEF). In cooperation with other UN agencies the FAO developed and promoted new hardy strains of grain which made possible substantial increases in food production in several countries, especially in Asia and Latin America, and some (e.g. India) became net exporters instead of net importers of food. Food productivity was also increased in consequence of campaigns to reduce the incidence of locusts, rinderpest, foot and mouth disease, and other scourges. The WHO waged successful campaigns against such diseases as smallpox, cholera, yellow fever, yaws and trachoma. UNICEF has had particular success in annually saving the lives of hundreds of thousands of Third World children through programmes for immunization and for provision of oral rehydration for those afflicted by diarrhoea.[13] In addition to these direct programmes of assistance the UN has made a major contribution to the work of raising public consciousness of key long-term development issues by organizing a series of international conferences on such subjects as the human environment (1972 in Stockholm), population (1974 in Bucharest), food (1974 in Rome), and human settlements (1976 in Vancouver).

Yet a third highlight of the work of the UN in the sixties and early seventies, in addition to successes in the field of armaments control and expansion of social and economic development programmes, was in relation to human rights. The period witnessed several important achievements in the process of building up a comprehensive international consensus on this issue. As observed earlier, the two basic Conventions on human rights (one civil and political; the other economic and social) were agreed (1966) and entered into force (1976). In response to the specific concerns of the Third World countries approval was given to a Declaration against Racial Discrimination (1963) and a related Convention (1965). A generally more enlightened climate also resulted in a Declaration on the Elimination of Discrimination against Women (1967) and a related Convention (1979).

A Time of Doubt, 1975–1985

After more than a decade of intense activity, discontent with the UN started to build up in each of the three main blocs of member countries:

By the early 1980s, the UN had sunk to a low ebb. The essential prerequisite for effective action – superpower willingness to work together in the Security Council – was absent. The US regarded the organization, with some justification, as an anti-American vitriol factory. Moscow had for years seen it as a propaganda arena, not a forum for serious business. The UN's Third World majority was disillusioned . . .[14]

In consequence there was to be a period lasting several years when the UN was virtually under siege, and there were even those who were asking if its days were numbered.

13 UNICEF was awarded the Nobel Peace Prize in 1965.

14 Anthony Parsons, UK Ambassador to the UN, 1979–1982, quoted in *World Press Review*, October 1988.

There were several broad reasons why the Western democracies seemed to be turning against what was essentially their own creation. One of these was undoubtedly the general disillusionment with big interventionist style government at all levels, local, national and international, which had been fashionable since the New Deal but which had recently shown signs of failing to deliver what had been promised – a theme discussed in Chapter 18. Such views first became prevalent in the United States and the United Kingdom.

A second broad factor was greater emphasis on military strength as the most effective way of achieving security and influence in the world, a reaction partly to the Russian invasion of Afghanistan in 1979, partly to the shift in the relative military balance on account of higher levels of armaments expenditure by Russia, and perhaps not least to the obvious limitations of the UN in acting as a force for peace. (A UN report in 1984 estimated that there had been about 150 armed conflicts in the world since 1945, in which 20 million had lost their lives.) This new hard-line attitude was reflected in such incidents as the refusal of the US Senate to ratify SALT II, the US refusal to accept the ruling of the World Court with regard to its mining of Nicaraguan harbours, the US invasion of Grenada, and the British military operation in the Falklands.

A third factor was a growing popular resentment against the Third World and against international development in particular. This was provoked by a series of matters including hostile rhetoric in the General Assembly, the actions of OPEC, and attacks on Western interests by Middle Eastern countries such as Iran and Libya. Objection was taken to the way the Third World bloc was able to ram through important initiatives in the General Assembly with little serious attempt to obtain the consensus of the Western countries, particularly the United States.[15] Specifically, there was objection to the proposed New International Economic Order designed to improve the lot of poorer countries at a price to be paid by the industrial countries (at a time when they were already having problems of their own with regard to increasing unemployment and high rates of inflation). There was similar resistance to the new Law at Sea Convention (1982), particularly those provisions setting aside the ocean floor beyond national jurisdiction as the common heritage of mankind and creating an International Sea-Bed Authority to administer it. However, the single most explosive act of the Third World lobby was undoubtedly the approval by the General

[15] Calculations show that by contrast with experience in the immediate post-war period, the US and the UN General Assembly were quite out of step, and that the US agreed with less than 20 percent of its votes (Riggs and Plano).

POPULATION GROWTH

A. Current annual percentage growth rates by continent, 1980–85

Africa	2.92
Americas – North	0.90
– Latin	2.27
Asia – East	1.22
– South	2.16
Europe	0.57
Oceania	1.51
World	1.67
More developed countries	0.60
Less developed countries	2.00

B. Current Annual Growth Rates According to Population Growth Grouping

Annual Percentage Growth Rate	No. of Nations and Dependencies	Total population in millions (1982)	Percentage of Total
less than 1%	33	346.1	7.6
1–2	40	1,618.9	35.4
2–3	49	1,704.2	37.3
3% or more	37	324.2	7.1
no data	30	574.7	12.6
Total (average 1.7)	**189**	**4,568.1**	**100.0**

C. Historical World Growth Rates over the last 1500 Years
Percentage per century

Century AD	Percentage Growth	Century	Percentage Growth	Century	Percentage Growth
6	5	11	20	16	28
7	5	12	12	17	12
8	5	13	–	18	45
9	10	14	–	19	80
10	10	15	21	20	140

Sources: Colin McEvedy and Richard Jones, *Atlast of World Population History*, Penguin 1985; *World Atlas 1985*.

Assembly in 1975 of a resolution declaring Zionism to be a form of racism.

This piece of mindless and counter-productive provocation was a turning point in United Nations affairs, especially in the United States, without in any way helping the Palestinians.[16]

TABLE 26

IMPACT OF POPULATION GROWTH ON STANDARDS OF LIVING

Percentage Growth in Real Per Capita Wealth for Selected Countries, 1960–1985

Continent	Country	Percentage Growth		Real GDP Percentage Per Capita	
		REAL GDP	POPULATION	1960–1985	AVERAGE PER ANNUM
Africa	Ghana	41.6	87.3	−24.4	−1.1
	Kenya	183.0	121.0	28.1	1.4
	Nigeria	145.6	114.3	14.6	0.6
Americas	Argentina	54.3	53.4	0.6	–
	Brazil	325.6	77.3	140.1	6.4
	Chile	90.2	59.9	19.0	0.8
	USA	115.3	32.4	62.6	2.5
Asia	China	191.0	53.4	89.7	4.1
	India	146.5	73.7	41.9	1.7
	Indonesia	280.8	72.5	120.8	4.8
	Japan	478.6	28.3	351.0	14.0
	Korea	686.4	66.2	373.2	14.9
	Philippines	191.1	99.5	45.9	1.8
Europe	France	169.5	20.8	123.1	4.9
	German Federal Republic	157.0	10.1	133.4	5.3
	Italy	156.9	15.1	123.2	4.9
	UK	76.1	8.2	62.8	2.5
Oceania	Australia	171.7	53.2	77.3	3.1

Source: International Financial Statistics, 1987, International Monetary Fund, Washington DC.

Disillusionment with international economic assistance stemmed not only from what was interpreted to be ungratefulness on the part of the recipients but also from a feeling that it was simply not working: despite the billions of dollars poured into aid, less-

[16] Brian Urquhart, Former UN Under-Secretary-General for Political Affairs, quoted in *World Watch,* July 1988.

developed countries seemed to be just as poor as ever. Much aid seemed to be stolen by corrupt politicians or spent on white elephants, and a failure to curb population growth negated whatever achievements there were.[17] The development agencies were accused of pushing projects which damaged the natural environment, hurt the interests of indigenous peoples and did not have local follow-up commitment and support.[18] In GATT, several industrial nations, though paying lip service to the principle of free trade, started to justify various sorts of protective measures, claiming unfair trading practices such as subsidization of exports. The IMF was criticized by both the left and the right. With the collapse of the par value system, the increase in oil prices in the seventies, and the Third World debt crisis of the eighties, the IMF seemed to lose whatever symmetry of influence it had ever had. Its influence on the rich countries seemed to become less at a time when its power in the Third World was growing because more countries were turning to it for conditional lending. The left charged the Fund with imposing Western 'free market' policies which were unnecessarily harsh especially on the poorest sections of the population. Even though the industrial countries had more influence in the IMF (and World Bank) than in the UN because of the weighted voting system, they nevertheless downplayed the organization along with the other UN agencies. One sign of this was that the main industrial countries (the G-7) began a practice of having regular summit meetings to coordinate economic policy separate from the formal framework of the IMF.

Soon the industrial countries were expressing dissatisfaction with the UN structure as such, accusing it of being inefficient, over-staffed[19] and in some instances, blatantly anti-Western. Several of the G-7 countries, which together paid more than 60 percent of the cost of the UN, felt they were not getting their money's worth. As they are a minority in the General Assembly which approves the budget

[17] A 1979 poll in the United States indicated that people 'often doubted aid's ability to . . . maintain peace'. In addition, they felt aid went to the wrong countries and did little to relieve poverty. A remarkable 91 percent felt that 'too much of our foreign assistance is kept by the leaders of poor countries and does not get to the people'. In the United Kingdom, a 1971 poll showed that 'two thirds thought that the UK provided more than its fair share . . . and almost 90 percent thought most of the problems in the poorer countries could be solved if the rich people in those countries helped their own people more'. In a 1974 poll in Germany, 'about two thirds of those asked had singled out aid as something to cut if budget cuts were needed'. (*Source: The IDA in Retrospect*, OUP 1982, p. 15).

[18] Disillusionment with international development was reflected in the amounts given, which fell from an actual average of 0.5 percent of GNP to 0.4.

[19] By the early eighties the UN and its agencies had about 60,000 regular staff compared with about 1,000 for the League. Though undoubtedly in need of trimming in some areas, the UN could hardly be called large when compared with the national public services of any one of the industrial countries.

they felt they had little control. The US Senate passed the Kassebaum amendment which required the US to reduce its regular contributions to the UN from 25 percent of the total to 20 percent.[20] Demands were made for retrenchment and as a gesture to show how exasperated they were with the most extreme cases the US and the UK terminated their membership of UNESCO.

Even before these criticisms started to crystallize the UN had made several efforts to reform. In 1974 it commissioned a group of experts, led by Richard Gardner of Columbia University, to make a report on the United Nations economic development organization and programmes. The report, completed the following year, stressed the need for more sharply focused direction and elimination of wasteful duplication of functions. To achieve this it recommended greater centralization and rationalization of the organization through such means as: (i) a strengthening of ECOSOC so that it would have authority to lay down priorities; (ii) the appointment of a new Director-General for International Economic Cooperation, second in rank only to the Secretary-General himself; (iii) a new United Nations Development Authority to consolidate all United Nations development programmes; and (iv) the replacement of expensive world conferences with small specialist groups for specific issues. However, these proposals were not accepted by the General Assembly, partly because many nations believed that in the process of reform they would lose influence and earmarked posts in the international bureaucracy.

The UN also made an effort to see what could be done to increase its effectiveness as a peace-keeping organization. In the late seventies two committees reviewed the issue. They discussed proposals: (i) to establish a new permanent commission to perform mediation and conciliation services; (ii) to establish a fact-finding committee of experts; (iii) to enhance the World Court; and (iv) to obtain agreement that the great powers not use the veto in cases involving peaceful settlement of disputes and threats to peace. One interesting proposal was to strengthen the General Assembly by making it more representative of the peoples of the world and of the realities of political power. This was to be achieved by means of a new 'bonded triad' system for voting. Under this system a resolution would only be deemed approved if it had the support of (a) the majority of member countries (as at present); (b) the nations representing a majority of the world's population; and (c) the nations contributing

---

[20] The US contribution to the regular UN budget had been reduced to 25 percent several years earlier as a result of a UN decision to establish maximum (25 percent) and minimum (0.01 percent) levels. Seventy-eight members, i.e. more than half the total, pay the minimum.

the major part of the UN's financial support. Some idea of the basic facts involved for such a scheme is shown in Table 27. Unfortunately, nothing came of these 'peace' reforms largely because of resistance by both superpowers.[21]

TABLE 27

SHARING THE COST OF THE UNITED NATIONS BETWEEN 157 MEMBERS
Percentage of Total Cost

Percentage of Total Contributed	Number of Member States						Amount Contributed
	AFRICA	AMERICAS	ASIA	EUROPE	OCEANIA	TOTAL	
Less than 0.1	47	28	22	5	5	107	1.90
0.10–0.99	4	4	13	13	1	35	13.51
1.00–4.99	–	2	–	7	1	10	22.30
5.00–9.99	–	–	–	2	–	2	14.63
10.00–19.99	–	–	1	1	–	2	22.66
20.00 & above	–	1	–	–	–	1	25.00
Total	51	35	36	28	7	157	
Amount Contributed	1.66	32.33	15.64	48.42	1.95		100.00

Note: The 10 largest contributors are

1	USA	25.00
2	USSR	11.82
3	Japan	10.84
4	Germany	8.26
5	France	6.37
6	UK	4.86
7	Italy	3.79
8	Canada	3.06
9	Spain	2.03
10	Netherlands	1.74
		77.77

78 countries make a minimum contribution of 0.01% of the total.

Source: The Statesman's Yearbook, 123rd edition, Macmillan 1986.

[21] However, one useful proposal which did win approval was that to establish a University of Peace. This was proposed in 1978 by Rodrigo Carazo, then President of Costa Rica. As a result land has already been set aside in Costa Rica for construction of the University, which will be built with voluntary contributions by governments, other organizations, and individuals.

Multilateralism: New Hope, 1985 to the Present

The remarkable improvement in East–West relations since the mid-1980s has presented the UN with an unprecedented number of opportunities to make valued contributions to the peace process and thereby enhance its own standing in the eyes of the world. The UN played a significant role in mediating the ceasefire between Iran and Iraq, the withdrawal of Russian troops from Afghanistan, and a settlement of the conflict relating to Namibia. It has also assisted with the reduction in tensions in the Western Sahara, in Cambodia, in Nicaragua, and even in Israel. In several of these cases the UN is providing monitoring or peace-keeping groups. Most notable is the arrangement for a 6,000-man peace force for Namibia, which has been given an unusually broad mandate to help with the transition to independence. The mandate provides not only for the maintenance of law and order (the contingent will include civilian police) and monitoring the withdrawal of foreign troops from the region, but also for giving of assistance in such matters as drafting a constitution and overseeing voter registration and elections. The award of the 1988 Nobel Peace Prize to the UN Peace-Keeping Forces was an indication of growing appreciation of the value of these services.

The UN has also been deeply involved in a whole series of advances in the area of disarmament. Under its auspices international agreement has been reached to extend the 1925 Geneva Protocol banning use of chemical weapons to cover production, stockpiling, and distribution as well. The problem of verification remains but an important advance has been made. The UN has also been associated to a greater or less degree with bilateral and regional arrangements recently agreed or under discussion. These have included: (i) the Intermediate Nuclear Forces Treaty (INF) between the USA and Russia which, for the first time, actually results in a reduction of nuclear arsenals (about 4 percent of the total); (ii) the talks on a Strategic Arms Limitation Treaty, which aim at a 50 percent reduction in strategic nuclear weapons; and (iii) negotiations for a reduction in the conventional armed forces of the two sides in Europe. In the offing are further significant possibilities: a comprehensive nuclear test ban treaty to cover underground testing and a treaty to limit manufacture of key elements needed for nuclear weapons (tritium and plutonium). Such arrangements could be reliably verified and would make a major contribution to elimination of the nuclear arms race.

Most encouraging also have been explicit statements by the Russian leadership that it wishes to give much more support to the

UN than in the past. In his speech to the UN General Assembly on 7 December 1988 Mr. Gorbachev said:

We feel that states must to some extent review their attitudes to the United Nations, this unique instrument without which world politics would be inconceivable today . . . Recent events have been making it increasingly clear that the world needs such an organization, and that the organization itself needs active involvement of all its members, their support for its initiatives and actions . . . World progress is only possible through a search for universal human consensus as we move forward to a new world order . . .

In support of this position the Soviet Union has taken steps to pay in full back-dues owed to the UN; it has expressed a willingness to accept the rulings of the World Court in human rights cases; and it has proposed reconstitution of the Military Staff Committee of the Security Council, as well as the placement of UN observers in areas of tension *before* violence occurs. Furthermore, it has indicated that it will modify its past practice of frequent rotation of Soviet staff in the UN Secretariat.

There is also evidence of renewed appreciation of the UN on the part of the Western nations, including the United States. Recent polls in the US show that 75 percent have a favourable view of the UN, a significant improvement over perceptions only a few years ago. This can be attributed not only to the peace services noted above but also to a more moderate tone in the General Assembly, reflecting a more pragmatic approach to problems on the part of the majority of Third World countries; the related issue of reform of several of the institutions; and, not least, a recognition of the unique role the UN can play in ameliorating world social and economic problems.

A key reform has been the agreement of the General Assembly that henceforth budgets will be approved on the basis of consensus rather than a simple two-thirds majority: this will allow the main contributors (the G-7 plus Russia) to have a much greater say in deciding on UN programmes and size of expenditures. Other recent trends which have gained general approval have included the depoliticization of UNESCO and conscious efforts on the part of the IMF and World Bank to respond positively to past criticism, e.g. better coordination between the two institutions, more concern for both the human and the natural environment by the World Bank, and for the poorest amongst the world's population by the IMF. A recent report on development and the environment prepared by a UN Commission headed by Gro Harlem Bruntland, Prime Minister of Norway, has received world-wide acclaim.

TABLE 28

MEMBERSHIP OF THE UNITED NATIONS ANALYSED BY POPULATION AND GROSS NATIONAL PRODUCT
157 Members,[1] 1983 Data

GNP in US$ Billions	Population in Millions								Percentage of Total	
	500+	200+	100+	50+	10+	1+	1⁻	TOTAL	COUNTRIES	GNP
3000+	0	1[2]	0	0	0	0	0	1	0.6	28.6
1000+	0	1[3]	1[4]	0	0	0	0	2	1.3	22.0
500+	0	0	0	3[5]	0	0	0	3	1.9	15.4
100+	2[6]	0	1[7]	2	6	1	0	16	7.6	19.8
50+	0	0	1[8]	1	9	5	0	16	10.2	7.0
10+	0	0	0	4	11	11	0	26	16.5	5.2
1+	0	0	0	0	12	41	12	65	41.6	1.9
0.1+	0	0	0	0	0	8	20	28	17.8	0.1
0.1⁻	0	0	0	0	0	4	0	4	2.5	0.0
Total	2	2	3	10	38	70	32	157[1]	100.0	100.0
Percentage of Total Countries	1.3	1.3	1.9	6.3	24.2	44.6	20.4	100.0		
Population	38.3	11.1	8.9	15.1	19.3	7.2	0.0	100.0		

[1] The official membership of the UN is 159, but this includes 3 for the USSR (USSR, Byelorussia and the Ukraine). There are 171 independent nations and states in the world. Of the 14 non-UN members the most important are North Korea, South Korea, Switzerland and Taiwan. The total world population in 1983 was about 4.6 billion and the total gross world product US$11,800 billion.
[2] USA
[3] USSR
[4] Japan
[5] France, Germany and the UK
[6] India and China
[7] Brazil
[8] Indonesia

Source: World Bank Atlas, 1985 and 'The World in Figures', The Economist, 1976.

Renewed appreciation of the value of the UN's unique economic and social services is particularly evident with regard to concerns about degradation of the natural environment. The UNEP is now receiving more enthusiastic support than at any time since its creation in 1974. Under its aegis, the nations of the world agreed in 1987 to the Montreal Protocol which it is calculated should result in

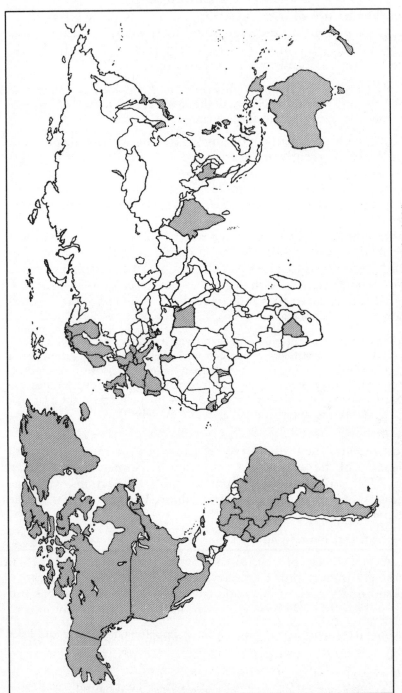

Nations with above-average practices with regard to Human Rights, (1984)

Source: Charles Humana, *World Human Rights Guide*, Pan Books, 1987

Based on 40 questions related to the Declaration of Human Rights and the two Covenants.

the worldwide use of ozone-depleting chemicals being reduced by some 30–40 percent by the year 2000. More radical measures may well prove necessary; nevertheless, as Hilary French of the World Watch Institute has said, this Protocol is the

first truly global treaty to deal with a threat to the global environment. It was also the first time the countries of the world agreed to impose controls on an industrial sector before all the evidence was in.[22]

Another useful agreement concerning a growing worldwide problem which has been recently sponsored by the UNEP is one to control international transfers of dangerous wastes. In addition, at the time of writing, plans are being mooted for an international treaty, to be administered by UNEP, to reduce global over-heating: the 'greenhouse' effect.

Other UN activities which have recently won acclaim have been in the field of health, notably the initiative of WHO in providing information on the global AIDS epidemic and its control, and in the field of human rights. With regard to the latter, it is increasingly appreciated that the treaties and conventions which have been agreed are not just pieces of paper:

The very existence of international standards may have a positive impact, particularly on governments concerned with their international reputation or those seeking grounds for altering their practices. More importantly, these standards may prove to be useful to citizens attempting to pressure their government into modifying its policies. In such cases, the fact that these standards are international and not merely those of a partisan, domestic political group may be of great importance.[23]

Most recently the President of France, when marking the fortieth anniversary of the Universal Declaration of Human Rights, called for a UN programme of human rights inspections and the publication of information on cases of abuse. His argument is simple and persuasive:

Silence nourishes oppression.

The general tenor of the times suggests that this will be an increasingly important activity for the UN in the coming years.

To summarize, recent developments in international relations and in the work of the UN have given grounds for increased optimism:

The United Nations is enjoying its most hopeful phase since the brief

---

[22] *World Watch*, July 1988.

[23] Jack Donnelly, quoted in *International Organization Magazine*, Autumn 1981.

euphoria when it was founded forty-three years ago.[24]

Multilateralism has proved itself far more capable of inspiring confidence and achieving results than any of the alternatives.[25]

However, some caution is in order. First, it has to be recognized that the present favourable state of affairs is very vulnerable to political shock – a change of policy by an important nation or group of nations could reverse recent advances almost overnight. The fragility of the situation is conveyed in the very terminology of the Secretary-General:

. . . sails of the small boat in which all the peoples of the earth were gathered seem to have caught a light but favorable wind.[26]

Second, it is clear that though there has been encouraging progress, the UN is still very far from being equal to the tasks at hand: the abolition of war between nations; a significant improvement in the economic well-being of the world's poorest; real protection of the environment; and proper enforcement of respect for basic human rights of all peoples.

A universal settlement is not around the corner . . . We are still a long way from a time when, as the French utopian theorist, Charles Fourier, put it, nations will 'dispute each other's excellence in the manufacture of little cakes'. But we are closer than we were.[27]

[24] Conor Cruise O'Brien writing in The Times of London, quoted in World Press Review, October 1988.

[25] Javier Perez de Cuellar, Secretary-General of the United Nations. Report to the United Nations, September 1988.

[26] Ibid.

[27] Martin Woollacott writing in the Guardian, quoted in World Press Review, October 1988.

PART III

The Future

CHAPTER 26

Where Do We Go From Here?

THE human race is rightly proud of its achievements in the arts and sciences. How the human spirit is raised by the beauty of music, painting, architecture, sculpture, literature, the theatre – all the arts and crafts in their variety and cultural diversity! So too is the mind expanded by contemplation of advances in science and technology, especially in the last two centuries.

What a piece of work is a man! How noble in reason! How infinite in faculty![1]

There is less pride, however, in achievements in political, social, and economic relationships, in large part because of the shock and horror of events in the twentieth century when apparently strong and civilized nations descended to the most barbaric behaviour. It has been a principal purpose of the first two parts of this book to draw attention to some of man's achievements in these fields and, while acknowledging the many failures, to show that here too there is much which merits our pride. The just society has by no means been achieved, but slowly, over time, there has been considerable progress in the right direction.

Although there is widespread scepticism today about the value of religion, especially in Western society, there is undeniable historical evidence that much of what has been achieved in moving towards the just society should be attributed to the direct or indirect impact of the world's great religions. They have immensely broadened man's vision of the universe and provided a sense of meaning, purpose and direction to life, encompassing such themes as the brotherhood of man and noble ethical standards of behaviour and thought. Undoubtedly this positive influence has been obscured because religious institutions have frequently led communities in directions which were contrary to their own principles and teachings; as a result some of the most terrible events in human history have been

[1] Shakespeare, *Hamlet*, Act II, scene ii.

attributable to religion. Nevertheless, the vision and principles which the great religions have brought are never entirely forgotten, and they have served as a standard by which people instinctively judge the behaviour of individuals and communities.

Though early civilizations were frequently brutal and cruel, they produced the first examples of themes essential to the just society. The great empires of the past (most notably those of China and Rome) gave proof of the benefits that flow from the maintenance of peace over a long period of time and over large areas. Ancient Greece provides an example of what can be achieved in a relatively free society where public issues can be openly discussed and a significant part of the population has some role in affairs of state. The revolt of Spartacus and the slaves of Rome was a milestone in the evolution of the collective consciousness of civilization. It is true that slavery would continue to be a recurring feature of civilization for another two thousand years, but it would be associated with a sense of unease. There was an unspoken awareness, sometimes weak, often fearful, but always there, that society could not be truly stable, peaceful and fruitful whilst it was built on the denial of the most basic freedoms to a part of the population. Similarly, the revolt of the Jews against the heavy-handed rule of Rome, though unsuccessful, showed that in the long run peace involves giving all peoples a right to express themselves freely through their own culture, a right to self-determination.

Slowly, over the centuries, man's consciousness of the idea of the just society and its basic requirements evolved. Then quite suddenly at the beginning of the nineteenth century the pace began to quicken, in step with technological innovations which made possible a great increase in the material wealth of mankind and the linking together of all communities into one world society. Progress towards a more just society was made on a series of interconnected fronts.

Political and social equality was the first. In the perspective of history, perhaps the most impressive advance will prove to have been the voluntary and almost total abolition of slavery, after thousands of years when nearly every major society considered it essential to the well-being of civilization. The widespread emergence of the national state, in which people are able to live according to their own culture and free of alien rule, took mankind another step forward. Of great significance, too, has been the replacement of authoritarian forms of government in many parts of the world with those that are constitutional and democratic, where ordinary people are not treated as children but are given an opportunity to participate in the management of their own public affairs. The growth of constitutional government has had reverberations even in countries where authoritarian forms of government remain, in the sense that these are increasingly sensitive about appearing, in the view of world opinion, to be oppressive and acting against the interest of their people, especially with regard to such issues as human rights.

The second 'front' where the pace of advance towards the just society has quickened in the last two centuries concerns elimination of poverty and a move towards greater equality in the distribution of material resources and services. These achievements in the economic sphere have come about partly as a result of a vast increase in total wealth, benefiting much of the world population, and partly as a result of the conscious effort of various movements – trade unions, cooperatives, socialism and the welfare state – to ensure greater economic justice and equal opportunity.

The conduct of international relations is the third arena where there has been considerable progress. International organizations have been established with the goal of bringing about world peace through such procedures as agreements to observe law in relations between states, collective security, disarmament, mediation of disputes, and negotiation of armistices between warring powers. Nations have taken steps to coordinate their policies concerning a whole range of economic and social fields for the benefit of all, and in particular to give financial and technical assistance to those countries that are economically less well off. For the first time in history there has been formed an international civil service, whose loyalty and outlook is governed to some degree at least by concern for the interest of all the nations of the world, not just that of their own countries. A multitude of non-governmental organizations, some with the highest professional and technical qualifications, have mobilized public support both to urge official bodies to maintain and increase levels of international cooperation, and to provide them with supplementary assistance. One of the greatest successes of the non-governmental organizations has been the development of a growing consciousness of and interest in the protection of basic human rights around the world.

Great as has been this progress towards the just society, there can be no question that far more has to be done, and done quickly, if there is not to be disaster on an unprecedented scale. In the political field the movement towards national self-determination, although nearly complete, has left a few areas where there is still enormous resentment against what is considered alien rule. In such situations, a sullen population will often give passive support to a passionate minority who engage in terrorism to publicize their feelings. Many nations which have achieved independence have allowed legitimate patriotism to become corrupted by greed and prejudice into a myopic chauvinism, leading to unnecessary conflict with internal minorities and external neighbours. Impressive as has been the advance of constitutional government, the majority of nations in the world still live under authoritarian forms of government, and many of those that are formally democratic are hampered by large-scale corruption and deep internal divisions. In some cases government has lost the power to maintain even minimum law and order, and the armed gangster rules the streets. Though democracy is undoubtedly an advance over autocracy, even the most advanced and well-established of democracies suffer from characteristics which detract from the well-being of their own people, not to speak of the well-being of the peoples of other nations. In particular there is a general tendency to a short-term perspective (i.e. a focus on the next election) and to promote sectional interest as a way of obtaining office. Though the foreign policy of the democracies is to some degree influenced by long-term ethical considerations, the major motivation is still short-term ruthless self-interest, and is often morally indistinguishable from the foreign policy of dictatorial governments.

These political failures are often linked to immense social and economic problems. Democracy does not easily survive today in conditions where there are large disparities in economic wealth within a nation. This is the case in many Third World nations, which despite all efforts are becoming poorer in relation to the rich countries. One aspect of the problem in these countries is a rapidly growing population amongst whom a virtually static level of resources has to be distributed. Another is the growing unwillingness of the rich countries to make the sacrifices necessary to help them, because of perceived failures of assistance given in the past, and, more important, increased concern for their own problems: high levels of unemployment, inflation, wastage of resources, pollution, and all the side effects of unadulterated materialism. The latter include widespread alcoholism and drug addiction, increased crime, and the breakdown of a sense of public duty and responsibility. Such symptoms of materialism are common to capitalist and socialist countries alike.

These political, social and economic problems come to a head on the international stage where the greatest failure of our time has been the continuation of armed conflict between nations despite the establishment of the United Nations. In the last year or two there has been a distinct cooling of international tensions, mainly as a consequence of improved relations between the two superpowers. Several wars have been stopped and there are better prospects for an end to the armaments race than at any time since 1945. Nevertheless, it should be cautioned that the foundations of the present *détente* are still far from firm. Until these foundations are permanently strengthened there will remain real risk of catastrophe on an unprecedented scale, either from conflict between the superpowers, accidental or otherwise, or as a result of the actions of the dozen or so other powers that have or may have access to weapons of mass destruction.

To conclude, humanity today faces challenges greater in magnitude and complexity than at any time since the beginning of civilization. Perhaps in the short run, with luck and good sense, we have a chance of muddling through and avoiding major disaster. In the long run, however, pragmatic muddling through in the traditional political fashion is not likely to be enough. The end result at best may be changes which are too modest and too late. There is a clear need to start thinking about a more thorough-going response to the great challenges – a response which will be needed over the long haul. The question is not just one of simple survival but of moving forward to a civilization which is prosperous and enlightened enough to provide every human being with the opportunity to reach his or her full potential. What is needed is a revival of that movement of progressive forces which has achieved so much in the past but which is now divided, directionless, and lacking in power because its supporters have dropped away out of weariness, disillusionment, and vulnerability to the seductive call of the materialistic philosophy which focuses on short-term selfish interest. Such a revival would involve:

(i) a unification of progressive forces, especially between those that put most emphasis on a free society with a democratic form of government and those which give the highest priority to the removal of the obstacles to human development that come from extremes of wealth and poverty;

(ii) a comprehensive programme which will give direction to the progressive movement and will respond to the major issues which face mankind today; and

(iii) a great awakening of popular enthusiasm and sustained commitment for such a programme, to provide the necessary power for its goals to be reached.

How can all this be achieved? The summary review of the most well-known progressive movements of the day in Part II of this book suggests that no one of them alone is able to fulfil all these requirements. There remain two alternatives. One is the development of some new movement, perhaps a syncretic philosophy, which will pull together all that is best from the movements of the past. Experience suggests that this will not work. It would no doubt involve, if taken seriously, some sort of international committee, which even with the best will in the world would take perhaps decades to come to a conclusion. And such a conclusion (if one were ever reached) would almost certainly represent a patched-together compromise representing the lowest common denominator by the time all the political bargaining had finished. This is not the type of programme likely to provide a real answer, or to arouse the long-term enthusiasm and commitment of a large part of the world's population.

That leaves the second alternative, which is to review the possibilities of progressive movements which have not so far been discussed. In taking this course the one movement which must surely attract immediate attention is the Bahá'í Faith. At first sight this may seem a strange choice, in view of the small number of its followers (about 4.7 million worldwide), its comparative obscurity until recently, and the fact that religion still has negative connotations for many. The suggestion is not made lightly, however; it is based on several reasons which it is believed have weight. Quite apart from the general point noted earlier that religion in its pure form has been the key progressive force in history, there are several specific aspects of the Bahá'í Faith which are relevant in this context. These include the comprehensiveness of its progressive approach to all the main problems which face mankind today, the great diversity of its adherents who are drawn from very nearly every nation in the world, and the fact that it is the oldest and most well-established movement for world peace and unity. In an age of instant communication the present small number of Bahá'ís is not necessarily a handicap. A movement in tune with the times cannot but attract millions when the issues become clear. In the light of these thoughts this book would be incomplete without a brief review of the Bahá'í Faith and its credentials as a progressive movement.

The Bahá'í method is not shrill and demanding; rather, it is in the manner of a gift offered to a king. In looking at this religion the peoples of the world are invited to strive for intellectual integrity, to make an independent and objective investigation to see if it makes sense and if it is the answer to the problems of the world. Unfettered investigation means being detached from views propagated by normal authority: tradition, the family, institutions. It means working matters out for oneself with all the tools available: reason, observation, intuition, meditation and prayer. It has to be recognized that this is indeed a difficult task and requires a great deal of concentration, especially to escape from the prison of time and place, for we are all deeply affected by the culture in which we have been raised. One example of such bias is the present-day common view of communism in the capitalist states, and vice-versa. Another is extreme scepticism about religion in a materialistic society.

The brief review of the Bahá'í Faith which follows has four parts. First, there is an examination of its broad vision of the universe to see whether this is likely to motivate change and improvement in society. Second, there is a summary of the Faith's programme of action as applied under present conditions to see if it is a practical approach to the building of a just society. Next there is a brief sketch of the long-term goal of the Faith, which is a new world society. Finally there is a short overview of the history of the Bahá'í community, to see what effect the Faith has on ordinary men and women in practice and whether this offers hope for the future.

In making this review some use will be made of quotations from the Bahá'í Writings. Many of these are from the Writings of Bahá'u'lláh (1817–1892), the Founder-Prophet of the Bahá'í Faith. Others are from the writings of Bahá'u'lláh's eldest son, 'Abdu'l-Bahá (1844–1921), whom He appointed to succeed Him as supreme guide of the Bahá'í community; and from Shoghi Effendi Rabbani (1896–1957), 'Abdu'l-Bahá's grandson whom He in turn appointed as His successor to the leadership of the Faith, with the title of Guardian. Following the death of Shoghi Effendi the world Bahá'í community has been directed by the Universal House of Justice, a world assembly elected by the international community every five years by secret ballot.

CHAPTER 27

The Big Picture

IN DISCUSSING the Bahá'í Faith's credentials as an effective world-embracing progressive movement there are two questions which require immediate attention.

The first of these relates to the fact that it is an independent religion with its own Prophet-Founder. It is not merely a sect of, say, Christianity or Islam. A large number of people, both religious and agnostic alike, are so used to the idea that all the familiar great religions are centuries old that they find it difficult to accept that one which is new can be a genuine revealed religion with the real power to change society. This is, of course, not very rational. Perhaps the most effective response is to review the evidence regarding the personality of the Founder, the quality of His teachings and their relevance to the needs of our time, and, above all, the impact there has been on His followers. These issues will be discussed briefly in the coming chapters.

The second question which arises when discussing a religion as a potential world progressive force is in a sense more fundamental: the widespread perception that all religion is contrary to science and therefore essentially a fraud. This is a view which has become common in parts of Europe and other Western countries in particular. This reaction is understandable. Most religions and their sects have beliefs and practices which indeed seem to be contrary to the evidence of science. Major forces in Christianity, in particular, have taken an aggressive stand against science, for instance in the persecution of Galileo when he produced scientific evidence that the earth revolved around the sun and not the reverse as the Church taught. More recently, attempts have been made to deny evolutionary theories and to maintain that the universe was literally made 6,000 years ago during a period of seven days. A long record of bloody quarrels about obscure theological issues, a belief in a static universe in which every man had his place which he should accept without question, and support for oppressive rulers, not to speak of corruption of religious institutions, have all combined to associate religion with superstition and reaction.

Science and Religion

Bahá'u'lláh said that truth is one, and that therefore religion and science cannot be in conflict. If some aspect of a religious teaching is clearly in conflict with concrete evidence provided by science, then that teaching is superstition and it is science which is correct. For this reason science does not oppose religion, but rather strengthens it by helping to clear away the superstition obscuring true religious teachings:

When religion, shorn of its superstitions, traditions and unintelligent dogmas, shows its conformity with science, then will there be a great unifying, cleansing force in the world which will sweep before it all wars, disagreements, discords and struggles – and then will mankind be united . . .[1]

The Bahá'í view is that science and religion are complementary; civilization requires both in order to progress. Religion is concerned with morals and spiritual requirements, and when it is weak, science, which helps with the material needs of man, is likely to become narrow in its view, arrogant and dangerous. On the other hand, when science is underdeveloped, the essence of religion can be veiled by ritual and superstition. It should be remembered, however, that in the short run at least, science is not necessarily objective:

Science is no inexorable march to truth, mediated by the collection of objective information and the destruction of ancient superstition. Scientists, as ordinary human beings, unconsciously reflect in their theories the social and political constraints of their times. As privileged members of society, more often than not they end up defending existing social arrangements as biologically foreordained.[2]

In this context it is perhaps useful to mention the Bahá'í view of the nature of the universe and of evolution, those particular stumbling-blocks of the Christian churches. The Bahá'í Writings refer to the vast size of the universe in both space and time. The universe is seen as consisting of units of energy which are continually forming and reforming into larger units of matter according to a universal law of attraction, repulsion, composition and decomposi-

1 'Abdu'l-Bahá, *Paris Talks*, p. 146.
2 Gould, *Ever Since Darwin*, p. 15. A classic example of scientific bias has been the use of evolutionary theory to justify the view that the white races are superior to others.

tion. The power of attraction organizes matter at several differing levels of complexity, of which the most primitive is the mineral. At a more sophisticated level it forms the vegetable, which has the power of growth and self-reproduction. At a still higher level is the animal which has the power of sensory perception. The highest and most complex form of matter is that which has not only the power of growth, reproduction and sensory perception, but also the ability to conceive ideas beyond itself – transcendental power. This is man. All levels of matter are forever changing and developing in relation to themselves and to the environment. Man himself has developed over an immense period of time from the most primitive beginnings, and in the process of evolution has passed through many different forms.

One distinctive aspect to the Bahá'í view of the evolution of man is the idea that he has always had the potential to be ultimately what he has become, just as the acorn, though humble in size and appearance, has the potential to become a mighty oak. From this perspective evolution not only results from ancestry and environment but involves also the fulfilment of inherent potential.

The clash of science and religion in the West inevitably led to science becoming involved in the old and ultimate question about the existence of God. The position of religion on this issue has been much stronger than on many subsidiary matters, and a whole range of rational arguments for belief in God have been presented. One is that the universe is in a constant state of movement and that there must have been some outside force – the First Cause – which set it in motion. Another is that the precise and detailed order of the universe, ranging from the galaxies to the atom, and culminating in the evolutionary process of nature towards higher forms of life, cannot be an accident – but must be the work of some intelligence far greater than man, the peak of creation. A recent refinement of this argument has been the calculation that the evolution of man has taken place in such a short span of time that the mathematics of chance indicate that it could not have been an accident. A third argument, going back to Plato, is that there must be some perfect standard, which is God, in order for us to realize that the things of this world are imperfect. Fourth is the argument of Immanuel Kant (1724–1804) in his *Critique of Pure Reason*, that as a practical matter any ethical system must ultimately depend on the decisive authority of some power greater than man.[3] A fifth argument is that there has always been in man an intuitive sense of God, even today despite massive campaigns by certain governments to eliminate it. This is too powerful and persistent to be dismissed, as it once was, as merely

[3] Hans Küng, *Does God Exist?*, p. 541.

a product of man's imagination in order to explain the forces of nature or to satisfy a need for a father figure to provide protection in an apparently hostile world.

Agnostics and atheists have been able to raise doubts about some of these arguments, but they have not been able to disprove them. Nor have they been able to demonstrate that the only alternative – that the universe is a pure accident – is as likely to be true. Nevertheless, disbelief in God is widespread. This does not appear to stem from conviction concerning the arguments (which are rarely discussed today anyway), but rather from a strong prejudice against religion as such, because of past experience with religious institutions and from the association of the idea of God with the unscientific and primitive anthropomorphic images projected for so long by churches when they were teaching ill-educated populations.

The Bahá'í Writings show that it is hardly surprising that man has difficulty understanding the idea of God, who is the Creator of a universe so vast and complex that it is in itself beyond man's comprehension. God is thus on a much higher plane of existence.

It is a self-evident fact that phenomenal existence can never grasp nor comprehend the ancient and essential reality . . . When we view the world of creation we discover differences in degree which make it impossible for the lower to comprehend the higher. For example, the mineral kingdom, no matter how much it may advance, can never comprehend the phenomena of the vegetable kingdom. Whatever development the vegetable may attain, it can have no message from nor come in touch with the kingdom of the animal . . . Likewise no matter how great the advancement of the animal it can have no idea of the human plane; no knowledge of intellect and spirit. Difference is an obstacle to this comprehension. A lower degree cannot comprehend a higher although all are in the same world of creation, whether mineral, vegetable or animal . . . Inasmuch as in the creational world which is phenomenal, difference of degree is an obstacle or hindrance to comprehension, how can the human being which is a created exigency, comprehend the ancient divine reality which is essential? This is impossible because the reality of divinity is sanctified beyond the comprehension of the created being man.[4]

Thus the Bahá'í Writings refer to God as that 'Unknowable Essence'. Though the essence of God is unknowable, the Writings maintain that there is evidence in the universe of the existence of God and that man has the capacity to see such evidence. The search for it, however, is not easy if the methods of search are confined to those used in the material realm, for such methods (empirical study, rational deduction, etc.) can give contradictory answers even about

---

4 'Abdu'l-Bahá, in *The Reality of Man*, pp. 53–4.

physical phenomena, let alone about the question of God. Even so, 'Abdu'l-Bahá did make the following statement to August Forel (1848–1931), the distinguished Swiss scientist[5] who subsequently became a Bahá'í, with respect to the rational argument of the 'First Cause' genre:

Now, formation is of three kinds and of three kinds only: accidental, necessary and voluntary. The coming together of the various constituent elements of beings cannot be accidental, for unto every effect there must be a cause. It cannot be compulsory, for then the formation must be an inherent property of the constituent parts and the inherent property of a thing can in no wise be dissociated from it, such as light that is the revealer of things, heat that causeth the expansion of elements and the (solar) rays which are the essential property of the sun. Thus under such circumstances the decomposition of any formation is impossible, for the inherent properties of a thing cannot be separated from it. The third formation remaineth and that is the voluntary one, that is, an unseen force described as the ancient Power, causeth these elements to come together, every formation giving rise to a distinct being.[6]

The Nature of Man

The task of searching for God is part of the process of developing our spiritual or higher qualities, and this point leads logically to discussion of the Bahá'í concept of the nature of man. In modern times all progressive movements have been initially motivated by a belief in the natural goodness of man – Rousseau's noble savage – which will be revealed once political, social and economic obstacles have been removed by reform or revolution. This optimistic view has been badly damaged in recent years because it does not seem to explain the experiences of our time, ranging from the holocaust of the Jews to the sometimes demoralizing effects of the welfare state on people. In reaction the prevailing view has swept around to the other extreme which sees man as essentially greedy, selfish, and aggressive. This is not far from the traditional Christian belief that man is innately sinful. It is certainly a view which undermines progressive movements, because it suggests that in the end nothing can be achieved. It is also unsatisfactory, because it too fails to explain human experience, such as the lives of the saints, the voluntary abolition of slavery, and the human rights movement.

The Bahá'í view lies in between these two extremes and embraces the concept that there are two sides to the nature of man. One side

[5] August Forel was a world-renowned psychiatrist, entomologist, anatomist, social reformer and peaceworker. His image appears on the present 1000-franc Swiss banknote.

[6] Quoted in *The Bahá'í Revelation*, pp. 225–6.

relates to his physical being – what he has in common with the animal and which motivates a drive to physical survival (the acquisition of the necessities of life: food, clothing, shelter) and the continuation of the species. The second side of his nature comes from those transcendental powers which distinguish him from the animal, and which find expression in love and concern for the well-being of others, and in a need for a meaning to life beyond mere physical existence. It is the Bahá'í view that the purpose of man is to develop this 'spiritual' side of his nature. When this happens man starts to fulfil his own destiny; he is noble, creative and happy, and the result is the advancement of civilization.

All men have been created to carry forward an ever-advancing civilization.[7]

When man fails to follow his true destiny and allows his higher nature to atrophy, then his physical side will become dominant; qualities which in moderation are necessary for his well-being become extreme and destructive. The qualities of physical preservation turn into selfishness, greed, material lust, laziness, lying, decadence, viciousness and violence, and society sinks into barbarism. Within limits – such as those imposed by time and place of birth, parents, mental and physical capability, health, accidents of nature – man has a free choice to follow the pull of either self. This means each person is responsible for his own actions. It is recognized that the lives of people vary greatly: some have much greater difficulties to contend with than others. What is important is not so much absolute standards, but how far the individual progresses toward the highest standards from the point of departure. Thus, much is expected in absolute terms from those who are fortunate in their circumstances.

This theme of the two sides to the nature of man is characterized on the one hand by optimism: a positive aspect which motivates a determination to advance civilization. At the same time it realistically puts responsibility on everyone to be on constant guard against dominance by his lower nature.

The view that the purpose of life is to develop the spiritual side of man's nature and in so doing to create an 'ever-advancing civilization', is seen in the context of a larger concept: a belief in a spiritual life after the physical existence has ended. Bahá'u'lláh said that man, in his physical existence, is given the opportunity to develop those spiritual qualities which he will require when he becomes a purely spiritual being. In the same way a child in the womb develops limbs,

---

[7] Bahá'u'lláh, *Gleanings*, p. 214.

eyes and ears for the time when he or she is born into the world. Of course, belief in a spiritual life after death is another casualty of the general scepticism with regard to religion, and again it is largely a reaction against simplistic teachings of the churches which have portrayed a heaven and a hell with almost physical qualities. The Bahá'í Writings say that the nature and joy of the future spiritual life is quite beyond anything man can experience as a physical being, and in consequence there is a limit to what he can learn from the Great Educators.

The nature of the soul after death can never be described, nor is it meet and permissible to reveal its whole character to the eyes of men . . . The purpose underlying their [the Messengers of God] revelation hath been to educate all men, that they may, at the hour of death, ascend, in the utmost purity and sanctity and with absolute detachment, to the throne of the Most High . . . The world beyond is as different from this world as this world is different from that of the child while still in the womb of its mother.[8]

The soul, like the mind, is abstract in the sense that it does not have a physical existence. It is reflected in the human body rather than forming part of it, and therefore it does not disintegrate at death. All people survive death, but at different levels of spirituality. The higher the level, the greater the understanding and joy in the creation of God. All become aware of their level after death, so that those who have only achieved a low level, because of their failure to grow when in the physical existence, will have cause for regret. This is the state which religions have called hell. Hell, too, is the state of mind of the man still living in the physical world who has allowed his spiritual qualities to wither away.

It should be added that Bahá'í teachings emphasise that man should not spend his life in contemplation of what is to come. His duty is to look to his life and actions during his physical existence. If he does this, the future spiritual life (which in any case can be only the subject of conjecture) will look after itself when the time comes.

This is not to say that man should cut himself off from all thought of God. On the contrary, he should seek God's assistance in the development of his spiritual qualities through meditation, prayer and fasting. Meditation frees man from his environment, liberates his mind from conscious direction, and allows it to contemplate the essence of reality. One specific act of meditation which Bahá'ís are enjoined to practise is to bring themselves to account at the end of each day. The very act of prayer, which is for the benefit of man, not God (who has no need of it) induces feelings of humility, detach-

8 Bahá'u'lláh, Gleanings, pp. 156–7.

ment, and contemplation of the things which really matter in life, and in so doing gives new strength.

Prayer and fasting is the cause of awakening and mindfulness and is conducive to protection and preserving from tests.[9]

This is particularly true of those prayers revealed by the Founders of the great religions, which always deal with the loftiest sentiments of man rather than those that are material or selfish:

Look not upon my hopes and my doings, nay rather look upon Thy will that hath encompassed the heavens and the earth.[10]

Because prayer is of such value in supporting the spiritual side of man's nature, it is a moral obligation for a Bahá'í to pray at least once a day. This should be at a time of alertness – such as at dawn – so that there is full consciousness of what is being said. Prayer is sometimes not easy at first for those who come from a non-religious background, but with time inhibitions pass away and there is a cleansing of the mind which comes from increased insight into the meaning of life.

Bahá'ís also observe a fast once a year for a period of nineteen days[11] during the month of March, when they abstain from food and drink between sunrise and sunset. The purpose of the Fast, an act of self-discipline, is to strengthen the sense of detachment from the material side of life, and at the same time to increase one's appreciation of those things which are daily taken for granted. 'Abdu'l-Bahá explained:

Fasting is a symbol. Fasting signifies abstinence from lust. Physical fasting is a symbol of that abstinence, and is a reminder: that is, just as a person abstains from physical appetites, he is to abstain from self-appetites and self-desires. But mere abstention from food has no effect on the spirit. It is only a symbol, a reminder. Otherwise it is of no importance.[12]

Discussion of the subject of life after death is closely linked with the question of pain – another reason for much doubt about the existence of God. Thus it is often argued that there cannot be a God because if He existed, He would not have subjected mankind to so much apparently unnecessary suffering. Concern about pain to this degree comes when existence is understood largely in physical terms.

[9] 'Abdu'l-Bahá, quoted in *The Divine Art of Living*, p. 27.

[10] Bahá'u'lláh, the Long Obligatory Prayer.

[11] A Bahá'í month; the Bahá'í calendar is described in Chapter 29.

[12] Quoted in Esslemont, *Bahá'u'lláh and the New Era*, p. 171.

Pain comes into perspective when seen in the context of the physical existence being a prelude to a spiritual afterlife. The Bahá'í Writings say that pain is an instrument of education, by which man can become detached and grow spiritually:

The mind and spirit of man advance when he is tried by suffering. The more the ground is ploughed the better the seed will grow, the better the harvest will be. Just as the plough furrows the earth deeply, purifying it of weeds and thistles, so suffering and tribulation free man from the petty affairs of this worldly life until he arrives at a state of complete detachment. His attitude in this world will be that of divine happiness. Man is, so to speak, unripe: the heat of the fire of suffering will mature him. Look back to the times past and you will find that the greatest men have suffered most.[13]

As C.S. Lewis pointed out, most of the suffering of man is caused by man himself. Negligence, ignorance, pride and selfishness attract pain to those who are responsible and for those who are around them, almost as a self-correcting spiritual law. If there is free will and if there is to be justice, there must be pain also. Pain has a purpose: it is a test for growth which calls for a vigorous response by the individual or by the community. The pain inflicted on men by the injustice of society is perhaps the greatest challenge of all, and the whole thrust of the Bahá'í community is to meet this challenge.

The best beloved of all things in My sight is justice.[14]

As has been observed already, belief in God and a spiritual after-life put the whole of material existence into perspective. The Bahá'í view is that everything that has been created by a good God must be good also. There is no evil as such in the world, only absence of good, just as darkness is the absence of light. Thus Bahá'ís, unlike adherents of some churches, do not feel weighed down by guilt. However, there is also belief that material things should be taken in moderation, for excess brings decreasing satisfaction (as expressed in the economic principle of marginal value) and may well be the cause of deprivation for someone else. It is important to keep a sense of proportion with material things. They can be enjoyed when the opportunity is there; but it is unwise and unhealthy to become attached to them. Their possession can be at best only ephemeral. Most important of all is the appreciation that the most profound sources of happiness are not to be found in material things but in matters of the spirit, the growth of the higher nature of man.

---

[13] 'Abdu'l-Bahá, Paris Talks, p. 178.
[14] Bahá'u'lláh, Hidden Words, Arabic no. 2.

The Cycles of Religions

Here, then, is something of the Bahá'í teachings on human nature. There remains one vital factor to complete the picture linking man to God. Bahá'ís believe that though man is free to choose between the pull of the two parts of his nature, there are limits beyond which he cannot develop his higher potential without external assistance, for it takes inspiration and imagination beyond anything he possesses to show him his own unsuspected potential. The normal sources of knowledge – empirical investigation, rational deduction and induction – are inadequate. The required inspiration and vision come at certain critical points in the cycles of history from great 'educators', or Manifestations of God, who have perspective and extraordinary insight into the meaning of life. There is nothing unnatural about the coming of these Educators. They come forward as part of what might be called a spiritual law, in response to the needs of society at the times of great moral confusion and despair which coincide with the decline of established beliefs, or because new circumstances have arisen for which traditional answers are no longer suitable. The Educators are the founders of the great religions. Many lived before recorded history; others have come to societies that have lost much of their record of the past. Those about whom we know at least a little are Noah, Abraham, Moses, Zoroaster, Krishna, Buddha, Jesus, and Muhammad.

The great Educators are distinctive in several respects. The first is the beauty and profundity of their teachings which if examined at their source, with scrupulous absence of prejudice, are clearly for the good of all mankind. Another is the example of their lives which fire love and respect in all men of sensibility. Like mirrors reflecting the light of the sun, the great Educators reflect the qualities of God in the manner of their lives. The depth of feeling they inspire is quite different from what may be felt about other men. The love that men may feel for a great artist or national hero is as nothing compared with what is felt for Jesus or Muhammad. Governments and established churches, seeing the influence of these Teachers as a threat to their own position, may try to repress them, but once they have made their claim to be the Educator for that age, they will never retract even unto death. Their followers, too, will risk all to break with the shackles of the past and to put into practice the new teachings, stumbling often, but nevertheless gloriously pressing forward to the highest attainments of life. This is the ultimate answer to the question of how we distinguish true prophets from the false.[15]

---

15 An example of a false prophet was Sebbati Zevi (see Chapter 2).

After religion's springtime comes the summer, when there is a phoenix-like rise of a new and more advanced civilization out of a previously moribund society. Thus, whatever may have been the weaknesses of early Christian society, no objective assessment could fail to remark on its progressiveness in terms of its humanity and its understanding of life as compared with the circus culture of Rome at the time of Tiberius and Caligula. The same thrust forward in the quality of society is noticeable in the Persia of Cyrus after Zoroaster, India after Buddha, the Kingdom of David after Moses, and the great Islamic civilization which followed Muhammad. It should be added that Bahá'u'lláh said that the rise of Greek civilization was in response to the teachings of the prophets of Israel.

Then comes the autumn. Over a period of time men gradually lose touch with the real nature of their Educator. They start to elaborate on his teachings, adding to them their own interpretations which soon carry the force of law. Parables, used by Educators to make a spiritual or moral point easier to understand and remember, are later read literally and the original point is lost. Different views evolve and quarrels break out, superstition becomes widespread and the true religious spirit begins to die. Men become hollow; they continue for a time to pay lip service to religion but their actions have less and less connection with their words. The fabric of society itself begins to weaken and tear. New conditions and problems arise for which there seems to be no answer. Winter has come. Then men begin to feel instinctively that something must happen to help society find its direction. It is time for the cycle of life to begin again and for a new Educator to appear with new teachings.

In the Bahá'í view, the teachings of each Educator have two broad aspects. First there are universal themes about man's relationship with God, his fellow human beings, and the universe at large: love, justice, detachment from personal desire, honesty, selflessness, faithfulness, humility, forgiveness, charity, obedience, mercy, trust-worthiness, sincerity, truthfulness, moderation. These themes are common to the teachings of all the Educators, and so in that sense each Educator is a Renewer, the means for the spiritual candle of mankind to burn brightly again after it has all but stuttered out. The second aspect is a group of social teachings which are the practical application of those general themes, adapted to the conditions of the time and the level of maturity of society. These are transitional and will be added to or replaced by subsequent Educators as circum-stances change.

Each divine revelation is divided into two parts. The first part is essential and belongs to the eternal world. It is the exposition of Divine truths and essential principles. It is the expression of the Love of God. This is one in all the religions, unchangeable and immutable. The second part is not eternal; it deals with practical life, transactions and business, and changes according to the evolution of man and the requirements of the time of each prophet . . . [16]

Some particular quality or teaching may be especially identified with an Educator, because of the circumstances of the time in which He lived. Thus Moses is associated with law, a vital requirement of a people setting up a new society in a strange land; Jesus, with love because of the need to temper the practices of religious leaders obsessed with the letter of the law rather than its spirit; Muhammad, with one God and one nation because of the extreme superstition and violent division of the Arab peoples amongst whom He taught. The teachings of each Educator will be, of course, ahead of the thinking of contemporary society, but not so far ahead that all men cannot understand them. They will be so much in tune with the needs of the time that should there be excessive resistance by government or a prejudiced people, the agony which society is then undergoing will become much greater.

As a pupil passes through a school, each teacher in turn builds on what the pupil was taught in his previous class. So too with the great Educators; each expresses the greatest love and respect for his predecessors, speaks of them as his equals, and far from destroying their work, strengthens and adds to it. Each has also had the vision to see that there would be a need for further educators after himself. Each in his teachings refers to his own return, not as a bodily reincarnation (as some mistakenly believe) but in the spirit. Sometimes the reference is to periodic returns, sometimes to one specific return when mankind would make a particularly significant advance in civilization (for instance what is referred to in the Bible as 'the time of the end'). Bahá'u'lláh himself said that as new problems arose in the distant future, new guidance would be needed and a new Educator would arise to provide it.

One of the most common criticisms of religion is its apparent division, as reflected in the existence of many different prophets and conflicting teachings, and with followers who claim that their particular version is the only truth. The Bahá'í theme of 'progressive revelation' points to a different conclusion. Religions are united by common universal themes, a progressive development of social teachings as civilization advances, and Founders whose attitudes to each other are characterized by respect and love. Apparent differ-

---

[16] 'Abdu'l-Bahá, quoted by Esslemont, *Bahá'u'lláh and the New Era*, pp. 117–18.

ences come from not recognizing the temporary nature of the social teachings of a religion, and from man-made additions to (and corruption of) the original pure teachings of the Founder. In the Bahá'í view 'progressive revelation' is the most significant force in history. Other approaches to history, such as that propounded by Karl Marx, may illumine certain aspects of man's experience, but what is important in the long run is the spiritual evolution of man: and this goes hand in hand with the development of the just society.

The Spiritual Dimension to the Progressive Movement

These underlying universal themes concerning the existence of God, the nature of man, a spiritual life after death, and the unity of religion are, it is suggested, factors which indicate the fundamentally progressive nature of the Bahá'í Faith. The very idea that the universe is in constant motion like society itself, and the consistent use of organic images rather than the mechanistic images of, say, eighteenth-century deists, suggests that inaction is contrary to the norm – very different from the medieval Christian picture of a static universe and society with every man obliged to stay in the station to which he was born and to accept life as it is. Belief in God induces a sense of humility and a protection against the hubris which the ancient Greeks so rightly warned about:

I testify at this moment, to my powerlessness and to Thy might, to my poverty and to Thy wealth . . . [17]

At the same time such belief develops a sense of responsibility because man is the highest creation of God, and a sense of unity of both the universe and of all men and women, the children of God. There is a clear statement of the purpose of life: to develop the nobler qualities and to help create an ever-advancing civilization. Even the most humble knows that he or she has a unique contribution to make to the building of the just society. Meditation and prayer help us to keep the vision in view. Knowledge of a spiritual life after death helps to give courage and frees us from material barriers to action. No 'pie in the sky' escapism here, but rather a freedom from a materialism which inevitably leads to the selfish and short-sighted philosophy of 'live for today for tomorrow we die' – a philosophy which is hardly likely to result in the just society. We cannot sit idly by while there is pain and suffering in the world, whether it is caused by nature or by man's injustice; it is our duty to ameliorate pain and suffering as best we can. And in these struggles we can be united at

[17] Bahá'u'lláh, the Short Obligatory Prayer.

the deepest level. The quarrel between science and religion is an illusion: a scientist can become a Bahá'í without having to split his mind into two separate and conflicting parts. Similarly there is no real division in religion. A Christian or a Muslim or a Buddhist becoming a Bahá'í does not give up love for Jesus, Muhammad or Buddha – on the contrary, the bonds are strengthened by greater understanding.

In proclaiming Himself to be the Messenger of God for this age, Bahá'u'lláh made the central theme of His teachings the need for all mankind to unite in order to avoid catastrophe and to continue the advancement of civilization. Until the nineteenth century such unity was not possible – or indeed necessary – because the world was divided into regions which had little or no contact with one another. Since then improvements in technology have revolutionized the situation so that all parts of the world are now linked together in a tight all-embracing web of communications. At the same time the major issues facing mankind – such as nuclear war, the environment, the economy, social habits and ethics – have become so extensive in scope that they can no longer be solved by individuals or even nations, but require cooperation at a world level. In the Bahá'í view, man has reached a critical point in history. He has to mature from a period of adolescence when he acquired great physical powers through the development of science, to a time of adulthood when he will learn to use these powers for the benefit of all. This requires a great strengthening of the sense of brotherhood and unity between all the peoples of the earth and the establishment of a world federal system which will put that spirit into effect by building a just society and enforcing universal peace.

Bahá'u'lláh did not confine His teachings to general exhortations or great themes about man's relationship with the universe and God. They also cover a wide range of practical guidelines for the achievement of world unity. It is recognized that the achievement of a just society will take time, and it is foreseen that there will be two distinct phases to the process. The first will be the 'Lesser Peace' when nations will have agreed to abolish war and settle disputes by peaceful means. The second will be the 'Most Great Peace' when the majority of the peoples of the world will have accepted His principles and teachings, and there is consequently a willingness to implement a truly just society. All the fundamental forces of history are pushing man in this direction; but there still exists the grave risk that the 'Lesser Peace' will not be achieved before mankind has undergone the trauma of another catastrophe, worse than anything ever experienced before, if there is not a major effort to overcome present divisions and address the real issues. Bahá'ís feel a responsibility to make their contribution, within the established system, to the resolution of these issues, as well as to bring about the 'Most Great Peace' in the longer term.

The Bahá'í teachings on society can be thus divided into two broad groups. Those that pertain to the period of the Lesser Peace include the changing of attitudes and the development of man's nobler and spiritual qualities, and also the evolution of a new model system of government demonstrating that a world system of administration can indeed work. These teachings will be discussed in Chapter 28. Later, in Chapter 29, there will be a brief discussion of the Bahá'í vision of a future world commonwealth and the coming of the 'Most Great Peace'.

Preparing for a Just Society

IN THIS chapter the present-day programme of action in the Bahá'í Faith is summarized to see if it is a practical approach to the building of a just society.

The Individual

Bahá'í guidelines for the individual in his relations with his fellow human beings are based on universal principles common to all the great religions. These may be divided into four groupings.

The first has to do with how we should view mankind. True religion urges us towards a deep sense that mankind is one family, that all are children of God, and that we are all, in essence, spiritual beings. As we all know only too well, some of our family are much harder to love than others. A practical approach to this problem is to understand that each one of us is at a different stage of spiritual growth, depending on the circumstances of our lives. By looking for the good qualities in others we both encourage their development and at the same time contribute to our own spiritual growth.

The second concerns putting these positive attitudes into action. We are enjoined to be kind to others, to be compassionate, especially to those who are unfortunate, to be forgiving of those who have committed wrongs, to be courteous, and to be generous, especially to those who are poor. In the Bahá'í Writings the principle of kindness is stressed by exhortation to beware of causing grief or despondency in the hearts of others. It is also quite clear that kindness is not to be confined to mankind but should be extended to animals and all living things. Courtesy, including the avoidance of bad language which degrades speaker and listener alike, is recommended as the 'lord of all virtues'. Generosity contributes to the goal of a just distribution of resources and the abolition of extremes of wealth and poverty – subjects which will be discussed more fully in Chapter 29.

The third group of guidelines concerns the cultivation of those qualities which will attract others. It is not enough to have a loving attitude: we must also make it easy for others to love us. Such qualities include trustworthiness, honesty and truthfulness, which 'Abdu'l-Bahá said is the 'foundation of all virtues'.

Finally, there is an emphasis in religion on taking steps to keep physically healthy so that we do not become a burden on the community and so that we can make a maximum contribution to its welfare. We are to treat the body as the temple of the soul. The Bahá'í Faith, like other religions, teaches moderation with regard to diet. It goes on to say that in the future, when conditions permit, diet should be based on grains and vegetables, and that meat would no longer be consumed – a teaching which has clear spiritual connotations as well as physical. Bahá'ís are urged to seek proper medical help when ill, to be physically clean (a practice which affects the spirit as well as the body), and to take sufficient exercise, recreation, and rest, though not beyond the point where it becomes a waste of time. It is pointed out that many illnesses are psychosomatic and sometimes such illnesses can be helped by prayer, meditation, and the influence of a person of high spirituality. Bahá'u'lláh added:

Yield not to grief and sorrow: they cause the greatest misery. Jealousy consumeth the body and anger doth burn the liver: avoid these two as you would a lion.[1]

These are broad principles essentially common to all the great religions. In the teachings of the Bahá'í Faith there are several refinements which receive special attention because of their particular relevance to conditions in modern society. Three of these relate to the first group – appropriate attitudes towards our fellow human beings.

The first of these is the need to make a conscious effort to abolish prejudice, which is a cause of disunity and conflict:

In every period, war has been waged in one country or another and that war was due to either religious prejudice, racial prejudice, political prejudice or patriotic prejudice . . . all prejudices are destructive of the human edifice. As long as these prejudices persist, the struggle for existence must remain dominant and bloodthirstiness and rapacity continue.[2]

The Universal House of Justice has developed this theme as follows:

Bahá'u'lláh tells us that prejudice in its various forms destroys the edifice of humanity. We are adjured by the Divine Messenger to eliminate all forms of prejudice from our lives. Our outer lives must show forth our beliefs. The world must see that, regardless of each passing whim or current fashion of

---

[1] Quoted in Esslemont, *Bahá'u'lláh and the New Era*, p. 103.

[2] 'Abdu'l-Bahá, quoted in *The Bahá'í Revelation*, p. 210.

the generality of mankind, the Bahá'í lives his life according to the tenets of his Faith. We must not allow the fear of rejection by our friends and neighbours to deter us from our goal: to live the Bahá'í life. Let us strive to blot out from our lives every last trace of prejudice – racial, religious, political, economic, national, tribal, class, culture, and that which is based on differences of education or age.[3]

It might be argued that prejudice is a particular problem of our time because there is more widespread and frequent contact between peoples of different cultures than ever before. Improvements in communications, and large-scale movements of peoples as immigrants, refugees, business travellers and tourists have brought people face to face with each other for the first time.

One of the most effective ways of abolishing prejudice is to learn to appreciate the diversity of culture in the world and to see it as an enrichment of our total experience. This mental attitude towards others receives special attention in the Bahá'í Writings:

Consider the flowers of the garden, though differing in kind, colour, form and shape, yet inasmuch as they are refreshed by the waters of one spring, revived by the breath of one wind, invigorated by the rays of one sun, this diversity increaseth their charm and addeth to their beauty. How unpleasing to the eye if all the flowers and plants, the leaves and blossoms, the fruits, the branches and the trees of that garden were all of the same shape and colour. Diversity of hues, form and shape enricheth and adorneth the garden, and heighteneth the effect thereof. In like manner, when divers shades of thought, temperament and character, are brought together under the power and influence of one central agency, the beauty and glory of human perfection will be revealed and made manifest.[4]

In speaking of the enrichment of society that comes from cultural diversity, the Bahá'í Writings make particular mention of those who have suffered extreme oppression, such as the African peoples and native Americans; they state that the sufferings of these peoples have made them more than usually sensitive, and that because of this they will make a special contribution to the spiritual illumination of a future world society.

Closely linked with these two themes is the Bahá'í principle of the equality of men and women. In the spiritual realm there is no difference between a woman and a man, and it is therefore not just for one to be treated as inferior to the other. Women play a vital role in society not only in their function as mothers of each generation, but also because if a just and peaceful society is to be achieved, there is

---

[3] Letter to all Bahá'í national spiritual assemblies, 13 July 1972. Quoted in *Lights of Guidance*, p. 408.

[4] 'Abdu'l-Bahá, quoted by Shoghi Effendi, *The Advent of Divine Justice*, pp. 45–6.

a need for the traditional feminine qualities of love and service to balance the traditional masculine qualities of force and aggressiveness.

The happiness of mankind will be realized when women and men co-ordinate and advance equally, for each is the complement and helpmeet of the other.[5]

Women are the equal of man in ability, but their subjugation in the past denied them education and training except in very narrow areas. Accordingly, the Bahá'í Writings say that women must be given equal education with men and the same curriculum. Indeed, they go further: if a choice has to be made, women should be given priority in education because they are the mothers of the next generation and 'first teachers of children'. It is interesting that this principle is becoming increasingly recognised in the world at large by those who are in the lead in the fight to eradicate disease, those who work with children, and those who are trying to improve food provision in the Third World. Women, say the Bahá'í Writings, should enjoy equal legal rights with men, equal social treatment and respect, equal job opportunities, and equal hearing and participation in councils of government.

There are two special refinements in Bahá'í teachings with regard to the second group of general principles, those pertaining to how we treat others. The first is the exhortation not to talk or listen to gossip or backbiting, because these have a deep, long-lasting detrimental effect on the soul:

. . . For the tongue is a smouldering fire and excess of speech a deadly poison. Material fire consumeth the body, whereas the fire of the tongue devoureth both heart and soul. The force of the former lasteth but for a time, whilst the effects of the latter endure a century.[6]

The second is one of the central concepts of the Bahá'í Faith. It is that the highest station a man can achieve is service to humanity:

This is worship: to serve mankind and to minister to the needs of the people. Service is prayer. A physician ministering to the sick, gently, tenderly, free from prejudice and believing in the solidarity of the human race, is giving praise.[7]

Service to mankind is particularly meritorious when it involves real sacrifice, because this contributes to the spiritual growth of both giver and receiver. Sacrifice is the real test of sincerity. It is the

---

[5] 'Abdu'l-Bahá, quoted in *Bahá'í World Faith*, p. 241.

[6] Bahá'u'lláh, *Kitáb-i-Íqán*, p. 193.

[7] 'Abdu'l-Bahá, quoted in Esslemont, *Bahá'u'lláh and the New Era*, p. 77.

ultimate test of whether or not one is willing to put conscious standards, hopes, and ideals before personal comfort.

Finally, there is one aspect of the Bahá'í teachings concerning the maintenance of physical health which is of special importance: the avoidance of all forms of drugs including alcohol:

The drinking of wine is . . . forbidden; for it is the cause of chronic diseases, weakeneth the nerves and consumeth the mind.[8]

. . . this wicked hashish extinguisheth the mind, freezeth the spirit, petrifieth the soul, wasteth the body and leaveth man frustrated and lost.[9]

The negative effects of drugs and alcohol, including their impact on the mind and spirit, have already been discussed in Chapter 19 in connection with the temperance movement. There are still many who argue that a little social drinking does no harm and may even be healthful. In the Bahá'í view the worldwide problem is too serious to make compromises of this sort which only serve to make drinking socially acceptable, for example to young people amongst whom will be the next generation of alcoholics, and to provide finance for the alcohol industry. Legalization of alcohol whilst making other drugs unlawful is also inconsistent; it gives the impression of special pleading and hypocrisy, and thereby encourages disrespect for the law and the taking of other drugs. In other words, 'social drinking' is both short-sighted and selfish. Its purpose – as with drug-taking – is to create an artificial euphoria, an escape from the harshness of life. The Bahá'í view is that people would be a lot happier if they spent their time and resources helping to build a more loving and just society. Consequently, the only exception the Bahá'í Writings make for drugs (including alcohol) is in case of medical need. It should be added that the smoking of tobacco is strongly discouraged as unclean and damaging to bodily health, but it is not forbidden, presumably because it, unlike alcohol and drugs, does not affect the mind and spirit.

The Family

Beyond the individual comes the family. As in the other great religions, the idea of family is upheld in the Bahá'í Faith, where it is seen as a basic building-block of society. Accordingly, men and women are enjoined to marry if they can find the right partner, and professional celibacy is deplored. The purpose of marriage and

[8] 'Abdu'l-Bahá, quoted by Shoghi Effendi, *The Advent of Divine Justice*, p. 27.

[9] 'Abdu'l-Bahá, quoted by Ghadirian, *In Search of Nirvana*, p. 70.

family is two-fold: (i) to produce children, and (ii) to promote the spiritual development of all family members. Thus marriage is described as 'a fortress of well-being and salvation'. It is within the bosom of the family that a child learns to have a loving relationship with others, and it is this habit which enables the child to have such an attitude when he or she grows up and goes out into the wider world.

Each member of the family has special rights and duties. One of the most important duties of parents is the education of their children:

. . . It is enjoined upon the father and the mother, as a duty, to strive with all effort to train the daughter and the son, to nurse them from the breast of knowledge and to rear them in the bosom of sciences and arts. Should they neglect this matter, they shall be held responsible and worthy of reproach in the presence of the stern Lord. This [to fail to educate a child] is a sin unpardonable, for they have made that poor babe a wanderer in the Sahara of ignorance, unfortunate and tormented; to remain during a lifetime a captive of ignorance and pride, negligent and without discernment. [10]

Parents are responsible for all aspects of their child's education, physical, mental and spiritual, of which the most important is the spiritual. Spiritual education should start at an early age and is then a particular responsibility of the mother because of her closeness to the child at that time in its life. Bahá'ís base their moral education on the teachings of their Faith, but children are also taught about other religions and philosophies as well, so as to increase understanding of and sympathy with others. There is no pressure put on children to follow their parents' faith for traditional reasons; it is recognised that each person must choose his own philosophy of how to live. Great emphasis is also placed on that aspect of intellectual education which will be of benefit to all society:

Knowledge is as wings to man's life, and a ladder for his ascent. Its acquisition is incumbent upon everyone. The knowledge of such sciences, however, should be acquired as can profit the peoples of the earth, and not those which begin with words and end with words. [11]

Bahá'ís try to raise their children with a balance between kindness and firmness, emphasising the encouragement of good qualities rather than focusing on faults, the father and mother trying to give a good example by their own behaviour and to be consistent. Parents

---

[10] 'Abdu'l-Bahá, *Tablets of Abdul-Baha*, Vol. III, pp. 578–9.

[11] Bahá'u'lláh, Tablet of Tajallíyát, *Tablets*, pp. 51–2. It is presumed that when Bahá'u'lláh talked of an education ending in mere words, He was referring in particular to the endless discussions in Iran amongst the mullas about obscure and useless theological issues.

should not beat their children or abuse them verbally: this will only make the children hate their home and so defeat the family's main purpose.

In view of the importance of the family as an instrument for the creation of the just society, it is not surprising that the Bahá'í Writings provide means for ensuring the strength and longevity of marriage, at the core of the family. The first principle of Bahá'í marriage is monogamy, a principle clearly related to the teachings about the equality of men and women. The fact that this is the first time in history that a great religion has been specific on this issue is perhaps another indicator that the time has come when there will be no more wars: polygamy has been considered justified in the past by the frequent shortage of men from deaths on the battlefield.

Another group of teachings relate to the preparation for marriage. Those searching for a marriage partner are advised to look first for spiritual qualities, because though physical attraction is important that alone will not ensure a lasting marriage. The qualities to be sought are loyalty, faithfulness, honesty, trustworthiness, generosity, absence of a jealous, possessive or domineering spirit, a willingness to work hard, and a balanced attitude to family economics, that is, being neither a spendthrift nor a miser. Such a person will have the strength to successfully handle the hard times as well as the good times. A sign of maturity is a sense of humour and an ability to laugh *with* others, not *at* others. A marriage relationship has the best chance of success if each partner is appreciative, sensitive, fundamentally at one with himself or herself, and if there is an understanding that what comes out of marriage will depend very much on what is put into it.

There are two important requirements relating to the marriage ceremony. The first is that the future man and wife state: 'We will all verily abide by the Will of God.' This means that the marriage is a spiritual contract involving God as well as the two partners, and that each partner submits to the will of God, not one partner to the will of the other! The second requirement is that prior assent to the marriage be given by both the two individuals concerned (not always the practice in the East, even today) and by all living parents (frequently not the case in modern Western society). This law helps to better assure that the partners are well suited by widening the number of those who have to make the decision. This is a responsibility which the parents are enjoined to take seriously. The law also serves to strengthen the wider family relationship and acts as a counter to the modern narrow nuclear family, where much of the richness of real family life has been lost, to the cost especially of the children.

After marriage the partners (and later the children) are encouraged to consult and pray together regularly and to avoid the autocratic style of family relationships which in the past has crushed both love and the spiritual development of parents and children alike. The sexual relationship between the parents is seen as a healthy and desirable means of strengthening the ties of marriage. For this reason, as well as the obvious danger sexual promiscuity has in promoting the lower or animal side of our nature, men and women alike should confine their sexual activity to marriage. The Bahá'í view of chastity goes beyond just abstinence from the physical act to include thoughts (which can often be detected by others), manners, posture, and style of dress. Sexual promiscuity only serves to create destructive comparisons and undermines trust. Predatory sexual attitudes not only affect the marriage partners but create division and mistrust in the wider community. It should be added that homo-sexuality is abhorred: however, the Bahá'í attitude is not one of self-righteous condemnation, but rather one of helping, in a loving way, someone who is in need of medical assistance and has a particular problem, which if addressed resolutely will lead to great spiritual growth. Divorce is permitted in the Bahá'í Faith but is strongly discouraged. It should be considered only when there is complete aversion between the marriage partners and in the light of the teaching that those who cause a divorce bear a heavy spiritual responsibility. If, after every effort, a couple feel unable to continue a marriage, they may apply to Bahá'í institutions for a divorce which will be granted after a year of patience during which they live in separate households and final opportunities are available for reconciliation.

Collective Action

The third dimension of the Bahá'í programme for a just society relates to the collective activities of the community and is one of the most distinctive features of the Faith. Most religions in the past have dealt almost exclusively with teachings for the individual, although (as noted in Chapter 10) Islam provided some guidance for the state, most notably in making specific provision for the poor. Christians, in particular, sometimes find it difficult to associate religion with community issues which go beyond one's immediate neighbour, yet clearly today the problems which face mankind (the threat of nuclear war, degradation of the environment, mass unemployment and poverty) are so profoundly complex and widespread that they cannot be solved by the individual – or indeed whole nations – acting in isolation, but require specific attention at the world community level. The application of individual ethics to collective action has not worked because the circumstances are different (for instance, balance between justice and mercy) and too much is left open for differences of opinion. Even the most highly motivated individual can become frustrated and corrupted by a political system which is amoral and badly structured. That religion now embraces teachings for collective activities is yet another sign of the need for man to recognize that he has reached the age of maturity.

A person coming across the Bahá'í Faith for the first time and being aware of its goal of creating a just world society and a permanent peace, might assume that Bahá'ís would be deeply involved in the political process. In fact, Bahá'ís are forbidden to take part in partisan politics. This is because Bahá'ís are very conscious that the conventional political system is obsolete: it is just not able to respond adequately to the needs of the time. In particular it fails to create a sense of the brotherhood of man and a unity of purpose and action – vital necessities, in the Bahá'í view, if the major problems of the world are to be solved. This is particularly so in relations between sovereign nations where each pursues its own short-term interest with little or no regard for its own long-term interest or that of the world community as a whole. Accordingly, Bahá'ís feel that the best service which they can render to the peoples of the world, especially bearing in mind the limited resources which they have available, is to establish and develop an alternative system of government within their own community which can be used as a model by the rest of the world. By taking this course Bahá'ís avoid the disunity that comes from the party political system, and are able to demonstrate that a united world community of great diversity is indeed possible.

This approach to politics does not imply that Bahá'ís have retreated into their own shell. On the contrary, they are very much concerned about what is going on in everyday life and perhaps have a better appreciation of the significance of events than most, because of their historical and world perspective. Thus they give support to other progressive movements working towards a just society, wherever they can avoid becoming involved in partisan politics: for instance, at the United Nations, in movements for peace, civil and human rights, the equality of men and women, education, health, the protection of the environment, and many others. As individuals Bahá'ís are free to vote in political elections, though they must refrain from publicising their position or campaigning for any individual or party. They are encouraged to vote for the individuals whom they judge to be most concerned with the welfare of all mankind, rather than for the straight party label. Bahá'ís may hold public office if the position is non-partisan and, as noted earlier, they tend to take up careers in fields which are of particular service to the community such as medicine, education, or agriculture.

Together with the Bahá'í position on non-involvement in party politics goes loyalty to legally established government as a matter of principle, even when a government is hostile to the Bahá'í community. This is a concrete example of practising what is preached about unity. How could Bahá'ís talk about establishing world unity if they themselves were to be quarrelling with established governments? This, of course, does not prevent them from distancing themselves from particular policies of government by stating clearly in public, if permitted, their own principles. The only government directive they are unable to obey is one which would require them to deny their Faith, a refusal which they will maintain even if it should mean death. This will be discussed more fully in Chapter 30 on the history of the Bahá'í community.

Because loyalty to government sometimes requires military service, it is perhaps appropriate to mention at this point the Bahá'í position on physical force. Bahá'í teachings are emphatically against personal violence, although *in extremis* when the state is not able to provide protection, a Bahá'í may use the minimum force necessary to defend himself and his family against criminal assault. He will not resist physical assault by representatives of the legal authorities. Bahá'ís should use every legal means to avoid serving in the military forces, especially combat arms which carry an obligation to kill, and should try instead to fulfil their duty to the state in community and non-combatant service where permitted. Yet Bahá'ís are not pacifists: as noted in Chapter 29, they recognize that there will be a need in the future for a world police force to protect the population against possible attack.

The alternative system of government established within the Bahá'í community is known as the Bahá'í Administrative Order. It has several distinctive and interesting features in the context of progress towards a just society. These include its organizational structure, its system of elections, its decision-making process, its handling of the question of authority, and its approach to financial matters. These features are discussed in turn in the following paragraphs.

Community Structure

Bahá'ís are organized into local communities at the village and town level, and come together at a minimum once every Bahá'í month (every 19 days),[12] to pray and receive spiritual sustenance, to discuss the affairs of the community and to strengthen social ties and friendships. All members of the community, children, youth, adults, male and female alike, take part in these 'Nineteen Day Feasts'. The local community elects every year, on the basis of adult suffrage, a local council, or 'spiritual assembly', to administer its affairs. The assembly is in constant touch with the grass roots of the community through the Nineteen Day Feast, when it communicates its own plans and listens to the views of one and all. Its main activities at present are the organization of programmes to make available information on the Faith and its principles to both individuals and to the general public; to enrol new Bahá'ís; to deepen the community in the teachings of the Faith; to hold children's classes; to provide for the general education of children where this is not the responsibility of the state or where a child does not have the support of its parents; to organize programmes for the social and economic development of the wider community (not just the Bahá'ís); to provide social services such as visiting the sick, the aged and the lonely; to keep in contact with local government authorities; to support local progressive activities such as peace movements; and to administer such personal services as conciliation efforts during divorce, marriage, and funeral arrangements.

Local communities of like culture or with commonality of history or geography are grouped together in national communities. The national community has its own 'secondary level' council or spiritual assembly which is elected for one-year terms by a national convention. The latter consists of delegates elected by the total national membership grouped by region or local community. The National Spiritual Assembly is responsible for helping to co-ordinate the activities of local communities, for leading national campaigns, and for providing various services such as publishing which, from the point of view of efficiency, are best centralized. It also has responsibility for handling relations with the national government and its agencies, and the national news media, as well as acting as a link between the local community and the third tier of the system.

The third level of the Bahá'í Administrative Order is a world assembly, the Universal House of Justice, which has its seat in Haifa, Israel, at the crossroads of the world from East to West and from North to South – the geographic and cultural world centre.[13] The

12 The Bahá'í calendar is described in Chapter 29.

13 As noted in Chapter 30, the Bahá'í World Centre was established in Haifa owing to events in the history of the Faith.

House of Justice is elected every five years by an international convention consisting of the members of all the national spiritual assemblies. Like the local and national spiritual assemblies, it presently has nine members. In addition to the co-ordinating and laying down of long-range plans for the world Bahá'í community, the House of Justice also has a legislative function. The basic authority and constitution governing the Bahá'í community lie in the Writings of Bahá'u'lláh, together with the interpretations made by 'Abdu'l-Bahá and Shoghi Effendi. These Writings are, of course, general in nature, being designed to give guidance to the entire world for at least one thousand years. Accordingly, the House of Justice has been given authority in Bahá'u'lláh's Writings to legislate supplementary guidance for the community in keeping with the spirit and principles given in the Bahá'í Writings.

An important point, and one which needs to be emphasized with regard to this system of government, is that no individual wields authority over another: there are no priests or presidents, prime ministers or mayors. Members of assemblies only have authority when acting together as an assembly. They have no special standing in the community as individuals just because they are members of the assembly. Officers of assemblies – chairmen, secretaries, treasurers – who are elected by the assembly do not have any special privilege; the chairman, for instance, acts more as a co-ordinator than as a leader, and normally will not express his or her opinion in discussion until everyone else has been heard.

In addition to the 'elective' pillar of the Administrative Order which starts at the local level – the base of the community – there is a parallel 'appointed' pillar to assist the Universal House of Justice, which starts at the top of the community and extends downwards. This second system consists of individual counsellors, distinguished in character and service, who are appointed by the Universal House of Justice for fixed terms, to give advice on the state of the community with regard to both its growth and its internal cohesion and maturity. Such counsellors have no executive or legislative function but their independent advisory role serves as a safeguard for the community in a way which might be paralleled roughly with the division of power in democratic systems. The counsellors, who are appointed for five-year terms at present, are grouped into regional boards with a co-ordinating centre in Haifa. They appoint auxiliary board members, who in turn have the help of assistants whom they appoint themselves. The elected branch of the system at national and local levels is encouraged to consult with the appointed branch, as indeed are individual members of the community.

Electoral system

The second interesting feature of the Bahá'í Administrative Order is the system of elections, which has not only the normal requirements of democracy (i.e. universal adult suffrage, secret ballot, and virtually no limit on who may be elected) but also some particularities of considerable importance to the goal of achieving a just society. First, when adult Bahá'ís (who all have a moral obligation to vote) come together for the election, they begin the proceedings with prayers and meditation on the importance of the election before the votes are cast. (Absentee voting, however, is permitted if an elector is unable to attend the meeting.) The goal is

to consider without the least trace of passion and prejudice, and irrespective of any material consideration, the names of only those who can best combine the necessary qualities of unquestioned loyalty, of selfless devotion, of a well-trained mind, of recognized ability and experience.[14]

The goal is to be achieved on the basis of active involvement in the community all the year round, a practice which develops experience and knowledge of the qualities of the members of the community. Second, there are no nominations, nor are attempts to sway opinion by electioneering permitted. Third, the elector is obliged to vote for all nine positions on the assembly; this has the effect of focusing attention on the body as a whole rather than on individuals. It requires consideration of the needs for change and/or continuity and of the desirability for diverse backgrounds and viewpoints to be represented: a membership including both men and women, young and old, rich and poor, black and white. Another important aspect of the electoral system is that when there is a tie for the last place, the community is encouraged to give priority to the one who comes from a group under-represented on the assembly. Finally, it should be mentioned that an assembly is responsible not just to those who elected it but to God Himself. This means upholding the principles of the Faith and taking into account the wider vision of a duty to preserve the heritage of the past, to protect the interest of future generations and to remember man's role as steward of the earth. The English philosopher Edmund Burke saw the importance of such a concept and urged members of parliament to a wider view of their duties than the immediate short-term interest of their constituents.

Decision-making

The third aspect of the Administrative Order, of critical importance

14 Shoghi Effendi, in *Bahá'í Administration*, p. 88.

to the search for the just society, is the process of consultation. This characteristic of Bahá'í decision-making differs from democratic debate in several key respects. Participants in a Bahá'í consultation are encouraged to be scientific in their approach: to establish first what is the problem; to ascertain the facts; to decide on the principles involved; to then discuss the matter; to come to a conclusion; and finally to see that it results in appropriate action. This all requires objectivity. Bahá'ís will strive to be detached from any idea which they personally have: they may offer a suggestion for general discussion and then as the consultation proceeds they decide which is the best idea, regardless of the originator. It is important to be frank and straight-forward so as not to overlook any issue, but at the same time there must be the utmost courtesy and consideration for others:

They must . . . proceed with the utmost devotion, courtesy, dignity, care and moderation to express their views. They must in every matter search out the truth and not insist upon their own opinion, for stubbornness and persistence in one's views will lead ultimately to discord and wrangling and the truth will remain hidden. The honoured members must with all freedom express their own thoughts, and it is in no wise permissible for one to belittle the thought of another . . .[15]

If these steps have been followed correctly at every stage, a unanimous decision usually results, and quite often an assembly will not be content until this has been achieved. However, decision by an absolute majority is permitted. Voting on an assembly should be a confidential matter. Another innovation is that once a decision has been made it should be supported by everyone on the assembly, and by the community, even if a particular individual thinks it wrong. In the Bahá'í view it is better in the long run to maintain unity even at the risk of making initial mistakes, because mistakes can usually be corrected but unity once lost is hard indeed to regain. If any individual in the community feels strongly about a decision, he can appeal to the assembly concerned to reconsider the matter, and if still not satisfied, can ask that the issue be reviewed by the assembly next higher in the hierarchy, even as far as the Universal House of Justice. In making such appeals he should, again in the interest of unity, seek to convince by the quality of his argument and not by the conventional political process of drumming up support from others. The issues discussed in a typical local community are still relatively minor for the most part, compared with those involved in the administration of a full system of local government. Nevertheless, the principles of consultation are still the same and large numbers of

[15] 'Abdu'l-Bahá, quoted in *The Local Spiritual Assembly*, p. 21.

people all around the world are gradually learning how to put them into practice so as to provide experience for use in the future on the biggest issues.

Handling authority

Discussions of the orderly approach to appeal in the consultative process leads logically to the fourth special aspect of the Bahá'í system of administration: the issue of authority and the relationship between rights and duties. In very broad terms the overriding concern of democracy, especially in the United States of America, is to protect the rights of citizens *vis-à-vis* the government. Authoritarian governments, by contrast, stress the duty of obedience. The Bahá'í view is that injustice comes about when either position is taken to extreme lengths, and that accordingly there is a need for a balance between the two: the golden mean. The preceding paragraphs have mentioned one important aspect of this principle: the rights of all members to be heard and to make orderly appeal on the one hand, and on the other the duty to abide eventually by the decision of the democratically-elected institutions of the community.

Another aspect of this principle concerns individuals and their observance of the moral laws of the Faith, which Bahá'u'lláh declared are there for protection, not for oppression.

True liberty consisteth in man's submission unto My commandments . . . Were men to observe that which We have sent down unto them from the Heaven of Revelation, they would, of a certainty, attain unto perfect liberty . . .[16]

Normally this is left entirely to the conscience of each individual. There is no self-righteous snooping either by other individuals or by institutions, so long as the matters remain private. However, when there is public, flagrant and wilful breaking of Bahá'í law the institutions have the right and the duty to intervene to protect the good name of the community. In such cases the assembly may counsel the person concerned and try to help him or her to overcome the problem, but if the behaviour persists, then it may have to apply sanctions. Such sanctions, which normally last until the errant behaviour has ceased, are called 'deprivation of administrative rights'. This means that the individual loses his community rights: voting in elections, contributing to the fund of the community (see below), and attendance at Feasts. It is a measure of the spiritual maturity already reached by the community that such sanctions,

---

[16] Bahá'u'lláh, *Gleanings*, p. 335.

which may seem decidedly mild by the standards of the outside world, should be taken very seriously by Bahá'ís.

Bahá'ís are free to express their own views in public so long as they make clear that they are personal opinions, as distinct from the official teachings of the Faith. Sanctions could be applied if such opinions amount to backbiting or support for some partisan political movement. The worst offence is to try to cause disunity in the community by attacking the position of the central figures of the Faith or its institutions. Anyone who has doubts on such matters is, of course, free to leave the community at any time and does not lose any friendship by doing so. But a person who seeks support within the community in attacking the bases of the community itself is undermining its very purpose and its special gift to the peoples of the world. In such circumstances the offending person may be expelled from the Bahá'í Faith by the Universal House of Justice as a 'covenant-breaker'. In that case members of the community (even members of the family of the covenant-breaker) are forbidden all contact with him or her, on pain of expulsion themselves. This sanction is for protection and not in any way vindictive. On the contrary, if a covenant-breaker expresses formal regret for past behaviour and renounces it for the future, he or she may be welcomed back into the community.

Financing

The last special aspect of the Bahá'í Administrative Order to be discussed here is the financing of communal activities. Up to the present much of the activity of the Faith has been conducted by the voluntary donation of time by members of the community. But clearly any organization, especially one on a worldwide basis and embracing a wide variety of different individual situations between rich and poor, needs financial resources in order to function and provide its services. The first principle involved in the financing of Bahá'í activity is that it is a privilege to contribute to the community's finances and so help build a new world order. Following this principle, the Faith does not accept any contributions from outside sources (i.e. not Bahá'í); if donations of this sort are received they are passed on to a charity named by the donor. Such a position means that the Faith does not indulge in offensive 'pan-handling' from the general public and is protected from any possibility of even the appearance of corruption.

The second principle is that giving to the 'Bahá'í Fund' is a moral obligation for Bahá'ís; the goal is to achieve universal participation on a regular basis, for this is viewed as a concrete sign of the community's commitment to the unity of mankind. From a spiritual point of view universal participation (including the giving of just a mite from each of the poorer members of the community) is preferable to a larger total sum donated by a rich minority. And there is no outside compulsion or pressure put on people. Once again there are principles of balance involved. On the one hand, Bahá'ís are urged not to put their personal financial position at risk by their contributions to the Fund; they should always first cover their outstanding debts. On the other hand, sacrifice – giving up something of value – in order to give to the Fund is considered highly meritorious. Having said all this, it should be added that contributions to the Fund are confidential, so that individuals are protected from direct outside pressure, and certainly no publicity is given to the names of the biggest contributors.

CHAPTER 29

A Vision of World Peace

THE Bahá'í teachings are not limited to individual guidelines and a new model advanced 'spiritual democracy'. They also embrace a vision of a future world commonwealth and a world civilization. Such a commonwealth will only be possible when the vast majority of the world's population voluntarily subscribe to Bahá'í principles – an event that Bahá'ís are confident will eventually happen, although they do not expect to see it happen overnight.[1] It is also recognised that for a long time to come – perhaps indefinitely – there will always be some who will cling to old ways. Such individuals and groups would be welcome in the commonwealth. There would, of course, be no coercion of them in any way, but they would be required to accept the laws generally applicable to society at that time, such as the outlawing of war and oppression of others. In attempting to give a quick sketch of such a commonwealth, it is perhaps useful to focus on two aspects of particular interest in the present overall context. The first is political and social unification on the basis of diversity. The second is the approach to a just distribution of resources in the economic field.

Political Unification

The key instrument envisaged for the achievement of unity in diversity in the political and social fields is a system of government interacting with the spiritual evolution of individuals in accordance with the principles now being applied within the Bahá'í community. The Writings indicate that the structure of government will be essentially a development or expansion of the Bahá'í Administrative Order. A world federal government will have legislative, executive, and judicial branches, backed up by a world police force. Elected

[1] Bahá'ís envisage a series of transitional steps, collectively known as the 'Lesser Peace' before the coming of the 'Most Great Peace' – a world commonwealth based on spiritual principles. One of the most significant early steps in this process would be a political agreement made by the nations of the world to end war as an instrument of international relations.

bodies in the administrative structure (all of which then would be called Houses of Justice even at national and local levels) will follow the electoral principles already discussed in Chapter 28 and all sections of the population will be represented on the basis of equal weighting. Consultative principles will be at the heart of all government activity. With a population becoming more advanced, generation by generation, in the practice of living according to the standards of the individual ethics discussed earlier, and with a government putting into practice Bahá'í collectivist principles with the approval of the people, it is reasonable to assume that the government will be able to rely to a great extent on voluntary compliance with, and execution of, its decisions. This suggests a minimum of bureaucracy. It is also clear from the Bahá'í Writings that a great deal of responsibility will be delegated to national and local bodies:

. . . The worldwide law of Bahá'u'lláh . . . repudiates excessive central-ization on one hand, and disclaims all attempts at uniformity on the other. Its watchword is unity in diversity . . . The principle of the oneness of mankind . . . calls for . . . a world organically unified in all the essential aspects of its life . . . infinite in the diversity of the national characteristics of its federated states.[2]

In some respects it is clear that the national level of administration will be less important than it is within the present political framework, which gives the national state more or less unrestricted sovereignty. On the one hand, general direction will be given to national governments by the world institutions, and on the other there will be a devolution of much responsibility to the local community where most day-to-day affairs will be administered. And, of course, two of the main bases of power in the national sovereign state – the armed forces and the foreign policy establish-ment – will be greatly reduced. It is interesting to note in this connection that Bahá'u'lláh originally only mentioned Houses of Justice at the world and local levels, and it was only later that 'Abdu'l-Bahá added provision for intermediary national bodies. It is also interesting that even today some of the larger Bahá'í communi-ties such as those in the USA and India are finding it necessary to set up administrative machinery at the provincial level (i.e. between the national and local levels) and the author would hazard that in a future world commonwealth the world federal government may legislate a fourth tier of assemblies for nations which are particularly large.

[2] Shoghi Effendi, 'The Goal of a New World Order', in *The World Order of Bahá'u'lláh*, pp. 41–3.

There are two other matters which might be mentioned in this connection. First, there are clear indications that the national groupings in a Bahá'í world commonwealth will differ in detail from present national boundaries so as to take account of the aspirations of cultural groups which are today minorities but which may wish in future for their own political entities. Second, there are, of course, certain areas where minorities are so interspersed with the majority that it would be impossible to carve out a territorial homeland for them where they could reside without massive relocation of population. In such circumstances a multi-cultural society will probably be the desire of all involved. If not, the desire for national self-expression may be achieved by a wide variety of other means, such as specialized local communities, possibly geopolitically separated, but federated for certain purposes. The possibilities with good will on all sides would seem to be numerous.

With regard to the functions of government, there are several issues emerging from the Writings which are of special interest to this discussion. There are first those matters which relate to the oldest and most elementary functions of government: defence and the maintenance of law and order. With the coming of world federation these two functions of protection will in effect merge into one. A key element of this merged function will be a world tribunal which:

. . . will adjudicate and deliver its compulsory and final verdict in all and any disputes that may arise between the various elements constituting this universal system . . . [3]

This would represent a logical and necessary step beyond the role and power of the present World Court and its predecessors. A second key element would be the world peace-keeping police force, already mentioned which would be the only significant armed group permitted. It would probably be very small by comparison with present-day national armies, and it would be sufficient only to defend the world community against any selfish interest which might arise. Local communities would have their own police forces sufficient to maintain law and order, and additionally there may be some need for a small central group under each national government. The important point, of course, is that such police forces would be the protectors of society, not oppressors as they are sometimes today, especially in authoritarian countries. Accordingly, it would be

[3] Shoghi Effendi, 'The Unfoldment of World Civilization', in *The World Order of Bahá'u'lláh*, p. 203.

expected that they would enjoy the whole-hearted support of those whom they protect.

Another aspect of law and order is the treatment of those individuals who breach the law. Though a Bahá'í society will eventually remove the environmental causes of crime (including poverty as discussed later in this chapter), as well as the conditions in which they fester, it is recognized that there will always be some who will be immature and anti-social, at least for some part of their lives. 'Abdu'l-Bahá made it clear that criminals have to be punished by the community so as to maintain public order. Punishment is needed both as a matter of justice with regard to the malefactor concerned, and as a deterrent to others. At all times these objectives should be kept clearly in mind so as to prevent passions rising which lead to feelings of vengeance and to unnecessary harshness. He said that the main thrust of public policy should not be repression of crime as such but removal of its causes by educating all people so that they will come to see crime as utterly abhorrent. Presumably this means that one factor in determining punishment should be the education of the criminal to help him also develop the spiritual side of his nature. Justice would also presumably require concern for the victim of the crime and compensation by either the criminal and/or the community. Incidentally, the Bahá'í Writings indicate that once a criminal has served his punishment his spiritual advance is no longer held back by his crime.

One of the key purposes of maintaining law and order is so that all members of the community are free to pursue their search for truth. Thus, in a Bahá'í commonwealth as in all open societies there would be room for great diversity of views and discussion. This, of course, requires socially responsible attitudes if it is to work. Recent history is replete with examples of open societies descending into anarchy when the basic rules are not followed. In this connection the Bahá'í Writings give due importance to the media which should be objective and free from prejudice, and should have a world point of view.

The press will, under such a system, while giving full scope to the expression of the diversified views and conditions of mankind, cease to be mischievously manipulated by vested interests, whether private or public, and will be liberated from the influence of contending governments and peoples.[4]

This is a principle of particular interest to citizens of Third World countries who today feel that they are unfairly portrayed in the all-

[4] Ibid. p. 204.

dominant Western media. The purpose of the news media would be to contribute to the process of education and to encourage the spiritual growth of society.

Freedom of thought and expression and self-disciplined freedom of the media lead logically to the subject of education which is seen as perhaps the most important of the social services to be provided by a future world commonwealth. Mention has already been made of the duty of parents with regard to the education of their children and of the responsibility of the local community. In a Bahá'í commonwealth the world federal government would bear ultimate responsibility for establishing a universal system of compulsory education, placing particular emphasis on spiritual growth as well as on the arts and sciences, though presumably administration of the system would be delegated to lower levels of the government hierarchy. An important aspect of spiritual education would be development of the sense that all peoples belong to one world family and an appreciation of the diversity of cultures. Spiritual studies would act as a unifying force which would give meaning to the whole process of education by focusing on the purpose of life and providing the universal principles which apply to the sciences and other branches of learning. The system of education would also restore the balance between intellectual learning and manual skills, giving recognition to the importance of each in the fully rounded human being. As noted earlier, learning is to benefit mankind and should not consist of studies which 'begin in words and end in words'. The object would be to raise up 'a new race of men', spiritually mature, and possessing an ever-inquiring view of the universe in its every aspect.

An important part of the curriculum of the world system of education would be a universal auxiliary language and script. Quite apart from the practical necessity for a world language in smooth and rapid communication, it is clear that language plays an important part in the growth of a sense of oneness in a people. The universality of Latin in the Roman Empire contributed much to the strength of that state, as has English to the unity of the United States. Disagreement over the principle of one language has been a source of major division in India. The Bahá'í Writings do not specify what would be the auxiliary world language, leaving it to the nations of the world to make the decision when they are ready. One alternative would be a completely new international language, and in this connection it may be remarked that 'Abdu'l-Bahá spoke favourably about 'Esperanto', whose advocates have for long had close contacts with Bahá'ís.[5] The

---

[5] Many Bahá'ís are members of Esperanto societies. Lidia Zamenhof, the daughter of Ludovic Zamenhof, the inventor of Esperanto, was a Bahá'í.

other alternative would be an existing national language. Such a choice today has obvious disadvantages because of perceptions of cultural imperialism and unfair advantage to one cultural group, but it could be that in the longer term such feelings will lessen and there might be agreement that a language with a long history and cultural richness would have an advantage over an artificial international language. It is to be stressed that in addition to a universal auxiliary language, the use of ethnic languages would also be encouraged in the Bahá'í system of education, so as to ensure the continuing vitality of local culture which is so important an aspect of the Bahá'í concept of world civilization. This objective would be made easier by the existence of a world auxiliary language because it would remove pressures on minority cultural groups to use the language of the majority cultural group in the area where they live.

The Bahá'í system of government would also be responsible for the provision of other social services (such as social security, health services, etc.) which would be available equally for all, and which would therefore contribute to the lessening of differences in wealth. Because of the basic Bahá'í principle that service is worship, and the particular concern for the well-being of the poor and the handicapped, it is to be expected that such services would be of the highest quality and would receive high social priority (see below). On the other hand, Bahá'í standards of morality, including honesty and the injunction against begging, should ensure that 'abuses' of social programmes would be minimal. It is clear that the administration of social services would be largely at the local level so as to enhance the 'human touch' in government. Hospitals and auxiliary medical units, homes for the aged and the handicapped, as well as educational and research facilities would be grouped in each village and town around a House of Worship (known to Bahá'ís as the 'dawning-place' of the remembrance of God's praise). The latter is specified in Bahá'í Writings as a nine-sided building surrounded by trees, fountains and gardens, open to adherents of all religions and beliefs for meditation and prayer.

The Economy

One useful way of summarizing Bahá'í teachings on economic issues is to group them under three broad headings of significance in any economic system: organization, the distribution of wealth, and the nature of its goods and services. With regard to organization, the underlying characteristics of the Bahá'í system are unity in diversity (as with the political and social aspects of the commonwealth) and encouragement both of co-operation and of individual initiative. Teachings on distribution of resources are governed by two broad principles of justice: (i) the abolition of excesses of wealth and poverty; and (ii) reward for those who contribute most to the welfare of society, and conversely the withholding of reward from those able-bodied who contribute little. Together, these principles indicate a great narrowing in the range of differences in material wealth of individuals as compared with the situation today both between nations and within nations. (For data on the present situation see Tables 7 and 20.) This does not, however, mean an attempt to achieve total economic equality. The Bahá'í Writings say that such equality is neither possible as a practical matter, nor indeed desirable from the point of view of the general interest. The nature of goods and services which might be expected in a Bahá'í commonwealth would be deeply influenced by consideration of man's spiritual requirements as well as basic material needs. In total, these themes amount to a shift in perception of economics as being primarily concerned with the gratification of short-term material desires to one in which an economy is directed towards the advancement of civilization and the all-round development of humanity. Often Bahá'ís describe the approach of their Faith as 'the spiritual solution of the economic problem'. The following paragraphs elaborate on these themes in a little more detail, taking each of the three broad subject categories in turn.

Economic organization

With regard to organization of the economy, it is clear that the public sector of a future Bahá'í world commonwealth will have a major role. One responsibility of the central organ of government would be to merge the various national economies into one true world economy so as to improve efficiency and equal opportunities for all peoples. In this connection the Bahá'í Writings speak of the need for genuine world free trade, a world system of communications, a world currency, a world system of weights and measures, and a world calendar.[6] Establishment of a unified world economy will

[6] Calendars, of course, have a considerable impact on the daily life of society. Today the world is divided by a multitude of calendars, each associated with some religion or other culture. These divisions, which are at the very least a cause of inefficiency, could be overcome by the adoption worldwide of the new calendar associated with the Bahá'í Faith, which alone advocates the unity of religions and cultures. This calendar dates from 1844, the year of the Declaration of the Báb, which officially marks the beginning of the Bahá'í Era (see Chapter 30). The calendar is based on the solar year which begins on the March Equinox. It is divided into nineteen months of nineteen days each, with four intercalary days to make up the year, except in leap years when a fifth intercalary is added. Each day starts at sunset. Each month is named after an attribute of God.

also be assisted by some of the principles already mentioned such as a universal compulsory education system and an auxiliary world language. Of course, establishment of a world free trade system would initially disrupt many existing patterns of production and distribution, and it would presumably be the responsibility of the world federal government, in accordance with principles of justice and concern for the welfare of all citizens, to make transitional arrangements so that the burden of change is shared equally by all, not just by those who lose their jobs, as is so often the case today. It is possible that such arrangements would include assistance with retraining and relocation. Whatever the means, it is clear that a world federal government would be in a better position to assist a transition than sovereign national states each acting by itself.

Creation of a world economy would also presumably thrust onto the world government responsibility for flattening out trade cycles, so as to prevent shortages and inflation during boom periods and unemployment during recessions. In this connection the Bahá'í Writings speak of the responsibility of each community to maintain a storehouse for surplus basic goods against times of shortage. The author would also hazard the suggestion that the problem of the trade cycle will be much lessened as the economy shifts more and more from production of goods to production of services (as discussed below) as the latter tend to be more stable in terms of both supply and demand.

Another important economic function of the federal government would be to ensure that the natural resources of the world are conserved, developed, and used for the benefit of all mankind and not just for those who happened to be located near them.[7]

The economic resources of the world will be organized, its sources of raw materials will be tapped and fully utilized, its markets will be co-ordinated and developed, and the distributions of its products will be equitably regulated . . . [8]

Besides these broad planning functions, and the social services mentioned earlier, it seems probable that in a world commonwealth

---

[7] One of the absurd and unjust consequences of the present system of sovereign states is that tremendous riches have accrued to small groups of people because they happen to live on top of oil deposits which they have done nothing to develop or produce whilst much of the rest of humanity lives at starvation level. This is only an extreme example. There are many other instances of peoples having had the good fortune to live in rich lands whose resources they have squandered and plundered, also without consideration of the idea that all mankind should benefit from the 'fruits of the earth'. Little has been agreed even with regard to the equitable sharing of the riches of the seas and oceans which belong to no nation.

[8] Shoghi Effendi, 'The Unfoldment of World Civilization', *The World Order of Bahá'u'lláh*, p. 204.

there would also be a place for public enterprises at the international, national, and local levels, especially in those fields where a single system might be the most rational (e.g. with regard to certain types of communication). Nevertheless, the general themes of decentralization and diversity, which run through descriptions of a Bahá'í commonwealth, suggest that most enterprises would be in the private sector. The Bahá'í system of value would further suggest that, in all likelihood, many enterprises in the private sector would be cooperatives, where the capital is owned by the workers or the consumers or both. It is also clear that there would be a place for the person who, for whatever reason, prefers to work for himself. The individual entrepreneur brings richness to society because he or she often finds that little extra service to perform which has been overlooked by larger enterprises. There is evidence, too, that the individual entrepreneur has been one of the main sources of innovation throughout history, and so contributes significantly to the dynamism and advancement of society. If the individual should hire others to work for him, he would be required by Bahá'í law to institute a profit-sharing scheme for them which would be registered with the local government so as to ensure fairness. As in every aspect of the collective life of the commonwealth, all enterprises employing more than one, whether state, cooperative, or profit-sharing, would be expected to manage their affairs in close consultation with all employed. On the other hand, the all-pervading atmosphere of co-operation would make it unnecessary and indeed inappropriate to maintain those present-day instruments of confrontation, the trade unions and employers' associations, strikes and lock-outs, some of which may have served a useful purpose in the past but would be obsolescent in a Bahá'í society.

Distribution of resources

Clearly much of this has a bearing on our second subject, the distribution of resources. There are also obvious implications in other teachings of the Bahá'í faith such as the equality of men and women, a universal education system, an auxiliary world language, the principle that work is worship, which all tend to have the effect of equalizing opportunities and thereby reducing extremes of wealth and poverty. This effect is reinforced by certain other teachings specifically aimed at achieving this goal. The first of these is the encouragement of the rich in particular to voluntarily give to the communal treasury for the benefit of all. Even in today's world voluntary giving to charity is widespread, and though no doubt there are ulterior motives for much of it (ego, tax avoidance, etc.), it surely cannot be denied that many philanthropists are inspired by motives of a more noble character. It is not unreasonable to expect that such practices would increase dramatically in a society which has been educated to a more profound view than generally exists today of the meaning and purpose of life.

The voluntary system of giving would be paralleled by a genuine progressive income tax system as discussed in Chapter 18. Progressive income tax systems have been implemented in many countries in recent decades, though their impact in reducing maldistribution of wealth has been severely weakened by tax loopholes and widespread tax avoidance. It is anticipated that in a Bahá'í society where there is unity about the goals of public expenditure, the rich would take pride in paying large taxes and thereby making a distinctive contribution to the achievement of these goals.[9] Taxes would not therefore be seen as a disencentive to work, as is so often the case today.

A third Bahá'í teaching of potential significance in reducing extremes of wealth and poverty concerns a personal will, which all are urged to prepare. Though there is no law as such on how wills are to distribute wealth, there are arrangements laid down in cases where a person dies intestate. These arrangements provide for the widespread distribution of the wealth of the deceased in set proportions between members of the family, the community, and – of special interest – the teacher. In other words, the common practice of excessive emphasis on direct descendants and in particular on primogeniture, which exacerbates economic differences, will be greatly reduced.

Another teaching bearing on this issue is the Bahá'í law against gambling, which presumably has been prompted by the fact that gambling has two undesirable consequences: (i) it is unjust to win something for nothing; and (ii) even more important, it can lead to loss of resources vital for the provision of the basic needs of the family.[10] This touches on another possible issue and that is the relative value placed on various occupations. The Bahá'í teachings do not make any specific statements on the subject, but certain conclusions may be inferred. For instance, the teaching profession is

[9] Many rationalize tax avoidance today on the grounds that they do not agree with the uses made of public funds. Some object to the welfare system which they assert subsidizes the lazy: others object to the vast sums spent on military matters which they see as far more than necessary for the security of the state.

[10] The subject of gambling needs further discussion. Any investment, for instance, is a gamble, yet some of the most risky investments serve a useful purpose in helping to bring about innovative improvements. Presumably such 'gambling' is legitimate provided the investor can afford to lose his investment and still provide the family with its basic needs.

particularly well regarded in the Bahá'í Writings, and it might be expected that remuneration rates of teachers would be relatively higher than now. This might be true too of others who are of great service to the community, especially those who do particularly unpleasant jobs, or jobs which involve special hardship or danger.

An issue of major relevance to the distribution of wealth is population size and its rate of growth. (See Table 25 for information on world population growth). The Bahá'í Faith does not have specific views on population policy. There are, however, certain principles with obvious bearing on the subject, most notably the emancipation and education of women and the high priority given to the abolition of poverty worldwide. The United Nations has stated that

improving the status of women may be the most effective and efficient solution to the population crisis. The formulation of population policy should include the full participation of women. (UN Conference on Population, 1984).[11]

The United Nations also endorses the view that a major factor in reducing population is to eliminate poverty, which creates a strong incentive for parents to have many children in the hope that at least one will survive to look after them in old age. This is in accord with Western experience, in which rising standards of living have led to a slow-down in population growth, indeed to absolute decline in total numbers in some cases. In addition, it should be noted that the Faith does not oppose use of contraceptive methods though it is apparent that those involving destruction of the foetus, such as abortion, are contrary to the spirit of the Faith, and should only be undertaken when the health of the mother is at risk. The Universal House of Justice has not laid down a policy on family planning but leaves it to the conscience of those involved. Furthermore, though one of the main purposes of Bahá'í marriage is the procreation of children, parents are encouraged to have only as many as they can provide with a good education.[12]

---

[11] *The Economist* for 13 June 1987 reported in connection with these issues that a survey in Third World village communities by Perdita Huston (Message from the Village) indicates that women generally want small families and it is the men who want many children. The same article states that in Nigeria mothers with primary education average 7.6 children, and those with secondary education, 3.9

[12] The author would suggest a few additional thoughts on the subject of population. First, it may well be that population size will not be a problem for a future world commonwealth (e.g. if it follows, God forbid, a major catastrophe). Second, if it is, then Bahá'ís can be expected to take account of social responsibilities in planning family size. Third, if nevertheless there is still a crisis, the world federal government would always be free, within the context of the Bahá'í Writings, to make appeals on the issue and to enact legislation to encourage smaller families until the situation has stabilised.

Goods and services

What types of goods and services might be expected of a Bahá'í economy? The general tone of the Bahá'í teachings and certain specific principles (such as the theme that the purpose of life is to develop the spiritual side of man's nature), give some quite definite clues. First, priority would surely be given to providing the whole world population with its basic needs with regard to food, clothing, shelter and medical care. It is interesting in this connection to note the specific statement in the Bahá'í Writings that agriculture, which provides for most of such basic needs on a renewable basis,[13] will play a central role in a Bahá'í economy. A central role for agriculture seems to imply a reversal of the present trend to urbanization, a goal of such development organizations as the World Bank, and a possibility made more feasible by computers and modern communications which allow people to work together without being physically in the same place. With more people in small communities and in the countryside, the spiritual advancement of society would be easier. Thus, on the one hand, there would be fewer in the big cities where people become anonymous in the crowd and thereby less responsive to social constraints. On the other hand, a life in the countryside makes for better appreciation of nature and the pulse of life, and this in itself focuses the mind and spirit on God and His purpose for man.

In addition to the basic material needs, high priority would certainly be given to those services which help to develop the spirit, mind and body: education, research, crafts, arts, sciences, active participation in sports,[14] parks, and the environment. On the other hand, it might be expected that there would be a reduction or elimination of certain other types of goods and services. Clearly the vast expenditures now devoted to military affairs will be drastically reduced, and the resources so released will be available for more constructive ends. Lands and other resources now used for the production of alcohol, tobacco and other drugs will similarly be released. The statements of 'Abdu'l-Bahá that the future diet will be mainly one of grains, fruits and vegetables suggests that much of the agricultural land now devoted to the production of meat will be switched to these products, a change which will greatly increase

---

[13] Many goods, including plastics, are today made from minerals and other non-renewable sources.

[14] It might be surmised that there would be special encouragement of team sports and those that do not centre on violent bodily contact, such as boxing.

efficiency in provision of protein.[15] One could also expect a major decrease in the production of useless luxuries, not so much through government decree as on account of changing values in society. A similar decrease might be expected in throw-away goods which waste resources and represent a lack of proper appreciation for the material world that has been provided by God for man's benefit. On the contrary, one might expect there to be a return to the appreciation of the high-quality goods that would result from producers taking a pride in their work and seeing it as worship of God.

A Realistic Vision?

In summarizing the social teachings of their Faith Bahá'ís will often draw attention to two underlying characteristics: the breadth of vision, and at the same time the down-to-earth realism. What is the basis for such claims?

The vision is of mankind achieving a permanent peace and a just world society. There are two aspects to this, as discussed in this chapter. First, there is a plan for a world federal government to maintain peace between nations. The purpose of such a peace is to provide an environment in which all the peoples of the world are free, indeed encouraged to develop to their full potential. By definition this means that the system of government cannot be dictatorial but must be an integral part of an open society.

Many of the Bahá'í social teachings contribute to this goal. Thus the teachings for individual development include intellectual integrity, love and concern for the well-being of others, appreciation of cultural diversity, and the need for universal participation in public affairs. The administrative structure of the government envisaged gives broad powers of planning and direction to the world organ but also provides for decentralisation of day-to-day administration, especially to the local level. The system of elections, including secret ballot and a hierarchy built up from below, is an important protection, as is the emphasis on choosing those who have shown themselves to be spiritually mature as well as able administrators, and from as wide a range of backgrounds as possible. The system is based on open consultation at every level, and between levels, including regular monthly meetings with the members of the local

---

[15] Reduced use of meat is not only conducive to efficiency and better health but is a response to a refinement of the spiritual side of man which would otherwise be retarded by the cruel and ugly business of slaughtering domestic animals for his benefit – in a sense a betrayal of trust. This thought also suggests that another side-effect would be reduced use of animal skins and furs for luxury clothing.

community. It allows for constant change in those who serve on governing bodies but in a stable, non-disruptive context.

One or two people have criticised the system as being undemocratic because it does not make provision for multiple political parties. But, the present writer suggests, the safeguards mentioned above are the key instruments for a free society. Political parties have only developed in Western democracy because of an absence of social solidarity.[16] The Bahá'í system has a potential for encouraging debate and change in the personnel of government which is certainly equal to that achieved where there are multiple political parties. In fact, the Bahá'í approach to government, with its emphasis on world unity, consultation with universal participation, and observance of high spiritual and social values is, in the view of the writer, a significant progressive advance beyond democracy.

The other part of the vision is a society enjoying a just economic system. Note has been made of the many provisions in the Bahá'í teachings to ensure the abolition of poverty and to reduce the range of differences in individual wealth. At the same time, individual initiative is to be encouraged and emphasis is put on voluntary contributions as well as compulsory taxation for the support of public activities. The focus of the economy would be to produce those goods and services which are essential for the physical well-being and which develop the all-round individual, especially the spiritual aspect. In a sense the economic teachings can be seen as a development of the best of both the capitalist system, with its emphasis on freedom and initiative, and the socialist system with its concern for equality and the protection of the poor, but with the addition of the vital religious dimension: the placing of material needs in the context of a wider picture of the nature, needs, and aspirations of the reality of man.

What about the down-to-earth realism of the teachings? Perhaps the most important theme is the idea that though historical forces will inevitably bring about world federation and peace, man is required to strive for it with all his might in order (i) to avoid catastrophe on the way, and (ii) to bring peace sooner than would otherwise be the case. The 'New Jerusalem' is not going to be a free gift from God coming down on a cloud. Socialists will recognize that there are certain parallels here with Karl Marx's theory of the historical inevitability of communism and of the necessity to struggle for it nevertheless.

[16] It might be added that a multi-party system does not necessarily mean rotation of governing parties, e.g. since 1946 in Japan one party has held office without break; this is also true of Italy except for the three years 1983–1986.

A second realistic aspect of the social teachings is the step-by-step approach. One example of this is the view that there will be a transitional 'Lesser Peace' before the 'Most Great Peace' is achieved. Another is the establishment of new methods of government in the Bahá'í community long before either form of peace (the Lesser or the Greater) comes into being. The workings of this system may seem very minor as yet, in the eyes of the world today, but they provide an opportunity for Bahá'ís to gain experience with such a system and to develop it so that it can be offered as an alternative working model when it is generally realized just how ineffective and obsolete is the existing political system. This is a more realistic and humble approach than sitting around with a perfect but untried blueprint of an ideal system, waiting for the day when the existing system collapses.

A third point of realism is the recognition that a just society will not come about by simply exhorting individuals to cultivate the nobler qualities alone, or by devising new ways of organizing collective action. What is needed is for individuals and government bodies alike to evolve simultaneously, so that each will interact with the other to create a progressive upward spiral. In this the Bahá'í Faith can claim to be unique. No other religion makes provision for a comprehensive plan of government for the whole world. No political system makes provision for developing the spiritual side of man and ultimately his nobler qualities.

Yet another realistic aspect is the balance between freedom and duties, a balance which has been essentially lost in democracy with a consequent negative impact on effectiveness. Bahá'u'lláh states that His laws are not there to limit man, but to protect him. Obedience to the established government once the process of consultation has taken place and appeals procedures followed is of vital necessity for the protection of the whole community. The Bahá'í Faith recognizes that there will always be some who are spiritually immature and do not accept their social obligations, and so provision has to be, and is, made for a world peace-keeping force and for the punishment of criminals. No idle dreams here about the perfectability of man.

Two other features of the Bahá'í social teachings should be mentioned in the context of realism: (i) the limitation on the power and authority of individuals, and (ii) the flexibility of the institutions. Throughout history, great leaders – whether political or religious[17] – have been one of the chief causes of misery for mankind. When

[17] This statement does not, of course, refer to the Founders of the great religions whose teachings and lives have shown that they exist on a far higher spiritual plane than ordinary men and women.

society was largely illiterate and uneducated, the leader (both spiritual and secular) was virtually a necessity. Many of them started with the highest motive: to save their people. Inevitably, however, power would corrupt. They thought they knew better than anyone else what was best and would resist anyone with different ideas, to the point of oppression. Subservient attitudes amongst others inflated the ego of the leader, and personal glory would often become his highest priority. There was also material temptation: his own luxury would become more important than food for the starving. Democracy has generally tempered the worst excesses of the cult of leadership; nevertheless, the problem is still very strong because the system still encourages and is dependent on individual competition for office. In the Bahá'í community there are no individual leaders in the government: all depends on collective action – as ensured by the very structure of assemblies, the election system and the process of consultation. There are indeed individuals who win a special regard on account of their services, spiritual qualities or scholarly erudition, and their views will be listened to with respect. But such views will be heard by an audience which has been educated to judge for itself in relation to the Writings of the Faith, and not to rely only on the advice of individuals.

Flexibility of institutional arrangements is clearly a necessary realistic approach, because of the wide range of circumstances that can occur between different societies and over a long period of time. The simplicity of the Bahá'í system of administration and its linkage with development of the spiritual side of man gives it a flexibility to adapt to all types of situation. Similarly the variety of approach in the economic teachings gives the possibility of different 'mixes' according to the wishes of each local or national community. It may be, for instance, that in a future world commonwealth, countries which had a socialist background would prefer to have a higher proportion of state enterprises than might be the case in countries which were formerly capitalist.

What all this amounts to from a Bahá'í perspective is a comprehensive set of social teachings which are consistent with, and logically developed from, the fundamental perspective of existence described in Chapter 27: man's nature, his relationship with God, and his purpose in life. At the same time, the writer suggests, Bahá'ís may see the progressive movements of the past as an important part of their cultural inheritance, and their Faith as a force which will unite all progressives around the world and give them the power to achieve the just society.

CHAPTER 30

The Programme in Action

IN reviewing the Bahá'í Faith certain basic questions spring to mind in trying to judge whether it has the power to inspire action; whether or not it is indeed the progressive movement of the future which will lead the way to the establishment of a just world society. Do these undoubtedly progressive teachings really have mass appeal to people of all backgrounds? Can the Faith substantiate its claim to be able to unite mankind? Are Bahá'ís fully committed to the vision of their Faith? Are they ready to make the necessary sacrifices? And can they remain united and strong in face of attack from outside and inside? Finally, what evidence is there that the Bahá'ís have in fact started to put their teachings into practice?

In order to answer these questions we need to turn to history and examine what has happened so far.

The Bahá'í Faith began at a time of expectation of a New Age and of the coming of a new Messenger of God among both Christians and Muslims. In the West calculations had been made from biblical prophecies (in Daniel, Isaiah, the Gospel of St. Matthew and the Revelation of St. John in particular) which seemed to indicate that the return of Christ, as promised, would occur in the year 1844. This calculation was taken particularly seriously by a group of Christians in the United States known as the Millerites. In the East the Shi'ih branch of Islam had traditions that the twelfth and last Imam would return in the year 1260 of the Muslim calendar (a thousand years after his disappearance), which corresponds to the year 1844 in the Gregorian calendar.

The Faith began in Iran, amongst a people who had once created one of the greatest civilizations of the world but had since sunk to the utmost depths of degradation. Their considerable talents and abilities were devoted to a culture of corruption, divisions, lies, violence, and routine casual cruelty. The noble religion of Islam, far from resisting this trend, was, in its decline, one of the major causes of it. The religious class was itself riddled with prejudice,[1] superstition, and all

[1] Some religious authorities even denied that women had souls.

the faults of the wider society. The monarchy and government were no better. Political and economic decline went hand in hand with the prevailing moral decadence, and the once mighty empire was itself an easy prey for neighbouring countries and marauding imperial powers.

On the night of 22–23 May 1844 a young man named Siyyid 'Alí-Muḥammad (1819–1850) declared to one who was seeking the new Messenger of God that He was the Forerunner of the Promised One of all ages and as such He took the title 'the Báb' or Gate.[2] This incident occurred in Shiraz, the city of roses and poets. The innate knowledge, sincerity, and nobility of character of the Báb soon attracted others who were also engaged in the spiritual search of the time, and they accepted His claims with joy. News of the Declaration swept across Iran and neighbouring areas where the Shi'ih sect was prevalent. Thousands from all classes of society, including the clergy and scholars, were drawn to the new movement. This aroused the ire of the religious hierarchy who saw it as a threat to their own power. The royal government also, after some initial hesitation, became fearful and joined the clergy in opposition to the movement. The Báb was put into prison in a remote part of the country and His followers were fiercely persecuted. Over the next few years several thousand were to be killed for their new Faith, some after the most brutal torture.

One of these was a young woman known today as Tahirih. Respected for her scholarship (unusual in a woman of her time and place) and for the beauty of her passionate poetry, she played a significant role in helping her fellow believers understand just how revolutionary was this new Faith – that it was not some modest reform movement within Islam. In particular, she drew attention to the impending emancipation of women by publicly unveiling herself (an unheard-of action in Islamic society) at a conference of the Báb's followers which was held at the hamlet of Badasht in June 1848.[3] When she was executed by strangulation some four years later her last words were reported to be:

You may kill me as soon as you like, but you cannot stop the emancipation of women.[4]

The Báb Himself, after a mock trial, was executed by firing squad on 9 July 1950 before a large crowd in the north-west city of Tabriz.

[2] It is of interest that the next day, 24 May 1844, Samuel Morse sent the first telegraph message from Washington DC to Baltimore which read 'What Hath God Wrought?'

[3] The year of revolutions in Europe.

[4] See Shoghi Effendi, God Passes By, p. 75.

This event was quite remarkable, for the first attempt at execution by a regiment of 750 men failed because every single bullet missed its target. After the smoke had cleared the Báb was found nearby dictating to His amanuensis, completing a task which had been previously interrupted by His guards. When He had finished He walked calmly back to the place of execution where a second regiment had been drawn up, and it was only then that His persecutors were able to carry out their intent.

The death of the Báb and of so many of His followers, including many of the most distinguished, threw the infant community into temporary disarray until those left started to gather strength from one of the few early followers of the Báb who did survive, Mírzá Husayn-'Alí (1817–1892), who took the title Bahá'u'lláh (the Glory of God). Bahá'u'lláh was the son of a minister of the Crown and had Himself been offered a position in government. However, He had preferred a simpler life, working to help the needy of His province where He was known as the 'Father of the Poor'. The Báb had made special arrangements in 1844 for news of His Declaration to be conveyed to Bahá'u'lláh, a Declaration which He, Bahá'u'lláh, accepted without hesitation. During the next few years He was imprisoned twice and subject to the bastinado, a particularly painful Iranian contribution to the torture culture which involves beating the soles of the feet with a cane. The second of His imprisonments was in the damp and filthy dungeon of the Siyáh-Chál, formerly an underground water reservoir. It was in this prison that Bahá'u'lláh had the intimation that it was He who was destined to be the Promised One. Eventually He was released from prison at the end of 1852. All His possessions were confiscated and He was sent into immediate exile. It is likely that He was saved from execution because He was one of the few Bábís from an aristocratic background (He was descended from the ancient line of Sassanian kings) and because of the efforts made on His behalf by the Russian minister in Iran, Prince Dolgorouki, a friend of the family.

Bahá'u'lláh spent the next ten years of His life in Baghdad in the neighbouring Ottoman Empire, save for a two-year interlude when He retreated into the mountains to meditate. It was during His stay in Baghdad that Bahá'u'lláh first addressed the world, in three books. The first was the *Hidden Words*, a series of verses in which God speaks to man about the human condition. The second, known as the *Seven Valleys*, describes the seven stages of the spiritual journey through the valleys of search, love, knowledge, unity, contentment, wonderment, and true poverty and absolute nothingness. The third was the *Book of Certitude*, in which He commented on the unknowable essence of God and laid forth the theme of 'progressive revelation (see p. 413). Under His guidance the small Bahá'í community in Baghdad became well-known for the quality of its spiritual life and the material detachment of its members who shared their few possessions. Many who had not previously had an opportunity to understand many of the teachings of the Faith, because of the brevity of the Báb's ministry and the difficulty of communication in a large undeveloped country, learnt for the first time the Bahá'í injunction to avoid politics and not under any circumstances to undertake violence (a sharp contrast with the practices of Islam at that time as well as today). Visitors from a variety of backgrounds were frequent. News of the growing prestige of the community reached Teheran and there was concern that the Faith, which the government thought it had crushed, was re-emerging. Pressure was put on the Ottoman government to move Bahá'u'lláh from the border region. On being told that He was to leave, Bahá'u'lláh called together the community, and in saying farewell told them for the first time of His claim to be the Messenger of God for this age.

The Ottoman government at first moved Bahá'u'lláh to Constantinople. However, He was soon sent to Adrianople, in the European part of the Empire, after further pressure from Iran which feared that if He stayed in the capital He would have undue influence on the government. Here He was to stay with a few of His followers for three years. This period was to be marred by an intensification of opposition (already displayed in Baghdad) on the part of Bahá'u'lláh's younger half-brother, a weak person persuaded by an ambitious companion to seek leadership for himself. There were several attempts to murder Bahá'u'lláh, one of which damaged His health for the rest of His life. When the community remained steady in its love for Bahá'u'lláh, His opponents changed their tactics, and set about alarming the Turkish authorities by suggesting that Bahá'u'lláh's liberal teachings would stir up nationalist sentiment among subject peoples of the Balkans, a matter about which the authorities were particularly sensitive. Suddenly in 1867, Bahá'u'lláh and His followers were moved once again, this time by sea to the fortress prison city of Akka (Acre) in Palestine, which was also a part of the Ottoman Empire at that time.

Whilst in Akka, Bahá'u'lláh completed a task He had begun in Adrianople. In a series of letters to the most powerful kings and rulers of the world He announced His claim to be the Messenger for this age, and called upon them to establish: (i) an international tribunal to arbitrate disputes between nations; (ii) an international

454	THE SEARCH FOR A JUST SOCIETY

police force; (iii) an auxiliary world language; and (iv) a compulsory system of education worldwide. They should also disarm, look after the poor, and establish constitutional governments. He particularly praised Queen Victoria for the constitutional form of government in Great Britain. He also wrote His *Book of Laws* laying down the main principles of the Faith; these were supplemented in a large number of additional letters or 'Tablets'. The *Book of Laws* and related documents include such principles as world federation, a world auxiliary language, a world currency, progressive taxation, profit-sharing, and equality of men and women – all very radical ideas for that time, even if some of them have since then become accepted in theory if not in practice. Another important work of this period was His *Book of the Covenant* in which He stated that His eldest son, 'Abdu'l-Bahá, should lead the community after His passing and would have the authority to interpret and clarify His Writings.

In the last few years of His life the Turks (many of whom had the deepest reverence for Him) allowed Bahá'u'lláh to leave His prison to live in a nearby mansion which had been obtained for Him by 'Abdu'l-Bahá. It was here that He was visited a short while before His passing (29 May 1892) by E.G. Browne, the English orientalist who was the only Westerner to leave a record of his impressions:

The face of Him on whom I gazed I can never forget, though I cannot describe it. Those piercing eyes seemed to read one's very soul; power and authority sat on that ample brow; while the deep lines on the forehead and face implied an age which the jet black hair and beard flowing down in indistinguishable luxuriance almost to the waist seemed to belie. No need to ask in whose presence I stood, as I bowed myself before one who is the object of a devotion and love which kings might envy and emperors sigh for in vain.[5]

'Abdu'l-Bahá (1844–1921) was a man of outstanding spiritual qualities, greatly loved by his Father who would speak of Him as the 'Master'. During Bahá'u'lláh's later years 'Abdu'l-Bahá had taken upon Himself the burden of most of His Father's administrative tasks, seeing most visitors on His behalf. For the first seventeen years after Bahá'u'lláh's passing 'Abdu'l-Bahá remained confined in Akka and its environs by the Ottoman government, which several times

---

[5] The views of the Bahá'í Faith held by Edward Granville Browne (1862–1924) fluctuated violently during the course of his life. Though much impressed as indicated by the above passage, he had reservations which derived first from being taken in by some crude forgeries put out by allies of Bahá'u'lláh's younger half-brother, and secondly, because he later felt that the Bahá'ís should have become involved in party politics and committed themselves to the new liberal constitutional movement in Persia. This showed that he had not understood the much greater vision of a new world civilization which is at the core of the Bahá'í Faith.

threatened His life as a result of misinformation fed to them by opponents of the Bahá'í Faith.

During these early years a Lebanese Bahá'í of Christian background, Ibrahim Khayru'lláh, went to the United States of his own accord to spread the Faith, and within a short while there were several hundred American Bahá'ís – the first Westerners to embrace the Faith. From 1898 onwards, small groups of them travelled to Akka to see 'Abdu'l-Bahá. It was in response to their questions that 'Abdu'l-Bahá clarified the relationship of the Bahá'í Faith to Christianity and other subjects of interest to Westerners. Some of His responses were recorded in the book *Some Answered Questions*.

'Abdu'l-Bahá had long wanted to visit the West Himself, and at last, in 1909, the opportunity came when He was set free by a new 'Young Turk' government. He had not been free since the age of nine when he had accompanied his Father into exile. Now it was as a man of sixty-five that He made preparation for this momentous journey. Forced to delay His departure by ill-health associated with His years of confinement, He set out at last in 1911 for Europe (France, Switzerland and Great Britain), and then in 1912 He undertook a major journey to North America. For some eight months He crossed the United States from coast to coast, with a visit to Canada. He met large numbers of people of all classes, men, women and children, from cabinet members to those on skid row, of different religions and political persuasions including socialists, radicals and trade unionists. He gave many public addresses expounding the Bahá'í perspective, but with rare mention of the Bahá'í Faith as such. His subject-matter included the need to abolish racial prejudice in the United States and the imminence of a great war between the nations. He told Christians they should accept Muhammad, and Jews that they should accept Jesus, because all religions were one. Many of His addresses in America and Europe are recorded in *The Promulgation of Universal Peace* and *Paris Talks*. His warmth, love, humour, simplicity, and wisdom attracted the hearts of thousands and gave new fire to the infant Bahá'í communities of the West.

Soon after He returned to Palestine the Great War broke out as He had predicted, and 'Abdu'l-Bahá was once again cut off from the Bahá'ís of the West. During this period He involved Himself in seeing to the needs of local people, an activity for which He was later to receive a knighthood from the British government. He also wrote a series of letters to the American and Canadian Bahá'ís in which He outlined plans for the spread of the Faith around the world. Towards the end of the war His life was once again put under threat by the Turkish authorities, but a rapid British advance, urged on by concerned people in London, drove the Turks northwards before any action had been taken against Him. When 'Abdu'l-Bahá died in November 1921 His funeral was attended by some 10,000 people drawn from all the religious groups of the region: Muslims, Christians, Druzes, Jews – an unprecedented event.

In His Will and Testament 'Abdu'l-Bahá stated that after His death the community should be led by His eldest grandson (He had no surviving sons), Shoghi Effendi Rabbani (born 1896), who was to bear the title of Guardian and would be authorized to interpret and expound the words of both Bahá'u'lláh and Himself. Shoghi Effendi was at that time a student at Oxford and his highest ambition had been to help with translation of the written works of Bahá'u'lláh into English. He was deeply shocked, not only by the untimely death of His beloved grandfather, but by the heavy responsibility suddenly thrust upon him. After a period of anguish he settled down to the task ordained, and for over thirty-five years, until his premature death in 1957, gave brilliant guidance to the Bahá'í world community.

Perhaps his greatest achievement was to nurture the young community of both West and East so that it learnt to abide by the highest moral standards and to establish and develop Bahá'í institutions which could be self-sustaining. The Guardian carried out this process by communication of letter and cable, and by meeting with Bahá'ís who came on pilgrimage to Haifa. When he judged the community was strong enough he launched a series of plans, beginning in 1937, whereby many Bahá'ís left their homelands to establish new centres in nearly every country of the world. By the time he died the Bahá'í Faith (which in 1921 had been largely confined to Iran and a few neighbouring countries in the Middle East, and to North America and a few tiny communities in Europe) had been established in around 200 independent nations and significant territories and islands. Contacts had also been made with first the League of Nations and then the United Nations where the Faith was recognized as an official non-governmental organization.

Translations into English of major Writings of Bahá'u'lláh, a dramatic and scholarly account of the history of the Faith during its first hundred years, and thousands of letters, in both English and Persian, flowed from the pen of the Guardian during these years. The development of the World Centre of the Bahá'í Faith on the slopes of Mount Carmel in Haifa (a process begun by 'Abdu'l-Bahá in accordance with the wishes of Bahá'u'lláh) was among the Guardian's continual cares. The most well-known building at the World Centre in the time of the Guardian was the Shrine that houses the remains of the Báb, brought secretly out of Iran during the ministry of 'Abdu'l-Bahá.

During the period of his last worldwide plan (1953–1963) the Guardian had envisaged a quadrupling of the number of national spiritual assemblies to 48, a number which he judged sufficient to elect the first Universal House of Justice. He had also revived and strengthened Bahá'u'lláh's institution of counsellors, by appointing a total of some twenty-seven 'Hands of the Cause'. When he died it was found that he had not appointed a successor to the position of Guardian, and it was understood in the event that he intended the Hands of the Cause, as a group, to manage the affairs of the community for a transitional period until such time as the Universal House of Justice had been elected at the end of the plan. And so it was. The election of the first Universal House of Justice in 1963 was preceded by a World Congress held at the Albert Hall in London which was attended by some 7,000 people from all over the world, drawn from an immense number of different cultural backgrounds including tribal people from Africa, Asia, the islands of the Pacific, and the Americas. In the writer's view it is not unreasonable to describe this Congress as the first real gathering of the ordinary peoples of the world in history (as distinct from meetings of diplomats, experts, and other 'professionals').

Since that first election nearly a quarter of a century ago, there have been a series of worldwide plans modelled on those of the Guardian and which have resulted in a steady strengthening, expansion and diversification of the Bahá'í community. By 1986 the community had 148 national spiritual assemblies (compared with 56 in 1963), and about 33,000 local spiritual assemblies. It was established in some 119,000 localities in 116 independent nations and 48 significant territories and islands (see Table 29). The total number of Bahá'ís worldwide was about 4.7 million, and included representatives from nearly 2,000 minority groups and tribes (in 1982).[6] Bahá'í material had been translated into over 700 languages and dialects (1982).

There has been a considerable effort, too, over the last twenty-five years, to expand the responsibilities of local assemblies and to deepen individual Bahá'ís in their understanding of the Faith and its purposes. As the community has become stronger it has been able to undertake a growing number of social and economic development projects both within the Bahá'í community and in the larger community as well, sometimes in cooperation with other develop-

[6] The article 'Religion: World Religious Statistics' in The 1988 Britannica Book of the Year states that the most global religions are Christianity, Islam and the Bahá'í Faith.

TABLE 29

STATISTICS ON THE BAHÁ'Í WORLD COMMUNITY
A. Growth Over Fifty Years

Number of:	1933[1]	1944[1]	1953	1963	1973	1986
National Spiritual Assemblies	9	8	12	56	113	148
Local Spiritual Assemblies	300	500	610	3,519	17,037	32,852
Localities where Bahá'ís reside	800	1,900	2,412	10,749	69,541	116,674
Independent nations where Bahá'ís reside					141	166
	46	77	128	250		
Significant territories and islands					194	48[3]

B. The Bahá'í Community in 1986 by Continent

Number of:	AFRICA	AMERICAS	ASIA	EUROPE	OCEANIA	TOTAL
National Spiritual Assemblies	43	41	26	21	17	148
Local Spiritual Assemblies	7,258	6,500	17,524	713	857	32,852
Localities where Bahá'ís reside[1]	35,612	26,586	48,730	2,844	2,902	116,674
Independent nations where Bahá'ís reside	51	35	36	33	11	166
Significant territories and islands where Bahá'ís reside	6	16	3	4	13	48
Indigenous tribes, races & ethnic groups represented in the Faith (1984)	1,250	340	250	22	250	2,112
No. of countries where Bahá'ís are 1 percent or more of the population	4	13	3	–	15	35

[1] Approximate figures only.

[2] Includes communities with Local Spiritual Assemblies.

[3] The figure is lower in 1986 because the term has been revised to approximate current geographical and political divisions. Previously the term covered divisions based on cultural, geographic and demographic factors.

Source: Department of Statistics, Bahá'í World Centre, June 1986.

ment institutions such as those of the United Nations and the Government of Canada. A major recent undertaking has been the issuing of a Statement on Peace in connection with the UN's

International Year of Peace, which has been presented to the UN
Secretary-General as well as to the heads of states of most nations,
and to a vast number of eminent persons in other public and private
positions.

These successes have been won against a background of violent
persecution of the Bahá'í community of Iran, which has been intense
ever since the establishment of the Islamic Republic in 1979. Terrible
as this has been – the worst persecution of the Bahá'ís since the last
century – it has resulted in an increased sense of solidarity and love
within the community and in a worldwide appreciation of the Bahá'í
Faith from all quarters and on a scale never before realized.

Let us now return to our questions at the beginning of this chapter.
At first sight there might be some doubt about the Faith's ability to
attract the peoples of the world; after all, 4.7 million adherents is
only a small proportion (0.1 percent) of the total world population of
about 4.8 billion, and compares unfavourably with the nominal
numbers claimed for the other great religions. A closer view of the
figures gives a different perspective. First, the rate of expansion of
the Faith is one of the fastest for any religion in the world,[7] and this
in the face of immense obstacles. Prejudice and blind adherence
to past values prevail on the part of many followers of the old
religions (particularly their leaders), while apathy, scepticism and
cynicism about religion in general characterise a society which is
predominantly materialistic in outlook. Despite this the number of
Bahá'ís compares favourably with the numbers attracted by the other
great religions in their first hundred years or so.[8] Further, experience
in the last fifty years suggests that when ideas catch the public
imagination they will sweep across the world like wildfire, helped on
by modern communications technology, and every effort of authority to stop them will fail. However, it is perhaps the diversity of the
peoples who are attracted to the Bahá'í Faith rather than absolute
numbers, which provide the most significant indication of its
potential power to unite the peoples of the world.

One of the most striking aspects of this diversity, which alone
would make the Faith unique, is its ability to attract peoples from
every religious background: Zoroastrian, Hindu, Buddhist, Jewish,
Christian and Muslim. This is in large part because the Faith fulfils

[7] In the twelve years 1974–1986, the number of Bahá'ís world-wide is estimated to have grown
by nearly 80 percent, or by 2 million. There are now 35 countries where the Bahá'ís are more
than one percent of the population.

[8] For instance, it is estimated that by the year 100 AD there were about 1 million Christians.
(David Barratt (ed.), *World Christian Encyclopedia*, Oxford University Press, 1982.)

the aspirations and the prophecies of their own traditions (with remarkable accuracy in some cases[9], and does not require them to give up belief in the founder figure of their former religion. The power of attraction of the Faith is indicated by the deep prejudice that has to be overcome when a Jew accepts the teaching to revere Jesus after nearly 2,000 years of Christian abuse, or when a Christian accepts Muhammad after centuries of poisonous stories and armed conflict. In the case of Muslims there is the additional factor that to become a Bahá'í can be personally dangerous, especially in Iran. Its appeal to peoples of religion is mirrored in its ability to attract scientists too (such as August Forel, or Richard St Barbe Baker, the pioneer environmentalist) because it does not require them to believe things which come into conflict with scientific knowledge, as well as agnostics and atheists who have come to recognize that a reductionist or materialistic view of the universe is incomplete and unsatisfactory.

A particular source of joy for the non-white races, tribes and minorities is the Bahá'í teaching and their practice with regard to equality of all mankind and appreciation of cultural diversity. For so long, millions of people were made to feel inferior by the Westerners' technology and administrative skills, a feeling frequently reinforced by Christian missionaries, critical of local customs, who taught that ancestors who had not even heard of Jesus would be damned for ever – a painful thought for anyone who cares about his family and its past. The Bahá'í Faith changes all this so that tribal peoples can once again hold their heads high and know that they and their cultures are valued equally with others in contributing to the richness of civilization. Thus, for instance, Central American Indians appreciate for the first time in centuries the great achievements of their Mayan forefathers. One of the most moving experiences the author has had, in this connection, was to hear a middle-aged black lady in Cape Town, South Africa, say that when she became a Bahá'í she became a person for the first time in her life. For some peoples, such as the North American Indians, the Faith has the additional force that it also fulfils prophecies of their traditional religion, and thus overcomes an understandable suspicion of outside religions which in the past have belittled and derided their culture. The community takes great pride in the fact that in North America there are now some 115 local spiritual assemblies on Indian reservations.

Another dimension of the Faith's diversity is its ability to bridge the generation gap in attracting both young people and their parents.

[9] e.g. as noted earlier, the timing of its coming from the viewpoint of Christianity and Shi'ih Islam.

Young people of the West come to the Faith because they seek idealism, a sense of purpose in life, an alternative to war, and a moral code that is strong and clear and makes sense. The latter aspect of the Faith also means a great deal to those parents who, appalled by the breakdown in moral standards in modern society, are frantically searching for some guidance for their children. Sometimes parents will be initially horrified to hear that their children have become Bahá'ís, fearing that it is yet another sect dividing families and promoting strange life-styles. When they find out what the Faith really stands for there is usually a change of heart. There are innumerable examples of parents following their children into the Faith – thus literally fulfilling Wordsworth's moral insight that the child is father of the man.

The Bahá'í teachings are obviously attractive to women, in promoting the principle of the equality of the sexes in all aspects of life. More profoundly, they make possible the reconciliation of life as a wage-earner with life as a mother and member of a family, and this offers particular support to women who are trying to find their place, since the sexual revolution, in a society which has not properly thought through the reality of sexual equality.

The Faith has also demonstrated its appeal for peoples of all classes in the West as in the East. From a Queen, Marie of Romania, or a Lady Blomfield in England, to professors at Yale or Oxford, to insurance agents, to clerks, to Devonshire fishermen, to share-croppers in the South of the United States; from artists such as the painter Mark Tobey or the potter Bernard Leach, to the film actress Carole Lombard or the jazz musician Dizzie Gillespie (to name but a few amongst many) – all kinds of people have committed themselves to the Bahá'í vision and identified themselves with this new Faith. The attraction extends into the political domain too; those with a conservative view of life appreciate the Faith's high moral standards and its emphasis on order; those who are liberal focus on its spirit of freedom, consultation, and independent investigation of the truth; whilst for those on the left there is the deep commitment and practical approach to the elimination of poverty world-wide, and the narrowing of economic differences.

One other aspect to the diversity of the Bahá'í community should be mentioned. As will be clear from the above remarks, many of those who come into the Bahá'í Faith already subscribe to the highest moral standards and social ideas; in the Faith they see a fulfilment of their hopes. But there are others, those who have experienced the harshest side of life, or who have suffered from all sorts of weaknesses such as addiction to alcohol and drugs. These have found in the Faith a haven where they will be helped by others to help themselves and where there will be no self-righteous bullying.

In a community of people of so many diverse backgrounds there will clearly be times in the process of growth when clashes of temperament will cause unhappiness which may even drive a person from the community. What is remarkable is that in so many instances such persons will eventually return, because once having had the experience of the Faith, the outside world seems cold, narrow, shallow, and empty.

What, then, can be said about the unity and degree of commitment of this diverse community to their ideals in the face of attack and demands for sacrifice? It is the experience of history that progressive movements which deserve to be taken seriously will always be persecuted by the established authorities, even if what is advocated is for the benefit of all, including those who stand so fiercely in opposition. Certainly the followers of all the great religions were persecuted in their early years, and the Bahá'í Faith is no exception. As with the other religions, it was the leading figures of the Faith who set the example of steadfastness in time of trial. The Báb suffered imprisonment for three years and then was martyred. Bahá'u'lláh was imprisoned, beaten, deprived of all His possessions and driven into exile for the rest of His life. 'Abdu'l-Bahá was imprisoned for forty years and threatened with death on several occasions.

These examples have prompted the deepest love on the part of Bahá'ís for the Central Figures of their Faith. Their commitment to the new teachings has inspired thousands of Bahá'ís to withstand persecution with fortitude. Such persecution has been most severe in the land where the Faith began, Iran, and it has been almost continuous since the first days. It was extremely savage in the middle of the nineteenth century when several thousand lost their lives. Though conditions generally improved thereafter, the threat to the community was constant, and as a result it had to conduct its activities with great caution. Periodically there would be outbreaks of violence as in 1874 (Isfahan), 1889 (Najafabad), 1891 (Yazd), 1896 (Turbat-i-Haydari), 1899 (Najafabad), 1903 (Rasht and Yazd),[10] 1926 (Jahrum), and 1955 when the royal government found it convenient to persecute the Bahá'ís in a nation-wide campaign aimed at appeasing the mullas. That campaign was only stopped after a worldwide public outcry and representation by the United Nations and several

[10] The Western press reported that 120 were massacred in Yazd alone on this occasion, including two who were blown from the mouth of a cannon. (M. Momen (ed.), *The Bábí and Bahá'í Religions, 1844–1944*, p. 298.)

national governments including that of President Eisenhower.

The situation became critical once again following the establishment of the Islamic Republic in 1979, whose representatives (including the Attorney-General) periodically stated that their intention was to 'wipe out' the Bahá'í community, the largest religious minority in Iran with an estimated population at that time of some 300,000–400,000. The new government undertook a comprehensive plan of destruction: execution so far of some 200 Bahá'ís;[11] torture; imprisonment (some 700 are still in prison at the time of writing); deprivation of property rights, jobs and pensions; denial of right to attend school or university; destruction of Bahá'í holy places and cemeteries.

What is distinctive about this persecution is that a Bahá'í can release himself from it by merely denying his Faith:[12] the choice is his in a way which was not true, for instance, of the Jews in Nazi Germany or the educated classes in Cambodia. Thousands of people, not only Bahá'ís, have been killed by the new regime. The case of the Bahá'ís is distinctive because they have specifically declared their loyalty and obedience to the government; thus when they were ordered, for instance, to dismantle their administrative system they did so immediately. By contrast most of the non-Bahá'ís executed, apart from a few genuine criminals, have been either identified with the Shah's government or have been suspected of armed opposition.

There is good reason for believing that the Bahá'í community would have suffered even more if there had not been a constant searchlight played on the issue by the outside world: the United Nations, national governments, human rights organizations and the news media. As it is, the regime has felt compelled to do much of its shameful work at night and in secret, and has put up a smoke screen of ridiculous charges, such as spying for Israel or the Western powers, to hide their real motives.[13]

The real offence is that the Faith is a new and living religion which has the power of attracting people from all backgrounds, including Islam. It is interesting, from the point of view of the progressive movement, that the teachings which seem to incense the mullas the most are first, the equality of men and women (thus the Bahá'ís are accused of prostitution and general sexual immorality), and second,

[11] The majority have been elected members of spiritual assemblies. Nearly all the members of two national spiritual assemblies have been executed or have disappeared without trace after arrest.

[12] As was proved in 1983 when there was a rare example of capitulation under great pressure and the man concerned was immediately set free.

[13] In one absurd case, for instance, an old country peasant was charged with spying offences.

the world perspective, which is considered unpatriotic. At one time they also accused the Bahá'ís of being communists.[14]

Though persecution has been the most severe in Iran, it has certainly not been confined to that country. In most Muslim states Bahá'ís have to be very cautious in their daily lives, and in some they have been imprisoned and threatened with death. The situation has been generally much better in the non-Muslim world, although there have been many instances of hostility on the part of individual Christians and occasionally Christian institutions. Thus Mayan Indians who became Bahá'ís in Central America were subsequently denied medical aid in church-run hospitals. Bahá'ís in Alaska have been sacked from public service positions as a result of intervention by Christian fundamentalists. Several clergymen are actually engaged in circulating material aimed at undermining the Bahá'í Faith.[15] There have been attacks initiated by political ideology too. As might be expected the Nazis tried to crush the German Bahá'í community, whose principles were clearly in direct opposition to Nazi ideology. In Russia after the 1917 Revolution the new Bolshevik government was at first tolerant of the small Bahá'í community, no doubt because it seemed very progressive compared with the Russian Orthodox Church, and it was only later during the general repression of the 1930s that the Bahá'ís were severely harassed.

The Bahá'í community has also survived attacks from within. As mentioned earlier, Bahá'u'lláh's own half-brother revolted against His leadership and for many years tried to foment opposition within the community. Very few followed him, as was attested by E.G. Browne after he had visited Iran in the 1890s and met various Bahá'í communities. He noted, incidentally, that the Azalis (followers of Bahá'u'lláh's half-brother) smoked opium like the rest of the population, whereas the true Bahá'ís did not. Bahá'u'lláh's half-brother himself died in loneliness in Cyprus in 1912 and was given a Muslim funeral. In the early years of His ministry 'Abdu'l-Bahá too had to face attacks by those who opposed His leadership. One such was Ibrahim Khayr'u'lláh, one of the first and most influential Bahá'í emissaries to the United States (see p. 455 above), who broke away

[14] This religious persecution is contrary to the teachings of Muhammad, as has been pointed out many times by Muslims and non-Muslims alike, e.g. in the article 'What Muslims Really Believe about Religious Liberty' by Mohammed Talbi, professor at the University of Tunis, which was published in the magazine *Liberty* in 1986. 'Let there be no compulsion in religion: Truth stands out clear from Error' (*Qur'án* 2: 256).

[15] Much of the Christian opposition comes from former missionaries to Iran who apparently envied the success of the Faith in that country compared with their own meagre results. Of course, from the Bahá'í perspective of progressive revelation it is not surprising that Christianity has had so little success in Islamic countries.

because he wanted to become co-head of the Bahá'í community, with responsibility for its Western wing. Very few followed him, even in America. Then there were those members of 'Abdu'l-Bahá's own family who wanted to use the property of the Faith for their private interest. Later there were periodic attempts to undermine the unity of the community during the ministry of the Guardian, partly because some older individuals thought they knew more than their new leader. Again, after his death, one of the Hands of the Cause (nearly ninety years old at the time and with fading mental faculties) claimed that he was the new Guardian. In all these cases, though there was much pain and anguish for the community, the effect was minimal and the 'covenant-breakers' soon broke away and sank into obscurity. These instances all serve to demonstrate the effectiveness of measures taken to ensure unity within the Bahá'í community, including the process of consultation for arriving at democratic decisions, the absence of individual leaders and the clear line of authority going back to the Bahá'í Writings, which are not open to interpretation by any one other than 'Abdu'l-Bahá and the Guardian. Whereas the Faith has much in common with the older great religions in its ability to withstand persecution from outside, it has already demonstrated a unique strength in being able to maintain unity in the face of internal assault.

Sacrifice for the Bahá'í cause has not been confined to resisting persecution and other attacks on the unity of the community. Large numbers have made considerable sacrifice either by service which has held back their career prospects or by unstinted voluntary giving to the funds of the community. Perhaps the greatest sacrifices have been made by the thousands who have left their homes to go and live in a strange country in order to help build up new communities. The Faith does not have a clergy or professional missionaries and relies entirely on the help of ordinary men and women for its diffusion. Such moves have often created difficulties in finding work, in health care, and in the education of children, to name only the most obvious, but it was such sacrifices which led to the creation of a world community in such a short time. In undertaking such assignments, Bahá'ís try to become integrated into their new environment, to act not as foreigners, but as servants to their new homeland. Their task is to help raise up new communities which will be self-sufficient and not dependent on them for leadership and guidance. Such 'pioneers' came for many years mainly from Iran, North America, and parts of Europe and Australasia. In recent times, however, as more and more national communities have become firmly established, the source of pioneers has greatly widened, so as to give an even broader multi-cultural aspect to a large number of national and local communities.

It was suggested at the beginning of this chapter that one more question should be asked of the history of the Faith: what has been achieved so far in putting into practice the programme of Bahá'u'lláh? What has been the result of this success in attracting such a diverse membership and of such sacrifice?

The first response must surely be to point to the very existence today of a system of functioning communities in virtually every country of the world (148 national spiritual assemblies), with firm roots in the countryside, the jungle, the desert, the islands of the seas, the town and the city. The majority of local communities are holding regular meetings, contributing to the funds, taking part in elections, and learning the process of consultation. They must overcome the problems familiar to voluntary workers the world over: lack of experience; small financial resources; distance, especially where transport facilities are weak or non-existent (as is often the case in local communities in the Third World); apathy with regard to local public affairs (as in many Western countries, and in places where there are centuries of expectation that public affairs are the responsibility of someone else). The effort is hard initially but it is working. The writer, for instance, has witnessed on several occasions the steady maturing of the art of consultation in local spiritual assemblies over only a year or two, although, of course, improvements are difficult to quantify. An immense amount needs still to be done; in particular there is a need in most communities to move closer to universal participation in all activities. The system can be seen at its best in the functioning of the Universal House of Justice (that unique body in the history of the world), and in the large number of international conferences held over the last few decades, which were not only genuine meetings of peoples from all around the world, but demonstrations of how such diverse groups can work together in harmony and unity of purpose.

Another significant achievement of the Faith has been its impact on the lives of the ordinary people of its communities. The emphasis on education, for instance, has resulted over time in a literacy rate amongst the Bahá'ís of Iran (who in terms of occupation and class were a rough cross-section of the population as a whole) well in excess of 90 percent, whereas the level for the rest of the population is no more than about 40 percent. Another sign of the impact of education is the growing number of Bahá'í children and young people for whom Bahá'í attitudes have become the norm; whose career choices are being made in the desire to be of service to humanity; and who are not crippled by negative attitudes inherited from the past. A report to the United Nations in connection with International Women's Year noted that in many countries Bahá'í women play an important part in the administration of their communities as assembly members and as assembly officers, in sharp contrast with other women in the same countries who are still in the main subjugated to their men in all public affairs as in the home.[16] A most notable success has been a significant lowering of the level of racial prejudice within the community as compared with outside. Bahá'ís have been constantly aware of the problem of deep-seated racial prejudices (described as the 'most challenging issue') since the visit of 'Abdu'l-Bahá to the United States in 1912, and it is of interest that the recent Statement on Peace made by the Universal House of Justice lists racial prejudice as first among the main causes of conflict in the world today, ahead even of extremes of wealth and poverty. A sign of success in this field has been the large number of inter-racial marriages in the community. Young people too have responded to the Bahá'í teachings in quite a remarkable way. Many young American Bahá'ís, for instance, previously involved in civil disobedience campaigns against the war in Vietnam, quietly did their compulsory military service after becoming Bahá'ís and for the most part were able to obtain non-combatant assignments. Just as impressive was the break-away from peer pressure – always an immensely powerful force over the young in particular – in a rejection of the fashion for promiscuous sex, alcohol, drugs, and unclean and unchaste styles of dress. Last, but not least, is the impression obtained when meeting with any Bahá'í community throughout the world, of a warm welcome and friendliness, a happy, relaxed atmosphere, and the absence of posturing and gossip. One can travel around the world, and at any place feel that one is at home with one's family.

Not that the community has achieved perfection. Imperfections abound, as they must do in any social community of people from every conceivable background, subject in their daily lives to all the pressures of a materialistic civilization. One of concern, for instance, is the fact that the community still has a relatively high rate of divorce in the West – not much lower than the prevailing rates in the world at large. The point is that the community aims at a high standard of behaviour, that in general standards are higher than in the outside world, and that they are improving all the time rather than declining.

[16] A recent study has shown that worldwide about 25 percent of the members of national spiritual assemblies are women. Within this world average the records of Africa, the Americas and Europe are above average and Asia is well below. Though still far below the ideal of 50 percent, the Baha'í record compares favourably with the figures given in Chapter 14 for women elected to political legislative assemblies and appointed to cabinet positions.

For many years the Bahá'í community poured nearly all its efforts into building a functioning worldwide community and in helping individual members of that community to cultivate the attitudes and qualities associated with the name 'Bahá'í'. This is a never-ending task, but after some sixty years of steady work it has been judged that a sound enough base is now established to allow the community to expand its activities into more direct service to the peoples of the world. Of course, the community has from its earliest days given its support to a large number of activities associated with other progressive organizations: the United Nations and movements for peace, human rights, equality of women, protection of the environment, and many others. Material has been published on such issues as the falsity of theories of racial superiority, on the education of children, the underlying oneness of the world's religions (the Bahá'ís were amongst the first to publish favourable and objective accounts of Islam in the West), the dangers of alcohol and other drugs, the unique Bahá'í decision-making process, and other themes. Bahá'í representatives have presented to the United Nations proposals for reform, including a world police force and compulsory arbitration of disputes, which would make it a more effective organization, as well as participating with consultative status in UN conferences and seminars on a multitude of subjects.[17] The Bahá'í community has also joined with the World Wide Fund for Nature in its initiative for the conservation of nature and the environment. The Bahá'ís of the United States have also been credited (by Jewish organizations) with playing a critical role in persuading the US Senate to approve, after over thirty years delay, the United Nations Genocide Convention. More recently the Canadian Bahá'í community played a key role in persuading participants in an Interfaith Programme for Public Awareness of Nuclear Issues to be impartial and free from partisan political involvement, with the result that public hearings on the issue were immensely more useful than they would otherwise have been, and in addition received government assistance.

The expansion now being undertaken by the community includes a worldwide programme of social and economic development projects such as establishing and maintaining schools, teacher training centres, agricultural stations where farmers are taught new methods of increasing productivity, primary health care, job training, language training for immigrants, and many others. There are also several community radio stations in Africa and North and

---

[17] The Bahá'í International Community is officially recognized as an international non-governmental organization of the UN and is accredited with consultative status with ECOSOC and UNICEF. It also has working relationships with other UN agencies and programmes, including UNEP, UNESCO, WHO, and FAO.

South America which exist to encourage local culture, to provide a notice-board for local events, and to give advice on the weather, farming methods, and medical matters. Such radio stations are staffed for the most part with local volunteers and broadcast in local languages. Most of these projects (in 1986 there were 703 in 79 countries), are small by the standards of official development programmes because Bahá'ís feel there is a need for a grass-roots approach so as to ensure success. Shortage of funds makes it necessary to adopt schemes which require little capital but which instead exploit the abundance of skills available in the Bahá'í community as a result of the emphasis on education and on crafts and professions which are of service to the community. The projects depend on a high degree of involvement by the recipients, who identify their own needs to start the ball rolling, and participate in the choice of project, construction, and management.

Another indication of the readiness of the Bahá'í community for a broadening range of activity in the public arena has been the Peace Statement issued in connection with the United Nations Year of Peace (1985–86). The statement draws attention to the choice which faces mankind: a peace after a catastrophe, or after a conscious and rational decision by the nations of the world. It points out that the greatest barrier to action is the prevailing pessimistic view that man is essentially aggressive and selfish and that therefore all peace efforts will end in failure. It argues that a lasting peace will require more than disarmament and treaties. There is a need to eliminate the root causes of conflict: racism, extremes of wealth and poverty, rampant nationalism, ignorance and prejudice, religious division. It calls for a system of education in which all are taught to see themselves as citizens of one world and for a meeting of all the world's leaders at which peace will be given the highest priority.

This short account of the history of the Bahá'í Faith and its achievements would seem, it is submitted to the reader, to give substance to the Bahá'í claim that theirs is not just a movement with fine principles. Rather it is a movement which has already demonstrated a deep commitment and unity of purpose in putting these principles into practice, inspired by love for Bahá'u'lláh, the Báb, 'Abdu'l-Bahá, and the Guardian and by their example. This is a community of ordinary men and women from all around the world, and their achievements demonstrate that the goals of the Bahá'í Faith are within the capability of mankind today. They invite all men and women to see for themselves. They appeal to progressive forces to unite, to join hands together, and march forward to achieve the greatest enterprise in history: the establishment of a just world society and a lasting peace.

World Population since the Beginning of Civilization

Year			Millions of People			
	AFRICA	AMERICAS	ASIA	EUROPE	OCEANIA	WORLD (rounded)
BC 4000						7
3000						14
2000						27
1000						50
AD 1	16	4.5	115	31	1	170
600	20	5	140	26	1.2	200
1000	33	9	185	36	1.5	265
1500	46	14	280	81	2	425
1700	61	13	415	120	2.3	610
1800	70	24	625	180	2.5	900
1850	81	59	795	265	2.25	1,200
1900	110	145	970	390	6.75	1,625
1950	205	325	1,450	515	14	2,500
1975	385	545	2,300	635	23	3,900
1984	537	658	2,887	676	24	4,800
Medium growth projection[1]						
2000	877	848	3,670	702	30	6,100
2025	1,643	1,134	4,614	741	40	8,200
2100 (stabilized population?)						9,000[2]

[1] Medium growth projection assumes the world population growth will drop from 1.67 percent per annum to 0.96 percent by 2025. If the rate only dropped to 1.29 percent then the world population by 2025 would be about 9.1 billion (high projection). If the annual growth rate dropped to 0.67 percent by 2025, then the world population in that year would be about 7.4 billion (*UN 1984 Population Report*).

[2] The medium growth projection indicates that the world population might stabilize at something near twice today's population. This is well below the theoretical limit of 20 billion which some scientists put on the earth's capacity. These projections assume no major catastrophe e.g. nuclear war, environmental or disease related. It has been pointed out that with regard to disease, the virus is the most threatening and difficult to counter.

Sources: Colin McEvedy and Richard Jones, *Atlas of World Population History*, Penguin, 1985; Jan Osmanczyk (ed), *Encyclopaedia of the UN and International Agreements*, Taylor & Francis, 1985.

Independent Nations and States of the World by Continent and Size of Population

Population in millions	Number of Nations & States						Percentage of Total	
	AFRICA	AMERICAS	ASIA	EUROPE	OCEANIA	TOTAL	COUNTRIES	POPULATION
200 & more	–	1	2	1	–	4	2.3	48.8
100–199	–	1	2	–	–	3	1.8	8.7
50–99	1	1	4	4	–	10	5.9	15.0
10–49	12	6	13	9	1	41	24.1	20.1
1–9	26	15	14	11	2	68	40.0	7.1
less than 1	12	11	4	8	9	44	25.9	0.3
Total	**51**	**35**	**39**	**33**	**12**	**170¹**	**100.0**	**100.0**

¹ Does not include the Vatican.

List of Nations and States

		Population in millions		
AFRICA	AMERICAS	ASIA	EUROPE	OCEANIA

Very large: 200 million and more

	234 USA	1022 China	272 USSR	
		733 India		

Large: 100–199 million

	130 Brazil	156 Indonesia		
		119 Japan		

Medium–large: 50–99 million

94 Nigeria	75 Mexico	95 Bangladesh	62 Germany FR	
		90 Pakistan	56 Italy	
		59 Vietnam	56 UK	
		52 Philippines	55 France	

Small–medium: 10–49 million

45 Egypt	29 Argentina	49 Thailand	38 Spain	15 Australia
34 Ethiopia	28 Colombia	47 Turkey	37 Poland	
32 Zaire	25 Canada	43 Iran	23 Romania	
31 South Africa	18 Peru	40 Korea R*	23 Yugoslavia	
21 Algeria	17 Venezuela	36 Burma	17 Germany DR	
21 Morocco	12 Chile	19 Korea PDR*	15 Czecho-	
21 Sudan		19 Taiwan*	slovakia	

APPENDIX 2
List of Nations and States

		Population in millions		
AFRICA	AMERICAS	ASIA	EUROPE	OCEANIA
20 Tanzania		17 Afghanistan	14 Netherlands	
19 Kenya		16 Nepal	11 Hungary	
14 Uganda		15 Iraq	10 Portugal	
13 Ghana		15 Malaysia		
13 Mozambique		15 Sri Lanka		
		10 Saudi Arabia		

Small: 1–9 million

AFRICA	AMERICAS	ASIA	EUROPE	OCEANIA
9 Cameroon	9 Cuba	9 Syria	10 Belgium	3 New Zealand
9 Ivory Coast	8 Ecuador	8 Yemen AR	9 Greece	3 Papua NG
9 Madagascar	8 Guatamala	6 Kampuchea	9 Bulgaria	
8 Angola	6 Bolivia	4 Israel	8 Austria	
8 Zimbabwe	6 Dominican R	4 Laos PDR	8 Sweden	
7 Burkina Faso	5 El Salvador	3 Jordan	6 Switzerland*	
7 Malawi	5 Haiti	3 Lebanon	5 Denmark	
7 Mali	4 Honduras	3 Singapore	5 Finland	
7 Tunisia	3 Nicaragua	2 Kuwait	4 Ireland	
6 Guinea	3 Paraguay	2 Mongolia	4 Norway	
6 Niger	3 Uruguay	2 Yemen PDR	3 Albania	
6 Rwanda	2 Costa Rica	1 Bhutan		
6 Senegal	2 Jamaica	1 Oman		
6 Zambia	2 Panama	1 United Arab Emirates		
5 Chad	1 Trinidad & Tobago			
5 Somalia				
4 Benin				
4 Burundi				
3 Libya				
3 Sierra Leone				
3 Togo				
2 Central African R				
2 Congo				
2 Liberia				
2 Mauritania				
1 Lesotho				

Mini States: less than 1 million

AFRICA	AMERICAS	ASIA	EUROPE	OCEANIA
.9 Mauritius	.8 Guyana	.4 Bahrain	.7 Cyprus	.7 Fiji
.9 Botswana	.4 Surinam	.3 Qatar	.4 Luxembourg	.3 Solomons
.9 Guinea Bissau	.3 Barbados	.2 Brunei	.4 Malta	.2 W. Samoa
.7 Gabon	.2 Bahamas	.2 Maldives	.2 Iceland	.1 Tonga*
.7 Gambia	.2 Belize		Liechtenstein*	.1 Vanuatu*
.7 Swaziland	.1 Antigua		Monaco*	.1 Kirabati*
.4 Comoros	.1 Dominica		Andorra*	Cook*
.4 Djibouti	.1 Grenada		San Marino*	Tuvalu*
.4 Equatorial Guinea	.1 Kitts-Nevis			Nauru*

List of Nations and States

		Population in millions		
AFRICA	AMERICAS	ASIA	EUROPE	OCEANIA
.3 Cape Verde	.1 St Lucia			
.1 Sao Tome	.1 St Vincent			
.1 Seychelles				

* 13 nations not members of the United Nations.

Overseas Dependencies and Islands

AFRICA	AMERICAS	ASIA	EUROPE	OCEANIA
.9 Namibia	3.3 Puerto Rico	5.3 Hong Kong	.1 Channel Is.	.1 French
.5 Reunion	.3 Guadeloupe	.3 Macao	.1 Greenland	Polynesia
.2 Spanish	.3 Martinique		.1 Isle of Man	.1 Guam
N. Africa	.2 Netherlands		Faroes	.1 New
.1 Sahara (West)	Antilles		Gibraltar	Guinea
Ascension	.1 French Guiana		Svalband	.1 Pacific Is.
Mayotte	.1 Virgin Is. (US)			Trust
St Helena	.1 Bermuda			Territory
	Anguilla			American
	Cayman			Samoa
	Falklands			Christmas
	(Malinas)			Is.
	Monserrat			Cocos Is.
	St Pierre &			Midway
	Miguelon			Johnson Is.
	Turks & Caicos			Niue
	Virgin Is. (UK)			Norfolk Is.
				Pitcairn
				Wake
				Wallis &
				Futuna
				Tokelau

No figure given for states, territories or islands with population of less than 50,000.

Source: World Bank Atlas, 1986.

APPENDIX 3

Winners of the Nobel Peace Prize
1901–1988

Year	Winner of Prize	Country	Profession	Service Rendered
1901	Henri Dunant & Red Cross	Switzerland	businessman	Founder of Red Cross
	Frédéric Passy	France	economist	Joint founder of Inter-Parliamentary Union
1902	Eli Ducammon	Switzerland	journalist, MP	General Secretary of International Peace Bureau
1903	Charles-Albert Gobat	Switzerland	lawyer, educator	General Secretary of International Peace Bureau
	William Cremer	Great Britain	trade unionist, MP	Secretary of International Arbitration League, joint founder of Inter-Parliamentary Union
1904	Institute of International Law			
1905	Bertha von Suttner	Austria	writer	Founder of Austrian Peace Society; wrote *Lay Down Your Arms*
1906	Theodore Roosevelt	USA	statesman	Helped bring Japanese–Russian peace at Treaty of Portsmouth
1907	Ernesto Teodoro Moneta	Italy	journalist	Presided over International Peace Conference in Milan (1906)
	Louis Renault	France	lawyer	Representative at Hague meetings; served on Hague Tribunal

Year	Name	Country	Profession	Description
1908	Klaus Pontus Arnoldson	Sweden	journalist, MP	A founder of Swedish Peace and Arbitration Association
	Fredik Bajer	Denmark	journalist, MP	A founder and first president of International Peace Bureau
1909	Auguste Beernaert	Belgium	statesman (Prime Minister)	Representative at Hague meetings; served on Hague Tribunal
	Paul Henri Benjamin Balluet	France	diplomat	Representative at Hague meetings; served on Hague Tribunal
1910	International Peace Bureau			
1911	Tobias Asser	Netherlands	lawyer	Head of Institute of International Law; representative at Hague Conferences
	Alfred Fried	Austria	journalist	Founder of German Peace Society; editor of *Peace Watch*
1912	Elihu Root	USA	statesman	Representative at 1907 Hague Conference; peace activities in Americas
1913	Henri La Fontaine	Belgium	lawyer	Founder of 'Centre Intellectual Mondial'; directed Peace Bureau; Hague meetings
1914–16	none given			
1917	Red Cross (2nd time)			
1918	none given			
1919	Woodrow Wilson	USA	statesman (President)	Main founder of League of Nations
1920	Leon Bourgeois	France	statesman	Chairman First (Hague) Commission of Arbitration; President of League Council
1921	Karl Branting	Sweden	statesman (Prime Minister)	Chairman of League Committee on Disarmament

Year	Winner of Prize	Country	Profession	Service Rendered
	Christian Lange	Norway	administrator	First Secretary-General of Nobel Committee; Secretary-General of Inter-Parliamentary Union; member Central Organization for a Lasting Peace
1922	Fridtjof Nansen & Nansen Office	Norway	explorer	League's High Commissioner for Refugees
1923–4	none given			
1925	Austen Chamberlain	Great Britain	statesman	Role in Treaty of Locarno
	Charles Dawes	USA	businessman	Dawes Plan for German reparations
1926	Aristide Briand	France	statesman (Prime Minister)	Role in Washington naval treaty, Locarno treaty, Kellogg-Briand Pack
	Gustave Stresemann	Germany	statesman (Chancellor)	Role in Treaty of Locarno and Dawes Plan
1927	Ferdinand Buisson	France	educator	A founder of the League of the Rights of Man
	Ludwig Quidde	Germany	educator	President, German Peace Society; role in Peace Congresses 1901 & 1905
1928	none given			
1929	Frank Kellogg	USA	statesman	Kellogg-Briand Pack outlawing war
1930	Nathan Söderblom	Sweden	theologian	Architect of ecumenical movement
1931	Jane Addams	USA	social worker	Chaired Women's Peace Party; President, International Congress of Women; President, International League for Peace and Freedom
	Nicholas Murray Butler	USA	educator	A Founder of the Carnegie Endowment for International Peace

Year	Name	Country	Profession	Description
1932	none given			
1933	Norman Angell	Great Britain	journalist, MP	Wrote *The Great Illusion*
1934	Arthur Henderson	Great Britain	statesman	Chairman of League's International Disarmament Conference
1935	Carl von Ossietzky	Germany	journalist	Exposed German rearmament programme; imprisoned
1936	Carlos Saavedra Lamas	Argentina	statesman	Role in Paraguay-Bolivia peace; presented Anti-War Pact to League of Nations
1937	Robert Cecil	Great Britain	statesman	President of UK League of Nations Union
1938	Nansen Office (2nd time)			
1939–42	none given			
1943	none given			
1944	Red Cross (3rd time)			
1945	Cordell Hull	USA	statesman	Called 'Father of the United Nations' (by President Roosevelt)
1946	Emily Balch	USA	educator	Secretary-General of Women's International League for Peace & Freedom
1946	John Mott	USA	educator	A founder of World's Student Christian Federation
1947	The Society of Friends (Quakers)			
1948	none given			
1949	John Boyd Orr	Great Britain	scientist	First Director-General of Food and Agriculture Organization
1950	Ralphe Bunche	USA	diplomat	UN mediator in Palestine

Year	Winner of Prize	Country	Profession	Service Rendered
1951	Leon Jouhaux	France	trade unionist	Role in founding ILO; first vice-president of International Federation of Trade Unions
1952	Albert Schweitzer	France	physician	Founder of medical centre at Lambarene, Belgian Congo
1953	George Marshall	USA	statesman, soldier	European Recovery Plan (Marshall Plan)
1954	UN High Commissioner for Refugees			
1955	none given			
1956	none given			
1957	Lester Pearson	Canada	statesman (Prime Minister)	Role in Korean Truce and partition of Palestine; biculturism in Canada
1958	Dominique Pire	Belgium	theologian	Founder of 'Aid to Displaced Persons and European Villages'
1959	Philip Noel-Baker	Great Britain	statesman	Role in League of Nations, United Nations and Food and Agriculture Organization
1960	Albert Lutuli	South Africa	chief	Non-violent campaign against apartheid
1961	Dag Hammarskjöld	Sweden	diplomat (Secretary-General of the United Nations)	Congo peace operation
1962	Linus Pauling		scientist	Organized world-wide petition of scientists against nuclear tests
1963	Red Cross (4th time)			
1964	Martin Luther King	USA	theologian	Non-violent campaign for civil rights in USA
1965	UN Children's Fund			
1966	none given			

Year	Name	Country/Organization	Profession	Achievement
1967	none given			
1968	René Cassin	France	lawyer	Main author with Eleanor Roosevelt of UN Declaration of Human Rights; a founder of UNESCO
1969	International Labour Organization			
1970	Norman Borlaug	USA	scientist	Developed new wheat strain leading to 'Green Revolution'
1971	Willy Brandt	Germany	statesman (Chancellor)	Work on easing East–West tensions
1972	none given			
1973	Henry Kissinger	USA	statesman	Ceasefire in Vietnam
1973	Le Duc Tho	Vietnam	statesman	Ceasefire in Vietnam
1974	Sean MacBride	Ireland	statesman	Work with International Commission of Jurists, Pontifical Commission on Justice & Peace, Amnesty International and other organizations
1974	Eisaku Sato	Japan	statesman	Normalization of relations with Korea; peaceful return to Japan of Okinawa
1975	Andrei Sakharov	USSR	scientist	Wrote *Progress, Peaceful Coexistence & Intellectual Freedom* (1968)
1976	Mairead Corrigan	Northern Ireland	volunteer social worker	Joint Founders of Northern Ireland Peace Movement
1976	Betty Williams	Northern Ireland	receptionist	
1977	Amnesty International			
1978	Menachem Begin	Israel	statesman (Prime Minister)	Treaty between Israel and Egypt
1978	Anwar Sadat	Egypt	statesman (President)	

Year	Winner of Prize	Country	Profession	Service Rendered
1979	Mother Teresa	Albania	nun	Work helping sick and dying in Calcutta
1980	Adolfo Perez Esquivel	Argentina	sculptor-architect	Work for human rights in Argentina; imprisoned
1981	UN High Commissioner for Refugees (2nd time)			
1982	Alfred Garcia Robles	Mexico	diplomat	Chairman UN Committee on Disarmament; work for nuclear free zone in Latin America
	Alva Myrdal	Sweden	sociologist, MP	Work on Geneva Disarmament Committee
1983	Lech Walesa	Poland	trade unionist	A founder of 'Solidarity', working for human rights
1984	Desmond Tutu	South Africa	theologian	Work for peaceful end to apartheid
1985	International Physicians for Prevention of Nuclear War			
1986	Elie Wiesel	USA	educator, journalist	Peace and human rights
1987	Oscar Arias	Costa Rica	statesman (President)	Central American Peace Plan
1988	UN Peace-Keeping Forces			

Text of the
Universal Declaration
of Human Rights

PREAMBLE

WHEREAS recognition of the inherent dignity and of the equal and inalienable rights of all members of the human family is the foundation of freedom, justice and peace in the world,

Whereas disregard and contempt for human rights have resulted in barbarous acts which have outraged the conscience of mankind, and the advent of a world in which human beings shall enjoy freedom of speech and belief and freedom from fear and want has been proclaimed as the highest aspiration of the common people,

Whereas it is essential, if man is not to be compelled to have recourse, as a last resort, to rebellion against tyranny and oppression, that human rights should be protected by the rule of law,

Whereas it is essential to promote the development of friendly relations between nations,

Whereas the peoples of the United Nations have in the Charter reaffirmed their faith in fundamental human rights, in the dignity and worth of the human person and in the equal rights of men and women and have determined to promote social progress and better standards of life in larger freedom,

Whereas Member States have pledged themselves to achieve, in co-operation with the United Nations, the promotion of universal respect for and observance of human rights and fundamental freedoms,

Whereas a common understanding of these rights and freedoms is of the greatest importance for the full realization of this pledge,

Now, therefore, THE GENERAL ASSEMBLY *proclaims*
THIS Universal Declaration of Human Rights as a common standard of achievement for all peoples and all nations, to the end that every individual and every organ of society, keeping this Declaration constantly in mind, shall strive by teaching and education to promote respect for these rights

and freedoms and by progressive measures, national and international, to secure their universal and effective recognition and observance, both among the peoples of Member States themselves and among the peoples of territories under their jurisdiction.

Article 1

All human beings are born free and equal in dignity and rights. They are endowed with reason and conscience and should act towards one another in a spirit of brotherhood.

Article 2

Everyone is entitled to all the rights and freedoms set forth in this Declaration, without distinction of any kind, such as race, colour, sex, language, religion, political or other opinion, national or social origin, property, birth or other status.
Furthermore, no distinction shall be made on the basis of the political, jurisdictional or international status of the country or territory to which a person belongs, whether it be independent, trust, non-self-governing or under any other limitation of sovereignty.

Article 3

Everyone has the right to life, liberty and security of person.

Article 4

No one shall be held in slavery or servitude; slavery and the slave trade shall be prohibited in all their forms.

Article 5

No one shall be subjected to torture or to cruel, inhuman or degrading treatment or punishment.

Article 6

Everyone has the right to recognition everywhere as a person before the law.

Article 7

All are equal before the law and are entitled without any discrimination to equal protection of the law. All are entitled to equal protection against any discrimination in violation of this Declaration and against any incitement to such discrimination.

Article 8

Everyone has the right to an effective remedy by the competent national tribunals for acts violating the fundamental rights granted him by the constitution or by law.

Article 9

No one shall be subjected to arbitrary arrest, detention or exile.

Article 10

Everyone is entitled in full equality to a fair and public hearing by an independent and impartial tribunal, in the determination of his rights and obligations and of any criminal charge against him.

Article 11

1. Everyone charged with a penal offence has the right to be presumed innocent until proved guilty according to law in a public trial at which he has had all the guarantees necessary for his defence.
2. No one shall be held guilty of any penal offence on account of any act or omission which did not constitute a penal offence, under national or international law, at the time when it was committed. Nor shall a heavier penalty be imposed than the one that was applicable at the time the penal offence was committed.

Article 12

No one shall be subjected to arbitrary interference with his privacy, family, home or correspondence, nor to attacks upon his honour and reputation. Everyone has the right to the protection of the law against such interference or attacks.

Article 13

1. Everyone has the right to freedom of movement and residence within the borders of each state.
2. Everyone has the right to leave any country, including his own, and to return to his country.

Article 14

1. Everyone has the right to seek and to enjoy in other countries asylum from persecution.
2. This right may not be invoked in the case of prosecutions genuinely arising from non-political crimes or from acts contrary to the purposes and principles of the United Nations.

Article 15

1. Everyone has the right to a nationality.
2. No one shall be arbitrarily deprived of his nationality nor denied the right to change his nationality.

Article 16

1. Men and women of full age, without any limitation due to race, nationality or religion, have the right to marry and to found a family. They are entitled to equal rights as to marriage, during marriage and at its dissolution.
2. Marriage shall be entered into only with the free and full consent of the intending spouses.
3. The family is the natural and fundamental group unit of society and is entitled to protection by society and the State.

Article 17

1. Everyone has the right to own property alone as well as in association with others.
2. No one shall be arbitrarily deprived of his property.

Article 18

Everyone has the right to freedom of thought, conscience and religion; this right includes freedom to change his religion or belief, and freedom, either alone or in community with others and in public or private, to manifest his religion or belief in teaching, practice, worship and observance.

Article 19

Everyone has the right to freedom of opinion and expression; this right includes freedom to hold opinions without interference and to seek, receive and impart information and ideas through any media and regardless of frontiers.

Article 20

1. Everyone has the right to freedom of peaceful assembly and association.
2. No one may be compelled to belong to an association.

Article 21

1. Everyone has the right to take part in the government of his country, directly or through freely chosen representatives.
2. Everyone has the right of equal access to public service in his country.
3. The will of the people shall be the basis of the authority of government; this will shall be expressed in periodic and genuine elections which shall be by universal and equal suffrage and shall be held by secret vote or by equivalent free voting procedures.

Article 22

Everyone, as a member of society, has the right to social security and is entitled to realization, through national effort and international co-operation and in accordance with the organization and resources of each State, of the economic, social and cultural rights indispensable for his dignity and the free development of his personality.

Article 23

1. Everyone has the right to work, to free choice of employment, to just and favourable conditions of work and to protection against unemployment.
2. Everyone, without any discrimination, has the right to equal pay for equal work.
3. Everyone who works has the right to just and favourable remuneration ensuring for himself and his family an existence worthy of human dignity, and supplemented, if necessary, by other means of social protection.
4. Everyone has the right to form and to join trade unions for the protection of his interests.

Article 24

Everyone has the right to rest and leisure, including reasonable limitation of working hours and periodic holidays with pay.

Article 25

1. Everyone has the right to a standard of living adequate for the health and well-being of himself and of his family, including food, clothing, housing and medical care and necessary social services, and the right to security in the event of unemployment, sickness, disability, widowhood, old age or other lack of livelihood in circumstances beyond his control.
2. Motherhood and childhood are entitled to special care and assistance. All children, whether born in or out of wedlock, shall enjoy the same social protection.

Article 26

1. Everyone has the right to education. Education shall be free, at least in the elementary and fundamental stages. Elementary education shall be compulsory. Technical and professional education shall be made generally available and higher education shall be equally accessible to all on the basis of merit.
2. Education shall be directed to the full development of the human personality and to the strengthening of respect for human rights and fundamental freedoms. It shall promote understanding, tolerance and friendship among all nations, racial or religious groups, and shall further the activities of the United Nations for the maintenance of peace.
3. Parents have a prior right to choose the kind of education that shall be given to their children.

Article 27

1. Everyone has the right freely to participate in the cultural life of the

community, to enjoy the arts and to share in scientific advancement and its benefits.

2. Everyone has the right to the protection of the moral and material interests resulting from any scientific, literary or artistic production of which he is the author.

Article 28

Everyone is entitled to a social and international order in which the rights and freedoms set forth in the Declaration can be fully realized.

Article 29

1. Everyone has duties to the community in which alone the free and full development of his personality is possible.
2. In the exercise of his rights and freedoms, everyone shall be subject only to such limitations as are determined by law solely for the purpose of securing due recognition and respect for the rights and freedoms of others and of meeting the just requirements of morality, public order and the general welfare in a democratic society.
3. These rights and freedoms may in no case be exercised contrary to the purposes and principles of the United Nations.

Article 30

Nothing in this Declaration may be interpreted as implying for any State, group or person any right to engage in any activity or to perform any act aimed at the destruction of any of the rights and freedoms set forth herein.

Select Bibliography

Paperback editions are cited where possible as more easily available for the interested reader to obtain.

PART I: THE PAST

Allen, J.W. *A History of Political Thought in the Sixteenth Century.* London: Methuen, 1960.

Ameer Ali, Syed. *The Spirit of Islam.* London: Christophers, 1935.

Balyuzi, H.M. *Muḥammad and the Course of Islám.* Oxford: George Ronald, 1976.

Barratt, David B. *World Christian Encyclopaedia.* Oxford: Oxford University Press, 1982.

Baumer, Franklin L. *Religion and the Rise of Scepticism.* New York: Harbinger, 1960.

Bradshaw, Jane. *Eight Major Religions in Britain.* London: Edward Arnold, 1979.

Bronowski, J. *The Ascent of Man.* Boston: Little, Brown, 1973.

Carus, Paul. *The Gospel of Buddha.* Tucson, Arizona: Omen Communications, 1973.

— and Nyanatiloka. *Buddha, His Life and Teachings.* New York: Crescent Books, n.d.

Cobb, Stanwood. *Islamic Contributions to Civilization.* Washington DC: Avalon Press, 1963.

Cole, W. Owen, and Piara Singh Sambhi. *Sikhism.* London: Ward Locke, 1973.

Crompton, Yorke. *Hinduism.* London: Ward Locke, 1971.

Durant, Will. and Arre. *The Age of Voltaire.* New York: Simon & Schuster, 1965.

— *Rousseau and Revolution.* New York: Simon & Schuster, 1967.

Eban, Abba. *My People.* New York, Random House, 1984.

Epstein, Isadore. *Judaism.* London: Pelican, 1973.

Fine, John V.A. *The Ancient Greeks.* Cambridge, Mass: Harvard University Press, 1983.

Fozdar, Jamshed. *The God of Buddha.* New York: Asia Publishing House, 1973.

Gail, Marzieh. *Six Lessons in Islám.* Wilmette, Illinois: Bahá'í Publishing Trust, 1957.

Goodwin, A. *The French Revolution*. London: Hutchinson, 1953.

Grousset, René. *The Rise and Splendor of the Chinese Empire*. Berkeley: University of California Press, 1953.

Hamilton, Edith. *The Greek Way*. New York: W.W. Norton, 1964.

Hampson, Norman. *The Enlightenment*. London: Penguin, 1981.

Hick, John. *The Existence of God*. New York: Macmillan, 1964.

— (ed). *The Myth of God Incarnate*. London: SCM, 1977.

Hill, Christopher. *The Century of Revolution, 1603–1714*. New York: W.W. Norton, 1961.

Hinnalls, John R.. and Eric J. Sharpe (eds). *Hinduism*. Newcastle: Oriel Press, 1972.

Hodgson, Marshall G.S. *The Venture of Islam*. Chicago: University of Chicago Press, 2 vols, 1974.

Hummells, John R. *Zoroastrianism and the Parsis*. London: Ward Locke, 1981.

Irving, Clive. *Crossroads of Civilization*. London: Weidenfeld & Nicolson, 1979.

Johnson, Paul. *A History of Christianity*. London: Atheneum, 1977.

Küng, Hans. *On Being a Christian*. New York: Doubleday, 1978.

— *Does God Exist?* New York: Doubleday, 1978.

Latourette, Kenneth Scott. *A History of Christianity*. New York: Harper & Row, 1953.

McEvedy, Colin, and Richard Jones. *Atlas of World Population History*. London: Penguin, 1985.

Middlekauf, Robert. *The Glorious Cause: The American Revolution, 1763–1789*. Oxford: Oxford University Press, 1982.

Momen, Moojan. *An Introduction to Shi'i Islam*. Oxford: George Ronald, 1985.

Moscati, Sabatino. *Ancient Semitic Civilizations*. New York: Putnam, 1957.

Norris, Richard. *Evolution and Human Nature*. New York: Putnam, 1983.

Parkes, James. *Whose Land?: A History of the People of Palestine*. London: Penguin, 1970.

Pritchard, James B. (ed). *The Ancient Near East*. Princeton, NJ: Princeton University Press, 1958.

Roberts, J.M. *History of the World*. London: Penguin, 1980.

Robertson, Roland (ed). *Sociology and Religion*. London: Penguin, 1981.

Rude, George. *Revolutionary Europe, 1783–1815*. London: Fontana, 1964.

Sen, K.M. *Hinduism*. London: Penguin, 1961.

Smith, William Cantwell. *The Meaning and End of Religion*. New York: Harper & Row, 1978.

Trager, James. *The People's Chronology*. New York: Holt Rinehard Winston, 1979.

Wells, Collin. *The Roman Empire*. Stanford, Ca: Stanford University Press, 1984.

Woodcock, George. *Mohandas Gandhi*. New York: Viking Press, 1971.

A. Greater Political and Social Equality

Atkinson, William C. *History of Spain and Portugal.* London: Penguin, 1960.

Bennett, Lerone, Jr. *Before the Mayflower: A History of the Negro in America, 1619–1964.* London: Penguin, 1966.

Billington, James. *Fire in the Minds of Man: Origins of the Revolutionary Faith.* New York: Basic Books, 1980.

Britton, Karl. *John Stuart Mill.* London: Penguin, 1953.

Brogan, Denis. *The Development of Modern France.* London: Hamish Hamilton, 1949.

Brown, Dee. *Bury My Heart at Wounded Knee.* New York: Bantam, 1972.

Bury, J.P.T. *France, 1814–1940,* London: Methuen, 1954.

Clark, Manning. *A Short History of Australia.* New York: Mentor, 1963.

Cranshaw, Edward. *The Shadow of the Winter Palace: Russia's Drift to Revolution, 1825–1917.* New York: Viking, 1976.

— *The Fall of the House of Hapsburg.* London: Penguin, 1984.

Crick, Bernard (ed). *Protest and Discontent.* London: Penguin, 1970.

Cunliffe, Marcus. *The Age of Expansion.* Springfield, Mass: G. and C. Merriam, 1974.

Davidson, Basil. *History of West Africa.* New York: Doubleday Anchor, 1966.

— *History of East and South Africa.* New York: Doubleday Anchor, 1969.

Davis, David Brun. *Slavery and Human Progress.* New York: Oxford University Press, 1984.

Eisler, Riane. *The Chalice and the Blade.* San Francisco: Harper & Row, 1987.

Goodwin, Michael. *Nineteenth Century Opinion.* London: Penguin, 1951.

Hampton, Christopher. *A Radical Reader, 1381–1914.* London: Penguin, 1984.

Hibbert, Christopher. *The Dragon Wakes: China and the West, 1793–1911.* London: Penguin, 1984.

Hobsbawn, E.J. *The Age of Revolution, 1789–1848.* New York: Mentor, 1962.

Hughes, Robert. *The Fatal Shore: The History of Transportation of Criminals to Australia, 1787–1860.* London: Collins, 1987.

Humphries, Christopher (ed). *A Radical Reader.* Pelican, 1984.

Maddock, Kenneth. *The Australian Aborigines.* London: Penguin, 1982.

McNaught, Kenneth. *History of Canada.* London: Penguin, 1969.

Midgely, Mary, and Judith Hughes. *Women's Choice: Philosophical Issues Facing Feminism.* New York: St. Martin's Press, 1983.

Moorehead, Alan. *Fatal Impact: An Account of the Invasion of the Pacific, 1767–1840.* London: Penguin, 1966.

Morgan, Edmund S. *Inventing the People: The Rise of Popular Sovereignty in England and America.* New York: Norton, 1988.

Morris, James. *Pax Britannica*. London: Faber & Faber, 3 vols, 1968–1978.

Morrison, Samuel Eliot, and Henry Steel Commanger. *The Growth of the American Republic*. New York: Oxford University Press, 2 vols, 1951.

Nozick, Robert. *Anarchy, State and Utopia*. New York: Basic Books, 1974.

Oates, Stephen B. *With Malice Towards None: A Life of Lincoln*. New York: Harper & Row, 1977.

O'Brien, Conor Cruise, and Maire O'Brien. *History of Ireland*. New York: Beckman House, 1972.

Oliver, Roland, and Michael Gowler. *Cambridge Encyclopedia of Africa*. Cambridge: Cambridge University Press, 1981.

Pendle, George. *History of Latin America*. London: Penguin, 1981.

Pollard, Sidney. *The Idea of Progress*. London: Penguin, 1971.

Rawley, James A. *The Transatlantic Slave Trade*. New York: W.W. Norton, 1981.

Rawls, John. *A Theory of Justice*. Cambridge, Mass: Harvard University Press, 1971.

Read, Waldeman, P. (ed). *Great Issues Concerning Freedom*. University of Utah Press, 1962.

Seager, Joni, and Ann Olson. *Women in the World: An International Atlas*. Sydney: Pan Books, 1986.

Seton Watson, Hugh. *The Decline of Imperial Russia*. London: Methuen, 1952.

Shirer, William L. *The Rise and Fall of the Third Reich*. Greenwich, Conn: Fawcett Crest, 1960.

Sinclair, Keith. *A History of New Zealand*. London, Penguin, 1976.

Sowell, Thomas. *Ethnic America*. New York: Basic Books, 1981.

Spear, Percival. *A History of India*. London: Penguin, 1965.

Storry, Richard. *A History of Modern Japan*. London: Penguin, 1960.

Sulzberger, C.L. *The Fall of Eagles*. New York: Crown, 1977.

Taylor, A.J.P. *The Course of German History*. London: Hamish Hamilton, 1951.

— *Bismarck*. London: Arrow Books, 1961.

— *The Hapsburg Monarchy*. London: Hamish Hamilton, 1951.

Tocqueville, de, Alexis. *Democracy in America*. New York: Vintage, 1945.

Tuchman, Barbara. *The Proud Tower: A Portrait of the World Before the War, 1890–1914*. New York: Macmillan, 1985.

Weeks, Kent. *Ombudsman and The World: A Comparative Analysis*. University of California, 1973.

Williams, Francis. *Dangerous Estate: The Anatomy of Newspapers*. London: Arrow, 1959.

B. Reducing Material Poverty

Arendt, Hannah. *On Revolution*. New York: Viking, 1965.

Bell, Daniel. *The Coming Post-Industrial Society*. New York: Basic Books, 1976.

Briggs, Asa. *Victorian Cities*. London: Penguin, 1968.
— *Social History of England*. London: Weidenfeld & Nicolson, 1983.
Brzezinski, Zbigniew. *The Grand Failure: The Birth and Death of Communism in the Twentieth Century*. New York: Scribners, 1989.
Carr, E.H. *The Bolshevik Revolution, 1917–1923*. London: Penguin, 3 vols, 1953.
Chesney, Kellow. *The Victorian Underworld*. New York: Schocken Books, 1972.
Clapham, J.H. *Economic Development of France and Germany, 1815–1914*. Cambridge: Cambridge University Press, 1961.
Cole, G.D.H., and Raymond Postage. *The Common People*. London: Methuen, 1938.
Commoner, Barry. *The Closing Circle*. New York: Bantam, 1974.
Conquest, Robert. *The Great Terror*. London: Penguin, 1968.
Daniel, W.W., and Francis Pintor. *Workplace Industrial Relations and Technical Change*. 1988.
Deutscher, Isaac, *Stalin: A Political Biography*. Oxford: Oxford University Press, 1961.
Galbraith, John Kenneth. *The Affluent Society*. Boston: Mentor, 1958.
Harrington, Michael. *The Accidental Century*. London: Penguin, 1966.
— *The Other America*. London: Penguin, 1966.
Harris, Nigel. *The Mandate of Heaven: Marx and Mao in Modern China*. New York: Quartet Books, 1978.
Hill, Christopher. *Lenin and the Russian Revolution*. London: Hodder & Stoughton, 1947.
Hirsch, Fred. *Social Limits to Growth*. Cambridge, Mass: Harvard University Press, 1976.
Hobsbawn, E.J. *Revolutionaries*. New York: Meridian, 1973.
— *Industry and Empire*. London: Penguin, 1977.
Hughes, Robert. *The Fatal Shore*. Collins, 1986.
Kutznets, Simon. *The Economic Growth of Nations*. Cambridge, Mass: Harvard University Press, 1971.
— *Growth Population and Income Distribution: Selected Essays*. New York: W.W. Norton, 1979.
Landemann, Albert. *A History of European Socialism*. New Haven, Mass: Yale University Press, 1983.
Lloyd, T.O. *Empire to Welfare State, 1906–1976*. Oxford: Oxford University Press, 1979.
Marwick, Arthur. *British Society Since 1945*. London: Penguin, 1982.
McCellan, David (ed). *Marx: The First Hundred Years*. Oxford: Fontana, 1983.
— *Marx: The Legacy*. London: British Broadcasting Corporation, 1983.
Moore, Barrington. *Injustice: The Social Basis of Obedience and Revolt*. London: MacMillan, 1979.
Pelling, Henry. *History of British Trade Unionism*. London: Penguin, 1963.
Radzinowiez, Sir Leon, and Joan King. *The Growth of Crime: The International Experience*. London: Hamish Hamilton, 1977.

Rostow, W.W. *The World Economy: History and Prospect*. Austin, Texas: University of Texas, 1978.

Sampson, Anthony. *Anatomy of Britain*. London: Hodder & Stoughton, 1965.

Stevensen, John. *British Society, 1914–1945*. London: Penguin, 1984.

Taylor, A.J.P. *Revolutions and Revolutionaries*. New York: Atheneum, 1978.

Taylor, Charles Lewis, and David Jodice. *World Handbook of Political and Social Indicators*. Yale: Yale University Press, 1983.

Thurow, Lester C. *The Zero-Sum Society*. New York: Basic Books, 1980.

Ward, Barbara, and René Dubois. *Only One Earth*. London: Penguin, 1976.

Williams, Raymond. *Culture and Society, 1780–1850*. London: Penguin, 1958.

Woodcock, George. *Anarchism*. London: Penguin, 1962.

C. From War to Peace

Ball, Desmond, and Andrew Mack. *The Future of Arms Control*. Australian National University, 1987.

Boyd, Andrew. *United Nations: Piety, Myth and Talk*. London: Penguin, 1964.

Brandt, Willy *et al. North–South: A Program for Survival*. Cambridge, Mass: M.I.T. Press, 1980.

Brown, Lester, R. *State of the World, 1988*. Washington, DC: World Watch Institute, 1988.

Bruntland, Gro Harlem, *et al. Our Common Future*. Oxford: World Commision on Environment and Development, 1987.

Cassen, Robert, and Associates. *Does Aid Work?* Oxford: Clarendon Press, 1986.

Clark, Grenville, and Louis Sohn. *World Peace Through World Law*. Chicago: World Without War Publications, 1984.

Conot, Robert E. *Justice at Nuremberg*. New York: Harper & Row, 1983.

Dougherty, James E., and Robert L. Pfaltzgraff, Jr. *Contending Theories of International Relations*. Philadelphia: Harper & Row, 1981.

Dyer, Gwynne, *War*. London: Bodley Head, 1985.

Falls, Cyril. *The Great War, 1914–1918*. New York: Perigee Books, 1959.

Ferenz, Benjamin. *A Common Sense Guide to World Peace*. New York: Oceana Publications, 1985.

Forster, Mark Arnold. *The World at War*. New York: Signet Books, 1974.

Franck, Thomas M. *Judging the World Court*. New York: Priority Press, 1986.

Hayter, Teresa. *Aid as Imperialism*. London: Penguin, 1971.

Hazzard, Shirley. *Defeat of an Ideal*. Boston: Little Brown & Co., 1973.

Heilbronner, Robert. *An Inquiry into the Human Prospect*. New York: Norton, 1975.

Heller, Peter. *The Implications of Fund Supported Adjustment Programs for Poverty: Experience in Selected Countries*. Washington, DC: International Monetary Fund, 1988.

Humana, Charles. *World Human Rights Guide*. London: Pan, 1987.

Ingram, Kenneth. *Years of Crisis*. London: George Allen & Unwin, 1946.

Kome, Penney, and Patrick Crean. *Peace, a Dream Unfolding*. California: Sierra Club Books, 1986.

Kuram, George Thomas. *The New Book of World Rankings*. New York: Facts on File Publications, 1984.

Laszlo, Ervin *et al*. *Goals for Mankind*. New York: E.P. Dutton, 1977.

— and Jong Yonl Yoo. *World Encyclopedia of Peace*. New York: Pergamon Press, 4 vols, 1986.

Mason, Edward S., and Robert E. Asher. *The World Bank*. Washington, DC: Brookings, 1973.

McNamara, Robert. *Blundering into Disaster*. New York: Pantheon, 1986.

Meier,, Gerald and Dudley Seers. *Pioneers in Development*. Oxford: Oxford University Press, 1984.

Miller, Lynn H. *Global Order: Values and Power in International Politics*. Boulder, Colorado: Westview Press, 1985.

Mische, Gerald and Patricia. *Toward a Human World Order*. New York: Paulist Press, 1977.

Morganthau, Hans J. *Politics Among Nations: The Struggle for Power and Peace*. New York: Alfred J. Knopf, 1967.

Morris, Charles R. *Iron Destinies, Lost Opportunities: The Arms Race Between the USA and the USSR, 1945–1987*. New York: Harper & Row, 1988.

Mueller, John. *The Obsolescence of Major War*. New York: Basic Books, 1989.

Myrdal, Gunnar. *The Challenge of World Poverty*. New York: Vintage, 1970.

Namier, L.B. *Europe in Decay*. London: MacMillan, 1950.

Ozmanecyk, Edmund Jan (ed). *Encyclopedia of the U.N. and International Agreements*. New York: Taylor & Frances, 1985.

Payer, Cheryl. *The World Bank: A Critical Analysis*. New York: Monthly Review, 1982.

Peccei, Aurelio. *One Hundred Pages for the Future*. London: Futura-McDonald, 1982.

Pitt, David, and Thomas Weiss. *The Nature of the UN Bureaucracies*. Boulder, Colorado: Westview Press, 1986.

Reardon, Betty A. *Sexism and the War System*. New York: Teachers College Press, 1985.

Riggs, Robert E., and Jack C. Plano. *The United Nations: International Organizations and World Politics*. Chicago: Dorsey Press, 1988.

Ross, John. *International Encyclopedia of Population*. New York: MacMillan, 1982.

Rovine Arthur W. *The First Fifty Years: The Secretary General in World Politics 1920–1970*. Leyden: A.W. Sychoff, 1970.

Sampson, Anthony. *The Arms Bazaar*. London: Coronet Books, 1977.

Schell, Jonathan. *The Fate of the Earth*. New York: Avon, 1982.

— *The Abolition*. New York: Avon, 1986.

Scott, Franklin, D. *World Migration in Modern Times*. New York n.d.

Sivard, Ruth Leger, *World Military and Social Expenditures, 1985*. Washington, DC: World Priorities Inc., 1985.

Stableford, Brian, and David Langford. *The Third Millennium: A History of the World ad 2000–3000*. London: Sidgwick & Jackson, 1985.

Stone: Julius. *Visions of World Order: Between State Power and Human Justice*. Baltimore: Johns Hopkins University Press, 1984.

Streeten, Paul. *First Things First*. Oxford: Oxford University Press, 1981.

Taylor, A.J.P. *The Struggle for Mastery in Europe*. Oxford: Oxford University Press, 1954.

— *The First World War*. London: Penguin, 1963.

— *The Troublemakers: Dissent over Foreign Policy, 1792–1939*. London: Penguin, 1971.

Thomson, David. *World History, 1914–1961*. Oxford: Oxford University Press, 1963.

Tofler, Alvin. *Future Shock*. New York: Bantam, 1974.

Tuchman, Barbara. *The Proud Tower*. New York: Macmillan, 1985.

U.S. State Department. *Country Reports on Human Rights Practices*. (Annual) Washington, DC.

Vries, de, Margaret. *The IMF in a Changing World, 1945–1985*. Washington, DC: IMF, 1986.

Walters, Frank P. *A History of the League of Nations*. Oxford: Oxford University Press, 1952.

Walworth, Arthur. *Woodrow Wilson*. London: Penguin, 1969.

Walzer, Michael. *Just and Unjust Wars*. London: Penguin, 1980.

Zimmern, Alfred. *The League of Nations and the Rule of Law*. London: MacMillan, 1939.

PART III: THE FUTURE

'Abdu'l-Bahá. *Paris Talks*. Addresses given by 'Abdu'l-Bahá in Paris in 1911–1912. London: Bahá'í Publishing Trust, 12th edn 1971.

— *The Promulgation of Universal Peace*. Wilmette, Illinois: Bahá'í Publishing Trust, 2nd edn 1982.

— *Some Answered Questions*. Wilmette, Illinois: Bahá'í Publishing Trust, 4th rev. edn 1981.

Bahá'í Electoral Process, The. Wilmette, Illinois: National Spiritual Assembly of the Bahá'ís of the United States, 1973.

Bahá'í Revelation, The. A compilation of the writings of Bahá'u'lláh and 'Abdu'l-Bahá. London: Bahá'í Publishing Trust, 1955.

Bahá'u'lláh. *Gleanings from the Writings of Bahá'u'lláh*. Translated by Shoghi Effendi. Wilmette, Illinois: Bahá'í Publishing Trust, rev. edn 1978.

— *Kitáb-i-Íqán. The Book of Certitude*. Translated by Shoghi Efffendi. Wilmette, Illinois: Bahá'í Publishing Trust, rev. edn 1974.

Divine Art of Living, The. A compilation of writings of Bahá'u'lláh and 'Abdu'l-Bahá by Mabel Hyde Paine. Wilmette, Illinois: Bahá'í Publishing Trust, rev. edn 1986.

Esslemont, J.E. *Bahá'u'lláh and the New Era*. London: Bahá'í Publishing Trust, rev. edn 1974.

Fortress of Well-Being, A: Bahá'í Teachings on Marriage. Wilmette, Illinois: National Spiritual Assembly of the Bahá'ís of the United States, 1973.

Ghadirian, A.M. *In Search of Nirvana: A New Perspective on Alcohol and Drug Dependency.* Oxford: George Ronald, rev. edn 1989.

Hatcher, William S. *The Science of Religion.* Ottawa: Association of Bahá'í Studies, 1977.

— and Douglas J. Martin. *The Bahá'í Faith: The Emerging Global Religion.* San Francisco: Harper & Row, 1984.

Hornby, Helen (ed). *Lights of Guidance: A Bahá'í Reference File.* New Delhi: Bahá'í Publishing Trust, 1983.

Huddleston, John. *The Earth is But One Country.* London: Bahá'í Publishing Trust, 2nd edn 1988.

Martin, Douglas J. *The Persecution of the Bahá'ís in Iran, 1844–1984.* Ottawa: Association of Bahá'í Studies, 1984.

Momen, Moojan. *The Bábí and Bahá'í Religions, 1844–1944: Some Contemporary Western Accounts.* Oxford: George Ronald, 1981.

Rinde, Beatrice C., and John B. Cornell. *Bahá'í Law.* Honolulu: National Spiritual Assembly of the Bahá'ís of Hawaii, 1973.

Shoghi Effendi. *The Advent of Divine Justice.* Wilmette, Illinois: Bahá'í Publishing Trust, 1939.

— *Bahá'í Administration.* Wilmette, Illinois: Bahá'í Publishing Trust, rev. edn 1974.

— *God Passes By.* Wilmette, Illinois: Bahá'í Publishing Trust, 1943.

— *The World Order of Bahá'u'lláh.* Wilmette, Illinois: Bahá'í Publishing Trust, 1965.

Smith, Peter. *The Babi and Baha'i Religions.* Cambridge: Cambridge University Press, 1987.

— *The Bahá'í Religion: A Short Introduction to its History and Teachings.* Oxford, George Ronald, 1988.

Teilhard de Chardin, Pierre. *The Future of Man.* London: Collins, 1982.

Tyson, J. *World Peace and World Government.* Oxford: George Ronald, 1986.

Universal House of Justice, The. *The Promise of World Peace.* London: Oneworld, 1985.

— *Bahá'í Education.* A Compilation. Wilmette, Illinois: Bahá'í Publishing Trust, 1977.

— *Consultation.* A Compilation. Wilmette, Illinois: Bahá'í Publishing Trust, 1980.

— *Women.* A Compilation. Ottawa: National Spiritual Assembly of the Bahá'ís of Canada, 1986.

Index

'Abbas the Great, 61
'Abbasids, 59, 60
'Abdu'l-Bahá, 401, 454–6, 462, illus.
   quotations from the writings of, 403–20 passim.
Abolition of Slavery Act (GB 1833), 86
Abolitionist Society, 85
Aborigines, 136
Abraham, 11, 12, 17, 52, 411
Abu Bakr, 58
accountability, 33, 50, 65, 74, 83, 119, 122, 136, 142, 174
Act of Congress (US 1884), 129
Act of Settlement (GB 1694), 68
Act of Union (GB & Ireland 1801), 110
Adam, 11, 12
Addams, Jane, 286, illus.
Addison Housing and Planning Act (GB 1919), 217
Aden, 116
administration, 112, 116, 140, 296, 426, 435, 446, 449
adversary system, 314
Aeschylus, 36
Africa, 5, 84, 105, 277, 295, 372
African Development Bank, 378
Afghanistan, 350–51, 360, 374
agriculture, 195, 209, 222, 263, 283, 364, 378, 445
aid targets, 375–6
AIDS, 390
Akbar the Great, 61
Alabama case, 280
Alaric the Goth, 42
Albigensians, 20, 48
alcohol, 8, 57, 254, 256–62, 469
Alcoholics Anonymous, 260
Alexander II, Czar, 93, 182, 276
Alexander the Great, 14, 19, 35
'Alí ibn Abú Talíb, 54, 58
Aliens and Sedition Acts (US 1789–1801), 160
Allende, Salvador, 196
Alliance for Progress, 378
Allies, 108, 139, 303, 331

al-Ma'mun the Great, 60
Alsace-Lorraine, 98, 294, 299, 305
Ambrose, 46
Amendments to the US Constitution, 91, 129, 149, 160, 243, 260
Amenhotep IV, 8
America, 5
American Association for the Advancement of Science, 265
American Congress (1826), 284
American Federation of Labor, 172
American Indians, 104, 120, 228, 261, 460
American Revolution, 72–4
American Society for the Propagation of Temperance, 258
American War of Independence, 75, 242
Amnesty International, 367
Amos, 14
Amritsar, 112
Amundsen, Roald, 102
Anabaptists, 49
Anarchists, 181
Angell, Norman, 286, 287
Anglican Church, 66, 229
Antarctic Treaty, 372–3
Anthony, Susan B., 149
Anti-Dühring: Socialism Utopian and Scientific, 187
anti-semitism, 50
Anti-Saloon League, 259
Anti-Slavery Society, 86
Antiochus IV, 15
Antiquities Act (US 1906), 266
apartheid, 342, 353
Arab countries, 118
arbitration, 273, 277–81, 311, 370
Archimedes, 36
architecture, 61, 219
Argentina, 104, 141
aristocracy, 74, 125, 186, 241
Aristotle, 36–7

armaments, 193, 272, 278, 304, 311, 315, 361; see also nuclear arms
armed forces, 78, 141, 273, 297, 306, 308, 348–9, 386
armed struggle, 116–17, 398
arms race, 281, 344, 399
Articles of Confederation (US 1781), 72
arts, 61, 395
Aryans, 22
Ashurbanipal, 10
Asian Development Bank, 378
assemblies, Bahá'í, 427, 457–8
assembly, 34, 69, 74, 121, 149, 151
Assembly, League of Nations, 312
Asoka the Great, 26
Association of South-East Asian Nations, 358
Assyrians, 9, 14
Athens, 33, 34
Atlantic Charter, 326
atomic bomb, 326
Aton, 11
Attlee, Clement, 173, 206, 210
audit, 123
Audobon Society, 265
Augustine, 45
Austen, Jane, 146
Australia, 105, 106, 120, 127, 191, 269
Australian Colonial Government Act (1850), 106
Austria, 97, 109, 137, 192, 275, 307, 323
Austro-Hungary, 95, 98, 102, 108, 243, 299, 303
authority, 63, 69, 431, 448
Automobile Workers' Union, 174
Avesta, 19
Axis powers, 323, 326, 342

Báb, The, 451–2, 462
Babeuf, Gracchus, 185, 188
Babylon, 8, 14, 94

Baghdad, 60
Bahá'í Faith, xv, 149, 400,
    402–8
    growth of, 458–9
    progressive nature of, xv,
    400, 416, 449, 469
Bahá'í
    Administrative Order,
    426–33, 434
    community, 401, 424–33,
    465–9
    daily life, 418–19
    and family, 421–4
    Fund, 432–3
    history, 450–58, 466
    House of Worship, 439
    International Convention,
    428, illus.
    law, 423, 431, 454
    method, 400
    teachings on human nature,
    406–10, 417–9
    view on economic issues,
    439–46
    view of government, 418,
    434–40
    view of universe, 403–6
    World Centre, 427, 456
    World Commonwealth, 440
    World Congress (1963), 457
    Writings, 401, 403, 407, 428,
    434, 445, 449, 456, 465
Bahá'u'lláh, 401, 415, 452–4,
    462
    quotations from the writings
    of, vi, 407, 462
Bajer, Frederick, 286, 287
Bakunin, Michael, 182
Balfour, Arthur, 260
Balkans, 102, 137, 294, 299
Balkan Wars, 102, 277
Bandaranaike, Siramavo, 151
Band of Hope, 260
Bandung Conference, 353
Bank of France, 193
Barnes, George, 314
Barnes, Thomas, 159
Baruch plan, 370
basic education, 197
Basques, 118
Bebel, August, 188
Beccaria, Cesare Bonesana, 233
Beecher Stowe, Harriet, 89,
    illus.
Belgium, 102–3, 117, 120, 172,
    243, 300, 305
Bellers, John, 273
Beneš, Eduard, 108
Bentham, Jeremy, 201, 210,
    234, 273
Berlin, 101, 349, 350
Berlin, Congress of (1884), 295
Bernadotte, King, 102
Bernard of Clairvaux, 48

Bessarabia, 101
Bevin, Ernest, 173
Bhagavad Gita, 22–3
Bhutan, 151
Bible, 49
bicameral system, 125, 133,
    134, 309
Biggs, Henry & Co., 180
bilateral agreements, 86, 97
Bill of Rights
    (GB 1689), 68
    (US 1791), 74, 339
biological weapons, 362, 374
Bismarck, Prince Otto von,
    97–8, 169, 198, 203, 209,
    299
Blacks, 228, 286, 288
Blanc, Louis, 186, 189, 206
Blanqui, Auguste, 186, 188
Bloom, Allan, 228
Boadicea, 146
Bon Marché, 180
bondage, 92
bonded triad system, 384
Boers, 107
Boer War, 107, 242, 288
Book of Certitude, 452–3
Book of My Covenant, 454
Book of Laws, 454
Bolivar, Simon, 104, 282
Bolivia, 104
Bolsheviks, 109, 139, 185,
    190–91, 302–3, 464
Booth, Charles, 202
Borgias, 49
Borgeois, Leon, 309
Boston Tea Party, 71
Bourbons, 87, 100, 104, 130
Bourgeois, Leon, 309
Boxer Rebellion, 115
Bradlaugh, Charles, 128
Brazil, 105, 120, 142, 269, 355,
    360
Bretons, 118
Briand, Aristide, 317
Bright, John, 147
Britain, 63–9, 85–6, 105,
    111–14, 116, 121, 123–4,
    126–9, 147–8, 158–60,
    165, 169–71, 176–8, 180,
    189–90, 192, 195, 200–25
    passim, 229–30, 235,
    237–9, 243, 263–5, 267,
    270, 275–6, 280, 284,
    290–91, 294–7, 309, 318,
    326, 331, 357, 360
British Broadcasting
    Corporation, 162, 184
Commonwealth, 105, 229,
    358
Empire, 27, 112, 116, 211,
    295
and Foreign School Society,
    229
Navy, 86, 105

North America Act (1867),
    106
Brontë sisters, 146
brotherhood of man, 4, 395,
    415, 425, 482
Brown, John, 90
Browne, E.G., 454, 464
Bruce Commission, 343
Bruntland, Gro Harlem, 151
Bruntland Report, 387
Brussels, 91, 190, 283
Bryan, William Jennings, 279
Buddha, Siddhatta Gautama, 3,
    25–6, 411
Buddhism, 19, 25–7, 29, 112
Bulgaria, 101, 102, 289, 305,
    306
Bundestag, 133
bureaucracy, 153, 194, 196
Bureau International de la Paix,
    286, 287
Burke, Edmund, 71, 78, 429
Burma, 142
Butler Education Act
    (GB 1944), 230
Byron, Lord, 288
Byzantium, 48, 58

Caesar Augustus, 40
Cadbury, George, 220
Calcutta, 222
calendar, 6, 28, 440
Caliphs, 47, 58–60
Calvin, John, 50
Canaanites, 12
Canada, 105–6, 153, 281
Canberra, 220, 359, 455
Capital, 187
capital, 181, 183, 233, 356
capitalism, 144, 167, 176, 187,
    211, 251–2, 346, 348, 447
capital punishment, 233–7
Caracalla, 42
Carazo, Rodrigo, 385
Carlos, King, 124
Carlsbad decrees, 132
Carnot, President, 182
Carson, Rachel, 226
Casablanca Conference, 326
caste system, 23, 24
Catherine the Great, 75, 146
Catholic Church, see Roman
    Catholic Church
Cavour, Camillo Benso di, 99
censorship, 37, 158, 161
Central Powers, 108, 299, 305,
    343
Central Rhine Commission,
    282
centralization, 192
Chadwick, Edwin, 210
Chamberlain, Joseph, 204, 216
Charlemagne, 47

charity, 205, 442–3
Chartists, 127, 147, 189
chemical weapons, 357, 362, 375, 386
Chernobyl, 351, 361
children, 209, 211, 222, 233, 237, 252, 420
Chile, 190
China, 5, 30–32, 95, 114–6, 118, 194, 225, 240, 294, 350, 360
Chou dynasty, 28
Christian Church, 45, 48, 49, 74, 113
Christianity, 19–20, 51, 61, 112, 200, 225, 296, 402, 464
Christians, 54, 61, 118, 190, 450, 455, 459
Christian evangelists, 202, 215
Christian Socialists, 177
church and state, 46–7, 64, 72
Churchill, Winston, 173, 326, 329
cinema, 161
citizenship, 39, 73, 119
City of God, The, 45
city planning, 219–21
Civilian Conservation Corps, 266
civilization, 6, 118, 315, 361, 396, 399, 403, 407, 412, 414, 439
civil disobedience, 113, 467
civil law, 87
civil rights, 67, 83, 91, 141, 149, 166, 202, 260, 286, 340, 425, 431
Civil Rights Acts (US), 141
civil service, 30, 76, 123, 124, 127, 129, 313, 397
Civil Service Reform Act (GB 1870), 127
civil war, 67, 115, 138, 141, 191, 357
Civil War, American, 90, 243
cleanliness, 57
Cleisthenes, 34
clergy, 77
Closing of the American Mind, The, 228
Club of Rome, 266
Coal Mines Regulation Act (GB 1860), 223
coalition, 121
Cobbett, William, 159
Cobden, Richard, 147, 291
Cochrane, Lord, 105
Code Napoleon, 130
Colbert, 184
Cold War, 346–52, 357, 368
collective action, 449
collectivism, 93, 145
collective security, 315, 321,

329, 368, 374
Colombia, 269
Colombo Plan, 378
colonial powers, 114, 117, 303, 354
colonies, 69, 91, 95, 105
colonization, 104
Combination Acts (GB 1800), 169
Commonwealth (of England), 67
Commune of Paris, 189
communism, communists, 124, 144, 169, 188, 191, 198, 320, 346, 348, 447
competition, 187, 197, 230
Compromise (Hapsburg 1867), 133
Compromise Agreement (1850) 89
confederation, 97
Condorcet, Marquis de, 87
Confucius, 29, illus.
Congo, 372
Congress (US), 72–3, 89, 123, 151
congress system, 342
conservation, 263–5
Conservative Party (GB), 116, 127
Constantine, Emperor, 45
Constantinople, 48
Constitution
  British, 128
  Canadian, 164
  Eastern European countries, 137
  French (1793), 78, 130; (1791), 226; (1815), 130–31
  German states, 132
  Irish, 137
  Italian, 150
  Piedmont (1848), 134
  South African, 107
  Soviet (1936), 143
  Spanish, 136
  United States, 72–3
  Weimar Republic, 150
constitutionalism, 137
constitutional monarchy, 64, 68, 105, 124
consultation, 46, 70, 137, 308, 309, 430–31, 435, 465, 466
consumer goods, 363
consumer society, 152, 166, 251–6
Continental Congresses (1774–6), 71
Convention on Pacific Settlement of International Disputes (1899), 279
cooperation, 277, 311, 361
cooperatives, 166–7, 176, 179, 183, 249, 344–5, 442

Cooperative Wholesale Society, 177
Corn Laws (GB), 285
Corrupt Practices Act (GB 1883), 128
corruption, 129, 137, 144, 357, 383
Corsica, 118
Costa Rica, 141, 359
costs, 196, 199, 241
councils, 26, 112
Council of Europe, 358
Council, League of Nations 312
Council of Nicaea, 46
covenants, 340, 344 see also United Nations
Cremer, William, 285, 287
Crete, 6
crime, 231, 254, 357, 398, 437
  against humanity, 327–8
  against peace, 327–8
Criminal Justice Act (GB 1848), 235
Crimean War, 93, 99, 213, 242, 277
Cripps, Stafford, 114
Cromwell, Oliver, 67, 110, 158
Crusades, 47, 48
Cuba, 194, 350
Cuban missile crisis, 349, 371
Cultural Revolution, 144, 194
culture, 94, 117, 188, 293, 296, 359, 395–6, 401, 419, 439
customs union, 97
Cyprus, 116, 118
Cyrus the Great, 10, 18–19
Czar, 134
Czechoslovakia, 108, 137, 139, 142, 307, 323, 349

Dana, Richard, 235
Darwin, Charles, 51
David, King, 13, 17, 43, 412
debate, 34
Debs, Eugene, 191
debt, 249, 281, 355–6, 383
decentralization, 142, 195, 345, 442
De Chardin, Teilhard, xiii
decision-making, 145, 429–31
Declaration of Independence (US 1776), 71, 88
Declaration of the Rights of Man (France 1789), 76, 339
Declaratory Act (US 1766), 70
decolonization, 116, 129, 139, 193
defence, 106, 138, 248, 295, 300, 345
Defoe, Daniel, 158
De Gaulle, General, 173

Delane, John Thadeus, 159
democratic socialists, 185
democracy, 33–6, 72, 83, 111,
    Ch.14, 194, 225, 227, 285,
    318, 326, 398, 429, 447,
    448–9
Denmark, 102, 110, 211
development aid, 376–7, 382–3
development, social and
    economic, 156, 375–6,
    380, 468–9
dialectical materialism, 187
Dickens, Charles, 202
Dickinson, Emily, 146
dictatorship, 105, 118, 130,
    137, 139, 140, 142, 185,
    188, 326
Diet
    German, 97, 132
    Hungarian, 98
Dinkard, 19
diplomacy, 311, 359
disarmament, 279, 309–10,
    317–19, 344, 369, 469
Disarmament Conference
    (1932), 318, 323
discrimination, 197, 340, 342,
    351
disputes, 271, 279, 315, 316,
    330, 334–5, 371, 372, 453
Disraeli, Benjamin, 101, 127,
    128, 147
distribution of resources, 397,
    417, 441, 442–4
diversity, 419, 435, 437, 459–60
divine right of kings, 68
division of labour, 187
divorce, 44, 254, 424, 467
Dix, Dorothy, 237
Dogger Bank, 279, 281
Dolfuss, Engelbert, 192
dominions, 106–7, 116
Dostoevsky, 231
Douglas, Stephen, 90
Douglass, Frederick, 89, illus.
Dred Scott decision, 90
drugs, 215, 240, 254, 262, 357,
    398, 421, 461, 468
drug traffic, 115, 262
Drummond, Eric, 313
Ducammon, Elie, 286, 287
Duma, 135
Dunant, Henri, 277, 287, illus.
Dumbarton Oaks, 330
Durham, Lord, 106
Dyer, Gwynne, 366

East Africa, 107
East Asia, 360
East Germany, 142
East India Company, 111
Eastern Europe, 137, 144, 193,
    208, 329, 343

economic
    cooperation, 326, 342
    equity, 179
    influence, 114
    justice, 397
    planning, 196, 441
    policy, 191, 195, 351, 440
    strength, 359, 360
    system, 447
Economist, The, 163
education, 18, 31, 57, 72, 75,
    139, 141, 143, 153–4, 165,
    185, 197, 224–31, 285, 340,
    356, 420, 422, 425, 438,
    443–4, 454, 466, 468, 485
Education Acts (GB), 159, 229
Edward I, 64
Egypt, 7, 12, 58, 107
election, xiv, 59, 68, 69, 77,
    120, 126, 127, 130, 429,
    435, 446, 457, 484
Electoral Reform Act
    (GB 1914), 148
electorate, 65, 77, 120–22,
    127–8, 131, 132, 134, 136,
    140, 148
Elijah, 14
Eliot, George, 146
Elizabeth I, 146
El Salvador, 104
Emancipation Declaration
    (US 1863), 90, 93
empire, 95, 110, 116, 272, 276,
    359, 396
Employee Share Ownership
    Plan (ESOP), 180
employers, 168–70, 175
Employers' Liability Act
    (GB 1880), 203
energy, 269, 355
Engels, Friedrich, 187
English Revolution, 49, 62, 67,
    242
Enlightenment, 74, 233
environment, 174, 253, 255,
    263–70, 362, 379, 390,
    415, 468
equality, 56, 67, 75, 76, 83,
    133, 140, 145, 154, 156,
    330, 396, 419, 420, 425,
    442, 454, 461, 468, 484
equal opportunity, xiv, 197,
    227
Equal Opportunities Act
    (US 1964), 208
Equal Rights Amendment
    (ERA), 152
equal weight, 128, 136, 140
Erasmus, 273
Eratosthenes, 36
Erfurt, Congress of, 189
Esperanto, 287, 438
Essay on Crime and Punishment,
    233

Essay on Slavery and Commerce
    of the Human Species, 85
Estates-General, 76
Estonia, 109
Ethiopia, 322
ethics, xiii, 3, 10, 18, 23, 25,
    28–9, 37, 43, 44, 50, 75,
    113, 157, 175, 181, 253,
    395, 403, 404, 422, 425,
    435, 461
Ethics, 37
Euclid, 36
Euripedes, 36
Euro-communists, 194
Europe, Europeans, 31, 45,
    103, 210, 233, 238, 257,
    265, 274, 276, 342, 360
European Common
    Market, 120
    Community, 142, 180, 208,
        245, 358, 377
    Court, 358
    Danube Commission, 282
    Human Rights Commission,
        358
    Parliament, 358
evangelism, 202
executive, 72, 77, 139
extremes of wealth and
    poverty, 142, 166, 176,
    180, 185, 250, 354, 398,
    399, 417, 439, 441, 469
evolution, 404
Ezekiel, 14

Fabian Society, 190, 197, 309
Factory Acts (GB), 223
Fair Deal, 208
Fair Labor Standards Act
    (US 1938), 206
family, 4, 9, 29, 152, 243, 252,
    254, 256, 421–4, 444, 483,
    484
family allowance 204
fascism, 169, 198, 325
fasting, 409
Fatimids, 60
Federal Public Health Service
    (US 1870), 211
federal system, 107, 132,
    144, 183, 415
Ferdinand, Archduke of
    Austro-Hungary, 300
Ferdinand of Bulgaria, 101
Ferry, Jules, 227
Fichte, Johann Gottlieb, 226
Fifth Monarchy men, 49
financial control, 133, 135
financial markets, 363
Finland, 109, 151, 260, 324
First Development Decade, 375

First World War, 108, 112, 137, 148, 150, 173, 191, 301–3, 325–6
Five Year Plan (Stalin), 192
Foch, Marshal, 308
food, 269, 378–9
Food and Agricultural Organization (FAO), 283, 336, 378, 468
Food and Drug Act (GB 1875) 211
Forel, August, 406
Fourteen Points, 108, 112, 303, 326
Fox, Charles, 298
Fox, James, 86
force, 79
forced labour, 92
Forrester, J.W., 266
Fourier, Charles, 182, 391
France, 103, 116, 120, 121, 123–4, 130, 150, 160, 189, 192, 196, 205, 211, 224, 226, 235, 243, 275, 276, 282, 310, 312
franchise, see suffrage
Franco, General, 138
Franco-Prussian War, 131, 300, 306
Frederick William I of Prussia, 225
Frederick William IV, 97
French
Empire, 131
National Insurance Co., 180
Republic, 131
Revolution: (1791), 74–9, 93, 94, 95, 99, 100, 103, 130, 185, 242, 276, 297; (1830), 130; (1848) 131, 186
freedom, 15, 33, 64, 67, 69, 93, 99, 142, 330, 339, 438, 448
of conscience, 340, 484
of information legislation, 140
of the press, 136, 140, 157, 161
of speech, 68, 122, 339
of thought, 75
free trade, 242, 251, 290–92, 440
frontiers, 117, 436
Fry, Elizabeth, 238
Fundamental Laws (Russia 1906), 135

Galbraith, John Kenneth, 254
Galileo, 51, 402
gambling, 57
Gandhi, Indira, 151
Gandhi, Mahatma, 24, 112–14, 141, illus.

garden city, 220
Gardner Report, 384
Garibaldi, Giuseppe, 99, 100, 285, 288
Gaskell, Elizabeth, 202
Gathas, 17
Gazette de Lausanne, 161
General
Act of Brussels, 91, 283
Assembly, see United Nations
Agreement on Trade and Tariffs (GATT), 337, 375, 383
Strike, 170, 172, 173
generation gap, 461
Geneva Protocol, 386
Genghis Khan, 300
genocide, 327
Genocide Convention, 341
George, Henry, 243
Germany, Germans, 95, 98, 113–14, 116, 133–4, 137, 150, 180, 203, 211, 218, 243, 267, 282, 303–7, 321
German
Federal Republic, 226
High Command, 302–3
Social Democratic Party, 189, 192, 290
Working Men's Association, 188
Ghana, 222
GI Bill, 227
Gillespie, Dizzie, 461
Gin Acts (GB 1751), 259
Gladstone, William, 101, 110, 147, 277
Glorious Revolution, 126
global corporations, 363
global perspective, 136, 365, 464
global village, 347, 361
Gobat, Charles A., 286, 287
God, 44, 46, 52, 55, 278, 404–6, 408, 410, 413, 440
Godwin, William, 182
Gompers, Samuel, 172, 314
goods and services, 188, 445
Gorbachev, Mikhael, 143, 195, 351, 387
Gotha, Congress of, 188
government, 29–30, 37, 75
aristocratic, 34, 37
authoritarian, 175, 233, 398
authority of, 69, 119
autocratic, 137, 139, 140, 144, 182, 185, 190, 370, 396–7
centralized, 72
constitutional, 94, 134, 135–6, 137, 139, 140, 158, 276, 285, 396–7, 398, 454
evolution of, 416

expenditure, 244–6, 247
federal, 72, 107, 132
financing of, 76
intervention, 380
local, 105–6, 126, 127, 130, 133, 135, 201, 216, 218, 430
military, 37, 71, 105, 143, 174
participation in, 64, 76, 83, 94, 119, 396–7, 484
republican, 67
rights and duties of, 69
revenues, 246
unitary, 107
world federal, 434–9, 441, 446
see also accountability, communism, democracy
governments, 344, 365, 366
Government of India Act (1919), 112–13
governor, 69, 105, 113
Gracchus brothers, 40
Grameen Bank, 156
Great Britain, see Britain
Great Depression, 199, 206, 264, 320, 337
Great Illusion, The, 286
Great Powers, 78, 99, 101, 103, 108, 275–81, 300, 307, 312, 320–21, 329, 359–60, 369, 371
Great Reform Act (GB 1832), 126, 128
Great Society, 207
Great War, see First World War
Greece, Ancient, 14–15, 33–8, 100, 224, 280
Greece, 100, 102, 144, 222
greenhouse effect, 208, 362, 390
Greens, 151, 267
Greenwood Housing Act (GB 1930), 217
Gregory VII, Pope, 47
Grenada, 380
Grotius, Hugo, 273
Group of Seven (G-7), 270, 353, 383
G-77, 353
guarantees, 73, 323–4
Guatemala, 104
Guizot, Francois, 226–7
Guptas, 27
Guru Nanak, 61

hadith, 55
Hadrian, 15
Hague, The, 280, 313
Hamilton, Alexander, 72
Hammarskjöld, Dag, 369
Hammurabi, 8, illus.

Han dynasty, 30, 42
Hanukkah, 15
Hands of the Cause, 457
Hapsburgs, 95, 98–9, 101, 133
Harappas, 22
Hardie, Keir, 190
Harper's Ferry, 90
Hárún ar-Rashíd, 61
Hayek, Friedrich von, 197
head of state, 124
health, 13, 156, 263, 418, 421, 439, see also public health
'Health for All by the Year 2000', 212
hedonism, 253
Henderson, Arthur, 318
Henry III of England, 64
Henry IV of Germany, 47
Henry VIII of England, 50
Hero, 36
Herod the Great, 15
Herodotus, 36
Hess, Rudolf, 326
Hidden Words, The, 452
Higher Education Act (US 1965), 227
Hill, Octavia, 216, 264, illus.
Hill, Roland, 283
Hippocrates, 36
history, 36
History of the World, 6
Hinduism, Hindus, 22–4, 61, 112–14, 140
Hiroshima, 361
Hitler, Adolf, 48, 109, 138, 193, 319, 323, 326
Hobbes, Thomas, 69
Hogarth, 257
Hollweg, Bethman, 302
Holocaust, 48
Holy Alliance, 276
Holy Roman Empire, 47, 95, 271
holy war, 55
Homer, 36
Home Rule, 112
L'Homme Libre, 186
Honduras, 104
hospitals, 213–15
hotline agreements, 378
House of Commons, 127, 128, 132, 148, 159, 192
House of Lords, 128, 243
House of Representatives, 73, 132
Houses of Parliament, 65
housing, 184, 210, 215–22, 251
How the Other Half Lives, 217
Howard, Ebenezer, 220
Howard, John, 238
Hudaybiyya, Treaty of, 54
hue and cry, 308, 309, 310
Hughes, William, 311–12
Hugo, Victor, 285

Hull, Cordell, 329
humanitarianism, 234
human nature, 411
human rights, 140, 143–4, 145, 273, 330, 338–42, 343, 351, 366–7, 390, 397, 425, 468
Human Rights Commission, see United Nations
Humboldt, Wilhelm von, 226
Hume, Joseph, 147
Hungary, Hungarians, 98–9, 133, 142, 288, 293, 307
Huskinson, William, 290
Huss, John, 49
Hyndman, H.M., 190

Ibis, 118
Ibrahim Pasha, 101
Iceland, 110
ICI, 180
Il Risorgimento, 99
Imams, 60
immigration, 222
imperialism, 51, 294–7
Imperial Preference, 284, 291
imprisonment, 233
income maintenance, 208
independence, 111, 114, 116, 117, 132, 193–4, 273, 311
India, 5, 105, 111, 118, 151, 231, 260, 360, 372, 378, 410, 438
Indian Councils Acts (1909), 112
Indian Mutiny, 111
indigenous populations, 105
individual liberty, 109, 123, 142
Indo-China, 116
Indonesia, 117, 118, 151, 269, 360, 372
industrial relations, 175
Industrial Revolution, 51, 165, 198, 251, 263
industry, 185
Indus Valley, 6
inertia, 327
infant mortality, 214
inflation, 138
injustice, 410, 431
Inquisition, 48
insurance, 168, 178, 202–4
intolerance, 61
Inter-American Development Bank (IDB), 378
Intermediate Nuclear Forces Treaty, 386
International Arbitration League, 285
Atomic Energy Agency (IAEA), 338, 372

Atomic Energy Commission, 370
Civil Aviation Agency (ICAO), 338
Chamber of Commerce, 287
civil service, 316, 335
Commission of Jurists, 367
commissions of inquiry, 279
conferences, 273
congresses, 275–8
Congress of Women, 286
Cooperative Alliance, 287
consultation, 310
Court of Justice, 330, 334, 344, 370–71, 436, illus.
development, 375, 380
Development Agency (IDA), 378
Development Corporation (IDC), 338
Finance Corporation (IFC), 338, 378
Institute of Agriculture, 283, 336
Institute of Law, 277, 285
institutions, 117, 118, 307, 315
Labour Organization (ILO), 92, 173, 224, 314, 336, 345
law, 277, 306, 307, 310, 330, 371
Monetary Fund, 337–8, 345, 375, 383
Office of Public Health, 283, 336
order, 486
organizations, 92, 397, 468
Parliamentary Union, 285
peace-keeping force, 317
Physicians for the Prevention of Nuclear War, 336
politics, 313
police force, 370, 454
Prize Court, 281
Red Cross Committee, 278
relations, 108, 145, 195, 276, 304, 346, 372, 390
Sea-Bed Authority, 380
Slavery Convention, 92
standards, 390
technical organizations, 282–4
Telecommunications Union (ITU), 282, 336
Telegraph Union, 282
tribunal, 453
Womens' Year, 341, 467
Workers' Congress, 287, 28(
Workers of the World (Wobblies), 183
International Herald Tribune, 163
Interpol, 315

intra-regional organizations, 284
Introduction to the Principles of Morals and Legislation, 234
investment, 179
Iran, 5, 117, 296, 360, 380, 386, 451, 459, 462, 466
Ireland, 110, 121, 137, 290
Irish Catholics, 118
Isaiah, 14
Israel, 16, 118, 353, 359
Israel-Arab wars, 355, 357, 371
Islam, 47, 52–62, 84, 112, 225, 359, 412, 451, 468
Islamic Republic of Iran, 459, 462
Italy, 99, 116, 120, 121, 134, 150, 243, 322, 353

Jackson, Robert, 328
Jacobins, 124
Jacquemyns, Gustave, 285
Jainism, Jains, 24
ben Jair, Eleazar, 15
Japan, 111, 115, 116, 256, 276, 294, 310, 312, 322, 351, 360, 363
Jaurès, Jean, 189, 192, *illus.*
Jay Treaty, 280
Jefferson, Thomas, 71
Jeremiah, 14
Jerusalem, 13, 15, 47, 54, 58
Jesus, 3, 19, 20, 43–4, 46, 50, 61, 411, 415, 455, 460
Jews, 14–15, 19, 42, 44, 48, 54, 55, 63, 94, 126, 141, 256, 293, 325, 327, 341, 396, 406, 455, 460, 463
jingoism, 160
jihad, 55
John, King of England, 63–4
John of Leyden, 49
John, King of Portugal, 105
Johnson, Lyndon, 207
Joseph, 12
Journal de Genève, 161
Judaism, 11–16, 19, *see also* Jews
judiciary, judicial system, 66, 72–3, 77, 139, 314, 328
Jungle, 211
jury system, 68, 73, 233
just society, xiii, 396, 415, 416, 425, 448, 449, 469
justice, 69, 314, 326, 437, 441
Justices of the Peace, 238
Justinian, 42

Kant, Immanuel, 273, 404
karma, 23
Kassebaum amendment, 384

Kay, William, 177
Kellogg, Frank, 317
Kellogg Pact (Pact of Paris, 1928), 316
Kenya, 116
Khrushchev, Nikita, 142
kibbutz, 178
King, Martin Luther, 141, *illus.*
Kingdom of the Two Sicilies, 134
Kingsley, Charles, 177, 202
Knights of Labor, 172
Korean War, 350
Koreas, two, 116, 331, 348–9, 369, 372, 388
Korea, South, 142, 364
Kossuth, Louis, 98, 288
Krishna, 22, 411
Kronstadt, 191
Kropotkin, Prince, 113, 182
Kurds, 117
Kushans, 27
Kuwait, 151

Labourers' Dwelling Act (GB 1875), 216
Labour Party (Australia), 191
Labour Party (GB), 114, 116, 170, 172, 190, 192, 195, 206
Laibach, Congress of, 275
laissez-faire, 29, 344
Land Lease, 377
land ownership, 185
language, 44, 94, 294, 359, 363
  universal auxiliary, 438, 441, 454
Langton, Stephen, 63
Lansdowne, Lord, 302
Lao Tze, 28
Latin America, 104, 276, 373, 378
Latvia, 109
law, 9, 28, 30, 42, 64, 67, 75, 76, 87, 94, 133, 277, 413, 431, *see also* rule of law
Law at Sea Convention (1982), 380
Lay Down Your Arms, 279, 286
Leach, Bernard, 461
leaders, 448–9, 469
League of Nations, 92, 304–5, Ch.22, 336, 342, 365
  Assembly, 312
  Council, 312, *illus.*
  Covenant, 307–11
  Permanent Court of Justice, 313–14
  Secretariat, 323–13
League of Nations, The: A Practical Suggestion, 309
Le Corbusier, 218

legislative assemblies, 106, 131, 140, 149, 151, 358
legislature, 72–3, 77, 105, 123, 124, 139
leisure, 252
Lenin, 138, 190–91, 228
Leopold of Saxe-Coburg, 103
Lesser Peace, 415, 434
Levellers, 67
Lever, W.H., 220
Leviticus, 13
Lewis, C.S., 410
liberalism, 132, 137, 289
Liberia, 89
Liberal Party (GB), 190, 192, 204, 243, 281
Liberté, Egalité, Fraternité, 77
liberty, 76
libraries, 228–9
Libya, 380
Liebknecht, William, 188
Liechtenstein, 335
life expectancy, 214, 231–2
life after death, 408
Ligue International et Permanent de la Paix, 284–5
Ligue International de la Paix et de la Liberté, 285
Limits to Growth, The, 266
Lincoln, Abraham, 74, 90, 326, *illus.*
list system, 121
Lister, Joseph, 213
literacy, 156, 161, 232, 466
Lithuania, 109
Lloyd George, David, 243
Locarno Pact, 316
Locke, John, 69, 71, 85, *illus.*
Loi Chapelier (1791), 169
Loi Tinguay (1850), 161
Lollards, 49
Lombard, Carole, 461
Lome Convention, 376
London Treaty (1930), 318
Los Angeles, 255
'lot', 273
Louis XVI, 77, 94
love, 413
loyalty, 68, 94, 179, 181, 368, 426, 463
Lunacy Act (GB 1845), 237
Luther, Martin, 49, 50

Maccabee Revolt, 15
MacDonald, Ramsay, 319
MacMillan, Harold, 116, 252
Madagascar, 269
Madison, James, 72
Magenta, Battle of, 100
magistrates, 35, 39
Magna Carta, 63, 69, 242, 339

Magyars, 134
Mahabarata, 22
Mahavira, 24
Maines, Esther, 149
Malawi, 222
Malthus, Thomas, 201
man, 395–410, 414, 447
Manchu dynasty, 31, 114
Manchuria, 115, 322
Maimonides, 16
management, 177, 178
mandates, 306, 307, 315
Manifestations of God, 411
Manichaeism, 20, 61
Manifesto of the Communist Party, 187
March Laws (Hungary 1848), 133
Marcus Aurelius, 38
Marie of Romania, 461
Marks & Spencer Ltd., 180
Maritime Transport Council, 308
marriage, 44, 148, 152, 157, 421, 423–4, 484
Married Women's Property Act (GB 1870), 147
Martel, Charles, 59
Marshall Aid, 377
martial law, 66
Marx, Karl, 3, 187, 188–9, 190, 258, 289, 414
Marxism, Marxists, 138, 250, 348
Masada, 15–16
Masaryk, Thomas, 108, 312, *illus.*
Mason-Dixon Line, 89
Massachusetts, 227, 258
Massachusetts Society for the Suppression of Intemperance, 258
materialism, 51, 143, 187, 253, 359, 398, 407, 414
mathematics, 7, 22, 28
Mathews, Theobald, 258
Mauryan dynasty, 26
Mazzini, Giuseppe, 99, 288
McCarthy hearings, 349
McCloy-Zonin agreement, 370
McNaghten Rules, 237
Mecca, 52–4
media, the, 124, 152, 157, 163, 437
mediation, 300, 308, 371
Medicare and Medicaid, 207, 210
medicine, 31
Medina, 53–4
meditation, 408
Meir, Golda, 151
membership of assemblies, 121
Mendès-France, Pierre, 261
Menes, King of Egypt, 7

Merchant Shipping Act (GB 1876), 223
Messengers of God, 44, 53–4
Messiah, 16
Mestivos, 104
Metternich, 130, 132, 275
Mexico, 6, 104, 269, 360
Mexico City, 222, 255
Micronesia, 334
micro-states, 117
militarism, 139
military, the, 272
military action, 333, 369
military strength, 94, 111, 115, 193, 233, 350, 359
Mill, John Stuart, 71
Millerand, Alexandre, 189
Mines Act (GB 1842), 223
Ming dynasty, 31
minimum income, 184, 199–200
minimum wage, 172, 204, 208
Minoans, 32
Missouri Compromise (US 1820), 89
Mithraism, 44
Mitterand, François, 390
Moghuls, 27
Molasses Act (GB 1733), 70
Moldavia, 100, 101
monarchy, 63–4, 66, 123, *see also* constitutional monarchy
Mondragon, 178
Mongols, 31, 61
monophysite theory, 46
monotheism, 8, 11, 44
Monroe Doctrine, 308, 310, 347
Montesquieu, 87, 233
Montfort, Simon de, 64
Montreal Protocol, 388
Morse, Samuel, 451
Moscow, 373
Moscow Limited Nuclear Test Ban Treaty (1963), 373
Moses, 3, 12, 16, 17, 411
Most Great Peace, 415–16, 434
Mothers Against Drunken Driving (MADD), 261
Mott, Lucretia, 149
muddling through, 399
Muhammad, 3, 20, 52–8, 84, 146, 411, 415, 455, 460, 464
multi-cultural society, 436, 460
multilateralism, 391
multi-party democracies, 143
Munich Agreement, 108, 323
Municipal Reform Act (GB 1835), 127
Muslims, 55–62, 113, 117, 460
Mussolini, Benito, 138, 323
Myceneans, 33

Nairobi Forward-Looking Strategies for the Advancement of Women, 145
Namibia, 334, 386
Napoleon Bonaparte (Napoleon I), 47, 79, 95, 99, 105, 226, 288
Napoleon III, 98, 99–100
Napoleonic Wars, 86, 93, 136
Nation, Carrie, 259
nationality, 483
nationalism, 83, 115–16, 139, 185, 293–4, 469
nationalization, 193, 195
National
    Assistance Act (GB 1948), 206–7
    Congress Party (India), 111, 113
    Conservation Conference (US 1907), 266
    Constituent Assembly (France 1789), 76
    Health Act (GB 1946), 206, 210
    Health Service (GB), 195
    Industry Recovery Act (US 1933), 170
    Insurance Act (GB 1946), 195, 206–7, 210
    Labor Relations Act (US 1935), 170
    Labor Relations Board (US), 171
    parks, 265
    Prohibition Party (US 1869), 258
    security, 138
    self-determination, 78, 83, Ch.13, 276, 288, 293, 296, 303, 305, 326, 396–7
    Socialist Party (NAZI), 48, 306, 319–20, 328
    Society for Promoting the Education of the People (GB 1811), 229
    sovereignty, 273, 277
    Trust Act (GB 1875), 264
    Union of Women's Suffrage Societies (GB), 148
    Women's Christian Temperance Union (US 1874), 259
Naturalization Act (GB 1870), 147
natural law, 8
natural justice, 310
natural rights, 71, 85
Navarino, Battle of, 101
Navigation Acts (GB 1653), 70, 290
Navy
    Brazilian, 105
    British, 86

Nazis, 48, 114, 150
Nazi-Soviet Pact, 109, 324
Nebuchadnezzar, 10
Netherlands, 117, 211
Neue Zürcher Zeitung, 161
neutrality, 298
Newcastle Commission, 229
New Deal, 170, 205–6, 218,
    219, 266, 380
New Delhi, 255
New England, 70
New Ideas on Peace (1907), 286
New International Economic
    Order, 380
New Testament, 45
New Towns Act (GB), 221
New York, 234, 255, 258, 285
New York Peace Society, 285
New Zealand, 106, 150, 191,
    195, 204, 245
News (1621), 158
newspapers, 158–61
Nicaea, Council of, 46
Nicaragua, 104, 380
Nigeria, 118
Nightingale, Florence, 213
Nineteen Day Feast, 427
Nirvana, 25
Noah, 8, 11–12, 411
Nobel, Alfred, 286
Nobel Peace Prize, 141, 286,
    329, 366, 367, 379, 386,
    App.3
Non-Aligned Movement, 353
non-governmental
    organizations (NGOS), 315,
    347, 365–7, 397, 456
Non-Proliferation Treaty
    (1968), 373–4
non-violence, 113, 183
North America, 274
North Atlantic Treaty
    Organization (NATO),
    349–50
North German Confederation,
    97
Northern Ireland, 110, 118
North-South axis, 346, 352–7
Norway, 102, 150
nuclear holocaust, 350
    power, 351
    powers, 331, 374
    tests, 374
    war, 361–2, 415
    weapons, 348, 349, 352, 360,
    361, 370, 372
    winter, 361
Nuclear Issues, Interfaith
    Programme for Public
    Awareness of, 468
Nuremberg Trials, 327–9

O'Higgins, Bernardo, 104

oil, 267, 347, 355, 363, 383
Old Testament prophets, 14
Oliver Twist, 202
ombudsman, 124, 136, 140
On Perpetual Peace, 273
opium trade, 115
Orange Free State, 107
Orleanists, 131
Organization
    of Economic Cooperation
    and Development (OECD),
    358
    for European Economic
    Cooperation (OEEC), 358
    of Petroleum Exporting
    Countries (OPEC), 355
Orthodox Church, 100
ostracism, 34
Ottoman Empire, 16, 95, 100,
    102, 108, 109, 288, 307,
    452
Outer Space Treaty (1967), 373
Owen Robert, 176, 189, 220,
    illus.
ozone layer, 268, 362

Pacific, 116
pacificism, pacifists, 285
pain, 409–10, 414
Paine, Thomas, 78, 289, *illus.*
Paix par le Droit, La, 285
Pakistan, 6, 114, 118, 372
Palestine, Palestinians, 11, 13,
    58, 382
Pan-American Conference
    (1889), 284
Pan-American Union, 284
Pankhurst, Christabel, 145, 148
Pankhurst, Emmeline, 148
Papal States, 100, 134
Papua, 118
Paris Talks, 455
Paris, Treaty of (1858), 101
parliament, 64–6, 102, 103,
    110, 123–4, 127, 130, 131,
    134, 172
Parliament Act (GB 1910), 128
Parsis, *see* Zoroastrians
Parthia, 19
Parti Ouvrier Français, 189
Passy, Frederic, 285, 287
Pasteur theory, 213
patriotism, 83, 98–9, 118, 194,
    293
Pax Britannica, 296
peace, 10, 144–5, 189, 272,
    275–6, 326, 337, 339, 343,
    358, 383, 415, 425, 446,
    469
    movements, 284–7, 308,
    319, 366, 400, 468

universal, 273, 330
    University of, 385
peaceful assembly, 74
Peaceful Nuclear Explosions
    Treaty, 376
peacekeeping force,
    international, 317
Peace of Amiens, 242
Pearl Harbour, 348
peasants, 93, 116, 194
Peasants' Rebellion, 65
Peel, Robert, 239, 242
Pepin, King of the Franks, 47
peoples' democracies, 124
perestroika, 144, 195
Permanent Court
    of Arbitration, 280
    of Justice, 313–4, 334,
    370–71
persecution, 462, 483
Persian Empire, 18, 20, 35, 58,
    412
Persian Gulf, 347
Pétain, Marshal, 150
Petition of Rights (GB 1628), 66
Philippines, 118
Philistines, 12
Phoenicians, 13
physicians, 212, 260
Piedmont, 99, 134, 376
picketing, 170
Pill, the, 252
Pinchot, Gifford, 265–6
Plato, 36–7, 185, 404
Plimsoll, Samuel, 223
Plimsoll line, 223
Poland, 108–9, 303, 305, 324,
    325
police, 238–9, 317, 321, 436, *see
    also* world police force
political rights, 340, 396
political systems, 425
Political Register, 159
Politics (Aristotle), 37
poll tax, 65, 129, 245
pollution, 255, 362, 398
polygamy, 56–7, 423
poor, the, 55, 63, 116, 120,
    185, 198, 202, 209, 242,
    252, 257, 286, 356, 378,
    387, 439
Poor Law Act (GB 1601),
    200–201
Poor Law Commission
    (GB), 210
Poor Law Reform Act
    (GB 1834), 201, 205
Pope, 46, 48, 63, 99, 273, 302
Popular Front (France), 193
population growth, 74, 201,
    256, 263, 269, 362, 378,
    381, 382–3, 444, 470
postal services, 282–3
post-industrial age, 196, 230

poverty, 139, 142, 153, 199,
    207, 215, 231
  elimination of, 124, 165, 177,
    225, 251, 272, 397, 444,
    see also extremes of wealth
    and poverty
Portugal, 85, 105, 117
power blocs, 361
powers, division of, 123
prayer, 408–9
Prebisch, Raul, 375–6
prejudice, 418–19, 469
presidency, 72, 124, 131
preventive health care, 210
pricing, 176–7, 195
priests, 19, 44, 50
primogeniture, 72
Principles of International Law,
    273
Prison Acts (GB 1830s), 238
prison reform, 257
privatization, 247
privilege, 75
productivity, 176, 364
profit, 181
profit-sharing, 176, 179–81,
    442
Progress and Poverty (1879), 243
progressive movement,
    399–400, 425, 449, 450,
    462, 469
progressive revelation, 413–14,
    453
prohibition, 259–60
*Project for the Perpetual Peace of
    Europe* (1713), 273
proletariat, 40, 124
Promise of World Peace, The
    (Peace Statement) (1985),
    458, 467, 469
*Promulgation of Universal Peace,
    The*, 455
property, 90, 91, 183, 187, 217
  ownership, 9, 65, 121,
    126–7, 178, 181, 219, 340,
    484
  qualifications, 128, 129
  rights, 56, 64, 76, 463
proportional representation,
    121
prostitution, 20, 157
protectionism, 320, 364, 383
Protestantism, 49–51, 68, 85,
    102–3
Proudhon, Pierre J., 183
Prussia, 97, 109, 225, 275, 298
Ptolemys, 14
public enterprise, 197, 442
public executions, 235
public good, 69
public health, 184, 198, 209–15,
    251, 379, 439
Public Health Act (GB 1848),
    210; (GB 1875), 211

Public Library Acts (GB 1850,
    1919), 229
Punic Wars, 39
punishment, 72, 231, 437, 483
Puritans, 67

Quakers (Society of Friends),
    72, 85, 285
Qur'án, 54

racism, 91, 112, 139, 141, 310,
    311–12, 341, 353, 382,
    455, 467, 468, 469
Radetsky, Marshall, 99
radio, 161
rape, 153
rearmament, 319
real politik, 194, 288
Reclamation Act (US), 266
Red Crescent, 278
Red Cross, 300, 304, 321
Red Cross Convention, 278
Redistribution Act (GB 1885),
    128
redistribution of wealth, 167
Red Lion, 278
referendum, 119–20, 130, 136,
    157
Reflections on Violence, 183
Reformation, 48, 110, 200
regional
  conventions, 140
  federations, 117
  institutions, 142, 358
Reichstag, 133, 134, 189, 294,
    302
Reith, John, 162
religion, 3, 27, 146, 188, 200,
    225, 256–7, 272, 287, 293,
    330, 395–6, 400, 403, 412,
    413, 417, 422, 455, 459
religious toleration, 26, 56, 67,
    72
Rent and Mortgage Interest
  Reductions Act (GB 1915),
    217
representative assembly, 136
Republic (Plato), 37, 185
Reuther, Walter, 174
revolution, 126, 185, 192
revolutionary socialism, 193
Rich, Charles, 279
Richelieu, 124
Riggles Brix, Evelyn, 237
Rights of Man, The, 78
Riis, Jacob, 217
Rio de Janeiro, 222
Rochdale Society of Equitable
  Pioneers (1844), 177
Romantic movement, 261
Roman Catholic Church, 100,
    126, 271

Roman, Romans, Ancient, 5,
    15, 20, 30, 39–42, 44, 84,
    210, 225, 396, 438
Romania, 101
Roosevelt
  Eleanor, 151–2, 339, *illus.*
  Franklin, 205, 218, 260, 326
  Theodore, 205, 265
Root, Elihu, 281
Rousseau, Jean-Jacques, 75, 87,
    271, 406
Rowntree, 180, 220
royal charter, 64
Royal Society for the
  Protection of Birds, 265
rule of law, 63, 83, 123, 139,
    142, 166, 278, 327, 369,
    397, 436, 482
rules of war, 272, 281, 328
Rush-Bagehot Agreement, 279
Russia, 93, 95, 109, 134, 137,
    142, 150, 191, 275, 278,
    295
Russian (Bolshevik)
  Revolution, 93, 109, 211,
    348–9
Russian Social Democratic
  Party, 190
Ruskin, John, 111, 216, 264
Russell, Bertrand, 366

Sagan, Carl, 366
St Ambrose, 46
St Barbe Baker, Richard, 460
St Francis, 45
St Germain, Treaty of, 307
St Paul, 44, 45
St Pierre, Charles de, 273
St Simon, 186
Saladin, 16, 47, 60
Salt, Titus, 220
sanctions, 311, 322, 333, 369,
    431–2
Sand, George, 146
San Francisco, 330
San Martin, José de, 104
San Marino, 335
*Sanitary Condition of the
    Labouring Population, The*,
    210
Sanskrit, 22
Sargon, King of Sumer, 8
Sassanians, 19
savings, 246
Scandinavia, 124, 218, 359
Schell, Jonathan, 366
Schleswig-Holstein, 97
Schoelcher, Victor, 87
Schumacher, E.F., 266
Schwarzenburg, Prince, 183
science, 402–3, 415
script, 7, 8, 22, 30
Scriptures, 50

sea-bed, 373, 374
Second Reform Act (GB 1867), 127–8
Second World War, 111, 116, 139, 150, 173, 217, 325–7
secret ballot, 120, 127
Secret Ballot Act (GB 1872), 127
segregation, 141
Selenka, Mme., 279
Seleucids, 14, 18
Self-Employed Women's Association, 156
self-defence, 55
Sellon, Jean-Jacques, 285
Senate
  French, 132
  Roman, 39–40
  United States, 73, 149, 320, 341, 374
Serbia, 101–2
serfdom, 83, 84, 92–3
service to humanity, 420, 425, 466
Seven Weeks War, 97
Severance Readjustment Act (US 1945), 219
Sèvres, Treaty of, 307
sex, 253–4, 424
Shaftesbury Acts (GB 1851), 216
Shaftesbury, Earl of, 223, illus.
Shah Bahram, 21
Shah of Persia, 296
Shang dynasty, 28
shares, 179
Shi'ism, 59, 60, 62, 450–51
Shoghi Effendi Rabbani, 401, 456
Shrine of the Báb, 456
Sia dynasty, 31
Siang dynasty, 31
Sicily, 276
Sièyes, Emmanuel Joseph, 76
Sikhism, Sikhs, 61, 117
Silent Spring, The, 266
sin, 406
Sinclair, Upton, 211
single transferable vote, 121
Six Acts (GB 1820), 169
Six Articles (Germany 1832), 132
slavery, 8, 28, 34–5, 38, 40, 53, 56, 72, 83, Ch.12, 129, 160, 223, 257, 276, 283, 288, 342, 396, 482
Slave Trade Abolition Act (GB 1807), 86
Slovenes, 109
Small Dwellings Acquisition Act (GB 1894), 219
Small is Beautiful, 266
Smith, Adam, 201, 291
Smuts, Jan, 309, 312
Sobieski, John, 109

social attitudes, 157
social contract, 69, 74
social justice, 139
social democracy, 190, 290, 345
Social Democratic Federation (GB), 190
Social Security Act (US 1935), 205
socialism, socialists, 136, 142, 166–7, Ch.17, 278, 301, 447
socialist bloc, 142
Socialist Democratic Party (Russia), 190
Socialist International, 289
Socialist Revolutionary Party (Russia), 190
Societé des Amis des Noirs, 87
Societé de la Paix, 285
Socrates, 35, 56, illus.
Soil Erosion Act (US), 266
Solferino, Battle of, 100, 277
solidarity, 288
Solomon, 13, 17
Some Answered Questions, 455
Somerset case (GB 1833), 85
Sorel, George, 183
soul, 37
South Africa, 105, 107
South America, 137, 262
South-East Asia, 246, 262
Southern Confederacy (US), 90
sovereignty, 74
Soviet Communist Party, 142–3
Soviet Union, 115, 118, 222, 227–8, 327, 347, 360, 368
Spain, 85, 95, 104, 136–7, 138–9, 193, 276
Spanish Civil War, 182
Sparta, 33–5
Spartacus, 41, 396
Special Drawing Right, 377
species of life, 270
Spectator, The, 158
Speenhamland, 201
Spence, Thomas, 189
spiritual life, 143, 255, 407–10, 417, 422, 438, 453
Sputnik, 350
Sri Lanka, 117
Stael, Mme. de, 146
Stalin, Joseph, 138, 142, 194, 196–7, 350
Stanton, Elizabeth Cady, 149, illus.
Star Chamber, 158
state
  cost of, 241–50
  and environment, 249, 263
  expenditure, 241–50
  intervention, 201
  as instrument of reform, 184
  ownership, 184, 192, 195

  protection, 120
  rights and duties of, 29, 37, 69
  role of, 181, 198
  role in education, 225
  role in eliminating poverty, 177, 249
  source of revenues, 246
State of Prisons in England and Wales, The (1777), 238
Stead, W.T., 279
Steele, Richard, 158
Stresemann, Gustav, 316
stock market takeovers, 175
Stoics, 38
Storting, 102
Strategic Arms Limitation Treaty (SALT), I AND II, 374, 380, 386
strikes, 169, 172, 179, 183, 184
Subjection of Women, The (1869), 147
subsidies, 200, 206, 209
Sudan, 6, 107, 118
suffrage, 65, 78, 120–40 passim, 146, 148–9, 150, 172, 185, 202, 225
Suffrage Committee, 147
Suffrage Movement, 147
Sulayman the Great, 61
Sumerians, 6, 8
Sunnis, 62
superpowers, 342, 347–8, 352, 360, 361, 372, 399
supply and demand, 177
Supreme Court (US), 90, 218, 239
Suttner, Bertha von, 279, 286, 287
Sweden, 102, 109, 161, 172, 193, 208, 222
Swarthmore College Peace Collection, 366
Switzerland, 33, 119, 120, 124, 151, 218, 267, 283, 298, 331, 335, 359, 388
syndicalism, 183

Taft Hartly Act (US 1947), 171
Tahirih, 149, 451
Taiwan, 331, 388
T'ang dynasty, 31
Tanzania, 196
Taoism, 28
Taylor, Telford, 329
taxation, 65, 66, 68, 69, 70, 73, 76, 122, 159, 241–50, 443, 454
technology, 186, 228, 248, 251, 261, 361, 395, 415
telecommunications, 333, 445
temperance movement, 145, 160, 256–61

Temperance Society of Saratoga, 258
Ten Commandments, 12
Ten Point Manifesto (Hungary), 98
Tennis Court Oath, 76
terrorism, 118, 192, 357, 397
Thailand, 142
Thant, U, 371
Thatcher, Margaret, 151
Theodosius, Emperor, 46
theology, 45–6
Third Estate, 76
Third World, 196, 199, 221–2, 224, 256, 341, 353–7, 375, 380, 387, 420, 437–8
third world war, 349
Thirty Years War, 300
Thomas-à-Becket, 46
Thoreau, Henri, 182
Thousand and One Nights, 60
Three Books on the Laws of War and Peace (1625), 273
Threshold Test Ban Treaty, 374
Thucydides, 36
Thugs, 23
Tibetans, 118
Tillett, Ben, 171
Times, The, 159
Timor, 118
Tito, Marshal, 353
Tlatelolco, Treaty of, 373
Trianon, Treaty of, 307
tribunals, 483
tobacco, 262
Tobey, Mark, 461
Toleration, Act of (GB 1689), 68, 126
Tolpuddle Martyrs, 169
Tolstoy, Leo, 113, 182
Tomorrow: A Peaceful Path to Real Reform (1898), 220
Torah, 14
torture, 28, 62, 75, 233, 342, 452, 463, 482
Town and Country Planning Act (GB 1908, 1946), 220–21
trade barriers, 363, 375
trade cycle, 172, 178, 181, 251, 441
Trade Disputes Act (GB 1906), 170
trade unions, 166, Ch.15, 342, 442, 485
Trade Unions Act (GB 1913), 170
Trade Union Congress (GB), 171
Trades Board Act (GB 1909), 204
trading system, 354, 363, 376
transport, 271

transportation, criminal, 235
travel, 44, 202
Treatise on Civil Government, 85
Tree, Seebohm, 202
tribal peoples, 460
Triennal Act (GB 1694), 68
troika, 369
Troppau, Congress of, 275
Trotsky, Leon, 192
Truman, Harry, 208
Trueblood, Benjamin, 279
trust, trustworthiness, 62
Turkey, 117, 118, 142, 305
Turner, Nat, 89
Two Treatises on Government, 69
Two Years Before the Mast, 235
Tzeng Tsu, 30

U'mar, 58
Umayyads, 58–9
Uncle Tom's Cabin, 89
unemployment, 168, 178, 193, 198, 201, 204–9 *passim*, 320, 356, 398
United Nations, 117, 120, 144, 268, 329–30, 342–3, 346–7, 379–84, 425, 444, 462, 468
agreements, 372–5
budget, 384–5, 387
Centre for Human Settlements (HABITAT), 338
Charter, 330–31, 338–9, 344, *illus.*
Conference on Trade and Development (UNCTAD), 365, 368
Commission on Human Rights, 339, 340
Commission on the Status of Women, 341
conventions, 341, 342
covenants, 340
Covenant on Civil and Political Rights, 340
Covenant on Economic and Social Rights, 340
Decade for Women, 156
Declaration on Human Rights, 339
Declaration on Elimination of Discrimination against Women, 341, 379
Development Authority, 384
Development Decades, 375
Development Program (UNDP), 378
disarmament commissions, 370
Economic and Social Council (ESOSOC), 330, 333–4, 339, 343, 345, 365, 384, 468

Education, Scientific and Cultural Organization (UNESCO), 230–31, 268, 337, 384, 387, 468
Environment Programme (UNEP), 268, 338, 388, 390, 468
FAO, *see* Food and Agricultural Organization
GATT, *see* General Agreement on Trades and Tariffs
General Assembly, 330, 331, 334, 335, 339, 342, 343, 344–5, 375, 387
Genocide Convention, 341
High Commission for Refugees, 338
International Children's Fund (UNICEF), 338, 356, 378–9, 468
IIA, *see* International Institute of Agriculture
ILO, *see* International Labour Organization
IMF, *see* International Monetary Fund
International Women's Year, 341
membership of, 373, 387
Military Staff Committee, 369, 387
and non-governmental organizations, 365
Peace-Keeping Forces, 386
Reconstruction and Rehabilitation Agency (UNRRA), 338
and refugees, 371–2
role: in disarmament, 369–70, 372, 386; in mediation, 371, 386; in peacekeeping, 371, 372, 384, 386; in monitoring ceasefires, 371
Secretary-General, 333, 335, 344, 366, 459
Secretariat, 330, 368, 369, 387, *illus.*
Security Council, 330, 331–3, 343, 344, 368, 369, *illus.*
specialized agencies, 336–8
staffing, 383
structure, 331–8
Trusteeship Council, 330, 334
Universal Declaration against Racial Discrimination, 341, 379
Universal Declaration of Human Rights, 92, 151, 208, 231, 233, 339–40
Universal Postal Union, 283, 308, 336

INDEX

University, 338
WHO, see World Health
  Organization
United States, 72–3, 88–91,
  129, 154, 169, 191, 205,
  207, 211, 217, 219, 221,
  227, 237–8, 243, 250, 253,
  258, 265, 284, 302, 310,
  312, 320, 326, 337, 368,
  380–82, 387, 455
United Socialist Labor Party,
  191
unity, 53, 55, 109, 415, 426
  in diversity, 435, 439
Universal House of Justice,
  The, 401, 418–9, 427, 430,
  444, 457, 466
Unlawful Oaths Act (GB 1797),
  169
urbanization, 210
Uruguay, 105
Utilitarians, 201, 202, 210, 215
Utrecht, Treaty of, 275

Vandals, 42
Vedic religion, 22, 24, 26
Veneto, 100
Venice, 99
Venezuela, 104
Venizelos, Eleutherios, 312
Verdun, Battle of, 301
Verona, Congress of, 275
Versailles, Treaty of, 173, 192,
  305–7, 310, 313, 321
veto, 333, 343, 368
Victor Emmanuel I, 100
Victor Emmanuel III, 283
Victoria, 87, 111, 454
Vienna, 192, 218
  Congress of (1815), 274
Vietnam, 162, 194, 350, 359,
  360, 372, 467
Vindication of the Rights of
  Women, A (1791), 147
Vishtaspa, King, 17
violence, 29, 61, 95, 113, 116,
  134, 153, 175, 188, 240,
  348, 387, 426, 453, 459,
  462
virtues, 417–18, 423
Voltaire, Jean-François Marie
  Arouet de, 74–5, 87, illus.
voting, xiv, 73, 77, 120–2, 140,
  145, 149, 157, 333, 334,
  343, 383–4, 429, 430

wages, 154, 168, 179, 181, 200,
  202, 204
Wallachia, 101
Walloons, 102
war, 273, 275, 297–8, 311,
  316–7, 357, 366, 418, 434

cost of, 242, 247
  see also nuclear war
Washington, George, 71
Washington Conference
  (1922), 115
Washington Naval Conference
  (1921), 317–18
Watt, James, 165
Webb-Kenyon Act (US 1913),
  259
wealth, 123, 187
Weimar Republic, 138, 150,
  226
welfare state, 152, 166–7, 184,
  Ch.18
Westminster system, 123, 129
Westphalia, Treaty of (1648),
  273, 275
What is the Third Estate?, 76
Whitbread, Samuel, 229
Whitman, Walt, 263
Wilberforce, William, 85
William of Orange, 68, 110
William of Prussia, 98
Willard, Frances, 257, 259,
  illus.
Wilson, Woodrow, 108, 243,
  302–3, 310, 321, 326, 365,
  illus.
Wollstonecraft, Mary, 147
Woman's Suffrage Committee
  (GB 1865), 147
women, 6, 10, 17, 23, 24, 35,
  52, 56, 57, 61, 216, 238,
  240, 252, 262, 298, 442,
  444, 467
  and access to credit, 156
  and development issues, 156
  education of, 153–4, 156,
    227, 229, 231
  emancipation of, 144–57,
    451, illus.
  in employment, 154
  equality of, 141, 145, 468
  and family, 152, 461
  and peace, 145, illus.
  and poverty, 153, 257
  and property, 147, 156
  and social reform, 257, 286
  and suffrage, 129, 146–7,
    149–51
  and state benefits, 156
  and violence, 153
  in the workplace, 154,
    222–4, 461
women's movement, 152
Women's Bank (India), 156
Women's Social and Political
  Union (GB 1903), 148
Women's World Banking, 156
work, 18, 50, 185, 442, 485
workers, 168, 179, 180, 187,
  188, 194, 196, 203, 252,
  289, 442

Workers' Compensation Act
  (GB 1897), 204
Workers' International, 182
workhouse, 201
working conditions, 184,
  222–4, 314
Works Progress
  Administration (US), 206
world
  citizens, 316
  commonwealth, 434, 440, 449
  court, 273, 280–81, 309
  currency, 377, 440, 454
  dominance, 349
  economy, 362–5, 375, 415,
    440
  federal government, 292,
    434–9, 441, 446, 454
  federation, 144, 273
  history, 272
  news media, 163
  order, 387, 486
  police force, 322, 426, 454,
    468
  trade, 337, 364, 376–7, 440
World
  Bank, 338, 343, 345, 383,
    387, 445
  Court, see International
    Court of Justice
  Economic Conference
    (1933), 320
  Food Council, 338
  Health Organization (WHO),
    212, 261, 336, 378, 468
  Meteorological Organization
    (WMO), 338
  Prohibition Conference
    (1909), 260
  Wide Fund for Nature
    (WWF), 269, 468
  Watch Institute, 390
World Dynamics, 266
Wycliffe, John, 48

Yugoslavia, 109, 194

Zaire, 117, 269, 369
Zamenhof, Ludovic, 287
Zanzibar, 92
Zarathrusta, see Zoroaster
Zemsto Laws (Russia 1864),
  135
Zevi, Sabbati, 16, 411
Zimmerman telegram, 302
Zimmern, Alfred, 198, 276,
  280
Zionism, 382
Zollverein, 291
Zoroaster, Zoroastrians, 3,
  17–21, 411
Zwingli, Huldreich, 49